# European Contract Law:
# Scots and South African Perspectives

EDINBURGH STUDIES IN LAW
VOLUME 2

# European Contract Law: Scots and South African Perspectives

*Edited by* Hector L MacQueen
*and* Reinhard Zimmermann

EDINBURGH UNIVERSITY PRESS

© The Edinburgh Law Review Trust and the Contributors, 2006

Edinburgh University Press Ltd
22 George Square, Edinburgh

Typeset in New Caledonia by
Koinonia, Manchester, and
printed and bound in Great Britain by
Antony Rowe Ltd, Chippenham, Wilts


A CIP record for this book is available from the British Library

ISBN 0 7486 2425 2 (hardback)

# Contents

# Preface

This volume set out initially to test the claim that, as combinations of Civil and Common Law influences, the mixed systems of contract law in Scotland and South Africa have in some sense anticipated the content of the Principles of European Contract Law (PECL) concluded and published in 2003 by the unofficial Commission on European Contract Law presided over by Professor Ole Lando (Copenhagen). In a way, therefore, the volume was supposed to build on the foundations laid by a trilogy of historical and comparative studies on Scots and South African law, culminating in a volume affectionately dubbed *Double Cross*, but in reality entitled *Mixed Legal Systems in Comparative Perspective: Property and Obligations in Scotland and South Africa* (2004). At the Edinburgh conference where the papers were first presented in December 2004, however, it became clear that the studies could and should go much further. For example, how far might the Scots and South African contract laws benefit from reform along the lines proposed by PECL? And given that PECL appeared likely to become the basis for some sort of European contract law (see further below), what criticisms might be made of it in the light of experiences made in Scotland and South Africa? Nor is PECL the only possible model for a European – or indeed global – contract law. Account has also to be taken of such projects as the (also unofficial) Code of Contract Law prepared by the Academy of European Law under the leadership of Professor Giuseppe Gandolfi (Pavia) and of the Principles of International Commercial Contracts (PICC) first published by UNIDROIT in 1994 and issued in a second edition in 2004.

The development and nature of PECL and the other instruments just mentioned are set out in Reinhard Zimmermann's opening paper, and therefore need not be further explained here. But it may also be helpful to readers to know something of the current official moves towards a European contract law within the European Union, which lend the critiques of PECL offered in this volume an especial urgency and significance.[1]

In July 2001 the European Commission issued a Communication to the Council and the European Parliament on European Contract Law (COM (2001) 398 final), seeking views on whether problems result from divergences in contract law between member states; whether the proper functioning of the Internal Market might be hindered by problems in relation to the conclusion, interpretation and application of cross-border contracts. The Commission was also interested in whether different national contract laws discourage or increase the costs of cross-border transactions. If concrete problems were identified, the Commission also wanted views on possible solutions, such as:

— leaving it to the market;
— promotion of the development of non-binding contract law principles such as the Principles of European Contract Law;
— review and improvement of existing EC legislation (the *acquis*) in the area to make it more coherent and/or adaptable;
— adoption of a European contract code at EC level.

In February 2003 the Commission issued a further Communication to the European Parliament and Council entitled *A More Coherent European Contract Law: An Action Plan* (COM (2003) 68 final). The Communication suggested a mix of non-regulatory and regulatory measures in order to solve the problems identified by its previous consultation, including:

— increasing the coherence of the Community *acquis* in contract law by means of what was called a Common Frame of Reference (CFR) for contract law;
— promoting the elaboration of EU-wide general contract terms;
— examining further whether problems in European contract law require non-sector-specific solutions such as an optional instrument on the subject.

A further Communication from the Commission to the European Parliament and Council, entitled *European Contract Law and the revision of the acquis: the way forward* was published in October 2004 (COM (2004) 651 final). The proposal for the development of a CFR was to be taken forward as a means of improving the quality and consistency of the *acquis* in the area of

---

1 Most of the Commission documents referred to in the following paragraphs can be accessed at http://europa.eu.int/comm/consumers/cons_int/safe_shop/fair_bus_pract/cont_law/index_en.htm.

contract law. The CFR was seen as a toolbox towards improvement of the quality and coherence of the *acquis* and future legislation, as well as its simplification. "The CFR will provide clear definitions of legal terms, fundamental principles and coherent model rules of contract law, drawing on the EC acquis and on best solutions found in Member States' legal orders" (para 2.1.1). It would, however, be a non-binding instrument, although the Commission reserved the right to consult again on this question when elaborating the CFR. The promotion of EU-wide standard terms and conditions is to be taken forward via a website which would be a platform for the exchange of information on such terms and conditions. Further, and in parallel with the development of the CFR, the Commission would continue to investigate the opportuneness of a non-sectoral-specific optional instrument on European contract law. The Commission said:

> Although it is premature to speculate about the possible outcome of the reflection, it is important to explain that it is neither the Commission's intention to propose a "European civil code" which would harmonise contract laws of Member States, nor should the reflections be seen as in any way calling into question the current approaches to promoting free circulation on the basis of flexible and efficient solutions (para 2.3).

The Commission has now (June 2005) contracted with a number of groups under the Sixth Framework programme to carry out the research needed for the preparation and elaboration of the CFR by 2007. The groups involved, to be known collectively as the CoPECL-Network of Excellence, are the following:

— Study Group on a European Civil Code (which seeks to build on PECL in many other areas of private law, including specific contracts, non-voluntary obligations, e-commerce, trusts, and transfer of property);
— Research Group on the Existing EC Private Law (the Acquis Group);
— Project Group on a restatement of European Insurance Contract Law (Insurance Group);
— Association Henri Capitant with the Société de Législation Comparée and the Conseil Supérieur du Notariat;
— Common Core of European Private Law Group;
— Research Group on the Economic Assessment of Contract Law Rules;
— Database Group of the Institute Charles Dumoulin, University of Paris (which is compiling a database of cases on European contract law);
— Academy of European Law, Trier (ERA).

The Network Co-ordinator is Professor Dr Hans Schulte-Nölke of the University of Bielefeld. Most of the Network groups are university-based (Edinburgh is among the universities involved). In order therefore to avoid the reproach of being merely an academic exercise, the work of the groups will be discussed and criticised in "stakeholder workshops" over the study period (a process which has indeed already begun). The stakeholders include representatives of business, consumers and legal practice. The overall aim will be to adopt a tried and tested CFR by 2009.

To date (June 2005), there have been two major reactions to these proposals in the United Kingdom. The first of these was the House of Lords European Union Committee's 12th Report of Session 2004–05, *European Contract Law – the way forward?* (HL Paper 95, 5 April 2005)[2]. Having taken evidence from a number of academic and practising lawyers, the Committee concluded that the CFR is to be welcomed in principle, and that in order to ensure its usability, industry, commerce, legal practitioners and consumers must be closely involved in the preparatory work.

The second significant response was the publication in March 2005 of a survey by the London law firm Clifford Chance, entitled *European Contract Law: what does business think?*.[3] Of the 175 businesses asked, 81.7 per cent would be likely or very likely to use an EU-wide contract law, although 74.3 per cent were against such a law being mandatory, and only 53.7 per cent believed it achievable in any event. The ability to choose the governing law of a contract was important to 83.4 per cent of respondents. 65 per cent found that there were obstacles, including legal differences, to cross-border trade in Europe, but only 27 per cent were actually deterred from doing such business as a result.

Of course, the proposals for the development of a European contract law by the methods being used by the Commission have met with severe criticism on policy and other grounds.[4] But even so it is evident that a European contract law is nearer to reality of a kind than ever before, and that policy critiques are not enough. There is also a need for technical and substantive assessment of the material such as PECL upon which the CFR will be based. This book seeks to provide just such criticism from the

2  See http://www.publications.parliament.uk/pa/ld200405/ldselect/ldeucom/95/9502.htm#evidence.

3  Accessible at http://www.cliffordchance.com/expertise/publications/details.aspx?FilterName= @URL&contentitemid=8354).

4  See, e.g., H Muir Watt, "European integration, legal diversity and the conflict of laws" (2005) 9 *Edinburgh LR* 6; J Smits (ed), *The Need for a European Contract Law: Empirical and Legal Perspectives* (2005).

perspective of Scots and South African contract lawyers, and it is offered to the debate without prejudice as to the deeper policy questions. At the same time it may help to inform Scots and South African lawyers about the substance of international developments in the field, and suggest ways in which our still vigorous and vital national laws may continue to be developed to remain in step with the needs of the day.

We are grateful to our fellow contributors for their prompt and efficient responses to our requests for the development of the papers which they presented in Edinburgh in December 2004, and to Elspeth Reid for much helpful guidance and support in bringing the volume forward to publication.

Hector L MacQueen and
Reinhard Zimmermann
*June 2005*

# List of Contributors

ERIC CLIVE is a Visiting Professor of Law in the University of Edinburgh.

JACQUES DU PLESSIS is a Professor of Private Law and Roman Law in the University of Stellenbosch.

A D M FORTE is Professor of Commercial Law in the University of Aberdeen.

SIEG EISELEN is Professor of Private Law in the University of South Africa.

CHARL HUGO is Professor of Mercantile Law in the University of Stellenbosch, and a pupil member of the Cape Bar.

MAX LOUBSER is a Professor of Private Law and Roman Law in the University of Stellenbosch.

GERHARD LUBBE is a Professor of Private Law and Roman Law in the University of Stellenbosch.

LAURA MACGREGOR is a Senior Lecturer in Law in the University of Edinburgh.

HECTOR MACQUEEN is Professor of Private Law in the University of Edinburgh.

TJAKIE NAUDÉ is Senior Lecturer in Law in the University of Stellenbosch.

GEO QUINOT is a Lecturer in Law in the University of Stellenbosch.

PHILIP SUTHERLAND is Professor of Mercantile Law in the University of Stellenbosch.

REINHARD ZIMMERMANN is Director of the Max Planck Institute for Foreign Private and Private International Law, Hamburg, and Professor of Private Law, Roman Law, and Comparative Law in the University of Regensburg.

# List of Abbreviations

**Part I: Books**

Bankton, *Institute*
Andrew McDouall, Lord Bankton, *An Institute of the Laws of Scotland in Civil Rights* (1751–53), reprinted by the Stair Society, vols 41–43 (1993–95)

Bell, *Commentaries*
George Joseph Bell, *Commentaries on the Law of Scotland and the Principles of Mercantile Jurisprudence*, 7th edn by J McLaren (1870; reprinted 1990)

Bell, *Principles*
George Joseph Bell, *Principles of the Law of Scotland*, 10th edn by W Guthrie (1899, reprinted 1989)

Brownsword et al, *Good Faith*
R Brownsword, N J Hird and G Howells (eds), *Good Faith in Contract: Concept and Context* (1999)

Busch et al, *PECL and Dutch Law*
D Busch, E Hondius, H van Kooten, H Schelhaas and W Schrama (eds), *Principles of European Contract Law and Dutch Law – A Commentary* (2002)

Christie, *Contract*
R H Christie, *The Law of Contract in South Africa*, 4th edn (2001)

De Wet & Van Wyk, *Kontraktereg*
J C de Wet and A H van Wyk, *Kontraktereg en Handelsreg*, 5th edn by A H van Wyk and G F Lubbe, 1992)

Erskine
John Erskine of Carnock, *An Institute of the Law of Scotland*, 8th edn by J B Nicholson (1871, reprinted 1989)

Forte, *Good Faith*
A D M Forte (ed), *Good Faith in Contract and Property* (1999)

Gloag, *Contract*
W M Gloag, *The Law of Contract: a Treatise on the Principles of Contract in the Law of Scotland*, 2nd edn (1929, reprinted 1986)

Grotius
Hugo de Groot, *Inleidinge tot de Hollandsche Rechts-geleerdheid* (eds F Dovring, H F W D Fischer, E M Meijers), 2nd edn (1965)

Hume, *Lectures*
Baron David Hume, *Lectures 1786–1822* (ed G C H Paton), Stair Society vols 5, 13, 15–19 (1939–58)

Hutchison et al, *Wille's Principles*
Dale Hutchison, Belinda van Heerden, D P Visser and C G van der Merwe, *Wille's Principles of South African Law*, 8th edn (1991)

Joubert, *Contract*
D J Joubert, *General Principles of the Law of Contract* (1987)

Kerr, *Agency*
A J Kerr, *The Law of Agency*, 3rd edn (1991)

Kerr, *Contract*
A J Kerr, *The Principles of the Law of Contract*, 6th edn (2002)

Kötz & Flessner, *European Contract Law*
H Kötz and A Flessner, *European Contract Law* (trans by T Weir), vol I (1997)

LAWSA
W A Joubert et al (eds), *The Law of South Africa* (1st and 2nd reissues) with cumulative supplements

Lubbe & Murray, *Contract*
G F Lubbe and C F Murray, *Farlam & Hathaway Contract – Cases, Materials and Commentary*, 3rd edn (1998)

McBryde, *Contract*
W W McBryde, *The Law of Contract in Scotland*, 2nd edn (2001)

MacQueen & Thomson, *Contract*
Hector L MacQueen and Joe Thomson, *Contract Law in Scotland* (2000)

PECL
O Lando and H Beale (eds), *Principles of European Contract Law*, vol 1,

parts I and II (2000); O Lando, E Clive, A Prüm and R Zimmermann (eds), *Principles of European Contract Law*, vol 2, part III (2003).

PICC
*Principles of International Commercial Contracts*, 2nd edn (2004)

PICC 1994
*Principles of International Commercial Contracts*, 1st edn (1994)

Reid & Zimmermann, *History*
Kenneth Reid and Reinhard Zimmermann (eds), *A History of Private Law in Scotland*, vols 1 (Introduction and Property) and 2 (Obligations) (2000)

Schmoeckel et al, *Historisch-kritisher Kommentar*
M Schmoeckel, J Rückert and R Zimmermann (eds), *Historisch-kritishcer Kommentar zum BGB*, vol I (2003)

Scott, *Cession*
S Scott, *Law of Cession*, 2nd edn (1991)

Smith, *Studies*
T B Smith, *Studies Critical and Comparative* (1962)

Smith, *Short Commentary*
T B Smith, *A Short Commentary on the Law of Scotland* (1962)

Stair, *Institutions*
James Dalrymple, 1st Viscount Stair, *Institutions of the Law of Scotland*, 6th edn by D M Walker (1981)

SME
T B Smith et al (eds), *The Laws of Scotland: Stair Memorial Encyclopaedia* (25 vols, 1987–96) with cumulative supplements and reissues

Treitel, *Contract*
G H Treitel, *The Law of Contract*, 11th edn (2000)

Treitel, *Remedies*
G H Treitel, *Remedies for Breach of Contract: A Comparative Account* (1988)

Van der Merwe et al, *Contract*
S W J van der Merwe, L F van Huyssteen, M F B Reinecke and G F Lubbe, *Contract: General Principles*, 2nd edn (2003)

Voet
Johannes Voet, *Commentarius ad Pandectas* (Hagae-Comitum, 1707)

Walker, *Contract*
D M Walker, *The Law of Contracts and Related Obligations in Scotland*, 3rd edn (1995)

Zimmermann, *Comparative Foundations*
Reinhard Zimmermann, *Comparative Foundations of Set-off and Prescription* (2002)

Zimmermann, *Obligations*
Reinhard Zimmermann, *The Law of Obligations: Roman Foundations of the Civilian Tradition* (1990; paperback edition, 1996)

Zimmermann, *Roman Law*
Reinhard Zimmermann, *Roman Law, Contemporary Law, European Law: The Civilian Tradition Today* (2001)

Zimmermann & Visser, *Southern Cross*
Reinhard Zimmermann and Daniel Visser (eds), *Southern Cross: Civil Law and Common Law in South Africa* (1996)

Zimmermann, Visser & Reid, *Mixed Legal Systems*
Reinhard Zimmermann, Daniel Visser and Kenneth Reid (eds), *Mixed Legal Systems in Comparative Perspective: Property and Obligations in Scotland and South Africa* (2004)

Zimmermann & Whittaker, *Good Faith*
Reinhard Zimmermann and Simon Whittaker (eds), *Good Faith in European Contract Law* (2000)

Zweigert & Kötz, *Comparative Law*
K. Zweigert and H. Kötz, *Introduction to Comparative Law*, 3rd edn, transl T Weir (1998)


## Part II: Other Abbreviations

| | |
|---|---|
| A | Appellate Division |
| ABGB | Allgemeines Bürgerliches Gesetzbuch |
| AC | Law Reports, Appeal Cases |
| ACJ | Acting Chief Justice |
| AD | Appellate Division; South African Law Reports, Appellate Division |
| Ad & El | Adolphus & Ellis's Reports, King's Bench and Queen's Bench |
| AJ | Acting Judge |

| | |
|---|---|
| AJA | Acting Judge of Appeal |
| AJCL | American Journal of Comparative Law |
| AJP | Acting Judge President |
| Alex | Alexander Severus |
| All ER | All England Reports |
| All SA | All South African Law Reports |
| App Cas | Law Reports, Appeal Cases, House of Lords |
| APS | Act(s) of the Parliament of Scotland (until 1707) |
| ASP | Act of the Scottish Parliament (from 1999) |
| B & C | Barnwall & Cresswell's King's Bench Reports |
| B & S | Best & Smith' Reports, Queen's Bench |
| BCLC | Butterworth's Company Law Cases |
| BCLR | Butterworth's Constitutional Law Reports |
| Bell App S | S Bell's Scotch Appeals, House of Lords |
| BGB | Bürgerliches Gesetzbuch |
| Bing | Bingham's Reports, Common Pleas |
| Bligh | Bligh's Reports, House of Lords |
| BMLR | Butterworth's Medico-Legal Reports |
| Bpk | Beperk (= Limited) |
| BS | Brown's Supplement, Court of Session reports |
| Buch | Buchanan's Reports, Cape Supreme Court |
| Buch AC | Buchanan's Appeal Cases, Cape Appeal Court |
| BW | Burgerlijk Wetboek |
| C | Cape Provincial Division |
| c(c) | chapter(s) (legislation) |
| C | *Codex Iustiniani* |
| CA | Court of Appeal |
| CA Mass | Court of Appeal, Massachusetts |
| Cambridge LJ | Cambridge Law Journal |
| Camp | Campbell's Nisi Prius Reports |
| CAQ | Cour d'Appel, Québec |
| Cardozo LR | Cardozo Law Review |
| CB | Common Bench Reports |
| CBNS | Common Bench Reports by Manning, Granger & Scott, New Series |
| CC | Constitutional Court, South Africa |
| Ch | Law Reports, Chancery Division |
| Ch D | Law Reports, Chancery Division |

| | |
|---|---|
| CILSA | The Comparative and International Law Journal of Southern Africa |
| CISG | Convention on the International Sale of Goods 1980 (Vienna Convention) |
| Civ | *Arrêt de la Chambre civile de la Cour de Cassation* |
| CJ | Chief Justice |
| Ck | South African Law Reports, Ciskei High Court |
| CLD | Commercial Law Reports (formerly Commercial Law Digest) |
| CLP | Current Legal Problems |
| CLR | Commonwealth Law Reports (Australia) |
| Co | Company |
| CP | Consultation Paper |
| CPD | Law Reports, Common Pleas Division; Cape Provincial Division; South African Law Reports, Cape Provincial Division |
| CSOH | Court of Session, Outer House |
| D | Dunlop's Session Cases; Durban and Coastal Local Division |
| D | Justinian's Digest |
| D & CLD | Durban and Coast Local Division |
| D(HL) | House of Lords Cases in Dunlop's Session Cases |
| DA | Dalloz, *Recueil Analytique de Jurisprudence et de Legislation* |
| DC Ill | District Court, Illinois |
| DC Pa | District Court, Pennsylvania |
| DP | Discussion Paper |
| E | Eastern Cape Local Division |
| EC | European Communities |
| EDC | Eastern District Court Reports, Cape of Good Hope |
| Edinburgh LR | Edinburgh Law Review |
| EDL | Eastern District Local Division Reports, Cape of Good Hope |
| EDLD | Eastern Districts Local Division |
| Edms | *Eiendoms* (=Proprietary) |
| ER | English Reports |
| ERPL | European Review of Private Law |
| EWCA Civ | Court of Appeal, Civil Division (England and Wales) |
| EWHC | High Court (England and Wales) |

| | |
|---|---|
| Ex | Law Reports, Exchequer |
| Ex D | Law Reports, Exchequer Division |
| F | Fraser's Session Cases |
| F Supp | Federal Supplement |
| F(HL) | House of Lords Cases in Fraser's Session Cases |
| FC | Faculty Collection, Court of Session; Federal Supreme Court of Southern Rhodesia |
| Foord | Foord's Reports, Cape Supreme Court |
| GWD | Green's Weekly Digest |
| Harvard LR | Harvard Law Review |
| HC | House of Commons |
| HCG | Reports of the High Court of Griqualand |
| HL | House of Lords |
| HLC | Clark's House of Lords Cases |
| HR | Hoge Raad |
| Hume | Hume's Decisions, Court of Session |
| Houston LR | Houston Law Review |
| ICLQ | International and Comparative Law Quarterly |
| ICR | Industrial Cases Reports |
| IH | Inner House |
| Inc | Incorporated |
| Inst | Justinian's Institutes |
| Irish Jur | Irish Jurist |
| IRLR | Industrial Relations Law Reports |
| Israel LR | Israel Law Review |
| J | Judge |
| JA | Judge of Appeal |
| JBL | Journal of Business Law |
| JE | Jurisprudence express |
| JLSS | Journal of the Law Society of Scotland |
| JP | Judge President |
| JR | Juridical Review |
| KB | Law Reports, King's Bench Division |
| LA | Lord Advocate |
| La LR | Louisiana Law Review |
| LAC | Labour Appeal Court |
| Law Com | Law Commission |
| LC | Lord Chancellor |
| LCJ | Lord Chief Justice |

| | |
|---|---|
| LJ | Lord Justice |
| LJC | Lord Justice Clerk |
| LJCP | Law Journal Reports, New Series, Common Pleas |
| LJEx | Law Journal Reports, Exchequer |
| Lloyd's Rep | Lloyd's Law Reports |
| LMCLQ | Lloyd's Maritime and Commercial Law Quarterly |
| LQR | Law Quarterly Review |
| LR CP | Law Reports, Common Pleas |
| LR QB | Law Reports, Queen's Bench |
| LT | Law Times Reports |
| M | Macpherson's Session Cases |
| Macq | Macqueen's House of Lords Reports |
| McGill LJ | McGill Law Journal |
| Memo | Memorandum |
| Menz | Menzies Reports, Cape Supreme Court |
| Mer | Merivale's Reports, Chancery |
| Michigan LR | Michigan Law Review |
| Mo | Missouri Supreme Court Reports |
| Mo App | Missouri Appeal Reports |
| Modern LR | Modern Law Review |
| Mor | Morison's Dictionary of Decisions, Court of Session |
| MR | Master of the Rolls |
| N | Natal Provincial Division |
| NC | Northern Cape Division |
| NJ | *Nederlandse Jurisprudentie* |
| NLR | Natal Law Reports |
| NO | *nomine officii* |
| NPD | South African Law Reports, Natal Provincial Division |
| NY | New York Reports |
| NZLR | New Zealand Law Reports |
| O | Orange Free State Provincial Division |
| OH | Outer House |
| OJ | Official Journal of the European Communities |
| Ont HCJ | High Court of Justice, Ontario |
| OPD | South African Law Reports, Orange Free State Provincial Division |
| OR | *Obligationenrecht* (Switzerland) |
| OR (2d) | Ontario Reports, Second Series (Canada) 1974–1991 |
| Oxford JLS | Oxford Journal of Legal Studies |

| | |
|---|---|
| PD | Law Reports, Probate, Divorce and Admiralty Division |
| PECL | Principles of European Contract Law |
| PICC | Principles of International Commercial Contracts |
| plc | Public limited company |
| pr | *principium* |
| Pty | Proprietary |
| Pvt | Private (Company) |
| QBD | Queen's Bench Division |
| R | Rettie's Session Cases; High Court of Rhodesia |
| R(HL) | House of Lords cases in Rettie's Session Cases |
| RA | High Court of Rhodesia, Appellate Division |
| RabelsZ | Rabels Zeitschrift für ausländisches und internationales Privatrecht |
| RAD | Rhodesia, Appellate Division |
| reg(s) | regulation(s) |
| rev | revised |
| RLR | Restitution Law Review |
| Rob | Robinson's Scotch Appeal Cases |
| S | P Shaw's Session Cases (NE indicates New Edition) |
| s | Section |
| SA | South African Law Reports |
| SA Merc LJ | South African Mercantile Law Journal |
| SAJHR | South African Journal on Human Rights |
| SALJ | South African Law Journal |
| SALR | Butterworth's South African Law Review |
| SAR | Reports of the High Court of the South African Republic |
| SC | Reports of the Cape Supreme Court; Session Cases |
| SC (HL) | House of Lords cases in Session Cases |
| SCA | Supreme Court of Appeal |
| SCLR | Scottish Civil Law Reports |
| Scot Law Com | Scottish Law Commission |
| SCR | Canada Law Reports, Supreme Court |
| SDNY | Southern District of New York |
| SE/SEC/SECLD | South Eastern Cape Local Division |
| Searle | Searle's Reports, Cape Supreme Court |
| SI | Statutory Instrument |
| SLPQ | Scottish Law & Practice Quarterly |
| SLR | Scottish Law Reporter |
| SLT | Scots Law Times |

| | |
|---|---|
| SLT (Lands Tr) | Lands Tribunal Reports in Scots Law Times |
| SLT (N) | Notes of Recent Decisions in Scots Law Times |
| SLT (News) | News Section in Scots Law Times |
| SLT (Notes) | Notes of Recent Decisions in Scots Law Times |
| SLT (Sh Ct) | Sheriff Court Reports in Scots Law Times |
| So | Southern Reporter |
| SPCB | Scottish Parliamentary Corporate Body |
| SR | High Court of Southern Rhodesia |
| Stellenbosch LR | Stellenbosch Law Review |
| sv | *sub voce* |
| SW | South Western Reporter |
| SWA | South African Law Reports, South West Africa Division |
| T | Transvaal Provincial Division |
| t/a | trading as |
| TH | Reports of the Witwatersrand High Court |
| THRHR | Tydskrif vir Hedendaagse Romeins-Hollandse Reg |
| Tk | South African Law Reports, Transkei High Court |
| TPD | South African Law Reports, Transvaal Provincial Division |
| TR | Tijdschrift voor Rechtsgeschiedenis |
| TS | Reports of the Transvaal Supreme Court |
| TSAR | Tydskrif vir die Suid-Afrikaanse Reg |
| Tulane LR | Tulane Law Review |
| UCC | Uniform Commercial Code |
| UKHL | United Kingdom, House of Lords |
| Ulp | Ulpian |
| US Dig | United States Digest |
| W | Witwatersrand Local Division |
| W& S | Wilson and Shaw's House of Lords Cases |
| WLD | South African Law Reports, Witwatersrand Local Division |
| WLR | Weekly Law Reports |
| Yale LJ | Yale Law Journal |
| ZEuP | Zeitschrift für Europäisches Privatrecht |
| ZfRV | Zeitschrift für Rechtsvergleichung |
| ZH/ZHC | Zimbabwe High Court |
| ZSS (RA) | Zeitschrift der Savigny-Stiftung für Rechtsgeschichte, Romanistische Abteilung |

# 1 *Ius Commune* and the Principles of European Contract Law: Contemporary Renewal of an Old Idea[*]

## *Reinhard Zimmermann*

[*] This is the text on which my opening lecture of the conference "Principles of European Contract Law: Another Mixed Legal System" on 2 Dec 2004 in Edinburgh was based. The manuscript, in turn, is based on an essay on the Principles of European Contract Law which is to be published, in late 2005, as part of a volume in honour of Hein Kötz. A German version has appeared in Dirk Heirbaut, Georges Martyn (eds), *Napoleons nalatenschap: Tweehonderd jaar Burgerlijk Wetboek in Belgie* (2005), pp. 377 ff.

## A. INTRODUCTION

This paper will focus on a key document within the process of the Europeanisation of private law legal scholarship, the Principles of European
Contract Law. I would like to demonstrate that these Principles can be seen
as a contemporary manifestation of a genuinely European tradition – a
tradition which used to be labelled *ius commune*. And I would like to argue
that they can serve as a catalyst for a Europeanisation of private law "from
within" and "from below" (as opposed to European legal unification by
means of legislation, i.e. unification "from outside" and "from above"). In a
way, therefore, the Principles mark the contours of a new European *ius commune* and can fulfil a function resembling that of its historical predecessor.
Before these arguments can be developed a few words have to be said about
the Principles of European Contract Law and about the old *ius commune*. It

should also be noted, at the outset, that this paper does not deal with private law in general but merely with one of its constituent elements: the law of contract. One reason for this is immediately obvious: the Principles of European Contract Law constitute the most advanced and internationally most widely noted academic project aiming at the Europeanisation of private law.[1] Similar sets of Principles for other areas of the law are only just beginning to be published.[2] This is hardly accidental. For, on the one hand, the law relating to commercial contracts has often tended to be the pacemaker for legal harmonisation.[3] On the other hand, most of the basic concepts and evaluations informing the law of contract have not been deeply affected by legal developments under the auspices of the age of legal nationalism. The differences between the national legal systems are largely on the level of technical detail.[4] In other areas of private law, the situation is more complex.[5]

---

1 See, e.g., R Zimmermann, "Konturen eines Europäischen Vertragsrechts" (1995) *Juristenzeitung* 477; H Beale, "The Principles of European Contract Law and Harmonization of the Laws of Contract", in *Festshrift til Ole Lando* (1997), 21; J Basedow (ed), *Europäische Vertragsrechtsvereinheitlichung und deutsches Recht* (2000); E Hondius, F Nieper et al, "Principles of European Contract Law" (2000) 17 *Nederlands Tijdschrift voor Burgerlijk Recht* 428; M W Hesselink & G J P de Vries, *Principles of European Contract Law* (2001); S Mazzamuto, C Castronovo et al, *Principi di diritto europeo dei contratti: spunti dell'edizione italiana, Europa e diritto privato* (2002), 847; cf also the bibliography in W Ernst & R Zimmermann (eds), *Zivilrechtswissenschaft und Schuldrechtsreform* (2001), 739.

2 A European Group on Tort Law, based in Vienna, has published a set of Principles of European Tort Law in 2004; see (2004) 12 *ZEuP* 427 ff; on which see H Koziol, "Die 'Principles of European Tort Law' der 'European Group on Tort Law'" (2004) 12 *ZEuP* 234 ff; R Zimmermann, "Principles of European Contract Law and Principles of European Tort Law: Comparison and Points of Contact" in H Koziol & B C Steininger (eds), *European Tort Law 2003* (2004), 2 ff. For first contours of the tort/delict regime of the Study Group on a European Civil Code, see J W G Blackie, "Tort/Delict in the Work of the European Civil Code Project of the Study Group on a European Civil Code", in R Zimmermann (ed), *Grundstrukturen eines Europäischen Deliktsrechts* (2003), 133.

3 See, e.g., for nineteenth-century German law, B Dölemeyer, in H Coing (ed), *Handbuch der Quellen und Literatur der neueren europäischen Privatrechtsgeschichte*, vol III/2 (1982), 1421; A J Kanning, *Unifying Commercial Laws of Nations-States* (2003), 46.

4 N Jansen, *Binnenmarkt, Privatrecht und europäische Identität* (2004), 23.

5 This even applies to closely related areas such as the law of delict. For many centuries, it had developed along similar lines. It constituted a *usus modernus* of Aquilian liability which was reconceptualised under the influence of Natural law theory. In spite of many differences in detail it retained an essentially European character. Unlike the law of contract, however, even in the eighteenth and nineteenth centuries the modernised version of Roman law was no longer really modern. For in its basic structure it was still essentially geared towards the sanctioning of private wrongs rather than the reasonable allocation of losses (see N Jansen, *Die Struktur des Haftungsrechts* (2003), §§ 4–6). This was a problem which European legal systems only started to grapple with in the course of the nineteenth century and at a time when the first wave of codifications had contributed to a national isolation of the legal discourse. As a result, the European legal landscape became considerably more patchy in this field than in that of contract law: see Jansen, *Binnenmarkt, Privatrecht und europäische Identität*, 33.

## B. THE PRINCIPLES OF EUROPEAN CONTRACT LAW

### (1) Scope and origin

The Principles of European Contract Law have been prepared by a Commission on European Contract Law.[6] This Commission – widely known as "Lando-Commission" – did not have any official status. It was based on a private initiative and consisted of (predominantly) academics from all member states of the European Union. The growth of the Commission paralleled that of the EU. In the end it consisted of twenty-three members; three of them came from Germany, two each from France, Italy, England and Scotland.[7] The Principles have been prepared in three stages.[8] Part I appeared in 1995, after thirteen years of deliberation.[9] Essentially, it deals with the modalities of performance, non-performance, remedies for non-performance, and a number of general questions such as application, general duties of behaviour in the course of a contractual relationship, and terminology. Work on Part II, which covers the formation of contracts, authority of agents, validity (including vices of consent but excluding illegality and immorality), interpretation, and contents and effects (including contracts in favour of a third party), lasted from 1992–1999. Part II has not been published separately, but was immediately integrated with a slightly redrafted version of Part I.[10] In 2003 a third, and final, part appeared.[11] It contains rules on plurality of parties, assignment of claims, substitution of new debtor and transfer of contract, set-off, prescription, illegality, conditions and capitalisation of interest. Part III was prepared between 1997 and 2002; unlike Part II, it has not been integrated with the existing set of Principles but has been published separately, for the time being.

---

6  O Lando & H Beale (eds), *Principles of European Contract Law, Parts I and II* (2000); O Lando, E Clive, A Prüm & R Zimmermann (eds), *Principles of European Contract Law, Part III* (2003) (PECL).

7  See the list in PECL, Part III, xiii–xiv.

8  This way of proceeding has left its traces in the Principles. Thus, for instance, they contain three different regimes concerning the restitution of benefits after failure of contracts; see R Zimmermann, "Restitutio in integrum: Die Rückabwicklung fehlgeschlagener Verträge nach den Principles of European Contract Law, den Unidroit Principles und dem Avant-projet eines Code Européen des Contrats", in *Festschrift für Ernst A Kramer* (2004), 735 ff.

9  PECL, Part I (1995).

10  Lando & Beale (note 6).

11  Lando et al (note 6).

## (2) Essential characteristics

Essential characteristics of the Principles of European Contract Law become apparent by comparison with another draft, also published in the name of a private group of European academics and also covering the field of contract law: the *Avant-projet* for a European Contract Code that has been published in the name of an *Accademia dei Giusprivatisti Europei*.[12] Very largely, the *Avant-projet* is the work of one man: Giuseppe Gandolfi, described on the title of the publication with too much modesty as "coordinator". The Academy did not have much more than a consultative function: it gave suggestions, commented on preliminary drafts and met occasionally in plenary sessions as well as in national sub-groups. But its members do not appear to have been involved in the actual drafting of the rules. With the Principles of European Contract Law matters were completely different. They are based on a joint effort. Of course, one or two "reporters" were responsible for the individual chapters. They had the task of preparing comparative position papers and draft articles and commentaries; and obviously these reporters, by virtue of their authority, competence, personality, and power of persuasion, have managed to mould "their" chapters to a greater or lesser extent. However, a number of different members of the Commission served as reporters. Also, the position papers and successive drafts had to be presented to the Commission as well as to a "Drafting Group" and were discussed, criticised, refined and referred back to the reporter several times by both bodies; finally they were passed in two "readings" by the Commission and subsequently checked again by another body, the Editing Group.

The *Avant-projet* takes its cue from two models. These models are the Italian Codice Civile (since it combines elements of French and German law)[13] and a Contract Code drawn up on behalf of the English Law Commission at the end of the 1960s (which, however, has neither been implemented nor even published in England).[14] The draftsmen of the Principles of European Contract Law, on the other hand, have made every effort not to

---

12 *Code Européen des Contrats*, edited on behalf on the Accademia dei Giusprivatisti by G Gandolfi (2000); on which see H J Sonnenberger, "Der Entwurf eines Europäischen Vertragsgesetzbuchs der Akademie Europäischer Privatrechtswissenschaftler – ein Meilenstein" (2001) *Recht der internationalen Wirtschaft* 409; F Sturm, "Der Entwurf eines Europäischen Vertragsgesetzbuchs" (2001) *Juristenzeitung* 1097; R Zimmermann, "Der 'Codice Gandolfi' als Modell eines einheitlichen Vertragsrechts für Europa?", in *Festschrift für Erik Jayme* (2004), 1401 ff.

13 See, e.g., for the law relating to breach of contract, C Resch, *Das italienische Privatrecht im Spannungsfeld von Code Civil und BGB* (2001).

14 H McGregor, *Contract Code drawn up on behalf of the English Law Commission* (1993) (published by Giuffré, Milano).

base their work on any individual national legal system. Their approach was more comparative in nature. They have attempted, as far as possible, to identify the common core of the contract law of all the EU member states and to create a workable system on that basis. Thus, in a way, they aimed at a restatement of European contract law.[15] At the same time, however, they realised that they were confronted with a more creative task than the draftsmen of the American Restatements. Divergences had to be resolved on the basis of a comparative evaluation of the experiences gathered in the national legal systems, by assessing and analysing European and international trends of legal development, or by employing other rational criteria.

### (3) Style and structure of publication

The Principles are also inspired by the Restatements of American Law as far as style and structure of their publication are concerned. Each volume contains the text of the Articles which the Commission has agreed upon. In addition, for every Article there is a commentary (including illustrations) and comparative notes; the latter inform the reader about the pertinent legal rules applicable in the EU member states but also take account of other sources of law, such as international Conventions. The publication of the *Avant-projet*, on the other hand, has a section entitled "rapports du coordinateur" which provides an account of the rules contained in the Codice Civile and the Contract Code, a survey of the solutions found in other European codifications, and a summary of the comments by the members of the Academy. The motivation for the individual rules contained in the *Avant-projet* is comparatively sparse. A notable feature of the *Avant-projet* is that it is published in French. The Articles contained in the Principles of European Contract Law have immediately been published in a French and an English version, even though English has otherwise been the language of publication. In the course of the deliberations of the Commission on European Contract Law great emphasis was placed on the possibility of expressing every term and concept used in the Principles in both French and English; the Commission was thus constantly aware of the danger of using a terminology indelibly shaped by the peculiarities of individual legal systems.

### (4) Rules or principles?

There is one other difference between the *Avant-projet* and the Principles which is, however, much less marked than may be thought at first glance. The

15  Lando & Beale (note 6), xxvi.

*Avant-projet* contains a set of rules which is designed to be implemented as a European Contract Code. The Commission on European Contract Law originally professed to do something else: they set out to draft "Principles" of European Contract Law. This can only mean that they did not aim at preparing a system of specific rules which might immediately be applied by courts of law.[16] Accordingly, the draftsmen of the Principles merely regard their work as a "first step" towards a future European Code of Contract Law.[17] At the same time, however, it must be acknowledged that in a whole variety of Chapters they have gone much further and have drafted sets of rules, rather than principles, which reach a level of specificity comparable to that of any national codification. This is true, in particular, of a number of Chapters of Part III.

## (5) The Unidroit Principles

Internationally, the Principles of European Contract Law compete with the Principles of International Commercial Contracts of Unidroit.[18] Both works are comparable in many respects. Thus, in particular, they have been prepared in a similar manner, they pursue similar aims,[19] and they have been drafted in a similar style. Like the Lando Commission the members of the working group of Unidroit have chosen the label "Principles" even though it does not quite correspond to what they have in fact done. In both cases the text of the Articles is accompanied by comments (though the draftsmen of the Unidroit Principles have refrained from adding comparative notes). There are two major differences in that (i) Unidroit pursues the aim of a global rather than European harmonisation of contract law, and (ii) the Unidroit project specifically deals with international commercial contracts while the Lando Commission has formulated principles of general contract law. In view of this it may appear to be surprising that the individual solutions

16  Rules, in the terminology widely used in methodological writing, set out legal consequences that follow when their conditions have been met. Principles are general standards that are to be observed because it is just, or fair, to do so. A principle does not necessitate a particular decision, a rule does. Principles have a relative weight which has to be taken into account when they intersect; one rule, on the other hand, cannot supersede another by virtue of its greater relative weight; see, R Dworkin, *Taking Rights Seriously* (1977), 22.

17  Lando & Beale (note 6), xxiii.

18  *Unidroit Principles of International Contracts* (1994); on which see M J Bonell, *An International Restatement of Contract Law*, 2nd edn (1997); E A Kramer, "Die Gültigkeit der Verträge nach den Principles of International Commercial Contracts" (1999) 7 *ZEuP* 209; J Basedow, "Die Unidroit-Prinzipien der internationalen Handelsverträge und das deutsche Recht", in *Gedächtnisschrift für Alexander Lüderitz* (2000), 1.

19  On the aims pursued by the Principles of European Contract Law, see Lando & Beale (note 6), xxi.

proposed by both sets of Principles do not very much differ from each other; in a number of areas they are virtually identical.[20] The dominance of European legal thinking even outside Europe may provide an explanation, as far as the first of the points mentioned above is concerned. As for (ii) it may perhaps be said that what is regarded as fair and reasonable for commercial contracts can very largely also be regarded as fair and reasonable for consumer contracts and vice versa. This confirms an observation on the development of modern sales law: the provisions in the Consumer Sales Directive 1999/44/ EC,[21] particularly those concerning the concept of conformity and the remedies in case of non-conformity, very largely mirror the rules contained in the UN Convention on the International Sale of Goods, even though the latter instrument specifically excludes consumer sales from its range of application.[22] The correspondence between these two international instruments will significantly contribute to the emergence of a common framework of reference for the discussion and development of the law of sale in Europe.[23] The same can be said, on the basis of a comparison between the Unidroit- and the Lando-Principles, for many central areas of the general law of contract.

## C. THE OLD *IUS COMMUNE*

### (1) A European legal tradition

The *ius commune*, the central point of reference for this paper, was the product of a dramatic and far-reaching cultural upheaval: the so-called Renaissance of the twelfth century.[24] First in Bologna, then also at other universities founded

---

20 See, for the topics dealt with in Part I of the PECL, R Zimmermann, "Konturen eines Europäischen Vertragsrechts" (1995) *Juristenzeitung* 477; generally, see A Hartkamp, "Principles of Contract Law", in A Hartkamp & M Hesselink et al (eds), *Towards a European Civil Code*, 3rd edn (2004) (henceforth Hartkamp & Hesselink, *Towards a European Civil Code*), 125 ff.

21 Easily accessible now in O Radley-Gardner, H Beale, R Zimmermann & R Schulze (eds), *Fundamental Texts on European Private Law* (2003) (henceforth Radley-Gardner et al, *Fundamental Texts*), 107.

22 Article 2 a) CISG. See S Grundmann, in M C Bianca & S Grundmann (eds), *EU Sales Directive: Commentary* (2002) (henceforth Bianca & Grundmann, *EU Sales Directive*), Introduction, nn 6, 22 ff.

23 See, most recently, the Principles of European Sales Law, the first contours of which are presented by V Heutger, "Konturen des Kaufrechtskonzeptes der Study Group on a European Civil Code – Ein Werkstattbericht" (2003) 11 *ERPL* 155.

24 On which see H J Berman, *Law and Revolution: The Formation of the Western Legal Tradition* (1983); E Cortese, *Il Rinascimento giuridico mediavale* (1992); generally on the *ius commune* see H Coing, *Die ursprüngliche Einheit der europäischen Rechtswissenschaft* (1968) (henceforth Coing, *Einheit*); H Coing, *Europäische Grundlagen des modernen Privatrechts* (1986); M Bellomo, *The Common Legal Past of Europe 1000–1800* (1995), 55; R C van Caenegem, *European Law in the Past and the Future* (2002), 13 ff, 24 ff.

on the same model, lawyers began systematically to penetrate the most important body of the Roman sources, the Digest (which had only recently been rediscovered) and to make it intellectually accessible. This was necessary, above all, because the Digest is not a systematically-structured piece of legislation or a textbook in the modern sense of the word, but a compilation of fragments from classical Roman legal writings, put together by Justinian in the sixth century. These writings themselves were full of controversy; furthermore, they originated from different stages of legal development. Nonetheless, the concepts, legal rules and maxims, systematic discoveries and models of argumentation from Roman law proved superior to the contemporary customary laws. Thus, the rationalisation of the law meant, to a significant degree, its Romanisation (and vice versa); and over the following centuries Roman law, as it had been moulded by Justinian and turned into a "legal science" (*Rechtswissenschaft*) by the lawyers of Bologna, conquered Europe. This was the "reception" of Roman law.[25] Three characteristic aspects may be emphasised.

The first of them is the truly European character of the tradition that was thus founded. Up until the time of the so-called *usus modernus pandectarum* in the seventeenth and eighteenth centuries, the whole of educated Europe formed a cultural unit; and law was a constituent part of that European culture.[26] This meant, for instance, that legal academics could receive their education in one country and accept a chair in another; that students were able to embark on a *peregrinatio academica* that could take them to a Dutch or French university, just as well as to a university in any of the many territories belonging to the Holy Roman Empire; and that the same textbooks and commentaries could be used in Alcala and Halle, in Orléans and Pavia, in Leiden, Oxford and Aberdeen.[27]

Secondly, the *ius commune* was distinguished by its inherent flexibility and capability of development. It thus became the basis of a European legal tradition. It was applied in practice and continued to be reinterpreted by successive

---

25 The standard account is by F Wieacker, *Privatrechtsgeschichte der Neuzeit*, 2nd edn (1967), 45 ff, 97 ff (trans by T Weir, *A History of Private Law in Europe* (1995)). For the significance of Roman law for European legal culture, see P Koschaker, *Europa und das römische Recht*, 4th edn (1966); R Zimmermann, "Europa und das römische Recht" (2002) 202 *Archiv für die civilistische Praxis* 243 ff. For an analysis of early modern German court practice, see P Oestmann, *Rechtsvielfalt vor Gericht* (2002).

26 This is the point of departure for H Coing's *opus magnum*, *Europäisches Privatrecht*, vol I (1985).

27 See, specifically for Roman-Dutch law, R Zimmermann, "Roman-Dutch Jurisprudence and its Contribution to European Private Law" (1992) 66 *Tulane LR* 1715; generally, see Coing, *Einheit* (note 24), 160 ff.

generations of jurists. In the process it was subject to a process of constant change and adaptation. It absorbed elements of Canon law and medieval moral theology, of mercantile custom and Natural law theory.[28] Moreover, it interacted with the local, regional and territorial laws applicable within a given area, and it took account of the requirements and value systems of contemporary society. Thus, the Roman law applied in early modern Europe was no longer the Roman law of antiquity; it was "Heutiges Römisches Recht", or an "usus modernus pandectarum".[29] In Holland it was dubbed Roman-Dutch law, in Friesland Roman-Frisian law and in Saxony *ius Romanum Saxonicum*. Many individual legal problems were solved differently by different lawyers at different times and in different parts of Europe. But these differences, by and large, were variations of a common theme, because the development of the law occurred within an established framework of sources and methods, of concepts, rules and arguments. It was a tradition marked as much by a considerable diversity as by a fundamental intellectual unity.[30]

## (2) *Ius commune* and codification

And finally: the *ius commune* constitutes a tradition which still informs our modern national legal systems.[31] This is not what many twentieth-century lawyers tended to think. "I simply do not believe that contemporary law has really grown from the old law, but I regard it as something new, created by the need of the present day and the sovereign will of the modern legislature", as an early twentieth-century German textbook writer expressed a widely held

---

28  R Zimmermann, *Roman Law, Contemporary Law, European Law: The Civilian Tradition Today* (2001) (henceforth Zimmermann, *Roman Law*), 158 ff.

29  See F C von Savigny, *System des heutigen Römischen Rechts*, eight vols (1840–1849); S Stryk, *Specimen usus moderni pandectarum* (first published between 1690 and 1712).

30  The theme is developed more fully in R Zimmermann, "The Civil Law in European Codes", in D L Carey Miller & R Zimmermann (eds), *The Civilian Tradition and Scots Law: Aberdeen Quincentenary Essays* (1997), 259 ff; and see, most recently, van Caenegem (note 24), *passim* (the subtitle of his book is, characteristically, *Unity and Diversity over Two Millennia*).

31  See, e.g., R Knütel, "Römisches Recht und deutsches Bürgerliches Recht", in W Ludwig (ed), *Die Antike in der europäischen Gegenwart* (1993), 43; D Johnston, "The Renewal of the Old" (1997) 56 *Cambridge LJ* 80; A Flessner, "Die Rechtsvergleichung als Kundin der Rechtsgeschichte" (1999) 7 *ZEuP* 513; E Bucher, "Rechtsüberlieferung und heutiges Recht" (2000) 8 *ZEuP* 394; E Picker, "Rechtsdogmatik und Rechtsgeschichte" (2001) 201 *Archiv für die civilistische Praxis* 763; J Gordley, "Why Look Backward" (2002) 50 *American Journal of Comparative Law* 657; A Bürge, "Das römische Recht als Grundlage für das Zivilrecht im künftigen Europa", in F Ranieri (ed), *Die Europäisierung der Rechtswissenschaft* (2002), 19; R Zimmermann, "Civil Code and Civil Law" (1994/5) 1 *Columbia Journal of European Law* 89; R Zimmermann, "Roman Law and the Harmonisation of Private Law in Europe", in Hartkamp & Hesselink, *Towards a European Civil Code*, 21 ff.

view after the German Civil Code had entered into force.[32] Lawyers in France or Austria, Prussia and the Netherlands had found similar words a century before, when the great codes of the age of Enlightenment had formally replaced the *ius commune*. A codification of private law, so it was assumed, contained a comprehensive and closed system of legal rules; it constituted an autonomous interpretational space. Thus, it contributed to a vertical as well as horizontal isolation of legal scholarship. The sense of continuity of the development of private law got lost. In reality, however, a code like the BGB has not been a radical turning point in German legal history.[33] For those who drafted the BGB did not, on a doctrinal level, intend their code to constitute a fresh start, a break with the past. On the contrary; they largely aimed at setting out, incorporating and consolidating "the legal achievements of centuries",[34] as they had been processed and refined by pandectist legal learning. Horst Heinrich Jakobs has, therefore, pointedly referred to the BGB as a codification "which does not contain the source of law in itself but has its source in the legal scholarship from which it was created".[35] And Bernhard Windscheid, the leading intellectual force behind the code, observed that the code "will be no more than a moment in the development, more tangible, certainly, than the ripple in a stream but, none the less, merely a ripple in the stream".[36] The BGB was designed to provide a framework for an "organically progressive legal science"[37] which was in itself an organic product of the Civilian tradition. It was in this spirit that the Imperial Court (*Reichsgericht*) started to interpret the BGB,[38] and it is in this spirit that we have learnt, once again, to question the radical separation

---

32 K Cosack, in H Planitz (ed), *Die Rechtswissenschaft der Gegenwart in Selbstdarstellungen*, vol I (1924), 16.

33 See R Zimmermann, "Das Bürgerliche Gesetzbuch und die Entwicklung des Bürgerlichen Rechts", in M Schmoeckel, J Rückert & R Zimmermann (eds), *Historisch-kritischer Kommentar zum BGB*, vol I (2003) (henceforth Schmoeckel et al, *Historisch-kritischer Kommentar*), Vor § 1, notes 1 ff with further references.

34 B Windscheid, "Die geschichtliche Schule in der Rechtswissenschaft", in B Windscheid, *Gesammelte Reden und Abhandlungen* (edited by P Oertmann) (1904), 75.

35 H H Jakobs, *Wissenschaft und Gesetzgebung im bürgerlichen Recht nach der Rechtsquellenlehre des 19. Jahrhunderts* (1983), 160. On the role of legal scholarship in the tradition of German law, see S Vogenauer, "An Empire of Light?: Learning and Lawmaking in the History of German Law" (2005) 2 *Cambridge LJ* 481

36 Windscheid (note 34), 76.

37 This was the vision of F C von Savigny, "Vom Beruf unserer Zeit für Gesetzgebung und Rechtswisenschaft", easily accessible today in H Hattenhauer (ed), *Thibaut und Savigny: Ihre programmatischen Schriften*, 2nd edn (2002), 126.

38 See the contributions to U Falk & H Mohnhaupt (eds), *Das bürgerliche Recht und seine Richter* (2000); Zimmermann, *Roman Law*, 53 ff.

between legal history and modern legal doctrine[39] and to rediscover that modern law cannot be understood in isolation; for the present is tied, indissolubly, to the past from which it has emerged.[40]

This is as true of the BGB as it is of the *Code Civil* and the other national codifications prevailing in modern Europe.[41] But it is equally true of the Principles of European Contract Law. They can be seen as the most recent fruit of a genuinely European legal experience.

## D. THE PRINCIPLES AS A CONTEMPORARY MANIFESTATION OF THE EUROPEAN LEGAL TRADITION

### (1) Common core

#### (a) Elements of contract law

In some respects the Principles do indeed specify a common core of the legal systems of the EU member states (to which Switzerland and Norway may be added). Basic concepts such as obligation, contract, damage, condition or solidarity may be mentioned in this context, and it is interesting to see that the French and English terminology is virtually identical in these five (and many other) cases. Reference may also be made to certain ideas fundamental to the understanding of contract law: a contract is concluded by way of offer and acceptance, the parties have to have the intention to be legally bound,[42] illegal and immoral contracts cannot be tolerated,[43] etc. But there are also individual requirements for specific legal rules which are identical in all Western European legal systems; set-off provides a good example, for it is generally agreed that the creditor of the one claim must be the debtor under the other, and vice versa (requirement of mutuality), that what the parties owe each other must be of the same kind, and that the cross-claim has to be due.[44] Of course, it must be borne in mind that the same concept can have a

---

39  On the development of which see Zimmermann, *Roman Law*, 22 ff.
40  See von Savigny (note 29), vol I, xiv f; F C von Savigny, "Ueber den Zweck dieser Zeitschrift" (1815) 1 *Zeitschrift für geschichtliche Rechtswissenschaft* 1.
41  For the *Code Civil*, see J Gordley, "Myths of the French Civil Code" (1994) 42 *American Journal of Comparative Law* 459.
42  On the reception in England, see A W B Simpson, "Innovation in Nineteenth Century Contract Law" (1975) 91 *LQR* 258 ff, 263 ff; J Gordley, *The Philosophical Origins of Modern Contract Doctrine* (1991), 139 ff, 175 ff; Zimmermann, *Obligations*, 571 f; generally, see H Kötz, *European Contract Law* (trans by T Weir), vol I (1997) (henceforth Kötz, *European Contract Law*), 16 ff (offer and acceptance), 71 ff (intention to enter a legal obligation).
43  Zimmermann, *Obligations*, 697 ff; Kötz, *European Contract Law*, 157 ff.
44  For details, see R Zimmermann, *Comparative Foundations of a European Law of Set-Off and Prescription* (2002) (henceforth Zimmermann, *Comparative Foundations*), 44 ff, 48 ff, 50 f.

somewhat different meaning in different legal systems and that a requirement such as the one that for a contract to come into existence the parties
must intend to be legally bound can have a different significance depending
on whether that legal system recognises other indicia of seriousness. Such
differences, however, are sometimes exaggerated. Thus, for example, it is
often said that the Anglo-American concept of contract does not so much
focus on the creation of obligations but on the creation of liability in case of
non-performance.[45] Yet, in Sir Guenter Treitel's textbook, a contract is
defined in words which are immediately comprehensible to Continental
lawyers, as "an agreement giving rise to obligations which are enforced or
recognised by law".[46] Some of these commonalities are based in the nature of
things (see, for example, the three requirements for set-off mentioned
above), whereas others are due to the fact that the respective doctrines derive
from the same historical roots; concerning the formation of contract these
roots lie in Natural law theory,[47] in other cases (the concept of an obligation,
or of a condition)[48] they reach back to Roman law.

### (b) Variations of a theme

It should have become apparent from what has been said about the nature of
the *ius commune* that it is of little interest to ask how many rules of Roman
law we find in the Principles. Roman law was the origin of much of modern
contract law but hardly any of its rules have survived in an unchanged form,
or have found an identical manifestation in all modern legal systems. Even
with regard to fairly abstract rules which are, in principle, agreed upon everywhere, we find subtle variations. The treatment of illegal and immoral contracts provides an example. All the rules contained in modern codifications
are based on Roman law: the *lex Non Dubium* of the Emperor Theodosius,
which elevated all statutory prohibitions to the status of *leges perfectae*,[49] and
the suppression of transactions *contra bonos mores* by the Roman jurists and
emperors.[50] Yet, while Article 20 I OR refers to "contracts with an illegal

---

45  This concept goes back to the pointed statements by O W Holmes, *The Common Law* (1881),
    297 ff.
46  Sir G Treitel, *The Law of Contract*, 10th edn (1999) (henceforth Treitel, *Contract*), 1. For a com-
    parative analysis see, most recently, C Coen, *Vertragsscheitern und Rückabwicklung* (2003),
    19 ff.
47  Gordley (note 42), 79 ff; and see D J Ibbetson, "Natural Law and Common Law" (2001) 5
    *Edinburgh LR* 15.
48  Zimmermann, *Obligations*, 1 ff, 716 ff.
49  Zimmermann, *Obligations*, 700 ff.
50  Zimmermann, *Obligations*, 706 ff.

content", § 134 BGB deals with a legal act "which violates a statutory prohibition" and Article 3:40(2) BW with the violation of a "mandatory rule of the law". The French and Italian codes relate the respective legal rule to their famous doctrines of *cause* or *causa*, though not in a completely identical manner ("The cause is illegal if it is prohibited by the law": Article 1133 Code Civil; "The causa is illegal if it is contrary to mandatory rules of law": Article 1343 Codice Civile). In Austria and Switzerland contracts infringing a statutory prohibition are void,[51] whereas § 134 BGB limits this sanction to cases where another legal consequence "does not follow from the statute". The Dutch code has a similar proviso though one referring to the intention of the statute.[52] Moreover, it renders a contract voidable rather than void where the mandatory rule of law which has been infringed merely aims at the protection of one of the parties to the contract. Infringement of the *boni mores* is dealt with in all the codes mentioned so far,[53] and it invariably leads to invalidity. In France, Italy and the Netherlands, however, *l'ordre public*, *l'ordine pubblico* and *openbare orde* are placed side by side with the *boni mores*.[54] English law distinguishes between statutory illegality and common law illegality; illegality at common law is said to exist, where a contract is against public policy.[55]

The Principles, too, retain the traditional bifurcation. On the one hand they declare a contract to be of no effect "to the extent that it is contrary to principles recognised as fundamental in the laws of the member states of the European Union".[56] This formulation is intended to avoid concepts such as the *boni mores* or public policy which carry a long history of different interpretations. On the other hand, the Principles deal with contracts infringing a "mandatory rule of law".[57] What is surprising, at first glance, is the great flexibility in determining the effect of statutory illegality. In the first place, regard must be had to the effect expressly prescribed in the mandatory rule of law itself. Where that rule does not expressly prescribe the effects of an infringement upon a contract, the contract may be declared to have full effect, to have some effect, to have no effect, or to be subject to modification. The decision has to be an appropriate and proportional response to the

---

51 Article 20 I OR; § 879 I ABGB.
52 Article 3:40(2) BW ("voor zover niet uit de strekking van de bepaling anders voortvloeit").
53 Article 1133 *Code Civil*; § 879 I ABGB; Article 20 I OR; § 138 BGB; Article 1343 *Codice Civile*; Article 3:40(1) BW.
54 Article 1133 *Code Civil*; Article 1343 *Codice Civile*; Article 3:40(1) BW.
55 See, e.g., E McKendrick, *Contract Law*, 5th edn (2003), ch 15.
56 Article 15:101 PECL.
57 Article 15:102 PECL.

infringement. A number of criteria are listed which have to be taken into account in this respect, among them the purpose of the rule which has been infringed and the seriousness of the infringement.[58] These criteria are also recognised in German law,[59] a country where the courts have arrogated to themselves a far-ranging discretion to decide about the invalidity or otherwise of transactions violating statutory prohibitions.[60] In particular, the courts do not confine themselves to the alternatives: validity or invalidity, but they also, under certain circumstances, uphold the contract in a modified form.[61] Basically, therefore, Article 15:102 PECL openly states what a rule like § 134 BGB hides behind a brief and clear-cut phrase. An inflexible rule along the lines of *"ex pacto illicito non oritur actio"* was also, incidentally, unknown to pre-Theodosian, classical Roman law where we find a graded system of *leges perfectae, leges minus quam perfectae* and *leges imperfectae.*[62]

## (c) Regulae iuris

At other places, however, the Principles contain a number of rules which can be regarded as modern versions of a *regula iuris* of the old *ius commune*. This is as true of the *contra proferentem* rule (interpretation of contract terms not individually negotiated against the party which has supplied them)[63] as it is of the provision that the true agreement prevails between parties who have concluded an apparent contract which was not intended to reflect their true agreement: *plus valere quod agitur quam quod simulate concipitur.*[64] A number of provisions in the law of extinctive prescription are based on a general principle coined or, at any rate, authoritatively established by Bartolus: *agere non valenti non currit praescriptio* (prescription does not run against a person who is unable to bring an action).[65] Thus, the running of the period of prescription is suspended as long as the creditor is prevented from pursuing his claim by an impediment which is beyond his control and which he could

---

58 Article 15:102(2), (3) PECL.

59 See O Jauernig, in O Jauernig (ed), *Bürgerliches Gesetzbuch*, 10th edn (2003), § 134 nn 14 f (purpose of the statute); H H Seiler, "Über verbotswidrige Rechtsgeschäfte (§ 134 BGB)", in *Gedächtnisschrift für Wolfgang Martens* (1987), 729 ff (seriousness of the infringement).

60 As analysed by Seiler (note 59), 725 ff.

61 F Dorn, in Schmoeckel et al, *Historisch-kritischer Kommentar*, §§ 134–137, nn 19 ff.

62 Zimmermann, *Obligations*, 697 ff.

63 Article 5:103 PECL; on the tradition of this rule, see Zimmermann, *Obligations*, 639 ff.

64 Article 6:103 PECL (according to the comparative notes to this rule it "is recognised in all Member States"); for the tradition, see Zimmermann, *Obligations*, 646 ff.

65 E Spiro, "Zur neueren Geschichte des Satzes 'agere non valenti non currit praescriptio'", in *Festschrift für Hans Lewald* (1953), 585 ff, 588; Zimmermann, *Comparative Foundations*, 132 f.

not reasonably have been expected to avoid or overcome.[66] The postponement of expiry in case of incapacity is based on the same notion,[67] as is the postponement of expiry in cases where either the creditor or the debtor has died,[68] and also the practically very important rule that the running of the period of prescription is suspended as long as the creditor does not know, and could not reasonably know of, the identity of the debtor, or the facts giving rise to his claim.[69] The regulation of partial invalidity contained in the Principles corresponds much better to the rule of *utile per inutile non vidiatur*[70] than § 139 BGB, for Article 15:103 PECL establishes a presumption that the remaining part of the contract continues to be valid. Since, however, this rule is subject to an equally far-ranging proviso as the contrary rule of § 139 BGB, both the Principles and German law effectively grant the judge a wide discretion to determine the consequences of partial invalidity according to reasonable interests of the parties.[71] This was also, in fact, the approach adopted by the classical Roman jurists.[72] Much less flexibility is displayed by German law in the application of § 817, 2 BGB, i.e. a codified version of *in pari turpitudine causa est melior possidentis*.[73] This is in marked contrast to the way the maxim was applied by the Roman jurists.[74] The Principles no longer contain a specific rule to this effect. Nonetheless, the idea of *in pari turpitudine* is hidden in the restitution rule of Article 15:104 PECL where the decision whether to grant restitution is made dependent upon criteria such as the purpose of the rule which has been infringed, the category of persons for whose protection the rule exists, and the seriousness of the infringement.[75]

---

66  Article 14:303 PECL.
67  Article 14:305 PECL.
68  Article 14:306 PECL.
69  Article 14:301 PECL; on which rule, see Zimmermann, *Comparative Foundations*, 106 f.
70  On which see Zimmermann, *Obligations*, 75 ff.
71  While, according to Article 15:103 PECL, the remaining part of the contract continues in effect "unless, giving due consideration to all the circumstances of the case, it is unreasonable to uphold it", § 139 BGB focuses on the (usually hypothetical) will of the parties when it states that the entire transaction is void "unless it may be assumed that it would have been entered into even without the invalid part"; see Dorn, in Schmoeckel et al, *Historisch-kritischer Kommentar*, §§ 139–141, n 18.
72  H H Seiler, "Utile per inutile non vitiatur", in *Festschrift für Max Kaser* (1976), 127 ff.
73  Zimmermann, *Obligations*, 863 ff.
74  H H Seiler, "§ 817 S 2 BGB und das römische Recht", in *Festschrift für Wilhelm Felgentraeger* (1969), 381 ff; Zimmermann, *Obligations*, 846 ff.
75  For an interesting account of the experiences of two mixed jurisdictions, see H MacQueen & A Cockrell, "Illegal Contracts", in R Zimmermann, D Visser & K Reid (eds), *Mixed Legal Systems in Comparative Perspective: Property and Obligations in Scotland and South Africa* (2004) (henceforth Zimmermann, Visser & Reid, *Mixed Legal Systems*), 143 ff. One of the authors, H MacQueen, was the reporter for the Chapter on illegality in the Land Commission.

## (d) Good faith

Most of the Latin legal maxims just mentioned have found their way into the modern national codifications. Thus, they belong to the common historical heritage of European private law. The same is true, to a large extent, for the principle contained in Article 1:201 PECL: "Each party must act in accordance with good faith and fair dealing." The tradition of this provision reaches back to one of the most fertile agents in the development of Roman law: the notion of *bona fides*.[76] Under the *ius commune*, it continued to constitute a vital mechanism for the implementation of substantive justice.[77] Also today, the principle of good faith in the exercise, performance and determination of contractual rights and duties is recognised in some or other form in all the legal systems of the European Union.[78] Many of them contain a general provision along the lines of Article 1:201 PECL. The significance attributed to these provisions can differ substantially, depending, *inter alia*, on which other doctrines are available to reach an equitable result.[79] The draftsmen of the Principles, too, have attempted to limit the recourse to Article 1:201 PECL by laying down a number of individual rules which can be seen as specific manifestations of the principles of good faith and, at the same time, of a common core of evaluations. Thus, each party owes to the other a duty to co-operate in order to give full effect to the contract;[80] parties have a duty not to enter into negotiations in the knowledge that they will not conclude a contract with the other side;[81] they may not disclose confidential information provided by the other party in the course of negotiations;[82] nor are they allowed to take advantage of each other's improvidence, ignorance, inexperience or lack of bargaining skills in a way which is grossly unfair.[83] The requirements of good faith and fair dealing play an important role in the implication of terms into a contract;[84] they provide support for rules like the ones on the quality of

---

76 S Whittaker & R Zimmermann, "Good Faith in European Contract Law: surveying the landscape", in R Zimmermann & S Whittaker (eds), *Good Faith in European Contract Law* (2000) (henceforth Zimmermann & Whittaker, *Good Faith*), 16 ff; and see, for a detailed account, M J Schermaier, "Bona fides in Roman contract law", in the same volume, 63 ff.

77 J Gordley, "Good faith in contract law in the medieval ius commune", in Zimmermann & Whittaker, *Good Faith*, 93 ff; F Ranieri, "Bonne foi et exercice du droit dans la tradition du civil law", 1998 *Revue internationale de droit comparé* 1055 ff.

78 See the case studies in Zimmermann & Whittaker, *Good Faith*, 143 ff.

79 See S Whittaker & R Zimmermann, "Coming to terms with good faith", in Zimmermann & Whittaker, *Good Faith*, 653 ff.

80 Article 1:202 PECL.

81 Article 2:301(2) PECL.

82 Article 2:302 PECL.

83 Article 4:109 PECL.

84 Article 6:102 PECL.

performance[85] or change of circumstances;[86] they allow a party to cure a non-conforming tender which has been made before the time for performance had arrived[87] and to refuse specific performance, if this would cause him unreasonable effort or expense.[88] The provisions on the postponement of the expiry of a period of prescription in case of negotiations[89] and on the interference with conditions[90] are also expressions of the principle of good faith.

## (2) Convergence and tradition

In a great number of cases legal rules and institutions have been developed under the *ius commune*, often on the basis of individual points of departure in the Roman sources, which have, as such, been unknown to the Romans or have even turned established principles on their head. *Pacta sunt servanda* provides an important example. The principle is recognised in all modern European legal systems, and thus also in the Principles, but it was established, in pointed contrast to the Roman maxim *ex nudo pacto non oritur actio*, by the medieval Canon lawyers.[91] In a number of cases the codes of the first great wave of codifications still reflect an older stage within the development of the *ius commune* whereas the codifications from around the time of 1900 contain the more modern solutions. They have been able to benefit from the results of pandectist legal scholarship which, in the famous words of Rudolf von Jhering, sometimes managed to move beyond Roman law by means of Roman law.[92] This can be illustrated by comparing the two most influential codifications of both periods, the French *Code Civil* and the German BGB. The solutions adopted by the BGB have often shaped the course of legal development – whether by way of legal scholarship or legislation – in other European countries and have sometimes even significantly influenced French law. Unsurprisingly, in these cases, the Principles endorse what can be regarded as the latest stage in the development of the *ius commune*.

---

85  Article 6:108 PECL.
86  Article 6:111 PECL.
87  Article 8:104 PECL.
88  Article 9:102(2)(b) PECL.
89  Article 14:304 PECL.
90  Article 16:102 PECL.
91  Zimmermann, *Obligations*, 537 ff; most recently, see P Landau, "Pacta sunt servanda: Zu den kanonistischen Grundlagen der Privatautonomie", in *"Ins Wasser geworfen und Ozeane durchquert": Festschrift für Knut Wolfgang Nörr* (2003), 457 ff.
92  R von Jhering, *Geist des römischen Rechts auf den verschiedenen Stufen seiner Entwicklung*, vol I, 6th edn (1907), 14.

## (a) Stipulatio alteri

This is true, for example, for the contract in favour of third parties.[93] Generations of jurists from the time of the Glossators had attempted, with much imagination and on the basis of some scattered indications in the Roman sources, to restrict, or possibly even unhinge, the Roman principle of *per extraneam personam nobis adquiri non potest*. But it was only in the seventeenth century that the great breakthrough towards the acceptance of the *stipulatio alteri* had taken place. For some time it was required, however, that the third party had to have accepted the right offered to him on account of the contract between the other two parties, and it was in the guise of this consensual construction that the contract in favour of third parties entered the Prussian, Bavarian and Saxonian codifications. The Austrian and French codes were even more conservative.[94] Thus, it was only the BGB that managed fully to emancipate itself from the Roman concept of an obligation as a *vinculum iuris* that attains its individuality by virtue of having been created between two specific parties and thus permitted the third party directly to acquire a right to claim under the contract in his favour.[95] Many subsequent codifications have received this model[96] and even the French courts have dropped, in the course of time, the restrictive requirements contained in Article 1165 *Code Civil*.[97] Thus, Article 6:110(1) PECL reflects a broad consensus among European legal systems[98] and one that can indeed be described as a "progressive development"[99] of the *ius commune*.

## (b) Direct representation

The concept of direct representation also had to struggle for many centuries against the Roman notion that nobody can be bound, or entitled, as a result of a contract concluded between two other parties.[100] By the end of the

---

93  For what follows, see Zimmermann, *Obligations*, 34 ff.

94  § 881 ABGB in its original form; Articles 1165, 1221 *Code Civil*.

95  § 328 BGB.

96  § 881 ABGB, as amended in 1916; Articles 410 f *Astikos Kodikas*; Article 1411 *Codice Civile*; Article 6:253 BW.

97  See K Zweigert & H Kötz, *An Introduction to Comparative Law* (trans by T Weir), 3rd edn (1998) (henceforth Zweigert & Kötz, *Comparative Law*), 462 ff; Zimmermann, *Obligations*, 44.

98  However, this principle is inappropriately jeopardised by Article 6:110(3) PECL; for criticism, see R Zimmermann, "Vertrag und Versprechen: Deutsches Recht und Principles of European Contract Law im Vergleich", in *Festschrift für Andreas Heldrich* (2005), 467 ff. For an implementation of the same basic idea which is both much clearer and more sensible, see the Unidroit Principles of International Commercial Contracts, as recently amended by Article 5.2.1.

99  Lando & Beale (note 6), xxiv.

100  For what follows, see Zimmermann, *Obligations*, 45 ff.

seventeenth century the struggle had essentially been won, and so the *Code Civil* does indeed recognise the possibility of direct representation. However, the draftsmen of the Code did not conceive of it as an independent legal institution in its own right but, following Pothier, as something associated with the contract of agency.[101] It was only in the course of the nineteenth century that Jhering and Laband introduced the conceptual distinction between the grant of authority and the legal relationship on the basis of which the agent is entitled to act for the principal.[102] The separation between what can be termed the external and the internal relationship characterises the regulation contained in the BGB, and the Greek, Italian and Dutch codes have followed suit.[103] In France, too, there has been a considerable modification of the traditional perspective; nearly every textbook on the law of obligations today contains an independent chapter on *représentation*.[104] The Principles, entirely in tune with the more modern codes, confine themselves to a regulation of the external relationship;[105] this is also, incidentally, in accordance with the Geneva Convention on Agency in the International Sale of Goods.[106]

### (c) Change of circumstances

Somewhat less straightforward was the development of an idea contained today in § 313 BGB (failure of the basis of a legal transaction).[107] Moral philosophers of antiquity had been the first to draw attention to the fact that, after conclusion of a contract, circumstances may arise which completely reverse the evaluation of the debtor's obligation: compliance with the contract can become a sin, non-compliance the debtor's moral duty. It was from this seed that in the high Middle Ages the doctrine of *clausula rebus sic stantibus* began to germinate. It blossomed in the sixteenth and seventeenth centuries but lost support from the eighteenth century onwards. The principle of *pacta sunt servanda* was now accentuated; and a general proviso *"rebus sic stantibus"* appeared to shake confidence in legal and commercial certainty. Thus, the

---

101  See, e.g., J Kleinschmidt, "Stellvertretungsrecht in Deutschland und Frankreich: Perspektiven für eine Rechtsvereinheitlichung" (2001) 9 *ZEuP* 700.
102  See Kötz, *European Contract Law*, 220 f; Zweigert & Kötz, *Comparative Law*, 434 f.
103  §§ 164 ff BGB; Articles 211 ff *Astikos Kodikas*; Articles 1387 ff *Codice Civile*; Articles 3:60 ff BW.
104  Kleinschmidt (2001) 9 *ZEuP* 700 f; Kötz, *European Contract Law*, 221.
105  Articles 3:101 ff PECL.
106  Radley-Gardner et al, *Fundamental Texts*, 283 ff. The Convention was concluded in 1983 but has not, as yet, entered into effect.
107  For what follows, see Zimmermann, *Obligations*, 579 ff.

*clausula* doctrine made its way neither into the *Code Civil* nor (in spite of Bernhard Windscheid's support for a modified version of it)[108] into the BGB. This very rigid point of view, until very recently, continued to prevail in France; for the *théorie de l'imprévision* was adopted only in administrative law and used to be rejected for dispute resolution in private law.[109] Only in the last few years has a certain relaxation occurred insofar as, in cases of a change of circumstances entailing a significant imbalance in the contractual allocation of rights and duties, the disadvantaged party is granted a right to ask for a renegotiation of the contract.[110] German courts, on the other hand, had started, soon after the BGB had entered into effect, to turn the decision of its drafts-men not to recognise the *clausula rebus sic stantibus* on its head;[111] in response to the problems posed by the consequences of the First World War on the performance of long-term contracts the doctrine of *Wegfall der Geschäfts-grundlage* was established by the Imperial Court on these foundations.[112] In the course of the "modernisation" of the German law of obligations[113] it was received into the Code. The Principles contain a rule which is very similar as far as both its structure and the evaluations supporting it are concerned.[114]

*(d) Determination of price*

Determination of the price is another problem area where French law appears to be out of step with modern legal development in Europe. Article 1108 *Code Civil* requires every contract to have "un objet certain". Object, in terms of this rule and in terms of Article 1129 is also, for instance, the counterperformance to be given for the performance of services, for the rent of an apartment, etc. Article 1591 *Code Civil* goes even further in requiring, for the contract of sale, that the purchase price has to be determined and indicated by the parties. The *Code Civil*, in this respect, is unmistakably

---

108  For Windscheid's presupposition doctrine (*Voraussetzungslehre*), see U Falk, *Ein Gelehrter wie Windscheid* (1989), 193 ff.

109  Zweigert & Kötz, *Comparative Law*, 524 ff.

110  B Fages, "Einige neuere Entwicklungen des französischen allgemeinen Vertragsrechts im Lichte der Grundregeln der Lando-Kommission" (2003) 11 ZEuP 519 f.

111  K Luig, "Die Kontinuität allgemeiner Rechtsgrundsätze: Das Beispiel der clausula rebus sic stantibus", in R Zimmermann, R Knütel & J P Meincke (eds), *Rechtsgeschichte und Privat-rechtsdogmatik* (2000), 171 ff.

112  J Emmert, *Auf der Suche nach den Grenzen vertraglicher Leistungspflichten* (2001), 247 ff; C Reiter, *Vertrag und Geschäftsgrundlage im deutschen und italienischen Recht* (2002), 36 ff.

113  On which see R Zimmermann, "Modernizing the German Law of Obligations?", in Peter Birks & Arianna Pretto (eds), *Themes in Comparative Law in Honour of Bernard Rudden* (2002), 265 ff.

114  Article 6:111 PECL.

influenced by the Roman *certum pretium* requirement.[115] According to Article 6:104 PECL, on the other hand, the parties are to be treated as having agreed on a reasonable price where the contract does not fix the price or the method of determining it. Where the price is to be determined by one party, and that party's determination is grossly unreasonable, a reasonable price has to be substituted.[116] The Principles thus follow, essentially, the more liberal regime laid down in § 315 BGB.[117] It is based on pandectist doctrine.[118] In the meantime, however, the *Assemblée plénière* of the *Cour de Cassation* has executed a spectacular volte face and no longer regards uncertainty of the price as an obstacle to the validity of a contract.[119] However, this new approach (which mirrors the rules contained in the Principles)[120] does not yet relate to the contract of sale which continues to be subject to the strict regime of Article 1591 *Code Civil*.

## (e) Conventional penalties

Contractual penalty provisions have always been regarded as permissible in the Civilian tradition.[121] What was disputed, for a long time, was whether even grossly excessive sums agreed upon by the parties have to be accepted as valid. The *Code Civil* used to leave determination of the amount of the penalty in the discretion of the parties.[122] The BGB, on the other hand, accepts a judicial right of reduction to a reasonable amount.[123] The decisive impulse towards recognition of such an exceptional right to modify a contractual provision was given by the medieval Canon lawyers.[124] This is the tradition

---

115  On which see  Zimmermann, *Obligations*, 253 ff.
116  Article 6:105 PECL.
117  At the same time, the Principles go further than Article 55 CISG. On the controversies preceding the adoption of that rule, and on the apparent contradiction between Article 55 CISG and Article 14 CISG, see G Hager, in P Schlechtriem, *Kommentar zum Einheitlichen Kaufrecht*, 3rd edn (2000) (henceforth Schlechtriem, *Kommentar*), Article 55, notes 1 ff; P Schlechtriem, in the same commentary, Article 14, notes 8 ff; cf also Kötz, *European Contract Law*, 18 f.
118  H-J Winter, *Die Bestimmung der Leistung durch den Vertragspartner oder Dritte (§§ 315 bis 319 BGB) unter besonderer Berücksichtigung der Rechtsprechung und Lehre des 19. Jahrhunderts*, Dr iur thesis, Frankfurt/Main (1979).
119  See Kötz, *European Contract Law*,  50 f; C Witz & G Wolter, "Das Ende der Problematik des unbestimmten Preises in Frankreich" (1996) 4 *ZEuP* 648 ff; Fages (2003) 11 *ZEuP* 521 ff.
120  Fages (2003) 11 *ZEuP* 523.
121  Zimmermann, *Obligations*, 95 ff.
122  See R-P Sossna, *Die Geschichte der Begrenzung von Vertragsstrafen* (1993), 144 ff. *Contra*: § 1336 II ABGB.
123  § 343 BGB.
124  Sossna (note 122), 64 ff. On the controversies surrounding the adoption of this "anomalous" right into the BGB, see Sossna, 165 ff.

which, apart from German law, has also moulded the respective provisions in the Greek, Italian and Dutch codes[125] and which now also finds its expression in Article 9:509 PECL. Even the French Code was revised in 1975 so as to allow a judicial reduction of excessive conventional penalties.[126]

## (f) Set-off

Set-off, according to Article 1290 *Code Civil* operates *ipso iure*: as soon as two obligations capable of being set off against each other confront each other, both of them are extinguished "de plein droit par la seule force de la loi, même à l'insu des débiteurs". This pronouncement is based on two sources from the *Corpus Juris Civilis*.[127] The BGB, on the contrary, requires set-off to be asserted by an extra-judicial, informal and unilateral declaration to the other party.[128] The draftsmen of the German code, in this respect, focused their attention on a Constitution by Justinian which appeared to indicate that set-off specifically had to be raised, or pleaded, by the defendant in the course of legal proceedings.[129] Above all, however, they based their decision on the case law of the Supreme Courts in Germany during the second half of the nineteenth century, where it had come to be recognised that even an extra-judicial declaration of the intention to set off two claims against each other had the effect of extinguishing these claims.[130] The German model of set-off subsequently gained acceptance in many European countries; it has been followed in Austrian law (in spite of the fact that § 1438 ABGB appears to endorse the *ipso iure* effect of set-off),[131] in Greece and in the Dutch Civil Code.[132] It also enjoys widespread support in Italian law.[133] French courts and legal writers have also found it impractical literally to implement the regime

---

125  Article 409 *Astikos Kodikas*; Article 1384 *Codice Civile*; Article 6:94 BW. For a comparative survey, see G H Treitel, *Remedies for Breach of Contract: A Comparative Account* (1988) (henceforth Treitel, *Remedies*), 223 ff; and see H Schelhaas, "The judicial power to reduce a penalty" (2004) 12 ZEuP 386 ff.

126  Article 1152 II *Code Civil*.

127  Inst IV, 6, 30; C 4, 31, 14 pr.; on the Justinianic law, see P Pichonnaz, *La compensation: Analyse historique et comparative des modes de compenser non conventionnels* (2001) (henceforth Pichonnaz, *La compensation*), 260 ff; on the development in France, see Pichonnaz, 386 ff.

128  § 388 BGB.

129  C 4, 31, 14, 1 ("Ita tamen compensationes obici iubemus"; "opponi compensationem").

130  On the development in Germany, see R Zimmermann, in R. Zimmermann, J Rückert & M Schmoeckel (eds), *Historisch-kritischer Kommentar zum BGB*, vol II (in preparation), (henceforth *Zimmermann et al, Historisch-kritischer Kommentar*) §§ 387–396, notes 12 ff.

131  See P Rummel, in P Rummel (ed), *Kommentar zum Allgemeinen bürgerlichen Gesetzbuch*, vol II, 2nd edn (1992), § 1438, nn 11 f; S Dullinger, *Handbuch der Aufrechnung* (1995), 96 ff.

132  Article 441 *Astikos Kodikas*; Articles 6:127 (1), 6:129 BW.

133  In spite of Article 1242 *Codice Civile*; see G Cian, "Hundert Jahre BGB aus italienischer Sicht" (1998) 6 ZEuP 220 f.

envisaged by Article 1290 *Code Civil*. Following the lead provided by pandectist scholarship they have effectively attributed decisive influence to the will of one of the parties to bring about the mutual extinction of the obligation.[134] As a result, there may indeed be said to be a "convergence avancée"[135] which is reflected in the provision of Article 13:104 PECL.

### (g) Other examples

In all the examples mentioned above the point of convergence is defined by developments which have moulded the last codification directly based on the old European *ius commune*. The list of such examples could easily be extended. Thus, for example, the Principles expressly reject the *causa* doctrine of the Romanistic legal family.[136] A party's right to terminate a contract for non-performance is to be exercised, just as in German law, by notice to the other party.[137] French law, on the other hand, traditionally requires court proceedings to effect termination.[138] Remarkably, however, the *Cour de Cassation* has recently recognised the possibility of an extra-judicial termination of the contract.[139] Contrary to French law, but as in § 254 BGB, contributory negligence and failure to reduce the loss suffered are treated alike.[140] Damages claims based on *culpa in contrahendo*, according to Articles 2:301 and 2:302 PECL, are regarded as a matter of contract law rather than delict. The fulfilment of a condition does not (as in French law) operate retrospectively but has prospective effect (as in German law).[141] In this latter instance neither the one nor the other solution can be said to have a greater historical legitimacy;[142] what can be said in favour of the German solution has been summed up by Bernhard Windscheid: retrospectivity is an awkward legal construct that should be avoided as far as possible.[143]

---

134  Pichonnaz, *La compensation*, 505 ff; Zimmermann, in Zimmermann et al, *Historisch-kritischer Kommentar* §§ 387–396, n 21.
135  Pichonnaz, *La compensation*, 601 ff.
136  See Article 2:101(1) ("without any further requirement"); Lando & Beale (note 6), 140.
137  Article 9:303 (1) PECL.
138  Article 1184 *Code Civil*; see Treitel, *Remedies*, 323 ff.
139  See Fages (2003) 11 *ZEuP* 523 f.
140  Articles 9:504 f PECL; for a comparative survey, see Treitel, *Remedies*, 179 ff; Lando & Beale (note 6), 447 f.
141  Article 16:103 PECL; for French law, see Article 1179 *Code Civil*; for German law, see § 158 BGB.
142  Zimmermann, *Obligations*, 726 ff.
143  B Windscheid, *Lehrbuch des Pandektenrechts*, vol II, 7th edn (1891), § 349, 4 (note 12 *in fine*).

## (3) International legal development

Set-off, conditions, conventional penalties, contracts in favour of a third party, the determination of the price: all of the doctrines discussed in the previous section belong to the traditional themes of the old *ius commune*. The Principles of European Contract Law, in these instances, take up and extend into contemporary European law centuries-old lines of development. They build on the historical experience of European private law. There are other areas of the law, however, where none of the codifications directly based on traditional Civilian doctrine contains a satisfactory set of rules. Here we have to look at more recent developments which, in spite of a far-reaching nationalisation of private law and private law scholarship, still occasionally display a common pattern. Comparative analysis of these patterns of development provides the basis for devising a modern uniform regime which can still be described as an attempt intellectually to penetrate, organically to adapt, rejuvenate, and bring up to date the legal material that has come down to us.[144] One of these areas is the law of extinctive prescription. Here we find in the old codifications (France, Austria, Germany) still the general prescription period of thirty years derived from the old *ius commune,* but also a bewildering variety of shorter periods for many special situations.[145] This regime has very widely been regarded as unsatisfactory: it is incoherent, unnecessarily complex, outdated, uncertain, unfair and inefficient.[146] Thus, for instance, in Germany the law of prescription was one of the central items of the agenda of modernising the law of obligations. If we look at the development of the law of prescription, at new enactments and proposed drafts in European countries as well as internationally, we find three dominant trends which fall in line with general considerations of policy.[147] In the first place, there is a clear tendency towards shorter periods of prescription. Secondly, there is an equally clear development favouring uniformity. And in the third place, and closely related to the general tendency towards shorter

---

144 Savigny (1815) 1 *Zeitschrift für geschichtliche Rechtswissenschaft* 6.

145 For Germany, see R Zimmermann, "Extinctive Prescription in German Law", in E Jayme (ed), *German National Reports in Civil Law Matters for the XIVth Congress of Comparative Law in Athens 1994* (1994), 153 ff; for further country reports, see E H Hondius (ed), *Extinctive Prescription: On the Limitation of Actions* (1995).

146 These are the words chosen, for England, by the Law Commission in its Consultation Paper No 151 (1998), entitled "Limitation of Actions", 241 ff. For France, see A Bénabent, "Le chaos du droit de la prescription extinctive", in *Mélanges dédiés à Louis Boyer* (1996), 123 ff; for Germany, see F Peters & R Zimmermann, "Verjährungsfristen", in Bundesminister der Justiz (ed), *Gutachten und Vorschläge zur Überarbeitung des Schuldrechts*, vol I (1981), 186 ff.

147 For what follows, see Zimmermann, *Comparative Foundations*, 76 ff.

periods of prescription, the idea has been gaining ground that prescription should not run unless the creditor knew (or ought reasonably to have known) about his claim. A fourth characteristic of a modern prescription regime, incidentally, follows from the latter point: a maximum period after which no claim may be brought, regardless of the creditor's knowledge, appears to be necessary as a counterbalance to the discoverability principle. The model sketched in these few lines provides the basis for the regulation contained in Chapter 14 of the Principles: more consistently so than in the BGB after the modernisation of the law of obligations[148] where we still find, for instance, a special regime for damages claims based on the seller's liability for latent defects.[149]

## (4) Uniform law

### (a) CISG and the European legal tradition

The most important text both documenting and shaping the international development in central areas of the law of obligations is the United Nations Convention on Contracts for the International Sale of Goods (CISG). It has been ratified, so far, by twelve of the EU member states.[150] This means that international commercial sales are governed by the same rules in the greater part of the European Union. Moreover, CISG has significantly influenced the Consumer Sales Directive[151] and it has played an important role in national law reforms concerning the law of sale and breach of contract.[152] Obviously,

---

148    For a comparative evaluation, see R Zimmermann, "Das neue deutsche Verjährungsrecht – ein Vorbild für Europa?", in I Koller, H Roth & R Zimmermann, *Schuldrechtsmodernisierungsgesetz 2002* (2002), 9 ff.

149    For criticism, see D Leenen, "Die Neuregelung der Verjährung" (2001) *Juristenzeitung* 552 ff; R Zimmermann, D Leenen, H-P Mansel & W Ernst, "Finis Litium? Zum Verjährungsrecht nach dem Regierungsentwurf eines Schuldrechtsmodernisierungsgesetzes" (2001) *Juristenzeitung* 688 ff. The matter has been solved more satisfactorily in the new Austrian law: §§ 932 ff ABGB; see R Welser, B Jud, *Die neue Gewährleistung, Kurzkommentar* (2001).

150    See the table of ratification in Radley-Gardner et al, *Fundamental Texts*, 239 f.

151    See S Grundmann, in Bianca & Grundmann, *EU Sales Directive*, Introduction, nn 1 ff; U Magnus, "The CISG's Impact on European Legislation", in F Ferrari (ed), *The 1980 Uniform Sales Law: Old Issues Revisited in the Light of Recent Experiences* (2003), 129 ff. The correspondence between these two international instruments will significantly contribute to the emergence of a common framework of reference for the development of sales law in Europe; see Heutger (2003) 11 *ERPL* 155 ff.

152    For Germany, see Bundesminister der Justiz (ed), *Abschlussbericht der Kommission zur Überarbeitung des Schuldrechts* (1992), 19 f; P Schlechtriem, "Rechtsvereinheitlichung in Europa und Schuldrechtsreform in Deutschland" (1993) 1 *ZEuP* 217 ff; P Schlechtriem, "10 Jahre CISG – Der Einfluss des UN-Kaufrechts auf die Entwicklung des deutschen und des internationalen Schuldrechts" (2001) 1 *Internationales Handelsrecht* 12 ff; generally, see the references in Schlechtriem, *Kommentar*, sub III. 4.

therefore, the draftsmen of the Principles have also been guided by an instrument which is not only of great significance today but can be seen as a contemporary emanation of a genuinely European tradition. It is based on the (Hague) Uniform Laws on the International Sale of Goods and on the Formation of Contracts for the International Sale of Goods. The driving force behind these Uniform Laws was Ernst Rabel: a scholar who always emphasised the vital connection between past and present, who consistently looked at legal history in order to comprehend the modern law[153] and who produced a treatise on the law of sale of goods which can still be seen as the model of a modern monograph which is historical and comparative at the same time.[154] With this monograph Rabel laid the foundations for the harmonisation of modern sales (and implicitly also central areas of general contract) law.

### (b) Breach of contract

No less than fifty-two of the 132 articles contained in the first two parts of PECL are modelled on a provision contained in CISG. Very often, however, there are phrasing changes or modifications.[155] Obviously, breach of contract and formation of contract are the two areas where the influence of CISG has been most prominent. The law relating to breach of contracts has been devised, in both texts, from the point of view of the remedies rather than of the different types of breach. The remedies of termination[156] and damages,[157] the concept of fundamental non-performance,[158] excuse due to an impediment beyond the debtor's control[159] and anticipatory non-performance[160] are essential structural elements taken over into the Principles from CISG. Specific performance is a problem before which CISG has capitulated;[161] the Principles have attempted to find a compromise solution bridging the differences between the Common Law and Civil Law approaches.[162] For the right to

153  R Zimmermann, "'In der Schule von Ludwig Mitteis': Ernst Rabels rechtshistorische Ursprünge" (2001) 65 *RabelsZ* 1 ff.
154  G Kegel, in G Kleinheyer & J Schröder (eds), *Deutsche und Europäische Juristen aus neun Jahrhunderten*, 4th edn (1996), 504.
155  See the table in H M Flechtner, "The CISG's Impact on International Unification Efforts: The Unidroit Principles of International Commercial Contracts and the Principles of European Contract Law", in Ferrari (note 151), 169 ff (181 ff).
156  Articles 9:301 ff PECL.
157  Articles 9:501 ff PECL.
158  Article 8:103 PECL.
159  Article 8:108 PECL.
160  Article 9:304 PECL.
161  See Article 28 CISG; on which, see U Huber, in Schlechtriem, *Kommentar*, Article 28, nn 1 ff.
162  Article 9:102 PECL.

withhold performance the Principles – in contrast to CISG[163] – present a uniform solution in the tradition of the *exceptio non adimpleti contractus*;[164] the rules on *restitutio in integrum* after termination for non-performance deviate from the unsatisfactory model in CISG[165] (though, in this instance, they happen to be even more unsatisfactory);[166] and price reduction has been turned into a general remedy which far exceeds the scope of application of Article 50 CISG.[167]

## (c) Formation of contracts

Concerning the mechanism for concluding a contract, both sets of rules very largely correspond to each other (requirements for an offer to become effective, revocation of an offer, requirements of an acceptance, modified acceptance, late acceptance, revocation of acceptance).[168] It is obvious that the draftsmen of the Principles have followed the lead provided by CISG. However, once again, they have modified a number of details and have also decided certain disputes arising from the application of CISG. One such dispute, which is of considerable practical importance, relates to the question whether the fixing of a time for acceptance makes an offer irrevocable. The compromise solution contained in Article 16(2) CISG can be interpreted differently by contracting parties from a country such as England where offers are always revocable and by offerors and offerees from a country such as Germany where an offeror is normally bound by his offer.[169] Article 2:202 PECL determines that a revocation of an offer is ineffective if it states a fixed time for its acceptance. This rule endorses the continental view: the fixing of a period for acceptance always renders an offer irrevocable.

---

163   But see now C Kern, "Ein einheitliches Zurückbehaltungsrecht im UN-Kaufrecht?" (2000) 8 *ZEuP* 837 ff.

164   Article 9:201 PECL. On the *exceptio non adimpleti contractus*, see W Ernst, *Die Einrede des nichterfüllten Vertrages* (2000).

165   Articles 81 ff CISG; for criticism, see U Magnus, in Staudinger, *Kommentar zum Bürgerlichen Gesetzbuch, Wiener UN-Kaufrecht* (Neubearbeitung 1999), Article 82, n 4; M Krebs, *Die Rückabwicklung im UN-Kaufrecht* (2000), 91 ff; H G Leser & R Hornung, in Schlechtriem, *Einheitlichen*, Article 82, nn 16 ff and Article 84, n 27a.

166   For criticism see Zimmermann (note 8).

167   Article 9:401 PECL. The Principles, insofar, reflect an international tendency; see A Sandrock, *Vertragswidrigkeit der Sachleistung* (2003), 209 ff.

168   For details, see E Luig, *Der internationale Vertragsschluss* (2002), 33 ff.

169   Schlechtriem, in Schlechtriem, *Kommentar*, Article 16, n 10; E Luig (note 168), 121 ff.

## (d) Other international Conventions

Obviously, therefore, the draftsmen of the Principles have critically examined the international Conventions establishing patches of uniform law, and
they have attempted productively to develop the ideas contained in these
instruments.[170] A similarly critical attitude has, however, also been adopted in
other areas of the law where we do not yet have genuinely international (or
European) texts providing a convenient starting point for critical reflection,
for occasionally the Principles have found and adopted an unconventional
solution which does not even reflect a prevailing view among the European
legal systems, let alone restate their common core. Even in these instances,
however, we can refer to a "progressive development"[171] within the intellectual framework established by the old *ius commune*. Two examples will
demonstrate this assertion.

## (5) "Progressive development"

### (a) Once again: set-off

Everywhere in Europe, except for Scandinavia, Ireland, and England and
Wales (i.e. in all countries where Roman law has been received in this respect),
set-off operates in one of two ways. Either both obligations are extinguished
*ipso iure* "from the day of their coexistence", or the right of set-off has to be
exercised by notice to the other party. Both obligations are then, however,
deemed to have expired at the moment at which, being suitable for set-off,
they first confronted each other.[172] The latter solution, as has been mentioned,
is the more modern one, and it is preferable for a number of reasons. However, it also suffers from a severe doctrinal flaw: the notion of retrospectivity.
Retrospectivity constituted an attempt, by nineteenth-century German legal
doctrine, to reconcile two divergent groups of Roman sources, one of them

---

170  This is true, particularly, for the United Nations Convention on the Assignment of Receivables
   in International Trade (reproduced in (2002) 10 *ZEuP* 860 ff; and see S V Bazinas, "Der Beitrag
   von Uncitral zur Vereinheitlichung der Rechtsvorschriften über Forderungsabtretungen: Das
   Übereinkommen der Vereinten Nationen über Abtretungen von Forderungen im
   internationalen Handel" (2002) 10  *ZEuP* 782 ff); for a comparative analysis, see H Eidenmüller, "Die Dogmatik der Zession vor dem Hintergrund der internationalen Entwicklung"
   (2004) 204 *Archiv für die civilistische Praxis* 457 ff. The United Nations Convention on the
   Limitation Period in the International Sale of Goods (printed in Radley-Gardner et al, *Fundamental Texts*, 269 ff) has only been relied upon in some respects; since it only deals with one
   specific type of claim, it does not provide a suitable model for a general prescription regime.
171  Lando & Beale (note 6), xxiv; see above, the text to note 99.
172  See the text to notes 127 ff above; on the development of the retrospectivity doctrine, see
   Zimmermann, in Zimmermann et al, *Historisch-kritischer Kommentar*, §§ 387–396, notes 14 ff,
   23 ff.

favouring set-off *ipso iure*, the other requiring an assertion of set-off.[173] In the course of time, the notion of retrospectivity has become firmly entrenched, in prevailing legal ideology, as an essential characteristic of a declaration of set-off.[174] Yet this notion is based on a centuries-old misunderstanding.[175] The phrase *ipso iure* appears to be of classical origin. It had been used, by the Roman jurists, in the special context of the banker's *agere cum compensatione*.[176] But the phrase had merely been intended to indicate that this type of set-off was not one effected by the judge. The banker himself was forced, by virtue of the formula granted to him by the *praetor*, to reduce his claim by the amount of the other party's counterclaim. The plaintiff was thus made *ipso iure*, i.e. by the law itself, to effect set-off. It is probable that Justinian also still attributed *ex nunc* effect to set-off.[177] The decisive turn came with the Glossators who reinterpreted set-off *ipso iure* as a form of set-off which occurred automatically, *sine facto hominis*. This misunderstanding still today casts its shadow on (as it would have been put in the nineteenth century) the "construction" of set-off in France and all the countries influenced by French law, but also in Germany[178] and the countries following German law.[179] From the sources compiled and edited by Jakobs and Schubert we now know that in the course of the deliberations leading up to the BGB Bernhard Windscheid had recommended the attribution of merely prospective effect to set-off;[180] and he had done so in spite of the fact that, as a pandectist scholar, he had previously made the intellectually most ambitious attempt to explain the tension between set-off *ipso iure* and the requirement that set-off had to be asserted.[181]

## (b) The unilateral promise

The other example is provided by Article 2:107 PECL which bluntly states: "A promise which is intended to be legally binding without acceptance is binding."[182] This is surprising in view of the fact that the great majority of

---

173  The text to notes 127 f above.
174  See Zimmermann, *Comparative Foundations*, 39 ff with references.
175  For what follows, see Pichonnaz (note 127), 9 ff (particularly 127 ff, 295 ff); Zimmermann, in Zimmermann et al, *Historisch-kritischer Kommentar*, §§ 387–396, notes 5 ff.
176  Paul D 16.2.21; C 4.31.4 (Alex.).
177  Pichonnaz, *La compensation*, 260 ff.
178  § 389 BGB.
179  Such as, most recently, Dutch law: Article 6:129 BW.
180  Zimmermann, in Zimmermann et al, *Historisch-kritischer Kommentar*, §§ 387–396, n 24.
181  B Windscheid & T Kipp, *Lehrbuch des Pandektenrechts*, 9th edn (1906), § 349.
182  For a systematic and comparative analysis of this provision, see Zimmermann (note 98), 478 ff.

European legal systems traditionally follows Hugo Grotius in requiring an acceptance before a promise can be regarded as legally binding.[183] Only exceptionally has a different view been adopted. In the BGB, for instance, special provision is made for the promise, by way of public notice, of "a reward for the performance of an act, in particular for the production of a result". It is known as *Auslobung*, a unilateral act which need not be accepted.[184] The Code, in this respect, endorsed a view propounded by a number of pandectist scholars:[185] a view for which there are but the faintest traces in the Roman sources.[186] On a much more general level, Grotius' view had been rejected by the most influential Institutional Writer in Scotland, Viscount Stair, who held a unilateral promise to be binding even if it has not been accepted by the promisee.[187] This is clearly based on Canon law.[188] The doctrine of promise, as expounded by Stair, has survived and remains part and parcel of Scots law.[189] And indeed, it may be asked why the release from an obligation, for example, should only be effective if the debtor has agreed to it. This is by no means self-evident, and the experience in German law has been that courts often get into trouble when attempting to establish whether an offer, on the part of the creditor, to conclude a contract of release has been accepted by the debtor.[190] Strangely, this obvious illustration of Article 2:107 PECL is not mentioned in the commentary to the rule.

183 H Grotius, *De jure belli ac pacis libri tres*, Amsterdami (1631), Lib. II, Cap. XI, § 14. Grotius' doctrine was based on L Lessius, *De iustitia et iure* (see Gordley (note 42), 80 f); via Pothier, it established itself in France and England: for France, see M Ferid & H J Sonnenberger, *Das Französische Zivilrecht*, 2nd edn (1994), vol I/1, 1 F 63; for England, see Simpson (1975) 91 *LQR* 259.

184 § 657 BGB. For the origin of this provision, see F P von Kübel, "Das einseitige Versprechen als Grund der Verpflichtung zur Erfüllung", in W Schubert (ed), *Die Vorlagen der Redaktoren für die erste Kommission zur Ausarbeitung des Entwurfs eines Bürgerlichen Gesetzbuches, Recht der Schuldverhältnisse, Teil 3* (1980), 1171 ff; F P von Kübel, "Einseitiges Versprechen", in Schubert, 475 ff. For a comparative overview, see R Zimmermann & P Hellwege, "Belohnungs-versprechen: 'pollicitatio', 'promise' oder 'offer'?: Schottisches Recht vor dem Hintergrund der europäischen Entwicklungen" (1998) 39 *ZfRV* 137; J Gordley, *The Enforceability of Promises in European Contract Law* (2001), 300 ff.

185 H Dernburg, *Pandekten*, 6th edn (1900), vol II, § 9; J Baron, *Pandekten*, 4th edn (1882), § 211.

186 Zimmermann, *Obligations*, 496 (n 15), 574 f.

187 Stair, *Institutions of the Law of Scotland*, 6th edn edited by D M Walker (1981), Book I, Title 10, §§ 3 f.

188 W D H Sellar, "Promise", in K Reid & R Zimmermann (eds), *A History of Private Law in Scotland* (2000) (henceforth Reid & Zimmermann, *History*), vol II, 252 ff.

189 Zimmermann & Hellwege (1998) 39 *ZfRV* 133 ff; Sellar (note 188), 267 ff, 277 ff; M Hogg, *Obligations* (2003), 36 ff.

190 For a detailed analysis, see now J Kleinschmidt, *Der Verzicht im Schuldrecht: Vertragsprinzip und einseitiges Rechtsgeschäft im deutschen und US-amerikanischen Recht* (2004).

## (c) Undue influence Civilian style

Article 2:107 PECL is not, incidentally, the only example for another inter-esting phenomenon: the re-emergence of certain solutions, or devices, adopted in the earlier *ius commune* which have subsequently come to be suppressed. Article 4:109 PECL can be mentioned in this context which grants a party the right to avoid a contract if, at the time of conclusion of the contract, that party was dependent on or had a relationship of trust with the other party and if the other party took advantage of the first party's situation in a way which is grossly unfair, or took an excessive benefit. This provision – which comple-ments a comparatively narrow doctrine of "threats", i.e. duress (England) or force and fear (Scotland)[191] – is clearly inspired by the English concept of "undue influence".[192] Contracts of suretyship concluded by close family members of the main debtor, and the resulting case law, have demonstrated the need for a similar rule also in Continental legal systems; in Germany, for example, the general *boni mores* provision of § 138 I BGB had to be resorted to in order to achieve satisfactory results.[193] The older *ius commune* had developed, on the basis of individual points of departure in the Roman sources, the notion of *metus reverentialis*.[194] Thus, according to the Accursian gloss, a married woman who sells or incumbers an object belonging to her under the influence of fear or reverence may revoke that transaction; the same applies to a clergyman who *"metu et reverentia episcopi"* renounces his prebend.[195] This is true even if there has been no threat of physical harm. A particularly vivid example of undue influence is reported by Matthaeus de Afflictis, though with regard to another type of legal transaction. A husband had secretly entered the room where his dying wife was engaged in making her will. He bent his head over hers ("posuit faciem super faciem Catherinae") and entreated and flattered her into making a legacy of immoveable property to himself. This legacy "metu reverentiali marito factum concurrentibus importunis precibus in damnum alterius" was subsequently held to be

---

191  Article 4:108 PECL.
192  On which see Treitel, *Contract*, 378 ff; *Royal Bank of Scotland v Etridge (No 2)* [2002] 2 AC 773.
193  M Habersack & R Zimmermann, "Legal Change in a Codified System: Recent Developments in German Suretyship Law" (1999) 3 *Edinburgh LR* 272 ff; A Stadler, in Jauernig (note 59), § 765, n 4.
194  Pap D 29, 6, 3; Ulp D 44, 5, 1, 6; Ulp D 50, 17, 4; C 2, 19 (20), 11. For details of what follows, see J du Plessis & R Zimmermann, "The Relevance of Reverence: Undue Influence Civilian Style" (2003) 10 *Maastricht Journal of European and Comparative Law* 345 ff.
195  Edition used: *Digestorum novum, seu pandectarum iuris civilis, tomus tertius*, Geneva (1625) (col 879).

invalid.[196] Via Pothier these ideas were received in England. The doctrine of undue influence, in turn, developed in England by the Court of Chancery, was subsequently reimported by Scots and South African courts into a Civilian legal environment.[197]

## E. THE PRINCIPLES AND RE-EUROPEANISATION OF PRIVATE LAW

### (1) A basic background text shaping national legal developments *imperio rationis*

It will have become clear by now that, as far as their substantive content is concerned, the Principles of European Contract Law do not constitute a replica of the old *ius commune*. They can, however, be regarded as an "organically progressive"[198] development of that old *ius commune*: as a contemporary adaptation of the legal material that has come down to us. This is completely in tune with the spirit of the old *ius commune* which depended for its vitality on the belief of the ongoing character of law, its capacity for growth over generations and centuries.[199] Pandectist legal science was not identical with the *usus modernus pandectarum* and the *usus modernus* was a far cry from the *usus antiquus*. But they were all part of the same tradition. Of course, in many respects there is a world of difference between the old *ius commune* and the Principles. The old *ius commune* was based on a body of sources of unparalleled richness and refinement. In comparison, the Principles must appear insipid, dreary, bland and lifeless. On the other hand, however, the great complexity of the legal sources of the old *ius commune* was the main reason for its decline. In the age of Enlightenment, it no longer appeared self-evidently right to apply a law that was riddled with contradictions, that had given rise to the most intricate doctrinal disputes, that was wedded to outdated and impractical *subtilitates* and that had been enacted by despotic rulers of another age. At about the same time another great advantage of the

---

196  M de Afflictis, *Decisionum sacri regni neapolitani consilii*, Francofurti (1600), *Decisio* LXIX; cf also I Menochius, *De praesumptionibus, coniecturis, signis et indiciis commentaria*, Lugduni (1608), *Liber* IV, *Praesumptio* XII, nn 8 f.

197  See J Story, *Commentaries on Equity Jurisprudence*, 3rd edn (by A E Randall), 1920, §§ 234 ff; G Lubbe, "Voidable Contracts", in R Zimmermann & D Visser (eds), *Southern Cross: Civil Law and Common Law in South Africa* (1996) (henceforth Zimmermann & Visser, *Southern Cross*), 296 ff; Du Plessis & Zimmermann (2003) 10 *Maastricht Journal of European and Comparative Law* 345 ff.

198  Savigny; see the text to note 37 above.

199  Berman (note 24), 9; and see above, the text to notes 28 ff.

old *ius commune* began to turn into a disadvantage. The language of the *ius commune* was Latin. It was the language that was understood by every learned lawyer who had received an academic legal training at any university in Europe. With the rise of the vernacular as an academic language the use of Latin was bound to be regarded as quaint and artificial. Dissemination of the Principles, of course, is not facilitated by a common language. English appears to be about to emerge as a kind of background language for international communication. Nonetheless, in countries like France or Germany legal literature written in English is not as readily received as it is in smaller nations such as the Netherlands. In order to become a foundational work of a truly European character the Principles therefore have to be translated into as many of the official European languages as possible. This process is under way at the moment.[200]

There are also, however, characteristic aspects which the Principles share with the old *ius commune* and which thus engender the hope that they can serve as a nucleus for the emergence of a renewed European legal scholarship. One which has been discussed above is their substantive content. Another is their source of legitimacy. The old *ius commune* was widely thought to apply *ratione imperii*.[201] But this was only true of certain parts of Europe. Moreover, in the middle of the seventeenth century it was clearly demonstrated that Roman law had not been made applicable by formal imperial enactment.[202] If it continued to apply, it did so because of its intrinsic qualities, i.e. *imperio rationis*. Particularly instructive is the situation prevailing in nineteenth-century Germany. A number of German territories still administered justice according to the contemporary, pandectist version of the Roman common law.[203] But even in the countries of codified law, the *ius commune* continued to contribute its underlying legal theory:[204] the codifications were always compared with, assessed and evaluated from the point of view of the *ius commune*. Pandectist legal scholarship very largely achieved a German unification on a scholarly level. Thus, it remained perfectly possible

---

200  G Rouhette, I de Lamberterie, D Tallon & C Witz, *Principes du droit Européen du contrat* (2003); C Castronovo, *Principi di diritto europeo dei contratti, Parte I e II* (2001); C von Bar & R Zimmermann, *Grundregeln des Europäischen Vertragsrechts, Teile I und II* (2003); P Barres Benlloch, J M Embid Irujo & F Martinez Sanz, *Principios de derecho contractual europeo, Partes I y II* (2003).

201  See Wieacker, *Privatrechtsgeschichte*, 97 ff.

202  See Wieacker, *Privatrechtsgeschichte*, 160 ff.

203  In 1890, about 14,416,000 (of a total of 50,000,000) inhabitants of the German Empire lived in areas where mainly the *ius commune* was applicable. See the map edited by D Klippel, *Deutsche Rechts- und Gerichtskarte* (1996), with an introduction by the editor.

204  Koschaker, *Europa und das römische Recht*, 292.

for a law professor to be called from Königsberg to Strasbourg, from Giessen to Vienna, or from Heidelberg to Leipzig. Nor were law students, as far as choice and change of universities were concerned, confined to the institutions of the state in which they later wanted to practise.

Nineteenth-century Roman common law was thus able to provide an intellectual bridge between the Prussian and the French, the Saxonian and the Austrian codes. It subtly influenced the way in which the various codes prevailing in different parts of Germany were understood and applied.[205] It decisively shaped all the codes of private law drafted or enacted in nineteenth-century Germany, down to the BGB of 1900. At the same time, the Roman common law was never static: it continued to be developed, to be refined and to be adjusted.

The Principles of European Contract Law have not been drafted by a body invested with any form of statutory authority. They do not constitute a formal source of law.[206] They are the product of scholarly work and thus they cannot have any other authority than their intrinsic merit. If they are to gain influence on the development of private law in Europe they can only do so *imperio rationis*: because they are perceived to provide solutions to legal problems which are both reasonable and free from national bias. It is important to note, in this respect, that the Commission drafting the Principles has consisted of lawyers from all member states of the European Union,[207] that no single legal system has been made the starting point from which the Principles are derived,[208] and that the process of drafting was not placed in the hands of one individual person.[209] The Principles, even though they constitute a kind of virtual law, nonetheless provide a neutral yardstick for an organic assimilation of the private law in Europe if they are used as a source of inspiration by the protagonists responsible for the development of European law, i.e. judges, legislators and professors.[210]

---

205  For the "pandectification" of the Prussian and Austrian codes, see the references in Zimmermann, *Roman Law*, 4ff. For the influence of pandectist scholarship outside Germany, see the references in R Zimmermann, "Savignys Vermächtnis" (1998) *Juristische Blätter* 276 (note 18).

206  For the implications, see C-W Canaris, "Die Stellung der 'Unidroit Principles' und der 'Principles of European Contract Law' im System der Rechtsquellen", in Basedow (note 1), 5 ff; R Michaels, "Privatautonomie und Privatkodifikation" (1998) 62 *RabelsZ* 580 ff.

207  Text following note 6 above.

208  Text following note 14 above

209  Text following note 12 above

210  R C van Caenegem, *Judges, Legislators and Professors* (1987); R C van Caenegem, *An Historical Introduction to Private Law* (1988), 170 ff.

## (2) Legislation

The disintegration of the old *ius commune* has led to the rise of the new discipline of comparative law. Originally, however, attention was confined nearly exclusively to foreign legislation. It was studied in order to improve the quality of one's own legislation. In its origins, therefore, the new discipline was one of comparative legislation (*législation comparée*): "La comparaison des lois étrangères est une étude de législation bien plus encore que de jurisconsulte."[211] Draftsmen of new legislation, in the course of the nineteenth century, usually looked at the way in which the problem at hand had been dealt with by the legislatures of other countries. This applied, at first, to the newly emerging areas of the law but subsequently also to codifications concerning the classical core areas of private law. The draftsmen of the BGB, for instance, very carefully took account of the French and Austrian codifications as well as of various other codes and draft codes in Germany and Switzerland. This tradition has continued throughout the twentieth century. The preparation of the new Dutch Civil Code provides another excellent example.[212] In recent years, uniform sales law has gained great significance as a pacemaker for national law reform. The various steps on the road towards modernising breach of contract and sale in German law have largely been inspired first by ULIS and then by CISG.[213] The Principles of European Contract Law constitute a model law which has the potential to attain a similar significance. It was one of the criticisms levelled against the so-called "Discussion Draft" of a statute for the modernisation of the German law of obligations, published in September 2000, that it failed to take account of more than ten years of legal development in Europe, as evidenced in the Dutch Civil Code, the Principles of European Contract Law and the Principles of International Commercial Contracts.[214] Thus, it was only in the final stages of the German reform process that the Principles were taken into consideration.[215]

---

211  See H Coing, "Rechtsvergleichung als Grundlage von Gesetzgebung im 19. Jahrhundert" (1978) 7 *Ius Commune* 160 ff; H Coing, *Europäisches Privatrecht*, vol II (1989), 56 ff; Zweigert & Kötz, *Comparative Law*, 48 ff; the quotation is from E-R Laboulaye, founder of the *Société de législation comparée*, the first association for comparative law in Europe; see Coing, *Europäisches Privatrecht II*, 61 and Coing, "Laboulaye" (1993) 1 *ZEuP* 519 ff.

212  U Drobnig, "Das neue niederländische bürgerliche Gesetzbuch aus vergleichender und deutscher Sicht" (1993) 1 *ERPL* 174.

213  Text to note 152 above.

214  B Dauner-Lieb, "Die geplante Schuldrechtsmodernisierung – Durchbruch oder Schnellschuss?" (2001) *Juristenzeitung* 15; U Huber, "Das geplante Recht der Leistungsstörungen", in Ernst & Zimmermann (note 1), 108 f; Zimmermann (note 113), 284 f.

215  Huber (note 214), 31 ff; C-W Canaris, "Die Reform des Rechts der Leistungsstörungen" (2001) *Juristenzeitung* 499 ff.

However, prescription was the only area of the law where they were able to exercise a significant influence; the German government specifically acknowledged to have adopted, in large parts, the model proposed in the Principles of European Contract Law.[216]

## (3) Courts of law

The existing national codes are interpreted, developed and adapted to new circumstances by the national courts of law. This is a process which has often changed the national systems of private law as dramatically as the intervention of the legislature. For some time already, it has been argued that the insights of comparative law have to play a role in this process.[217] The then President of the German Federal Supreme Court, Walter Odersky, has even gone further by advocating what he calls a harmonising method of interpretation: the national judge, in the process of applying his own national law, may legitimately be guided by the consideration that a particular solution would serve the harmonisation of European law. With the increasing European integration this argument should gain an ever increasing weight.[218] At the same time, however, Odersky also pointed at the difficulties posed by this approach.[219] Even for the judges of national supreme courts it is virtually impossible to establish the legal position on a particular point in all the other EU member states. Sometimes he will be able to turn to the pertinent legal literature which, however, is not always easy to find and is also not usually aimed at the harmonisation of European law. The Principles, apart from textbooks and source books on European contract law,[220] could play a very significant role in this respect, for they provide a beacon, established on the basis of comparative research and international co-operation, which can serve to guide the interpretation and development of the national legal systems. In Germany this idea does not appear, so far, to have gained acceptance; this is hardly surprising in view of the fact that even the "normal"

---

216 "Bericht des Rechtsausschusses, BT-Drucksache 14/7052", easily accessible in C-W Canaris (ed), *Schuldrechtsmodernisierung 2002* (2002), 1051 ff (1066); cf also "Begründung der Bundesregierung zum Entwurf eines Gesetzes zur Modernisierung des Schuldrechts, BT-Drucksache 6857", in Canaris 569 ff, 600, 612 f. For a comparative analysis, see Zimmermann (note 148), 9 ff.

217 See, e.g., K Zweigert, "Rechtsvergleichung als universale Interpretationsmethode" (1949/50) 15 *RabelsZ* 5 ff; Zweigert & Kötz, *Comparative Law*, 18 ff.

218 W Odersky, "Harmonisierende Auslegung und europäische Rechtskultur" (1994) 2 *ZEuP* 1 ff.

219 Odersky (1994) 2 *ZEuP* 4.

220 Kötz, *European Contract Law*; H Beale, A Hartkamp, H Kötz & D Tallon, *Cases, Materials and Text on Contract Law* (2002).

comparative interpretation is practised but rarely.[221] Many Continental lawyers will be surprised to see that the House of Lords was one of the first European Supreme Courts to refer to the Principles. This happened in a decision of 2001 dealing with the notion of "good faith" in the context of the Unfair Terms in Consumer Contracts Regulations.[222] In the Netherlands a number of conclusions by various Advocate-Generals have invoked the Principles, but the Hoge Raad does not yet appear to have quoted them.[223]

## (4) Legal scholarship

In the first place, however, it is the task of legal scholarship to take note of the Principles, to provide critical comment and discussion, and intellectually to relate them to the various national legal systems. This does not have to be, and indeed should not be, a one-way process. For as much as national legal developments have to be evaluated against the yardstick provided by the Principles, the Principles may not pass muster when they are evaluated against the background of national legal experiences which have been gathered over a long period and by sophisticated courts and legal writers. There are a number of deficiencies in the Principles. Thus, for example, the Principles contain in their three parts three sets of rules dealing with restitution of benefits received under a contract that has been avoided, that has turned out to be invalid or that has been terminated.[224] This triplication of rules as well as the differences between them are not justifiable. Moreover, one of these regimes is based on an outmoded model, whereas the other two leave important questions unregulated.[225] More instances could be mentioned where the Principles lack consistency or where they will have to be

221 S Vogenauer, *Die Auslegung von Gesetzen in England und auf dem Kontinent: Eine rechtsvergleichende Untersuchung der Rechtsprechung und ihrer historischen Grundlagen*, vol I (2001), 43 with further references. For a comparative overview, see U Drobnig & S van Erp (eds), *The Use of Comparative Law by Courts* (1999); for Scotland, see H L MacQueen, "Mixing it? Comparative Law in the Scottish Courts" (2003) 11 *ERPL* 735 ff.

222 *Director-General of Fair Trading v First National Bank* [2002] 1 AC 481 (HL) at 500 per Lord Steyn and 502 per Lord Hope. On this decision, see S Whittaker, "Assessing the fairness of contract terms: the parties' 'essential bargain', its regulatory context and the significance of the requirement of good faith" (2004) 12 *ZEuP* 75 ff.

223 The minority in a decision of the Swedish Supreme Court has referred to Article 2:205(1) PECL: 2000 *Nytt Juridiskt Arkiv* 747. I am grateful to Mr Justice Torgny Håstad for the reference.

224 Articles 4:115, 9:305 ff, 15:104 PECL.

225 For criticism, see Zimmermann (note 8); generally, see P Hellwege, *Die Rückabwicklung gegenseitiger Verträge als einheitliches Problem: Deutsches, englisches und schottisches Recht in historisch-vergleichender Perspektive* (2004).

refined and specified.[226] In many other cases, however, the comparison will reveal quirks and idiosyncracies of the national legal systems and will lead to a reappraisal of the latter. For Germany the process of comparative assessment was initiated at a symposium on "Unification of European Contract Law and German Law" which was held in the Hamburg Max Planck Institute in 1999;[227] it was designed to re-establish the intellectual contact between private law legal doctrine and comparative law under the auspices of the Principles of European Contract Law and the Principles of International Commercial Contracts. At the most recent biannual meeting of the association of German-speaking professors of private law the Principles of European Contract Law featured prominently in two of the four lectures, the one dealing with breach of contract,[228] the other with the law of assignment of claims.[229] In the latter paper the technical quality and internal consistency of Chapter 11 of the Principles were emphasised and, on that basis, a number of changes to the German law of cession were recommended. Unfortunately, however, the Principles have not yet worked their way into the general textbooks and commentaries on German private law. Dutch writers, on the other hand, refer to the Principles almost as a matter of routine even if they merely deal with a question of Dutch law. And a recent collection of texts, cases and materials on English contract law invokes the Principles on a number of occasions even though it specifically does not describe itself as a book on comparative law.[230] Another very interesting initiative has been taken in the Netherlands. Five authors have systematically examined their own legal system from the point of view of the Principles and have thus, by using a supranational frame of reference, made Dutch law more easily accessible to foreign lawyers.[231]

---

226 For criticism concerning Article 6:110 PECL (Stipulation in Favour of a Third Party), see Zimmermann (note 98), 478.

227 Basedow (note 1). For France, see now P Rémy-Corlay & D Fenouillet (eds), *Les concepts contractuels francais à l'heure des Principes de droit européen des contrats* (2003).

228 H-P Mansel, "Die Kaufrechtsreform in Europa und die Dogmatik des Leistungsstörungsrechts" (2004) 204 *Archiv für die civilistische Praxis* 396 ff. Cf. also R Zimmermann, "Remedies for Non-Performance: The revised German Law of Obligations, viewed against the Background of the Principles of European Contract Law" (2002) 6 *Edinburgh LR* 271 ff.

229 Eidenmüller (2004) 204 *Archiv für die civilistische Praxis* 457 ff.

230 E McKendrick, *Contract Law: Text, Cases and Materials* (2003), 55 f, 102, 133, 276 f, 552, 615 f and more frequently; cf. in particular 417 f. For Scotland, see the remarks by MacQueen (2003) 11 *ERPL* 751 on two recent texts on contract law that have drawn significantly on the Principles: H L MacQueen & J Thomson, *Contract Law in Scotland* (2000) (a student book) and W W McBryde, *The Law of Contract in Scotland*, 2nd edn (2001) (a practitioner work).

231 D Busch, E Hondius, H van Kooten, H Schelhaas & W Schrama, *The Principles of European Contract Law and Dutch Law: A Commentary* (2002). Cf also D Busch and E Hondius, "Ein neues Vertragsrecht für Europa: Die Principles of European Contract Law aus niederländischer Sicht" (2001) 9 *ZEuP* 223 ff.

## (5) Autonomous convergence

Occasionally, today, we also witness what may be called a process of autonomous, or spontaneous, harmonisation of European contract law. Bertrand Fages has recently drawn attention to a number of significant developments, instigated by the Cour de Cassation, which have pragmatically steered French contract law in a direction coinciding with that adopted by the European Principles.[232] Particularly significant, in this respect, are the growing prominence of the principle of good faith, the new approach towards the determination of price, and the recognition of an extra-judicial way of terminating contracts after breach of contract. These developments cannot be credited to the Principles which have probably not been present in the judges' minds. But if French courts take their bearings by a point of reference which has, independently, also been identified by the Principles, this may be taken as a confirmation of the approach adopted in the Principles. Another example of an autonomous convergence may be provided by the English law on limitation of actions, as soon as the report of the Law Commission presented in July 2001 is implemented; this report proposes a regime which, in many essential features, resembles the model proposed by the Principles.[233]

## (6) Legal training

Legislators, judges and professors have been, and still are, the protagonists of legal development in Europe. Their minds have been, and still are, shaped by the legal training they have received. The intellectual unity of the old *ius commune* was very largely provided by a training based on the same legal sources. Today, too, the Europeanisation of private law decisively depends on a Europeanisation of the legal training provided in the various universities throughout Europe.[234] Once again, the Principles can play a very important role in this respect. They provide a nucleus around which a general theory of European contract law can crystallise: a general theory which can conceivably attain the same position as the *ius commune* in the lecture rooms of

---

232  Fages (2003) 11 *ZEuP* 514 ff.
233  Report on Limitation of Actions (Law Com No 270, 2001).
234  See F Ranieri, "Der europäische Jurist: Rechtshistorisches Forschungsthema und rechtspolitische Aufgabe" (1990) 17 *Ius Commune* 9 ff; H Kötz, "Europäische Juristenausbildung" (1993) 1 *ZEuP* 268 ff; R Goode, "The European Law School" (1993) 13 *Legal Studies* 1 ff; B Grossfeld, "Europäisches Recht und Rechtsstudium" (1993) *Juristische Schulung* 710 ff; B de Witte & C Forder (eds), *The Common Law of Europe and the Future of Legal Education* (1992); A Flessner, "Deutsche Juristenausbildung" (1996) *Juristenzeitung* 689 ff; P Häberle, "Der Europäische Jurist" (2002) 50 *Jahrbuch des öffentlichen Rechts der Gegenwart* 123 ff.

nineteenth-century German universities. "Neither the Prussian Code, nor the law of the Code Civil or that of the Badisches Landrecht, nor indeed the law of the Saxonian Civil Code became the focal point for legal training in the universities of the respective states" as it is stated in a memorandum of 1896.[235] It was the training in the *ius commune* that was regarded as suitable to provide a sufficient introduction to the understanding of the codified laws. Thus, "the possibility existed that the Prussian, Saxonian or the native of Baden could receive his educational background in law at a university in a different state, as long as he acquired, at the end of his studies, some more specific ... knowledge of the legal system which ... he might be required to apply for the rest of his life". Our position today is different in some respects. But the vision of a European legal training in spite of the variety of national systems of law very much resembles what was reality in earlier times. Why should it not be possible, today, to make the Principles the starting point for courses in contract law in Germany as much as in France or England? The students would then become familiar with a common frame of reference which would enable them to appreciate the contours of their own legal system much more clearly and, at the same time, facilitate access to the others.

## F. CONCLUSION

All in all, it is obvious today that the discussions concerning a European contract law have considerably intensified over the last few years.[236] The main actors on the stage of the institutionalised Europe, i.e. Council, Commission and Parliament of the European Union, have even envisaged the possibility of a codification of European contract law. Whether, eventually, such a step will be taken or not, the academic community would neglect its duty if it did not set out to prepare, refine and critically examine the intellectual foundations for a European contract law. The Principles are an attempt to establish such foundations. They should be taken into consideration not only by comparative lawyers but, particularly, by all those engaged in shaping and elucidating national legal doctrine. The Principles may sharpen an awareness

---

235 E Friedberg, *Die künftige Gestaltung des deutschen Rechtsstudiums nach den Beschlüssen der Eisenacher Konferenz* (1996), 7 f.

236 See Jansen, *Binnenmarkt: Privatrecht und europäische Identität*, 2 ff (with references); most recently, see D Staudenmayer, "Ein optionelles Instrument im Europäischen Vertragsrecht" (2003) 11 *ZEuP* 828 ff; C von Bar & S Swann, "Response to the Action Plan on European Contract Law: A More Coherent European Contract Law (COM (2003) 63)" (2003) 11 *ERPL* 595 ff.

for the peculiarities of the national legal systems and provide inspiration for their interpretation and development. Thus, they can serve as a catalyst for a "soft" harmonisation of the European legal systems. Soft harmonisation would appear, in the short and medium term, to be the preferable alternative to central regulation, and the one in tune with the tradition of the old *ius commune*.[237] At the same time, it may pave the way towards a codification which is as widely accepted in Europe as the *Code Civil* in France or the BGB in Germany.

---

237 Zimmermann (1998) *Juristische Blätter* 273 ff; Zimmermann, "Roman Law and the Harmonisation of Private Law in Europe" (note 31), 21 ff; for a different view, see O Lando, "Why Codify the European Law of Contract" (1997) 5 *ERPL* 525 ff; O Lando, "The Principles of European Contract Law after Year 2000", in F Werro (ed), *New Perspectives on European Private Law* (1998), 59 ff; W Tilmann, "Eine Privatrechtskodifikation für die Europäische Gemeinschaft", in P-C Müller-Graff (ed), *Gemeinsames Privatrecht in der Europäischen Gemeinschaft*, 2nd edn (1999), 579 ff; J Basedow, "Das BGB im künftigen europäischen Privatrecht: Der hybride Kodex" (2000) 200 *Archiv für die civilistische Praxis* 445 ff; J Basedow, "Codification of Private Law in the European Union: The Making of a Hybrid" (2001) 9 *ERPL* 35 ff. For a balanced assessment of the debate, see W van Gerven, "A Common Law for Europe: The Future Meeting the Past?" (2001) 9 *ERPL* 485 ff.

# 2 Good Faith

## Hector L MacQueen

## A. GOOD FAITH AND FAIR DEALING IN PECL

Good faith is a powerful concept in PECL. Almost from the outset, Article 1:201 PECL declares that "each party must act in accordance with good faith and fair dealing", and that this "duty" may not be excluded or limited by the parties. Comment A says that the Article "sets forth a basic principle running through the Principles", while Comment B adds: "Its purpose is to enforce community standards of decency, fairness and reasonableness in commercial transactions." Even the recognition of parties' freedom to enter into a contract and determine its contents is made "subject to the requirements of good faith and fair dealing" (Article 1:102 PECL). Amongst the various purposes for which the Principles are to be interpreted and developed, "the need to promote good faith and fair dealing" is listed first, ahead of "certainty in contractual relationships and uniformity of application" (Article 1:106 PECL).

The constant conjunction in PECL of good faith with fair dealing indicates that overall an objective standard is intended, rather than a subjective one of simple honesty. Comment E to Article 1:201 PECL says:

"Good faith" means honesty and fairness in mind, which are subjective concepts. ... "Fair dealing" means observance of fairness in fact which is an objective test ...[1]

There are links to other concepts in PECL. Comment A says that Article 1:201 PECL is a companion to the Article on usages, which makes binding between the parties agreed, established or generally applicable and reasonable usages and practices (Article 1:105 PECL). In this way are ideas about "community standards", as well as the standards the parties set themselves, articulated in the actual text. Article 1:202 PECL, which immediately follows the article stating the good faith obligation of the parties, further imposes on them a duty to co-operate to give full effect to the contract (although unlike good faith and fair dealing this duty is not expressly made unexcludable or unlimitable). Article 1:302 PECL says that "reasonableness [another frequently used concept in the Principles] is to be judged by what persons acting in good faith and in the same situation as the parties would consider to be reasonable".

The application of good faith and fair dealing is fleshed out in several more specific provisions, although Comment B to Article 1:201 PECL points out that the concept is "broader than any of these specific applications". Thus, while parties negotiating a contract are not liable for failure to reach an agreement, negotiating or breaking off negotiations contrary to good faith and fair dealing leads to liability for the losses caused to the other party. There is such liability if a party enters into or continues negotiations with no real intention of reaching an agreement with the other party (Article 2:301 PECL).[2] Good faith and fair dealing may also require a negotiating party to disclose information to the other party, otherwise any resultant contract may be avoided (Article 4:107 PECL). The requirement will typically arise for a party who has special expertise on the matter in issue, and account will also be taken of the cost of acquiring the information, whether the other party could reasonably acquire the information for itself, and the apparent importance of the information to the other party (Article 4:107(3) PECL).

Good faith and fair dealing are also among the "relevant circumstances" to which regard is to be had in interpreting the contract (Article 5:102 PECL), although it is difficult to see either as a "circumstance" comparable with some of the other matters listed in the Article.[3] Terms stemming from good faith

---

1 "Good faith" sometimes appears on its own in PECL: see e.g. Articles 1:302, 3:201(3).

2 See also Article 6:111(3) PECL (damages may be awarded for loss suffered through a party refusing to negotiate or breaking off negotiations contrary to good faith and fair dealing where contract has become excessively onerous as a result of change of circumstances since the contract was concluded).

3 In his contribution to this volume (at 202) Professor Clive points out that good faith and fair dealing are "considerations" rather than "circumstances".

and fair dealing may be implied (Article 6:102 PECL). Since this power is not limited to consistency with the express terms, freedom of contract may here be subject to good faith and fair dealing requirements. The Comments do not refer to this, however, seeing the main function of the implied term as filling gaps in the contract. If, contrary to duties of good faith and fair dealing or co-operation, a party prevents or brings about the fulfilment of a condition, to the respective disadvantage or advantage of the other party, the condition is to be deemed either fulfilled or unfulfilled, as the case may be (Article 16:102 PECL).

A court may also regulate the provisions of the contract to be in accordance with the demands of good faith and fair dealing. Here again we see freedom of contract being hemmed in by good faith and fair dealing. In cases where one party had taken advantage of another's relative weakness or susceptibility to influence in a way that was grossly unfair or took excessive benefit, courts are empowered to adapt a contract to bring it into accordance with what might have been agreed had the requirements of good faith and fair dealing been followed (Article 4:109 PECL). Terms not individually negotiated (i.e. in standard form contracts) may be avoided if, "contrary to good faith and fair dealing", they cause a "significant imbalance in the parties' rights and obligations under the contract" (Article 4:110 PECL). But the remedies of avoidance and damages for mistake and incorrect information (misrepresentation) may be excluded unless to do so is contrary to good faith and fair dealing (Article 4:118 PECL).[4] Likewise remedies for non-performance may be excluded or restricted unless it would be contrary to good faith and fair dealing to invoke the exclusion or restriction (Article 8:109 PECL).

All this seems to stand in clear contrast to the classical Common Law view against general duties of good faith in contracts, succinctly expressed by Bingham LJ in a well-known dictum: "English law has characteristically com-mitted itself to no such overriding principle but has developed piecemeal solutions in response to demonstrated problems of unfairness."[5] Equally well known is Lord Ackner's remark in *Walford v Miles* – "the concept of a duty to carry on negotiations in good faith is inherently repugnant to the adversarial position of the parties when involved in negotiations"[6] – almost diametrically opposite to the position expressed in Articles 1:201 and 1:202 as well as in

---

4 Note that the remedies for fraud, threats and excessive benefit or unfair advantage-taking may never be excluded or restricted: Article 4:118(1) PECL.

5 *Interfoto Picture Library Ltd v Stiletto Visual Programmes Ltd* [1989] QB 433 at 439.

6 *Walford v Miles* [1992] 2 AC 128 at 138. For further argument against a general principle of good faith in contract negotiation, see S A Smith, *Contract Theory* (2004), 197–207.

Article 2:301 PECL. Commentators such as Michael Bridge argue that the imposition of a general standard of good faith would undermine commercial certainty to an unacceptable degree, and that "it is better to confront particular problems than to adopt a general ethical imperative. ... The purpose of legislation should not be to make a moral demonstration."[7] He questions the machinery by which community values should be introduced into private litigation (the judiciary at all, but especially lower levels), and wonders how the relevant community is to be defined. Common Law doubts about good faith led to the well-known compromise of Article 7.1 CISG: "In the interpretation of this Convention, regard is to be had to ... the observance of good faith in international trade." But nevertheless, outside England good faith has been gaining increasing acceptance and prominence in the Common Law world, most notably in the Uniform Commercial Code's duty of good faith in performance (§ 2–103 UCC), and also in Australian, New Zealand and Canadian court decisions.[8]

Observing the UCC obligation of good faith in performance highlights one further point about PECL: the almost complete lack of reference to good faith and fair dealing in the chapters on performance, non-performance and remedies for non-performance. As we have already seen, however, this lack cannot be read as meaning that good faith and fair dealing are excluded from, or irrelevant to, these chapters. So the Comments link to good faith principles the limits on the remedy of specific performance in Article 9:102 PECL, and the aggrieved party's duty to mitigate loss flowing from the other's non-performance (Article 9:505 PECL).[9] Again, Comment B to Article 1:201 PECL notes that the Article

> may take precedence over other provisions of these Principles when a strict adherence to them would lead to a manifestly unjust result. Thus, even if the non-performance of an obligation is fundamental because strict compliance with the obligation is of the essence of the contract under Article 8:103, a party would not be permitted to terminate because of a trivial breach of the obligation.

---

7 M Bridge, "Good faith in commercial contracts", in R Brownsword, N J Hird & G Howells (eds), *Good Faith in Contract: Concept and Context* (1999) (henceforth Brownsword et al, *Good Faith*), 143.

8 See A F Mason, "Contract, good faith and equitable standards in fair dealing" (2000) 116 *LQR* 66. Cf J W Carter & E Peden, "Good faith in Australian contract law" (2003) 19 *Journal of Contract Law* 155. For judicious analyses of the current state of development in English law, see J Stapleton, "Good faith in private law" (1999) 49 *CLP* 1; R Brownsword, *Contract Law: Themes for the Twenty-First Century* (2000), ch 5, and E McKendrick, *Contract Law*, 6th edn (2005), 264–269.

9 See Comments A and D to Article 1:201 PECL.

On the other hand, Comment H to the same Article notes that good faith is dependent "to some extent" upon what the parties have agreed. So parties may agree "that even a technical breach may entitle the aggrieved party to refuse performance, when, for instance, its agents can ascertain a technical breach but not whether it is a trifle or not". There is some tension between Comments B and H, and it is perhaps a pity that there is nothing in the texts of the relevant Articles to make the position clearer.

Hugh Beale has argued that the concept of good faith and fair dealing is used in a variety of inconsistent ways in PECL. While the concept is not of itself a source for development of the Principles, something more than "not bad faith" is meant. But under Article 1:106 PECL regard is to be had, not only to good faith and fair dealing, but also, as we have seen above, to certainty in contractual relationships and uniformity of application. Article 1:102 PECL may appear to create an over-arching principle and role for good faith; but, suggests Beale, the many other Articles providing for more specific controls based on good faith would be unnecessary if Article 1:102 PECL did have this effect. In general, good faith and fair dealing in PECL appear to exclude the unreasonable rather than to impose a duty to be reasonable. They are at their most positive in relation to implied terms (Article 6:102 PECL), with regard to the duty to co-operate (Article 1:202 PECL), and with regard to invalidity (see e.g. Article 4:107 PECL). When good faith and reasonableness are juxtaposed, as in Article 1:302 PECL, they seem not to be very different from each other. There is an overall lack of consistency, and Beale proposes a tidying-up exercise to clarify what is intended by the concepts of good faith and dealing in PECL before they become part of the Common Frame of Reference now proposed by the European Commission. It should be made explicit that good faith is not an over-arching standard or principle for the whole of PECL, but is rather a standard used within particular rules. Good faith should be visibly an excluder principle only (i.e. merely excluding the unreasonable rather than imposing positive standards of conduct). Finally, a suitably defined standard of "reasonableness" should be used for the imposition of positive duties.[10]

---

10 H Beale, "General clauses and specific rules in the Principles of European Contract Law: the 'good faith' clause", in S Grundmann & D Mazeaud (eds), *General Clauses and Standards in European Contract Law – Comparative Law, EC Law and Codification* (forthcoming), ch 12. I am grateful to Professor Beale for letting me see his paper in advance of publication and discussing it with me. Note that Stapleton (1999) 49 *CLP* 1 at 8, 10–12, argues that reasonableness is a more demanding standard than good faith.

Beale's argument contributes to more general anxieties that may be felt about the significance of the good faith principle in PECL. Why, for example, when the House of Lords drew for the first time upon PECL to help in determining the meaning of the concept of good faith as used in the Unfair Terms Directive of 1993,[11] did their Lordships not find the Principles more useful? For both Lords Steyn and Hope, PECL seemed merely to confirm the diversity of the ways in which the concept of good faith is applied in the various European legal systems, with a range of factors – in particular, the availability of other doctrines and the scope assigned to them – affecting its reach.[12] Thus the House was free to develop its own understanding of the concept in the case before them.[13] Then again, Eric Clive has said that PECL might be used as a basis for codifying the Scots law of contract, while also expressing doubts about whether a general principle of good faith would serve any useful purpose in such a codification.[14]

## B. GOOD FAITH IN MIXED LEGAL SYSTEMS GENERALLY

The starting point for the next three sections of this paper is a claim which I and others have often made over the last few years: that the contract laws of the world's uncodified mixed legal systems (in which Common Law and Civil Law sources, rules, concepts and methods have interacted for long periods) often show striking parallels with the results of PECL. The particular interest of this lies in the way the substance of the uncodified mixed systems is developed by decisions in cases, that is, from the decisions about actual disputes as distinct from academic systematisation.[15] But the picture on good faith coming out of the uncodified mixed systems turns out to be quite distinct from the PECL one, although not exactly like that of English law

11  *Director-General of Fair Trading v First National Bank* [2002] 1 AC 481 at 500, 502. Lord Hope of Craighead also refers to PECL in his speech in *R v Immigration Officer at Prague Airport, ex parte European Roma Rights Centre* [2004] UKHL 55, [2005] 2 WLR 1, para 59.

12  See also Zimmermann & Whittaker, *Good Faith*, 653–701.

13  Note too that the Law Commissions' Report on Unfair Terms in Contract (Law Com No 292; Scot Law Com No 199 (2005)) recommends that the Directive control of good faith should be transposed into new legislation in the UK as a test of fairness and reasonableness, without any reference to good faith.

14  Eric Clive, "The Scottish Civil Code project" in H L MacQueen et al, *Regional Private Laws and Codification in Europe* (2003) at 93, 95.

15  See e.g. R Zimmermann, *Roman Law, Contemporary Law, European Law: The Civilian Tradition Today* (2001) (henceforth Zimmermann, *Roman Law*), especially at 126–177; H L MacQueen, *Scots Law and the Road to the New Ius Commune* (Ius Commune Lectures on European Private Law, 1, 2000) (also available in the *Electronic Journal of Comparative Law*, vol 4.4 (Dec 2000), *http://www.ejcl.org/ejcl/44/art44–1.html*.

either. In neither Scots nor South African contract law is there an active general principle of good faith. The most recent commentators on the subject, Fritz Brand and Douglas Brodie, observe that

> in both systems the role of good faith is to inform and explain the rules of the law of contract and, when necessary, to provide the basis for amending these rules. In neither of the two systems, however, is good faith recognized as an independent or free-floating basis for the setting aside or amendment of a contract.[16]

The same view has been taken even more recently in an obiter dictum of Lord Hope of Craighead in the House of Lords:

> [G]ood faith in Scottish contract law, as in South African law, is generally an underlying principle of an explanatory and legitimating rather than an active or creative nature.[17]

I want to ask what, if any, significance these observations about Scots and South African law may have for principles of good faith and their possible European development and application. Do they support general scepticism about a wide-ranging principle of good faith in any future European contract law, or indicate a gap in the laws of these mixed systems?

Although this paper will focus most on the *uncodified* mixed legal systems (i.e. Scotland and South Africa), good faith in the codified mixed systems (Louisiana, Quebec and Israel) can also be taken into account. Their codes all now state an explicit general principle of good faith. But in each case an interesting history lies behind the present law.

## C. THE CODIFIED MIXED SYSTEMS

### (1) Louisiana

Article 1759 of the Louisiana Civil Code, which appears in the general section on obligations, and so is not limited to contracts, is headed "Good Faith" and states:

> Good faith shall govern the conduct of the obligor and the obligee in whatever pertains to the obligation.

But this Article was only introduced into the Louisiana Code in 1984.

---

16  F Brand & D Brodie, "Good faith in contract law", in Zimmermann, Visser & Reid, *Mixed Legal Systems*, 116.

17  *R v Immigration Officer at Prague Airport, ex parte European Roma Rights Centre* [2004] UKHL 55, [2005] 2 WLR 1, para 60. See also Lord Hope of Craighead, "The place of a mixed system in the Common Law world" (2001) 35 *Israel LR* 1–23 at 16.

Previously there had been only Article 1901 of the 1870 Code, which had appeared in virtually the same words in the 1808 Digest of the Civil Laws (Article 34) and the 1825 Code (Article 1895). Under the heading, "Law for the parties; performance in good faith", Article 1901 ran as follows:

> Agreements legally entered into have the effect of laws on those who have formed them. They can not be revoked, unless by mutual consent of the parties, or for causes acknowledged by law. They must be performed with good faith.

Article 1901 and its predecessors were ultimately derived from the French Code Civil of 1804, which provided – and provides – in its Article 1134 that, in addition to being the private law of the parties, contracts must be performed in good faith.

As well as introducing the general good faith clause in Article 1759, the 1984 revisions of the Louisiana Code transformed the wording but not the substance of the former Article 1901 into what is now Article 1983:

> **Law for the parties; performance in good faith**
> Contracts have the effect of law for the parties and may be dissolved only through the consent of the parties or on grounds provided by law. Contracts must be performed in good faith.

The leading commentator on obligations on the Louisiana Civil Code, Saul Litvinoff, writes as follows about good faith:

> Perhaps good faith emerges with more clarity out of a contrast with its opposite. Thus, if in general terms *bad faith* consists in the intention of obtaining an unfair advantage at another's expense, even if an advantage results for one who acts without that intention, the lack of such intention constitutes good faith, even if an advantage results for one who acts without that intention. The duty that the law imposes upon parties to perform their contracts in good faith is but a consequence of the more general duty of obligors and obligees to govern their conduct by good faith in whatever pertains to the obligation (art 1983). The duty to observe good faith is thus part and parcel of an overriding obligation of good faith that amounts to a very strong general principle (art 1759). It is however in the field of conventional obligations, that is, those willingly entered by the parties to contracts, where good faith has been explored and expounded in a livelier and more complex fashion, *perhaps because the overriding nature of the principle of good faith has only recently been recognized.*[18]

---

18  S Litvinoff, *Louisiana Civil Law Treatise Volume 5: The Law of Obligations*, 2nd edn (2001), § 1.8 (second emphasis HLM). Note also § 1.14, and cf A A Levasseur, *Louisiana Law of Obligations in General: A Précis* (1988), 28–29 ("an inductive reasoning led to the inclusion of LSA-CC Art 1759. From a series of extant Code articles, a general principle was extracted and placed in such a manner as to govern all obligations. ... All in all, the novelty and the merit of [Art 1759] reside[s] only in the formal existence [it] vest[s] on the article [itself] whereas [its] substance has long been of the essence of the law of obligations").

Litvinoff has more recently expounded the potential significance of the over-riding obligation of good faith in an article in the *Tulane Law Review* which, however, draws more heavily on comparative law from Europe and else-where in the USA, than on actual Louisiana case law.[19] He shows that good faith gives rise to duties not expressly contemplated by parties in their agree-ments, and is not limited to performance. The article suggests that the juris-prudence of good faith is not very well developed in Louisiana, save where its good faith in performance requirement can be elaborated upon from the extensive case law on the equivalent provision in the Uniform Commercial Code, §1–203. Litvinoff argues that good faith as well as an express codal provision recognising detrimental reliance as a source of obligation[20] allows the court to remedy *culpa in contrahendo*;[21] and that it may enable the courts to deal with impracticability as well as impossibility, and to extend the scope of lesion. Good faith cannot be confined to the opposite of bad faith, or be presumed in the absence of bad faith; and it could regulate the exercise of contractual discretions. Litvinoff concludes, still looking to the future: "[A] wider judicial freedom to revise contracts may be the ultimate product of the twentieth-century expansion of the requirement of good faith."[22]

The gate is therefore open to a much wider use of an overriding principle of good faith, but the Louisiana courts have not yet passed through. The concept is frequently referred to in the jurisprudence but has seldom been the sole or pre-eminent basis for a judicial decision. There is no sign yet of a decision developing a doctrine akin to *culpa in contrahendo*. Typically it is Article 1983 (contract to be performed in good faith) which is used or cited in the cases,[23] while references to the more general, new, Article 1759 seem often to be in conjunction with citations of Article 1983.[24] In *Badalamenti v Jefferson Guaranty Bank*[25] and *Nicholas v Allstate Insurance Co*[26] it was held that application of Article 1759 could not affect the meaning of a clear and

19  S Litvinoff, "Good faith" (1997) 71 *Tulane LR* 1645.
20  Article 1967 Louisiana Civil Code.
21  See also on this S Herman, "Detrimental reliance in Louisiana law – past, present, and future (?): the code drafter's perspective" (1984) 58 *Tulane LR* 707 at 744–747.
22  Litvinoff (1997) 71 *Tulane LR* 1645 at 1674.
23  See e.g. *MKM LLC v Rebstock Marine Transportation Inc* 776 So 2d 460 (2000); *Levin v May* 887 So 2d 497 (2004).
24  See e.g. the cases cited in the next three footnotes, and *King v Parish National Bank* 885 So 2d 540 (2004) (finding that the requirement of good faith could not render enforceable an oral credit agreement where statute required such agreements to be in writing; see also on this *Aaron v Landcraft Inc* 2005 La App LEXIS 616, which, however, refers only to Article 1759).
25  759 So 2d 274 (2000) (bank's duty of disclosure to borrowers providing pledge).
26  739 So 2d 830 (1999) (malicious termination of "at-will" employment contract).

unambiguous contract. But in another case where the contract was either silent or open-ended, it fell to be interpreted in accordance with good faith.[27] Perhaps more remarkably, in *Bieber-Guillory v Aswell*[28] the Court of Appeal, Third Circuit, remanded for trial a reconventional claim that what were alleged to be excessive charges for services rendered, were contrary to good faith under Article 1759.

## (2) Quebec

Like its Louisiana forebear, the Civil Code of Lower Canada 1866 drew upon the French Code of 1804 but, "enacted at a time when economic liberalism prevailed",[29] contained no provision on good faith. Instead it confined itself to allowing the addition to a contract, beyond what was express in it, "what is incident to it according to its nature and in conformity with usage, equity or law" (Article 1024). It is in the new Quebec Civil Code 1992 (implemented in 1994) that we find the following articles:

### Article 6
Every person is bound to exercise his civil rights in good faith.

### Article 1375
The parties [to a contract] shall conduct themselves in good faith both at the time the obligation is created and at the time it is performed or extinguished.

Article 7 also prohibits the exercise of rights "in an excessive and unreasonable manner contrary to the requirements of good faith". But under Article 2805, restating Article 2202 of the old code, good faith is always presumed, unless the law expressly requires that it be proved.

The leading Quebec jurist, Paul Crépeau, called the new provisions on good faith "a spectacular evolution of the civil law", resulting from "the fact that Quebec has joined an international trend that is striving to bring a new sense of morality to contract law".[30] He says that good faith was first revived in Quebec by "a strong line of cases, originating mostly from the Supreme Court of Canada, [giving] new life to the long-forgotten term 'equity' in article 1024 of the Civil Code of Lower Canada ... in allowing good faith to play, as the source of implied obligations, a fundamental role in the *performance* of

---

27 *Kite v Gus Kaplan Inc* 747 So 2d 503 (1999) (landlord's right to change premises leased to tenant limited to providing space reasonably comparable with previous premises).
28 723 So 2d 1145 (1998).
29 Paul-A Crépeau, *The UNIDROIT Principles and the Civil Code of Québec: Shared Values* (1998) (henceforth Crépeau, *The UNIDROIT Principles and the Civil Code of Québec*), 49.
30 Crépeau, *The UNIDROIT Principles and the Civil Code of Québec*, 53.

contracts."[31] The legislature in Article 1375 has opened up the possibility of extending good faith to many more aspects of contract, without spelling out much in the way of detail; Crépeau suggests that good faith has a role in each case where the Code does not include a specific rule directed to a precise situation. "One must hope", he says, "that the courts will take up the mandate to recognize the variety of precontractual, contractual and even 'post-contractual' instances in which good faith should play a predominant role in the regulation of legal relations."[32]

A search of recent Quebec decisions on the Canadian Legal Information Institute website[33] and in the *Annuaire de Jurisprudence et de doctrine du Québec* suggests that the mandate offered by the concept of good faith has indeed been taken up in the courts, with Articles 6, 7 and 1375 often cited together, and resultant duties of disclosure, co-operation and loyalty being highlighted, especially in the context of contractual performance and termination. Because the principle of good faith permeates the whole of the law of obligations, the courts can deal with breach of the duty by way of any of the sanctions known to the civil law. Good faith is also closely linked to other concepts and techniques available in the Code, such as equity (Article 1434), or the regulation of abusive and penal clauses (Articles 1437, 1623).[34] But the presumption of good faith means that the concept functions mainly to exclude bad faith rather than to impose new standards of behaviour on contracting parties; for example, it has not been used to deal with cases of

31 Crépeau, *The UNIDROIT Principles and the Civil Code of Québec*, 52. The cases cited are: *National Bank of Canada v Soucisse* [1981] 2 SCR 339 (bank's duty of full disclosure to sureties); *Bank of Montreal v Kuet Leong Ng* [1989] 2 SCR 429 (employee's duty of good faith to employer); *Houle v National Bank of Canada* [1990] 3 SCR 122 (bank's duty of good faith to customer); *Bank of Montreal v Bail Ltd* [1992] 2 SCR 554 (obligation of information between contracting parties). To the list might now be added *CIBC Mortgage Corp v Vasquez* [2002] 3 SCR 168 and *Banque national de Paris (Canada) v 165836 Canada Inc* [2004] 2 SCR 45 (both Quebec cases, kindly brought to my attention by Professor Madeleine Cantin-Cumyn).

32 Crépeau, *The UNIDROIT Principles and the Civil Code of Québec*, 57. For the lack of a *culpa in contrahendo* doctrine before the 1992 Code, see P Legrand, "Quebec", in E H Hondius (ed), *Pre-Contractual Liability: Reports to the XIIIth Congress of the International Academy of Comparative Law* (1991), 273–296, and B Lefebvre, "La bonne foi dans la formation du contrat" (1992) 37 *McGill LJ* 1053 at 1056–1058.

33 The website is *http://www.canlii.org/*.

34 See J-L Baudouin & P-G Jobin, *Les Obligations*, 5th edn (1998), paras 86–123 (a 6th edn is imminent); (1996) 26(2) *Revue de droit de l'Université de Sherbrooke* (special issue on the subject of good faith); B Lefebvre, *La bonne foi dans la formation des contrats* (1998); J-L Baudouin, "Justice et équilibre: la nouvelle moralité contractuelle du droit civil québécois", in *Etudes offertes á Jacques Ghestin: le contrat au début du XXIe siècle* (2001), 29–44; D Lluelles, "La bonne foi dans l'exécution des contrats et la problématique des sanctions" (2004) 83 *Canadian Bar Review* 181. I owe several of these references to the kindness of Professor Madeleine Cantin-Cumyn and Judge Jean-Louis Baudouin.

hardship (or *imprévision*).[35] Although commentators are clear that the duty of good faith entails potential liability (including damages liability) for bad faith in pre-contractual negotiations,[36] there has yet to be a judicial decision to this effect in Quebec.[37] In a case coming from Ontario, and therefore reflecting the Canadian Common Law tradition, the Supreme Court of Canada has denied the existence of a tortious duty of care in contract negotiations.[38] But there seems no reason to suppose that this decision will have any impact on developments in Quebec.

## (3) Israel

The Israeli Contracts (General Part) Law 1973 provides that "An obligation or right arising out of a contract shall be fulfilled or exercised in customary manner and in good faith."[39] There is also a specific provision for *culpa in contrahendo*: "In negotiating a contract, a person shall act in customary manner and in good faith."[40] The elevation of the duty to act in good faith to the rank of an overriding principle in the formation and performance of contracts nicely illustrates the character of Israel's mixity – that of a Common Law system being Civilianised by a group of jurists who, in the first generation after the Second World War, "were predominantly Jewish jurists who had been trained in continental Europe (particularly Germany, Austria and Italy) and who had fled from Nazi tyranny to Mandatory Palestine in the 1930s. Despite their experiences in Fascist-dominated Europe, these jurists retained a strong affinity for continental private law."[41] In the thirty years of the good

---

35 For discussion of the Article 2805 presumption see contributions by Lefebvre (at 329–335) and Karim (429–454) in (1996) 26(2) *Revue de droit de l'Université de Sherbrooke*.

36 See, in addition to other works cited in note 34, Lefebvre, *La bonne foi dans la formation des contrats*, 111–163; V Karim, "La règle de la bonne foi prévue dans l'article 1375 du Code civil du Québec: sa portée et les sanctions qui en découlent" (2000) 41 *Les Cahiers de Droit* 435, and M A Grégoire, "Les sanctions de l'obligation de bonne foi lors de la formation et de l'elaboration du contrat" (2002) 104 *Revue du Notariat* 173.

37 There have been cases where the courts have recognised the possibility of liability for abuse of the right to withdraw from negotiations but found it not to apply on the particular facts. See e.g. *Jolicoeur v Rainville*, JE 2000–201, and *Compagnie France Film Inc v Imax Corporation*, JE 2002–5, both CAQ. I am grateful to Professor Daniel Jutras for drawing my attention to these cases.

38 *Martel Building Ltd v Canada* (2000) 12 SCR 860, discussed in P Giliker, "A role for tort in pre-contractual negotiations? An examination of English, French and Canadian law" (2003) 52 *ICLQ* 969. Note that the court (at para 73) expressly declined to comment on the existence of a duty of good faith in pre-contractual negotiations.

39 Section 39.

40 Section 12(a).

41 S Goldstein in V V Palmer, *Mixed Jurisdictions Worldwide: The Third Legal Family* (2001), 450 (see also for more detail S Goldstein, "Israel: creating a new legal system from different sources by jurists of different backgrounds", in E Örücü, E Attwooll & S Coyle (eds), *Studies in Legal Systems: Mixed and Mixing* (1996), 147).

faith provisions in Israel, it is clear that the courts have taken a vigorous approach to the introduction of equity in contract law by way of good faith, and that in particular the provision on pre-contractual liability has been much used.[42] Nili Cohen however observes:

> The operation of the duty of good faith in Israeli case law is actually translated to categories of bad faith. The duty of good faith serves as an 'excluder' mechanism: it does not provide for guidelines for positive conduct of good faith, rather it categorises negative conduct which is incompatible with the standard of good faith.[43]

## D. UNCODIFIED MIXED SYSTEMS

### (1) Scotland

In contrast to the present state of Louisiana, Quebec and Israeli law, there can be no doubt that, if there is a general principle of good faith in Scots contract law, it has been almost entirely latent and inarticulate until now. Indeed, there are judicial *dicta* against such a principle, at least insofar as it might connote a duty to take another's interests into account, or a power to strike down a bargain as unfair.[44] Professor McBryde has written in the leading Scottish text:

> It is clear that certain rights under a contract cannot be acquired by a person who is in bad faith. That is what centuries of case law [has] established. It would be a different proposition to require a person to show that they were in good faith. In entering into a contract knowledge of a contracting party has had relevance in the context of fraud or misrepresentation or error, but otherwise the tendency has been to construe the contract, not to apply a general concept of good faith. In the context of breach of contract the generally accepted position is that bona fides is not a defence to a claim for breach of a mercantile contract. A bad motive in termination of a contract is irrelevant. Damages are not increased because the contract breaker was in bad faith, although in exceptional cases the law may be changing. Nevertheless if a concept of bad faith were to develop it might be possible to

---

42 See S Renner, "Israeli contract law – recent trends and evolution" (1995) 29 *Israel LR* 360; G Shalev, "Israel", in E H Hondius, *Pre-Contractual Liability: Reports to the XIIIth Congress of the International Academy of Comparative Law* (1991), 179–194; A M Rabello, "Culpa in contrahendo and good faith in the formation of contract: precontractual liability in Israeli law", in Rabello (ed), *Essays on European Law and Israel* (1996); N Cohen, "The effect of the duty of good faith on a previously common law system: the experience of Israeli law", in Brownsword et al, *Good Faith*, 189–212. See also Cohen's "Pre-contractual duties: two freedoms and the contract to negotiate", in J Beatson & D Friedmann (eds), *Good Faith and Fault in Contract Law* (1995), 25–56.

43 Cohen, in Brownsword et al, *Good Faith* at 209.

44 See for a collection of such *dicta* J M Thomson, "Good faith in contracting: a sceptical view", in Forte, *Good Faith*, 64–65, 68–69, 70–71. See also Thomson, "Judicial control of unfair contract terms", in Reid & Zimmermann, *History*, vol 2, 157–174.

attack any underhand dealing. In effect the law of contract might have come full circle to the time before the development of the doctrines of facility and circumvention, undue influence and fraudulent or unfair preferences in bankruptcy.[45]

But in *Smith v Bank of Scotland*,[46] decided by the House of Lords in 1997, the leading speech of Lord Clyde referred to "the broad principle in the field of contract law of fair dealing in good faith".[47] He then used this principle to avoid a personal guarantee, applying in Scots law the protection of a guarantor against unfair pressure (undue influence or misrepresentation) resulting from close personal relationship (marriage) with the person whose debts were being guaranteed; a protection created earlier in English law by the House of Lords in *Barclays Bank plc v O'Brien*.[48] As a result, the creditor in a guarantee is bound to take steps to ensure that the guarantor is not improperly affected by conduct of the person whose debts are to be guaranteed.[49] Good faith was used to this end in *Smith* because the equity of constructive notice and the doctrine of presumed undue influence deployed in *O'Brien* is said to be unknown to Scots law. In subsequent decisions,[50] the Scottish courts have preferred to continue to use the broad principle of good faith rather than adopt the detailed guidance for creditors developed in English law by the House of Lords in *Royal Bank of Scotland v Etridge*.[51] The preference for a broad principled approach over "matters of ritual, the blind performance of which will secure the avoidance of doom",[52] is probably to be explained by a reluctance to find the bank's omission of one of the many steps set out in *Etridge* enough of itself to avoid the guarantee.[53]

45 McBryde, *Contract*, para 1-33. Compare the rather different analysis in H L MacQueen, "Good faith in the Scots law of contract: an undisclosed principle?", in Forte, *Good Faith* at 13–17. See also T M Taylor, "Bona et mala fides", in *Encyclopaedia of the Laws of Scotland*, vol 2 (1927); and two works of T B Smith: *British Justice: The Scottish Contribution* (1961), 177–179, and *Short Commentary on the Laws of Scotland* (1962), 297–298, 835–837.

46 1997 SC (HL) 111.

47 Per Lord Clyde at 121B–C. A similar *dictum* is found in the earlier case of *Trade Development Bank v David W Haig (Bellshill) Ltd* 1983 SLT 510 at 517 per Lord President Emslie.

48 [1994] 1 AC 180.

49 Note that the same result is reached in Article 4:111 PECL; see further the contribution to this volume of Professor du Plessis (171–174).

50 See G J Junor, "The dust settling: *Smith v Bank of Scotland*" 1999 *JR* 67; S M Eden, "Cautionary tales – the continued development of *Smith v Bank of Scotland*" (2003) 7 *Edinburgh LR* 107; Eden, "More cautionary tales" (2004) 8 *Edinburgh LR* 276.

51 [2002] 2 AC 773.

52 *Etridge* at 817, per Lord Clyde (para 95).

53 *Clydesdale Bank v Black* 2002 SC 555 (where the guarantor argued that the bank had fallen foul of the *Etridge* requirements by not holding a meeting with her outwith her husband's presence at which they warned her about the consequences of signing the document and advised her to obtain independent legal advice; but she had in fact taken such advice, the content of which she did not disclose in her pleadings).

Lord Clyde based his assertion about good faith in contract, not upon any historical or comparative analysis of Scots law, but upon the authority of comparatively modern property law cases dealing with the problem of "double sales".[54] The aptness of this for contract law is doubtful, since good faith in property is a much more subjective matter than in contract.[55] But there is in fact some good old authority for general contractual obligations of good faith in Scots law. The Civilian heritage meant that certain contracts (sale being the prime example) were always *bona fide*, but this was increasingly generalised to all contracts in the eighteenth and early nineteenth centuries, by authoritative writers such as Bankton, Kames and Bell.[56] *Bona fides* was actively deployed in judicial decisions of the period as well.[57] In *Whitson v Neilson & Co*,[58] for example, N ordered 200 tons of flax, to be obtained from Riga and imported in two ships by the seller W, for delivery in the following July and August. The first ship arrived back on 23 August, but N declined to take delivery until the full quantity was available. The second ship arrived on 29 August, but the state of the tides prevented it entering harbour before 2 September. W told N that he would begin unloading the second ship by way of lighters, starting on 30 August; but N continued to refuse to take delivery, unless the whole quantity could be delivered before the end of August. In the end, the flax was delivered on 1 September but N stated that since the original contract was now terminated they would pay only the current market price, which was £700 less than the contract one. W, who was insolvent, raised an action for the balance, to which the Court of Session held he was entitled. The contract was to be construed *bona fide*, and the seller had offered sufficient *bona fide* implement. "If we were compelled to go to the utmost strictness in *bona fide* contracts," said Lord Alloway, in an interesting inversion of modern arguments *against* good faith in contract, "I do not know where there would be an end of it."[59] Lord Glenlee, who was worried about taking "more liberties with the terms of mercantile contracts than it [is] safe

---

54 *Rodger (Builders) Ltd v Fawdry* 1950 SC 483; *Trade Development Bank v David W Haig (Bellshill) Ltd* 1983 SLT 510.

55 This observation also holds good for Professor McBryde's observation (quoted in text accompanying note 45 above) that certain rights cannot be acquired under a contract by a party in bad faith.

56 See A D M Forte, "Good faith and utmost good faith", in Forte, *Good Faith* at 77–79, 96–97; see also at 13 n 32 (MacQueen).

57 See, in addition to the case cited in the next note, *Smith v Bank of Scotland* (1829) 7 S 244.

58 (1828) 6 S 579. The case was brought to my attention by the Aberdeen PhD thesis of Mohammed Al Othman, of which I was external examiner in January 2005. For the declining authority of the case later in the nineteenth century, see McBryde, *Contract*, 1st edn (1987), 331 n 74 (not in the 2nd edition); see also Gloag, *Contract*, 283 n 2.

59 (1828) 6 S 579 at 584.

to do",[60] nonetheless thought the contract did not stipulate for delivery to be *complete* before the end of August. *Bona fides* meant that ambiguous contracts were given common sense constructions. Lord Pitmilly looked for the "fair meaning"[61] of the bargain; and the Lord Justice-Clerk could "see no authority for holding, that if there was a hundredweight to deliver at twelve o'clock at night of the 31st, the purchasers could get quit of the bargain."[62] The contract in this case was one of sale, and so one of *bona fides* in the Civilian tradition; but nonetheless the case shows the concept of good faith being deployed in an active way in a commercial context – termination of contract for literal non-performance – which today some at least might see as controversial.[63]

It was probably later nineteenth-century will and *laissez faire* theories that sterilised any potential good faith might have had to become an active doctrine in Scots law.[64] But cases and writers did develop concepts of terms to be applied generally in all types of contract unless there was express contrary provision or specific implication in certain kinds of contract. For example, an 1881 House of Lords authority is still cited for a duty on contracting parties to do all that is necessary to be done on their part to ensure that the contract is carried out.[65] And writers have accepted such implications as requirements that contracts be carried out within a reasonable time; that one party does not do anything to prevent completion of performance by the other or otherwise derogate from the contract; and that discretionary powers under a contract are exercised reasonably.[66] The doctrine of undue influence, which was first borrowed (with some discrimination) from English law in 1879,[67] also looks like a product of good faith under another name.

---

60  At 584.

61  At 585.

62  At 586. The Lord Justice-Clerk, lapsing into anti-semitism, adds (at 586): "To hold this would be a judaical construction which should not be introduced into bona fide contracts."

63  Compare the Privy Council's decision in *Union Eagle Ltd v Golden Achievement Ltd* [1997] AC 514, where the contract was held terminable when a purchaser tendered payment 10 minutes after the contractually stipulated time. A deposit was also forfeited. See further E McKendrick, "Good faith: a matter of principle?", in Forte, *Good Faith*, 56–58, and Bridge, in Brownsword et al, *Good Faith*, 150–162 (discussing termination in commodities contracts under English law). See also Zimmermann & Whittaker, *Good Faith*, discussions of case nos 6, 7, 8, and 24.

64  See Thomson, in Forte, *Good Faith* at 64–69, 70–71; S C Styles, "Good faith: a principled matter", also in Forte, *Good Faith* at 165–166.

65  *Mackay v Dick and Stevenson* (1881) 8 R (HL) 37 at 40 per Lord Blackburn. Gloag, *Contract*, 280; McBryde, *Contract*, 483; SME, vol 15, paras 6, 714 (where this is summarised as a duty to co-operate).

66  See MacQueen, in Forte, *Good Faith* at 16, and MacQueen & Thomson, *Contract*, para 3.34, for the authorities. For further comment on discretionary powers, mainly in the employment context, see Brand & Brodie, in Zimmermann, Visser & Reid, *Mixed Legal Systems* at 109–112.

67  *Gray v Binny* (1879) 7 R 332.

It remains to be seen, however, whether twenty-first century courts, also encouraged by the use of the principle in EU-inspired legislation such as that on unfair terms in consumer contracts,[68] will take good faith beyond its present realm of personal guarantees into other areas of contemporary contract law. So far, there has not been much sign of that. In *Macari v Celtic Football and Athletic Club Ltd*,[69] a leading case on the mutual obligations of trust and confidence (or good faith?) in employment contracts, it was argued that the employer's bad faith in seeking to undermine the employee's position disabled the former from eventually terminating the latter's contract. But the court held that the employer's conduct, and the final dismissal, had been justified and reasonable in all the circumstances, and therefore it never really reached the legal question of the relevance or otherwise of bad motive in cases of termination of contract for breach.[70] Possibly, however, good faith might explain why the employee's right to withhold performance in respect of his employer's undoubted breach of contract was denied, since he was picking and choosing amongst his obligations as to which ones he would perform.[71] *Walford v Miles*,[72] which denied the existence of obligations to negotiate in good faith in English law, was not applied by Lord Hamilton in *McCall's Entertainments v South Ayrshire Council*,[73] but the relevant aspect of *Walford* was not so much the good faith point as the question of the enforceability of agreements to negotiate. In *McCall's Entertainments* an agreement to negotiate a sale under an option in a lease was held to be enforceable because there was provision for an arbiter to fix the price if the parties could not; good faith was not in issue.[74] And in *W S Karoulias SA v Drambuie Liqueur Co Ltd*,[75] a case involving a Scottish company and its Greek distributor in which questions arose about whether or not negotiations had concluded a new contract between the parties, neither the arguments of counsel nor the opinion of Lord Clarke took account of the possibility that good faith in negotiations might mean that there was some liability regardless of contract. Indeed, Lord Clarke said: "[W]hat the court is looking for is

---

68 Unfair Terms in Consumer Contracts Regulations 1999 (SI 1999/2083), implementing Directive of 1993.

69 1999 SC 628.

70 Contrary to Professor McBryde's comment about its irrelevance, quoted above, text accompanying note 45.

71 J M Thomson, "An unsuitable case for suspension?" (1999) 3 *Edinburgh LR* 394.

72 [1992] 2 AC 128.

73 1998 SLT 1403.

74 Although it might well have been: see the sequel to the case after a proof had been held, *McCall's Entertainments v South Ayrshire Council (No 2)* 1998 SLT 1423.

75 2004 GWD 31–638.

whether or not the parties have reached finality in their agreement. The question is whether or not the parties have passed beyond negotiation and have a concluded agreement."[76] After proof Lord Clarke affirmed that there was indeed no contract, albeit that Drambuie had been guilty of "stringing along" Karoulias while intending to contract with a third party.[77] Neither counsel nor the judge argued that there was liability in Scots law comparable to that which Article 2:301(2) PECL would have imposed on such facts.

For the time being, at least, good faith remains at best an underlying principle of Scots contract law, which "enables the identification and solution of problems which the existing rules do not, or seem unable to reach. ... The principle also provides a basis upon which existing rules inconsistent with it can be criticised and reformed, whether judicially or by legislation."[78] I have suggested in particular that good faith would help us to make sense of an inchoate *culpa in contrahendo* doctrine to be found in a series of cases stretching back to *Walker v Milne* [79] (the "Melville Monument" case) in 1823, and also perhaps enable the courts to develop the precedents a little way beyond the very narrow scope they currently receive in the courts.[80] But I have also argued that while good faith underlies or explains much of our contract law, it has not been necessary to use it actively to fill gaps in the law; and given the extent of existing statutory protection for weaker contracting parties, I should be hesitant about its use to add yet further equity into that particular branch of contract law.

In December 2004 news broke of an action raised against the Scottish Parliamentary Corporate Body by one of the unsuccessful tenderers for the building of the Scottish Parliament.[81] The gist of the claim is that the tenderer was wrongfully excluded from the tender competition in its final stages before the award of the contract. Part of the background is also that the ultimately

---

76  At para 33. Note also *Robertson Group (Construction) Ltd v Amey-Miller (Edinburgh) Joint Venture* [2005] CSOH 60, in which a pre-contractual letter of intent was held to be "a contract of an essentially temporary nature", accepted by commencement of work in accordance with the letter's instructions (para 1).

77  2005 SLT 813.

78  MacQueen, in Forte, *Good Faith* at 18, 19.

79  (1823) 2 S 379. See also the comment of J Blackie, "Good faith and the doctrine of personal bar" (in Forte, *Good Faith*) on *Walker* and the line of nineteenth-century cases descending therefrom: "These cases (and others later) are so full of references to good faith and bad faith that it is clear beyond a peradventure that this is what they are about" (at 155).

80  MacQueen, in Forte, *Good Faith* at 22–33. For the current position see *Dawson International plc v Coats Paton plc* 1988 SLT 854. For comparative source material from Europe see H Beale, A Hartkamp, H Kötz & D Tallon, *Cases, Materials and Text on Contract Law* (2002), ch 2.2.

81  See BBC News Online 22 Dec 2004 (*http://news.bbc.co.uk/1/hi/scotland/4118801.stm*) and 2 Feb 2005 (*http://news.bbc.co.uk/1/hi/scotland/4229151.stm*).

successful tenderer had been first excluded, and then, having adjusted its tender, readmitted to the competition at the behest of the civil servant running the project at that stage.[82] The claim seems to be based upon possible breaches of European Union public procurement rules rather than upon any common law notions of good faith or *culpa in contrahendo*.[83] The advantage the public procurement rules may offer over any common law liability is the recovery of damages based upon loss of the contract profit, as distinct from the reimbursement of wasted or reliance expenditure which is as far as the previous Scottish cases go by way of remedy. It thus does not seem very likely that the Scottish Parliament case will provide an opportunity for belated recognition of good faith duties in pre-contractual negotiations. Indeed, it looks as though the first issue to be addressed is that of prescription, since the alleged breaches of duty took place more than five years before the action was raised in December 2004.[84] On the other hand, the public procurement rules demonstrate a recognition of the validity of pre-contractual obligations in at least some cases; and while public body contracts may be particularly strong cases for insisting on the existence of such obligations,[85] it does not follow that the private, and in particular the commercial, sector should be wholly free of them.

82 For the factual background so far as publicly known at the time the action was raised, see the Final Report of the Holyrood Inquiry as conducted by Lord Fraser of Carmyllie QC (Sept 2004, accessible at *http://www.holyroodinquiry.org/FINAL_report/report.htm*), ch 7. Note in particular Lord Fraser's comment in his conclusions that "[i]t does however appear to me, on elementary considerations of fairness as between competing tenderers, that if one tenderer was effectively permitted to change a very material aspect of the financial basis upon which its tender was submitted that is an opportunity which should have been afforded to the others."

83 For the procurement rules, see SME, vol 3, para 17 (note also Cumulative Service and Service Update); Chitty on Contracts, 29th edn (2004), vol I, ch 10(7). Note too that on 16 March 2005 the European Commission announced an investigation of possible breaches of the procurement rules: see its press release at *http://europa.eu.int/rapid/pressReleasesAction.do?reference=IP/05/314&format=HTML&aged=0&language=EN&guiLanguage=en*.

84 There is also an issue about whether the SPCB is the correct, or the only, possible defender, given that the contract was awarded by the Scottish Office before the SPCB came into existence. But see Scotland Act 1998, s 23.

85 See the comments of Finn J in *Hughes Aircraft Systems Ltd v Airservices Australia* (1997) 146 ALR 1 at 37–42. I cannot here resist also quoting a splendid letter to the *Scotsman* newspaper by Mr Ian Arnott, published on 2 Dec 2004 under the heading, "Building on Good Faith", in which he commented critically on the findings of the Civil Service Commissioner that the civil servants involved in the Scottish Parliament building project were blameless since all their decisions were taken in good faith. Mr Arnott said: "There may be no universal definition of what constitutes good faith, but there is a general understanding of what it means, and the commissioner's concept seems to be elastic to an unusual degree and certainly questionable." Amongst other subsequent scathing remarks, Mr Arnott added, with particular pertinence to the present discussion: "Was it good faith that bent the rules of tendering to allow the reintroduction and appointment of a previously rejected firm of contract managers?" Perhaps in due course the progress of the Court of Session action will give Mr Arnott a greater sense of justice being seen to be done.

## (2) South Africa

As already noted above, observations about good faith as an underlying rather than an active principle of contract law hold good for the main other un-codified mixed jurisdiction, South Africa.[86] In a study of good faith published in 1999, Dale Hutchison concluded:

> [I]t seems reasonably clear that South African law has no general doctrine of good faith. By that I mean that good faith is not an independent or free-floating principle that the courts can employ directly to justify intervention in contractual relationships on the grounds of unreasonableness or unfairness. ... [G]ood faith may be regarded as an ethical value or controlling principle, based on community standards of decency and fairness, that underlies and informs the substantive law of contract. It finds expression in various technical rules and doctrines, defines their form, content and field of application and provides them with a moral and theoretical foundation. Good faith thus has a creative, a controlling and a legitimating or explanatory function. It is not, however, the only value or principle that underlies the law of contract. ... [T]he influence of good faith in the law of contract is merely of an indirect nature, in that the concept is usually if not always mediated by some other, more technical doctrinal device. Thus, for example, while good faith does not empower a court directly to supplement the terms of a contract, or to limit their operation, it might in appropriate cases enable the court to achieve these same results indirectly, through the use of devices such as implied terms and the public policy rule.[87]

In South Africa, however, the existence and scope of open-ended norms such as good faith in contract law seems to be more hotly disputed than in Scotland.[88] As Hutchison noted, there were one or two judges prepared to go further than his conclusion. In *Eerste Nasionale Bank van Suidelike Afrika Bpk v Saayman NO*,[89] the facts of which were comparable in some respects to the *O'Brien*, *Smith* and *Etridge* cases described earlier, a sick old woman stood as surety to a bank for the debts of her son. The woman's daughter was subsequently appointed her curatrix and obtained an order from the court that the suretyship was unenforceable. The majority decided the case on the basis of the woman's lack of capacity, but Olivier JA founded his concurring decision squarely on a doctrine of good faith. In *Mort NO v Henry Shields-*

---

86 See R Zimmermann, "Good faith and equity", in Zimmermann & Visser, *Southern Cross*, esp at 239–255.

87 D Hutchison, "Good faith in the South African law of contract", in Brownsword et al, *Good Faith*, 213–242 at 229–231.

88 See e.g. Zimmermann, in Zimmermann & Visser, *Southern Cross*; A Cockrell, "Second-guessing the exercise of contractual power on rationality grounds" [1997] *Acta Juridica* 26; J Lewis, "Fairness in South African contract law" (2003) 120 *SALJ* 330; G Lubbe, "Taking fundamental rights seriously: the Bill of Rights and its implications for the development of contract law" (2004) 121 *SALJ* 395.

89 1997 (4) SA 302 (SCA).

*Chiat*[90] Davis J argued that the constitutional obligation to develop the common law in accordance with the rights of equality and dignity required the courts to establish an active doctrine of good faith; a view which prompted Hutchison to comment:

> [T]o reach directly for the baton of good faith would be to confess to a want of technical expertise or creativity. Palm-tree justice no doubt has its virtues, but as lawyers we should adhere to the ideal of justice according to law.[91]

Eventually, however, the Supreme Court of Appeal (SCA) expressly followed Hutchison when confirming twice in 2002[92] that the 1996 Constitution did not require the development of a good faith doctrine in contract law. In *Brisley v Drotsky*[93] the SCA held that the common law *Shifren* doctrine – an entrenchment clause in a contract providing that all amendments to the contract had to comply with specified formalities is binding[94] – remained in force, even although the contract in question (a lease) and the clause were embodied in a standard form purchased by the landlord in a shop, and were never the subject of negotiation, disclosure or legal advice between the parties.[95] The landlord was seeking to evict the tenant for breaches of the lease conditions, although previously he had taken no action in response to similar breaches by the tenant and might therefore, without the *Shifren* clause, have been taken to have accepted an implicit variation of the lease. The court rejected an argument that the principle of good faith could prevent invocation of the *Shifren* clause because it was in all the circumstances unreasonable, unfair and contrary to good faith. The judgment of Olivier JA in *Eerste Nasionale Bank* was disapproved. The court accepted Dale Hutchison's understanding of the legitimating and explanatory role of good faith, but observed that this did not override other important considerations such as freedom of contract. The court also did not take Hutchison's preferred, rule-based, route – "limiting the *Shifren* principle, possibly by recognizing exceptional circumstances where the principle will not apply, certainly by employing and developing concepts such as waiver, estoppel and pactum de non petendo".[96]

---

90  2001 (1) SA 464 (C) at 474–475.
91  "Non-variation clauses in contract: any escape from the *Shifren* straitjacket?" (2001) 118 *SALJ* 720.
92  *Brisley v Drotsky* 2002 (4) SA 1 (SCA) at paras 33–36; *Afrox Healthcare Bpk v Strydom* 2002 (6) SA 21 (SCA), para 18.
93  2002 (4) SA 1 (SCA).
94  *SA Sentrale Ko-op Graanmaatskappy Bpk v Shifren* 1964 (4) SA 760 (A).
95  On these facts in Scotland, it is submitted, the clause would have been subjected to the fairness and reasonableness tests of the Unfair Contract Terms Act 1977, s 17.
96  Hutchison (2001) 118 *SALJ* 720 at 745.

In *Afrox Healthcare v Strydom*,[97] an exclusion clause in a hospital treatment contract was challenged as contrary to public policy and good faith by a
patient who had suffered irreparable harm in a hospital operation as a result
of a nurse's negligence in dressing his wounds. The challenge was dismissed,
the court finding that the contractual relationship was not an unequal one,
that good faith was not in itself a ground for invalidating contracts,[98] and that
the clause did not promote negligent conduct contrary to the respondent's
constitutional right of access to health care; other factors, such as the hospital's
need to maintain its professional reputation, would ensure promotion of the
right to health. Moreover freedom of contract had to be taken into account.

The Supreme Court of Appeal has been criticised for being insufficiently
radical in its approach to contractual freedom under the Constitution.[99] But I
have some sympathy with the judges, at least in the *Afrox* case, where what
was really being sought was a regime for control of exclusion clauses –
something peculiarly apt for legislative rather than judicial innovation. Even
more so where, as in South Africa, the legislature has not yet chosen to act
upon a recent Law Commission report on the subject,[100] and it is clear that
there are significantly divided counsels on the subject. It is one thing to use
an *existing* doctrine of good faith to "radiate" human right principles, as
happens in Germany and Israel;[101] quite another, I would suggest, to *invent* such
an open-ended doctrine as a human right or as required by other human rights.

Having said that, there was perhaps one other avenue open to the South
African judges with regard to the particular kind of exclusion clause in question:
viz, an exclusion of liability for death or personal injury. That was the active
public policy doctrine which has evolved in South African contract law since
the 1980s. The doctrine has been used to attack unacceptable contract terms

---

97  2002 (6) SA 21 (SCA).

98  See also on this *BOE Bank Bpk v Van Zyl* 2002 (5) SA 165 (C): bank able to enforce surety
     against father-in-law of principal debtor; no duress or undue influence; and no overarching
     principle of good faith or improper procurement of consensus recognised in South Africa by
     SCA; a lower court would need direction before it could make the change.

99  See e.g. D D Tladi, "Breathing constitutional values into the law of contract: freedom of contract
     and the Constitution" (2002) 35 *De Jure* 306; D Tladi, "One step forward, two steps back for
     constitutionalising the common law: *Afrox Health Care v Strydom*" (2002) 17 *South African
     Public Law* 472; Lewis (2003) 120 *SALJ* 330; Lubbe (2004) 121 *SALJ* 395.

100 South African Law Commission Report, Project 47, Unreasonable Stipulations in Contracts and
     the Rectification of Contracts (April 1998).

101 See A Flessner, "Freedom of contract and constitutional law in Germany", in A M Rabello & P
     Sarcevic (eds), *Freedom of Contract and Constitutional Law* (1998); A Barak, "Constitutional
     human rights and private law", in D Friedmann & D Barak-Erez (eds), *Human Rights in Private
     Law* (2001) at 40 (good faith a means of introducing human rights principles into Israeli
     contract law, especially equality).

since the well-known case of *Sasfin v Beukes* in 1989,[102] and it was put into play in *Afrox*, failing because only one basis for doing so was put forward, viz certain provisions of the Constitution which did not point clearly to the conclusion sought. Alfred Cockrell and I have argued that public policy falls to be distinguished from good faith. The latter is essentially concerned with the relationship of the contracting parties, albeit applying external community standards to them, while public policy deals with more general issues such as the prevention of crime and wrongs, the protection of marriage and family life, the right to work, and the proper administration of justice. South African law has a much more dynamic concept of public policy than Scotland, where there has been what Cockrell and I call a "hardening of the categories"; it offers some interesting lessons for PECL, a point to which I will briefly return below.[103]

The Supreme Court of Appeal has reaffirmed, but also developed, its basic stance on good faith in its most recent discussion of the subject, in *South African Forestry Co Ltd v York Timbers Ltd*.[104] The case involved contracts for the supply of logs from SAFCOL plantations to the defendants' sawmills. The contracts, which were to continue for an unspecified period, contained mechanisms for the revision of prices from time to time, and for termination should the parties be unable to agree new prices. But the contract was later amended so that in the event of disagreement over price revision the matter was to be referred to a Government Minister who was empowered to refer the dispute on to arbitration if he were of the opinion that no agreement could be reached. There was also provision for the Minister to settle disputes about other terms subject to revision, but if his decision was unacceptable to the sawmill company, the contract would continue on the old terms, but subject to termination after five years. The sawmill company also had the right to terminate the contract at any time on one year's written notice, while should the Minister at any stage be of the opinion that it would be in the interest of the wood industry or of the country as a whole to terminate the contract, then SAFCOL would be entitled to cancel the contract on giving the sawmill company written notice of at least five years. The policy behind this remarkably unbalanced contract was to encourage private sector investment in the sector, with long-term agreements giving investors in a capital-intensive industry time to recoup their investment, as well as some security of tenure.[105]

---

102  1989 (1) SA 1 (A).
103  See H MacQueen & A Cockrell, "Illegal contracts", in Zimmermann, Visser & Reid, *Mixed Legal Systems*, esp at 171–175; and further below, final paragraph of this article.
104  2005 (3) SA 323 (SCA).
105  See para [3] of Brand JA's judgment.

For many years SAFCOL sought price revision under their contract with York; but they were frustrated, or strung along, by an adroit series of manouevres by York, which enabled the latter to continue to sell its timber in the market at prices up to 60 per cent lower than those of competitors who had agreed price revisions with SAFCOL under other contracts. SAFCOL had great difficulty in persuading the relevant Minister to become involved, and finally went to court to seek an order that the York contracts had been terminated. Their claim was based upon breach by York of an implied term in the contracts, to the effect that York would act in accordance with the dictates of reasonableness, fairness and good faith when SAFCOL sought price revisions under the contract.

Giving the judgment of the court, Brand JA rejected SAFCOL's contentions. He reaffirmed the approach to good faith in the *Brisley* and *Afrox* cases as an underlying value; to allow good faith a more active role would undermine certainty to an unacceptable degree. A term could be implied on the basis of good faith, but not to override what the parties had intended as that could be derived from interpretation of the contract's express terms.

But Brand JA then went on to say that "in the interpretation process, the notions of fairness and good faith ... have a role to play", and continued (para 32):

> While a court is not entitled to superimpose on the clearly expressed intention of the parties its notion of fairness, the position is different when a contract is ambiguous. In such a case the principle that all contracts are governed by good faith is applied and the intention of the parties is determined on the basis that they negotiated with one another in good faith. [33] Having regard to the provisions of clause 3.2 it is clear that it confers the right upon a party (in this instance, Safcol) who found it impossible to come to an agreement on revision of price, firstly, to approach the Minister as a preliminary step to arbitration and, secondly, to refer the matter to arbitration if the Minister should express the opinion that no agreement could be reached. Although the clause does not expressly impose any duty or obligation on the other party (York) the corollary of the rights conferred upon Safcol is an obligation or duty on the part of York not to frustrate Safcol in the exercise of these rights. This follows logically from the structure of the rights and duties the parties themselves created. [34] However, had there been any interpretative ambiguity as to the existence of such a duty or obligation on the part of York, it is removed by considerations of reasonableness, fairness and good faith. In other words, even where the logical consequences of the rights and duties may not necessitate such an inference, the underlying principle of good faith requires its importation.

Brand JA then went on to say that York had indeed frustrated and delayed SAFCOL in the exercise of its rights:

by pretending that it was prepared to negotiate; by contending that it was possible to reach agreement whereas obviously it was not; by contending, contrary to the whole scheme of the agreements revealed by clauses 3.2 and 4.2, that revised prices could not be negotiated before the terms of the long term contracts had been settled; by raising contentions which can only be described as absurd, as for example, that a reference to the Minister was inappropriate where the parties were in agreement on the principle that there should be price revision, thus creating an obvious deadlock; by insisting upon the Minister's involvement only to raise the objection subsequently that Safcol had approached the wrong Minister and that the Minister should recuse himself on grounds of bias.

All this, the judge concluded, amounted to such repudiation as to justify SAFCOL in terminating the contract.

The case shows that to say good faith has an underlying rather than a creative role in the law of contract need not imply judicial passivity in the face of bad faith behaviour that is seemingly not prohibited by the contract's express terms. It is a good illustration of what PECL would call having regard to good faith and fair dealing in the interpretation of a contract (Article 5:102 PECL), and perhaps also an instance of the duty of contracting parties to co-operate to give full effect to the contract (Article 1:202 PECL). There are also elements of fundamental non-performance under Article 8:103 PECL, that is, intentional non-performance substantially depriving the aggrieved party of what it was entitled to expect under the contract, and giving that party reason to believe that it could not rely on the other's future performance. There is a comparison with a Scottish decision in a construction case, *Scottish Power v Kvaerner Construction*,[106] where a sub-contractor (SP) recovered damages from a main contractor (K) for disruption and delay to its work caused by the latter. The decision was based upon implied terms that K would not hinder or prevent SP from carrying out their obligations in a regular and orderly manner; that K would take all reasonable steps to enable SP to carry out their work in an orderly manner; and that K would provide such information as ought reasonably to be known to K and required by SP so as to enable SP to fulfil their obligations. The court also indicated that while implied terms could not contradict express terms, they could deal with the same subject area.[107]

A final observation from South Africa is the current lack of any developed doctrine akin to *culpa in contrahendo* or 'Melville monument' liability in Scots law. But in *Transnet Ltd v Goodman Brothers (Pty) Ltd*[108] it was held

---

106   1999 SLT 721. See also *E & J Glasgow Ltd v UGC Estates Ltd* [2005] CSOH 63.
107   Compare, however, *Thomson v Thomas Muir (Waste Management) Ltd* 1995 SLT 403 (described in MacQueen & Thomson, *Contract*, para 3.37).
108   2001 (1) SA 853 (SCA).

that the Constitution required a government-owned corporation to provide an unsuccessful tenderer with reasons why another had been preferred, while in *Transnet Ltd v Sechaba Photoscan (Pty) Ltd* [109] the same corporation was ordered to pay damages including loss of prospective profit to another unsuccessful tenderer, in a tender process admitted to have been irregular, fraudulent and dishonest. In yet another case involving Transnet, the Supreme Court of Appeal held that an agreement to negotiate in good faith was enforceable. [110]

## E. LESSONS

What lessons are to be drawn from all this mixed system material? One is obvious: in all the systems there is current, active debate about good faith in contract, along with relevant activity in legislation, the courts and legal practice. This is a significant subject, and it is right that there should also be discussion about it at a European level. Further, if European legal development moves forward by way of instruments, whether legislative or "soft law" in character, specific reference in them to good faith is highly likely. Indeed, such reference is already frequently made: see the Unfair Terms, Commercial Agents and Distance Selling Directives, for example. The UNIDROIT PICC 2004 also use the concept of good faith and fair dealing similarly to PECL (although the differences between the two instruments deserve more exploration than is possible here). [111] The European Code of Contract prepared by the Pavia Academy of European Private Lawyers gives good faith a significant role in pre-contractual liability (Article 6), implying terms (Article 32), interpretation (Article 39(1)), determining the effects of the contract (Article 44), performance (Article 75), and suspension of performance

---

109 2005 (1) SA 299 (SCA).

110 *Southernport Developments (Pty) Ltd v Transnet Ltd* 2005 (2) SA 202 (SCA).

111 Thus, although each party must act in accordance with good faith and fair dealing in international trade and the duty is non-excludable (Article 1.7 PICC), freedom and sanctity of contract are not made subject to good faith (Articles 1.1, 1.3 PICC). Liability in negotiations depends on "bad faith" (Article 2.1.15 PICC), and in general direct reference to good faith is avoided in particular clauses (although see Articles 4.8 (supplying omitted terms) and 5.1.2 PICC (implied obligations)). The right to terminate is controlled through the concept of fundamental non-performance rather than good faith, and parties' right to require strict compliance is unaffected (Article 7.3.1 PICC). Exemption clauses can be struck down only if grossly unfair (Article 7.1.6 PICC). In general the Principles appear to prefer to speak of "reasonableness": see Chapter 4 (interpretation), and Articles 5.1.3 (co-operation) and 6.2.3 PICC (hardship renegotiations).

(Article 108); but, notably, there is no over-arching principle.[112] As a final footnote, it may be observed that the draft Code of Contract Law prepared for the Law Commissions of England and Scotland by Harvey McGregor between 1967 and 1971 also provided for an obligation of good faith in performance, albeit in terms of requiring fair dealing.[113]

All the codified mixed systems also use an express concept of good faith, and the intention seems to be to cover against gaps in the code and create flexibility for the future. Louisiana, Quebec and Israel all have a very general provision alongside other, more specific, ones. Louisiana and Quebec ultimately go back to French influence for their more specific provisions on good faith in performance – but the former's approach to this may well be more influenced by USA UCC § 1–203 (good faith in performance only). Neither Louisiana nor Quebec has anything akin to Israel's provision on *culpa in contrahendo*, but each thinks that their general clauses will do the trick if necessary. In all three jurisdictions a process of Civilianisation is readily discernible in the modern developments of texts on good faith; but there is also a concern to increase the scope for contractual equity in the courts. The courts appear to use good faith alongside the ordinary rules of contract and obligations, however, supporting and supplementing rather than altogether displacing them.

The contrasting lack of an explicit general principle in the uncodified systems may be explicable by their case law basis for contract, and the typical reluctance of the judiciary to do more than is necessary to decide the case before them. A contract law built up from cases is more likely than a code to be a system of fairly specific rules. Such rules may be latently informed by good faith, but the judge is unlikely to take good faith very often as the major premise justifying the conclusion of the case. In the main this system works reasonably well; but every now and then the judges need a helping hand from the legislature and commentators before all the issues can be addressed – for example, with regard to unfair contract terms, extortionate credit bargains (recently in the news in England[114]) and the like. *Culpa in contrahendo* may

---

112  I have used the translation published in September 2004 as a special issue of the *Edinburgh Law Review*, under the title *European Code of Contract*.

113  H McGregor, *Contract Code drawn up on behalf of the English Law Commission* (1993), section 201. See further McGregor, "The codification of contracts in England and Scotland", in A M Rabello (ed), *Aequitas and Equity: Equity in Civil Law and Mixed Jurisdictions* (1997).

114  See the decision to set aside an extortionate credit bargain reported on BBC News Online 28 Oct 2004: *http://news.bbc.co.uk/1/hi/england/merseyside/3962963.stm*. A UK Government Bill to amend the law on extortionate credit bargains is currently before the Westminster Parliament (see further Professor du Plessis' contribution to this volume, at 165 n 74).

be another such area, although the creation of such a liability would meet opposition from many at least in British legal as well as business circles.

By and large, good faith appears to be primarily an "excluder" in all the mixed systems, working to prevent bad faith (or perhaps more accurately, unreasonableness) more than to impose positive requirements of behaviour on contracting parties. The main exception noted in this paper is the sequence of cases in Scotland beginning with *Smith v Bank of Scotland*, under which the courts have required banks to achieve certain standards of conduct in their dealings with prospective guarantors where they have a close personal relationship with the debtor whose debts are to be guaranteed. In doing this, the courts have taken into account the banks' own Code of Practice on the matter – in the language of PECL, they have referred to generally applicable and reasonable usages and practices. But even here the courts have looked at all the circumstances, so that, for example, it was not fatal to the guarantee's enforceability for the bank to have failed to advise the prospective guarantor away from her matrimonial home that she needed to take independent legal advice, when she had anyway taken such advice and moreover had not disclosed its substance to the court where she was seeking to reduce the guarantee.[115]

Against this background, what should be done in European contract law? There is a debate already about this on the Continent, and I want here to pick out some recent contributions to that discussion. The Dutch scholar Martijn Hesselink argues that there is no need for a general principle of good faith in a European contract code, so long as the rules already developed on the basis of good faith are clearly articulated and formulated as rules in the system.[116] If a general principle is left in, its function should mainly be to remind judges of the need to develop the law by way of interpretation, correction and supplementation of contracts; in Zimmermann's words, "an invitation, or reminder, for courts to do what they do anyway: to develop the law in accordance with the perceived needs of their times".[117] Hein Kötz has a similar, but more positive, view of the role to be played by good faith in European contract law. In an article in which he sets out to allay English lawyers' fear of good faith, he argues that it is a mechanism by which judicial decisions develop the law incrementally and case by case (the *Fallgruppen* approach of German law). Kötz concludes: "An open texture calling for judicial amplification

---

115 *Clydesdale Bank v Black* 2002 SC 555.
116 M Hesselink, "The concept of good faith", in A Hartkamp et al, *Towards a European Civil Code*, 3rd edn (2004), 471–498.
117 Zimmermann, *Roman Law*, 176.

seems preferable because the whole project [*of a European Civil Code/ Contract Law*] might fail unless European judges were left with an area of play larger perhaps than that acceptable in any national legal system."[118] Finally, Matthias Storme argues that while judicial activism should be contained by the formulation of as many precise rules as possible, an open-ended rule of good faith which is more than just the absence of bad faith, is needed in European contract law, because good faith cannot be exhausted as a source of more specific norms, and may also act as a corrective against the way rules originally based on good faith subsequently develop.[119] Thus, I think, he would allow Articles 1:102 and 1:106 PECL to co-exist with more precise rules (such as Article 4:110 PECL) also invoking good faith in their text. Further, the specific instances of good faith in the code give guidance as to the scope of the general norm. Perhaps too this refutes Hugh Beale's argument that Article 1:102 PECL cannot be meant as an over-arching clause because there are more specific controls elsewhere in PECL.[120] Storme suggests that the real issue is judicial activism: how to encourage it, without having too much of it. He thinks the answer may lie in the approach of the Swiss Civil Code, requiring the judge exercising discretion to do so by way of a formulation of a rule:

> If no relevant provision can be found in a statute, the judge must decide in accordance with the customary law and, in its absence, in accordance with the rule which he would, were he the legislator, adopt. In so doing he must pay attention to accepted doctrine and tradition.[121]

From all this, I draw the message that a general good faith principle (or equivalent) should and probably will be included in a European contract code or restatement or Common Frame of Reference, as a way of enabling judges to meet the probability that cases will arise which will be at best incompletely provided for by whatever more specific rules there may be. It will have to be a *European* principle, not one based upon any notion of the concept found in any given legal system within the European Union; and its

---

118  H Kötz, "Towards a European Civil Code: the duty of good faith", in P Cane & J Stapleton (eds), *The Law of Obligations: Essays in Celebration of John Fleming* (1998) at 258.
119  "Good faith and contents of contracts in European private law", in S Espiau & A Vaquer Aloy, *Bases of a European Contract Law* (2003), 17–30.
120  See above, text accompanying note 10.
121  Article 1 paras 2 and 3 Swiss Civil Code. Cf the approach to equity often found in Louisiana courts: V V Palmer, *The Louisiana Civilian Experience* (2005), 249–250, esp at n 98. See also Stapleton (1999) 49 *CLP* 1 at 28–35, arguing that recognition of good faith also entails the deployment of "incidence" rules, identifying relevant factors in determining when the requirement bites *and* when it does not.

role will be determined in the first place by the other specific rules in the *European* system. Good faith should be seen, not so much as an over-arching as an underlying principle, much as it is at present in Scots and South African law. As an underlying principle, its role will be mainly to exclude bad faith, possibly attached to a presumption of good faith akin to that found in Article 2805 of the Quebec Civil Code.[122] But the principle can in some circumstances be the basis for new rules (e.g. like that in the *Smith* case in Scots law) or re-rationalisations of existing authority or rules to develop them further (as with my suggestions for *culpa in contrahendo* in Scots law); or simply a guideline in the application of existing rules.

Whether this is quite what PECL gives us is perhaps a moot point. My general impression, despite Hugh Beale's arguments to the contrary, is that Article 1:201 PECL *is* intended to be an over-arching principle, capable of over-powering rather than just tempering freedom of contract; and that the appearance of good faith in other, more specific, articles must be seen, as suggested by Matthias Storme, as simply showing places where the drafters found it especially helpful to reinforce the strong role good faith is intended to play throughout the Principles. Having said that, it is unfortunate that in some areas where it would be very important to know whether or not good faith had a part to play, such as termination for non-performance, there is nothing specific in the black-letter text, and the ambiguous comments on the matter are placed at a considerable distance from the actual Articles on termination. Beale's point about the need to revise PECL to make the general approach more explicit, whether it be an over-arching or an underlying one, is therefore well made in general, and needs, like good faith itself, to be taken seriously. Indeed, I find myself in agreement with what I take from his paper to be his preferred position on the question of good faith, seeing it as primarily an important underlying principle, albeit certainly not a wholly inactive or inert one.

A final observation concerns the interaction between the good faith principle, whatever its content and role, and the "public policy" clause in PECL:

### Article 15:101: Contracts Contrary To Fundamental Principles
A contract is of no effect to the extent that it is contrary to principles recognised as fundamental in the laws of the Member States of the European Union.

---

122  See above, text accompanying notes 29–30. Stapleton (1999) 49 *CLP* 1 at 17–20, argues in favour of a presumption of good faith. See also Article 1:201 PECL Comment F.

As already indicated, there is a fundamental difference between good faith and public policy, lying essentially between the former's concentration upon the relationship of the contracting parties and the latter's concern with broader social issues. So fundamental principles are concerned with human rights as expressed in the European Convention on Human Rights and the European Constitution, as well as basic legal ideas which are widespread in the European Union, such as hostility to interference with the processes of justice and to restraints upon personal liberty or the right to work, as well as support for contemporary understandings of family life and morality. Public policy is also confined to the invalidation of contracts and does not impose positive obligations and liabilities in the manner sometimes achieved by way of good faith. But it is rather important that, if there are two general clauses of this kind operative within European contract law, their respective territories and bounds are fairly clearly set out. By comparison with good faith, discussion of public policy in the European Union has scarcely begun. But this too is a discussion we need to have.

# 3 Offer, Acceptance and the Moment of Contract Formation

## Geo Quinot

A.  INTRODUCTION
B.  THE OFFER AND ACCEPTANCE MODEL
C.  CONTRACT FORMATION *INTER ABSENTES*
(1)  Development in Scotland
(2)  Development in South Africa
(3)  Justification and problems
(4)  The PECL approach
(5)  Comparison
D.  CONCLUSION

## A. INTRODUCTION

It was the Natural lawyers of the seventeenth century, especially in France, who developed the concept of *consensus* as the basis of modern contract law.[1] Roman-Dutch authorities embraced this notion and further accepted that *consensus* can be analysed in terms of two declarations of will, i.e. offer and acceptance.[2] These Civilian concepts also had a profound influence on the development of contract law in the Common Law. In England, especially, Pothier's writings on the subject became influential and resulted in the adoption of the offer and acceptance analysis.[3] English jurists in turn further developed and refined offer and acceptance to a model of contract formation.[4]

The offer and acceptance model is a standard feature of modern contract law in South Africa and Scotland.[5] Typically of both these mixed legal

---

1 Zimmermann, *Obligations*, 559 ff.
2 Zimmermann, *Obligations*, 567–569; D Hutchison, "Contract formation", in Zimmermann & Visser, *Southern Cross*, 173.
3 Zimmermann, *Obligations*, 569 ff.
4 Hutchison, in Zimmermann & Visser, *Southern Cross*, 173.
5 McBryde, *Contract*, 123–161; SME, vol 15, para 619; Gloag, *Contract*, 24–27; Walker, *Contract*, para 7.1; MacQueen & Thomson, *Contract*, 39; Van der Merwe et al, *Kontraktereg*, ch 3; Kerr, *Contract*, 61–129; Christie, *Contract*, 32–88.

systems, the model was received from Civilian sources, but has been significantly influenced by the Common Law.[6] As such, the offer and acceptance model presents an interesting subject matter for a comparative analysis of the newly formulated PECL[7] viewed against the mixed legal systems of South Africa and Scotland. The focus in this paper is specifically on that aspect of the Scots and South African model that represents the most evident Common Law influence, namely the rules pertaining to *inter absentes* contracting and specifically the so-called postal rule.[8] The goal of the analysis is on the one hand to determine to what extent PECL can be likened to mixed legal systems such as South Africa and Scotland. On the other hand, and perhaps more importantly, it is to see whether any reciprocal lessons can be learned. Part B starts off the discussion with a comparison of the general offer and acceptance models found in the three systems. Part C then focuses specifically on the approach to *inter absentes* contracting, and it begins with the situation in Scots and South African law (1) and (2). That is followed by a more general discussion of the justification traditionally advanced for the adoption of the postal rule of contract formation and the problems emerging from the application of this rule: C(3). Part C(4) sets out the specific approach to *inter absentes* contracting adopted by PECL. Subsequently, the rules developed in Scots and South African law are compared to those adopted by PECL. Finally, some conclusions will be drawn.

## B. THE OFFER AND ACCEPTANCE MODEL

In both Scots and South African law offer and acceptance are regarded as the most basic conceptual tool in analysing the formation of contracts.[9] Both systems, however, recognise that the analysis in terms of offer and acceptance is only a tool and not a prerequisite for determining whether a contract is formed.[10] Commentators have convincingly shown that there are many instances of contracting where the formation of the contract cannot

---

6  Hutchison, in Zimmermann & Visser, *Southern Cross*, 173–174; J E du Plessis, "Common Law influences on the law of contract and unjustified enrichment in some mixed legal systems" (2003) 78 *Tulane LR* 219 at 230; McBryde, *Contract*, 7–11; G F Lubbe, "Formation of contract" in Reid & Zimmermann, *History*, vol 2, 44.

7  PECL, Chapter 2 Section 2.

8  This is also sometimes referred to as the mailbox rule or dispatch rule.

9  Stair, *Institutions*, 1.10.3 ("So then an offer accepted is a contract, because it is the deed of two, the offerer and accepter"); De Wet & van Wyk, *Kontraktereg*, vol 1, 32; Van der Merwe et al, *Kontraktereg*, 52; McBryde, *Contract*, 123; MacQueen & Thomson, *Contract*, 39.

10  De Wet & Van Wyk, *Kontraktereg*, 32–33; McBryde, *Contract*, 124–125; Gloag, *Contract*, 44; Van der Merwe et al, *Kontraktereg*, 52–53; MacQueen & Thomson, *Contract*, 39, 54–55.

satisfactorily be analysed by way of offer and acceptance.[11] Nevertheless, the model is widely used to determine whether a contract has come into existence and what the content of that contract is.

PECL also adopts the offer and acceptance model in analysing the conclusion of contracts. However, they go further than Scots and South African law. Article 2:211 PECL states that the rules on offer and acceptance contained in PECL Chapter 2 Section 2 also apply "with appropriate adaptations" to instances of contracting that do not follow the offer and acceptance model.[12] Yet it is difficult to see how that is going to work. Take, for example, the case of protracted negotiations between the parties, with a multitude of documents exchanged. It may not always be possible (or realistic) to subject such process to an offer and acceptance analysis, especially where the end result is the signing of a document recording the agreement between the parties and drawn up by a third party.[13] Can the rules regarding the revocation of offers[14] and acceptances[15] be applied to such cases to prohibit one party walking away from the transaction prior to signing the agreement?[16] However, PECL does not elevate offer and acceptance to requirements for the conclusion of a contract; to that extent, they are in line with Scots and South African law. Article 2:101 PECL states that the conditions for the conclusion of a contract are an intention by both parties to be legally bound and sufficient agreement between these parties "without any further requirement"[17] including "requirements as to form".[18] This provision is also important in that it confirms that PECL does not require consideration or *causa* for an agreement to be binding.[19] Once again, therefore, by requiring nothing more than offer and acceptance to create a binding contract, PECL is similar to Scots and South African law.[20]

11  See note 10 above; Zweigert & Kötz, *Comparative Law*, 356–357.
12  Article 2:211 PECL.
13  See De Wet & Van Wyk, *Kontraktereg*, 32; Zweigert & Kötz, *Comparative Law*, 356–357; MacQueen & Thomson, *Contract*, 39.
14  Article 2:202 PECL read with Article 1:303 PECL.
15  Article 2:205 PECL read with Article 1:303 PECL.
16  PECL provide detailed rules for negotiations prior to contract formation in Chapter 2 Section 3, so that it may not be necessary to resort to offer and acceptance rules in the stated scenario. The present example can be solved with reference to Article 2:301 PECL that provides for breaking off negotiations.
17  Article 2:101(1) PECL.
18  Article 2:101(2) PECL. This position is confirmed by Article 2:107 PECL, which states that a promise which is intended to be binding without acceptance is binding, read with Article 1:107 PECL which applies the Principles by analogy to unilateral promises.
19  See the notes to Article 2:101 PECL.
20  McBryde, *Contract*, 123; Hutchison, in Zimmermann & Visser, *Southern Cross*, 166–173.

The offer and acceptance model adopted by PECL conforms in general terms to the Scots and South African models. Offers have to be made with the intention that acceptance will create a binding contract,[21] it has to be sufficiently certain to form a contract,[22] must be communicated to the offeree(s),[23] and need not be made to a specific offeree.[24] Whether a specific statement by the offeror will amount to an offer or simply an invitation to make an offer[25] will in Scots and South African law depend on the circumstances of the particular case and principally on the intention of the offeror.[26] In this regard it has been stated in both South African and Scots law that the display of goods in a shop with prices attached to them does not amount to an offer, but only to an invitation to make an offer.[27] PECL adopts a different approach to such cases. Although the distinction between offers and invitations to make offers will have to be determined with reference to the general requirements for offers stated in PECL,[28] a special rule is laid down for the display and advertisement of goods and services by professional suppliers.[29] In terms of this provision such proposals to supply goods or services at a stated price will be presumed to be an offer. The presumed offer will, however, be subject to availability of stock, or the supplier's capacity to render the service. PECL's approach differs from the Scots and South African position only with regard to the burden of proof. In Scots and South African law the party claiming that a contract has come into existence by a purported acceptance of an offer contained in the advertisement or display will have to show that the advertisement or display did in fact amount to an offer. Under PECL, in contrast, the party claiming that no contract has come into existence under

21 Article 2:201(1)(a) PECL; Van der Merwe et al, *Kontraktereg*, 54; McBryde, *Contract*,128; SME, vol 15, paras 615, 616, 620; Gloag, *Contract,* 16–17, 24–25; Walker, *Contract,* para 7.6; MacQueen & Thomson, *Contract,* 40.

22 Article 2:201(1)(b) PECL; Van der Merwe et al, *Kontraktereg*, 55; McBryde, *Contract,* 128; SME, vol 15, para 620; Walker, *Contract,* para 7.6; MacQueen & Thomson, *Contract,* 40.

23 Article 2:201(2) PECL; Van der Merwe et al, *Kontraktereg*, 59; McBryde, *Contract,*134–135; SME, vol 15, paras 628–630; Gloag, *Contract,* 16–17; Walker, *Contract,* paras 7.7, 7.45, 7.46; MacQueen & Thomson, *Contract,* 44.

24 Article 2:201(2) PECL; Van der Merwe et al, *Kontraktereg*, 54; McBryde, *Contract,*132–133; SME, vol 15, para 627; Gloag, *Contract,* 22; Walker, *Contract,* para 7.19; MacQueen & Thomson, *Contract,* 44–45.

25 In Scots law this is often referred to as an invitation to treat: SME, vol 15, para 620.

26 Van der Merwe et al, *Kontraktereg*, 55–56; McBryde, *Contract,* 128–131; SME, vol 15, paras 620–626; Gloag, *Contract,* 21–24; Walker, *Contract,* paras 7.7–7.13; MacQueen & Thomson, *Contract,* 40–44.

27 *Crawley v Rex* 1909 TS 1105; *Campbell v Ker* 24 Feb 1810 FC referred to in SME, vol 15, para 621; McBryde, *Contract,* 129; Walker, *Contract,* para 7.9; MacQueen & Thomson, *Contract,* 42.

28 Article 2:201(1) and (2) PECL.

29 Article 2:201(3) PECL.

these circumstances will have to show that the advertisement or display did not amount to an offer.[30] Like South African and Scots law, PECL allows for offers to be revoked prior to acceptance.[31]

Under all three systems any unequivocal indication of assent to the offer will amount to an acceptance.[32] Such indication may be either by words or conduct, but must come from the offeree.[33] Generally, the acceptance must simply indicate assent to all the terms and conditions of the offer.[34] In each system this general statement presents a somewhat simplified view of the model, and exceptions to the general position are recognised, allowing for some variance between offer and acceptance.[35] In keeping with the general position, and subject to the exceptions just noted, anything more or less than simple consent to the terms of the offer will amount to a rejection of the offer, and will constitute a counter-offer under all three systems.[36]

From the above discussion, it seems that there is a fair amount of similarity between PECL on the one hand and Scots and South African law on the other, as far as the general characteristics of the offer and acceptance model are concerned. This is not surprising in the light of the shared use of the model in Civil and Common Law systems noted above. More interesting though, for present purposes, is PECL's approach to *inter absentes* contracting. As also noted above, it is in this aspect of the principally Civilian offer and acceptance model that our mixed legal systems show significant Common Law influence. In analysing the "mixed character" of PECL, it is to this aspect of the model that we therefore have to turn our attention.

---

30  An alternative defence would be that the condition under which the presumed offer was made was not fulfilled, i.e. that the stock of goods or capacity to supply the services was exhausted prior to the other party's purported acceptance of that offer.

31  Article 2:202 PECL. Van der Merwe et al, *Kontraktereg,* 57; McBryde, *Contract,* 140; SME, vol 15, para 647; Gloag, *Contract,* 37; Walker, *Contract,* para 7.32; MacQueen & Thomson, *Contract,* 45.

32  Article 2:204 PECL; McBryde, *Contract,* 145; SME, vol 15, para 631; Gloag, *Contract,* 26–30; Walker, *Contract,* paras 7.38–7.39; Van der Merwe et al, *Kontraktereg,* 58–60; MacQueen & Thomson, *Contract,* 46.

33  Article 2:204(1) PECL; McBryde, *Contract,* 145–147, 156; SME, vol 15, paras 631, 632, 638; Gloag, *Contract,* 26–30; Walker, *Contract,* paras 7.38, 7.45, 7.48, 7.66; Van der Merwe et al, *Kontraktereg,* 63–64; MacQueen & Thomson, *Contract,* 46, 47–48.

34  Articles 2:204 and 2:208 PECL; McBryde, *Contract,* 150; SME, vol 15, para 635; Gloag, *Contract,* 39–42; Walker, *Contract,* para 7.49; Van der Merwe et al, *Kontraktereg,* 59–60; MacQueen & Thomson, *Contract,* 46.

35  In the light of Professor Forte's chapter on the battle of the forms, this aspect of offer and acceptance will not be discussed here.

36  Article 2:208(1) PECL; McBryde, *Contract,* 152; SME, vol 15, para 635; Gloag, *Contract,* 39; Walker, *Contract,* para 7.49; Van der Merwe et al, *Kontraktereg* 59–60; MacQueen & Thomson, *Contract,* 46.

## C. CONTRACT FORMATION *INTER ABSENTES*

When parties contract *inter praesentes* it is not difficult to discover the moment and place of contracting as evidenced by offer and acceptance. Since the moment when the offeree indicates her acceptance of the offer coincides with the moment when the offeror learns of such acceptance,[37] that moment naturally constitutes the time of contracting. However, when parties contract *inter absentes* the offer and acceptance model can lead to significant difficulties in establishing the time and place of contracting. At what exact moment during the process of contract formation does the contract come into being?[38]

At least four theories have been advanced to address this question:[39]

1. The declaration theory states that the contract comes into existence when the offeree declares her acceptance of the offer.
2. The expedition theory holds that the moment of contracting is when the acceptance is dispatched to the offeror.
3. The reception theory focuses on the key moment as the one when the acceptance reaches the offeror, that is when it is delivered to his address. The offeror may not necessarily be aware that the acceptance has reached him.
4. The information theory states that the contract will be formed only when the offeror becomes aware of the acceptance.

The Roman-Dutch authorities differed about which of these theories to adopt.[40] Grotius advocated the information theory, but subject to the intention of the parties.[41] Huber, in contrast, favoured the declaration theory and expressly rejected Grotius' view.[42] Voet seems to have supported either the reception or the information theory.[43] The early Scots Institutional Writers,

---

37 I am leaving aside the situation where the parties negotiate *inter praesentes*, but for some reason the acceptance does not come to the attention of the offeror, e.g. the offeror does not hear the offeree.

38 The answer to this question is also of utmost importance for conflict of law purposes. The *locus contractus* is often dispositive in conflict of law questions: see C F Forsyth, *Private International Law: The modern Roman-Dutch law including the jurisdiction of the high courts*, 4th edn (2003), 303–325.

39 *Cape Explosive Works Ltd v South African Oil & Fat Industries Ltd* 1921 CPD 244 at 256; Van der Merwe et al, *Kontraktereg*, 53 n 9; Hutchison, in Zimmermann & Visser, *Southern Cross*, 174; E Kahn, "Some mysteries of offer and acceptance" (1955) 72 *SALJ* 246 at 254–255.

40 See the discussions in *The Fern Gold Mining Co v Tobias* (1890) 3 SAR 134 at 137–138; *Cape Explosive* (note 39) at 257–258; Hutchison, in Zimmermann & Visser, *Southern Cross*, 174.

41 Grotius, *De jure belli ac pacis*, 2.11.15 (transl F W Kelsey, 1925).

42 *Cape Explosive* (note 39) at 258; Hutchison, in Zimmermann & Visser, *Southern Cross*, 174.

43 Voet, *Commentarius ad Pandectas*, 5.1.73 (transl P Gane, 1956).

notably Stair, did not express an opinion on the point.[44] In both South Africa and Scotland it was thus left to the courts to develop an appropriate approach to contract formation *inter absentes*, without much guidance from the traditional sources.

## (1) Development in Scotland

It is a clear rule of Scots law that an acceptance must be communicated to the offeror before a contract will come into existence.[45] However, it is considerably less clear whether this rule in fact adopts the reception or information theory in Scots law. Scottish case law does not seem to provide an unequivocal answer in this regard.[46] In contrast, English courts appear to have opted for the information theory.[47] On the strength of the *Entores* judgment, in particular, a number of academic commentators have argued that the information theory also applies in Scots law.[48] However, there are also strong dissenting voices favouring the reception theory.[49] It is clear, however, that the offeror may prescribe a method of acceptance and thereby either waive

---

44  *Thomson v James* (1855) 18 D 1 at 12–13; see Lubbe, in Reid & Zimmermann, *History*, vol 2, 38; du Plessis (2003) 78 *Tulane LR* 219 at 231. Although there is reference to Bell's *Commentaries* in the early Scottish case of *Dunlop v Higgins* [1848] 1 HLC 381 as authority for the proposition that the expedition theory applies in Scotland, Bell's statements have been interpreted as referring to English rather than Scots law (Huntley, *Contract*, 137).

45  *Thomson v James* at 1; McBryde, *Contract*, 157; SME, vol 15, para 641; Gloag, *Contract*, 28; Walker, *Contract*, para 7.55; Hogg, *Obligations*, 44; Huntley, *Contract*, 129; MacQueen & Thomson, *Contract*, 48.

46  Hogg, *Obligations*, 45. This uncertainty is augmented by the position pertaining to the revocation of offers in an *inter absentes* context. Although the clear rule seems to be that such revocation will only be effective if it is communicated to the offeree before acceptance, it is less clear what is meant with "communication" in this respect. In *Burnley v Alford* (1919) 2 SLT 123 it was said that as a general rule a revocation of an offer must be "brought to the knowledge or mind of the party holding the offer" to be effective, i.e. applying the information theory, but that such rule is not of rigid application and that mere delivery to the address of the offeree may suffice in certain circumstances, i.e. applying the reception theory.

47  *Entores Ltd v Miles Far East Corporation* [1955] 2 QB 327 at 332 per Denning LJ; *Brinkibon Ltd v Stahag Stahl und Stahlwarenhandelsgesselschaft mbH* [1982] 1 All ER 293, HL.

48  SME, vol 15, para 643; Walker, *Contract*, paras 7.55, 7.63; Huntley, *Contract*, 129–131; see also Hogg, *Obligations*, 45; MacQueen & Thomson, *Contract*, 49, 52; Gloag, *Contract*, 28, 38.

49  A notable dissent from the above view is the argument presented by Professor McBryde (*Contract* at 157–158) that knowledge on the part of the offeror is not a requirement for the existence of a contract. He argues that the offeree need have only an intention to accept and have moved beyond the deliberative stage. The focus should thus be on the actions of the offeree and particularly whether she has indicated an irrevocable intention to be bound. McBryde further states that indications to the contrary in the case law, requiring actual knowledge on the part of the offeror, are remnants of the (now outdated) adherence to a subjective basis of contractual liability. See also Hogg, *Obligations*, 45 ("Putting the written acceptance through the offeror's letterbox would be sufficient to constitute acceptance").

the requirement of knowledge/receipt of acceptance, or expressly require knowledge.[50] Generally the contract will only come into existence once the offeree has complied with such specific requirements.[51]

The position regarding postal contracts[52] is significantly different from the one set out above. The application of the expedition theory to postal contracts was incorporated into Scots law by the House of Lords decision in *Dunlop v Higgins*.[53] This development was strongly influenced by English law, where the expedition theory was adopted for postal contracts in the well-known 1818 case of *Adams v Lindsell*.[54] Thus, in *Dunlop v Higgins* Lord Cottenham LC relied on two English cases, i.e. *Adams v Lindsell* and *Stocken v Collen*,[55] for his conclusion that a postal contract is formed upon dispatch of the letter of acceptance.[56] He simply asserted that the law is the same for Scotland on the strength of Bell's *Commentaries*.[57] The classic case, which settled the "postal rule"[58] in Scots law, was *Thomson v James*.[59] In that case the defender offered to purchase the pursuer's estate per letter. The pursuer accepted the offer likewise per letter. Before the acceptance was delivered to the offeror, but after posting thereof by the offeree, the offeror sent a letter retracting his offer. The court held that a valid contract had come into existence.

The scope of the postal rule in Scots law is, however, far from clear.[60] While the position in English law seems to be settled that the contract will come into existence upon posting of the letter of acceptance even if the letter

---

50  SME, vol 15, para 637; McBryde, *Contract*, 145–147; Hogg, *Obligations*, 45; Gloag, *Contract*, 34–35; Walker, *Contract*, para 7.56; MacQueen & Thomson, *Contract*, 48–49. This is not to suggest that the offeror has an unlimited capacity to prescribe any mode of acceptance. The offeror cannot prescribe all types of action as constituting acceptance, especially where acceptance is to be in the form of conduct rather than express communication. Also, apart from exceptional circumstances, silence cannot be prescribed as constituting acceptance. In this regard see McBryde, *Contract*, 146–150; SME, vol 15, paras 637–640; Gloag, *Contract*, 28–29; MacQueen & Thomson, *Contract*, 48–49.

51  See note 50 above.

52  Postal contracts, in this context, are contracts concluded completely by means of the post, that is where both offer and acceptance are made by means of letters sent by post.

53  Huntley, *Contract*, 136–137; SME, vol 15, para 644; Lubbe, in Reid & Zimmermann, *History*, vol 2, 35.

54  (1818) 1 B & Ald 681. See further S Gardner, "Trashing with Trollope: a deconstruction of the postal rules in contract" (1992) 12 *Oxford JLS* 170; Lubbe, in Reid & Zimmermann, *History*, vol 2, 35 n 378.

55  (1841) 7 Mee and Wels 515.

56  At 400.

57  At 400.

58  As the application of the expedition theory in cases concerning postal contracts became known.

59  (1855) 18 D1.

60  See Report on Formation of Contract: Scottish Law and the United Nations Convention on Contracts for the International Sale of Goods (Scot Law Com No 144, 1993), para 4.4.

never reaches the offeror,[61] serious doubts exist about this for Scots law.[62] Logically, the adoption of the expedition theory in postal contracts should rule out the possibility of retraction of an acceptance already posted. However, some commentators have read the case of *Countess of Dunmore v Alexander*[63] as holding that an acceptance, once posted, may indeed be retracted should the retraction reach the offeror either before or at least at the same time as the acceptance.[64] Others have doubted whether this is the correct reading of the case.[65] Since *Countess of Dunmore* preceded the adoption of the postal rule in Scots law it has also been argued that it has been overruled by the decisions accepting the postal rule.[66] It is also not altogether clear whether the postal rule also applies to other forms of *inter absentes* contracting in Scots law. In English law the rule has been applied to acceptance by telegram,[67] but not by telephone and telex.[68] It remains to be seen whether this will be followed in Scots law.[69]

Most recently, the Scottish Law Commission has published a report on contract formation in Scots law containing a recommendation that the postal rule be abolished in Scots law.[70] The report noted the many anomalies created by the rule and the large measure of uncertainty associated with the rule in Scots law.[71] It furthermore pointed out that all consultees in the commission's deliberations leading up to the report supported a change of the postal rule and that none of them put forward any argument in favour of

61  *Household Fire and Carriage Accident Insurance Co v Grant* (1879) 4 Ex D 216, CA.

62  *Higgins & Sons v Dunlop, Wilson & Co* (1847) 9 D 1407 at 1414 per Lord Fullerton; *Thomson v James* (note 45) at 12 per Lord President McNeill; *Mason v Benhar Coal Co* (1882) 9 R 883 per Lord Shand; Gloag, *Contract*, 34; Walker, *Contract*, para 7.60; SME, vol 15, para 644; MacQueen & Thomson, *Contract*, 50.

63  (1830) 9 S 190.

64  See SME, vol 15, para 644; Gloag, *Contract*, 38; MacQueen & Thomson, *Contract*, 51.

65  SME, vol 15, para 644; Walker, *Contract*, para 7.69; Huntley, *Contract*, 149.

66  Walker, *Contract*, para 7.69 with specific reference to the remarks in *Thomson v James* (note 45) at 13 per Lord President McNeill and 25 per Lord Deas, doubting *Countess of Dunmore*; MacQueen & Thomson, *Contract*, 51. Similar uncertainty exists regarding the retraction of an offer made through the post when such retraction objectively reaches the offeree prior to dispatch of the acceptance, but only comes to the attention of the offeree after such dispatch. See note 46 above for a discussion of *Burnley v Alford*.

67  *Stevenson v McLean* (1880) 5 QBD 346; *Bruner v Moore* [1904] 1 Ch 305.

68  See the *Entores* and *Brinkibon* cases, both note 47.

69  As noted above, note 47 and accompanying text, Scottish commentators have found these English cases particularly persuasive regarding the adoption of the information theory in Scots law. McBryde, *Contract* at 160 also notes that the reasoning for the adoption of the postal rule in *Thomson v James* is not restricted to posting and may therefore lead Scottish courts to extend the rule to other forms of *inter absentes* communication. See also Hogg, *Obligations*, 46.

70  Report on Formation of Contract (Scot Law Com No 144, 1993), paras 4.4–4.7.

71  At para 4.4.

the rule.[72] However, the Commission's recommendation that the rule be abolished was by no means a new development in Scottish law reform. As long ago as 1977 the Scottish Law Commission had published a consultative memorandum on contract formation that suggested the abolition of the postal rule.[73] Although the suggestion had been favourably received[74] it had not been taken further at that time.[75] The matter was only raised again when the adoption of the United Nations Convention for the International Sale of Goods into Scots law was considered.[76] In this context the Commission recommended that the postal rule be replaced by CISG's receipt rule.[77] Subject to alternative arrangement between the parties, this rule is supposed to apply to all contracts concluded *inter absentes*.[78] Although the Commission's recommendations included a draft Bill, no legislation has followed as yet. For the time being, therefore, the postal rule remains in place in Scotland.

## (2) Development in South Africa

The South African courts have generally adopted the information theory as the default approach for contract formation. As early as 1915 the Appellate Division of the Supreme Court of South Africa stated: "Under ordinary circumstances the direct communication of the acceptance to the person making the offer is essential to the constitution of a contractual *vinculum*."[79] The court added that the offeror may dispense with this requirement and indicate another method of acceptance.[80] This position is now fairly well entrenched in South African law.[81]

---

72  At para 4.6.

73  Formation of Contract (Scot Law Com Memorandum No 36, 1977).

74  See Report on Formation of Contract (Scot Law Com No 144, 1993), para 4.6.

75  Scot Law Com No 144 (1993), para 1.2.

76  At para 1.7.

77  At para 4.7.

78   At paras 2.11, 4.2–4.4.

79  *Bloom v American Swiss Watch Co* 1915 AD 100 at 102.

80  *Bloom* at 102. See also *Dietrichsen v Dietrichsen* 1911 TPD 486, predating that case, where Wessels J came to similar conclusions.

81  *Laws v Rutherford* 1924 AD 261; *Driftwood Properties (Pty) Ltd v McLean* 1971 (3) SA 591 (A); *S v Henckert* 1981 (3) SA 445 (A); *Westinghouse Brake & Equipment (Pty) Ltd v Bilger Engineering (Pty) Ltd* 1986 (2) SA 555 (A); *Amcoal Collieries Ltd v Truter* 1990 (1) SA 1 (A); *Seef Commercial & Industrial Properties (Pty) Ltd v Silberman* 2001 (3) SA 952 (SCA); *Smeiman v Volkersz* 1954 (4) SA 170 (C); *Tel Peda Investigation Bureau (Pty) Ltd v Van Zyl* 1965 (4) SA 475 (E); *Millman v Klein* 1986 (1) SA 465 (C); *Lines v Liberty Life Association of Africa Ltd* 1990 (3) SA 268 (T); *De Jager v Burger* 1994 (1) SA 402 (C); *Ideal Fastener Corporation CC v Book Vision (Pty) Ltd (t/a Colour Graphic)* 2001 (3) SA 1028 (D); Van der Merwe et al, *Kontraktereg*, 53 ff; Kerr, *Contract*, 111; Christie, *Contract*, 76; Hutchison, in Zimmermann & Visser, *Southern Cross*, 177, 180; De Wet & Van Wyk, *Kontraktereg*, 37; Lubbe & Murray, *Contract*, 40.

The single exception to the information theory's sway in South Africa is the application of the expedition theory to postal contracts. This exception is one of the best examples of the direct influence of English law on the South African law of contract. In the light of the uncertainty amongst Roman-Dutch authorities regarding the appropriate theory concerning *inter absentes* contract formation, the unanimity reached in English law in the early nineteenth century of applying the expedition theory to postal contracts[82] has been too tempting for South African judges to resist. Early cases, such as the *Fern Gold Mining* case,[83] *Bal v Van Staden*[84] and *Naude v Malcolm*,[85] all pointed towards increasing English law influence on the issue. The leading case of *Cape Explosive Works Ltd v South African Oil & Fat Industries Ltd* was decided in 1921.[86] The contracts at issue had both been concluded through the mail, the offerors mailing their offers from the Transvaal and Natal Provinces respectively and the offeree mailing its acceptance in both instances from the Cape Province. The defendants argued that, since the acceptances were only communicated to them outside the Cape Province, the contracts were also concluded outside that province, in line with the information theory. Kotzé JP discussed the opinions of the Roman-Dutch authorities in some detail and came to the conclusion that no single approach can be discerned in Roman-Dutch law.[87] His analysis of the more recent discussion of the issue confirmed that the difference in opinion continued in most foreign jurisdictions such as Dutch, French and German law.[88] In contrast, the judge noted that English law unequivocally adopted the expedition theory in the case of postal contracts such as the one before the court.[89] His analysis of the early South African cases on point indicated a leaning towards the English rule, but confirmed that the issue had not been decided in South Africa.[90] Accordingly, he laid down the principle that postal contracts will come into existence in South Africa upon the dispatch of the acceptance. Thus, in other words, he adopted the expedition theory.[91] Kotzé JP made clear in his judgment that he accepted the expedition theory as a result of its

---

82  See note 54 above.
83  *Fern Gold Mining* (note 40) at 138.
84  1902 TS 128.
85  (1902) 19 SC 482.
86  1921 CPD 244.
87  1921 CPD 244 at 256–258.
88  At 258–261.
89  At 261–262, where the judge specifically referred to *inter alia Adams v Lindsell* and *Dunlop v Higgins*. He further noted that American and Scots law follow the English rule, at 262–263, 266.
90  1921 CPD 244, at 263–264.
91  At 266. See also Searle J's general endorsement of this approach at 276.

"practical convenience"[92] and because it is in the best "interest of commerce and the activities of men in their dealings and intercourse with one another".[93] This justification followed the express recognition by the judge that the information theory is theoretically the soundest one.[94]

The Appellate Division in *Kergeulen Sealing & Whaling Co Ltd v Commissioner for Inland Revenue*[95] seemingly confirmed the adoption in the *Cape Explosive Works* case of the expedition theory for postal contracts. Since then, it has become an established principle of South African law.[96] However, South African courts have been reluctant to extend the operation of the expedition theory beyond the narrow limits identified in *Cape Explosive*.[97] Apart from postal contracts it has been applied to contracts concluded by telegram[98] and telefax.[99] Although the expedition theory was initially applied to telephonic communication as well,[100] the courts have since rejected this approach and applied the information theory to such instances, in line with the general default position.[101] Most recently the Supreme Court

---

92  At 266.

93  At 265.

94  At 264–265.

95  1939 AD 487 (henceforth *Kergeulen*). There is some dispute as to whether *Kergeulen* can be read as binding confirmation of the expedition theory in cases concerning postal contracts. Some commentators have argued that the confirmation of *Cape Explosive* in *Kergeulen* was *obiter* since the latter case did not involve a true postal contract as contemplated in *Cape Explosive*: see Flemming J's opinion in *Hawkins v Contract, Design Centre (Cape Town)* 1983 (4) SA 296 (T) at 300–301; J P Vorster, "Waar kom 'n kontrak inter absentes gesluit tot stand?" 1984 *TSAR* 196; Van der Merwe et al, *Kontraktereg*, 67 (noting that the confirmation may have been *obiter*); *contra* Kerr, *Contract*, 118–119.

96  *A to Z Bazaars (Pty) Ltd v Minister of Agriculture* 1975 (3) SA 468 (AD) at 476; see also Kerr, *Contract*, 120.

97  *Cape Explosive Works* (note 87) at 266 ("we should now lay down that, where in the ordinary course the Post Office is used as the channel of communication, and a written offer is made, the offer becomes a contract on the posting of the letter of acceptance").

98  *Yates v Dalton* 1938 EDL 177; Christie, *Contract*, 85–87; Kahn (1955) 72 *SALJ* 246 at 263–266.

99  *Ex parte Jamieson: In Re Jamieson v Sabingo* 2001(2) SA 775 (W). Note, however, the comment in Van der Merwe et al, *Kontraktereg*, 71 that Willis J's application of the expedition theory to telefax cases is "neither convincing nor authoritative" and the references in note 129 to English cases which treated telefax communication as instantaneous and thus subject to the "normal" information theory. T Pistorius, "Formation of Internet contracts: an analysis of the contractual and security issues" (1999) 11 *SA Merc LJ* 282 at 288 argues, however, that modern technology has indeed brought telefax communication closer to postal contracts than instantaneous communication such as telephone and that the relevant English cases should therefore be read as being "obsolete". It follows that, in her view, the expedition theory was correctly applied to telefax cases in the *Jamieson* case.

100  *Wolmer v Rees* 1935 TPD 319; C Turpin, "Acceptance of offer: instantaneous communication" (1956) 73 *SALJ* 77; Kahn (1955) 72 *SALJ* 246 at 267.

101  *Tel Peda Investigation Bureau (Pty) Ltd v Van Zyl* 1965 (4) SA 475 (E) confirmed as the correct approach in *S v Henckert* 1981 (3) SA 445 (A); M C J Olmesdahl, "Unheralded demise of Wolmer versus Rees" (1984) 101 *SALJ* 545; A J Kerr, "Contracts by telex and by telephone:

of Appeal has (indirectly) cast doubt on the use of the expedition theory in postal contracts. In *Kaap Suiwelkoöperasie Bpk v Louw*[102] the court simply applied the information theory[103] in a postal contract context, without any reference to the expedition theory. In that case the respondent's membership in the appellant's co-operative at a particular date depended on whether agreement had been reached between the parties as to the date of resignation of the respondent.[104] The respondent had sent several letters to the appellant in which he conveyed his wish to resign at the earliest possible date.[105] The appellant accepted this request (characterised by the court as an offer of early resignation[106]) at its annual general meeting on 11 and 12 August 1992.[107] Such acceptance was communicated to the respondent in a letter dated 31 August 1992.[108] Despite the clear postal nature of the case,[109] the court came to the conclusion that an agreement had come into existence regarding termination of the respondent's membership *after* receipt by the respondent of the appellant's letter of 31 August 1992.[110] The statement that the contract only came into existence *after* receipt of the letter[111] and not *upon* receipt seems to suggest that the court had the information theory in mind rather than the reception theory.[112] However, irrespective of whether the court applied the information theory or the reception theory, the important point to note is that the court did not apply the expedition theory.

---

when and where entered into" (1982) 99 *SALJ* 642; E Kahn, "Contracts by telephone" (1966) 83 *SALJ* 5; P M Nienaber, "Vonnisbespreking: Tel Peda Investigation Bureau (Pty) Ltd v Van Zyl, Easten Cape Division, 6 November 1964" (1965) 28 *THRHR* 67.

102  2001 (2) SA 80 (SCA).

103  It is not completely clear from the judgment whether the court applied the information theory or the reception theory. Van der Merwe et al, *Kontraktereg*, 67 n 101 seem to suggest that the reception theory was applied. However, for the reasons set out below, I think that the information theory was applied.

104  At para 20.

105  At para 24.

106  At para 24.

107  At para 17.

108  At para 17.

109  From the judgment it seems that "the Post Office [was] used as the [exclusive] channel of communication" (in the words of *Cape Explosive Works* (note 86) at 266), *Kaap Suiwelkoöperasie* (note 102) at paras 1, 11–17.

110  At paras 24 - 26.

111  At para 25.

112  This conclusion seems to me to be strengthened by the court's emphasis on the respondent's knowledge of the acceptance in para 25.

## (3) Justification and problems

Many reasons have been advanced for using the expedition theory to determine the time and place of *inter absentes* contracting. Most of these illustrate the struggle to justify a departure from strict adherence to *consensus* as the basis of contractual liability. One of the first reasons advanced was that by using the post to make the offer, the offeror by implication authorises the offeree also to use the post for her acceptance. Consequently, the Post Office became the agent of both parties, and as soon as the offeree mailed her acceptance the offeror became aware of it through his agent, the Post Office.[113] This reasoning was examined and expressly rejected in South Africa in the *Cape Explosive Works* case.[114] However, implied authorisation has remained an important rationale behind the use of the expedition theory for postal contracts.[115] It has at times been linked to the principle that the offeror may dictate the method of acceptance.[116] When the offeror uses the post the offer contains an implied term, that the posting of the acceptance will suffice to create a contract.[117] Commentators have criticised this reasoning for being based on an unjustifiable fiction.[118]

Another reason, which has been advanced in both South Africa and Scotland, is the perceived practical convenience of adopting the expedition theory in cases involving postal contracts.[119] There can be no doubt that this convenience is experienced particularly on the part of the offeree.[120] It is

---

113  *Thomson v James* at 11; Gardner (1992) 12 *Oxford JLS* 170 at 173; Kahn (1955) 72 *SALJ* 246 at 256; Huntley, *Contract*, 136; Walker, *Contract*, para 7.63.

114  *Cape Explosive Works* (note 86) at 262. See also the criticism of this rationale in Scots law in McBryde, *Contract*, 159–160; Huntley, *Contract*, 136; Walker, *Contract*, para 7.63.

115  Lubbe & Murray, *Contract*, 68; Gloag, *Contract*, 34.

116  Lubbe & Murray, *Contract*, 68; Gloag, *Contract*, 34.

117  Lubbe & Murray, *Contract*, 68; Gloag, *Contract*, 34; Van der Merwe et al, *Kontraktereg*, 67; De Wet & Van Wyk, *Kontraktereg*, 39–40; Kahn (1955) 72 *SALJ* 246 at 256–257; Anonymous, "Smeiman revisited" (1955) 72 *SALJ* 308 at 309; SME, vol 15, para 644; Gloag, *Contract*, 34; Huntley, *Contract*, 136.

118  Van der Merwe et al, *Kontraktereg*, 67; De Wet & Van Wyk, *Kontraktereg*, 39–40; Anonymous (1955) 72 *SALJ* 308 at 309; Huntley, *Contract*, 136.

119  *Cape Explosive* at 265–266; *Kergeulen* at 504–505; Gardner (1992) 12 *Oxford JLS* 170 at 173–176; Huntley, *Contract*, 136; Gloag, *Contract*, 34; Walker, *Contract*, para 7.63.

120  *A to Z Bazaars* (note 96) at 476; Van der Merwe et al, *Kontraktereg*, 67; De Wet & Van Wyk, *Kontraktereg*, 41; Gardner (1992) 12 *Oxford JLS* 170 at 173–174, 177; Kahn (1955) 72 *SALJ* 246 at 256; Report on Formation of Contract (Scot Law Com No 144, 1993), para 4.5. Peter Goodrich has argued that the postal rule had its origin in early marriage contracts in English law. The protection it affords specifically to the offeree thus represents the "law's protection of women up until the point of entry into the effective completion of the marriage contract". Such protection may now seem arbitrary "only because of the erasure of the face of the offeree; it has been forgotten that it was a woman who put a letter of acceptance in the post" (P Goodrich, "Habermas and the postal rule" (1996) 17 *Cardozo LR* 1457 at 1470, 1472).

convenient for her that when she mails her acceptance she may be certain that a contract has come into existence. In this sense, the adoption of the expedition theory also has a risk-allocation function. The risk of loss of the letter of acceptance in the mail is placed on the offeror.[121] This may be seen to be justified in view of the fact that it was the offeror who initiated negotiations through the mail.[122] The rule also protects the offeree against a revocation of the offer by the offeror prior to the acceptance reaching the offeror, but subsequent to the declaration of such acceptance.[123] Since revocation of an offer is always possible in English law as a result of the requirement of consideration, there is a perceived need to protect the offeree in such instances. The expedition theory affords this protection. In South African and Scots law this need is less pronounced. Since neither of these systems require consideration as an element of contract formation it is much easier to create irrevocable offers.[124] Furthermore, the expedition theory is convenient in that the time and place at which the letter of acceptance was committed to the postal service can be objectively determined, and consequently also the time and place of contracting.[125] Yet

---

121 McBryde, *Contract*, 159; Walker, *Contract*, para 7.64; Van der Merwe et al, *Kontraktereg*, 68; Gardner (1992) 12 *Oxford JLS* 170 at 74; Anonymous (1955) 72 *SALJ* 308 at 309.

122 McBryde, *Contract*, 159; Van der Merwe et al, *Kontraktereg*, 69; De Wet & Van Wyk, *Kontraktereg*, 41; Anonymous (1955) 72 *SALJ* 308 at 309.

123 MacQueen & Thomson, *Contract*, 53.

124 In Scotland offers can be made irrevocable by a mere promise to such effect by the offeror. This is because Scots law recognises a promise as a binding obligation: *Littlejohn v Hadwen* (1882) 20 SLR 5; *A & G Paterson Ltd v Highland Railway Co* 1927 SC (HL) 32; Gloag, *Contract*, 25; MacQueen & Thomson, *Contract*, 45. In South Africa the position seems to be that offers cannot be made irrevocable by a mere declaration to such effect on the part of the offeror. Agreement, i.e. offer and acceptance, on the issue of irrevocability is still required before the main offer will be irrevocable. The absence of a requirement of consideration, however, opens up the possibility that agreement can be reached on the irrevocability of the main offer without any *quid pro quo* from the offeree. See, however, the South African case of *Building Material Manufacturers Ltd v Marais* 1990 (1) SA 243 (O) which Christie, *Contract*, 59 reads as authority for the proposition that offers can be made irrevocable by mere declaration in South African law. Van der Merwe et al, *Kontraktereg*, 79 n 179, argue that the offer to keep the main offer open in that case was accepted by mere receipt of the former in line with the intention of the parties. De Wet has also noted that this justification for the adoption of the expedition theory should be treated with circumspection, since the moment the contract comes into existence and the moment up to when the offeror can revoke his offer should not be equated as this justification by implication does. According to De Wet these moments differ. While a contract will generally come into existence when the offeror learns of the acceptance, he can only retract his offer up to the moment when the offeree starts declaring her acceptance, which even precedes the dispatch of the acceptance (De Wet & Van Wyk, *Kontraktereg*, 33, 40).

125 De Wet & Van Wyk, *Kontraktereg*, 39 n 135; Kahn (1955) 72 *SALJ* 246 at 256. This also helps to prevent fraud since the offeror will not be able to avoid the contract by simply stating that he did not receive the acceptance when in fact he did: Gardner (1992) 12 *Oxford JLS* 170 at 174.

other commentators have suggested that the "real" reason for adopting the expedition theory in these instances is historical in nature.[126]

One final explanation that deserves mention is that contract formation at the moment of posting may be based on an objective standard of contractual liability in the form of reasonable reliance.[127] The argument here, especially in South African law, is that the use of the expedition theory for postal contracts must be seen as a corrective principle basing liability on objective grounds because the will theory of contract yields harsh or unfair results.[128] If the reliability of the postal service is accepted it may be said that the offeree has a legitimate expectation that the negotiations are finalised at the moment when the acceptance is posted. Hence, the expedition theory bases contractual liability on that reliance.[129]

Despite the justifications formulated for the adoption of the expedition theory in postal contract cases, this theory does not solve all problems relating to offer and acceptance *inter absentes*. When a letter of acceptance does not reach the offeror due to error on the part of the offeree,[130] no contract seems to come into existence.[131] This seems to be an exception to the application of the expedition theory. However, it is difficult to see how such situations should be treated in light of the expedition theory. Is there a

---

126  Gardner (1992) 12 *Oxford JLS* 170 at 176, 178–192 (where it is noted that the development of the postal acceptance rule in English law can be explained with reference to historical factors such as the popular perception of posting as being equivalent to delivery following the postal reforms of the 1840s in England, the questioning of that perception following the introduction of telephones in the 1870s and the development of the concept of limited liability companies and associated mass company flotations of the 1860s and 1870s); Van der Merwe et al, *Kontraktereg*, 68. Goodrich (1996) 17 *Cardozo LR* 1457 at 1473, on the other hand, has argued that the rule had its origin in early marriage contracts in English law and that the protection it affords to the offeree "recollects an institutional history, an unconscious structure within which it would be ethically absurd to allow the man to escape his duties and dishonourable in the extreme to leave a woman in suspense or unprotected".

127  Lubbe & Murray, *Contract*, 67–68; Van der Merwe et al, *Kontraktereg*, 69; Lubbe, in Reid & Zimmermann, *History*, vol 2, 36, 38.

128  Also see Goodrich (1996) 17 *Cardozo LR* 1457 at 1466–1467 ("While the rule of full communication suggests a linguistically unrealistic ideology of consensus, the postal rule introduces the objective possibility of the non-arrival of the letter, and faces the consequences of that failure of delivery or non-communication which constantly threatens to undermine the subjective theory of contracts").

129  Lubbe & Murray, *Contract*, 67–68; Van der Merwe et al, *Kontraktereg*, 69; Lubbe, in Reid & Zimmermann, *History*, vol 2, 36, 38. See, however, the doubt cast on the reasonableness of this reliance in Report on Contract Formation (Scot Law Com No 144, 1993), para 4.5.

130  For example, if the offeree incorrectly addressed the letter.

131  Kahn (1955) 72 *SALJ* 246 at 257; Christie, *Contract*, 84; Kerr, *Contract*, 120; *Levben Products (Pty) Ltd v Alexander Films (SA) (Pty) Ltd* 1959 (3) SA 208 (SR); McBryde, *Contract*, 159; Walker, *Contract*, para 7.64 (noting, however, that there seems to be no Scottish case to confirm such outcome).

general exception to the application of the expedition theory to postal contracts in all instances where the offeree makes a mistake in committing the acceptance to the postal service?[132] Must a court therefore also enquire into the correctness of the acceptance's expedition before concluding that the contract has come into existence at the moment of dispatch? Alternatively, does the exception only apply to cases where the acceptance was in fact not received? If this is the case, what is the legal position between posting and receipt or non-receipt, if the applicable theory can only be determined after the latter event?

Another significant problem following the adoption of the expedition theory is the effect of communications subsequent to the dispatch of the acceptance and overtaking the latter.[133] In South African law it seems, as a matter of logic, that such overtaking communication cannot neutralise the acceptance so that a binding contract has come into existence.[134] However, such logical conclusion is not beyond doubt and the Supreme Court of Appeal has questioned whether this should be the appropriate result.[135] In Scotland the position seems to be that the overtaking communication is effective, which presents a logical conundrum since the expedition theory holds that the contract comes into existence at the time when the acceptance is posted.[136]

132  The court in *Levben Products* at least seems to suggest that such exception only occurs where the mistake is of a serious nature, causing non-delivery of the acceptance. McBryde argues that the postal rule should not apply to cases where the offeree made a mistake in dispatching the acceptance (*Contract*, 159). See notes 61–62 and accompanying text above on whether the operation of the postal rule is qualified in Scots law by the requirement that the acceptance must in fact be received. A similar mistake analysis seems to be employed in Scots law to determine the effectiveness of a revocation of a postal offer prior to the dispatch of the acceptance. See note 46 above for a discussion of *Burnley v Alford* where it was held, in a postal contract context, that the revocation of an offer was effective despite the dispatch of an acceptance after receipt of the revocation, but prior to knowledge of that revocation reaching the offeree. It seems that mistake on the part of the offeree resulting in his lack of knowledge of the revocation, and the absence of mistake on the part of the offeror in this regard, played a significant role in the court's conclusion. See also *Thomson v James* at 11; MacQueen & Thomson, *Contract*, 50–51.

133  For example, if the offeree telephones the offeror after the former has posted her acceptance but before the latter has received it, and informs the offeror that she withdraws her acceptance.

134  Kerr, *Contract*, 121; Hutchison, in Zimmermann & Visser, *Southern Cross*, 179; this was also the conclusion of the court *a quo* in *A to Z Bazaars (Pty) Ltd v Minister of Agriculture* 1974 (4) SA 392 (C).

135  *A to Z Bazaars* 1975 (3) SA 468 (D) at 476; see also Christie, *Contract*, 84; Kahn (1955) 72 *SALJ* 246 at 261.

136  See notes 63–66 and accompanying text above.

## (4) The PECL approach

Article 2:205(1) PECL states that the contract will be concluded once "the acceptance reaches the offeror". When this provision is read with Article 1:303 PECL, it becomes clear that the reception theory as defined above has been adopted. Article 1:303(3) PECL provides that "a notice" reaches the offeror when it is delivered to his address; hence actual knowledge of the acceptance is not required. This position is confirmed in the comment to Article 1:303 PECL where it is stated that "[i]t is not necessary that the notice should actually have come to the addressee's attention".[137] Paragraph (6) furthermore states that "notice" as used in the Article includes the communication of an acceptance, thereby removing any doubt that the position stated in Article 1:303 PECL applies to contract formation as well.

Article 2:205(2) PECL confirms that the above position also holds true for cases where acceptance is in the form of conduct. However, Article 2:205(3) PECL creates an important exception to the general application of the reception theory. It states that if by virtue of the offer, or established practice between the parties, or usage, acceptance may take another form without notice to the offeror, the contract will come into existence when the offeree starts to express her acceptance in that form. This exception clearly allows the offeror to waive the requirement of a notice of acceptance. It is interesting to note that while Article 2:205 PECL thus provides for something *less* than notice of acceptance to the offeror, it does not provide for something *more* than such notice for the formation of a contract. From Article 2:205 PECL alone it would therefore seem that the offeror cannot require actual knowledge of the acceptance on his part before the contract will be concluded. It is submitted, however, that this option is open to the offeror. PECL is generally non-mandatory in nature[138] and thus allow for the exclusion or derogation of any of their non-mandatory provisions;[139] and there is no reason to assume that Article 2:205 should be mandatory. Alternatively, the offeror may merely state actual knowledge of acceptance as an essential term or condition of the proposed contract with the result that no contract will come into existence before such condition has been fulfilled.[140]

---

137   This is in curious conflict with the statement in the "Survey of Chapters 1–9", published in the first volume of PECL (at xxxi), that "[t]he contract will become binding once the acceptance … has become known to the offeror".
138   "Survey of Chapters 1–9", xxix.
139   Article 1:102(2) PECL.
140   Article 2:103(2) PECL.

Although it follows logically from the adoption of the reception theory that the offeree can neutralise her acceptance by an overtaking communication, PECL expressly confirms the effectiveness of such withdrawal.[141] It furthermore states that, should the acceptance reach the offeror at the same time as the withdrawal, the acceptance will not be effective.[142]

## (5) Comparison

From the aforesaid it is clear that PECL differs significantly from the position in Scotland and South Africa regarding *inter absentes* contracting. As a point of departure they do not differentiate between *inter absentes* and *inter praesentes* contracting. For both scenarios they adopt the reception theory requiring only formal delivery of acceptance to the offeror for contract formation. No exception is made for postal contracts.

I would suggest that the approach adopted by PECL is superior in a number of ways to the position in South Africa and Scotland. As a point of departure it entails a single default rule for all instances, subject only to variation by the parties themselves. This approach does away with the need for tenuous classifications of various forms of communication in order to establish the applicable rule of contract formation. As a number of commentators have indicated, it may not be particularly easy (or even possible) to classify more recent forms of communication into the categories of instantaneous and non-instantaneous.[143] The adoption of a universal rule that does not rely on such distinctions is clearly preferable. Such an approach has the added advantage of being perfectly clear, hence advancing legal and commercial certainty.[144] In adopting a universal rule, PECL's approach seems to accord much better with the "predilection for reasoning on general principle" of both South African and Scots law than "a more casuistic approach", in which a rule seems to "focus on the postal contract as a special case".[145]

One of the biggest changes brought about by replacing the postal rule and the information theory with the reception theory is that the risk of the acceptance not reaching the offeror is largely shifted to the offeree. This new

---

141　Article 1:303(5) PECL.

142　Article 1:303(5) PECL.

143　Gardner (1992) 12 *Oxford JLS* 170 at 192–194; Pistorius (1999) 11 *SA Merc LJ* 282 at 288–290; L Davies, "Contract formation on the Internet: shattering a few myths" in L Edwards & C Waelde (eds), *Law and the Internet: Regulating Cyberspace* (1997), 104–115; Christie, *Contract*, 87–88; Van der Merwe et al, *Kontraktereg*, 71–75.

144　For an affirmation of the importance of these factors in contract law, see Brand JA's remarks in *South African Forestry Co Ltd v York Timbers Ltd* 2005 (3) SA 323 (SCA) at para 27.

145　Lubbe, in Reid & Zimmermann, *History*, vol 2, 38.

allocation of risk seems to be much more in line with the reality of modern trade than the allocation under the postal rule and information theory. It is now incumbent on the offeree to ensure that her acceptance reaches the offeror's address. This seems to be reasonable since the offeree is undoubtedly better placed to ensure such receipt, and a number of mechanisms are available to her to confirm delivery.[146] Furthermore, since she knows that she has dispatched her acceptance she can ask the offeror whether he has received it. None of these mechanisms is available to the offeror, who does not even necessarily know that an acceptance has been dispatched.[147]

Although the reception theory to some extent shifts the risk to the offeree compared to the postal rule, it does not do so in an unreasonable manner. For under the reception theory, the offeree merely has to prove the delivery of the acceptance to the offeror. She does not have to prove, as she would have to under the information theory, that the offeror has actually become aware of the acceptance.

PECL does not, however, allocate all risk in the period between dispatch and receipt to the offeree. The offeree is protected against any revocation of the offer during this period. Article 2:202(1) PECL states that revocation of an offer will only be effective if it reaches the offeree before dispatch of the acceptance. Once the offeree has formulated and dispatched her acceptance she has the certainty that the offeror can no longer nullify her actions by revoking his offer.[148] This bar on revocation of course places the offeror at a certain inconvenience: he may not be aware of the dispatch of the acceptance but is, at the same time, unable to revoke his offer. Thus, he is left in a period of uncertainty. However, on the one hand, he may opt out of the reception theory;[149] on the other hand, he is protected by the requirement that the acceptance must reach the offeror within the time limit fixed by the offer or, in the absence of an express time limit, within a reasonable time.[150] It is important to note in this regard that PECL requires the acceptance to *reach* the offeror within a reasonable time and not simply that it must be dispatched

---

146 Most modern postal services offer delivery confirmation and tracking services by means of which the addressor can at any moment establish the location of his or her posted item.

147 See Report on Contract Formation (Scot Law Com No 144, 1993), para 4.5.

148 This splitting of the moment of contract formation and revocation of the offer was also advanced by De Wet as an appropriate way of addressing some of the problems experienced with *inter absentes* contracting. De Wet, however, identified the two relevant moments as expedition (for the purposes of the moment of contract formation; this is in line with the postal rule), and as the moment the offeree starts to express her acceptance (from which time revocation is no longer possible): De Wet & Van Wyk, *Kontraktereg*, 40.

149 See notes 138–140 and accompanying text above.

150 Article 2:206 PECL.

within a reasonable time.[151] The risk of an unreasonable delay between dispatch and receipt is thus placed on the offeree.

A late acceptance[152] may, however, still be effective. If the acceptance is late due to the offeree's fault, it will not be effective, unless the offeror notifies the offeree that he consents to the late acceptance: in other words, unless he waives the time limit fixed in the offer or the reasonable time limit implied by law.[153] A similar result may ensue in South African and Scots law when an offeror consents to a late acceptance by notice to the offeree. However, the route to the result is different. The late acceptance will be treated as a counter-offer that the original offeror can accept with the result of a contract coming into existence. The moment of contract formation under this construction will be when the original offeror's notice of his acceptance of the late acceptance reaches the original offeree. In contrast, in terms of PECL the contract is concluded when the original (late) acceptance reaches the offeror, subject to the offeror's notice. If the late acceptance is not due to the offeree's fault, but to some other delay, a contract will come into existence at receipt of the late acceptance *except* if the offeror notifies the offeree that he considers the late acceptance as ineffective.[154] The risk of a delay in transmission is still on the offeree, but a positive duty is placed on the offeror to communicate the ineffectiveness of the late acceptance to the offeree. In this way the offeree's position is somewhat improved. The combination of these mechanisms ensures the protection of the expectations of both parties. The offeror can expect to receive an acceptance within a reasonable time, failing which he has a choice whether he wants to be bound. The offeree will know whether she dispatched her acceptance in time and, if she did, she can expect to be bound, or informed if that is not the case; and hence any uncertainty is reduced to a minimum.

The reception theory places the risks emanating from the offeror's sphere of control on the offeror in contrast to the information theory, which places such risks on the offeree. Once the acceptance has been physically delivered to the offeror's address a contract comes into existence and the offeree is protected. The offeror subsequently bears the risk that such delivery may not come to his attention. This seems equally reasonable since the offeror is better placed to reduce such risk. The approach adopted by PECL therefore

---

151  Article 2:206 PECL.
152  That is, an acceptance that reaches the offeror after the time limit set by the offer or after an unreasonable delay.
153  Article 2:207(1) PECL.
154  Article 2:207(2) PECL.

seems to achieve a much more balanced allocation of risks between the parties than that achieved currently in Scotland and South Africa.

Another convincing reason for doing away with the postal rule is the objective approach to contractual liability adopted by PECL.[155] The approach to *inter absentes* contract formation adopted by PECL is part and parcel of favouring objective liability. As noted above,[156] especially in South African law,[157] the postal rule can be explained as a corrective to the subjective theory of contractual liability. It thus protects the reasonable reliance of the offeree that a contract has come into existence. In the light of the otherwise harsh results that might flow from a strict adherence to the will theory of contract,[158] this seems a sensible approach to adopt.[159] PECL, however, protects the offeree's reliance in a much more fundamental and comprehensive manner. In fact both parties' reliance seems to be accommodated in an integrated and balanced fashion throughout the regime adopted by PECL.

## D. CONCLUSION

PECL embraces the offer and acceptance model for contract formation found in most Western legal systems today. In rejecting both consideration and *causa* as requirements for contract formation PECL endorses the offer and acceptance model as the primary and sole vehicle for analysing the parties' interaction to establish whether, and when, a contract has come into existence. PECL is closely aligned to both Scots and South African law in this regard. However, the model developed by PECL is in a number of respects more refined and distinctively more modern than those found in Scots and South African law. One specific aspect of PECL's model that seems significantly superior to that found in the former two systems is its treatment of *inter absentes* contracting, and specifically the absence of the postal rule in that model.

The reception of the postal rule in South African and Scots law has been described as undesirable and is not viewed in either system as an unqualified

---

155  Article 2:102 PECL, read with Article 5:101 PECL.

156  See notes 127–129 and accompanying text above.

157  Since Scots law adopts a more objective approach to contractual liability, the postal rule does not serve as a corrective to a subjective approach. However, the development of the postal rule in Scotland seems to go hand in hand with the recognition of objective contractual liability so that there is also in Scotland a link between adopting objective contractual liability and following the postal rule: see Lubbe, in Reid & Zimmermann, *History*, vol 2, 36; Hogg, *Obligations*, 21.

158  See Hogg, *Obligations*, 20; Van der Merwe et al, *Kontraktereg*, 28–30; Lubbe & Murray, *Contract*, 108 ff.

159  See also Goodrich's remarks quoted above, note 128.

success.[160] Certainly the rule is open to much criticism both from practical and principled perspectives. From the practical side neither the ambit of the rule nor its relationship to the retraction of offers and acceptances is altogether clear. From the point of view of principle, the rule does not sit well with the subjective approach to contract formation followed in South Africa, and in both systems it seems to represent a departure from reliance on general principles in favour of casuistic rules focusing on special cases.[161] In England, the rule's country of origin, these difficulties are counterbalanced by the need to protect the offeree against an unfair revocation of the offer and the difficulty in creating irrevocable offers resulting from the doctrine of consideration. However, neither Scots nor South African law experience such need or difficulty. Both systems have developed fairly sophisticated methods to create irrevocable offers.

Despite these misgivings about the reception of the postal rule, it seems to me that, at least in South Africa, the rule cannot simply be dismissed as a knee-jerk reaction to commercial developments of a bygone era precipitated by convenience and certainty in an influential foreign jurisdiction. The presence of the postal rule points to a different need experienced in South African law: a corrective to the subjective theory of contract formation. Under the postal rule, the contract is not based on the true meeting of the parties' minds, but rather on the reliance of one of the parties, the offeree. Scots law in contrast experiences no such need since it accepts an objective theory of contract formation. It can therefore simply reject the postal rule in favour of a receipt rule. This is in line with the principle of an objective determination of *consensus* as basis of contractual liability linked to the requirement that acceptance be communicated to be effective. South African law, in contrast, cannot at present simply reject the postal rule. Its place would then be taken by the default information theory with resultant hardship to the offeree. The South African model would have to be replaced in its entirety by that adopted by PECL. As I have argued above, that model seems to protect the interests of both parties effectively. It represents a well-balanced regime for all forms of contracting, treating *inter praesentes* and *inter absentes* contracting alike. More importantly, at least for the South African context, it seems to protect a more realistic reliance on the part of the offeree, namely that the offeror will take note of an acceptance once it has been delivered.

---

160  Du Plessis (2003) 78 *Tulane LR* 219 at 232–233.
161  See Lubbe, in Reid & Zimmermann, *History*, vol 2 at 38.

Overall, the offer and acceptance model adopted in PECL shows more similarity than difference compared to those found in Scots and South African law. However, from a comparative point of view, the importance lies in the difference. In this respect I would suggest that the PECL model represents an evolution of the Scots and South African models, rather than any radical departure from them. As such it provides Scots and South African lawyers with the foretaste of a possible and, I would suggest, highly desirable future.

# 4 The Battle of Forms

## A D M Forte

## A. THE CASUS BELLI

A battle of forms arises where each of the parties to what they at least perceive as a contract have employed their own standard terms of trading or business. In the case of an anticipated sale of goods, the buyer's purchase order and the seller's acknowledgment of order will be on terms drafted in advance: perhaps by a representative trade association or by the parties' respective legal advisers. If all goes well the goods will be dispatched and paid for and nothing more will be heard of the matter. If this happy scenario does not ensue, however – perhaps, for example, the buyer feels that the goods do not conform to specification or are defective in quality – the parties may turn to their respective standard forms and point to terms therein which they consider to be resolutive of the dispute. In particular the seller may stand on a clause in its acknowledgment of order which excludes liability for the non-conformity alleged[1] and point to another which neutralises any

---

1 In Scots law a business-to-business contract concluded on the standard terms of one of the contracting parties does not prevent exclusion of liability for breach of contract so long as fair and reasonable: Unfair Contract Terms Act 1977, s 17. However, if both parties deal on the basis of their respective standard forms, and those forms can be read together, it would seem that the Act

contrary term in the buyer's purchase order. For example:

> We shall not be liable in respect of defects and we shall not be liable for loss of profits, detention or other consequential damage or expenses. It is a term of this acknowledgment of order that it shall represent the entire agreement between the Purchaser and the Vendor.

Not to be outdone the buyer will point to a counteractive term of its own:

> The Company recognises that the Vendor may use its own acknowledgment of order form. Therefore any provisions in the form of acceptance used which modify, conflict with or contradict any provision of the contract or order shall be deemed to be waived unless expressly agreed to in writing by the Company and signed by an authorised representative.[2]

Both of these clauses paramount are of course anticipatory. Buyer and seller have realised that some of their respective standard forms may clash. Therefore both seek to neutralise such differences by asserting the exclusive application of their contract terms. The buyer states that its terms will prevail no matter what the seller's terms are. The seller states that the converse will obtain. Both parties are content to accept that they have a contract and proceed to performance. The seller delivers the goods to the buyer and the latter pays for these. Then the dispute arises and only at this stage do the differences in the two sets of standard forms assume importance.

## B. NATURE OF THE BATTLE: CONSENSUS OR CONTENT?

From a United Kingdom perspective there are, broadly speaking, two possible approaches to the battle of forms. The first is to confine one's thinking safely within the box of orthodox or classical formation theory. This approach emphasises the central requirement of *consensus* or agreement and ascertains its presence or absence by reference to the conventional constructs of offer and acceptance. The buyer's purchase order is taken to represent its offer to acquire goods from the seller. But because some (or even all) of the general conditions of the seller's acknowledgment of order form conflict with or vary

---

does not apply. Under recent proposals for reform of the law on unfair contract terms, a distinction will be observed between business contracts and "small business contracts". The former will remain, in effect, subject to the current rules; the latter, however, will be treated in a more protectionist manner than at present: Report on Unfair Terms in Contracts (Law Com No 292, Scot Law Com No 199, 2005), 57–77. It does not appear to be the case, however, that the proposed legislation addresses the situation where both parties use standard forms.

2 These examples are based on the terms used by buyer and seller in *Uniroyal Ltd v Miller & Co Ltd* 1985 SLT 101.

the terms in the offer, the second form cannot be regarded as an acceptance of the first. Instead, the seller's form represents its rejection of the buyer's offer and may be treated by the latter as a counter-offer. For brevity's sake, this is often referred to as a "qualified acceptance".[3] At this stage, therefore, after incongruent forms have been exchanged, the "acceptance" does not mirror image the offer and so there is no contract concluded between the parties.

## C. THINKING INSIDE THE BOX: ORTHODOX FORMATION THEORY, OBJECTIVITY AND THE BATTLE OF FORMS

What has been described as the "classic Scots authority"[4] on the battle of forms is an Outer House case – *Uniroyal Ltd v Miller & Co Ltd*.[5] Whether it merits the accolade of "authority" is, however, debatable and some examination of the cases generally is necessary at this point.[6] The first of these decisions is not Scottish, but because of its importance to the debate on battle of forms and since it was referred to in argument in both of the Scottish cases which will be discussed, some mention here is helpful.

*Butler Machine Tool Co Ltd v Ex-Cell-O Corpn (England) Ltd*[7] involved the sale by the plaintiffs, Butler Machine Tool, of an item of machinery known as a plane-miller to the defendants, Ex-Cell-O. The sequence of events was as follows. On 23 May 1969 the seller quoted a price for the sale of a plane-miller. The reverse side of this form contained sixteen conditions, of which the two relevant to the litigation are reproduced here:

[1] All orders are accepted only upon and subject to the terms set out in our quotation and the following conditions. These terms and conditions shall prevail over any terms and conditions in the buyer's order.

[3] Prices are based on present day costs of manufacture and design and having

3 *Wolf and Wolf v Forfar Potato Co* 1984 SLT 100. For a detailed criticism of the construct of the qualified acceptance, see A D M Forte, "The qualified acceptance: a revisionist view of the fundamentals of commercial contract formation in Scots law" (1995) 1 *Contemporary Issues in Law* 43. For a challenging analysis of the mirror-image theory of contract formation, see M M Siems, "Unevenly formed contracts: ignoring the mirror of offer and acceptance" (2004) 12 *ERPL* 771.

4 M Hogg and G Lubbe, "Formation of contract", in Zimmermann, Visser & Reid, *Mixed Legal Systems*, 34–65 at 58, n 159.

5 1985 SLT 101.

6 For a more detailed examination of this case as a decision on both battle of forms and letters of intent see A D M Forte & H L MacQueen, "Contract procedure, contract formation and the battle of forms" (1986) 31 *JLSS* 224. Note also, in connection with battle of forms, McBryde, *Contract*, 153–156.

7 [1979 1 All ER 965. Note also *OTM Ltd v Hydranautics* [1981] 2 Lloyd's Rep 211.

regard to the delivery quoted and uncertainty as to the cost of labour, materials, etc during the period of manufacture, we regret that we have no alternative but to make it a condition of acceptance of order that goods will be charged at prices ruling upon date of delivery.

On 27 May 1969 the buyer placed a written order for the machine employing its own standard form. This stated that its terms and conditions were to apply. There were several terms which differed from those in the seller's quotation; and at the bottom of the buyer's order form was a tear-off slip which read:

Acknowledgment: Please sign and return to Ex-Cell-O. We accept your order on the terms and conditions stated thereon – and undertake to deliver by – Date – signed.

The seller responded to the buyer's order form on 5 June 1969, affirming that delivery of the machine would be as per its quotation of 23 May, and returning, dated and signed, the buyer's acknowledgment of order form. By the delivery date, however, the seller maintained that costs had risen and so it claimed more than the price originally quoted under reference to the price variation provision in the quotation of 23 May. The buyer refused to pay the revised figure and the seller raised an action for payment.

On an analysis of these facts, the majority in the Court of Appeal found that the seller's quotation of 23 May was an offer; but that as the buyer's order of 27 May contained terms which varied those in the offer, it was not an acceptance thereof but a counter-offer which the seller accepted by returning the acknowledgment of order form duly signed. That being so, a contract was concluded on the buyer's terms and conditions. However, the judges were most certainly not *ad idem* as to why the buyer's terms triumphed. Lord Denning MR, thinking outside the box, favoured an holistic approach to the forms passing between parties. One should abandon the orthodox contract formation analysis of such documents; establish if there is agreement on the material points;[8] and, if there is, determine which of the remaining terms are congruent and which conflict. Conflicting terms would be knocked out, and any remaining gaps filled by implying appropriate terms.

---

8  Lord Denning expressed much the same view earlier in *Port Sudan Cotton Co v Govindaswamy Chettiar & Sons* [1977] 2 Lloyd's Rep 5 at 10: "I do not much like the analysis in the text-books of inquiring whether there was an offer and acceptance, or a counter-offer, and so forth. I prefer to examine the whole of the documents ... and decide from them whether the parties did reach an agreement upon all material terms in such circumstances that the proper inference is that they agreed to be bound by those terms from that time onwards". He repeated this in *Gibson v Manchester City Council* [1978] 1 WLR 520 at 523. On appeal, however, the House of Lords took the opportunity to disapprove of this approach generally, though conceding that there could be "exceptional" circumstances where it might be appropriate: [1979] 1 WLR 297.

Consequently, how one classified the signed acknowledgment of order was irrelevant and unnecessary for a finding that a contract existed. Lawton and Bridge LJJ, on the other hand, were of a distinctly more conservative view. For the former the battle of forms was one to be fought "on classical 18th century lines". The latter, in agreement, made plain that a battle of forms was governed by the "classical doctrine" of contract formation in which "a counter-offer amounts to a rejection of the offer and puts an end to the effect of the offer".

These two approaches, the holistic and the classical or orthodox, are of course radically different. The former (that of Lord Denning) is a two-stage process which asks first if the parties have a contract, and answers this by considering the forms exchanged in order to discover if agreement has been reached on "all material points". This usually produces a finding that "there is a contract as soon as the last of the forms is sent and received without objection being taken to it".[9] If this is indeed the case, the second stage is to elicit the terms of this contract. Orthodox analysis, on the other hand, subsumes content within the formation issue and any resultant contract will be concluded on the terms imposed by the party who fires off the last form.[10] The more radical approach espoused by Lord Denning, therefore, divorces content from formation and does not produce an inevitable finding that the party who fires the last shot must win. But it is not simply a matter of choosing one or other of these approaches, which, in the instant case, produced the same result. Rather the application of orthodox contract formation analysis to a battle of forms, with its implicit stress on objectively determined agreement, carries with it the risk that no contract may be found to exist: a risk that a court faced with a dispute between commercial parties might be reluctant to run.[11] Indeed, such a finding might have been produced in *Butler Machine Tool Co Ltd v Ex-Cell-O Corpn (England) Ltd.*

As already noted, the seller's letter of 5 June 1969, enclosing the buyer's acknowledgment of order, expressly stipulated that the plane-miller was to

---

9  At 968 per Lord Denning MR.

10  Note also *British Road Services v Arthur Crutchley* [1968] 1 All ER 811.

11  Objectivity can be understood in different senses. The sense in which the objective analysis referred to in the text is to be understood is what has been termed "detached objectivity" – i.e., the perspective of a reasonable person looking at what has transpired: see W Howarth, "The meaning of objectivity in contract" (1984) 100 *LQR* 265. Cf J Vorster, "A comment on the meaning of objectivity in contract" (1987) 103 *LQR* 274. Note also Lord Steyn, "Contract law: fulfilling the expectations of reasonable men" (1997) 113 *LQR* 433. Just as this approach may result in a finding of no contract, so too, paradoxically, it carries the risk that a contract may be deemed to have been concluded contrary to the expectations, intention, and business procedures of the contracting parties: Forte and MacQueen (1986) 31 *JLSS* 224 at 228.

be supplied "in accordance with" its quotation of 23 May. From the seller's perspective, therefore, this letter was intended to reinstate the standard terms in its quotation of 23 May. If, however, the Court of Appeal agreed with this submission, it meant that on receipt of that letter plus the enclosed acknowledgment of order form, the buyer now had two documents before it which were mutually contradictory. The first, the seller's letter, was a counter-offer; the second, the buyer's form, was its own earlier counter-offer to purchase the goods – albeit duly signed by the seller. On an objective analysis[12] of this highly ambivalent situation, where the offeree holds what may be construed as a counter-offer, or, possibly an acceptance, together with what clearly is a counter-offer, both of which arrived at the same time, it is hard to disagree with Bridge LJ that "the parties never were *ad idem*".[13] To avoid such a result the wording of the letter of 5 June was construed restrictively as referring only to the price and identity of the machine to be supplied and not to the standard terms and conditions on the reverse of the quotation of 23 May. The somewhat procrustean moulding of the facts to produce a finding that there was a contract in this case suggests that orthodox contract formation analysis affords a rather crude model for solving the battle of forms;[14] and that of Lord Denning appears the more attractive. It may be objected that in *Butler Machine Tool Co Ltd v Ex-Cell-O Corpn (England) Ltd* Lord Denning did not actually adhere to his own model since the parties did not agree on a "material point", namely price.[15] This is not a persuasive stance. The seller quoted a price and the buyer accepted that figure. What the latter objected to was the price variation clause. Consequently, the dispute was only concerned with whether or not a term permitting variation of the agreed price should apply.

　　*Butler Machine Tool Co Ltd v Ex-Cell-O Corpn (England) Ltd* was referred to in argument in two Scottish cases which may be thought of as involving in some respects a battle of forms; though in both the judges did not regard them as such. The first of these is a decision of the Sheriff Principal of North Strathclyde: *Roofcare Ltd v Gillies*.[16] There the pursuers, Roofcare Ltd,

---

12　In the sense of detached objectivity.

13　At 970.

14　In *New Zealand Shipping Co Ltd v A M Satterthwaite & Co Ltd* [1975] AC 154 Lord Wilberforce observed at 167 that "English law, having committed itself to a rather technical and schematic doctrine of contract, in application takes a practical approach, often at the cost of *forcing the facts to fit uneasily into the marked slots of offer, acceptance* and consideration" (emphasis ADMF).

15　E McKendrick, *Contract Law: Text, Cases, and Materials*, 2nd edn (2005) (henceforth McKendrick, *Contract Law: Text, Cases, and Materials*) at 99.

16　1984 SLT (Sh Ct) 8.

quoted for roofing repairs to the house of the defender, Gillies. The quotation contained this condition:

> This quotation is made subject to the undernoted terms and conditions and no alterations, exclusions, additions, or qualifications to the quotation and specification will be made unless confirmed in writing by Roofcare.

Roofcare Ltd's terms and conditions did not oblige it to make the premises wind and watertight. But Gillies' written acceptance of the quotation stipulated that the repairs had to do so. This elicited no response from Roofcare Ltd. Gillies then ordered Roofcare Ltd to do the job. After the repairs were effected, however, Gillies refused to pay, alleging that leaking still occurred. It was argued for Gillies that (1) there was no contract since there was no *consensus ad idem*; and (2) that if there was a contract, then the condition in his acceptance stipulating that the roofs be made wind and watertight was a term of that contract. Neither argument found favour with the Sheriff Principal. Roofcare Ltd had offered to do the work on its terms alone, unless it consented, in writing, to a proposed variation by the offeree. Although just such a variation was proposed, the offeror did not consent to it. At this stage, therefore, there was no contract; but when Gillies instructed Roofcare Ltd to proceed "it was on the basis that the unaccepted qualification or condition did not apply".[17] *Butler Machine Tool Co Ltd v Ex-Cell-O Corpn (England) Ltd* was rightly distinguished on its facts: this case is not a battle of forms one. Nonetheless it is significant to the debate about the battle of forms, since the term under discussion was a clause paramount whereby the offeror intended to trump any terms to the contrary in the offeree's acceptance: which it successfully did. Moreover, although the contract here was for the supply of services, it echoes the judgment of Leggatt LJ in another case concerning the sale of goods:

> If express terms are to govern a contract of sale, a buyer would expect to buy goods upon the seller's terms, unless supplanted by the buyer's own.[18]

This, it has been argued, indicates that where a seller (or supplier) will not budge from reliance on its own terms, and does not react to proposals for change by the other party, any resulting contract is concluded on its terms.[19] *Roofcare Ltd v Gillies*, therefore, provides a measure of support for the view that "in some cases the battle is won by the man who gets the blow in first".[20]

17 1984 SLT (Sh Ct) 8 at 9 per Sheriff Principal Bennett.
18 *Hitchins (Hatfield) Ltd v H Butterworth Ltd*, unreported, Court of Appeal, 25 Feb 1995.
19 McKendrick, *Contract Law: Text, Cases, and Materials*, 99.
20 *Butler Machine Tool Co Ltd v Ex-Cell-O Corpn (England) Ltd* [1979] 1 All ER 965 at 968 per Lord Denning MR.

The next case to be examined, however, does not; and it is this case which, as already noted, has been described as the "classic Scots authority" on the battle of forms.[21]

*Butler Machine Tool Co Ltd v Ex-Cell-O Corpn (England) Ltd* featured in the arguments for both sides in *Uniroyal Ltd v Miller & Co Ltd*.[22] The sequence of relevant events was as follows. On 8 February 1974 the defenders, Miller & Co Ltd, quoted for the sale of steel rolls to the pursuers, Uniroyal Ltd. The reverse side of this form set out the seller's terms and conditions. On 23 May 1974 the buyer sent its purchase order which contained its standard terms. One of these was a clause paramount:

> The [Company] recognises that the Vendor may use its own form of acknowledgement. Therefore, any provisions of the form of acceptance used which modify, conflict with, or contradict any provision of the contract or order shall be deemed to be waived unless expressly agreed to in writing by [the Company] and signed by an authorised representative.

On 7 June 1974 the seller "accepted" this form, but its own acknowledgement of order form stated:

> We shall not be liable in respect of defects and we shall not be liable for loss of profits, detention or other consequential damage or expenses.

One of the substantive terms in this last document excluded liability for loss of profits or other consequential loss. The seller then delivered the goods and the buyer took delivery of and paid for these. A dispute subsequently arose about the quality of the goods and both parties stood upon their respective standard terms and conditions.

Although the Lord Ordinary thought that it made no difference whether he followed Lord Denning's approach in *Butler Machine Tool Co Ltd v Ex-Cell-O Corpn (England) Ltd* or that of Lawton and Bridge LJJ, he reached his decision on the basis of orthodox formation principles. The purchase order was an offer, and the acknowledgment of order, because it contained a revised price and specified a delivery date, was a counter-offer. At this stage therefore the parties were not *ad idem* on the matter of price and price was an essential (or material) term in contracts for the sale of goods. A contract was only concluded when the buyer took delivery and paid for the goods. This meant that the buyer's conduct indicated its acceptance of the seller's counter-offer and, consequently, that the seller's terms prevailed over those of the

21  Hogg & Lubbe, in Zimmermann, Visser & Reid, *Mixed Legal Systems* at 58 n 159.
22  1985 SLT 101.

buyer. Unfortunately the judgment is fraught with difficulties. In the first place the Lord Ordinary's view that price is an essential term in a contract for the sale of goods does not square either with s 8(1) and (2) of the Sale of Goods Act 1979, which provides for payment of a reasonable price where this is not determined by the contract or a course of dealings, or with a subsequent decision of the First Division to the effect that where an agreement is incomplete, but performance has followed, then terms, particularly as to price, may readily be implied to remedy the omission.[23] Then there is the matter of the delivery date. The judge's attitude to this was ambivalent. He did not think that a term stipulating the delivery date was, in itself, essential; nonetheless, the fact that there was such a term gave "weight to the view that the acknowledgment of order was not an unqualified acceptance of the purchase order".[24] However, in the case of commercial contracts the date or time of delivery is generally regarded as being an essential contract term.[25] And this view is reflected in the case of international sales by Article 19(3) CISG, which regards "place and time of delivery" as material contract terms. To like effect are the Comments to Article 2.1.22 PICC.[26] Finally, there is the judge's view that he was not dealing with a "simple" battle of forms case: a type of case which, in his opinion, was one where "the result of such a battle might have been a complicated and abstruse matter to determine".[27] *Butler Machine Tool Co Ltd v Ex-Cell-O Corpn (England) Ltd* was, he thought, just such a case. Quite why this startling conclusion was reached in a matter litigated on almost a decade after goods had been delivered and paid for, and where the only point in issue was whether or not the seller's exclusion of liability for consequential loss prevailed over the buyer's terms which preserved that liability, is impossible to understand.

With due respect to the view of the Lord Ordinary, *Uniroyal Ltd v Miller & Co Ltd* is a classic battle of forms case. What it is not, however, is the "classic Scots authority" on battle of forms. To the extent that it upholds the view that the party who fires the last shot wins the battle of forms, it differs from *Roofcare Ltd v Gillies* which suggests that the first shot may win the battle. Consequently, as an Outer House decision commands no greater respect than that of a sheriff court, the best that can be said is that it is

---

23 *Avintair Ltd v Ryder Airline Services Ltd* 1994 SC 270. Note also G D L Cameron, "Consensus in dissensus" 1995 SLT (News) 132.
24 1985 SLT 101 at 106.
25 *Bunge Corpn v Tradax Export SA* [1981] 1WLR 711. Note also *The Honam Jade* [1991] 1 Lloyd's Rep 38. See also R M Goode, *Commercial Law*, 3rd edn (2004) at 270.
26 Comment 3, Illustration 1. See further below, text accompanying notes 68–74.
27 At 106.

presently unclear in Scots law which party's form, first or last, will win that battle.

It is interesting in this context to note a degree of parallelism with South Africa. The South African law of contract seems to have tended to ignore the battle of forms debate. One writer expresses the opinion that if a contract exists at all it may be hard to determine its content.[28] The most recent edition of Christie[29] does not refer to *Butler Machine Tool Co v Ex-Cell-O Corpn (England) Ltd*, and makes no mention of the "battle of forms" either as a term or as a discrete problem. However, the brief yet complex analysis of the case law by Hogg and Lubbe suggests that while a South African battle of forms case might be analysed in terms of orthodox contract formation theory (which would produce a victory for the firer of the last shot),[30] overall the law "reflects an approach which places the emphasis less on the concurrence of declarations and manifested consent than on disagreement and induced reliance".[31] For example, in *Bok Clothing Manufacturers (Pty) Ltd v Lady Land (Pty) Ltd*,[32] the issue was whether or not the seller could rely on a retention of title clause. Although the parties had done business since 1977, it was only in 1980 that this clause appeared in the terms and conditions found on the reverse of the seller's order forms. Reference to this term was also, however, in the seller's invoices and in "the legend at the bottom of the order form[s]". As Hogg and Lubbe point out, "the court eschewed an analysis in terms of the rules of offer and acceptance and the "last shot rule",[33] preferring an approach based on the rules relating to the incorporation of contract terms.[34] In *Guncrete (Pty) Ltd v Scharrighuisen Construction (Pty) Ltd*,[35] the issue was whether or not terms found in the main contract between the defendants and the building owner, and empowering the site engineer to vary or cancel work, applied to a subcontract between the defendants and the plaintiffs. In response to the latter's tender the defendants counter-offered,

---

28  Kerr, *Contract* 6th edn (2002), 77.
29  Published in 2001.
30  Citing *Ideal Fastener Corpn CC v Book Vision (Pty) Ltd (t/a Colour Graphic)* 2001 (3) SA 1028 (D); *Seef Commercial and Industrial Properties (Pty) Ltd v Silberman* 2001 (3) SA 952 (SCA).
31  Hogg & Lubbe, in Zimmermann, Visser & Reid, *Mixed Legal Systems*, 58–59.
32  1982 (2) SA 565 (C).
33  Hogg & Lubbe, in Zimmermann, Visser & Reid, *Mixed Legal Systems*, 58–59.
34  On the facts the judge found that it was unfair to incorporate a term which was so onerous and contained an element of surprise. His reasoning is reminiscent of that in *Interfoto Picture Library Ltd v Stiletto Visual Programmes Ltd* [1989] QB 433, though that case was not referred to. One may doubt, however, whether a retention of title clause in a contract between a trade seller and a trade buyer is either onerous or surprising.
35  1996 (2) SA 682 (N).

accepting the tender subject to the above term of the main contract being one of the subcontract. The plaintiffs subsequently conducted themselves in a manner which implied that they accepted the counter-offer and, indeed, judgment was given in their favour on that basis. According to Hogg and Lubbe this decision did not turn on whether there was a contract between contractor and subcontractor, but "on an objective principle of reasonable reliance".[36] With respect, neither of these two decisions commends itself as a model for the resolution of the battle of forms. Indeed neither case involved a battle of forms.

The first, it is true, is correct in inferring that incorporation is an issue of content and not formation. But the rules regarding incorporation of terms are essentially designed to promote fair dealing – particularly in the context of consumer contracts. The basis on which a term is not to be included in a contract where an incorporation approach is adopted is premised upon its unfairness: consequently, seller's term X is not a term of the contract because it is unfair and the law, for policy reasons, does not permit the inclusion of unfair terms. However, in a classic battle of forms case between business parties of proportionate bargaining power substantive fairness of contract terms should not be an issue which the law encourages either of the parties to plead easily.[37] Furthermore, one cannot assume that the battle of forms is confined to cases involving terms which are considered to be objectionable on the ground of unfairness. Is there anything inherently unfair in retention of title or price-variation clauses? The battle of forms centres on terms that are different and mutually incompatible: seller's term X is negated by buyer's term Y. The question here is – what is to be done with such terms?

There is, however, one useful point which incorporation analysis can highlight; and that is the element of (unfair) surprise caused by the manner in which the term is incorporated. And this is something to which I will return when discussing the treatment of clauses paramount.

The second case, with its stress on objectivity, is more problematic. The contract was made on the main contractor's terms because the subcontractor reacted in a manner which would induce a reasonable person to believe that it "was assenting to the terms proposed by the other party".[38] The difficulty

36  Hogg & Lubbe, in Zimmermann, Visser & Reid, *Mixed Legal Systems*, 59.
37  This is what the two Law Commissions discovered when they proposed extending the grounds of challenge available under the Unfair Terms in Consumer Contracts Regulations 1999 (SI 1999/2083) to business-to-business contracts (Law Com No 292, Scot Law Com No 199) at 61 – "businesses value certainty above protection and, with the exception of small businesses, neither need nor want additional protection".
38  At 686 per Alexander J, quoting Blackburn J in *Smith v Hughes* (1871) LR 6 QB 597 at 607.

with this approach, however, is its recourse to the objectivity paradigm and the connected problem of which variant of that paradigm is to be used.[39] Added to this is the possibility that whichever variant is resorted to, the conclusion may be that there is no contract. This presents no difficulty where performance has not yet taken place; but is scarcely satisfactory where it is otherwise. A further consequence of this approach, if applied to a true battle of forms situation, would be to distance South African contract law from the position adopted by the international commercial harmonising measures which will be discussed later in this essay.

## D. FIGHTING THE BATTLE OF FORMS UNDER SCOTS LAW: A CRITIQUE

The notes to the Comment to Article 2:209 PECL observe that the last shot theory represents the "prevailing view" in Scotland in relation to the winning of the battle of forms.[40] As a statement of the stance taken by some scholars, this is correct:[41] though the justification for taking it, as has been suggested, is rather slight. Certainly for those who do espouse it, or who see the battle of forms as being resolved on a "traditional approach",[42] this manner of tackling the problem in Scots law has the merit of simplicity. The buyer's purchase order is its offer to acquire goods from the seller. The seller's acknowledgment of order form represents its rejection of the seller's offer and its own counter-offer: at this point not only is there no contract between buyer and seller, but the buyer's offer has also ceased to exist, having been killed off by the seller's qualified acceptance.[43] However, the seller then does what both parties want: it delivers the goods. And the buyer then does what the seller wishes; it takes delivery of the goods and pays for these. The buyer's conduct here is treated as acceptance; and as acceptance of the counter-offer made by the seller in the acknowledgment of order form. Thus the battle of forms has been resolved upon an orthodox contract formation analysis as in *Uniroyal Ltd v Miller & Co Ltd*.[44]

---

39  Above note 10.
40  Article 2:209 PECL, Note 2(b).
41  SME, vol 15, para 636 note 2.
42  McBryde, *Contract*, para 6–105.
43  *Wolf and Wolf v Forfar Potato Co* 1984 SLT 100; *Rutterford Ltd v Allied Breweries Ltd* 1990 SLT 249; *Findlater v Mann* 1990 SLT 465.
44  1985 SLT 101. Note also, to similar effect, *Chitton Bros v S Eker Ltd* unreported, Outer House, 8 July 1980. However, in *Roofcare v Gillies* 1984 SLT (Sh Ct) 8 the first shot rule was applied. Non-Scottish readers may care to note that the decisions in *Uniroyal Ltd v Miller & Co Ltd* and

At least five incidents of this analysis are, however, overlooked in its application. First, it produces only one conclusion where it is applied; and that is that the party who fires off the last form in the battle of forms always wins. Second, the winner's victory is always gained by default. It does not matter that the party who fires the first form appreciates the outcome produced by the orthodox analysis and actively seeks to displace it by the inclusion of a clause paramount.[45] Consequently, in the context of sales transactions the seller will always have the edge over the buyer.[46] Third, although the clause paramount may offer an opportunity to negotiate a solution to points of difference between the two sets of terms, thereby reinforcing the message that the first party's terms are otherwise to prevail, the second party may ignore these; safe in the knowledge that the law will support what is basically quite unreasonable behaviour. Fourth, the orthodox analysis injects a substantial dose of uncertainty into commercial activities. The parties' understanding is that they have a contract; they would find the suggestion that they do not ludicrous. Their only point of disagreement is whether the particular term in issue does or does not apply. The orthodox analysis queries the parties' understanding and resolves the problem of contractual content by deconstructing that understanding. As such it is not only quite inimical to the *lex mercatoria* principle of *favor contractus*, and must therefore be accounted a positive disadvantage in cross-border contracting,[47] but it is also contrary to the policy principle of Scots law that "the essence of commerce is making bargains", and that "unenforceable arrangements are the exception and not the rule".[48]

Fifth, and finally, the orthodox analysis has a clear and negative impact on transaction costs. Standard forms represent an economically efficient means

---

*Chitton Bros v Eker* were those of Outer House judges in the Court of Session and that such decisions do not have a higher authority than those delivered by a sheriff. Thus the case law goes either way in Scotland: a point overlooked in the Comment to Article 2:209 PECL.

45  A point recognised by Lord Denning MR in *Butler Machine Tool Co Ltd v Ex-Cel-O Corporation (England) Ltd* [1979] 1 All ER 965, CA. The Dutch Civil Code provides that it is the first shot which wins the battle: *Hardstaal Holdings BV v NN* (2001) C99/315HR.

46  C Sukurs, "Harmonizing the battle of the forms: a comparison of the United States, Canada, and the United Nations Convention on Contracts for the International Sale of Goods" (2001) 34 *Vanderbilt Journal of Transnational Law* 1481 at 1487.

47  G Baron, "Do the UNIDROIT Principles of International Commercial Contracts form a new *lex mercatoria*?" http://www.cisg.law.pace.edu/cisg/biblio/baron.html.

48  *R & J Dempster v Motherwell Bridge and Engineering Co Ltd* 1964 SC 308 at 328 per Lord President Clyde. To like effect was Lord Guthrie at 332: "The object of our law of contract is to facilitate the transactions of commercial men, and not to create obstacles in the way of solving practical problems arising out of the circumstances confronting them, or to expose them to unnecessary pitfalls".

of doing business. The initial outlay is in legal fees to the draftsperson. Thereafter the forms may be signed and dispatched by "underlings".[49] Transaction costs would, however, rise were it to become necessary for each "underling" to scrutinise every form sent by another "underling" in order to detect minor differences.[50] The clause paramount may therefore be viewed as promoting rather than impeding economic efficiency. But the clause paramount, whether in the first shot or the last, is certainly not immune from criticism either. The clause is essentially adhesive in nature; and the refusal to do business save on one's own terms represents a take it or leave it approach. To some extent this rather leonine clause may be mitigated if negotiation of different terms is conceded as a means of shifting the position of the party insisting on its terms alone, but such negotiation may not always stand much chance of changing that party's mind. Consequently, in dealings between commercial parties, although there is nothing intrinsically unfair about wishing to have one's own contract terms prevail, given that the purpose of a clause paramount is to negate all of the other party's terms, it is not unreasonable to argue that it must do so in clear terms and above all in a prominent fashion. This, as we shall see, is a feature of some of the models to be considered next.

## E. THINKING OUTSIDE THE BOX: MODEL SOLUTIONS TO THE BATTLE OF FORMS

A number of solutions to the problem of the battle of forms exist. Perhaps the best known of these are to be found in the US Uniform Commercial Code (UCC); CISG; UNIDROIT PICC; and PECL. From a United Kingdom (and that includes a specifically Scottish) perspective, each represents a different approach from that adopted domestically. None, however, adopt quite the same approach and so a measure of comparison[51] must be drawn before any evaluation may be attempted.

---

49 The terminology is that of J White & R S Summers, *Uniform Commercial Code* (1988), 23; however the sentiment was one shared by UNCITRAL in drafting CISG: *Yearbook of the United Nations Commission on International Trade Law*, vol 9 (1978), 92.

50 D A Levin & E B Rubert, "Beyond UCC Section 2–207: should Professor Murray's proposed revision be adopted?" (1992) 11 *Journal of Law and Commerce* 175 at 188.

51 For a broad comparative perspective, see E Jacobs, "The battle of the forms: standard term contracts in comparative perspective" (1985) 34 *ICLQ* 297; A T von Mehren, "The battle of forms: a comparative view" (1990) 38 *American Journal of Comparative Law* 265.

## (1) The UCC

### § 2–207 UCC [extant]

(1) A definite and seasonable expression of acceptance … which is sent within a reasonable time operates as an acceptance even though it states terms additional to or different from those offered or agreed upon, unless acceptance is expressly made conditional on assent to the additional or different terms

(2) The additional terms are to be construed as proposals for addition to the contract. Between merchants such terms become part of the contract unless:
   (a) the offer expressly limits acceptance to the terms of the offer;
   (b) they materially alter it; or
   (c) notification of objection to them has already been given or is given within a reasonable time after notice of them is received.

(3) Conduct by both parties which recognizes the existence of a contract is sufficient to establish a contract for sale although the writings of the parties do not otherwise establish a contract. In such case the terms of the particular contract consist of those terms on which the writings of the parties agree, together with any supplementary terms incorporated under any other provisions of this Act.

### § 2–207 UCC [proposed]

If (i) conduct by both parties recognizes the existence of a contract although their records do not otherwise establish a contract, (ii) a contract is formed by offer and acceptance, or (iii) a contract formed in any manner is confirmed by a record that contains terms additional to or different from those in the contract being confirmed, the terms of the contract subject to Section 2–202 are:
(a)  terms that appear in the records of both parties;
(b)  terms, whether in the record or not, to which both parties agree; and
(c)  terms supplied or incorporated under any provision of this Act.

So far as the UCC is concerned, the current provision on battle of forms is on the way out. The effect of § 2–207 UCC, as it stands, may be summarised very briefly. Subsection (1) rejects the equiparation of qualified acceptance and counter-offer just because some terms of the "acceptance" do not mirror image those of the offer.[52] But this exception to orthodox formation analysis hangs on two criteria being met. First, despite the presence of additional or differing terms, an objective view of the facts must reveal that a contract has been concluded.[53] Second, the offeror may forestall conclusion by providing that it must first assent to such additional or differing terms.[54] If these hurdles are overcome, the content of the contract is then determined by subsection (2). Incorporation is not automatic, however. A clause paramount in the offer

---

52  To like effect is Restatement, Second, Contracts, Articles 38(2), 39, 59, and 61. Note also, as examples, *Roto-Lith Ltd v F P Bartlett & Co*, CA Mass 1962, 297 F 2d 497; *Howard Construction Co v Jeff-Cole Quarries Inc*, Mo App 1983, 669 SW 2d 221.

53  *US Industries Inc v Semco Manufacturing Inc* 1977 CA 8 Mo, 562 Mo 2d 1061.

54  Such a precondition will not be easily inferred: *Reaction Molding Techniques Inc v General Electric Co*, DC Pa 1984, 588 F Supp 1280.

which makes clear that only a *de plano* acceptance will be tolerated renders the offeree's attempt to incorporate its terms, whether additional or differing, nugatory. There will be a contract, but its content will be determined by the offer. Subsection (3) is something of a longstop where documentary exchanges between parties do not disclose a concluded contract. But if buyer and seller behave in a manner which indicates their belief, which is consistent with commercial reality, that they have a contract, then the law respects that belief. In this case the content of the contract is a mixture of those terms which the documentary exchanges reveal to have been agreed, supplemented if need be by terms implied by the UCC in sales contracts.

§ 2–207 UCC remains predicated upon a core requirement that a contract must exist either in fact or in belief. Nevertheless, its purpose is to determine the issue of content when the parties' terms differ in some respects. Its suggested replacement rests upon the same requirement and continues to espouse that objective. There is, however, an important difference between proposed and extant § 2–207 UCC. I have already noted that extant § 2–207 UCC recognises the effect of a clause paramount in the offer. Proposed § 2–207 UCC[55] does not. By implication it appears to reject the automatic effect of the clause paramount (the first shot) and also orthodox formation analysis (the last shot). Consequently, a battle of forms cannot, automatically, be won by either the party who fires the first shot or the party who fires the last. Where the response to an offer containing a clause paramount is a counter-offer, there is no presumption that the offeror agrees to contract on the counter-offeror's terms. If the parties move to performance, the contract will comprise those terms on which the parties have agreed (including terms not found in the documentary record) and terms "supplied or incorporated" by the UCC. A final brief comment: proposed § 2–207 UCC is not restricted to battle of forms situations and is generally applicable to contracts for the sale of goods.

## (2) CISG[56]

### Article 19 CISG

(1) A reply to an offer which purports to be an acceptance but contains additions, limitations or other modifications is a rejection of the offer and constitutes a counter-offer.

---

55 2002 revision.
56 See generally, F Vergne, "The 'battle of the forms' under the 1980 United Nations Convention on Contracts for the International Sale of Goods" (1985) 33 *American Journal of Comparative Law* 233; C Moccia, "The United Nations Convention on Contracts for the International Sale of Goods and the 'battle of the forms'" (1989–90) 13 *Fordham International Law Journal* 649; Forte (1995) 1 *Contemporary Issues in Law* 43 at 62–65.

(2) However, a reply to an offer which purports to be an acceptance but contains additional or different terms which do not materially alter the terms of the offer constitutes an acceptance, unless the offeror, without undue delay, objects orally to the discrepancy or dispatches a notice to that effect. If he does not so object, the terms of the contract are the terms of the offer with the modifications contained in the acceptance.

(3) Additional or different terms relating among other things to the price, payment, quality and quantity of the goods, place and time of delivery, extent of one party's liability to the other, or the settlement of disputes are considered to alter the terms of the offer materially.

The Scottish Law Commission has proposed that certain provisions of CISG should serve as a model for reform of the law of contract formation.[57] Indeed Article 7(1) and (2) of the Uniform Law on the Formation of Contracts for the International Sales of Goods 1964, which are substantially the same in content as Article 19(1) and (2) CISG, were given effect in the United Kingdom by the Uniform Laws on International Sales Act 1967, section 2(1) in respect of international sales of goods. So the Scottish Law Commission's proposal was scarcely radical. As far as the problem of the battle of forms is concerned, this is most unfortunate. If § 2–207 UCC extant can be described as an "amphibious tank that was originally designed to fight in swamps but was ultimately sent to fight in the desert",[58] then Article 19 CISG is an amphibious tank that was designed to sink in those swamps. In modern parlance it "talks the talk". But we may enquire does it "walk the walk"? To be blunt – I think not.

Article 19(1) CISG is fundamentally premised on the orthodox analysis of contract formation: the mirror image rule.[59] As a result, additional or differing terms in the response to an offer cannot in principle permit that response to be viewed as anything other than a rejection and counter-offer.[60] Such terms are not to be viewed as proposals for modification of the offer's terms.

---

57  Report on Formation of Contract: Scottish Law and the United Nations Convention on Contracts for the International Sale of Goods (Scot Law Com No 144, 1993) at para 1.10.

58  White & Summers, *Uniform Commercial Code* at 24.

59  Sukurs (2001) 34 *Vanderbilt Journal of Transnational Law* 1481 at 1496. UNCITRAL considered the viewpoint that what ultimately emerged as Article 19(2) CISG should be deleted since it altered the mirror image approach. This proposal was rejected, though only "after considerable deliberation" (*Yearbook of the United Nations Commission on International Trade Law*, vol 9 (1978), 42–43). A working group subsequently recommended the addition of a version of what is now Article 19(3) CISG; but stated that its "first preference" was the deletion of what is now Article 19(2) CISG since this "contradicted the basis principle", set out in what is now Article 19(1) CISG, "that an acceptance must agree with the terms of an offer" (*Yearbook of the United Nations Commission on International Trade Law*, vol 9 (1978), 43).

60  As was the case in the CISG's ill-fated predecessor, the 1964 Hague Uniform Law on the Formation of Contracts for the Sale of Goods, Article 7(1).

It is of course true that Article 19(2) CISG permits minor variations so long as the offeror does not object; but any *material* variation of the offer quite simply precludes the formation of a contract for the sale of goods. Here there is an instant and stark contrast with § 2–207 UCC, which regards materiality as relevant to the content of a contract but not to its formation. The converse is true of Article 19(1) CISG. And when we turn to consider terms which would preclude the formation of a contract because they constitute material alterations, Article 19(3) presents a list which is not only extensive but which is also questionable in some instances and not exhaustive. Consequently, the scope for departure from the mirror image rule is too severely restricted: a point which the Scottish Law Commission concedes.[61] That said, particularly in relation to "additional terms", the Article is less circumscribed than it may first appear. Thus terms implied by trade usage,[62] and therefore implicit in an acceptance of an offer which makes no mention thereof, will not prevent conclusion of a contract and will form part of its contents.

Article 19 CISG is directed at the situation where parties have spotted additions or variations, have not proceeded to performance, and are wrangling over whether or not they have a contract. But what if after having exchanged standard forms of offer and acceptance, and having performed their respective parts of the bargain, a problem arises which is referable to diverging terms in the documents exchanged? Since Article 18(3) CISG permits conclusion of a contract on the basis of performance, and since the seller's standard acknowledgment of order form would be treated by Article 19(1) CISG as its counter-offer, the buyer by taking the goods and making payment of the price has accepted the counter-offer and the contract would be on its terms. In other words, the seller who fires the last shot automatically wins the battle of forms.[63] This is quite simply not an acceptable solution to the problem.

Article 19(2) CISG represents a compromise between those legal systems that require the application of a strict mirror image rule, and those that adopt a more relaxed position re immaterial or ancillary variations of the offer's

---

61  Scot Law Com No 144 (1993) at para 4.19.

62  M Schmidt-Kessel, in P Schlechtriem & I Schwenzer (eds), *Commentary on the UN Convention on the International Sale of Goods*, 2nd edn (2005) at 139.

63  This appears to be the result reached by an American court in *Magellan International Corp v Salzgitter Handel GmbH*, DC Ill, 1999, US Dist Lexis 19386. Note also *Filanto SpA v Chilewich International Corp*, SDNY 1992, 789 F Supp 1229; R S Rendell, "The new UN Convention on International Sales Contracts: an overview" (1989) 15 *Brooklyn Journal of International Law* 23 at 29.

terms.[64] Scots law with its rejection of the concept of essential and inessential terms in offers[65] falls into the former category. However, in comparison with the UCC in both its present and future manifestations, it merely tinkers with orthodox formation analysis. The Scottish Law Commission regards it as close to the orthodox model and the features which would seem to commend it to them all relate to the point that the legislation proposed would require virtually no practical change to current Scots law.[66] This attitude contrasts strongly with that in the United States where it has been very persuasively argued that CISG should not be used as a paradigm for revision of the UCC.[67] Again in contrast to the approach of either extant or proposed § 2–207 UCC, Article 19 CISG is inconsistent with the modalities of modern commerce. As a formation-based approach, it queries commercial understanding of the contracting process and is therefore unduly paternalistic. Furthermore, as already mentioned, it is economically inefficient, producing a negative impact on transaction costs. The American model facilitates commerce; and the proposed revision, by eliminating first or last strike victories, is conducive to future business relations between disputants. CISG, on the other hand, by adherence to the contract formation approach to battle of forms not only produces an almost certain winner in the party who fires last but, thanks to its restrictive interpretation of immateriality, is more conducive to a finding of no contract rather than a determination of contractual content. If Scots law is to be reformed in this area, I would hope that CISG is no longer considered to represent the ideal model.

## (3) PICC

Article 2.1.22 PICC
Where both parties use standard terms and reach agreement except on those terms, a contract is concluded on the basis of the agreed terms and of any standard terms which are common in substance unless one party clearly indicates in advance, or later and without undue delay informs the other party, that it does not intend to be bound by such a contract.

Article 2.1.22 PICC[68] represents a simple yet elegant approach to the battle

---

64 A M Garro, "Reconciliation of legal traditions in the UN Convention on Contracts for the International Sale of Goods" (1989) 23 *International Law* 443 at 462–463.
65 *Rutterford Ltd v Allied Breweries Ltd* 1990 SLT 249.
66 Scot Law Com No 144 (1993) at para 4.19.
67 H D Gabriel, "The inapplicability of the United Nations Convention on the International Sale of Goods as a model for revision of Article Two of the Uniform Commercial Code" (1998) 72 *Tulane LR* 1995.
68 Although the 2004 version of PICC is a revision of the 1994 original, Article 2.1.22 of the 2004 Principles is a verbatim reproduction of Article 2.22 of that original.

of forms. Essentially it requires us to envisage a situation in which a distinction can be drawn between the non-standard (i.e. variable) terms and the standard (i.e. general) terms in the purchase order and acknowledgment of order. The former will normally, I think, refer to price, payment, and delivery:[69] clearly matters which vary from transaction to transaction. The latter may be on the reverse side of the document containing the variable terms, or in an accompanying document. If the parties can be shown to be agreed on the variable terms, then the fact that their general terms may differ does not prevent conclusion of a contract, the terms of which are the agreed variable terms plus those general terms that "are common in substance". General terms which conflict are simply discarded under the "knock-out" principle. It will be noted that the CISG approach does not require conduct to perfect the bargain. A contract is concluded by the documentary exchange itself. In this respect Article 2.1.22 PICC departs from UCC § 2–207(3) UCC but is consistent with Article 19 CISG and Article 2:209 PECL.

Article 2.1.22 PICC recognises the twin problems produced by the mirror image rule, namely that there may be no concluded contract; and that if there is, then it must be on the terms found in the last shot fired.[70] It further recognises commercial reality by concluding that where standard form offers generate standard form acceptances, with neither buyer nor seller being "aware of [any] conflict between their respective general terms", then neither should be permitted thereafter either to challenge the existence of a contract between them or to maintain that it is the terms of the last shot which determine the contract's content.[71] However, the last shot may still win the battle where it contains a clause paramount. The justification for this last position would seem to be its adhesive nature. The seller has drawn its line in the sand, accept its terms of business or proceed no further with the proposed transaction. If the buyer performs its part of the bargain, the contract is concluded on the seller's terms alone. A buyer may, however, pre-empt such a strike by declaring that a contract may only be concluded on its terms. But whether the clause paramount is pre-emptive or reactive, it must be "clearly indicate[d]" to the other party. The Comment to Article 2.1.22 PICC is somewhat equivocal on this point; but appears reluctant to concede that clauses paramount found in the general terms and conditions themselves might satisfy the publicity requirement.

---

69  These are the terms identified in Comment 3, Illustration 1. PECL adds to these terms relating to description of performance: Comment A.
70  Comment 2.
71  Comment 3.

If, for example, one applies Article 2.1.22 PICC to the facts of *Uniroyal Ltd v Miller & Co Ltd*,[72] in which the clauses paramount appeared only in the parties' general terms but were not referred to otherwise, then neither would apply.[73] If, on the other hand, the buyer (Uniroyal) had included their clause paramount along with other variable terms (such as price and time and place of delivery) on the face of their purchase order, the seller's acceptance, regardless of what its standard terms provided, would have concluded a contract on the buyer's terms.[74] So here the first shot would have prevailed. It did not of course because on the approach taken, the last shot rule was applied.

Article 2.1.22 PICC is quite unlike Article 19 CISG. The latter is mired in an approach to the battle of forms which is predicated on the orthodox formation analysis; and by virtue of that connection is condemned to the last shot principle if indeed there is a finding that a contract has been concluded. From an international convention concerned with cross-border contracts one would expect a philosophy designed more to promote enforceability than to impede it and Article 19 CISG, like Scots law, is at positive odds with the principle of *favor contractus* which may be accounted part of the modern *lex mercatoria*. Article 2.1.22 PICC is quite a radical shift away from orthodox theory; which it implicitly recognises as productive of these extreme results. Indeed its preservation of the clause paramount, but only where there has been clear satisfaction of a prominent visibility prerequisite, seems to sit well with the requirement under English (and I would venture Scots) law, that terms which radically alter the basic expectations of a contracting party must be specifically drawn to the attention of that party.[75]

Perhaps the only major expression of dissatisfaction which might be levelled at Article 2.1.22 PICC concerns the effect of clauses paramount. The first point, of course, is that by permitting these adhesive terms one reinforces potential inequalities of economic strength between buyers and sellers. One wonders whether the requirement of fair dealing "in international trade"[76] might not yet be interpreted to encompass abuse of bargaining power. PICC appears to condone the practice, provided the strike is publicised and visible. While it is true that a clause paramount may come as a surprise to one of the parties, the clause is primarily objectionable on policy grounds. True,

72  1985 SLT 101.

73  Comment 3, Illustration 2.

74  Comment 3, Illustration 3.

75  *Interfoto Picture Library Ltd v Stiletto Visual Programmes Ltd* [1989] QB 433; *Montgomery Litho Ltd v Maxwell* 2000 SC 56.

76  Article 1.7 PICC.

the recipient of a document in these terms may "inform the other party that it does not intend to be bound by such a contract", but this produces a dysfunctional solution at least in terms of cross-border trade. In this respect the policy underpinning proposed § 2–207 UCC is to be preferred.

## (4) PECL

There is *consensus* that Article 2:209 PECL and PICC are basically the same.[77] This is perhaps debatable. There is also a view that Article 2:209 PECL "has adopted the common-law [sic] approach".[78] This is not debatable; it is simply bizarre. Were Article 2:209 PECL to be applied to the facts of *Uniroyal Ltd v Miller & Co Ltd*[79] the seller (Miller & Co Ltd) would not have won by virtue of firing the last shot. But nor would the buyer (Uniroyal Ltd) have won on the basis of having fired the first shot. Because both parties asserted the paramountcy of their respective standard terms, thereby indicating their unwillingness to be bound by the other's standard terms, neither set of standard terms would have prevailed. Instead, their contract would have comprised the essential terms of their contract, upon which their agreement would be patent, together with those general terms which were "common in substance"; the standard terms which conflicted with each other would cancel or knock each other out.

But it "will not always be easy to decide", the Comment tells us, whether terms really are "common in substance".[80] The illustration provided by the Comment deals with an arbitration clause which occurs in both purchase and acknowledgment of order forms. But whereas one form stipulates that arbitration will take place in London, the other states that it will be in Sweden.[81] This is a classic problem which is replicated where parties specify different courts to hear any potential dispute: for example, the seller specifies the "Commercial Court in London" and the buyer a "Court in London".[82] The

---

77 PECL, Notes 2(a); M J Bonnell, "The UNIDROIT Principles of International Commercial Contracts and the Principles of European Contract Law: similar rules for the same purposes?" (1996) 26 *Uniform Law Review* 229; M P Viscasillas, "The formation of contracts and the Principles of European Contract Law" (2001) 13 *Pace International Law Review* 371.

78 Viscasillas, (2001) 13 *Pace International L Rev* 371 at 389. The same writer asserts that this is equally true of Article 2.22 PICC (1994 edition).

79 1985 SLT 101.

80 Comment C2.

81 Illustration 2.

82 For a case in which the seller's offer insisted that disputes were to be resolved by arbitration in California, and the buyer's acceptance stipulated for their resolution by arbitration in the United Kingdom, see *OTM Ltd v Hydranautics* [1981] 2 Lloyd's Rep 211.

statement in the Comment – "it is the identity in result not in formulation that counts" – suggests to me that the term should not be interpreted literally but teleologically or purposively instead, which would, I think, mean that one should overlook the fact that the places of arbitration differ and recognise that because the parties' common purpose was to avoid litigation and submit disputes to arbitration the two clauses have a common substance. But this is not the result which the illustration endorses: "Although offer and acceptance have in common that they both refer to arbitration, the clauses are not 'common in substance' and accordingly neither of the places of arbitration are agreed on." There is no doubt that the place of arbitration can be important and may have been chosen deliberately and with care depending, for example, upon whether there is a light or hard review of arbitral decisions by the courts of the place where arbitration takes place. Ultimately this may be a matter which will require litigation to determine if this clause remains in the contract or must be discarded.

Another complication arises where the buyer or seller respectively includes a clause paramount in the variable terms of the offer or the acceptance. Under Article 2.1.22 PICC a clause paramount will be effective provided that it appears in the variable terms of the form and satisfies a prominent visibility requirement. This does not appear to be quite the PECL approach.[83] If one of the parties expressly stipulates, but not in the general terms of the form, that it will not be bound by terms other than its own, then no contract comes into being.[84] By implication, however, if the clause paramount is one of the general terms then a contract will be capable of conclusion. A similar term in the general terms of the response of the other party will disappear on the knock-out principle since these two clauses paramount are irreconcilable. However, there is also a fall-back position. This operates where after forms have been exchanged one party notifies the other "without delay" that it does not want to be bound by the contract.[85] Suppose that the buyer's offer includes this clause :

> Any provisions in the form of acceptance used which modify, conflict with or contradict any provision of the contract or order shall be deemed to be waived unless expressly agreed to in writing by the Company and signed by an authorised representative.

83  Article 2:209(2) PECL.
84  Article 2:209(a) PECL.
85  Article 2:209(b) PECL.

Under Article 2.1.22 PICC there would be a contract if this clause paramount was not part of the buyer's standard conditions. Under Article 2:209(2) PECL, however, there would not. Under Article 2.1.22 PICC there would still be a contract if this clause was found in the buyer's standard conditions but the clause paramount would be disregarded. The same result would occur under Article 2:209(2)(a) PECL. PICC, therefore, adheres more closely to the *favor contractus* principle than does PECL in this regard. One wonders why PECL has not here lived up to its belief that a "contract may be formed by the exchange of general conditions"?[86]

## F. PECL AS THE WAY FORWARD?

Several things are very clear. The first is that as a national legal system Scots law treats the battle of forms in a fragmented fashion in that the cases do not suggest a uniform response to the question – does the first or the last shot prevail? Second, Scots law does not appreciate that the battle of forms is a matter of contract content, not of contract formation. Third, there has been no judicial recognition so far that orthodox formation analysis is ill-suited to the reality of modern commerce, contract procedure, and commercial expectations.[87] A fourth concern is that despite the volume of cross-border commerce within the European Union, there is no uniform approach to the battle of forms among the member states.[88] Under Dutch law the first shot rule has been applied;[89] in the United Kingdom the last shot rule has been assumed to prevail;[90] and under Austrian and German law the knock-out rule seems to be preferred.[91] In Spain, however, the position appears to be unclear and in Sweden opinion is against the application of any single approach. But problems are relatively easy to articulate in this context; solutions are more difficult. How does PECL fit into the reformist debate?

Article 2:209 PECL is not flawless; and some of these flaws have been mentioned here. However, the provision is based on the fundamentally

---

86 Comment C1.

87 On the gap between judicial perceptions of commercial expectations and the reality, see S Styles, "Good faith: a principled matter" in A D M Forte, *Good Faith*, 157 at 170–171.

88 See E Hondius & C Mahé, "The battle of forms: towards a uniform solution" (1997–98) 10 *Journal. of Contract Law* 268.

89 Article 6:225(3) BW.

90 *Uniroyal Ltd v Miller & Co Ltd* 1985 SLT 101; *British Road Services v Arthur Crutchley* [1968] 1 All ER 811; *Butler Machine Tool Co Ltd v Ex-Cell-O Corp (England) Ltd* [1979] 1 All ER 965, CA. As noted in the text earlier, Article 19 CISG also embraces the last shot doctrine.

91 Note also Article 2.1.22 PICC; and proposed § 2–207 UCC.

sound premise that the battle of forms is a contents question and not a formation issue. In addition, it is more reflective of commercial reality than the approach taken by my own legal system. On the other hand, PECL is no more than a model law which has no force in the member states and may (or may not) provide a template for a European Union-wide contract code.[92] However, it is just as important to remember that PECL, as it stands, provides a useful point of reference for judges or legislators wishing to develop the law.[93] Moreover, PECL has been considered by the Scottish Law Commission in connection with the reform of the law on penalty clauses and the payment of interest on debts and damages.[94] This is important because the Commission's conception of the Scots law of contract is one which is both modernist and integrationist in spirit:

> Scots law has a tradition of being receptive to the best international legal developments, given the obvious advantages for Scottish traders, lawyers and arbiters in having our internal law the same as the law which is now widely applied throughout the world in relation to contracts for the international sale of goods.[95]

At that time, however, the model upon which the Commission pinned its hopes, at least in relation to the battle of forms, was CISG. For the reasons argued for above, in my opinion the PECL model is to be preferred; and it is to be hoped that should the matter arise for adjudication in the future, a Scottish court will recognise that the battle of forms is not yet a resolved and settled area of law, and will pay serious consideration to disposing of the issue on the basis of the approach taken in Article 2:209 PECL.

92  PECL, vol 1, Introduction.
93  House of Lords decisions in which reference has been made to PECL are: *Director-General of Fair Trading v First National Bank* [2002] 1 AC 481; *Shogun Finance Ltd v Hudson* [2004] 1 AC 919; *R v Immigration Officer at Prague Airport, ex parte European Roma Rights Centre* [2005] 2 WLR 1.
94  See, e.g., Report on Penalty Clauses (Scot Law Com No 171, 1999); Discussion Paper on Interest on Debt and Damages No 127 (2005).
95  Scot Law Com No 144 at para 1.7. For a rather similar argument in favour of harmonising national and international rules, see J Hellner, "The UN Convention on the International Sale of Goods: its influence on national sales and contract law", in R Cranston & R Goode (eds), *Commercial and Consumer Law. National and International Dimensions* (1993), 40 at 42.

# 5 Agency

## *Laura Macgregor*

## A. INTRODUCTION

A chapter on agency occupies a somewhat unique position in a book of this type. First, agency is often considered to be more properly part of commercial rather than contract law. This commercial background must be borne in mind. Agency transactions are increasingly likely to be international in nature, particularly as agents cross borders within Europe, benefiting from the protection of European Directives as they do so.[1] This international context makes the prospect of uniform rules for agency transactions throughout Europe an extremely important one for agency lawyers. It is not difficult to see the pressing argument in favour of developing Scots agency principles in line with PECL.

The second reason why this chapter may differ from others in this book is the extent of English influence which has operated on both Scots and South African law. English law has been so dominant in matters commercial that both Scots and South African agency law bear a strong resemblance to English law. One would imagine that the same could not be said of PECL, being a collaboration between jurists from both Civilian and Common Law countries. Nevertheless, as this chapter should illustrate, English agency principles have been so influential that they have left an obvious mark on PECL, perhaps to a greater extent than one might have anticipated.

Providing a full flavour of the entirety of agency law in each of the systems studied is a task which would require a great deal more space than is available in this book. Two concepts only are discussed in this chapter: apparent authority and the availability of direct actions between principal and third party where the principal is undisclosed. There are compelling reasons for choosing those particular concepts. Perhaps most importantly, the issue of direct actions forms one of the "fault lines" between the Common and the Civil Law. Such actions, part of English law for at least three hundred years,[2] were originally rejected by Civil Law countries, being recognised there only relatively recently and in a piecemeal and limited fashion.[3] The presence of direct actions in PECL is therefore of immediate interest to the agency lawyer. They are additionally worthy of attention because the English version, the undisclosed principal doctrine, is highly controversial. As is

---

1 See EC Council Directive 86/653/EC (OJ 1986, L382/17) on the co-ordination of the laws of member states relating to self-employed commercial agents.
2 R Powell, "Contractual agency in Roman law and English law" (1956) *SALR* 41 at 49
3 The extent to which such actions are available in other European countries is summarised in the Notes to Articles 3:302 and 3:303 PECL.

explored in more detail below, many argue that the English version fails adequately to take account of the third party's interests. This may be because the principles of English agency law developed largely during the eighteenth century, at a time when protection of reasonable reliance by third parties was not a high priority. Suffused as PECL is with overriding concepts of good faith, it would not be surprising if the versions contained in PECL shift the balance towards greater third-party protection. The extent to which this is the case is explored below.

The other concept analysed here, apparent authority, shares the same English heritage as the concept of the undisclosed principal. Despite the fact that its rationale appears to be the protection of third parties through the operation of an estoppel, its requirements are so rigorous that it often operates in the principal's favour. The same issue of the lack of third-party protection therefore arises. Apparent authority differs from the direct actions in that it is not, at least to the same extent, a "fault line" between the Common Law and the Civil Law. Many European systems have developed their own solutions to the problem which the Common Law solves using apparent authority.[4] Again, the version of apparent authority appearing in PECL owes much to English law. The focus for discussion is therefore the innovations on English law contained within PECL, and how useful those might be for Scots and South African lawyers.

## B. APPARENT AUTHORITY

### (1) Definition?

Where apparent authority is relevant, the agent lacks the authority to do what he is purporting to do. Lacking such authority, he cannot create a contract between the principal and the third party. However, it is important to consider the conduct of the principal. The principal may have misled the third party as to the extent of the agent's authority. Using the terminology of English law, misleading the third party in this way is treated as a representation. The third party may rely on the representation and suffer loss as a result. If the third party can successfully prove each of these elements of representation, reliance and loss, an estoppel is created in his favour. If the third party sues the principal, the principal is estopped from denying that the agent was properly authorised. This provides the third party with protection in cases where the agent is acting beyond the confines of his authority.

---

4 Such solutions are summarised in Note 5 to Article 3:201 PECL.

Despite what one would imagine the case to be, in practice the rules of apparent authority tend to operate in favour of the principal. This is due to the emphasis which estoppel places on the voluntary conduct of the principal in the form of a representation. It is often difficult to prove that a valid representation has been made. Any number of factors may have contributed to form the third party's impression of the agent's authority: for example, a representation by the agent himself,[5] or the surrounding circumstances as a whole, including the appointment of the agent to a specific role. Thus, it is probably unrealistic to seek to tie the third party's impression exclusively to the conduct of the principal. As a result, many commentators are in favour of a shift in the balance away from the protection of the principal's interests and towards further third-party protection,[6] perhaps by focusing on the "agent's conduct, as seen from the third party's perspective, rather than the principal's conduct in creating the appearance of authority".[7] Basing apparent authority on estoppel brings with it a high degree of emphasis on the principal's representation as the most important factual cause of the loss. It may be that apparent authority requires to be rationalised in a manner which does not utilise estoppel in order to rectify the potential bias in favour of the principal.

## (2) South African law

In this section and the section on Scots law which follows it, full summaries of the South African and Scots principles of apparent authority are not provided. Rather, the sections focus on some key conclusions, borne out by a comparison of the two legal systems.

In contrast to Scottish law, South African law has benefited from analysis

---

5 A representation by the agent himself as to the extent of his authority would be an insufficient basis for a case of apparent authority: see F M B Reynolds, *Bowstead & Reynolds on the Law of Agency*, 17th edn (2002) (henceforth *Bowstead & Reynolds*) at para 8-022, and *Armagas Ltd v Mundogas SA* [1986] 1 AC 717.

6 See, e.g., I Brown, "The agent's apparent authority: paradigm or paradox?" [1995] *JBL* 360. This is probably also the motivation behind the wider approach exhibited in the English case of *First Energy (UK) Ltd v Hungarian International Bank Ltd* [1993] 2 Lloyd's Rep 194, particularly by Lord Steyn. He emphasises the protection of the third party's reasonable expectations at several points during his judgment: see at 196, 204. He explores the same theme in judgments in other cases: see *Darlington Borough Council v Wiltshier Northern Ltd* [1995] 3 All ER 895 at 903–904; and in published articles: see "Fulfilling the reasonable expectations of honest men" (1997) 113 *LQR* 433 and "Written contracts: to what extent may evidence control language?" (1998) 51 *CLP* 23. Reynolds too prefers this theme as the underlying basis of apparent authority: see F M B Reynolds, "The ultimate apparent authority" (1994) 110 *LQR* 21 at 22: "This doctrine, which may depend on estoppel but is probably better based on the same reasoning which holds contracting parties to the objective appearances of intention which they create…"

7 Brown [1995] *JBL* 360 at 372.

in some recent cases where the courts, including the Supreme Court of Appeal, have had the opportunity to identify the separate elements of an apparent authority case. Quoting from an earlier judgment by Schutz JA,[8] Nienaber JA approved the following requirements for a case of apparent authority in *Glofinco v Absa Bank Ltd (t/a United Bank)*:[9]

1. a representation by words or conduct;
2. made by [the principal] and not merely by [the agent], that he had the authority to act as he did;
3. a representation in a form such that [the principal] should reasonably have expected that outsiders would act on the strength of it;
4. reliance by [the third party] on the representation;
5. the reasonableness of such reliance;
6. consequent prejudice to [the third party].[10]

This formulation of apparent authority appears to be firmly rooted in estoppel by representation. Indeed, one could even argue that, because of the emphasis placed on estoppel, the South African version is "more English than the English version". This is because it remains doubtful in English law whether apparent authority is, in fact, a form of estoppel. It is true that there are high profile English cases in which clear statements are made linking apparent authority with estoppel.[11] One example is the speech of Lord Diplock in *Freeman and Lockyer v Buckhurst Park Properties (Mangal) Ltd*,[12] which has become the touchstone for this type of case in England[13] and in Scotland.[14] However, on the basis of research carried out to date into English agency law, it is impossible to state with confidence that apparent authority is a form of estoppel by representation, or even to confirm whether estoppel by representation developed before apparent authority or vice versa. Whilst Reynolds takes the view that some apparent authority cases "even seem to

---

8  *NBS Bank Ltd v Cape Produce Co (Pty) Ltd* 2002 (1) SA 396 (SCA) at 412C=E.

9  2002 (6) SA 470 (SCA) at 479–480.

10  2002 (6) SA 470 (SCA) at 479.

11  See Slade J in *Rama Corporation v Proved Tin and General Investments Ltd* [1952] 2 QB 147 at 149–150. Slade J's judgment is widely cited; however, it could be argued that, as a first instance judgment, it has had a disproportionate impact on this area of law.

12  [1964] 2 QB 480 at 502.

13  *Bowstead & Reynolds*, at para 8–014, indicates that Lord Diplock's judgment is "constantly cited". See also B S Markesinis & R J C Munday, *An Outline of the Law of Agency*, 4th edn (1998) at 37.

14  See, e.g., *British Bata Shoe Co Ltd v Double M Shah Ltd* 1980 SC 311 at 317 per Lord Jauncey; *Dornier GmbH v Cannon* 1991 SC 310 at 317 per Lord Cowie; *Bank of Scotland v Brunswick Developments (1987) Ltd (No 2)* 1998 SLT 439 at 443–444 per Lord President Rodger; *John Davidson (Pipes) Ltd v First Engineering Ltd* 2001 SCLR 73 at 77 per Lord Macfadyen.

figure among the origins of the general doctrine of estoppel",[15] others have suggested that apparent authority cases predate the development of estoppel.[16] By contrast, in South African law, the basis in estoppel is much clearer than it is in English law. Despite the importance of estoppel in the South African concept, it would not be correct fully to equate South African law with English law. It must be remembered that South Africa has its own version of estoppel.

Closer reference to the South African version of apparent authority also reveals some differences from English law. The most striking element of the South African definition is the presence of an extra requirement which is part of neither English nor Scots law.[17] In South African law, a representation must be in such a form that the principal should reasonably have expected that outsiders would act on the strength of it.[18] At first glance, this may appear to be a relatively minor difference. However, it is notable that this extra requirement works in the principal's favour. The principal is judged by reference to the conduct of the reasonable person, and only if a reasonable person would expect the representation to be acted on will it be relevant. The South African concept therefore appears to be more protective of the principal than its English equivalent. To this extent South African law appears to go against the current international trend by adding an extra factor which favours the principal.

### (3) Scots law

Reference to the few modern Scots cases on apparent authority creates the impression that Scots law has simply "lifted" the concept from English law. In one recent case, Lord President Rodger, referring to what the parties to the case had agreed, stated:

---

15 *Bowstead & Reynolds*, at para 8–029, cites as examples *Pickering v Busk* (1812) 15 East 38; *Pickard v Sears* (1837) 6 Ad & El 469 and *Freeman v Cooke* (1848) 2 Ex 654. Montrose also tended towards this view: see "The basis of the power of an agent in cases of actual and apparent authority" (1938) 16 *Canadian Bar Review* 757 at 787.

16 See W W Cook, "Estoppel as applied to agency" (1903) 15 *Harvard LR* 324 at 325, which is favoured by G H L Fridman, *The Law of Agency*, 7th edn (1996) (henceforth Fridman, *Agency*) at 120.

17 Nor is this a requirement of the version of apparent authority which appears in Article 2.2.5 PICC.

18 *Monzali v Smith* 1929 AD 382; *Quinn and Co Ltd v Witwatersrand Military Institute* 1953 (1) SA 155 (T) at 159E–F; *Connock's (SA) Motor Co Ltd v Sentraal Westelike Ko-operatiewe Mpy Bpk* 1964 (2) SA 47 (T) at 51A; *NBS Bank Ltd v Cape Produce Co (Pty) Ltd* 2002 (1) SA 396 (SCA) at 412D.

[T]he law in England and Scotland on apparent or ostensible authority is the same and in particular ... in both systems it is built on the doctrine which is known as estoppel in English law and personal bar in Scots law.[19]

However, in contrast to the approach of the South African courts,[20] the Scottish courts have not sought to make use of the native Scottish concept of personal bar in order to create a distinctive Scottish concept of apparent authority. Instead, English case law, and particularly *Freeman and Lockyer v Buckhurst Park Properties (Mangal) Ltd*,[21] is simply applied *in toto*. This ignores the fact, recently confirmed in a leading Scottish case on personal bar,[22] that personal bar differs from estoppel in significant respects. As a result, any differences between the Scots and English principles of apparent authority which might arise because of differences between estoppel and personal bar are obscured. The reason for the reluctance to delve too far into Scots personal bar may be that, until recently, only one rather dated textbook analysing the area was available.[23]

## (4) PECL

### (a) An estoppel or not?

Article 3:201 PECL deals with apparent authority under the heading "Express, Implied and Apparent Authority". Apparent authority is covered in sub-paragraph (3) which states that:

A person is to be treated as having granted authority to an apparent agent if the person's statements or conduct induce the third party reasonably and in good faith to believe that the apparent agent has been granted authority for the act performed by it.

Whether this Article creates an estoppel is a difficult question to answer. The opening words, "A person is to be *treated as having granted authority* if", appear to focus entirely on the principal, and to suggest that an estoppel only

---

19  *Bank of Scotland v Brunswick Developments (1987) Ltd (No 2)* 1998 SLT 439 at 443–444 per Lord President Rodger. See also the other Scottish cases cited in note 14 above, where Lord Diplock's speech from *Freeman and Lockyer v Buckhurst Properties (Mangal) Ltd* [1964] 2 QB 480 at 502 is used as the main authority.

20  An example is *Glofinco v Absa Bank Ltd (t/a United Bank)* 2002 (6) SA 470 (SCA) at 479–480.

21  [1964] 2 QB 480 at 502.

22  *William Grant & Sons Ltd v Glen Catrine Bonded Warehouse Ltd* 2001 SC 901 at 944 per Lord Clarke (where he approves Lord Keith in *Armia Ltd v Daejan Developments Ltd* 1979 SC (HL) 56 at 72) and per Lord President Rodger at 915.

23  J Rankine, *A Treatise on the Law of Personal Bar in Scotland* (1921). This situation will shortly change with the publication of the Scottish Universities Law Institute text on Personal Bar by John Blackie and Elspeth Reid. The author is grateful to Professor Blackie and Ms Reid for advance sight of their chapter on agency.

is intended. If so, the result is that the principal is barred from denying the grant of authority to the agent in a question with a third party. The fact that Article 3:201 PECL contains further conditions redolent of estoppel seems to support this interpretation: for example, it requires a type of representation by the principal which induces reasonable reliance by the third party. There is, however, no reference to the type of loss which the third party must suffer, which is an issue which would normally be covered were this an estoppel.

There is an equally persuasive argument that Article 3:201 PECL is not based on estoppel. The language seems to indicate that, as an established fact, authority has actually been granted to the agent. One could infer from the context that, if the criteria are fulfilled, the agent will benefit from full authority. This inference might arise from the fact that the other types of authority covered in Article 3:201 PECL, i.e. express and implied authority, are both types of actual authority. Actual authority is, of course, sufficient to enable the agent to create contractual relations between the principal and the third party. Comment D seems to put it beyond doubt that this interpretation is the correct one:

> An agent who has apparent authority will have power to bind the principal as much as if the agent had express authority.

It is important to be able to ascertain whether or not Article 3:201 PECL is based on estoppel. If so, then the agent will have failed to conclude a contract between principal and third party. If, however, it is rather in the nature of a deemed grant of authority, then a valid contract will have been formed. If the third party is bound by a contract with the principal, then he can make use of the full range of contractual remedies for breach including specific implement/ performance. If this provision is intended to be an estoppel only, then there is a strong argument that, logically, no action for implement should be available. There is, of course, no contract to implement, given that the agent, not being authorised, could not have created a contract. If an action of implement were available, it could only be so on the basis of a legal fiction.

It is very difficult to say whether an action of implement would be available in this situation in Scots and South African law. Looking at the latter first, the leading text emphasises that where estoppel is used in a situation which would otherwise be contractual, there is no *consensus* and therefore no agreement.[24] That being the case, one would imagine that specific performance

---

24 J C Sonnekus, *The Law of Estoppel in South Africa* (2000) at 196

would not be available.[25] It is even more difficult to reach a conclusion on this point in Scots law. No cases have been found in which the third party actually raises an action of implement on this footing. One can say, therefore, that the point is subject to doubt in both legal systems. If PECL does provide a route which does not rely on estoppel, then it is an improvement on Scots and South African law. The third party has the protection of a valid contract, and the full panoply of contractual remedies that come with it.[26]

### (b) Words or conduct on part of principal

PECL recognises that impressions may be created through conduct as well as words. This is equally the case in Scots[27] and South African law.[28] Indeed, as has been judicially noted in both Scotland and England, in the vast majority of cases the representation will be made through conduct rather than words.[29] In both Scots and South African law the conduct may actually involve silence or an omission to act where a duty to speak or act was present.[30] In both also the conduct may simply involve appointing the agent to a particular position.[31] This very broad approach is welcome, and it is hoped that a similar approach will be taken under PECL. The impression which the third party gains of the agent's authority is highly likely to have been created by a number of different

---

25  A comparison can be made with the concept of *rei interventus* (the forerunner of s 1(3) and (4) of the Requirements of Writing (Scotland) Act 1995). This concept prevented a party from relying on the absence of necessary formalities for a contract where his actings resulted in him being personally barred from denying the existence of the contract. Thus, although, in theory, the personal bar operated simply to prevent the party from denying the existence of the contract, the actual practical effect was to set up a contract.

26  It is interesting to note that Article 2.2.5 PICC retains estoppel as a basis.

27  *Dornier GmbH v Cannon* 1991 SC 310.

28  A J Kerr, *The Law of Agency*, 3rd edn (1991) (henceforth Kerr, *Agency*) at 118–119; *Quinn and Co Ltd v Witwatersrand Military Institute* 1953 (1) SA 155 (T) at 160C–E, 161F–G.

29  See *Dornier GmbH v Cannon* 1991 SC 310 at 314 per Lord President Hope, where he approves a *dictum* of Lord Diplock which suggests that the most common form of representation is one by conduct, "namely by permitting the agent to act in the management or conduct of the principal's business" (*Freeman and Lockyer v Buckhurst Park Properties (Mangal) Ltd* [1964] 2 QB 480 at 503).

30  For South African law see *Universal Stores Ltd v OK Bazaars (1929) Ltd* 1973 (4) SA 747 (A) at 761C per Rumpff JA. For Scots law see E Reid, "Personal bar: case-law in search of principle" (2003) 7 *Edinburgh LR* 340 at 352, 361; *Cairncross v Lorimer* (1860) 3 Macq 827 at 829 per Lord Campbell LC; *William Grant & Sons Ltd v Glen Catrine Bonded Warehouse Ltd* 2001 SC 901 at 925 per Lord President Rodger.

31  For South African law see Kerr, *Agency* at 118; *Quinn and Co Ltd v Witwatersrand Military Institute* 1953 (1) SA 155 (T) at 159F–H; *Reed NO v Sager's Motors (Pty) Ltd* 1970 (1) SA 521 (RAD) at 349; *Seniors Service (Pty) Ltd v Nyoni* 1987 (2) SA 762 (ZSC). For Scots law see *Dornier GmbH v Cannon* 1991 SC 310 at 314 per Lord President Hope, where he approves the *dictum* of Lord Diplock in *Freeman and Lockyer v Buckhurst Park Properties (Mangal) Ltd* [1964] 2 QB 480 at 530.

factors, one of which may be the agent's appointment to that job. PECL does not define relevant conduct on the part of the principal. This would, perhaps, be to expect too much from PECL in view of its nature as a code rather than detailed legislation extrapolated from case law.

### (c) Reasonableness requirement/good faith on part of third party

As already stated, the criteria which appear in Article 3:201 PECL are very similar to those which would apply were it an estoppel. The principal's statements or conduct must induce the third party "reasonably and in good faith" to believe in the agent's authority. The requirement of reasonableness is already present in Scots[32] and South African law.[33] A development of this idea, also present in both legal systems, is that the unusual nature of the transaction may prevent the third party from arguing that his reliance was reasonable.[34] The requirement of good faith is present in neither Scots nor South African law. Whether its addition would add anything to the current reasonableness requirement is debatable. However, one can hardly object to its addition. Its appearance is also not at all surprising in PECL, suffused as the Principles are with duties of good faith.[35]

### (d) Reliance by third party

PECL retains the link between the third party's loss and the principal's con-duct: the third party must have *relied* on the principal's conduct. As already stated, many academics urge that the third party's reasonable expectations ought to be protected, howsoever caused. PECL has not taken this route, and this balanced solution is preferable. The imposition of a type of "strict liability" on the principal for the agent's conduct would not be justifiable. Analogies with vicarious liability in the law of delict or tort are not apposite. Such situations require extreme solutions as a result of the more serious invasion of the victim's physical integrity and for reasons of social policy, in protecting through the employer's compulsory insurance scheme those injured at work. To impose strict liability in an agency situation could have

---

32 See Gloag, *Contract*, at 152, citing *Paterson Bros v Gladstone* (1891) 18 R 403 and *Hayman v American Cotton Co* (1907) 45 SLR 207.

33 *Quinn and Co Ltd v Witwatersrand Military Institute* 1953 (1) SA 155 (T); *Monzali v Smith* 1929 AD 382 at 389.

34 *Glofinco v Absa Bank Ltd (t/a United Bank)* 2002 (6) SA 470 (SCA) at 496; *British Bata Shoe Co v Double M Shah Ltd* 1980 SC 311 at 318 per Lord Jauncey; *Dornier GMBH v Cannon* 1991 SC 310 at 315; *Kerry v Handel, Garth & Co* (1905) 21 Sh Ct Rep 106 at 109 per Sheriff Henderson.

35 See the contribution by H L MacQueen to this volume.

adverse economic consequences, even extending to reluctance on the part of principals to use agents.

## (e) Causation

As in estoppel, the causal nexus between the statements or conduct and the third party's belief is retained. Again this protects the principal by ensuring that his actions are the true cause of the loss.

## (f) Loss

The type of loss which the third party must suffer in order to raise a successful action is not specified in Article 3:201 PECL. This is an issue of some complexity in English, South African and Scots law. In English law, it appears to be an issue which differentiates apparent authority from estoppel by representation in general. Whereas estoppel by representation appears to require an actual loss, change of position in reliance on the representation only is sufficient for apparent authority.[36] This change of position will usually be entering into a contract in reliance on the representation.[37] However, the English texts focus on a change of position alone, without proceeding further to analyse the extent of loss which is caused by that change of position.[38] The requirement is therefore a relatively easy one for the third party to fulfil.

The South African requirement appears to be a more difficult one for the third party to fulfil. David Yuill usefully examines both the type of prejudice necessary and the time at which it must be suffered.[39] According to him, the third party must prove that he has altered his position to his prejudice.[40] Thus, in contrast to English law, real prejudice or loss is a requirement. Other writers disagree, asserting that, as in English law, a change of position alone is sufficient.[41] Case law does, however, appear to support Yuill's view that real prejudice is required, although that term is given a wide interpretation.[42]

36 Fridman, *Agency* at 49; *Bowstead & Reynolds* at para 8-026; S Wilken, *Law of Waiver, Variation and Estoppel* 2nd edn (2002) at para 16.12.
37 *Bowstead & Reynolds* at para 8–026.
38 Fridman, *Agency* at 49; *Bowstead & Reynolds* at para 8–026.
39 These arguments are made in an unpublished article by David Yuill, "Unauthorised agency in South African law", on file with the author. The author would like to express her thanks to Mr Yuill for sight of the article.
40 Yuill, "Unauthorised agency" (forthcoming) at 16.
41 D H Bester, "The scope of an agent's power of representation" (1972) 89 *SALJ* 49 at 56; Kerr, *Agency* at 139.
42 Yuill, "Unauthorised agency" (forthcoming) at 16; citing *Jonker v Boland Bank Pks Bpk* 2000 (1) SA 542 (O); *Hosken Employee Benefits (Pty) Ltd v Slabe* 1992 (4) SA 183 (W) at 191C–D.

With regard to timing, Yuill suggests that prejudice must be measured, not when the change of position occurs, but rather by looking forward to the prejudice which the third party would suffer if the principal successfully denied that the agent was authorised.[43] It is, of course, unnecessary for the issue of timing to be analysed in English law because of the focus on a change of position only rather than any real detriment.[44]

In Scotland there is no real analysis of this issue in an agency context. In the context of a recent case on personal bar, Lord President Rodger indicated that the loss is "that which would flow from the change of position if the assumption were deserted that led to it".[45] The approach is similar to the South African one: Lord Rodger seems to envisage a change of position which actually results in some degree of prejudice. His approach also shares the South African view as to the time at which loss must be measured: the relevant time is the moment when the principal seeks to withdraw from the so-called contract.

PECL, by omitting to specify the degree of loss or time at which it is measured, avoids these rather intricate questions. Whether or not this approach is welcome is debatable. It does seem to leave a court a wide discretion as to the questions of extent of loss and time at which it must be suffered. One wonders just how the court would cope with such open questions. It may be that, because PECL has not opted to take the estoppel route, any degree of loss on the part of the third party will be treated as relevant. If so, one can cautiously welcome the PECL solution as likely to act in a manner which is beneficial to the third party.

## (g) Notice requirement

Finally, PECL provides the third party with a further, more general, weapon in his armoury where doubt exists over the extent of the agent's authority. Article 3:208 PECL contains a mechanism which allows the third party to obtain clarification of the existence or otherwise of the agent's authority. It applies only where the third party's doubt as to the agent's authority has been caused by statements or conduct of the principal.[46] The third party is entitled to send either written confirmation to, or request ratification from, the

---

43 J E De Villiers & J C Mackintosh, *The Law of Agency in South Africa*, 3rd edn by J M Silke (1981) at 449.

44 Fridman, *Agency* at 49l; *Bowstead & Reynolds* at para 8–026.

45 *William Grant & Sons Ltd v Glen Catrine Bonded Warhouse Ltd* 2001 SC 901 at 921 per Lord President Rodger, citing with approval Dixon J's definition in *Grundt v Great Boulder Pty Gold Mines Ltd* (1937) 59 CLR 641 at 674.

46 Comment B adds that the third party's belief in the authorisation of the agent must be reasonable and *bona fide*.

principal. Exactly what is being "confirmed" is not specified, although one would assume that it is the third party's confirmation that he considers the agent to be authorised. A request for ratification, by contrast, would seem to indicate the opposite, namely that the third party is aware of the agent's lack of authority and is requesting the principal to rectify the situation.[47] The principal is then bound to respond to either request "without delay" and, if he fails in this, the agent is treated as being authorised.

This provision does not appear to be particularly well drafted. The confirmation route seems more appropriate looking at the matter from the third party's perspective. It appears to permit the third party to "crystallise" the agent's authority simply by sending the notice, even if the authority was not, in fact, present. The result will, of course, be the creation of an actual contract between principal and third party. The ratification route, in theory, should actually require further action by the principal: he is being requested to ratify. One wonders therefore why the third party would ever choose the ratification route, which requires action on the principal's part, rather than the confirmation route, which does not. However, this point should not be overstressed. The value of both routes lies in the short timescale within which the principal must respond, either by objecting to the confirmation or refusing the ratification request. On the whole this provision is a useful tool for the third party. It goes some way towards shifting the balance towards third party protection. There is an element of recognition that the principal is at fault for the doubt which has been created, and must be encouraged to eliminate that doubt as quickly as possible.

In summary, on apparent authority PECL provides Scots and South African lawyers with a very balanced and useful solution. This is especially so if, as appears to be the case, the PECL formulation is not based on estoppel.

## C. UNDISCLOSED PRINCIPAL: THE DIRECT ACTION

### (1) Nature of problem

Where the doctrine of the undisclosed principal operates, in contrast to the situation of apparent authority, the problem is not the agent's lack of authority. Rather, the agent is fully authorised. The controversy lies in the fact that a principal may instruct an agent to act on his behalf but without disclosing to the third party either the principal's identity or even the fact that

---

47 Comment C does not help to clarify this point. It simply states that the request for confirmation and ratification "amount to the same thing".

a principal/agent relationship exists. The third party is under the impression that he is contracting with the "agent" as a principal. The real principal may, however, emerge at a later date in order to sue the third party directly.

As is the case with apparent authority, this doctrine can operate harshly against the third party. It favours the principal unduly by allowing him to choose whether, and when, to enter the frame in order to sue the third party directly. It is true that the third party equally has the option of a direct action against the principal. However, in practice, the third party's option is much more limited. It is only available once the third party knows of the principal's existence. The principal will only emerge if it is in his interests to do so. Thus, the third party is usually unaware of the existence of a principal and is therefore unlikely to invoke an independent direct action. Practically, he is more likely to use it as a response to an action by an emerging principal, for example to avail himself against the principal of those defences and set-offs which he originally had against the so-called "agent". This may go some way towards explaining why there are far fewer reported cases which concern the third party's direct action as opposed to the principal's direct action.

Whether this situation involves any real unfairness to the third party is, however, a question of some complexity. On the one hand, the third party, when sued by the principal, is only called upon to do exactly what he contracted to do, i.e. perform, but to a different person. In the famous English case of *Keighley Maxsted & Co v Durant* Lord Lindley indicated that it was generally a matter of indifference to a third party whether an undisclosed principal was in existence or not.[48] He implies that in most commercial contracts the identity of the other contracting party will not be an important issue to the third party. However, this case was decided in 1901, and one must query whether commercial parties remain "indifferent" today as to the identity of their contracting parties.[49] Permitting an undisclosed principal to intervene certainly appears to upset the type of commercial risk assessment that parties make when they conclude contracts. When he enters into a contract the third party will assess his risks by reference to a particular contracting party. When it turns out that that person was secretly acting as an agent, then that risk assessment is rendered futile. If contracts are about risk assessment, then the undisclosed principal's ability to intervene represents a significant erosion of the third party's contractual rights.

It is perhaps important to clarify how this unusual doctrine arose. It is accepted that the current English version grew from the more limited basis

48 [1901] AC 240 at 261.
49 Cf T Cheng-Han, "Undisclosed principals and contract" (2004) 120 *LQR* 480 at 484, 504.

of providing the principal with a direct action against the third party in the event of the agent's bankruptcy. To give such a direct action to the principal where the agent is insolvent may or may not be justifiable. To extend the doctrine beyond the confines of insolvency takes matters much further. The modern doctrine gives to the principal an unlimited right to a direct action. One must query whether this extensive right is justified.

## (2) South African law

The most striking aspect of the South African doctrine is the evident judicial motivation to limit the doctrine. The case of *Cullinan v Noordkaaplandse Aartappelkernmoerkwekers Koöperasie Beperk.*[50] is perhaps the most visible example of this. In a judgment delivered by Potgieter JA, the Appellate Division accepted the practical effectiveness[51] of the doctrine, but refused to apply it to permit intervention by more than one undisclosed principal in the context of one contract. Potgieter JA explained:

> one should proceed from the premise that the doctrine ... rests on dubious grounds and that it in any case offends against the basic principles of our law of contract, viz that only the real parties to a contract incur duties and acquire rights thereunder.[52]

In consequence, he suggested that it would be

> undesirable to extend the ambit of the doctrine ... to such an extent that an agent can lawfully contract with a third party on behalf of more than one undisclosed principal who on the strength of such contract can obtain rights and incur obligations.[53]

The Appellate Division was also motivated by a desire to avoid the practical difficulties which would be caused for the right of election were several undisclosed principals to be given the right to intervene. The third party would be forced to elect to sue either the agent or a number of principals whom he would be required to sue separately for his *pro rata* share. Clearly this would place the third party in a situation of undesirable complexity.

Thus, in this case the Appellate Division, at the same time as accepting that the doctrine is an established and workable part of South African law, sought to constrain rather than expand it. Although the court supported its view by reference to the rule against cession of a portion of a right of action,

50  1972 (1) SA 761 (A).
51  1972 (1) SA 761 (A) at 768E.
52  1972 (1) SA 761 (A) at 770B.
53  1972 (1) SA 761 (A) at 770B.

it seems clear from the language used that the main motivation was concern for the position of the third party.

Another case which exhibits a similar motivation is *Karstein v Moribe*.[54] Here, the Transvaal Provincial Division refused to allow the undisclosed principal to intervene where to do so would turn a contract, valid at the point of formation, into an illegal contract. Ackermann J did not limit himself to the discussion of the area of illegal contracts. Quoting at length from Potgieter JA's opinion in *Cullinan*, Ackermann J identified the ratio for restriction of the doctrine in that case as the fear of prejudice to the third party. In an extensive review of academic writings, not only from South Africa but also from, *inter alia*, England and Scotland,[55] he concluded:

> There is much to be said, in my view, for the opinions of the learned writers I have referred to above that the limitation of the undisclosed principal's right to intervene is one based on broad considerations of equity.[56]

One may conclude, therefore, that the South African judiciary have applied the doctrine of the undisclosed principal with great care, mindful of its status as an exception to established principles of contract law, and careful to constrain it as much as possible. The doctrine emerges as possessing a clearer equitable basis than its equivalents in English or Scots law.

## (3) Scots law

In contrast to South African law, Scots law suffers from a lack of modern case law in which the judiciary have had an opportunity to consider and perhaps refine the doctrine. As a result, it is probably more interesting for the Scots lawyer to consider South African law than vice versa. There has been nothing in Scots law akin to the South African attempts to place the concept on a more equitable basis.

It seems likely that the concept is one which was received into Scots law from English law. Little convincing evidence is available which would accurately date the emergence of the concept in England. Only Powell amongst the English commentators ventures a view, stating that "[t]here is no clear case of an undisclosed principal before the eighteenth century."[57] The leading Scottish cases date from the late nineteenth and twentieth centuries and rely

---

54 1982 (2) SA 282 (T).
55 1982 (2) SA 282 (T) at 295 (where he refers, *inter alia*, to Walker, *Contract*, 1st edn (1979), 425–426).
56 1982 (2) SA 282 (T) at 299.
57 R Powell (1956) *SALR* 41 at 49.

either on English cases, or, instead, the works of Bell, who, in turn, relied on English cases.[58] It should at least be mentioned in this context that a wealth of analysis on agency and mandate exists in the works of the Scottish Institutional Writers. The author has explored elsewhere the possibility that Scots law did, in fact, develop its own native concept of the undisclosed principal.[59] It is true to say, however, that the benefits of the works of the Institutional Writers in this respect have been almost wholly lost by the application of English authorities in the leading Scottish cases.

## (4) PECL

### (a) General

Article 3:102 PECL classifies representation into direct and indirect, with the latter being dealt with in Section 3. One might question whether the retention of this classification is justifiable. The term "indirect representation" evokes what is the traditionally Civilian attitude, refusing to recognise direct actions between principal and third party. As the main thrust of the Articles which follow is to create direct actions, the use of the term "indirect representation" is misconceived.[60] Nevertheless, Article 3:301(1) PECL proceeds to classify indirect representation into two types. Paragraph (b) equates with the undisclosed principal, whereas paragraph (a) is the equivalent of what is known in most European countries as "commission agency". As the latter is not part of English law, and therefore did not become part of Scots or South African law, it will not be analysed here.[61]

### (b) Clarification of types of contract formed

PECL takes an important step forward in its clarification of the parties to the contract formed when an intermediary[62] acts on behalf of, but not in the

---

58  See, e.g., *Meier v Kuchenmeister* (1881) 8 R 642 at 644–645 per Lord Justice-Clerk Moncreiff; *Wester Moffat Colliery Co Ltd v A Jeffrey & Co* 1911 SC 346 at 351 per Lord Ardwall; *A F Craig & Co Ltd v Blackater* 1923 SC 472 at 482–483 per Lord Justice-Clerk Alness and at 485 per Lord Ormidale. See also Bell, *Commentaries* I, 537 (where only one Scottish case, *Hood v Cochrane* 16 Jan 1818 FC, is cited in addition to English cases).

59  L J Macgregor, "Agency and mandate", *SME Reissue* (2002), paras 5–17

60  This term has been dropped from the version which appears in Article 2.2.4 PICC.

61  Whether English law recognises the concept of the commission agent is analysed by D Busch in "Indirect representation and the Lando Principles: an analysis of some problem areas from the perspective of English law" (1999) 7 *ERPL* 319 at 341–346. He identifies some English cases which could be interpreted as forming a basis for the existence of the commission agent in English law, but his overall conclusion is that there is no strong evidence suggesting that this is the case.

62  Where indirect agency is at issue, PECL uses the term "intermediary" rather than "agent," see Comment A to Article 3:301 PECL.

name of, a principal. Article 3:301(1) PECL states that "the intermediary and the third party are bound to each other". The comment indicates that this conclusion follows because the intermediary did not act in the name of the principal. This point is far from clear in English law. Some assert that this is the case.[63] The debate rages on, however, and, very recently, others have appeared in print arguing that a contract is formed from the outset between the principal and third party notwithstanding the fact that the principal is completely unknown to the third party at that stage.[64] South African and Scots law appear to adopt a stance similar to PECL on this point. Nonetheless, in both the Scots and South African legal systems it is more common to see commentators assert that this is the correct approach rather than prove it by reference to case law.[65]

The approach asserting that a contract is formed between intermediary/ agent and third party must be preferred here. It would stretch ideas of *consensus in idem* too far to hold that a contract is formed between principal and third party where the third party is completely unaware of the existence of the principal. English analyses stress the fact that the agent is fully authorised to make such a contract, and justify its stance on that point alone. This emphasis completely fails to consider the issue from the third party's perspective. PECL makes a significant contribution by adopting what is the most logical conclusion and clearing up any doubt on the matter.

The direct actions of the principal and the third party emerge as exceptions to the general rule in PECL that the intermediary is bound to the third party.[66] Thus, where the principal is entitled to sue, he exercises against the third party the rights which the intermediary has acquired on his behalf,[67]

---

63 *Welsh Development Agency v Export Finance Co Ltd* [1992] BCLC 148. R Powell forcefully argues to this effect: see in particular his description of this point as "an obvious fact" in *The Law of Agency*, 2nd edn (1961) at 151 (see also 158, 267). This is also the argument posed by A L Goodhart & C J Hamson "Undisclosed principals in contract" (1932) 4 *Cambridge LJ* 320.

64 See Cheng-Han (2004) 120 *LQR* 480 at 496. See also *Keighley Maxsted & Co v Durant* [1901] AC 240 at 261 per Lord Lindley.

65 For South African law see J C de Wet (rev B P Wanda) "Agency and representation" in *LAWSA*, vol 1 (second reissue 2003) at para 228. This is also the view of the writer of the previous edition rev A G du Plessis, first reissue 1993) at paras 154, 155. For Scots law see *Meier v Kuchenmeister* (1881) 8 R 642 at 646 per Lord Young; J J Gow, *Mercantile and Industrial Law of Scotland* (1964) at 525; Macgregor, "Agency and mandate", *SME Reissue*, para 149.

66 It is interesting to note how similar the direct actions are to the formulation which appears in the Dutch Civil Code. This is acknowledged in note 2 to Article 3:302 PECL and illustrated well by D Busch, E Hondius, H van Kooten, H Schelhaas & W Schrama (eds), *The Principles of European Contract Law and Dutch Law: A Commentary* (2002) (henceforth Busch et al, *PECL and Dutch Law*).

67 Article 3:302(b) PECL.

and where the third party is entitled to sue, he exercises against the principal the rights which he had against the intermediary.[68]

## (c) When direct actions may be exercised

Under PECL, in contrast to the position in Scots and South African law, the principal/third party is not entitled to exercise a direct action as and when he wishes. Intervention is only possible in three situations: where the intermediary becomes insolvent, commits a fundamental non-performance towards the principal/third party, or commits what could be described as an anticipatory fundamental non-performance towards the principal/third party.[69]

PECL has not opted, therefore, to limit the exercise of the direct actions to situations of the intermediary's insolvency only. Fundamental non-performance, defined in Article 8:103 PECL, is clearly a key issue.[70] Non-performance of an obligation is fundamental to the contract in three types of case, namely where:

(a)  strict compliance with the obligation is of the essence of the contract; or

(b)  the non-performance substantially deprives the aggrieved party of what it was entitled to expect under the contract, unless the other party did not foresee and could not reasonably have foreseen that result; or

(c)  the non-performance is intentional and gives the aggrieved party reason to believe that it cannot rely on the other party's future performance.

"Fundamental non-performance" is a concept within PECL which is relevant not just to agency situations, but rather to contractual situations in general. Nonetheless, because it has an impact on the exercise of the direct actions, it is useful to analyse it briefly here.[71] The similarity of criteria (a) and (b) to English law is striking and Note 1 confirms that fundamental non-performance corresponds "closely to English law". The notes identify the English sources of the concepts appearing in (a), (b) and (c) in Article 8:103 PECL: (a) corresponds to *Bunge Corp v Tradax Export SA*,[72] where a similar test was used to identify a condition as opposed to a warranty; (b) to *Hong Kong Fir Shipping Co Ltd v Kawasaki Kisen Kaisha Ltd*,[73] where Lord

---

68  Article 3:303(b) PECL.
69  Articles 3:302 and 3:303 PECL.
70  See the contribution by T Naudé, "Termination for breach of contract" to this volume, at 282.
71  Naudé, in this volume, at 282.
72  [1981] 1 WLR 711.
73  [1962] 2 QB 26.

Diplock outlined a broadly similar test to define what was a breach of an intermediate term;[74] and (c) takes as its reference point section 31(2) of the Sale of Goods Act 1979.

There is, however, an important difference between Article 8:103(c) PECL and English law. Article 8:103(c) PECL is confined to cases of intentional breach. The motivation of the party in breach is, of course, not usually relevant in Scots or English law. This therefore introduces a Civilian flavour to the idea of fundamental non-performance. This provision has not simply been included as an indicator that the party in breach is likely to carry out a further breach in the future. Such a role for an intentional breach is unnecessary in the context of agency: the possibility of an anticipatory breach is already included in Articles 3:302 and 3:303 PECL. The role of this provision is therefore more general. Presumably the aim is to allow certain minor breaches to be actionable, if they are rendered more serious by an improper motive on the part of the contract breaker. This is consistent with the overall role of good faith in PECL as a whole.

Apart from the inclusion of intentional breach in Article 8:103(c) PECL, the concept of "fundamental non-performance" appearing within PECL is essentially an English one, and the question which therefore arises is whether Scots and South African law would find it a useful model. Scots law expressly rejected the English categorisation into condition and warranty (the intermediate term being a later addition)[75] at least as early as 1874.[76] Although there is some evidence of the South African courts using the terms "condition" and "warranty" to describe the importance of a contractual term, Christie counsels against this usage, not least because of the confusion caused by the fact that both terms have several different meanings.[77] Both Scots and South African law use the concept of a material or fundamental breach. In Scotland, what constitutes a material breach is a notoriously ambiguous question, the relevant cases rather unhelpfully indicating that whether a breach is material or not is a question of fact. It has been stated that "[t]he question is the nature of the breach rather than its consequences, although these may illustrate materiality."[78] Thus, the Scottish judiciary has quite a wide discretion on this issue.

---

74  [1962] 2 QB 26 at 72.
75  [1962] 2 QB 26.
76  *Turnbull v McLean & Co* (1874) 1 R 730.
77  Christie, *Contract* at 598.
78  McBryde, *Contract* at 511.

Although not adopting the same unitary approach to breach as Scots law, materiality is important in South African law, as Naude has illustrated here and elsewhere.[79] Her analysis of Scots and South African case law leads her to suggest that the factors which appear in Article 8:103 PECL are used by Scots and South African courts in order to decide whether the breach is material or not.[80] She therefore welcomes Article 8:103 PECL because it encourages Scots and South African lawyers to formulate more explicitly the factors that courts consider to establish materiality.[81] Thus, although Article 8:103 PECL, with its resemblance to English law, might at first glance appear to be some distance away from Scots and South African law, this is not necessarily the case. It is, however, inevitable that any attempt to identify all of the factors which might render a breach either material or fundamental is likely to fall short in some way. Article 8:103 PECL could therefore be criticised as lacking the flexibility possessed by Scots and South African law. One must also take into account the inevitable difficulty inherent in applying what appear to be new criteria, even if, at the end of the day, they would also be part of the assessment of a material breach in our native systems.

Looking at the terms of Article 8:103 PECL as a whole, the important question must be whether the PECL scheme is, as it would first appear, narrower than the Scots and South African direct actions. It is difficult to think of a situation in which the principal or third party would want to sue which would not be covered by PECL's current formulation. Both non-performance and anticipatory non-performance are included. The only rather unlikely situation which might not be covered under PECL would be where the principal/third party wanted to use a direct action simply because the "target" had a better financial reputation than the agent. The difference between PECL and Scots/South African law therefore boils down to the difference between material breach and the less flexible and possibly narrower concept of fundamental non-performance appearing within PECL. Much would depend upon how this concept was interpreted. The conclusion must, therefore, be that the PECL formulation is not substantially narrower than that appearing in Scots or South African law.

---

79 Naudé, in this volume, particularly at 283; and see also T Naudé & G Lubbe, "Cancellation for 'material'" or 'fundamental' breach: a comparative analysis of South African law, the UN Convention on Contracts for the International Sale of Goods (CISG) and the UNIDROIT Principles of International Commercial Contracts" (2001) 3 *Stellenbosch LR* 371.

80 Naudé, in this volume at 284.

81 Naudé, in this volume at 285.

## D. UNDISCLOSED PRINCIPAL: THE NOTICE REQUIREMENT

### (1) General

Article 3:304 PECL applies a notice requirement to the exercise of the direct actions. Before exercising a direct action, the party bringing the action must inform the "target" of the action that he intends to do so. Thus the principal intending to exercise a direct action against the third party must serve notice of his intention to do so on the third party, and vice versa in relation to the third party exercising his direct action on the principal. There is no requirement that the notice be in writing.

Whether serving a notice has a substantive effect rather than simply alerting the "target" to an impending action is a difficult question. Comment A to this Article indicates that serving notice crystallises the moment at which the "transfer or delegation becomes effective". In other words, where, for example, the principal is exercising a direct action, the notice marks the point at which the principal "steps into" the contract originally concluded between intermediary and third party. The language used by PECL in the comment, "transfer or delegation", is very imprecise and this is perhaps not surprising. Exactly what happens to the contractual structure when the principal intervenes is a question which has never been resolved in English law. Clearly, it is not a valid assignation or delegation of rights. The drafters of PECL have accepted the prevailing view that the transfer of rights cannot be explained using normal contractual principles. The ability to exercise a direct action under PECL must be accepted as an anomaly and, as in English law, justified purely on the basis of commercial convenience.[82]

### (2) Interplay with rules on election

PECL is silent on an issue which has received a good deal of attention in Scots and South African law. This is the operation of the rules on election. Both Scots and South African law emphasise that the party exercising a direct action must elect which of the other two parties to sue, and, having made that election, cannot additionally sue the other party if the initial case failed fully to compensate him.[83] Liability is described as "alternative" in both of those

---

82  Fridman, *Agency* at 254; *Bowstead & Reynolds* at para 8–071.

83  In Scots law see, e.g., Macgregor, "Agency and mandate", *SME Reissue*, paras 155–156; A F Phillips, "Agency: some elections and reflections" 1993 *JR* 133. For South African law see *Natal Trading and Milling Co Ltd v Inglis* 1925 TPD 724 and *Talacchi v The Master* 1997 (1) SA 702 (T) and comment by Wanda, *LAWSA*, vol 1 (2002 reissue) at para 232.

legal systems.[84] In one of the leading South African cases it was stated that "once the cause of action against either of the two is exhausted by reason of a judgment taken, there can be no room in principle for enforcing that same claim against the other".[85] It is not clear under PECL whether, once notice has been served on the "target" that an action is impending, a further action would be available against the intermediary to recover any sums which remain uncompensated. Those more familiar with the position under English, Scots and South African law would tend to the, probably emphatic, view that a further action could not be available. However, the provisions concerning the direct actions under PECL are, in general, very similar to those contained in the Dutch Civil Code.[86] In Dutch law, where the third party is exercising his direct action, the intermediary is not released by an unsuccessful, or partially successful, action against the principal.[87] The principal and the intermediary remain jointly liable. Dutch authors have urged that PECL should be interpreted in the same way.[88] This interpretation is, however, not convincing, given that PECL is entirely silent on the question. Dutch law contains no similar protection for the principal – only the third party has the ability to sue first the principal and then the intermediary.

### (3) Effect of performance to wrong party

The notice requirement also tackles the practical problems which can ensue where doubt exists as to whom the principal/third party should perform. There is always a possibility that, for example, the third party may perform to the agent at a time when the principal has become disclosed and seeks performance to be rendered to him. This possibility arises because it is often difficult to pinpoint exactly when the principal emerges. He will probably be disclosed, not through a single definite act, but rather through a combination of facts and circumstances. That being the case, the third party may, for a time, be in some doubt as to whether to perform to the agent or to the newly emergent principal. Say, for example, that after such an ambiguous disclosure the third party tenders performance to the agent and this is closely followed

---

84 For Scots law see Gloag, *Contract* at 140; *David Logan & Sons Ltd v Schuldt* (1903) 10 SLT 598; *British Bata Shoe Co v Double M Shah Ltd* 1980 SC 311. For South African law see *Talacchi v The Master* 1997 (1) SA 702 (T) at 709 per Vorster AJ.

85 *Talacchi v The Master* 1997 (1) SA 702 (T) at 709 per Vorster AJ.

86 See Note 2 to Article 3:302 PECL and comment by Busch et al, *PECL and Dutch Law* at 176–190.

87 Article 7:421 BW.

88 Busch et al, *PECL and Dutch Law* at 189.

by the agent's insolvency. One would have to consider whether it would be fair to force the third party to render further performance to the principal. PECL does not provide an answer to this question. However, the effect of the notice requirement in Article 3:304 PECL avoids this becoming an issue. The emerging principal is forced unequivocally to indicate that the direct action is about to be exercised. Thus notified, the third party would be foolish to perform to the intermediary, and one would assume that the third party could be asked to pay again if he had ignored such a notice from the principal. Similarly, by serving notice on the principal that he is about to exercise a direct action, the third party avoids the possibility of the principal performing to the intermediary.

Scots and South African law do not, of course, contain such a notice requirement. The clarification of the actual legal effect of prior performance which is provided by PECL is therefore useful. Dealing first of all with the situation where the principal has already paid the agent, and the third party nevertheless calls on the undisclosed principal to pay, the Scots approach is confused. This appears to be a direct result of the application of English law, which has veered between two approaches: a wider approach, stipulating that the principal may be called upon to pay twice provided that the state of account between principal and agent is not altered to the prejudice of the principal;[89] and a narrower one stipulating that the matter is resolved by estoppel, as a result of which the principal can be called upon to pay again unless the third party has induced the principal into paying.[90] The application of estoppel reasoning to this situation has been criticised by the author elsewhere.[91] Where the third party is unaware of the existence of the undisclosed principal, it is difficult to see how he could have induced the principal to settle with the agent. Nevertheless, Bell, relying only on English cases, indicated that Scots law rested on personal bar.[92] The leading Scottish case appears, however, to favour the wider rule stated above.[93]

There appears to be very little South African authority on this issue. Wanda refers to a case[94] which suggests that the principal cannot be forced to pay again, before rejecting this approach.[95]

---

89  *Thomson v Davenport* (1829) 9 B & C 78.
90  *Heald v Kenworthy* (1855) 24 LJ Ex 76, 10 Ex 739; *Irvine & Co v Watson* (1874) QBD 414.
91  See the explanation in Macgregor, "Agency and mandate", *SME Reissue* at para 163.
92  Bell, *Commentaries*, I, 537.
93  *Bennett v Inveresk Paper Co* (1891) 18 R 975.
94  *O'Leary v Harbord* (1888) 5 HCG 1.
95  Wanda, *LAWSA*, vol 1 (2002 reissue) at 232.

Turning now to the principal's direct action and the question of whether the third party's payment to the agent absolves him, or whether in Scots and South African law he may be called upon to pay again, there must be an even stronger argument that the third party is absolved from liability. This appears to be the stance of both Scots[96] and South African law.[97] English cases which apply estoppel as a solution to this situation, in a manner similar to that described above in the context of the principal being required to pay again, should be rejected.[98]

Whether a party who has already paid the agent can be called upon to pay again is clearly a difficult issue in Scots and South African law. By seeking, through the notice requirement, to avoid such a situation ever arising, PECL offers an attractive solution.

### (4) Summary of comments on notice requirement

Notice requirements like that to be found in Article 3:304 PECL are common throughout the Principles.[99] This one obviously serves a useful purpose. The disadvantages of notices should nevertheless be borne in mind. The ability to transact business with the minimum of expense and loss of time is a high priority for commercial parties. Where a notice requirement applies, such parties will tend to consult solicitors for advice concerning the drafting of a notice, being unwilling to take the responsibility of ensuring that the notice is appropriately worded (although no specific form is stipulated in Article 3:304 PECL). One could accuse PECL of introducing an unduly cumbersome mechanism into an area which is characterised by practical ease in English law. Despite these practical objections, the notice requirement is welcome. The moment at which the change in the identity of the contracting parties occurs must be identified in some way, as the Scots and South African rules on election illustrate. The disadvantages are perhaps the price to pay for the continued use of the doctrine of the undisclosed principal.

One further point can be made about the notice requirement in Article 3:304 PECL. As stated above, the third party will very rarely institute an independent action against a previously undisclosed but now disclosed

---

96 Gloag, *Contract* at 130–131.

97 Wanda, *LAWSA*, vol 1 (2002 reissue), para 230, indicates that there is no South African case which is directly in point on this issue, but makes reference to Innes CJ in *Symon v Brecker* 1904 TS 745 at 747 where he states that "payment to the agent would be a full discharge; the principal could not demand payment over again".

98 *Ramazotti v Bowring* (1859) 7 CBNS 851; *Drakeford v Piercy* (1866) 7 B & S 515.

99 See, e.g., the third party's ability through a notice to obtain confirmation of the agent's authority in Article 3:208 PECL.

principal. This is because the principal is unlikely to emerge unless it is in his interests to do so. As a result, it will almost always be the case that the principal is exercising a direct action against the third party, and the third party is exercising a right to counterclaim. Given the rare incidence of third party direct actions, the third party will use the notice requirement equally rarely. Presumably the third party would not be required to serve notice on the principal if he was counterclaiming. To require otherwise would seem superfluous – the third party is already being sued by the principal and is simply reacting to the principal's case. Nevertheless, there might be an argument that the third party is still under an obligation in terms of Article 3:304 PECL to serve notice on the principal that he intends to counterclaim. In order to avoid any doubt on the issue, it would have been preferable had this point been covered in Article 3:304 PECL.

## E. UNDISCLOSED PRINCIPAL: AVAILABILITY OF DEFENCES AND COMPENSATION/SET OFF

### (1) Exercise of principal's direct action

As stated above, the essence of the principal's direct action is found in Article 3:302(b) PECL: he is entitled to exercise against the third party the rights acquired on his behalf by the intermediary. The Article also deals with the defences which the third party can exercise against the principal if sued by the principal. Whether the reference to defences includes rights to claim compensation/set-off is not specified[100] but may be assumed.[101] As can be expected, the guiding principle is that the third party should be in no better or worse position than he would have been in had the principal not emerged. Article 3:302(b) PECL therefore provides that the principal will be subject to any defences which the third party may set up against the intermediary. Whilst this seems to be a sensible approach, it is interesting to note that English law provides the third party with more protection than PECL in this type of situation.[102] In addition to the ability to exercise against the principal all defences which he would have had against the agent, the third party is also

---

100  See the wording of Articles 3:302(b) and 3:303(b) PECL.
101  A similar assumption is made by the authors of Busch et al, *PECL and Dutch Law* at 179, 185; although subject to one reservation which is commented on at note 106 below. It should be recalled that these provisions in PECL are very similar to those contained in the Dutch Civil Code.
102  An excellent and very full comparison of the protections provided by PECL and those provided by English law can be found in Busch et al, *PECL and Dutch Law* at 332–334.

entitled to set up against the principal all defences he would have had against the *principal*, had the principal himself and not the agent made the contract.[103] This additional right of the third party can only be rationalised on the basis that English law treats the contract as formed between principal and third party from the outset although, as already discussed, there is little agreement on this point. PECL specifically rejects this analysis, and therefore it would not be appropriate to include this additional protection for the third party in Article 3:302(b) PECL. The approach of PECL in this respect is the same as that which currently exists under Scots[104] and South African law.[105] There is no evidence in either system of the additional right provided by English law. As such, the attitude of PECL is likely to be acceptable to both jurisdictions.

## (2) Exercise of third party's direct action

The provisions concerning the use of defences where the third party exercises his direct action are not exact reflections of those which apply where the principal exercises his direct action. In terms of Article 3:303(b) PECL the principal who is subject to a direct action from the third party can utilise two sets of defences: first the defences which the intermediary had against the third party; and secondly the defences which the principal had against the intermediary. The first set of defences is uncontroversial – again, the aim is to minimise the impact of the exercise of the direct action. The third party would have been subject to such defences had he sued the intermediary, and so should remain subject to them in the event of suing the principal.[106] However, the second set is more controversial. The emergence of the principal is a surprise to the third party. Not having asked to be put in this situation, it seems slightly unfair to subject him to issues existing between the principal and the intermediary of which he can have had no notice. Comment E to Article 3:303(b) PECL justifies this approach by pointing out that the "principal has a pre-existing underlying relationship with the intermediary". This is in contrast to the situation where the principal's direct action is being exercised: the third party has no pre-existing relationship with the intermediary,

---

103  *Bowstead & Reynolds* at 432–433.

104  *Bennett v Inveresk Paper Co* (1891) 18 R 975. In relation to rights to claim compensation see Gloag, *Contract* at 131–132.

105  Wanda, *LAWSA*, vol 1 at 230.

106  This is, however, the one reservation expressed by Busch et al, *PECL and Dutch Law* at 185, in relation to whether the word "defences" in Articles 3:302(b) and 3:303(b) PECL always includes rights to set off. In their opinion, although the principal can exercise against the third party the defences which the intermediary would have had against the third party, it is not clear whether this would include rights of set–off.

hence the lack of a similar provision in Article 3:302 PECL. Again, it is interesting to note that PECL, in taking this stance, is more severe on the third party than English law would be. In English law, where the principal is sued by the third party, he is not entitled to set off against the third party a claim that he has against the agent,[107] nor plead any defence that he had against the agent.[108]

No Scots cases have been found exploring the same question, perhaps because, as noted above, the third party, not knowing of the principal's existence, exercises his direct action rarely, and usually in the form of a counterclaim. South African law appears to be equally ambiguous. Kerr notes that: "In *Natal Trading & Milling Co Ltd v Inglis* it was stated that the third party's election to sue the principal is said to be 'subject to such equities ... as the occasion may give rise to'"; but no examples are given.[109] Apparently this point has not been explored in either Scots or South African law. The door is therefore open for both jurisdictions to follow either PECL, with its more severe approach towards the third party, or English law, with its more lenient approach.

## F. CONCLUSION

The PECL framework for indirect representation and apparent authority is likely, on the whole, to be acceptable to Scots and South African lawyers. It is clear that the Common Law has been highly influential in the modelling of the PECL provisions, and, as a result, they are similar to both Scots and South African law. The main improvements which PECL has made are procedural rather than substantive. Examples of such welcome improvements include the rejection of estoppel as a basis for apparent authority, the clarification of the parties to the contract, and use of the notice requirement in the exercise of the direct actions in indirect representation. The PECL scheme is, however, a relatively "traditional" one. PECL offers no significant gains in third party protection. It may be that to make such gains would involve too radical a scheme to be acceptable to those drafting PECL. Some relatively minor criticisms have been made in the course of this chapter: for example, the lack of any reference to election is regrettable. The PECL scheme, in general, emerges as practical, workable and sensible, and one which could be adopted by Scots or South African law with relative ease.

---

107  *Waring v Favenck* (1807) 1 Camp 85; *Kymer v Suwercropp* (1807) 1 Camp 109.
108  Busch et al, *PECL and Dutch Law*, 333.
109  Kerr, *Agency* at 271, citing *Natal Trading & Milling Co Ltd v Inglis* 1925 TPD 724 at 727.

# 6 Threats and Excessive Benefits or Unfair Advantage

## *Jacques du Plessis**

## A. INTRODUCTION

Chapter 4 of PECL deals with certain factors that affect the validity of a contract. These include[1] threats (Article 4:108 PECL) and excessive benefit

---

* This paper was presented at the Oxford University Comparative Law Discussion Group on 3 Dec 2004, as well as at the conference for this volume in Edinburgh. I would like to express my gratitude to the organisers of these events for their respective invitations and to the participants for their valuable comments.

1  The other factors are initial impossibility (Article 4:102 PECL), mistake (Articles 4:103–4:106 PECL), fraud (Article 4:107 PECL) and unfair terms not individually negotiated (Article 4:110 PECL). Chapter 4 does not deal with invalidity arising from illegality, immorality or lack of capacity (Article 4:101 PECL), for which see Chapter 15.

or unfair advantage (Article 4:109 PECL).[2] The close relationship between these factors has been appreciated for some time – as long ago as 1937 Professor John P Dawson argued forcefully that the problem of economic duress in particular cannot be divorced from the larger problem of the fair exchange.[3] In that essay Dawson stressed that an appreciation of the development of these concepts in Civil Law systems could help Common lawyers understand certain developments in their own system. But here the aims are somewhat different. The first aim is to test the proposition that many of the solutions found by the draftsmen of PECL have been anticipated in the mixed systems of South Africa and/or Scotland, while the second aim is to evaluate the laws of contract of these systems from a comparative perspective. This could reveal either the need to modify PECL in the light of the experiences of the mixed systems, or to draw lessons from PECL for their further development.[4]

## B. ARTICLE 4:108 PECL: THREATS

Two areas of the Scots law of force and fear and the South African law of duress merit comparison with Article 4:108 PECL. The first of these areas concerns the effect which the force and fear or duress have on the victim and the second with the conduct of the wrongdoer.[5]

### (1) The effect on the victim: the quality of the fear and reasonableness of the conduct

In line with a number of modern Civilian systems,[6] Article 4:108 PECL does

2 Cf J P Dawson, "Economic duress and the fair exchange in French and German law" (1937) 11 *Tulane LR* 345 at 346.

3 (1937) 11 *Tulane LR* 345 at 346; (1937) 12 *Tulane LR* 42.

4 On the historical development of the concepts of force and fear or *metus*, as well as undue influence in mixed legal systems, see G F Lubbe, "Voidable contracts", in Zimmermann & Visser, *Southern Cross*, 261; J E du Plessis, "Force and fear", in Reid & Zimmermann, *History*, 101–128. For a comparison of the relevant Scots and South African law see J E du Plessis and W W McBryde, "Defects of consent" in Zimmermann, Visser & Reid, *Mixed Legal Systems*, 117–142.

5 Depending on the emphasis placed on these two dimensions of duress, it is possible to group legal systems into two categories. It has been said that systems primarily focusing on the effect on the victim are "result oriented", while systems focusing on the conduct of the person responsible for the duress are "means oriented". See E A Kramer & T Probst, "Defects in the contracting process", *International Encyclopedia of Comparative Law*, vol VII/11 (2001) (henceforth Kramer & Probst, "Defects in the contracting process"), para 387 n 1640. In this context the distinction drawn in A Wertheimer, *Coercion* (1987), between the "choice" and "proposal" prongs of coercion, is also relevant. The "choice" prong focuses on the effect on the victim, while the "proposal" prong focuses on the means used.

6 See, e.g., § 123 BGB; Article 3:44 BW; on the limited number of modern codes that do refer to fear, see Kramer & Probst, "Defects in the contracting process", para 362.

not require that the victim acted under fear (*metus*).[7] It is only said that threats of a certain quality must have "led" the victim to contract. This indicates that a causal link should exist between the threat and the contract, without any fear necessarily being present. Unlike earlier Civilian authority, Article 4:108 PECL therefore does not explicitly link force/threats (*vis*) with the effect of fear (*metus*). The mixed systems, in turn, still remain faithful to the earlier Civilian approach by regarding fear as a requirement of a claim of "force and fear" or duress. It is quite clear, though, that it is not sufficient for victims to allege that they were afraid. The mixed systems require the fear to be of a certain quality.

### (a)  The overborne will approach

First, some Scottish judgments maintain that fear has to "overpower" the mind of the victim. These judgments then refer to certain English authorities which maintain that duress requires the victim's will to be "overborne" and that his consent should be "vitiated".[8] This "overborne" or "vitiated" will or consent theory has been severely criticised in the Common Law.[9] A major objection has been that duress does not vitiate consent in the sense that the victim's will is destroyed.[10] The victim acts willingly in the sense that he intentionally brings about a certain result. But the victim does not act willingly in the sense that he desires such a result. These objections to the overborne will theory have also been raised in the Scottish context.[11] In fact the influence of

---

7 It seems warranted not to require fear where the threat in any event so inconvenienced or irritated the victim that he was induced into concluding the contract (but cf Kramer & Probst, "Defects in the contracting process", paras 421, 443, who seem to maintain that the emotion of fear is essential to provide the causal link between the threat and conclusion of the contract). If the victim's will had indeed been vitiated in the sense of being rendered totally nugatory, he would also not be bound, but then other provisions come into play (see Articles 2:101 and 2:102 PECL on the intention requirement, as well as the Comment accompanying Article 4:108 PECL). The subjection of a person to actual physical violence, as opposed to threatened violence, but without vitiating his will (e.g., through imprisonment) is rather problematic – PECL, like some Civil Law systems, pass it over in silence (see Kramer & Probst, "Defects in the contracting process", para 393 n 1669).

8 See *Hislop v Dickson Motors (Forres) Ltd* 1978 SLT (Notes) 73 at 75; *Mahmood v Mahmood* 1993 SLT 589 at 592B; du Plessis, in Reid & Zimmermann, *History*, 106–107 especially n 41; du Plessis and McBryde, in Zimmermann, Visser & Reid, *Mixed Legal Systems*, 125.

9 See P S Atiyah, "Economic duress and the overborne will" (1982) 98 *LQR* 197; R Halson, "Opportunism, economic duress and contractual modifications" (1991) 107 *LQR* 649 at 665 ff. On the general decline of the theory, see Kramer & Probst, "Defects in the contracting process", para 363.

10 See the speech of Lord Simon of Glaisdale in *Lynch v DPP of Northern Ireland* [1975] AC 653 at 695.

11 In response to an article by A Thompson, "Economic duress" 1985 *SLT (News)* 84, Professor Ewan McKendrick commented that, "[g]iven these criticisms of the overborne will theory, it

English upon Scots law is rather ironical in this respect. The roots of the Scots law of force and fear are Civilian. And one of the basic tenets of the Roman law of (*vis et*) *metus* was the statement by Paulus in D 4.2.21.5 that "that which is willed under compulsion is nonetheless willed" (*voluntas coacta tamen voluntas est*), a principle which has gained general acceptance in the Civilian tradition.[12] Even English lawyers have come to prefer this principle to the overborne will approach. For example, Paulus's text was expressly referred to in *Lynch v Director of Public Prosecutions of Northern Ireland*.[13] The experience of Scots law in being influenced by English law in this particular context has therefore not been positive. The challenge, as modern Civilian systems and PECL, as well as a number of Common Law lawyers have come to accept, is rather to determine what circumstances lead a person to do something that he does not desire to do, and especially what threats of harm contribute to this result.

But one qualification has to be added to the criticism above of the overborne will theory. It is only warranted if the portrayal of the "overborne will" or "vitiated will" as one characterised by an absence of consent is indeed accurate. According to the most recent (11th) edition of Professor Treitel's *Law of Contract*,

> [t]he view that consent is 'vitiated' has been criticised but the criticism appears to be based on a misrepresentation of it: what it seems to mean is, not that consent is negatived, but that it has been improperly obtained.[14]

In the case of *The Universe Sentinel*,[15] for example, there would only be economic duress vitiating the consent to agree to make certain payments if the threat was *illegitimate*. Upon such an analysis, the position in English law, and presumably Scots law, would be closer to that of PECL and modern Civilian systems than has traditionally been understood.

---

should cause the Scottish lawyer grave concern that it still appears to form the basis of force and fear" ("Economic duress – a reply" 1985 *SLT* (*News*) 277).

12  See Kramer & Probst, "Defects in the contracting process", para 363.

13  [1975] AC 653 – Lord Simon tellingly adding that "I do not cite this merely for antiquarian interest" (694 ff).

14  At 405.

15  *Universe Tankships Inc of Monrovia v International Transport Workers' Federation, The Universe Sentinel* [1983] 1 AC 366.

## (b) Reasonable fear

A second, closely related dimension of the victim's position is the requirement in both South African and Scots law of the victim's fear to have been
"reasonable".[16] This requirement originated in Roman law, which valued
resoluteness highly, and embodied it in the *homo constantissimus*.[17] Roman
law in turn apparently influenced early English law. For example, Bracton's
treatment of duress, borrowed from the Glossators, refers to the standard of
the constant man.[18] However, over time this standard declined in popularity.
By the end of the nineteenth century, English law clearly had departed from
the notion that the fear had to be such as "would impel a person of ordinary
courage and resolution to yield to it",[19] while in the Civil Law context the
drafters of the German Civil Code rejected the notion that the victim's fear
should be reasonable.[20] A key consideration underlying this decision was that
it is precisely the weak person whom the legal order should protect.

Against the background of these developments we can proceed to examine
the requirement in Article 4:108 PECL that a claim should be refused if the
victim had a "reasonable alternative" to enter into the contract. The
implication is that persons should not simply submit to threats, but that they
should display a measure of constancy.[21] Ultimately, systems can of course
differ about the extent to which they expect some resistance from those faced
with threats of harm. German law, for example, does not enquire whether a
reasonable third party in the position of the victim would have done the
same, had alternative courses of conduct been available.[22] Whether such a
requirement should be imposed essentially involves a value judgment.

But it may be that the "absence of a reasonable alternative" requirement
can serve another, somewhat disguised, purpose. According to Comment E
to Article 4:108 PECL, the absence of a reasonable alternative "suggests that
the threat was *not the real reason* for the threatened party agreeing to the

---

16 See J E du Plessis, *Compulsion and Restitution* (2004) (henceforth Du Plessis, *Compulsion and Restitution*), 38–39, 101, 130.

17 Gai D 4.2.6.

18 Bracton, *De Legibus et Consuetudinibus Angliae* (S E Thorne ed, 1958) folios 16b and 103b (pp 64 and 296 in the Thorne edition); compare Azo, *Summa Codicis* (1552) 2.19 no 3, and further see J P Dawson, "Economic duress – an essay in perspective" (1947) 45(3) *Michigan LR* 253 at 255; T Schindler, *Rechtsgeschäftliche Entscheidungsfreiheit und Drohung – die englische duress-Lehre in rechtsvergleichender Perspektive* (2005) (henceforth Schindler, *Rechtsgeschäftliche Entscheidungsfreiheit und Drohung*), 68–69.

19 Cf *Scott, falsely called Sebright v Sebright* (1886) 12 PD at 21, 24.

20 B Mugdan (ed), *Die gesammten Materialien zum Bürgerlichen Gesetzbuch für das Deutsche Reich*, vol 1 (1899), 208; see Schindler, *Rechtsgeschäftliche Entscheidungsfreiheit und Drohung*, 25.

21 See Halson (1991) 107 *LQR* 649 at 669.

22 Schindler, *Rechtsgeschäftliche Entscheidungsfreiheit und Drohung*, 27.

demand" (own emphasis). This indicates that the purpose of the no "reasonable alternative" requirement may be to assist, in a rather roundabout manner, with determining that a causal link exists between a threat and the decision of the victim to conclude a contract.[23] There are further indications that the question whether the absence of a reasonable alternative requirement serves this function is also of central importance in modern English law. [24]

These developments are also relevant to mixed systems. They too have to establish more clearly why it is necessary to disqualify the victim whose fear is not reasonable or who does not avail himself of reasonable alternatives. And they especially need to determine whether requirements such as these do not merely indirectly indicate that an insufficient causal link exists between threat and conduct.[25] In the South African context it can for example be argued that the purpose of the reasonable fear requirement is to determine causality.[26] However, this does not mean that all duress issues should be reduced to merely identifying a wrongful threat and then causally linking it to the victim's conduct. In this regard lawyers in mixed systems as well as those interested in PECL would do well to follow debates in English law about the relevance of the absence of a reasonable alternative when dealing with *economic* duress. It may well be that in this context a greater justification exists for requiring that the victim should display resilience, compared to the traditional cases of threats of physical harm.[27] Such a differentiated approach deserves serious consideration by those who need to apply the reasonable fear requirement of mixed systems and the absence of reasonable alternative requirement of PECL.

## (2) Nature of the threats and affected interests

According to Article 4:108 PECL the threat has to be either wrongful in itself, or it must be wrongful to use the threat as a means to obtain the conclusion of the contract. Such an abstract, threat-based approach is typical of modern Civilian systems.[28] However, it is obviously vague and needs to be fleshed out.[29]

---

23 See Schindler, *Rechtsgeschäftliche Entscheidungsfreiheit und Drohung*, 217–218.
24 See D Nolan, "Economic duress and the availability of a reasonable alternative (Huyton *v* Peter Cremer)" (2000) 8 *RLR* 105 at 112–113.
25 See generally Du Plessis, *Compulsion and Restitution*, 130.
26 Du Plessis, *Compulsion and Restitution*, 130.
27 See the analysis of the economic duress case *Huyton SA v Peter Cremer GmbH and Co* [1999] 1 Lloyd's Rep 620 in Nolan (2000) 8 *RLR* 105 at 112–113; cf also S A Smith, "Contracting under pressure: a theory of duress" (1997) 56 *Cambridge LJ* 343.
28 Kramer & Probst, "Defects in the contracting process", para 387.
29 Kramer & Probst, "Defects in the contracting process", para 415, referring to an approach of "statutory silence".

The question now arises whether mixed systems, which are well acquainted with this abstract approach,[30] and which have also demonstrated that at times they are able to flesh out general principles by resorting to Common Law authority,[31] have anything of value to offer in this context. Here it is of particular interest that a limited number of cases on economic duress have generated a wealth of analysis in Common Law jurisdictions.[32] Unfortunately, it has not been appreciated in mixed systems that, without blindly following English law, guidance may be obtained from these analyses of threats of economic harm.[33] This is somewhat ironical given that English lawyers increasingly appreciate that an *unlawful* threat is a cornerstone of economic duress.[34] Had mixed systems been more creative in resorting to Common Law materials in this context, they could have provided valuable guidance in fleshing out the abstract requirement in Article 4:108 PECL that a threat has to be wrongful in itself or has to have a wrongful purpose.[35]

---

30  South African law requires a "threat or intimidation" which is "unlawful or *contra bonos mores*" (see *Broodryk v Smuts* NO 1942 TPD 47, *BOE Bank v Van Zyl* 2002 (5) SA 165(C) paras 36 ff, 49 ff; *Shoprite Checkers (Pty) Ltd v Jardim* 2004 (1) SA 502 (O), while Scots law recognises that the method of instilling fear has to be illegal or unwarrantable, or, conversely, that a lawful threat cannot be actionable; see Du Plessis and McBryde, in Zimmermann, Visser & Reid, *Mixed Legal Systems*, 127.

31  A notable example is the South African law of delict.

32  This is not to say that Civilian systems do not recognise that cases of economic duress fall within the scope of unlawful threats – but, as Kramer & Probst remark, the statutory basis for economic duress in Civilian systems does not make it any easier to decide whether it renders a contract voidable ("Defects in the contracting process", para 419); also see A Hadjiani, "Duress and undue influence in English and German contract law: a comparative study on vitiating factors in Common and Civil Law" 2002 *Oxford University Comparative Law Forum* 1 at http://ouclf. iuscomp.org, part IV (b) (cc) (accessed on 31 March 2005).

33  In both *Hendricks v Barnett* 1975 (1) SA 765 (N) and *Van den Berg and Kie Rekenkundige Beamptes v Boomprops* 1028 BK 1999 (1) SA 780 (T) the requirement that the threat has to be *contra bonos mores* could have been given greater meaning through creative use of comparable English material without having to accept that South African law has taken over English legal principles relating to duress, and economic duress in particular, or that such principles should necessarily determine legal developments in South Africa. South African courts are obliged to apply the English law of economic duress in admiralty law (see *Malilang v MV Houda Pearl* 1986 (2) SA 714 (A)). The Namibian Labour Court did not sufficiently appreciate in *Vlasiu v President of the Republic of Namibia* 1994 R 332 (LC) that *Malilang* was an admiralty case, and that English law consequently had to be applied.

34  Treitel, *Contract*, 405–406; J Cartwright, *Unequal Bargaining* (1991) (henceforth Cartwright, *Unequal Bargaining*), 163 ff; J Cartwright, "Defects of consent and security of contract: French and English law compared", in P Birks and A Pretto (eds), *Themes in Comparative Law in Honour of Bernard Rudden* (2002), 153 at 162. It should be noted, though, that the threat must still have a "coercive effect": "no particular type of threat is regarded as *ipso facto* having such effect or being incapable, as a matter of law, of producing it".

35  See Note 2 to Article 4:108 PECL (vol 1, 260).

## C. ARTICLE 4:109 PECL: EXCESSIVE BENEFIT OR UNFAIR ADVANTAGE

### (1) Introduction

In the previous section it was relatively easy to link a specific provision of PECL, namely Article 4:108 PECL on threats, with specific areas of Scots and South African law, namely force and fear and duress, respectively. Unfortunately, the position is not that simple when dealing with Article 4:109 PECL. The heading "excessive benefit or unfair advantage" is somewhat misleading. The Article does not only deal with the essentially "substantive" matters of excessive benefit or unfair advantage. It also contains other "procedural" requirements. As the definition indicates, the aggrieved party had to be in some position of weakness which the other party either knew about or should have known about, and then took advantage of. It is only after this subtle shift in emphasis that it becomes clearer that Article 4:109 PECL can be linked to certain grounds for avoiding contracts in mixed legal systems. These grounds are undue influence in both Scots law and South African law, and facility and circumvention in Scots law.

### (2) Anticipating Article 4:109 PECL – undue influence in mixed legal systems

In line with the aims of this volume, it will first be enquired whether Article 4:109 PECL has been anticipated in the mixed systems of South Africa and/ or Scotland. To answer this question, some insight into their respective historical backgrounds is necessary. The story has already been told else-where,[36] and only the following summary needs to be provided.

In the latter half of the nineteenth century, the need was felt in both Scotland and South Africa to provide relief in certain situations that could not easily be accommodated under the existing defects of consent.[37] These were situations where the parties stood in an unequal relationship, involving some influence of the one over the other, but where there was neither a threat of harm or *metus*, nor conduct that could be described as fraudulent or involving *dolus*. Scots law further recognised an off-shoot of fraud called "facility and circumvention", but this ground for relief was only available where a

---

36　See Du Plessis & McBryde, in Reid & Zimmermann, *History*, 117–142.

37　See Du Plessis & McBryde, in Reid & Zimmermann, *History*, 128 ff; Lubbe, in Zimmermann & Visser, *Southern Cross*, 287. In South Africa, the reception was rather tentative and undue influence was only clearly recognised in *Armstrong v Magid* 1937 AD 260 (see Lubbe, in Zimmermann & Visser, *Southern Cross*, 288; *Preller v Jordaan* 1956 (1) SA 483 (A) at 506).

person took advantage of the weak-mindedness or facility of another, and thereby induced a disadvantageous contract.[38] Facility and circumvention was not present in cases where advantage was taken of the natural affection or trust of someone who was not weak-minded or facile. To fill this gap,[39] Scots law, like South African law subsequently, drew on the English law of undue influence and recognised it as a new and independent ground for attacking the validity of a contract.[40] Curiously though, neither mixed system makes use of the presumptions which play such an important role in cases of undue influence in the Common Law.

Upon returning to PECL, it becomes apparent that in situations which do not qualify as threats under Article 4:108 PECL or as fraud under Article 4:107 PECL, recourse can be had to Article 4:109 PECL in cases of taking advantage of situations of dependence and trust, i.e. situations comparable to those covered by undue influence. However, Article 4:109 PECL also covers circumstances that cannot easily be brought home under undue influence in these systems – for example, if a party at the time of the conclusion of the contract was in economic distress or had urgent needs, was improvident, ignorant, inexperienced or lacking in bargaining skill. The first question can therefore only partially be answered positively: Article 4:109 PECL has been anticipated by the mixed systems, but only to the extent that it covers undue influence.[41]

### (3) Learning from Article 4:109 PECL: cases of weakness falling outside undue influence

A second aim of the volume is to adopt the comparative yardstick to establish whether the mixed systems and PECL can learn from each other's experiences. In the present context, a question of particular interest is how mixed systems should deal with cases of weakness which are covered by Article 4:109 PECL, but do not fall under undue influence. Again some comparative and historical background is useful, especially for determining what constructs in the Civil and Common Law traditions are at play in this context.

---

38  See McBryde, *Contract*, paras 16–01 ff.
39  On "gap-filling" as a way to develop mixed legal systems, see J E du Plessis, "Common Law influences on the law of contract and unjustified enrichment in some mixed legal systems" (2003) 78 *Tulane LR* 219 at 248.
40  As far as the actions of the wrongdoer are concerned, South African law requires unscrupulous conduct, which Scots law does not, although it can be expected that such conduct would usually be present.
41  See J du Plessis and R Zimmermann, "The relevance of reverence: undue influence Civilian style" (2003) 10 *Maastricht Journal of European and Comparative Law* 345 at 346, 378.

*(a) Article 4:109 PECL from a Civilian perspective: laesio enormis and usury*

Some Continental European legal systems recognise that the substantive disproportion between the values of performances may influence the validity of a contract – in other words, they still subscribe to the modern equivalents of the doctrine of *laesio enormis*. However, other systems, such as German law, provide only relief if the conclusion of an excessively one-sided or unfair contract was accompanied by certain procedural problems – most notably taking advantage of certain types of weakness or vulnerability. This is also the approach followed in Article 4:109 PECL. To understand this type of approach better, it is helpful to examine the German experience more closely. And to understand this experience the clock should be turned back to the late nineteenth century,[42] when drafting Commissions of the new German Civil Code were engaged in serious deliberations as to whether a provision on *laesio enormis* should be included in the code. They knew that there had been unfortunate experiences with its application, especially with determining when it may be renounced. The Commission then decided not to include such provision – as Dawson has put it, "Germany's protracted experience with *laesio enormis* produced a profound disbelief in this arithmetical standard of fairness".[43] But, as Dawson also pointed out:

> The doctrine of *laesio enormis* was indeed condemned. What proved harder to destroy was the central core of ideas which had there achieved inadequate expression. Before the final publication of the German Civil Code these ideas were unexpectedly to reappear in a new form but under a very old name. The idea that was to be appropriated for the purpose was the idea of usury.[44]

In 1880 German criminal law was reformed to combat some unpleasant experiences with the abolition of usury rules.[45] The reform initially only prohibited loans at an excessive return, but in 1893 it was extended to cover every type of transaction that served the same economic purpose. The penal provisions of the legislation had a curious feature. Mere substantive excess was not enough. The contract also had to be concluded as a result of certain

---

42  See generally Dawson (1937) 11 *Tulane LR* 345 at 370, 375–376; (1937) 12 *Tulane LR* 42 at 48 ff; J P Dawson, "Unconscionable coercion: the German version" (1976) 89 *Harvard LR* 1041 at 1052 ff; K Luig, "Vertragsfreiheit und Äquivalenzprinzip im gemeinen Recht und im BGB. Bemerkungen zur Vorgeschichte des § 138 II BGB", in C Bergfeld (ed), *Aspekte europäischer Rechtsgeschichte, Festgabe für Helmut Coing zum 70. Geburtstag* (Ius Commune Sonderhefte 17, Frankfurt/Main, 1982), 171; H-P Haferkamp, in Schmoeckel et al, *Historisch-kritischer Kommentar*, vol 1 Allgemeiner Teil (2003), § 138, nn 12–13.

43  See Dawson (1937) 11 *Tulane LR* 345 at 375 f (referring to Motive, in Mugdan, *Die gesammten Materialien zum Bürgerlichen Gesetzbuch für das Deutsche Reich*, vol 2 (1899), 321).

44  Dawson (1937) 11 *Tulane LR* 345 at 376.

45  See Luig, in Bergfeld, *Aspekte europäischer Rechtsgeschichte*, 182 ff.

types of weakness.[46] It is from this approach that the *Reichstag* took its lead. At the eleventh hour, after the drafting Commission had completed its work, the centre and left wings of the *Reichstag* pushed for the introduction of similar restrictions on usury (or *Wucher*) in the Civil Code. The new provision on *Wucher* was then latched on to the general prohibition in §138(1) BGB of transactions that offend good morals (i.e. are *gegen die gute Sitten*). The location of the new §138(2) BGB in the Code is significant: in essence, it only deals with a concrete instance of transactions that offend good morals. Today, after a reform in 1976, it reads as follows:

> In particular, voidness attaches to a legal transaction, whereby one person through exploitation of the distressed situation [*Zwangslage*], inexperience [*Unerfahrenheit*], lack of the ability to form a sound judgment [*Mangel an Urteilsvermögen*] or grave weakness of will [*erhebliche Willensschwäche*] of another, causes economic advantages to be promised or granted to himself or to a third party in exchange for a performance, and these advantages exceed the value of the performance to such an extent that, under the circumstances, there is a striking disproportion between them.[47]

It did not take the German courts long to realise that §138(2) BGB did not adequately take account of cases where a person was mentally weak without being insane. The courts therefore expanded the illegality requirement of §138(1) BGB to cover these cases that were analogous to those falling under §138(2) BGB.[48] In addition, §138(1) BGB could be made to cover situations where disadvantageous contracts were concluded by economically inferior or pressurised parties, or by parties who had been subjected to undue solicitations.[49] In this way German law could now also provide relief in situations comparable to those covered by the Common Law of undue influence.[50]

Nowadays a number of Continental codes contain provisions comparable to §138(2) and the extensions to §138(1) BGB.[51] For example, the drafters of

46 The inequality between performance and counterperformance had to be achieved through "exploitation of the necessity [*Notlage*], thoughtlessness [*Leichtsinn*] or inexperience [*Unerfahrenheit*] of the other party. See Dawson, (1937) 12 *Tulane LR* 42 at 48 ff; Zimmermann, *Obligations*, 175 f; Zimmermann, *The New German Law of Obligations: Historical and Comparative Perspective* (forthcoming henceforth Zimmermann, *The New German Law of Obligations*), ch 5, II.7.

47 See Zimmermann, *Obligations*, 176; Zweigert & Kötz, *Comparative Law*, 330; Dawson (1976) 89 *Harvard LR* 1041 at 1052. Before 1976, § 138 II BGB had defined the instances of weakness in the way set out in note 46.

48 See Dawson (1937) 12 *Tulane LR* 41 at 64 f; Dawson (1976) 89 *Harvard LR* 1041 at 1061; on "wucherähnliche Geschäfte", see Rolf Sack, in J von Staudinger, *Kommentar zum Bürgerlichen Gesetzbuch* (revised edition 2003), § 138 nn 228 ff.

49 See Dawson (1937) 12 *Tulane LR* 41 at 64–68; Zimmermann, *The New German Law of Obligations*, ch 5, VI.1.b) and c).

50 Dawson (1937) 12 *Tulane LR* at 64; Hadjiani, 2002 *Oxford University Comparative Law Forum*, VII, IX.

the New Dutch Civil Code have been directly inspired by the German § 138, as well as the English law of undue influence, when they decided to adopt abuse of circumstances, independently from threats and fraud, as a ground for attacking the validity of a contract.[52]

From this short overview it should be apparent that from the perspective of some Civilian systems, Article 4:109 PECL in terms of both its structure and approach can be regarded as a modern manifestation of the earlier prohibitions of usury, rather than *laesio enormis*.

### (b) Article 4:109 PECL from a Common Law perspective: undue influence and unconscionability

From the Comment and Notes to Article 4:109 PECL it is apparent that the drafters were not only mindful of Continental positions in the law of lesion and usury, but also of certain parallel developments in the Common Law.[53] These are undue influence, which we have already touched upon, and unconscionability.[54] To appreciate the relevance of unconscionability in the present context, a historical perspective is again of value.

It was shown above that in the middle of the nineteenth century, the relaxation of usury laws in Germany gave rise to abuses that had to be righted by legislative reform. Significantly, after a long agitation, usury laws were at that time also relaxed in Britain,[55] only to give rise to similar problems. Unconscionability, which was an established instrument for protecting weak persons who concluded usurious transactions, then came into greater prominence. Although it is rather difficult for an outsider to grasp its ambit, the impression is that unconscionability protects persons, sometimes described

---

51 See PECL, vol 1, 264–265; see Article 3:44(4) BW; Articles 1447, 1448 of the Italian Codice Civile; Articles 282–283 of the Portuguese Código Civil; Article 118 of the Luxembourg Code Civil.

52 Article 3:44(4) PECL ("A person who knows or should know that another is being induced to execute a juridical act as a result of special circumstances – such as state of necessity, dependency, wantonness, abnormal mental condition or inexperience – and who promotes the creation of that juridical act, although what he knows or ought to know should prevent him therefrom, commits an abuse of circumstances"). As to its background, see C J van Zeben and J W du Pon (eds), *Parlementaire Geschiedenis van het Nieuwe Burgerlijk Wetboek* (1981), 203, 210; A S Hartkamp, "Das neue niederländische Bürgerliche Gesetzbuch aus europäischer Sicht" (1993) 57 *RabelsZ* 664 at 673.

53 PECL, vol 1, 264 f.

54 Cf Treitel, *Contract*, 420 ff; Cartwright, *Unequal Bargaining*, 197 ff; J Beatson, *Anson's Law of Contract*, 28th edn (2002) (henceforth Beatson, *Anson's Law of Contract*), 296–298.

55 See *Alec Lobb (Garages) Ltd v Total Oil (Great Britain) Ltd* [1983] 1 WLR 87 (henceforth *Lobb v Total Oil*), 94; for the background to the repeal of these laws see P S Atiyah, *The Rise and Fall of Freedom of Contract* (1979) (henceforth Atiyah, *Rise and Fall of Freedom of Contract*), 550–551.

as the "poor and ignorant",[56] who have been exploited and entered into oppressive contracts.[57] This is done by a presumption of impropriety, which then has to be rebutted by the party seeking to enforce the contract.[58]

It should be noted that we again are not dealing with relief purely on the basis that a contract is unfair in its substance or content.[59] As in the case of undue influence, or the modern German law of usury for that matter, it is a combination of substantive and procedural requirements that have to be met before relief can be provided.

### (c) Article 4:109 PECL and the current position in mixed systems

From the above overview, it should be apparent that some Civil Law and Common Law constructs give relief in situations of weakness which do not fall under undue influence, duress or fraud. The fate of these and comparable constructs in the mixed systems will now be examined, starting with *laesio enormis*.

Although Roman-Dutch law inherited the doctrine of *laesio enormis* from post-classical Roman law, it was rejected in the Cape and Natal in the late nineteenth century, at roughly the same time as undue influence was on the rise. Subsequently *laesio enormis* was abolished by statute in the whole of South Africa.[60] This was done after the Appellate Division had severely criticised the doctrine, branding it as "redolent of the *cerebrina aequitas* of Constantinople and Berytus" and as "inherently arbitrary and preposterous".[61] Incidentally, to some it appeared rather odd that a system which could reject *laesio enormis* could at the same time embrace undue influence.[62] For example, Professor J C de Wet of the Stellenbosch Law Faculty caustically remarked that:

---

56  Apparently, these disabilities are nowadays interpreted more liberally (see *Cresswell v Potter* [1978] 1 WLR 255; *Watkin v Watson-Smith*, The Times, 3 July 1986; Cartwright, *Unequal Bargaining*, 202; K N Scott, "Evolving equity and the presumption of undue influence" (2002) 18 *Journal of Contract Law* 236 at 241 n 33; but cf also Beatson, *Anson's Law of Contract*, 298. Treitel refers to unfair advantage being taken "of a person who is poor, ignorant or weak-minded, *or is for some other reason in need of special protection*" (*Contract*, 421, own emphasis).

57  It has been said that the contract has to be so oppressive that it "shocks the conscience of the court" (*Lobb v Total Oil*; Scott (2002) 18 *Journal of Contract Law* 236 at 241).

58  See Treitel, *Contract*, 420.

59  On the general rejection in English law of providing relief purely on this basis, see S A Smith, "In defence of substantive fairness" (1996) 112 *LQR* 138; but cf D Capper, "Undue influence and unconscionability: a rationalisation" (1998) 114 *LQR* 479 at 501.

60  Section 25 of the General Law Amendment Act 32 of 1952.

61  *Tjollo Ateljees (Eins) Bpk v Small* 1949 (1) SA 856 (A) at 862–863.

62  *Preller v Jordaan* 1956 (1) SA 483 (A), the *locus classicus*, which placed the final stamp of approval on undue influence, was decided only four years after the abolition of *laesio enormis*.

in the light of the abolition of *laesio enormis* it is quite puzzling that the Appellate Division pampers the doctrine of undue influence. The courts took off the shepherd's cloak of Justinian, or is it now Diocletian, and put on the cloak of Father Christmas.[63]

But, as we have seen, this comparison is rather unfair, since undue influence, unlike *laesio enormis*, contains substantive as well as procedural requirements. Nowadays, it is clear in South African law that a contractual term cannot be avoided merely because it substantively gives a party an "excessive benefit". A contractual term may of course be illegal if its content or purpose is contrary to public policy, but this requirement is interpreted narrowly – in essence, the impropriety of the transaction and the element of public harm must be manifest.[64] A term generally is not illegal merely because one party obtains a benefit which is considered excessive. A contractual term would also be illegal if it is contrary to statute, and in this regard there are a number of statutory regulations, such as the limitations on usury by the prescription of maximum interest rates[65] and on certain terms in credit agreements.[66] Through applying the illegality test, the courts may protect weak parties, for example, employees entering into restraint of trade agreements, or borrowers who were required to provide security to the extent that they were virtually enslaved by their creditors.[67] But such protection is at best indirect, or a by-product of the regulation of the substance of the contract.

So far as concerns giving more concrete protection to weak parties by resorting to the notion of good faith, the South African Supreme Court of Appeal is adopting a careful approach, and is especially wary of a free-floating principle to which courts might resort whenever they feel that they do not want to enforce a contract.[68] It is not entirely surprising that the South African Law Commission has suggested some rather bold legislative reforms. This has taken the form of a potentially far-reaching Bill on the Control of Unreasonableness, Unconscionableness [sic] or Oppressiveness in Contracts or Terms.[69]

---

63 De Wet and Van Wyk, *Kontraktereg*, 53 and n 211 (translation JEduP).
64 See *Botha (now Griessel) v Finanscredit (Pty) Ltd* 1989 (3) SA 773 (A); *Sasfin v Beukes* 1989 (1) SA 1 (A).
65 Usury Act 73 of 1968; on earlier cases dealing with usury, see L F Van Huyssteen, *Onbehoorlike Beïnvloeding en Misbruik van Omstandighede in die Suid-Afrikaanse Verbintenisreg* (1980) (henceforth Van Huyssteen, *Onbehoorlike Beïnvloeding*), 119–121.
66 Credit Agreements Act 75 of 1980.
67 See *Sasfin (Pty) Ltd v Beukes* 1989 (1) SA 1 (A). On the possibility that unequal bargaining positions may have a bearing on determining the reasonableness of a restraint in English law, see Cartwright, *Unequal Bargaining*, 205.
68 Cf *Brisley v Drotsky* 2002 (4) SA 1 (SCA).
69 See South African Law Commission, Project 47 Report on Unreasonable Stipulations in Contracts and the Rectification of Contracts (April 1998), Annexure A (213 ff).

This Bill *inter alia* provides that a court can strike down any contract or contractual term if the way in which it has come about is "unreasonable, unconscionable or oppressive". The guidelines supposed to assist a court in reaching its decision include lack of relative bargaining power (2(a)), and lack of intelligibility (2(h)). However, at present the fate of the Bill is uncertain.

As far as Scots law is concerned, the position is not that different. *Laesio enormis* had already been rejected in the seventeenth century by Stair.[70] At present, the mere fact that a contractual term is harsh still does not affect its invalidity. It is only in a number of exceptional cases that, as Professor McBryde has put it, there is "spasmodic control"; it relates to minors' contracts, penalty clauses, leonine partnerships, moneylending and irritancies.[71] Nothing has come of a proposal by the Scottish Law Commission more than twenty-five years ago that a new ground for annulment of obligations styled "lesion" should be introduced, which was defined in terms of taking unfair advantage of a person's weak personal or economic position.[72] The idea was that this ground would exist alongside error and threats, but replace facility and circumvention, undue influence and extortion (in the sense of exploiting another's necessity).

Under Scots law, contractual terms can also be invalid if found to be contrary to public policy, or *contra bonos mores*. Statutory control is further exercised over unfair contract terms,[73] and certain credit agreements – more specifically, section 137 of the Consumer Credit Act 1974 enables a court which finds a credit bargain extortionate to reopen it so as to do justice between the parties.[74] Of interest in the present context is that in deter-

---

70 Stair, *Institutions*, 1.10.14 ("But the question is here, Whether in these contracts there be a moral necessity to keep an exact equality, that whosoever *ex post facto*, shall be found to have made an unequal bargain, the gainer ought to repair the loser. In this the Romans did not notice every inequality, but that which was enorm, above the half of the just value; which our custom alloweth not").

71 McBryde, *Contract*, para 17–22.

72 Defective Consent and Consequential Matters (Scot Law Com Memorandum No 42, 1978), vol 1, paras 1.56 ff, vol 2, paras 3.120 ff.

73 See the Unfair Contract Terms Act 1977 (c 50); Unfair Terms in Consumer Contracts Regulations (SI 1999/2083), which came into effect on 1 Oct 1999; although these regulations appear to focus on substantive unfairness, it has been argued that the regulations are not primarily concerned with substantive fairness but with the prevention of unfair surprises and the absence of real choice (Beatson, *Anson's Law of Contract*, 305). The English and Scottish Law Commissions have recently published a Report proposing a simpler law of unfair contract terms, by combining the 1977 Act and the 1999 Regulations and widening the control over non-negotiated terms in business-to-business contracts to protect small businesses: see Report on Unfair Terms in Contracts, Law Com No 292, Scot Law Com No 199 (2005).

74 Section 137. The provisions are under review. A Government Consumer Credit Bill, under which the current ss 137–140 would have been repealed, with a new set of ss 140A–D introduced to govern "unfair relationships" between debtors and creditors, fell in April 2005 when a General Election was called before the Bill had completed its parliamentary course. The Bill was, however, reintroduced following the election.

mining whether a credit bargain is extortionate, section 138 of the 1974 Act provides that regard shall be had to, *inter alia*, the prevailing interest rates, the debtor's age, experience, business capacity, state of health and extent to which he was under financial pressure, and his relationship to the creditor.[75] It should be apparent that, in the limited context of credit bargains, we are dealing with a set of circumstances that bear some resemblance to situations covered by Article 4:109 PECL. But crucially, section 138 only applies to credit bargains and not to contractual bargains in general.

Finally, Scottish courts, under English influence, have recognised that good faith can play a prominent role when considering whether parties should be made to bear the consequences of improperly obtained consent if they do not take at least some steps to protect their contracting partners. I will return to this matter when three-party issues are considered in the context of Article 4:111 PECL below.

### (d) Article 4:109 PECL and the future development of mixed legal systems

The overview above shows that mixed systems were progressive by adopting undue influence, but that they were also somewhat conservative by not providing relief in other cases of weakness, such as necessity, improvidence, ignorance or inexperience. Two questions now arise. The first is whether Scots and South African law should also provide relief in these cases and the second, on the assumption that the first question is answered positively, is whether there are suitable instruments with which to promote this end.

1. As far as the first question is concerned, it is simply not clear why taking advantage of a person's economic distress, urgent needs, improvidence, ignorance, inexperience or inability to bargain is qualitatively so different from the protected case of taking advantage of another's trust and confidence. These are all instances of taking advantage of weakness or vulnerability that may not have been created by the party seeking to enforce the contract, but are now consciously used to conclude a disadvantageous contract.

It is also not clear why the fact that the exploitation relates to one type of contract, rather than another, should necessarily influence whether relief is to be granted.[76] For example, why should protection be afforded to weak parties who conclude extortionate credit bargains due to inexperience and financial pressure under section 138 of the Consumer Credit Act, but not to

---

75 Section 138.

76 But cf J Cartwright, "Taking stock of O'Brien" (1999) 7 *RLR* 1 at 15, on the need for taking the special context of suretyship into account when determining whether third parties should bear the consequences of vitiated consent.

parties who suffer similar weaknesses and then conclude other transactions that are equally extortionate? It will be recalled that this type of anomaly was removed when the reformers of German law more than a century ago introduced §138 of the new Civil Code. This provision broadened the scope of "usury" (and incidentally by so doing reverted to its medieval meaning)[77] to include a variety of substantively disadvantageous transactions concluded as a result of certain types of weakness. This is also the approach of Article 4:109 PECL, which applies to contracts in general, without any specific regimes for sales, loans, providing services, suretyship contracts, and so forth.

2. Once it is accepted that an argument can be made for broadening the scope of protection, the second question arises of how this can best be achieved. One possibility is, of course, to introduce broad legislative provisions, such as Article 4:109 PECL. However, as indicated above, the legislative route has thus far not been very promising. This naturally shifts the focus to judicial development of institutions that might either be transplanted from other jurisdictions, or already form part of the existing non-statutory law. Here a number of vehicles for change can be considered.

It is not necessary to deal at length with the vehicle of unconscionability. There are at least two rather serious obstacles in the way of transplanting it into mixed jurisdictions. The first is that the climate in mixed systems is at present not conducive for such a wholesale reception. In the nineteenth and early twentieth centuries, judges were rather free to incorporate features of the Common Law into the existing law.[78] Nowadays, the judiciaries of the mixed systems, although certainly not hostile to the comparative method, are more conscious of developing domestic law.[79]

The second obstacle relates to the track record of the doctrine itself. It has not only been applied rarely,[80] but has given rise to a remarkable divergence in views on its relationship with undue influence – especially on the extent to which unconscionability and undue influence are "plaintiff"- or "defendant"-based, and whether the one should be subsumed under the other.[81] There is

77 See Atiyah, *Rise and Fall of Freedom of Contract*, 65.
78 Even then, use was not made of the opportunity: see *Taylor v Hoddard* (1886) 2 SAR 78; Van Huyssteen, *Onbehoorlike Beïnvloeding*, 120.
79 See Section D below on how in *Smith v Bank of Scotland* 1997 SC (HL) 111 the House of Lords resorted to the principle of good faith to impose duties on creditors to warn cautioners, with a view to achieving an outcome similar to that reached in the English case of *Barclays Bank plc v O'Brien* [1994] 1 AC 180 through recourse to constructive notice.
80 It is not clear why this is so (cf Capper (1998) 114 *LQR* 479; but cf Lubbe & Murray, *Contract*, 389 on the general inability of weak parties to conduct litigation).
81 The positions are summarised in Capper (1998) 114 *LQR* 479. Some have argued strongly in favour of distinguishing between undue influence and unconscionability, on the basis that the

every reason to believe that if mixed systems were ever to receive the Common Law doctrine of "unconscionability", similar demarcation problems would arise.

The second possible vehicle for change is the law of illegality. It has been shown that the German codification rejected *laesio enormis*, but subsumed "usury" and related cases where a substantively disadvantageous contract was concluded due to the exploitation of specific forms of weakness under § 138 BGB, which requires that a transaction should not be contrary to public morals.

Given that mixed systems have jettisoned *laesio enormis* and further have a very limited, statutory conception of usury, it can be asked whether they may use the legality requirement to provide relief in these other cases of weakness. Again, the answer is that the prospects for such a development seem limited. Apart from the obvious fact that German law achieved this outcome through some rather bold legislation, illegality in the mixed systems in any event generally relates to the substance or content of the contract, and not to the manner in which it was concluded.[82] It is of course true that by finding that the substance or purpose of a contract is contrary to public policy, protection can be afforded to an exploited weak party. But, as indicated above, such protection is essentially a by-product of controlling of the substance of the contract.

This brings us to the third possible vehicle for change, namely the law of undue influence. Certain features make this a more appealing alternative[83] than the previous two. Unlike unconscionability, it nowadays is firmly

---

former is "plaintiff"-sided, and requires impaired autonomy or consent, rather than improper exploitation by the defendant (cf P Birks & N-Y Chin, "On the nature of undue influence", in J Beatson & D Friedmann (eds), *Good Faith and Fault in Contract* (1995), 57; also see P Birks, "Undue influence as wrongful exploitation" (2004) 120 *LQR* 34, drawing on *Hammond v Osborn* [2002] EWCA Civ 885; but see Scott (2002) 18 *Journal of Contract Law* 236 at 239 on the negative implications of *Etridge* for this view). Others have argued that undue influence (see Capper (1998) 114 *LQR* 479), or even undue influence and economic duress (A Phang, "Undue influence methodology, sources and linkages" [1995] *Journal of Business Law* 552) can be subsumed under a general doctrine of unconscionability. Apparently, the broader scope given to unconscionability in Australia has given rise to a decrease in the significance of undue influence. For demarcation problems see further M Chen-Wishart's analysis of *Credit Lyonnais Bank Nederland NV v Burch* [1997] 1 All ER 144 ("The O'Brien principle and substantive unfairness" (1997) 56 *Cambridge LJ* 60).

82 See *Barnard v Barnard* 2000 (3) SA 741 (C) at 753–754; Van Huyssteen, *Onbehoorlike Beïnvloeding*, 133–134. But procedural problems are not irrelevant – see *Afrox Healthcare Bpk v Strydom* 2002 (6) SA 21 (A) at para [12] on the possibility that inequality of bargaining power can be *a factor* in determining whether an agreement is contrary to the public interest (also see Christie, *Contract*, 416).

83 On such a facilitative function of undue influence, see Van Huyssteen, *Onbehoorlike Beïnvloeding*, 126–141.

established in mixed legal systems, even though it is of Common Law origin. And unlike illegality, it also incorporates the key procedural elements of weakness and advantage-taking. What would be required is the analogous extension of the abuse of relationships of influence or dependence to taking advantage of analogous situations of weakness. In the Scottish context, in particular, such a development could accommodate facility and circumvention, which seems to lead a rather idiosyncratic life as an off-shoot of fraud. Perhaps "undue advantage taking", or the Dutch label of "abuse of circumstances" would better describe these cases. In this context it is also of interest that, as indicated above, some English lawyers have proposed a merger of undue influence and unconscionability,[84] or at least have begun to argue that there may be practical benefits associated with identifying a principle underlying them.[85] More specifically, it is appreciated that such a principle may guide the development of existing categories by indicating their underlying function and purpose, and therefore promote, rather than undermine, legal certainty.[86]

From the perspective of an outsider, it is of particular interest that the requirements of relational inequality, unconscionable conduct, and transactional imbalance have been identified as cornerstones of a possible future unified law of undue influence and unconscionability. This type of approach bears a more than superficial resemblance to that of Article 4:109 PECL, which contains the elements of weakness of the one party in relation to the other, and taking advantage in a grossly unfair manner, or taking an excessive benefit. There seems to be no reason why mixed systems cannot also be guided by such underlying principles when developing the existing law.[87]

Developing such a broader ground of undue influence would of course not be without its difficulties. More specifically, it will have to be made clear how the procedural and substantive components of such an extended notion of undue influence have to be balanced. Unfortunately, it is rather difficult to obtain clear guidance from Article 4:109 PECL in this respect. This provision

---

84  See note 81 above.

85  See e.g. Cartwright, *Unequal Bargaining*, 220; Beatson, *Anson's Law of Contract*, 298–299; but cf Treitel, *Contract*, 422 at n 21.

86  See Capper (1998) 114 *LQR* 503; S M Waddams "Unconscionability in contracts" (1976) 39 *Modern LR* 369.

87  On the absence of guiding principles, see also McBryde, *Contract*, para 17–22; Lubbe & Murray, *Contract*, 388. Applying such principles would, e.g., explain why in a case like *Lombard v Pongola Sugar Milling Co Ltd* 1963 (4) SA 860 (A) the contract had to be enforced: the mere existence of inequality of bargaining power between the farmer and the company is not sufficient; the company's conduct as well as the extent to which the farmer was disadvantaged also have to be weighed up before it can be determined that there is no liability.

differs from the approach of a number of Continental codes because it does not require an excessive benefit. A victim would also be assisted if advantage were to be taken of his situation in a way that was "grossly unfair".

But when and how should this test of taking a "grossly unfair" advantage be applied? This challenge is also faced by Dutch law, which provides relief in cases of "abuse of circumstances", without requiring excessive benefit.[88] This approach was already followed prior to the new code – the *locus classicus* is *Van Elmbt v Feierabend*.[89] There it was held that a contract of sale of an aged widow's house to her selfish adviser was void because it had been concluded while she was very dependent on him, in financial and mental distress, and the adviser knew that she wanted to keep the house at all costs. It was not found that the transaction objectively had to be financially disadvantageous.[90] I must confess, though, that it is not at all easy to discern from this case what exactly the circumstances were that warranted providing relief to the widow.

Although this is only a tentative suggestion, it does seem as if a lesson can be learnt here from English law. If I understand it correctly, the element of disadvantage is less important when dealing with undue influence than with unconscionability, where it is required that the transaction must "shock the conscience of the court".[91] One is drawn to the conclusion that English law appreciates that the type and degree of procedural impropriety affects the extent to which substantive disadvantage is required. This conclusion could be of value when applying Article 4:109 PECL, as well as any extended notion of undue influence in the mixed systems. It shows that even though it may be desirable to provide relief by extending the category of cases of weakness, there may still be a need to adopt a nuanced approach when determining the extent to which substantive detriment should be required.

A second and final difficulty relates to establishing the boundaries between such an extended notion of undue influence on the one hand, and force and fear or duress on the other. It will be recalled that at the outset mention was made of this link. Examples of at least a partial conflation of duress and undue influence are the notion of "coercion" developed by the American moral

88 See the comparison and evaluation of Article 4:109 PECL by M M van Rossum, in Busch et al, *PECL and Dutch Law*, 213; Comment E read with Note 5 to PECL, vol 1, 265.

89 HR 29 May 1964, NJ 1965, 104; further see HR 27 March 1992, NJ 1992, 377.

90 According to the Hoge Raad, abuse of circumstances can arise if making use by one party of circumstances in which the other party finds himself has led the other party to conclude an agreement which, if he had not been in such circumstances, he would not have concluded in view of detriment associated with it for him. Objective detriment is not required.

91 See *Etridge (No 2)* [2001] 3 WLR 1021 at 1032; Scott (2002) 18 *Journal of Contract Law* 236 at 242.

92 Alan Wertheimer, *Coercion* (1987).

philosopher Wertheimer,[92] as well as, to a certain extent, the doctrine of inequality of bargaining power created by Lord Denning.[93] However, as Professor Honoré has pointed out in a review of Wertheimer's book, a problem with this very broad notion of coercion is that there may be sound reasons to differentiate between these categories. The question whether the victim has a reasonable alternative traditionally is only asked in the context of duress, and is not really relevant in the defective capacity cases.[94] And finally, it may well be that a lesser degree of harm should be required in the duress cases, compared to undue influence. Both these distinctions are borne out by PECL.

## D. ARTICLE 4:111 PECL: THIRD PERSONS

Determining the extent to which third persons may be made to bear the consequences of the type of defects of consent under review is a highly complex matter. The focus here will only be on Article 4:111(2)(e) PECL.[95] This provision relates to a fact pattern which has given rise to some of the most heated debates in modern contract doctrine – that of one party providing security for the debts of another closely related party (usually a spouse) in favour of a third party (usually a financial institution). This fact pattern, which due to the inventiveness of some Australian feminists has come to be described as "sexually transmitted debt",[96] has received particular attention in Scots law. I will therefore only focus on the development in that jurisdiction.[97]

---

93 *Lloyds Bank Ltd v Bundy* [1975] QB 326.

94 See A M Honoré, "A theory of coercion" (1999) 10 *Oxford JLS* 94 at 99; also cf Halson (1991) 107 *LQR* 649 at 658–659, who states that the early development of undue influence in equity "was not haunted by the spectre of the constant man".

95 For more general comment to Article 4:111 PECL, see J Hijma, in Busch et al, *PECL and Dutch Law*, 218–220. The effect of duress emanating from a third person who is not a party to the contract or an agent is disputed in the two systems, but the favoured view seems to be that the validity of the contract can be challenged (see *Trustee Savings Bank v Balloch* 1983 SLT 240; *Broodryk v Smuts NO* 1942 TPD 47 at 52; but cf Lubbe & Murray, *Contract*, 365, who argue for uniformity with the position under misrepresentation, where the contract would be valid). But it has not been made clear to what extent the party seeking to enforce the contract either has to know, or reasonably is supposed to know, about the duress.

96 See G Gretton, "Sexually transmitted debt" 1999 *TSAR* 419.

97 In South African law it is settled that where the victim (A) confers a benefit under a contract with a person exerting undue influence (B), and B in turn confers the benefit on a *bona fide* third party (C), C obtains valid title. However, Article 4:111(2)(e) PECL covers the situation where the party who acts improperly (B) leads the victim (A) to contract with a party (C), who knew or ought to have known of the relevant facts. Traditionally, it is said that in South African law, A would only have a claim against C if C *knew* about the undue influence of B (see Christie, *Contract*, 361). However, the minority judgment of Oliver JA in *Eerste Nasionale Bank NO v Saayman van Suidelike Afrika Bpk* 1997 (4) SA 302 (SCA) lends itself to the interpretation that good faith demands that A could have a claim against C even though C did not have such knowledge.

Traditionally, Scots law visited the consequences of undue influence on a third party where there was proof that the third party had known of facts and circumstances indicating that undue influence had in fact been exercised.[98] However, in *Smith v Bank of Scotland*[99] the House of Lords held that good faith requires, in the surety example above, the third party bank to take steps in the interest of the surety[100] – more specifically, the bank has "to warn the potential cautioner [surety] of the consequences of entering into the proposed cautionary obligation and to advise him or her to take independent advice".[101] Actual knowledge of undue influence is not a requirement for such a duty to arise; to use the language of PECL, this duty would arise in cases where one can say that the bank "ought to have known" of the relevant facts. There is no doubt that this position was adopted to bring Scots law in line with the English decision of *Barclays Bank plc v O'Brien*,[102] where, by recourse to the concept of notice, it was held that third parties such as banks can be adversely affected if they have "constructive notice" of certain vitiating circumstances. Since the concept of notice is based on equitable principles, a different justification for this development had to be found in Scots law. The House of Lords then followed the path closest to equity that is available in Scots law, namely that of the need to display good faith in the creation of contracts.[103]

It is clear, though, that Scottish courts are not going to follow the English lead blindly – an approach in line with some prophetic suggestions made by Professor Ewan McKendrick.[104] Of particular concern in Scotland has been the idea that banks should not merely warn and advise the potential surety to take advice, but should "bring home" to that person the risks of the transaction. The detailed steps that creditors are supposed to take according to the English case of *Royal Bank of Scotland plc v Etridge (No 2)*[105] have been described as "difficult to reconcile with the normal approach of Scots law to questions of good faith".[106] It further seems as if the extension is also restricted to contracts of caution, which traditionally impose specific duties on the

---

98  See the judgment of Lord Hope in *Mumford v Bank of Scotland; Smith v Bank of Scotland* 1996 SLT 392.
99  1997 SC (HL) 111.
100  1997 SC (HL) 111 at 118.
101  1997 SC (HL) 111 at 122.
102  [1994] 1 AC 180.
103  1997 SC (HL) 111 at 121.
104  E McKendrick, "The undue influence of English law?", in *Essays Wilson*, 214 ff.
105  [2002] 2 AC 773.
106  *Clydesdale Bank plc v Black* 2002 SC 555 at para 31.

creditor – an approach which apparently has also found favour in Common Law circles.[107] It would therefore seem as if Scottish courts are intent on developing their own, more conservative approach to the problem.[108]

Curiously, even though both mixed systems adopted the Common Law of undue influence, they, like Article 4:109 PECL, do not make any use of presumptions in three-party, or even two party situations.[109] It is not clear why this is so. In a recent paper, Reinhard Zimmermann and I have argued that use of presumptions in this context is not at all unusual in the Civilian tradition.[110] It was already appreciated in the Middle Ages that the severe problems of proof faced by persons who were in reverence or awe of another and then subjected to improper influence or advantage-taking could be alleviated by presumptions of fear or *metus reverentialis*. The mixed systems therefore can hardly object to making use of presumptions on the basis that it is incompatible with the Civilian heritage.

Furthermore, and this is also of interest when evaluating PECL, it is not only the modern Common Law which makes use of presumptions, but also modern Civilian systems such as German and Dutch law. Under German law, if a suretyship agreement concluded by close relatives of the debtor has unbearable financial consequences for the debtor, it is presumed that the creditor has exploited the typical relationship between such parties in a manner that can be regarded as *contra bonos mores*. The creditor would then have to indicate that the suretyship is based on an autonomous decision of the surety which has not been influenced by the emotional bond with the debtor – for example, if the surety had a personal interest in the granting of the loan.[111] Ignorance of the surety being overstrained would also be a ground for rebuttal, although the creditor would not be able to rely on this ground if he fails to take certain steps to enquire about the value of the security, thereby deliberately preventing knowledge of the surety's inability to perform from being obtained.[112]

---

107  See J Cartwright (1999) 7 *RLR* 1 at 14 f, on limiting the *O'Brien* doctrine to the surety contract; as to the background see G J Junor, "The dust settling: Smith *v* Bank of Scotland" 1999 *JR* 67.

108  See Du Plessis and McBryde, in Zimmermann, Visser & Reid, *Mixed Legal Systems*, 131.

109  See *Mumford v Bank of Scotland; Smith v Bank of Scotland* 1996 SLT 392; *Miller v Miller* 1965 (4) SA 458 (C).

110  Du Plessis & Zimmermann (2004) 10 *Maastricht Journal of European and Comparative Law* 345.

111  M Habersack, *Münchener Kommentar zum Bürgerlichen Gesetzbuch*, 4th edn, vol 5 (henceforth Habersack, *Münchener Kommentar*), vol 5, 4th edn (2004), § 765 rdnr 23–28; M Habersack & R Zimmermann, "Legal change in a codified system: recent developments in German suretyship law" (1999) 3 *Edinburgh LR* 272 at 282; for arguments in favour of the use of presumptions in Dutch law, see A S Hartkamp, *Verbintenissenrecht – deel II Algemene Leer der Overeenkomsten* 11th edn (2001), para 216a.

112  Habersack, *Münchener Kommentar*, § 765, n 25.

From the perspective of South African law, it is especially significant that the greater protection of the surety in German law was a direct consequence of a finding by the Federal Constitutional Court that when applying general provisions of the Civil Code such as § 138 BGB, due attention must be paid to the protection afforded by the Basic Law to the private autonomy of individuals.[113] In 1996 South Africa adopted a new Constitution[114] which contains a horizontally operative Bill of Rights. This Bill not only protects specific rights but also, less directly, certain values, such as individual autonomy.[115] It may well be that effective protection of this value would ultimately require adopting much more progressive measures than those recognised at present,[116] but without "unduly disturbing the existing doctrinal machinery or creating wholesale legal uncertainty".[117] And in determining what amounts to effective protection, it would seem as if valuable guidance can be obtained from the experiences of other jurisdictions with the application of presumptions, as well as the imposition of duties to warn and advise, on third parties who seek to enforce potentially onerous transactions. These are still early days, but perhaps there is also a lesson here for those who are interested in refining PECL, and especially in determining whether the failure of the bank to take steps gives rise to an inference that it "ought to have known of the relevant facts", and thus should be liable under Article 4:111 PECL.

## E. CONCLUSIONS

As indicated at the outset, one aim of this volume is to determine whether the solutions found by the draftsmen of PECL have been anticipated in the two mixed systems. As we have seen, one such instance is the reception of the Common Law of undue influence to fill a gap between the Civil Law of force and fear/duress and fraud. In this way mixed systems have reached an outcome which is now at least partially also achieved by Article 4:109 PECL. But mixed systems have also at times missed opportunities, which could have resulted in them anticipating developments in PECL. They do not generally provide relief in cases of what is called unconscionability under the Common Law, whereas cases of necessity and ignorance are also brought home under

113   See M Habersack & R Zimmermann (1999) 3 *Edinburgh LR* 272 at 276 f.
114   Act 108 of 1996.
115   See judgment of Cameron JA in *Brisley v Drotsky* 2002 (4) SA 1 (SCA), para 94.
116   See G F Lubbe, "Taking fundamental rights seriously: The Bill of Rights and its implications for the development of contract law" (2004) 121 *SALJ* 395 at 407 f.
117   (2004) 121 *SALJ* at 408.

Article 4:109 PECL. And although there does not seem to be a problem in either of the mixed systems with recognising that threats of economic harm can be unlawful,[118] these systems have hardly made use of the opportunity to give greater scope to the notion of unlawfulness by drawing on the Common Law of economic duress. Such a development could have been an interesting precursor to the assimilation in Article 4:108 PECL of the Civil Law and Common Law of threats of physical as well as economic harm under the broad requirement that the threat has to be wrongful.

A second aim of this volume is to evaluate the respective positions adopted in the mixed systems compared to PECL. In this regard it was pointed out that the overborne will theory has had an unfortunate effect on the Scots law of force and fear, whereas Article 4:109 PECL avoids such problems by (merely) requiring that a wrongful threat must have led or influenced a party to conclude the contract.[119] But lessons can also be learned from the mixed systems which may assist in refining PECL. When dealing with three-party problems under Article 4:111 PECL, the experiences of Scottish courts in determining whether third parties should bear the consequences of undue influence and related situations are particularly instructive. However, as we have seen, it may well be that both the mixed systems and PECL could benefit from reconsidering their refusal to assist weak parties by making use of presumptions of impropriety.

---

118  See McBryde, *Contract*, para 17–04; Christie, *Contract*, 353–354; Du Plessis, *Compulsion and Restitution*, 68 ff, 102, 131 ff. The statement in the Notes to Article 4:108 that "economic duress has not yet been recognised in ... Scots law" (see PECL, vol 1, 260) is therefore incorrect, inasmuch as it suggests that Scots law does not recognise that threats of economic harm can give rise to force and fear.

119  Also see PECL, vol 1, 259–260 (Comment D, Note 1 to Article 4:108 PECL).

# 7 Interpretation

## Eric Clive

# A. INTRODUCTION

Given the statement in the Introduction to PECL to the effect that one of the benefits offered by them "is to provide a bridge between the civil law and the common law"[1] it is of some interest, particularly for those from so-called "mixed systems" like Scotland and South Africa, to try to detect major influences on parts of PECL. Are the PECL rules predominantly Civil Law, predominantly Common Law, or "mixed"? I will therefore consider the PECL rules on interpretation from this point of view before turning to what are for me more interesting questions – namely whether the PECL rules on interpretation are acceptable rules, and how they compare with the rules in Scottish and South African law.

# B. THE PECL RULES: CIVIL LAW, COMMON LAW OR MIXED?

## (1) The PECL rules

The PECL rules for the interpretation of contracts are to be found in Chapter 5. The more general rules are in Articles 5:101 and 5:107 PECL. Article 5:101 provides that

(1) A contract is to be interpreted according to the common intention of the parties even if this differs from the literal meaning of the words.

(2) If it is established that one party intended the contract to have a particular meaning, and at the time of the conclusion of the contract the other party could not have been unaware of the first party's intention, the contract is to be interpreted in the way intended by the first party.

(3) If an intention cannot be established according to (1) or (2), the contract is to be interpreted according to the meaning that reasonable persons of the same kind as the parties would give to it in the same circumstances.

Article 5:107 PECL provides that terms are to be interpreted in the light of the whole contract in which they appear.

These general rules are supplemented by an Article spelling out what circumstances are to be taken into account in interpreting a contract.[2] These include the preliminary negotiations; the conduct of the parties, even subsequent to the conclusion of the contract; the nature and purpose of the

---

1 PECL, vol 1, xxiii.
2 Article 5:102 PECL.

contract; usages; and good faith and fair dealing. There are further Articles containing some rules of preference for cases of doubt.[3] These Articles contain, for example, the *contra proferentem* rule, a rule giving preference to individually negotiated terms over standard terms, a rule giving preference to an interpretation which renders the terms of the contract lawful or effective, and a rule giving a preference to the linguistic version in which the contract was originally drawn up.

## (2) Civilian influences?

There is no doubt that at first sight the PECL rules contain much that is distinctly Civilian. The first rule in Article 5:101 PECL – that a contract is to be interpreted according to the common intention of the parties even if this differs from the literal meaning of the words – comes from Papinian, via Pothier and the French Civil Code. Papinian says the intention of the parties should be regarded rather than the mere words used.[4] Pothier states that "One should, in contracts, seek what was the common intention of the parties, rather than the grammatical sense of the terms".[5] The French Civil Code is almost identical: it provides in Article 1156 that "One should look for the common intention of the contracting parties, rather than stop at the literal meaning of the terms used". The Italian Civil Code begins its treatment of interpretation of contracts in the same way.[6]

In Article 5:102 PECL the open-ended nature of the circumstances which can be taken into account also looks more Civilian than Common Law. This is particularly true of the reference to the preliminary negotiations, to subsequent conduct of the parties and to good faith and fair dealing. The Italian Civil Code, for example, provides that in order to ascertain the common intent of the parties "the general course of their behaviour, including that subsequent to the conclusion of the contract", is to be taken into account.[7] The Spanish Civil Code has a similar provision.[8] The German

---

3 Articles 5:103–5:107 PECL.
4 D 50.16.219 (*"In conventionibus contrahentium voluntatem potius quam verba spectari placuit."*).
5 Robert Joseph Pothier, *Traité des Obligations*, in *Oeuvres de Pothier* (ed M Bugnet, 1861) (henceforth Pothier, *Traité des Obligations*), 91 ("On doit, dans les conventions, rechercher quelle a été la commune intention des parties contractantes, plutôt que le sens grammatical des termes").
6 Article 1362, first sentence: "That which was the common intention of the parties, not limited to the literal meaning of the words, shall be sought in interpreting the contract" (from the translation by Beltramo, Longo and Merryman, *The Italian Civil Code* (1969)).
7 Article 1362, second sentence.
8 Article 1282.

BGB places particular stress on good faith and usage in the interpretation of contracts.[9] The Italian Civil Code also says that the contract is to be interpreted "in accordance with good faith".[10]

Most of the later Articles on interpretation can also be seen to have Civilian origins. Versions of the rule in Article 5:102 PECL on having regard to the nature and purpose of the contract, the rule in Article 5:103 PECL on interpretation *contra proferentem*, the rule in Article 5:105 PECL on reference to the contract as a whole, and the rule in Article 5:106 PECL on preferring a construction which renders the terms of a contract lawful or effective can be found in the Digest.[11] From there they made their way into Pothier,[12] the French Civil Code[13] and several other civil codes.[14]

In short, it is not difficult to find Civilian origins for most of the provisions in Chapter 5 of PECL.

### (3) English influences?

Article 5:101(2) PECL deals with the situation where one party intended the contract to have a particular meaning and the other party could not have been unaware of that intention. The contract is then interpreted in accordance with that intention. The Notes to that provision in PECL state that this rule is found in English law but not in a number of Civilian systems. Do we have here a distinctively English influence? Probably not. It is true that certain English decisions[15] proceed on the basis of a similar approach. It is also true that Chitty on Contracts advocates such a rule, in the context of a discussion of mistake.[16] But it could hardly be said to have been a well-recognised rule in the English law on the interpretation of contracts at the time when PECL was being formulated. It seems doubtful that the origin of the rule was English law.[17]

---

9 § 157.

10 Article 1366.

11 D 50.17.67; D 12.1.3; D 1.3.24; D 34.5.26 (27); and D 45.1.80.

12 *Traité des Obligations*, 92, 93, 96, 97.

13 Articles 1157, 1158, 1161, 1162.

14 Articles 1363, 1367, 1369, 1370 of the Italian Civil Code; Articles 1284, 1285, 1286, 1288 of the Spanish Civil Code.

15 See e.g. *Hartog v Colin & Shields* [1939] 3 All ER 566 (hare skins offered at so much per pound. Should have been clear to offeree that offeror meant so much per piece. Offeree nonetheless accepted. Offeree not allowed to found on contract as written). Reference can also be made to the House of Lords case of *Sutton & Co v Ciceri* (1890) 15 AC 144, (1890) 17 R(HL) 40 which, although a Scottish case, did not proceed on any speciality of Scottish law.

16 29th edn (2004), paras 5-068–5-075.

17 The immediate origin appears to have been CISG but, in essence, the rule is an application of the principle of good faith in the interpretation of contracts.

The Notes to the third paragraph of Article 5:101 PECL say that the paragraph is similar to the basic rule in English law. That is true, but the rule is not exclusively English and it seems doubtful whether English law was the main origin of the rule.

In short, there is not much in Chapter 5 of PECL that has an immediately recognisable English law origin.

### (4) The American Restatement

There are certain similarities between the PECL rules on interpretation and the rules in the American Law Institute's Restatement of the law on contracts.[18] The Restatement has a rule to the effect that if the parties have attached the same meaning to an agreement or term, it is interpreted in accordance with that meaning.[19] This is followed by a rule for the situation where one party knew or had reason to know of a meaning attached by the other.[20] The similarity with the first two provisions of Article 5:101 PECL is striking. The Restatement also has secondary rules rather similar to those in PECL.[21]

### (5) United Nations Convention on the International Sale of Goods

The second two paragraphs of Article 5:101 PECL seem remarkably similar to the first two paragraphs of Article 8 of the UN Convention on Contracts for the International Sale of Goods. Article 8 provides that:

(1) statements made by and other conduct of a party are to be interpreted according to his intent where the other party knew or could not have been unaware what that intent was.
(2) If the preceding paragraph is not applicable, statements made by and other conduct of a party are to be interpreted according to the understanding that a reasonable person of the same kind as the other party would have had in the same circumstances.

There are also some similarities between Article 5:102 PECL and Article 8(3) of the Convention which provides that:

[Iin determining the intention of a party or the understanding a reasonable person would have had, due consideration is to be given to all relevant circumstances of the case including the negotiations, any practices which the parties have established between themselves, usages and any subsequent conduct of the parties.

18 *Restatement of the Law Second: Contracts 2d.*
19 Article 201(1).
20 Article 201(2).
21 Articles 202 and 203. Compare, in particular, Article 203(d) with Article 5:104 PECL.

## (6) Preliminary conclusion

The preliminary conclusion is that Chapter 5 of PECL seems on the surface to be predominantly Civilian with a substantial dash of international and American.

## (7) Further considerations

If, however, we probe deeper we find a more complex picture.

### (a) Is English law really so different?

First of all, English law is more like the PECL rules than might be thought.

One point worth noting is that many of the leading accounts and leading cases on the interpretation of contracts in English law deal only with the interpretation of formal written contracts. The rules on less formal contracts are bound to be much more flexible and much more like the PECL rules. For one thing, the distinction between the contract and the negotiations cannot be so clearly drawn: in many informal contracts the contract has to be spelled out of the negotiations.

Judges and textbook writers frequently refer to the primacy of the common intention of the parties. For example, in a recent House of Lords case Lord Bingham said that "the object of the court is to give effect to what the parties intended." [22] In a much older case the court said that in interpreting a contract "greater regard is to be had to the intention of the parties than to any particular words which they may have used in the expression of their intent." [23] Chitty on Contracts states that "[t]he object of all construction of the terms of a written agreement is to discover therefrom the intention of the parties to the agreement." [24] It is true of course that the cases and writers almost always go on to stress that the intention of the parties must be sought by an objective interpretation of the terms used, read in the light of the whole contract and the relevant surrounding circumstances, but the starting point is often the intention of the parties. [25] Moreover, the common intention of the parties is what rules in matters of rectification of written contracts. [26] And a

---

22 *Bank of Credit and Commerce International v Ali* [2002] 1 AC 251 at 259 (henceforth *BCCI v Ali*).

23 *Ford v Beech* (1848) 11 QB 852 at 866.

24 29th edn (2004), para 12–042.

25 Often, but not always. For example, in what is now the classic and dominant statement of the rules on the interpretation of contracts in English law, Lord Hoffmann does not mention the common intention of the parties: see *Investors Compensation Scheme v West Bromwich Building Society* [1998] 1 WLR 896 (henceforth *Investors Compensation Scheme*).

26 See Chitty on Contracts, 29th edn (2004), para 12–000.

common intention may give rise to an estoppel by convention, which would personally bar the parties from founding on the objective meaning of the relevant contract terms.[27] Even more directly, the actual common intention may be decisive as a simple matter of interpretation if the parties have contracted on the basis that an agreed meaning is to be given to a particular expression.[28] So the first rule in Article 5:101 PECL is not so totally alien to English law as might be supposed. It just expresses as a primary rule what in English law would be regarded as an exception or as something to be used for the purposes of special safety mechanisms.

We have already seen that the second paragraph of Article 5:101 PECL (on the situation where one party knows of a special meaning attached by the other) has its parallels in English law, even if they tend to be treated under the heading of mistake.[29] And the objective approach in the third paragraph of Article 5:101 PECL causes no problems for English law. Indeed this paragraph brings PECL and English law close together in those many cases where the parties had no actual intentions at all on the meaning of a term.

So far as Article 5:102 PECL, on relevant circumstances, is concerned, there has been a dramatic shift in English law in recent years. The traditional approach of refusing to admit extrinsic evidence where the terms of a written contract were unambiguous has been changed. The courts are now willing to look at relevant surrounding circumstances even where there is no ambiguity on the face of the contract. It is now generally recognised that meaning depends on context and that the context of contractual terms includes not only the whole of the document or documents in which they appear but also the factual matrix in which the contract was entered into. In *Mannai Investment Co Ltd v Eagle Star Insurance* in 1997 Lord Hoffmann said that the old "restriction on the use of background had been quietly dropped".[30] Apart from some special rules on prior negotiations and subjective declarations of intention, commercial contracts would be construed in the light of all the background which could reasonably have been expected to have been available

---

27  See Lord Hoffmann, "The intolerable wrestle with words and meaning" (1997) 114 *SALJ* 656.

28  *The Karen Oltmann* [1976] 2 Lloyd's Rep 708 at 713. Note also Lord Hoffmann's statements to the effect that the background which can be taken into account in interpreting a contractual document can include "proved common assumptions which were in fact quite mistaken": *Investors Compensation Scheme* (note 25) as modified in *BCCI v Ali* (note 22) at 269.

29  See e.g. *Centrovincial Estates plc v Merchant Investors Assurance Ltd* [1983] Com LR 158, Chitty on Contracts, 29th edn (2004), paras 5-063, 5-068–5-075.

30  *Mannai Investment Co Ltd v Eagle Star Insurance* [1997] AC 749 (henceforth *Mannai*). This case concerned a unilateral notice by a tenant which said 12 January when it should have said 13 January. The court held that any reasonable landlord would have realised that 13 January was meant and interpreted the notice accordingly.

to the parties in order to ascertain what would objectively have been understood to have been their intention. He went on to say that:

> [t]he fact that the words are capable of a literal application is no obstacle to evidence which demonstrates what a reasonable person with knowledge of the background would have understood the parties to mean, even if this compels one to say that they used the wrong words.

Lord Bingham stated the modern English approach to the interpretation of contracts very clearly in the case of *Bank of Credit and Commerce International v Ali* in 2002:[31]

> To ascertain the intention of the parties the court reads the terms of the contract as a whole, giving the words used their ordinary natural meaning in the context of the agreement, the parties' relationship and all the relevant facts surrounding the transaction so far as known to the parties.

Even in relation to prior negotiations there are exceptions to the exclusionary approach. Negotiations can, for example, be considered in order to identify the circumstances in which the contract was intended to apply, the factual background known to the parties, or the genesis and objective aim of the transaction.[32] Even more importantly, negotiations and prior declarations of intention can be taken into account in proceedings for rectification of the terms of the contract. What this means is that the objection to admitting this type of evidence turns out to be procedural rather than substantive. Evidence of negotiations can be used by a two-step process even in those cases where it cannot be used directly for interpretation.

So far as the secondary rules of interpretation are concerned, English law is very similar to Articles 5:103 to 5:107 PECL. The fact that some of these rules are obviously derived from Roman law does not mean that they are not also now part of English law. English law is itself a mixed system.

So, it seems clear that although the PECL rules on interpretation do not look very much like English law at first sight they are in fact not very different in substance. The differences relate to matters of emphasis, evidence and procedure. English law makes objective interpretation the primary rule rather than the fall-back rule; it is unusually restrictive in relation to the admissibility of evidence of prior negotiations and subsequent conduct; and, in many situations, it requires some things which could be done by straight interpretation under PECL to be done by special procedures or doctrines.

---

31 [2002] 1 AC 251 at 259.
32 *Prenn v Simmonds* [1971] 1 WLR 1381 (henceforth *Prenn v Simmonds*).

## (b) Are Civilian systems so similar to PECL and each other?

If English law is more like PECL than might be supposed, it can also be said that Civilian systems are less like PECL and indeed less like each other than might be supposed. So far as the main rules of interpretation of contracts are concerned, Roman law already reflected a tension between literal interpretation and a more liberal contextual interpretation. The prevailing approach varied over time, the general movement being from literal to liberal.[33] In the Digest we find both approaches represented. Papinian's rather subjective approach has already been mentioned but Paulus says that when there is no ambiguity in the words used the question of the underlying intention of the parties is irrelevant.[34] Modern Civilian systems reflect the same tension. We have seen that Article 1156 of the French Civil Code concentrates on the common intention of the contracting parties, rather than the literal meaning of the terms used. But the French courts have recognised and developed a doctrine of "clear and precise terms"[35] which is to the effect that if the terms of a contract are unambiguous they must generally receive effect as written.[36] Some books on contract begin their treatment of interpretation with the "clear and precise terms" rule rather than the code provision.[37] The whole approach to interpretation under current French doctrine is rather more objective than the terms of the Civil Code would suggest.[38] The position in Italian law is similar.[39] Some accounts of the Italian law as currently applied read almost like accounts of English law. For example, one recent introductory book on private law explains that the scope of interpretation is *not* to enquire into "some inner will, or contemplation shared by both parties but not expressly set forth" but is to enquire into the meaning of the words used and other relevant facts.[40] The Spanish Civil Code begins its rules on the interpretation of contracts with the provision that if the terms of a contract are clear and leave no doubt as to the intention of the contracting parties their literal meaning is legally relevant.[41] This is then qualified by a provision to the

---

33  See Zimmermann, *Obligations*, 634.
34  D 32.25.1 (*"Cum in verbis nulla ambiguitas est, non debet admitti voluntatis quaestio"*).
35  *"Termes clairs et précis"*.
36  Civ 19 janv 1942, DA 1942 *Jurisprudence* 107. However, a literal application of a "clear and precise clause" can be rejected if it appears to be the result of a manifest error and against the parties' certain common intention. See Weill & Terré, *Les Obligations*, 4th edn (1986), para 365.
37  See e.g. J Schmidt-Szalewski, *Droit des Contrats* (1989) at 293.
38  See e.g. A Weill & F Terré, *Les Obligations*, 4th edn (1986), para 362.
39  Article 1362 Italian Civil Code; M Bianca, *Dirritto Civile, vol III, Il Contratto*, 2nd edn (2000), 420.
40  G Iudica & P Zatti, *Language and Rules of Italian Private Law: An Introduction* (trans J Funck) (2003).
41  Article 1281.

effect that if the words appear to be contrary to the evident intention of the parties the latter prevails,[42] but the order of treatment is interesting. Some Civilian systems keep the legal rules on interpretation deliberately short on the view that there is no point in stating fairly obvious and often contradictory rules for the guidance of interpreters. In Germany the BGB says that contracts are to be interpreted according to the requirements of good faith, giving consideration to common usage.[43] It says little else: it does not contain the various canons of construction found in a number of other civil codes. The new Dutch Civil Code is also very brief.[44] The rules in these systems do not look at all like the PECL rules.

### (8) Conclusion on PECL as a mixed system

The PECL rules on the interpretation of contracts cannot reasonably be categorised as Civilian or Common Law. Nor can they be categorised as a simple mixture of the two. They are, however, mixed in the sense that, like all sophisticated modern systems, they involve a mixture of approaches to the main rules on interpretation. All such systems have to operate within a narrow range of acceptable options and have to take the same considerations into account. There are different ways of balancing conflicting considerations and presenting the results. At any one time within any one system different people will have different views on the best way. Prevailing opinions are likely to change over time within any one system. Systems – even systems within the same legal "family" – are likely to differ between themselves on the best way of setting out the relevant rules. PECL represents one way. The important question is not whether the PECL rules are mixed rules in any traditional sense but whether they are good rules.

## C. PECL RULES IN RELATION TO SCOTTISH AND SOUTH AFRICAN LAW

### (1) Introduction

What has been said in the last paragraph applies also to the Scottish and South African laws on the interpretation of contracts. They have been exposed to Roman law and English law influences but, more importantly, have had to

---

42 Article 1281, second sentence.
43 § 157 BGB.
44 See Article 3:35 BW.

balance conflicting policy considerations.[45] Divisions of opinion, shifts of opinion and tensions are apparent in both systems.[46] It may be that adoption of the PECL rules would provide a coherent and principled way out of some current difficulties.

This is not the place for a full account of the relevant Scottish and South African laws. Such accounts have been given elsewhere.[47] For present purposes some general impressions coupled with notes on points of particular relevance to the PECL rules must suffice.

## (2) General impressions

The current Scottish law on the interpretation of contracts is similar to English law. Leading English cases and *dicta* on interpretation, including the important *dicta* of Lord Hoffmann on the importance of interpreting words in their context and in the light of relevant background circumstances,[48] are cited as highly persuasive authorities.[49] As in English law, there is authority for the view that if the parties contract on an agreed basis that a term is to have an unusual meaning, that meaning will prevail over the ordinary meaning of the term.[50] There is also authority for the view that "an error of expression will not necessarily prevent the court from giving effect to the true intention of the parties".[51] And there is clear House of Lords authority for the proposition that, if one party attaches a particular meaning to an expression

---

45  See C Lewis, "Interpretation of contracts" in Zimmermann & Visser, *Southern Cross*, 195–216; E Clive, "Interpretation" in Reid & Zimmermann, *History*, vol 2, 47–71.

46  For a comparison of both systems which brings out clearly the shifts and differences of opinion and the tensions, see L J Macgregor & C Lewis, "Interpretation of contract", in Zimmermann, Visser & Reid, *Mixed Legal Systems*, 66–93. For Scotland, see also MacQueen & Thomson, *Contract*, 110–117 (which begins with the traditional objective approach and then proceeds to ask about a "change in approach") and the Scottish Law Commission's Report on Interpretation in Private Law (Scot Law Com No 160, 1997), which is critical of the extent to which the current law is dominated by restrictive and complicated rules of evidence. For South Africa, see e.g. Hutchison et al, *Wille's Principles*, 461–462 (which sets out the traditional approach, based on the exclusion of extrinsic evidence, and then observes that "in more recent times a trend of judicial thought has emerged in favour of a more liberal approach to interpretation"). See also Lewis, in Zimmermann & Visser, *Southern Cross*, 195–216.

47  In addition to the standard texts, see Macgregor & Lewis, in Zimmermann, Visser & Reid, *Mixed Legal Systems*, 66–93; Lewis, in Zimmermann & Visser, *Southern Cross*, 195–216 and Clive, in Reid & Zimmermann, *History*, 47–71. For Scottish law, see also Scot Law Com No 160 (1997).

48  *Investors Compensation Scheme* (note 25); *Mannai*.

49  See e.g. *Bank of Scotland v Dunedin Property Investment Co* 1998 SC 657 at 661, 670, 677 (henceforth *BoS v Dunedin*); *Bank of Scotland v Junior* 1999 SCLR 284; *Lindsay Plant Ltd v Norwest Group plc* 2000 SC 93 at 98; *Project Fishing International v CEPO Ltd* 2002 SC 534 at 539 (henceforth *Project Fishing*).

50  See *Hunter v Barron's Trustees* (1886) 13 R 883.

51  See *Project Fishing* (note 49).

and the other knows this or could reasonably be expected to have known it, and concludes the contract without saying anything on the point, that meaning will prevail.[52] In the absence of any such special features the contract will be interpreted objectively. The basic Scottish rules are therefore perfectly compatible with the PECL rules although, as in English law, the emphasis often appears to be different. The recommendations of the Scottish Law Commission on the substantive law on the above matters are also perfectly compatible with the PECL rules although again the emphasis and order of treatment are slightly different.[53]

The current South African law also seems basically similar to English law.[54] English cases and *dicta* are occasionally cited,[55] although to a lesser extent than in Scotland. There is much more overt reference to Roman law than there is in Scotland.[56] The Civilian background is worn more openly on the sleeve. Nonetheless the basic approach, after some difference of opinion, seems now to be rather literal and objective. A recent statement is as follows (citations omitted).

> According to our ... law a policy of insurance must be construed like any other written contract so as to give effect to the intention of the parties as expressed in the terms of the policy, considered as a whole. The terms are to be understood in their plain, ordinary and popular sense unless it is evident from the context that the parties intended them to have a different meaning, or unless they have by known usage of trade, or the like, acquired a peculiar sense distinct from their popular meaning. If the ordinary sense of the words necessarily leads to some absurdity or to some repugnance or inconsistency with the rest of the contract, then the court may modify the words just so much as to avoid that absurdity or inconsistency but no more. It must also be borne in mind that very few words bear a single meaning, and the "ordinary" meaning of words appearing in a contract will necessarily depend upon the context in which they are used, their interrelation and the nature of the transaction as it appears from the entire contract. It is essential to have regard to the context in which the word or phrase is used with its interrelation to the contract as a whole, including the nature and purpose of the contract.[57]

---

52 *Sutton & Co v Ciceri* (1890) 17 R (HL) 40, (1890) 15 AC 144.

53 See Scot Law Com No 160 (1997). The Commission begins with the rule on objective interpretation but this is explained by the fact that its rules were framed for all juridical acts. The special rules for contracts are presented as exceptions to the general rule of objective interpretation.

54 See Lewis, in Zimmermann & Visser, *Southern Cross*, 195–216.

55 For recent examples see e.g. the references to *Smith v Hughes* (1871) LR 6 QB 597 in *HNR Properties CC v Standard Bank of South Africa Ltd* 2004 (4) SA 471 (SCA) and in the *MV Navigator* 2004 (5) SA 10 (CPD). See also the brief reference to *Investors Compensation Scheme* in *Uitenhage Transitional Local Council v South African Revenue Service* 2004 (1) SA 292 (SCA).

56 See e.g. the quotations from Justinian's Digest in Hutchison et al, *Wille's Principles*, 461–462.

57 *Metcash Trading Ltd v Credit Guarantee Insurance Corporation of Africa Ltd* Case No 96/2003, heard 9 March 2004, delivered 25 March 2004. For other recent statements see *Holland Life Assurance Co Ltd v G J Van der Merwe NO* Case No 569/2003, heard 19 Nov 2004, delivered 30 Nov 2004 and *Aktiebolaget Hässle v Triomed (Pty) Ltd* 2003 (1) SA 155 (SCA), para 1. See also *Coopers & Lybrand v Bryant* 1995 (3) SA 761 (A) at 768A–B (henceforth *Coopers & Lybrand*).

As in Scottish law, however, it seems that if the parties have attached a special and unusual meaning to an expression in their contract that meaning will prevail over the ordinary or dictionary meaning in a question between the parties.

> Even if a word has a plain and ordinary meaning, but the parties at the time the contract was made both understood it to have a different meaning, the latter meaning is binding on them though not on innocent third parties.[58]

It would be surprising if this principle were not equally applicable to the situation where one party attached a special meaning to an expression and the other party knew this, or could reasonably be expected to have known it, but said nothing.

In both systems rules restricting the admissibility of extrinsic evidence in the interpretation of written contracts play an important role. In both systems these restrictive rules are under challenge and seem to be in an unstable state.

### (3) Must there be ambiguity before extrinsic evidence is admissible?

There is no such requirement in PECL. There probably was such a require-ment in Scottish law, subject to exceptions, "ambiguity" being construed widely so as to include uncertainty.[59] The requirement was criticised by the Scottish Law Commission as illogical, unnecessary and troublesome.[60] It can probably be assumed that there is now no such requirement. It seems that the judicial abolition of it by the House of Lords in English cases in the late 1990s[61] will be regarded as settling the law of Scotland on this point in the direction recommended by the Scottish Law Commission.[62]

The traditional view in South African law has also been that there has to be ambiguity or sufficient uncertainty before extrinsic evidence will be admitted

---

58  Hutchison et al, *Wille's Principles*, 464. Similar statements can be found in other books. See Macgregor & Lewis, in Zimmermann, Visser & Reid, *Mixed Legal Systems*, 76.

59  For the confused and unsatisfactory state of the authorities on this point, see Macgregor & Lewis, in Zimmermann, Visser & Reid, *Mixed Legal Systems*, 80. One of the most curious features of the old law was the distinction between latent and patent ambiguities. This came in from English law but is probably no longer part of that law. See *Wickman Tools Ltd v Schuler AG* [1974] AC 235 at 268 by Lord Simon of Glaisdale, and K Lewison, *The Interpretation of Contracts*, 3rd edn (2004), para 8.02.

60  Scot Law Com No 160 (1997), paras 2.13–2.14. Illogical because meaning often depends on background. Unnecessary because if there is an arguable dispute about the interpretation of an expression it will usually be possible to find ambiguity. Troublesome because it merely adds another stage to the dispute-solving process, a stage where the courts find it difficult to be consistent.

61  *Investors Compensation Scheme* (note 25); *Mannai* (note 30).

62  See the cases cited in note 49 above.

for the interpretation of a written contract.[63] However, this view has been under challenge for some time. It is now said that a court may always be informed of the "background circumstances under which the contract was concluded, such as the relationship in which the parties stood to one another at the time of contracting."[64] A distinction is drawn between such "background circumstances" and "surrounding circumstances", the latter being admissible only in the event of ambiguity or sufficient uncertainty,[65] but the nature of the distinction is not entirely clear[66] and the question has been asked why evidence of relevant surrounding circumstances should not be admissible in all cases.[67] It remains to be seen whether, and if so how, the obvious tension in this area of the law will be resolved.

## (4) Negotiations

In Scottish law evidence of negotiations or prior communings is still, as a rule, regarded as inadmissible in the interpretation of a written contract.[68] There seem to be several reasons for this continuing restriction. Each is plausible in some cases but they do not justify a blanket exclusion for all cases. First, it is said that reference to negotiations will be "unhelpful".[69] This is often true: it will not help an interpreter to be told of abandoned negotiating positions which cast no light on the meaning of expressions in the final agreement. However, that is not always true: there are cases where reference to particular parts of the negotiations can elucidate the meaning which both parties attached, or must have attached, to a particular expression.[70] Secondly, it may be said that in drawing up a formal written contract the parties must have intended the wording of that contract to supersede anything said in the negotiations. That will often be true, but not always. Parties may not include

---

63 See Hutchison et al, *Wille's Principles*, 461–462 and, for a more recent statement, *Rane Investments Trust v Commissioner, South African Revenue Service* 2003 (6) SA 332 (SCA) at 346.

64 Hutchison et al, *Wille's Principles*, 462.

65 See *HNR Properties CC v Standard Bank of South Africa Ltd* 2004 (4) SA 471 (SCA) at 478 – court can look at "background circumstances or, in the event of ambiguity, surrounding circumstances".

66 Contrast the statements in *Delmas Milling Co Ltd v Du Plessis* 1955 (3) SA 447 (A) with those in *Coopers & Lybrand* (note 57) at 768A-B. And see Macgregor & Lewis, in Zimmermann, Visser & Reid, *Mixed Legal Systems*, 82.

67 See *Cinema City (Pty) Ltd v Morgenstern Family Estates (Pty) Ltd* 1980 (1) SA 796 (AD) at 804 per Jansen JA. See also Hutchison et al, *Wille's Principles*, 462 and Lewis, in Zimmermann & Visser, *Southern Cross*, 195 -216.

68 *BoS v Dunedin* (note 49) at 661.

69 *Prenn v Simmonds* (note 32).

70 A point made in S C Smith, "Making sense of contracts" 1999 *SLT (News)* 307 at 311.

everything of relevance from the negotiations in their final written contract: they may not have intended to supersede the excluded material: they may simply not have realised that it would turn out to be important. Thirdly, it may be said that the exclusion of reference to negotiations saves expense. That will often be true, but not always. If evidence of surrounding circumstances is admissible anyway, it is not clear that expense will always be saved by excluding evidence of negotiations. Sometimes reference to the negotiations would provide a clear and direct answer to the question in dispute. And justice and party autonomy are relevant as well as expense. If the parties just wanted *any decision* they could toss a coin. Fourthly, it may be said that allowing evidence of negotiations is likely to be unfair to third parties, who have no knowledge of what went on during negotiations. That will occasionally be true, but not often. There are many cases where the dispute is only between the parties to the contract. The protection of third parties is a separate issue and can be otherwise accommodated. This fourth argument also goes too far. It would suggest that in a question with third parties no surrounding circumstances at all should be considered unless they could have been known to a hypothetical third party.

Not surprisingly, it is recognised in the existing Scottish law that there are exceptions to the rule excluding evidence of prior communings. Such evidence can be used if the parties themselves refer to the negotiations to supplement the terms of the contract.[71] It can be used to identify the subject-matter of the contract.[72] And, significantly, it can be used to prove the state of knowledge of the parties at the time of contracting.[73] This last exception suggests that the rule excluding negotiations cannot survive. It makes no sense to allow reference to prior communings to show that the parties knew that one of them was planning to incur costs of a certain type but not to allow such reference to show that the parties had agreed in the course of the negotiations that the expression would cover costs of that type. It is worth mentioning also that negotiations can be referred to in order to demonstrate that the parties had deliberately rejected a solution which would have had the same effect as one possible meaning of an expression in their contract.[74] This too casts doubt on the survivability of the rule excluding evidence of negotiations. If negotiations can be used to prove a negative common intention as to the meaning of an expression why should they not be used to prove a positive

---

71  See e.g. *Bovis Construction Ltd v Whatlings Construction Ltd* 1994 SLT 865.
72  See e.g. *Houldsworth v Gordon Cumming* 1910 SC (HL) 49.
73  *BoS v Dunedin* (note 49).
74  See *Hunter v Livingston Development Corporation* 1986 SC (HL) 31.

common intention?[75] It is obvious too that the rule excluding evidence of negotiations has no application in those cases where the contract has to be spelled out of the negotiations.

What seems clear in the current state of Scottish law is that, in practice, evidence of negotiations is much more widely admitted than it used to be.[76]

In its report on Interpretation in Private Law the Scottish Law Commission recommended that evidence of negotiations should continue to be inadmissible for the purpose of interpreting a contract objectively – i.e. in any case where there was no argument that the parties or one of them had attached a special meaning to an expression.[77] However, the Commission did not rule out the use of negotiations where there was a question as to whether the parties (or one of them with the actual or constructive knowledge of the other) had attached a special meaning to an expression.[78] The Commission's recommendation was thus half-way between the existing Scottish (and English) approach and the PECL approach. It would have been an improvement on the existing law. It is arguable, however, that the Commission did not go far enough in allowing evidence of negotiations. As between the parties to a contract, reference to negotiations may sometimes be helpful for the purpose of arriving at an objective determination of a reasonable or commercially sensible meaning even in a case where neither party claims that any special meaning was attached to an expression. Indeed it can be seen with hindsight that the Commission's recommendation is narrower in some respects than the existing law, where negotiations can be referred to in order to show the state of knowledge of the parties.[79] The PECL solution seems preferable

South African law appears to be more flexible than the existing Scottish law on the use of negotiations. There is authority for saying that if there is sufficient ambiguity or uncertainty to allow in evidence of "surrounding circumstances"[80] then evidence of negotiations and correspondence between the parties will be admissible as part of those circumstances.[81] The policy considerations are the same as in relation to Scotland.

---

75 This point is also made in D W McLauchlan "Common assumptions and contract interpretation" (1997) 113 *LQR* 237 with reference to the Australian case of *Codelfa Construction Pty Ltd v State Rail Authority of New South Wales* (1982) 149 CLR 337 where it was held to be permissible to allow evidence that the "parties had united in rejecting" a particular meaning.

76 See e.g. *City Wall Properties (Scotland) Ltd v Pearl Assurance plc* 2004 SC 214 at 225.

77 Paras 2.19–2.22, 8.11.

78 Paras 3.19, 8.12.

79 *BoS v Dunedin* (note 49).

80 As opposed to "background circumstances". See above, text accompanying note ??.

81 *Coopers & Lybrand* (note 57) at 768A–B. And see Macgregor & Lewis, in Zimmermann, Visser & Reid, *Mixed Legal Systems*, 83–85.

## (5) Subsequent conduct

There is a line of Scottish authority which clearly allowed evidence of subsequent conduct to be admitted to establish what must have been, at the time of contracting, the common intention of the parties as to the meaning of an expression in their contract.[82] These cases have never been expressly overruled but it seems that in practice Scottish judges now tend to follow statements in English House of Lords decisions[83] to the effect that reference to subsequent conduct is inadmissible for the purposes of interpreting a contract.[84] Whether this change of approach is wise is open to question. Consider the facts of an old Scottish case. The parties had entered into a formal contract for the lease of land. The period of the lease was to begin and end at Whitsunday. At the end of the lease the question arose as to what was meant by that term. The normal meaning would have been 15 May. The tenant argued that the parties had used the term to mean 26 May.[85] It was proved that the landlord had given, and the tenant had taken, possession on 26 May. The court held, unanimously and without any apparent difficulty, that this subsequent conduct established that the parties had used Whitsunday to mean 26 May. Lord Young said:

> [I]t is proved to demonstration what the parties did mean … for the landlord gave, and the tenant took, possession of the subjects let upon 26th May 1866, thereby shewing clearly what they meant by the term of Whitsunday.[86]

It is difficult to believe that the result would have been better if evidence of the parties' subsequent conduct had been held inadmissible.[87]

South African law also appears to be rather less restrictive than English law in relation to subsequent conduct. The court can have regard to post-contractual conduct for the purposes of interpretation if there is ambiguity or

---

82  The Scottish Law Commission listed fourteen cases, from 1830 to 1957, in its Discussion Paper No 101 on Interpretation in Private Law (1996) at para 7.14 n 233.

83  *Whitworth Street Estates (Manchester) Ltd v James Miller & Partners Ltd* [1970] AC 583; *Wickman Tools Ltd v Schuler AG* [1974] AC 235.

84  See e.g. *Cameron (Scotland) Ltd v Melville Dundas Ltd* 2001 SCLR 691. The current Scottish approach has been criticised. See Professor McBryde's Comment to the case just cited, and Macgregor & Lewis, in Zimmermann, Visser & Reid, *Mixed Legal Systems*, 86.

85  It was alleged that this was in accordance with local custom but the court did not decide the case on the basis of local custom.

86  *Hunter v Barron's Trustees* (1886) 13 R 883 at 891.

87  Under the Scottish Law Commission's recommendations, evidence of subsequent conduct would have been admissible in this type of case. The Commission did not, however, think that subsequent conduct would be relevant to a purely objective interpretation of a contract. See Scot Law Com No 160 (1997), paras 2.24–2.29, 8.13.

sufficient uncertainty.[88] The requirement of ambiguity or uncertainty seems suspect on policy grounds.

There is South African authority for the point that a court will have regard to the subsequent conduct of the parties in deciding whether a contract is a sham or simulate transaction.[89] In this context it was said that the court would seek to ascertain the true intention of the parties from all relevant circumstances, including the manner in which the contract was implemented. The question in this type of case is slightly different from the question in an interpretation case[90] but nonetheless this line of authority supports the view that subsequent conduct may be relevant for the purposes of ascertaining the common intention of the parties at the time of conclusion of the contract.[91]

## D. ASSESSMENT OF THE PECL RULES

### (1) Considerations which have to be taken into account

The main considerations which any legal system has to take into account in framing rules for the interpretation of contracts seem to me to be these:

1.  The need to respect the autonomy of the contracting parties: it is for the parties to determine the contents of their contract: it is not for a court to make a new contract for the parties.
2.  The need for rationality and common sense and consistency in the law. It would be irrational and contrary to common sense to interpret words without regard to their context. It might be regarded as inconsistent to use one approach in deciding whether a contract had been formed but another approach in interpreting the contract once formed.[92]
3.  The need to avoid unnecessary unfairness. It would, for example, be widely regarded as unfair to allow a party to give the impression that a term was being used in one sense, to allow the other party to rely on

88  See *Rane Investments Trust v Commissioner, South African Revenue Service* 2003 (6) SA 332 (SCA) and Hutchison et al, *Wille's Principles*, 464: "Where ... the terms of a contract are ambiguous or vague, but the conduct of the parties shows that they have both given the same meaning to the words used the court will give effect to that meaning."

89  *Michau v Maize Board* 2003 (6) SA 459 (SCA).

90  In a simulation case the question is not what the parties meant by an expression but what legal effect they intended their contract to have.

91  A similar point is made in G McMeel "Prior negotiations and subsequent conduct – the next step forward for contractual interpretation" (2003) 119 *LQR* 272, by reference to *Agnew v CIR* [2001] 2 AC 710, where it was held that subsequent conduct was admissible to see whether a contract was a sham.

92  See Lewis, in Zimmermann & Visser, *Southern Cross*, 195–216 and Scot Law Com No 160 (1997), para 3.8.

that sense, and then to turn round later and say that the term should be given some quite different sense. This consideration often finds expression in notions of good faith or personal bar or estoppel but it can also come into play directly in interpretation.

4. The need to protect reasonable reliance of the parties and third parties. Those who have relied in good faith on an apparent meaning should not be prejudiced by an interpretation based on intentions or circumstances of which they did not know and could not reasonably be expected to know.

5. The need for a measure of certainty and predictability in legal relationships. This is sometimes said to favour an objective approach to interpretation but it also suggests that the rules on interpretation themselves should be clear and consistent. They should not be vague and full of ill-defined exceptions and sub-exceptions.

6. The desirability of keeping the scope and length and cost of legal proceedings within reasonable bounds. This consideration is often reflected in doctrines to the effect that if the words of a written contract are clear there is no need to go beyond them.

7. The desirability of imposing some discipline on those drafting contracts. Drafters should not be encouraged to be lax: they might be so encouraged if the courts were to look for actual intention and ignore the words used in a written contract.

## (2) Important policy choices

There are several basic policy choices to be made in drafting a set of rules on interpretation.

### (a) Scope

Should the rules include or exclude rules on the implication of terms? PECL deals separately with implied terms. Article 6:102 PECL provides that:

> In addition to the express terms, a contract may contain implied terms which stem from
>     (a) the intention of the parties;
>     (b) the nature and purpose of the contract; and
>     (c) good faith and fair dealing.

This seems to be the correct approach.[93] The process of interpretation begins only when the terms of the contract have been determined.

---

93 It was also the approach taken in Scot Law Com No 160 (1997), para 1.6. See also *Bank of Scotland v Junior* 1999 SCLR 284 at 291D–E per Lord Penrose.

## (b) Rules of law or rules of evidence?

Should the problems of interpretation be tackled by substantive rules or rules of evidence? PECL has chosen substantive rules. This was also the approach recommended by the Scottish Law Commission, which thought that the major defect in the Scottish law on this subject was that it tried to solve the problems by arbitrary and complicated rules of evidence.[94] The Commission pointed out that contracts have to be interpreted outside court proceedings as well as in court proceedings. It recommended that the only rule of evidence in this area should be that relevant evidence is admissible and irrelevant evidence is inadmissible.[95] At European level the merits of this approach are even more obvious. It would be very difficult to persuade the representatives of twenty-five European countries that the way to solve problems of interpretation was to begin by rules excluding certain types of potentially relevant evidence for the purposes of court proceedings but not necessarily for arbitration proceedings or other situations where interpretation might be an issue.

## (c) One-step or two-step process?

By a two-step process I mean primarily the process available in English and Scottish law whereby a written contract which fails to express the common intention of the parties can first be rectified and then interpreted in its rectified form. It seems clear that this two-step process would be difficult to support as a solution at European level. It would be based on the assumption that a rectification procedure is available in all EU countries and is the same in all of them; alternatively it would mean that a unified European rectification procedure would have to be devised. The assumption would be unwarranted and the device would be difficult to realise. Moreover it would be difficult to argue at the European level that one solution should apply to important written contracts which might justify expensive rectification procedures and another solution to all other contracts.[96] Only the one-step process seems suitable for the purposes of model European rules on the interpretation of contracts.

---

94 Scot Law Com No 160 (1997), paras 1.2, 8.1–8.8.
95 This is already the rule in relation to rectification of documents in Scottish law: see the Law Reform (Miscellaneous Provisions) (Scotland) Act 1985, s 8(2).
96 There may also be technical barriers to rectification in some cases. For example, in English law there may have to be a mistake before there can be rectification: see McLauchlan (1997) 113 *LQR* 237. This is not a requirement in Scottish law: see the Law Reform (Miscellaneous Provisions) (Scotland) Act 1985, s 8. For another case where there was a technical reason why rectification could not be used, see *AXZS Industries v AF Dreyer (Pty) Ltd* 2004 (4) SA 186 (W).

Similar observations apply to the other possible two-step process of interpreting a contract objectively and then saying that the parties are personally barred or estopped from exercising rights based on that interpretation. It would be difficult to persuade a European audience of the merits of this approach as opposed to a straight one-step interpretation approach. Why not simply say "As between you, the contracting parties, this term means what you both intended it to mean" rather than "This term means what we say it means but you are not allowed to act on that basis"?

### (d) One rule for all contracts or different rules for different types?

The practical question here is whether the same rules of interpretation should apply to all contracts whether or not the terms are embodied or recorded in writing. PECL has one set of rules for all contracts. The word "contract" in Chapter 5 generally means a contractual agreement, not a contractual document.[97] A unified approach seems the better approach.[98] There are millions of contracts which are never recorded in writing. Their terms may, however, be recorded or provable in other ways and they may require interpretation. A non-unified approach also gives rise to questions of classification: what counts as a written contract? One of the implications of a unified approach is that the law on the rectification of documents cannot be relied on as a safety valve. Another is that restrictive rules of evidence applying only to contracts reduced to writing cannot be used to solve all interpretation problems. A unified approach does not mean that the fact that a contract has been deliberately reduced to formal writing must be regarded as irrelevant. On the contrary, it would be a highly relevant circumstance to be taken into account and would lead any interpreter to be most reluctant to depart from the ordinary meaning of the words which the parties had used to set out their agreement.

### (e) Subjective or objective starting point?

It is quite clear that any reasonable set of rules will need to balance subjective and objective considerations. What is not so clear is whether it is better to begin with a reference to the common intention of the parties and then

---

97 There are references, e.g., to a contract being "concluded". One concludes an agreement, but not a document. However, in Article 5:107 PECL on linguistic discrepancies the reference to a "contract drawn up in two or more language versions" seems to use "contract" in the sense of a contract document.

98 This was the approach recommended by the Scottish Law Commission: see Scot Law Com No 160 (1997), para 1.9.

supplement that, as PECL does, or to begin with a principle of objective interpretation and then qualify that, as some European systems currently do.

The answer to the question depends partly on whether one is drafting rules for the interpretation of contracts or rules for the interpretation of all juridical acts. In the latter case it would be better to begin with an objective principle, because it seems clear that the maker of a unilateral juridical act cannot reasonably expect it to be interpreted according to his or her subjective intention if that was never made known to the addressee and if the addressee could not reasonably be expected to have known of it. In the case of contracts there is a free choice because the reference to the *common* intention of the parties generally avoids the problems of protecting reliance interests as between the parties. In my view the expression "common intention" implies that the parties have communicated with each other sufficiently to form a common intention: a common intention is not the same as identical uncommunicated individual intentions. There is nothing unconscionable in allowing either party to rely on the parties' common intention in this sense. Of course, different considerations apply if third parties are involved but that is a special case. I come back to that later. In most cases it is only the parties to the contract who are involved.

## (3) Main PECL rules assessed

### (a) Rule in Article 5:101(1) PECL

It seems to me that the Lando Commission's decision to begin with common intention is defensible. If the common intention of the parties as to the meaning of an expression in their contract is admitted or proved it would be hard to justify ignoring it and foisting some other contract on the parties. If this is so, then there is much to be said for making common intention the primary rule. It better expresses the regard which the law has for the autonomy of the parties. It is moreover the prevailing European and international approach. It is the approach adopted, for example, in the Unidroit Principles of International Commercial Contracts. It would have been possible to reverse the order of paragraphs (1) and (3) of Article 5:101 PECL and to say something like

> [i]n cases where neither of the following paragraphs applies a contract is to be interpreted according to the meaning which a reasonable third person would give to it in the circumstances.

That order of treatment could be justified on the ground that the situations where the parties have a common intention as to the meaning of terms used in their contract which differs from the ordinary meaning of those terms are likely to be rare and exceptional. There is something to be said for beginning with the ordinary case and then dealing with the exceptional case. However, there are arguments both ways on this, and the order of treatment does not greatly matter.

What does matter is that it has to be made clear that where the parties have formed a common intention as to the meaning of an expression used in their contract, that meaning should prevail in all questions between them.

The key case which has to be considered is the following. The parties agree before the contract is concluded that a certain expression is to be used in a certain sense. They do not, however, state that in the contract itself. Their prior agreement is admitted by both parties or can be proved by evidence. Surely any legal system with any regard for fairness would, in a question between the parties, give effect to the parties' common intention in this type of case and would not allow one of the parties to found on a different meaning objectively arrived at. English law, in spite of its general preference for an objective approach, would allow the agreed basis to prevail if there is any ambiguity on the point in the contract,[99] and the requirement of ambiguity now seems dubious in the light of recent developments,[100] and in the light of common sense.[101]

So the rule in Article 5:101 PECL seems justifiable, even if it need not necessarily have been the opening rule.

### (b) Rule in Article 5:101(2) PECL

Basic considerations of fairness seem fully to justify the rule in the second paragraph of Article 5:101 PECL for the case where one party has used an expression in a particular sense and the other party could not have been unaware of this and concludes a contract without putting forward any other meaning. It would be contrary to good faith and fair dealing to allow the second party to argue later that a different objective interpretation of the expression ought to be adopted.

Again we can consider a key case. Suppose that a builder sends a written offer to do some work. On looking over a copy of the offer after it has been posted the builder notices a mistake. He phones up the customer and says: "There is a mistake in the offer I've just posted to you. When I say 'square

---

99  *The Karen Oltmann* [1976] 2 Lloyd's Rep 708 at 713.
100  *Investors Compensation Scheme* (note 25); *Mannai* (note 30).
101  See McLauchlan (1997) 113 *LQR* 237 at 243.

feet' I mean "linear feet."' The customer says "Do you want to send a new offer?" The builder says "No. As long as you realise what is meant that is fine." The customer sends a written acceptance of the offer without mentioning this point. The phone call was recorded. Under PECL the contract would be read as referring to linear feet. This seems reasonable.

It is perhaps worth noting that if paragraph (2) of Article 5:101 PECL is accepted as sound policy then paragraph (1) has to be accepted too. The case where both parties agree on a meaning for an expression is just one type of case where one party uses an expression in a particular sense and the other knows of this. Indeed a suitably drafted paragraph (2) would render paragraph (1) unnecessary.[102] That is not to say that it is undesirable to have paragraph (1) separately expressed as a general rule.

### (c) Rule in Article 5:101(3) PECL

The third paragraph in Article 5:101 PECL seems necessary and useful. It meets the criticism that rules based only on the idea of common intention are unrealistic because in many cases the parties will not have formed any common intention as to the meaning of the expression under consideration.

### (d) Rules in Article 5:102 PECL

Article 5:102 PECL is not an exhaustive list and it might be argued that this sort of illustrative list is unnecessary because it merely states the obvious, given the general underlying criterion that circumstances relevant to the point in dispute should be taken into account and irrelevant circumstances should not be.[103] I have some sympathy with that view in general. Nonetheless it seems to me that in this instance the list is useful, given the difference in legal systems regarding preliminary negotiations and subsequent conduct.

So far as negotiations are concerned it seems clear that these may sometimes be relevant to a determination, for the purposes of paragraph (1) of Article 5:101 PECL, of whether the parties had a common intention as to the meaning of a term. And clearly it will be necessary to consider negotiations if one party claims that paragraph (2) of Article 5:101 PECL applies. The negotiations may also shed light on the factual background with reference to which the parties contracted and so may occasionally be relevant for the

---

102  This solution is the one adopted by CISG and the one recommended for Scottish law by the Scottish Law Commission. See Scot Law Com No 160 (1997), para 3.13.

103  See C-W Canaris & H C Grigoleit, "Interpretation of contracts", in A Hartkamp et al (eds), *Towards a European Civil Code*, 445–469 at 456.

purposes of paragraph (3) of Article 5:101 PECL. It has been explained in the House of Lords that the general exclusion of reference to negotiations in English law is not for any technical reasons but just because it is thought that such evidence will not be helpful.[104] That, however, will clearly not always be true in relation to the principal rules of interpretation in PECL. Of course, much of the negotiating history *will* generally be irrelevant to the point in dispute and it is in nobody's interests to increase the cost of litigation by allowing in a great mass of irrelevant evidence – but there are perhaps better ways of excluding irrelevant evidence than having a blanket rule which also excludes relevant evidence.

A similar point can be made about subsequent conduct. Often this will be irrelevant or inconclusive. It may just suggest that the parties have departed from the contract or chosen to ignore the contract. But sometimes subsequent conduct may cast a light backwards on what the knowledge or common intention of the parties must have been at the time of conclusion of the contract and then it would be relevant.

### (e) Other rules

I do not propose to say anything about the other rules in Chapter 5 of PECL, partly because of lack of space, but partly because they seem uncontroversial. The drafters of PECL are, in my view, to be commended for not including more rules of preference. Most such rules state the obvious or cause more problems than they solve. For example, a rule to the effect that, unless a different intention is indicated, ordinary words are to be given their ordinary meaning and technical words their technical meaning seems so obvious as to be unnecessary.[105] Nobody would think of adopting any other approach.

### (f) Some criticisms

One criticism of the PECL rules is that they deal inadequately with unilateral juridical acts. Article 1:107 PECL says that the Principles apply with appropriate modifications to unilateral promises and to other statements and conduct indicating intention. It is quite clear, however, that important modifications are needed before the rules on the interpretation of contracts can be applied to unilateral juridical acts. The common intention of the parties cannot be used as a criterion, and an objective approach is necessary in order to protect reliance interests. The rather offhand way in which

---

104  *Prenn v Simmonds* (note 32).
105  There is a rule to this effect in the American Restatement, section 202(3).

unilateral juridical acts are dealt with in PECL is perhaps excusable, or at least understandable, given that the primary focus was contract law but this is a matter which may have to be dealt with if the PECL rules are used as the basis for an instrument of wider application.

Another criticism of the PECL rules is that they do not make any express provision for the reliance interests of third parties. It might perhaps be argued that the reference to good faith and fair dealing can be used to protect the reliance interests of third parties but an express provision would seem preferable. This is not an easy question and it might have been better to tackle it overtly. What seems reasonably clear is that if the contract is of a type which is intended from the outset to be relied on by third parties then an objective interpretation should apply. Third parties should not be bound by an interpretation based on intentions or circumstances of which they had no knowledge and could not reasonably be expected to have had knowledge. Into this category would fall negotiable instruments and contracts registered in the land registers and creating rights and obligations intended to run with the land. There are no doubt other similar cases. What, however, of the position of assignees under ordinary contracts? Here the considerations seem rather different. The reliance interests of the debtor also have to be considered. The debtor does not need to consent to an assignment and should not be exposed to a greater liability as a result of the assignment than existed before. The principle that the assignee has no better rights than the assignor is a useful one. It has to be remembered that an assignee runs various risks in taking an assignment of a right under a contract. The contract may have been varied by the parties. There may have been partial perform-ance. In general the assignee is protected from such risks by rights against the assignor.[106] There seems no reason why the same approach should not be used in relation to interpretation.[107]

Criticisms can also be made of the drafting of Chapter 5. For example, there is a lack of consistency as to what it is that is being interpreted. Sometimes the reference is to the contract, sometimes to clauses, sometimes to terms and once to terms and expressions. Strictly speaking it is perhaps expressions used by the parties that are interpreted. The expression "could not have been unaware" is suspect. It has a respectable pedigree in the UN Convention on Contracts for the International Sale of Goods but it is nonetheless rather unsatisfactory. If it means "knew" why not say so? If it

---

106  See Article 11:204 PECL.
107  This was the approach recommended by the Scottish Law Commission: see Scot Law Com No 160 (1997), para 3.17 n 23.

means "could reasonably be expected to have known" why not say so? The reference to "reasonable persons of the same kind as the parties" also comes from the UN Sales Convention but is also an unhappy one, for several reasons. The fictitious referees are unnecessary. "Of the same kind" is curious. Why not just say "the meaning which would reasonably be given to it in the circumstances"? The beginning of Article 5:102 PECL should perhaps be permissive rather than directory: it should say "regard may be had" to the listed circumstances. Nobody would wish to force an interpreter to have regard to circumstances which were of no relevance to the issue under consideration. The reference to good faith and fair dealing seems to be misplaced. Good faith and fair dealing are not relevant circumstances but relevant considerations. It might be preferable to bring this provision out into a separate Article.

These criticisms are, however, minor ones. They do not affect the conclusion that the PECL rules on interpretation seem preferable to the existing Scottish and South African rules.

# 8 Third-Party Contracts

## Philip Sutherland

## A. BACKGROUND

A third-party contract is concluded where one person, the debtor or promisor, agrees with another, the promisee, to perform an obligation to a third party. Third party contracts are now enforced in most jurisdictions.[1] Under the influence of the Civil Law, they are recognised in the two mixed legal systems of South Africa and Scotland as well as in Article 6:110 PECL.

In the past the doctrine of privity of contract combined with the doctrine of consideration stood in the way of recognition of such contracts in England.[2]

---

1 France: Article 1121 Code Civil; New Zealand: Contracts (Privity) Act 1982; Netherlands: Article 6:254 BW; Queensland: Property Law Act 1974, s 55; USA: Restatement of Contract (Second) s 302; Western Australia: Property Law Act 1969, s 11(2), (3). See further Privity of Contract: Contracts for the Benefit of Third Parties (Law Com Consultation Paper 121, 1991) (henceforth Law Com CP 121) appendix; PECL, vol 1, 322 n 1.
2 *Tweddle v Atkinson* (1861) 1 B & S 393; *Dunlop v Selfridge* [1915] AC 847; *Drive Yourself Hire*

Both mixed legal systems have been contrasted with English law in this respect.[3] If the law in England had continued on this path, it would have been difficult to find the type of common ground that is necessary for a proper comparative analysis. However, English law underwent radical change in 1999 and it now recognises a highly sophisticated third-party contract in terms of a new statute which is the product of a comprehensive comparative investigation of Continental as well as Commonwealth sources.[4] Suddenly the mixed legal systems are playing catch-up. In this contribution the rules on third-party contracts in Scotland, South Africa, PECL and England will be compared from the perspective of a lawyer whose home system is a mixed one.

## B. WHY SHOULD THE LAW ALLOW THIRD-PARTY CONTRACTS TO BE ENFORCED?

According to the principle of privity of contract, a contract may create rights and obligations only for the parties who conclude it. Hence, a person who is not a party to a contract cannot derive rights, duties or contractual remedies from it.[5] A third-party contract negates this principle. The promisor undertakes to the promisee to perform an obligation to the third party and the third party then receives rights by virtue of the contract between promisor and promisee.

---

Co (London) Ltd v Strutt [1954] 1 QB 250 at 272 (criticised (1954) 70 LQR 467); Midland Silicones Ltd v Scrutton Ltd [1962] AC 446, discussed by M P Furmston, "Return to Dunlop v Selfridge?" (1960) 23 Modern LR 373; Beswick v Beswick [1968] AC 58; Woodar Investment Development Ltd v Wimpey Construction (UK) Ltd [1980] 1 WLR 277; R Merkin, Privity of Contract (2000) (henceforth Merkin, Privity), paras 1.25 ff; Law Com CP 121, paras 2.11–2.16; Privity of Contract: Contracts for the Benefit of Third Parties (Law Com No 242, 1996) (henceforth Law Com No 242), paras 2.1–2.7; R Flannigan, "Privity: the end of an era (error)" (1987) 103 LQR 564 at 564–572; Treitel, Contract, 587, 588–590.

3  Alfred McAlpine Construction Ltd v Panatown Ltd [2001] 1 AC 518 (henceforth Panatown) at 527, 534; Carmichael v Carmichael's Executrix 1919 SC 636 (henceforth Carmichael (CS)) at 656; Carmichael v Carmichael's Executrix 1919 SC (HL) 195 (henceforth Carmichael (HL)) at 198; T B Smith, "Jus quaesitum tertio: remedies of the "tertius" in Scottish Law" 1956 JR 3 at 3–4; H L MacQueen, "Third party rights in contract: jus quaesitum tertio", in Reid & Zimmermann, History, vol 2 at 220–221; Tradesmen's Benefit Society v Du Preez (1887) 5 SC 269 (henceforth Tradesmen's Benefit Society) at 276; McCullogh v Fernwood Estate Ltd 1920 AD 204 (henceforth McCullogh) at 206; D-Jay Corporation CC v Investor Management Services (Pty) Ltd 2000 (2) SA 755 (W) at 762; P Sutherland & D Johnston, "Contracts for the benefit of third parties", in Zimmermann, Visser & Reid, Mixed Legal Systems at 208, 211.

4  Contracts (Rights of Third Parties) Act 1999. The Act had a long gestation: see Law Revision Committee Sixth Interim Report (Cmd 5449, 1937); Law Com CP 121, paras 1.1–1.3; Law Com No 242, paras 1.3–1.10; Merkin, Privity, paras 5.7–5.13. Treitel, Contract at 580, 651 stresses that the Act did not reject, but merely created exceptions to, the doctrine of privity of contract.

5  Law Com CP 121, para 1.1.

The principle of privity of contract, at least insofar as it prevents third-party contracts, has been thoroughly discredited.[6] Even in England, where this aspect of the doctrine of privity of contract survived the longest, "[t]he affirmation of privity was effected with at the very least little enthusiasm and in some cases with the utmost reluctance".[7] Third-party contracts are useful in non-commercial transactions and important in commercial relations.[8] Personal and commercial relations are complex and they do not always respect the boundaries of privity of contract. Nevertheless, privity of contract has stunted the development of third-party contracts even in the Civil Law countries,[9] as well as in the mixed legal systems like South Africa and Scotland that have long histories of recognising them. The arguments for privity of contract therefore have to be evaluated in greater detail.

It has been averred that privity of contract has to protect the contracting parties,[10] that contracts are personal and that third parties have no place in enforcing them. But it is impossible to think why contracting parties should not be able to invite a third party into their contract if that is their wish. It will sometimes be difficult to determine when contracting parties intend to create rights for third parties.[11] This may lead to contractual gate-crashing, but the determination of the intention of contracting parties is a general contract law problem that is not more or less acute in this context. There is no reason why the liberal principle of privity of contract should not be trumped by another liberal principle: freedom of contract.[12]

Perhaps there is a further liberal sentiment that informs privity of contract. It may be that privity of contract is aimed at protecting third parties against the consequences of contracts that are concluded between other parties. Contractual liability is created by means of agreement or consent.

---

6 Law Com CP 121, paras 1.2, 2.16, 4.1 ff.

7 Merkin, *Privity*, para 1.34; *Beswick* at 72; *The Pioneer Container* [1994] 2 AC 324 at 335; *Darlington Borough Council v Wiltshier Northern Ltd* [1995] 1 WLR 68 (henceforth *Darlington Borough Council*) at 76; Flannigan (1987) 103 *LQR* 564 at 572 ff (esp the list at 581–582); Law Com No 242, paras 1.1, 2.63 (esp n 163), 2.64–2.69. See Law Com CP 121, para 1.2.

8 *Panatown* (note 3) at 538–539, 544 per Lord Goff; Furmston (1960) 23 *Modern LR* 373 at 376; Law Com No 242, paras 3.9–3.27; McBryde, *Contract*, para 10–02 (with reference to Christie, *Contract*, 3rd edn (1996), 291).

9 SME, vol 15, para 826; *Tradesmen's Benefit Society* (note 3), 272–278; J C De Wet, *Die Ontwikkeling van die Ooreenkoms ten Behoewe van 'n Derde* (Leiden PhD, 1940; henceforth De Wet, *Die Ontwikkeling*), 4–146; L Getz, "Contracts for the benefit of third parties" 1962 *Acta Juridica* 38 at 38–39; De Wet & Van Wyk, *Kontraktereg*, 93–94; Kerr, *Contract*, 88 n 228; Sutherland & Johnston, in Zimmermann, Visser & Reid, *Mixed Legal Systems* at 210–211.

10 See also Treitel, *Contract* at 588.

11 See the minority to the proposals in Law Com CP 121 discussed in Law Com No 242, para 1.7.

12 *Darlington Borough Council* (note 7) at 76; *Panatown* at 544.

Third parties should not be burdened by an agreement concluded between others.[13] Yet, third-party contracts will not offend against this principle because they concern only rights. Perhaps it may be suggested that rights should also not be foisted onto third parties; that third parties might be offended or prejudiced even by the mere acquisition of unwanted rights.[14] But will this ever be the case? Rights may of course have negative tax or other consequences for third parties. However, the automatic acquisition of third-party rights cannot harm a third party if he is allowed to reject rights granted in his favour.[15]

In England it was decided that third-party contracts conflict with the doctrine of valuable consideration. Indeed, the doctrines of privity of contract and valuable consideration have not been clearly separated in the Common Law.[16] However, the doctrine of valuable consideration is a Common Law phenomenon. It is not part of Scots[17] or South African law.[18] Still, third-party contracts and this doctrine are not necessarily incompatible. In the nineteenth century Lord de Villiers, the then Chief Justice of the Cape, was intent on accommodating both the doctrine of consideration and third-party contracts in the law of that colony. He decided that consideration does not have to move from the third party, to allow him to enforce his right against the promisor.[19] The new English Act has adopted a similar approach. Accordingly it has abandoned only this element of the doctrine of valuable consideration.[20]

---

13  *Darlington Borough Council* (note 7) at 76; Law Com CP 121, paras 5.36. 6.17; Law Com No 242, paras 2.1, 2.63, 10.24; Treitel, *Contract* at 580, 588; F R Malan, "Gedagtes oor die beding ten behoewe van 'n derde" (1976) 9 *De Iure* 85 at 85–86 (although he thinks that a normal offer is not made here); J C Sonnekus, "Enkele opmerkings om die beding ten behoewe van 'n derde" 1999 *TSAR* 594 at 598; Sutherland & Johnston, in Zimmermann, Visser & Reid, *Mixed Legal Systems* at 209.

14  *Crookes NO v Watson* 1956 (1) SA 277 (A) (henceforth *Crookes*) at 292; Sonnekus, 1999 *TSAR* 594 at 598.

15  See below text accompanying notes 42–49. See also Contracts (Rights of Third Parties) Act 1999, s 7(1); Law Com CP 121, para 5.39, Law Com No 242 at 12.3; Merkin, *Privity*, para 5.57. In England third party rights will not affect any other rights of the third party.

16  See the cases mentioned above in note 2 as well as *Panatown* (note 3) at 544; Law Com CP 121, paras 2.5–2.10; Law Com No 242, paras 6.3–6.8; Flannigan (1987) 103 *LQR* 564 at 568; Merkin, *Privity*, paras 1.35–1.36, 5.50–5.53; Sutherland & Johnston, in Zimmermann, Visser & Reid, *Mixed Legal Systems* at 211.

17  Smith, 1956 *JR* 3 at 3–5; McBryde, *Contract*, para 2–02, on gratuitous promise. See *Tradesmen's Benefit Society* (note 3) at 275 where this is recognised.

18  *Conradie v Rossouw* 1919 AD 279; Christie, *Contract*, 81.

19  *Tradesmen's Benefit Society* (note 3) at 278; Getz, 1962 *Acta Juridica* 38 at 38. For criticism of this type of approach in England, see Law Com CP 121, para 2.7; Furmston (1960) 23 *Modern LR* 373 at 384; Flannigan (1987) 103 *LQR* 564 at 568. But see Merkin, *Privity*, paras 1.21 ff.

20  Although only by necessary implication (Merkin, *Privity*, para 5.52). Thus, gratuitous promises may not be made unless they form part of third-party contracts (Merkin, *Privity*, para 5.53).

Next, and in some ways related to the first point, it may be said that the tripartite relationships established in terms of third-party contracts are unmanageable and that adequate and clear rules cannot be made in order to address these difficulties.[21] Third-party contracts cannot be recognised without establishing an intricate set of rules for dealing with them. But this area of law is no more convoluted than many others. The benefits of allowing third-party contracts seem to outweigh the disadvantage of creating a relatively complex set of rules.

Once it is realised that there is a need for third-party contracts, the previous argument can succeed only if other legal devices can effectively fulfil the same functions as third-party contracts.[22] In the past, several devices have been used to achieve the same ends as such contracts.[23] However, the evasion of the doctrine of privity of contract for pragmatic reasons often leads to abuse and the skewed development of other legal concepts.[24] Moreover, a legal system that does not recognise a third-party contract will not adequately protect parties who are not able to obtain proper legal advice on how to avoid the principle of privity of contract.[25] Experience in England has shown that other legal phenomena cannot always fill the void left by a strict principle of privity of contract and that the creation of a range of exceptions to it merely causes confusion.

The English Contracts (Rights of Third Parties) Act 1999 is a testimony to the importance of recognising third-party contracts. However, the analysis below points out the problematic areas that will have to be addressed by every law on third-party contracts.


## C. WHEN AND HOW SHOULD A THIRD PARTY ACQUIRE RIGHT OR BENEFIT FROM CONTRACT BETWEEN OTHERS?

Logically, the third party to a true third-party contract should acquire a right directly from the contract between the debtor and promisor,[26] as is the case in

---

21 See the minority that opposed the proposals in Law Com CP 121, discussed in Law Com No 242, para 1.7.
22 See again the minority that opposed the proposals in Law Com CP 121, discussed in Law Com No 242, para 1.7.
23 Law Com CP 121, paras 3.1–3.56; Law Com No 242, paras 2.8–2.62; Merkin, *Privity*, para 1.31, ch 2; Treitel, *Contract* at 626–651.
24 *Swain v The Law Society* [1983] 1 AC 598; *Panatown* (note 3) at 535; Law Com No 242, para 1.8; *Clark Contracts v Burrel Construction* 2003 SLT (Sh Ct) 73 (henceforth *Clark Contracts*), para 37.
25 Law Com CP 121, para 4.4; Law Com No 242, para 1.8.
26 See the three types of contracts distinguished by De Wet, *Ontwikkeling* at 140–141.

England[27] and PECL.[28] In the PECL comments it is stated that the third party will acquire a right only if the promisee notifies him of the benefit.[29] However, this conclusion is not justified by the text of PECL. Such an approach would be illogical and cause grave and unnecessary uncertainty for third parties.

Under the influence of the Roman-Dutch author Hugo Grotius,[30] the South African courts have determined that a third party will acquire a benefit from a contract between others only if he has accepted it.[31] What South Africans call a *stipulatio alteri* is really a complex of two contracts, the contract between the promisee and promisor according to which the promisor agrees with the promisee to keep open an offer to the third party and the second between the promisor and third party which comes into existence when the third party accepts the offer which the promisor has made to him.[32] The South African third-party contract that operates in this manner fits in easily with the ordinary principles of contract law. Many of the general objections to third-party contracts mentioned above are avoided. But J C de Wet correctly criticised this construction for not being a third-party contract at all.[33] The objection to the two-contract approach is not just theoretical. In many situations, acceptance will have to be artificially constructed to allow a third party a claim. The main problem in South Africa is that most courts and commentators, especially De Wet, have viewed the two-contract approach and the true contract for the benefit of a third party as mutually exclusive alternatives. But why should it not be possible for a legal system to accommodate

27  See Contracts (Rights of Third Parties) Act 1999, s 1.
28  Article 6:110(1) PECL.
29  Comment H to Article 6:110 PECL.
30  *De Iure Belli ac Pacis*, II.11.18. See also Grotius, *Introduction to Roman-Dutch Law*, III.3.37, III.3.38.
31  *Tradesmen's Benefit Society* (note 3) at 278; *McCullogh* (note 3) at 206, 215; *Hofer v Kevitt* 1998 (1) SA 382 (SCA) at 386; *Warricker v Liberty Life Association of Africa Ltd* 2003 (6) SA 272 (W), paras 8–10.
32  *Pieterse v Shrosbree* 2005 (1) SA 309 (SCA), para 9; *Kynochs Ltd v Transvaal Silver and Base Metals Ltd* 1922 WLD 71 (henceforth *Kynochs*) at 77; *Gayather v Rajkali* 1947 (4) SA 706 (D) at 708; *George Ruggier and Co v Brook* 1966 (1) SA 17 (N) at 23; R G McKerron, "The juristic nature of contracts for the benefit of third persons" (1929) 46 *SALJ* 387 at 394–396; Joubert, *Contract* at 189; Christie, *Contract* at 308; Sutherland & Johnston, in Zimmermann, Visser & Reid, *Mixed Legal Systems* at 215; Van der Merwe et al, *Contract* at 244–245, 247–251 where the authors accept that there is some authority for this approach although they prefer an alternative explanation for third-party contracts. See *Mpakathi v Kghotso* 2003 (3) SA 429 (W), paras 9–19 where a *stipulatio alteri* was clearly regarded as two contracts.
33  De Wet, *Ontwikkeling* at 152; De Wet & Van Wyk, *Kontraktereg* at 94–97; R Brownsword & D Hutchison, "Beyond promissory principles and protective pragmatism", in P Kincaid (ed), *Privity: Private Justice or Public Regulation* (2001) (henceforth Kincaid, *Privity*) at 133 ff, 141; Sutherland & Johnston, in Zimmermann, Visser & Reid, *Mixed Legal Systems* at 213–214.

both?[34] According to a true third-party contract the third party acquires his right from the valid contract between debtor and promisee. Where the South African two-contract device is intended, the question is whether there was a valid offer by the promisee and acceptance by the third party.[35] Both rights and duties, or burdens, for a third party can be established here.[36] However, from a terminological point of view, it seems strange to call this device a *stipulatio alteri* or third-party contract. It should rather be labelled a third-party option.[37]

In Scotland a third party automatically acquires rights from the *ius quaesitum tertio*.[38] The acquisition of the third party's rights does not depend on his assent.[39] According to Scots law, under the influence of the Institutional Writer Stair, even unilateral promises may be enforced.[40] Hence, it has often been suggested that the foundation of the *ius quaesitum tertio* in Scotland is unilateral promise or *pollicitatio*.[41] But this proposal has not found clear judicial support and is unconvincing. In a system where unilateral promises are recognised, the need for third-party contracts is reduced, but where there is a unilateral promise, there is no need to speak of a "third-party contract". Again a true third-party contract should be regarded as a unique device for creating rights for a third party.[42]

South African and Scots law show that third party contracts are *sui generis*. Attempts to equate them with other more familiar legal phenomena only lead to confusion. Still, Scots law pertinently asks a fundamental question about

---

34 Sutherland & Johnston, in Zimmermann, Visser & Reid, *Mixed Legal Systems* at 215.

35 See Merkin, *Privity*, para 5.22. If the two-contract device is used, it may be possible in South Africa to obtain rights on the basis of reasonable reliance, even if the stipulator did not intend to grant such rights. In the true third-party contract this is inconceivable: see in England Law Com CP 121, para 5.9. Only the reasonable reliance of the contracting parties is relevant.

36 See below, text accompanying notes 58–61.

37 See *Malelane Suikerkorporasie (Edms) Bpk v Streak* 1970 (4) SA 478 (T) at 482 where an analogy with an option was drawn; *Kynochs* (note 32) at 77 where reference was made to a standing offer; McKerron (1929) 46 *SALJ* 387 at 395; M J Oosthuisen, "Die aanspreeklikheid van die maatskappypromotor by voorinlywingskontrakte", 1986 *TSAR* 360 at 363; Kerr, *Contract* at 85–86.

38 Although the third party often acquires a limited right initially: see below, text accompanying notes 101–109.

39 *Finnie v Glasgow and South Western Railway Co* (1857) 3 Macq 75 (henceforth *Finnie*) at 90.

40 McBryde, *Contract*, para 2–02. In Scotland Stair, *Institutions*, 1.10.4, explicitly rejected the opposing view of Grotius.

41 Smith, 1956 *JR* 3 at 16, 21; D I C Ashton Cross, "Bare promise in Scots law" 1957 *JR* 138 at 145–146; D N MacCormick, "*Jus quaesitum tertio*: Stair v Dunedin" 1970 *JR* 228 at 233–234; MacQueen, in Reid & Zimmermann, *History*, vol 2 at 221, 223; SME, vol 15, para 827 (but see para 828).

42 A Rodger, "Molina, Stair and the *jus quaesitum tertio*" 1969 *JR* 34 and 128 (two parts) at 141–144; McBryde, *Contract*, para 10–07; *Finnie* (note 39) at 89–90 per Lord Wensleydale; see Sutherland & Johnston, in Zimmermann, Visser & Reid, *Mixed Legal Systems* at 216–217.

the law of contract. Very few systems recognise unilateral promise while most embrace third-party contracts, but why should a legal system not recognise unilateral promise if it allows two parties to create benefits for third parties?[43]

Although consent of or acceptance by a third party should not be necessary for the creation of a right created in a contract between other parties, such a right should of course not be force-fed to a third party, who should be able to renounce it.[44] The third party's renunciation should cause the right to fall away *ab initio*.[45] This issue is seldom raised in Scotland,[46] but in South Africa even De Wet, who did not regard acceptance as a necessary requirement for establishing rights for third parties, nevertheless stressed that the third party has the power to reject a right created for him by others.[47] This is clearly set out in PECL.[48] The English Act is strangely silent on the matter of rejection but it is inconceivable that renunciation will not be possible in England.[49]

Moreover, there are some difficult questions that will have to be answered with regard to how and when renunciation of rights by third parties should be possible. None of them are answered properly by the legal systems under discussion. In answering these questions, the objective should be to protect the third party who has received an unsolicited right. The risk of uncertainty created by third-party contracts should be on the contracting parties, not the third party.

In which way should it be possible to renounce a right? According to the comments to Article 6:110 PECL, notice of rejection has to be given to the debtor. Formal notice of renunciation of a third-party right provides clear proof of rejection and it is advisable that third parties reject rights contracted in their favour in this manner. But it is doubted whether such formalism should be necessary to enable a third party to rid himself of an unwanted right and whether this statement is justified by the text of PECL.

Should a third party be required to exercise his power of renunciation within a particular or reasonable time, or should he have a continuing power

---

43 Article 2:107 PECL does so. See also Merkin, *Privity*, para 5.22.
44 See also above, text accompanying note 14.
45 In South Africa the Supreme Court of Appeal has apparently attempted to side-step problems of repudiation by an insolvent beneficiary in the law of succession: *Wessels v De Jager* 2000 (4) SA 924 (SCA). But this case has often been criticised.
46 See McBryde, *Contract*, para 10–32; Smith, 1956 *JR* 3 at 15; MacQueen, in Reid & Zimmermann, *History*, vol 2 at 224.
47 De Wet & Van Wyk, *Kontraktereg*, at 104, 108–109.
48 Article 6:110(2) PECL; Comment G.
49 See the discussion of rejection in Law Com No 242, paras 11.6–11.11; Merkin, *Privity*, para 5.62.

to reject the right bargained in his favour? Third parties should lose their powers of renunciation only if they have either accepted rights or have created the impression that they have done so.

Renunciation of a right by the third party may have drastic consequences if there is a quasi-reciprocal relationship between the promisor and promisee in the sense that the promisee has to perform to the promisor in exchange for the latter's performance to the third party. Should rejection be possible in these situations and, if so, what should its effect be on the relationship between the contracting parties?[50] The existence of an element of reciprocity should not deprive a third party of his power to reject the third-party right. In England, although this has not been set out in legislation, the promisee apparently will then be entitled to claim performance from the promisee but will be liable to the promisor; and this may also be the case in Scotland.[51] However, this should be merely the default position. The contracting parties should be allowed to depart from it where performance that was intended for the third party cannot or should not be made to the promisee. In such circumstances the parties will have to agree either that the promisee will no longer be liable to the promisor or that he has to perform despite the termination of the promisor's duty to render performance.

## D. WHAT BENEFITS WILL THIRD PARTIES RECEIVE FROM THIRD-PARTY CONTRACTS?

Only narrowly defined benefits may be granted to third parties in terms of third-party contracts.[52] For simplicity, reference has thus far been made only to the acquisition of rights by third parties but immunities also may be derived from contracts concluded between others.[53] It has been pointed out in England that a contract between A and B according to which A agrees that he will not bring a particular claim against C can also be directly enforced by C even though C does not obtain a right in the true sense in this situation.[54]

The formulation of legislative provisions for dealing with third-party contracts is difficult because benefits may consist of both rights and immunities.

---

50 See Merkin, *Privity*, para 5.62 on the distinction that was previously drawn.

51 Law Com No 242, paras 11.7–11.8; Merkin, *Privity*, para 5.62. See below, text accompanying notes 101–109, on the right of the promisee.

52 Law Com No 242, para 10.24 (although the Contracts (Rights of Third Parties) Act 1999, s 1(1)(a) does not make this clear: see Merkin, *Privity*, para 5.25).

53 SME, vol 15, para 840; McBryde, *Contract*, para 10–10.

54 Merkin, *Privity*, para 5.15; Law Com CP 121, paras 5.17–5.18; Law Com No 242, paras 10.24 ff. See Contracts (Rights of Third Parties) Act 1999, s 1(6) and Merkin, *Privity*, para 5.46.

The new English Act mostly refers to the third party's ability to enforce a "term" in the contract, but this causes uncertainty.[55] It would be more accurate to refer to benefits and then to define that word as rights and immunities, or to speak directly of rights and immunities in the legislation.[56] PECL refers only to the third party's rights.[57] This term is too narrow and is not ideal; but it probably can be interpreted to include immunities.

Duties or other burdens may not be imposed upon third parties in terms of a third-party contract,[58] although a right can be granted subject to a condition that the third party will have to render some performance if he wants to enforce it.[59] The third party will be adequately protected in these situations. The condition cannot be directly enforced, and the third party will be subjected to it only if he intends to take the benefit. However, it may be difficult to determine where the line lies between contracts that impose conditional benefits and ones that lay down duties, especially where drafting is done by laymen.

In South Africa, a third party may become subject to duties in terms of a *stipulatio alteri*. This is the primary advantage of the two-contract approach.[60] Through it, reciprocal contracts may be concluded with third parties. In true third-party contracts, promisees often have to perform duties that are established in exchange for undertakings by debtors to provide third-party benefits. This has led to many conflicts between third parties and promisees in Scotland.[61] The South African two-contract device can be used effectively to prevent many of these conflicts.

---

55  But see Contracts (Rights of Third Parties) Act 1999, s 1(6), which speaks of "benefit".
56  Many of the problems discussed by Merkin, *Privity*, paras 5.30–5.32, 5.47 can be addressed more easily by legislation that is so worded.
57  Article 6:110(1) PECL.
58  This is never stated in the modern legislation because it is too obvious a point: Merkin, *Privity*, paras 4.1, 5.14. See the problems that this principle will cause in cases where reciprocity is required, SME, vol 15, para 830. See above, text accompanying note 14.
59  SME, vol 15, para 830; Contracts (Rights of Third Parties) Act 1999, s 1(4); Law Com CP 121, paras 5.36 ff; Law Com No 242, para 10.25; Merkin, *Privity*, paras 5.43–5.45. See also Contracts (Rights of Third Parties) Act 1999, s 8, on the application of arbitration clauses to the rights obtained by third parties: also *Nisshin Shipping Co Ltd v Cleaves & Co Ltd* [2004] 1 Lloyd's Rep 38.
60  McKerron (1929) 46 *SALJ* 387 at 390, 393–394; Sutherland & Johnston, in Zimmermann, Visser & Reid, *Mixed Legal Systems* at 219; Christie, *Contract* at 305–307; *Crookes* (note 14) at 291 with reference to *Jankelow v Binder Gering and Co* 1927 TPD 364; *Malelane Suikerkorporasie (Edms) Bpk v Streak* 1970 (4) SA 478 (T) at 481–482; *Total South Africa (Pty) Ltd v Bekker* 1992 (1) SA 617 (A) at 625; *Unitrans Freight (Pty) Ltd v Santam Ltd* 2004 (6) SA 21 (SCA), para 14; *Pieterse v Shrosbree* 2005 (1) SA 309 (SCA), para 9 and *Wimbledon Lodge (Pty) Ltd v Gore* 2003 (5) SA 315 (SCA), para 54; Brownsword & Hutchison, in Kincaid, *Privity* at 140; Van der Merwe, *Contract* at 244. See also *Sage Life Ltd v Van der Merwe* 2001 (2) SA 166 (W) at 168.
61  See below, text accompanying notes 101–109.

## E. DIRECT OR INDIRECT BENEFITS FOR THIRD PARTIES

A third party cannot acquire legal remedies from a contract between other parties merely because that contract benefits him.[62] Where A concludes a contract of sale with B, and B in turn agrees with C to sell the same *merx* to C, no direct contractual bond arises between A and C.[63] An agreement between A and B that A may perform the obligation that he owes B to a third party C, called an *adiectus solutionis causa* in South Africa, will cause A to be freed from his obligation to B if he performs to C; but again C will not acquire any right against A in these circumstances.[64]

The third party should obtain legal remedies from a contract between others only if the contracting parties intend it.[65] It may be difficult to determine when contracting parties have this intention. Both PECL[66] and the English Act[67] attempt to address these problems although they are not very successful in doing so. Both determine that a third party will acquire rights if the contract expressly so provides. However, it is difficult to understand why this obvious point needs to be made in a statute.[68] It is also not quite clear when exactly a contract expressly grants a third party a right.

Furthermore, the English Act creates a presumption,[69] that a term purporting to create third-party benefits will be deemed enforceable by the third party, unless "on the proper construction of the contract it appears that the parties did not intend the term to be enforceable by the third party".[70] This

---

62  Law Com CP 121 at para 2.17; Treitel, *Contract* at 653; Gloag, *Contract* at 235, 237; Smith, 1956 *JR* 3 at 8; McBryde, *Contract*, para 10–11; SME, vol 15, para 835; H L MacQueen, "Third party rights in contract: English reform and Scottish concerns" (1997) *Edinburgh LR* 488 at 490–491. See cases listed above at note 60, esp *Sage Life Ltd v Van der Merwe* 2001 (2) SA 166 (W) at 168.

63  Merkin, *Privity*, para 5.33; McBryde, *Contract*, para 10–11. See *Jankelow v Binder Gering and Co* 1927 TPD 364 at 368.

64  *Mondorp Eiendomsagentskap (Edms) Bpk v Kemp en De Beer* 1979 (4) SA 74 (A) at 88; *Barnett v Abe Swersky & Associates* 1986 (4) SA 407 (C) at 411; *Mpakathi v Kghotso* 2003 (3) SA 429 (W), para 14; Christie, *Contract* at 304. See generally on this legal device Lubbe & Murray, *Contract* at 708–709. See also Comment F to Article 6:110 PECL (at 319), and Comment C (at 318); Gloag, *Contract* at 238.

65  Law Com CP 121, paras 2.19, 5.8 ff; Comment F to Article 6:110 PECL (at 319); Gloag, *Contract* at 235; Smith, 1956 *JR* 3 at 7, 10; McBryde, *Contract*, paras 10–10, 10–12; SME, vol 15, para 835; and the South African cases mentioned above at note 60.

66  Article 6:110(1) PECL.

67  Contracts (Rights of Third Parties) Act 1999, s 1(1), (2); Law Com CP 121, paras 5.8–5.15; Law Com No 242, ch 7; Merkin, *Privity*, paras 5.24 ff.

68  See the explanation of Treitel, *Contract* at 652.

69  Merkin, *Privity*, paras 5.27 ff; Law Com No 242, para 7.1.7.

70  Contracts (Rights of Third Parties) Act 1999, s 1(1)(b) read with s 1(2). See *Laemthong International Lines Co Ltd v Artis* [2005] All ER (D) 50; [2005] 1 Lloyd's Rep 100; *Kharegat v Deloitte & Touche LLP* [2004] EWHC 1767 (QB) at para 54; *Nisshin Shipping Co Ltd v Cleaves & Co Ltd* [2004] 1 Lloyd's Rep 38.

presumption may be useful in a system that previously applied a strict principle of privity of contract, such as England; but this type of rule will cause only confusion in jurisdictions that are familiar with third-party contracts.[71]

The PECL rule, that a third party also will acquire a right in his favour if "such an agreement is to be inferred from the purpose of the contract or the circumstances of the case",[72] is preferable to the English one. But this provision is also not perfect. There is perhaps a need to reiterate that third-party contracts can also be tacitly concluded,[73] but it is not quite clear why the determination of whether a tacit third-party contract has been concluded cannot be left to general contract law principles.

All legal systems have sophisticated rules for determining the intention of contracting parties. Ultimately these rules should be applied in deciding whether contracting parties have concluded third-party contracts.[74] Care should be taken to keep third-party contracts within their proper sphere of operation. It is often said that a proper approach to third-party contracts will facilitate claims by delictual claimants who have suffered pure economic loss, such as disappointed beneficiaries,[75] or persons who have made statements on which third parties have relied. However, the scope for the operation of third-party contracts in these situations ought to be narrow. Third-party contracts should not be abused in order to correct deficiencies in the law of delict,[76] although these contracts are important in creating a smooth transition from contract to delict.

## F. WHO WILL ACQUIRE RIGHTS FROM THIRD-PARTY CONTRACTS?

Once it is established that the contracting parties intended a third-party contract, the beneficiary of the contract must be identified. Normally, it will be relatively easy to determine the parties to a contract. After all, the contracting parties actually conclude the contract. This is not true of third party contracts.

---

71 Although a similar provision may be necessary in Scotland where Gloag, *Contract* at 236, has remarked that there is a presumption against third-party contracts; see Sutherland & Johnston, in Zimmermann, Visser & Reid, *Mixed Legal Systems* at 233.

72 Article 6:110(1) PECL.

73 See MacQueen, in Reid & Zimmermann, *History*, vol 2 at 233–234; McBryde, *Contract*, para 10–12; Gloag, *Contract* at 236; Christie, *Contract* at 307.

74 Treitel, *Contract* at 653; Smith, 1956 *JR* 3 at 7, 10; SME, vol 15, para 835.

75 See Law Com CP 121, paras 3.12 ff; SME, vol 15, para 838; Brownsword & Hutchison, in Kincaid, *Privity* at 138; *Ries v Boland Bank PKS Ltd* 2000 (4) SA 955 (C) at 963.

76 Law Com CP 121, paras 1.17 ff.

In England[77] and PECL further guidance is given. Section 1(3) of the Contracts (Rights of Third Parties) Act 1999 determines that "the third party must be expressly identified in the contract by name, as a member of a class or as answering a particular description". This type of provision does not appear to play any useful role and can only serve to confuse matters. The statement in PECL,[78] that the third party need not be identified at the time the agreement is concluded, is sufficient. It has not always been clear in the past in Scotland whether beneficiaries have to be identified in the third-party contract.[79] A plain legislative statement such as the one in PECL may help to settle the matter.

According to all four systems under discussion, it is possible to conclude a third-party contract in favour of a party who does not exist at the time when the contract is concluded. The contract will be valid from the outset but the third party will only acquire a right to claim performance once he comes into existence.[80] In England, South Africa and Scotland, a principal who did not exist at the time when an agent concluded a contract in his favour cannot ratify that contract even once it has come into being.[81] It is accordingly impossible to conclude a pre-incorporation contract as representative for a company that is to be incorporated. Third-party contracts nevertheless may be utilised to achieve the same result,[82] although a reciprocal contract in favour of a company that does not yet exist can only be concluded by utilising the South African two-contract device.[83]

---

77 Law Com CP 121, para 5.19; Law Com No 242, paras 8.1 ff; Merkin, *Privity*, paras 5.33–5.36. See *Kharegat v Deloitte & Touche LLP* [2004] EWHC 1767 (QB), para 54.

78 Article 6:110(1) PECL and Comment D (at 318–319).

79 *Peddie v Brown* (1857) 3 Macq 65 at 70–71; McBryde, *Contract*, paras 10-16–10-19, but see paras 10-18 and 10-19; SME, vol 15, para 833; See also Merkin, *Privity*, paras 5.33 ff; Law Com CP 121, para 5.19. A *stipulatio alteri* in South Africa may be concluded in favour of a class: Van der Merwe, *Contract* at 245.

80 Specifically confirmed in England: see Contracts (Rights of Third Parties) Act 1999, s 1(3). See also Law Com CP 121, paras 5.20, 6.8; Law Com No 242, paras 8.5 ff; Treitel, *Contract*, 655. See also MacQueen, in Reid & Zimmermann, *History*, vol 2 at 249–250; Van der Merwe, *Contract* at 245.

81 The *locus classicus* in this area is *Kelner v Baxter* (1866) LR 2 CP 174, accepted in South Africa in *Nordis Construction Co (Pty) Ltd v Theron Burke & Isaac* 1972 (2) SA 535 (D & CLD); *Heathfield v Maqelepo* 2004 (2) SA 636 (SCA), para 13; and in Scotland in *Tinnevelley Sugar Refining Co Ltd v Mirrlees, Watson and Yaryan Co Ltd* (1894) 21 R 1009.

82 Merkin, *Privity*, para 5.38; Law Com No 242, paras 8.9 ff Most South African cases on third-party contracts concern this issue: see e.g. *McCullogh* (note 3), esp at 208–209; *Wimbledon Lodge (Pty) Ltd v Gore* 2003 (5) SA 315 (SCA), para 59. In Scotland in *Cumming v Quartzag Ltd* 1980 SC 276 at 285 the South African solution was discussed but not correctly understood: see MacQueen (1997) *Edinburgh LR* 488 at 491; H L MacQueen, "Promoters' contracts, agency and the *ius quaesitum tertio*" 1982 *SLT (News)* 257–261; SME, vol 15, para 834 n 8. See also McBryde, *Contract*, para 10–14.

83 *Nine Hundred Umgeni Road (Pty) Ltd v Bali* 1986 (1) SA 1 (A); Sutherland & Johnston, in Zimmermann, Visser & Reid, *Mixed Legal Systems* at 221.

## G. AMENDMENT OR TERMINATION OF THIRD-PARTY BENEFITS WITHOUT THIRD PARTY'S CONSENT

True third-party rights are created by agreement between the contracting parties but the third party is not a party, or at least not an active party, to this contract. The agreement between the promisor and promisee, as such, is an insufficient justification for not allowing variation or termination of the third party's right.[84] Nevertheless, the third party may be prejudiced if his right were to remain in this tenuous state; it will never be safe for him to rely on it. There needs to be a point at which the right of the third party becomes fixed.[85] Of course a contract cannot be fixed to the extent that it is no longer open to any amendment. But the English Act correctly states that the consent of the third party will be necessary once this point has been reached.[86]

The English Act accordingly determines that the contacting parties may agree to vary or rescind rights of the third party, unless the third party relies on those rights.[87] Theoretically this is the ideal cut-off point;[88] but it is often difficult to establish the point in time from when the third party can be taken to have relied reasonably on his rights. For this pragmatic reason the English Act allows the third party also to settle his rights by acceptance.[89] This part of the English Act shows some similarities with the position in South Africa. Before acceptance, the South African promisee and promisor will also be able to vary or rescind the benefits that the third party will receive by agreement between them.[90] However, the role of acceptance in England should not be confused with acceptance of a *stipulatio alteri* as it has been understood in South Africa. In South Africa, acceptance creates the third party right.[91] In the true third-party contract, acceptance merely entrenches it.

The broad approach to variation and rescission in England can be endorsed, but some of the more detailed aspects of this part of the English Act

---

84 Law Com CP 121, paras 5.27 ff

85 MacQueen, in Reid & Zimmermann, *History*, vol 2 at 249, and in (1997) *Edinburgh LR* 488 at 490, speaks of crystallisation.

86 Law Com No 242, paras 9.45–9.47; Merkin, *Privity*, para 5.86.

87 Contracts (Rights of Third Parties) Act 1999, s 2(1)(b), (1)(c). See Lord Salvesen in *Carmichael* (CS) at 636, 649 who focused on intimation.

88 See Getz, 1962 *Acta Juridica* 38 at 50–53, for South Africa.

89 Contracts (Rights of Third Parties) Act 1999, s 2(1)(a); *Precis 521 plc v William M Mercer Ltd* [2005] EWCA Civ 114, para 39 on acceptance of exemption clauses.

90 *Van der Planck v Otto* 1912 AD 353 at 366; *Commissioner for Inland Revenue v Crewe* 1943 AD 656 at 674–675; *Crookes* (note 14) at 285–287; *Cape Produce Co (PE) (Pty) Ltd v Dal Maso* 2001 (2) SA 182 (W) at 188; McKerron (1929) 46 *SALJ* 387 at 389–390. See also Christie, *Contract* at 310 (especially his analysis of the contrary statement in *Commissioner for Inland Revenue v Crewe* 1943 AD 656 at 675).

91 See above, text accompanying note 30.

are open to criticism. Third parties may think that they are already protected if they rely on a third-party contract. They may feel that acceptance and reliance are alternatives and that, accordingly, there will be no need for acceptance once there is reliance. However, acceptance will strengthen the third party's position as the burden of proof will be relaxed.[92] The two mechanisms for fixing third-party rights should not be stated as equal alternatives as is done in England.

Further, the Act requires that assent be communicated to the promisor; but is this notice requirement not too narrow? If the only function of acceptance is to settle the third-party right, it should suffice if it is made to the promisee.[93] Indeed, conflicts in third-party contracts often arise between the promisee and the third party because the promisee causes third-party rights to be rescinded.[94] It may be as important for the promisee to know whether the right can be amended or withdrawn as for the promisor. PECL allows notice to either the promisor or promisee.[95]

Again, the difficulties of determining when a third party relies on the rights created for him by the contracting parties is exacerbated by the wording of the relevant provisions in the English Act. Section 2(1) determines that variation or rescission will no longer be possible where the promisor (1) is aware that the third party has relied on the benefit;[96] or (2) should reasonably have foreseen the reliance and the third party has in fact relied on the benefit.[97] This focuses too much on the state of mind of the promisor. Variation in England will require agreement between the contracting parties.[98] The question whether the third party has acquired a settled right should rather be judged from the perspective of the third party. The right should be regarded as settled if the reliance of the third party is reasonable. The question whether the promisor knew or reasonably should have known that the third party relied on the benefit should be considered in determining whether reliance is reasonable.

At least the English Act is correct in not requiring detrimental reliance.[99] Where the contract for the benefit of the third party creates immunity against any liability that may arise from a particular range of activities, there will be

92 Law Com No 242, paras 9.29, 9.32, 9.36; Merkin, *Privity*, paras 5.75, 5.80, 5.82, 5.85.
93 See De Wet & Van Wyk, *Kontraktereg* at 95; Getz, 1962 *Acta Juridica* 38 at 44.
94 See the Scottish cases cited below, text accompanying notes 101–109. See for England below, text accompanying notes 139–142.
95 Article 6:110(3)(b) PECL.
96 Contracts (Rights of Third Parties) Act 1999, s 2(1)(b).
97 Contracts (Rights of Third Parties) Act 1999, s 2(1)(c).
98 See the reasons for this, Law Com No 242, para 9.27. It may be possible for a promisee to deprive a third party of a claim by bringing a claim himself: see below text accompanying notes 139–142.
99 Merkin, *Privity*, paras 5.75, 5.83.

reliance once the third party, who knows of the immunity, commences activities within the sphere in which he has immunity. It will not be necessary for him to perform an act that would otherwise lead to liability.[100]

In most cases in Scotland the agreement between promisor and promisee will create initially a mere title to sue in favour of the third party.[101] The third party will obtain the claim himself or a settled claim only once the contract has become irrevocable. Irrevocability will be "a condition, not a consequence, of the expression of the *jus* in favour of the third party".[102] It is not quite clear in Scotland what this title to sue means;[103] but it is certain that the promisee will have a stronger claim to performance than the third party, if the promisee decides to claim it. In reality the promisee will deprive the third party of his claim by doing so.[104] A promisee has a similar power in England up to the point where the right becomes settled,[105] although Scots law does not as a general rule allow the promisor and promisee to vary or rescind the right of the third party by agreement as is the case in England.[106] The *ius quaesitum tertio* will become irrevocable on delivery of the document in which the right is set out, or its equivalent.[107] This rule developed in the context of conflicts between promisees and third parties. It has been more or less successful in resolving such disputes, but only because the delivery requirement has been widely interpreted.[108] Scots law correctly distinguishes between the requirements for the third party's right to bring a claim and for the right becoming fixed. Yet the Scottish irrevocability rule seems to be an imperfect tool for fixing rights. The right to sue, which the third party acquires before the *ius quaesitum tertio* becomes irrevocable, is not the type

100  Merkin, *Privity*, para 5.83.
101  *Carmichael* (HL) (note 3) at 197–198; Gloag, *Contract* at 68, 235; see also MacQueen, in Reid & Zimmermann, *History*, vol 2 at 246, 250, and Sutherland & Johnston, in Zimmermann, Visser & Reid, *Mixed Legal Systems* at 223–224. For cases where claims that were allowed without reference to the delivery requirement, see *Carmichael* (HL) (note 3) at 198. See Merkin, *Privity*, para 5.26
102  *Carmichael* (CS) (note 3) at 645–646, 652; *Carmichael* (HL) (note 3) at 200.
103  McBryde, *Contract*, para 10–03.
104  This is not revocation in the strict sense: McBryde, *Contract*, paras 10-27–10-29.
105  See below, text accompanying notes 139–142.
106  See Law Com CP 121, para 5.27 n 50 on the position in Scots law with reference to *Blumer v Scott* (1874) 1 R 379 (although it will be possible to provide for such variation by agreement: see below, text accompanying note 126).
107  See on the delivery requirement *Hill v Hill* (1755) Mor 11580; *Jarvie's Trustee v Jarvie's Trustees* (1887) 14 R 411; *Cameron's Trustees v Cameron* 1907 SC 407; *Carmichael* (CS) (note 3) at 643–647, 653; McBryde, *Contract*, paras 4-07, 4-32–4-44.
108  *Carmichael* (HL) (note 3) at 203 per Lord Dunedin; and see at 205–207 per Lord Shaw of Dunfermline; *Allan's Trustees v Lord Advocate* 1971 SC (HL) 45; Gloag, *Contract* at 68–69; SME, vol 15, paras 829–830; Sutherland & Johnston, in Zimmermann, Visser & Reid, *Mixed Legal Systems* at 228–229.

of strong right that is normally established by a third-party contract. Pretending that the cut-off point is determined with reference to delivery merely draws attention away from what should actually be the cut-off point, namely the reliance of the third party.[109]

PECL agrees with Scots law and differs from English law. It allows the promisee unilaterally to withdraw the right granted to the third party before the cut-off point,[110] unless the former has agreed with the third party not to do so.[111] In the comments to PECL it is stated that the contracting parties may agree to amend or revoke the third party's right.[112] But this statement is not borne out by the text of PECL, and is not well thought through. For instance, it does not state until when this power will exist.

Nevertheless, there are important differences between PECL and Scots law. Revocation will no longer be possible if the third party has given notice of acceptance to either the promisor or promisee.[113] As in England, acceptance will stabilise the third party's right. But, in distinction from England, the right will become irrevocable only on that basis and notice of acceptance can be given to either the promisor or promisee.[114] The English approach seems preferable on the first issue, and the stance taken in PECL seems better on the second.

Under PECL the revocation will require notice to the promisor.[115] In the comments it is stated that acceptance need not be express;[116] but it is not stated how this will relate to the notice requirement in PECL. It is understandable that notice to the promisor is required. The promisor should know whether and to whom he should perform; but it may be asked whether the third party cannot also expect to receive such notice, especially because the reliance of the third party is not protected in PECL.

Moreover, PECL provides specifically[117] that the promisee may settle the third party's right by notifying the third party accordingly. The notice requirement is probably intended to ensure that the third party will know

---

109 The Scottish Law Commission has proposed that the delivery requirement be abandoned: Constitution and Proof of Voluntary Obligations: Stipulations in Favour of Third Parties (Scot Law Com Memorandum No 38, 1977), para 36. But something should be put in its place: see also the criticism of McBryde, *Contract*, para 4-36; and MacQueen (1997) 1 *Edinburgh LR* 488 at 490.

110 Article 6:110(3) PECL.

111 Comment H (at 321).

112 Comment H (at 320).

113 Article 6:110(3)(b) PECL.

114 See above, text accompanying notes 87–95.

115 Article 6:110(3) PECL; Comment G (at 320).

116 Comment G (at 321). See also J Kerr Wylie, "Contracts in favour of third parties" (1943) 7 *THRHR* 94 at 115, criticised by Getz, 1962 *Acta Juridica* 38 at 48.

117 Article 6:110(3)(a) PECL.

when to protect himself by giving notice of acceptance himself. But why should the third party not receive protection from variation even without notice?

Of course contracting parties should be allowed to depart from these regimes. The English Act makes clear that the rules regarding variation and rescission are merely default rules.[118] The contracting parties may by their agreement be given a power to rescind or vary rights of the third party even in situations where the third party's benefit would otherwise have been settled in terms of section 2(1). The promisee may be given the power to change the beneficiary of the third-party benefit or to alter its terms.[119] The agreement may allow variation or rescission only with the consent of the third party in situations where it would not be required in terms of section 2(1).

The English Act does not expressly provide that unilateral powers of rescission and variation may be given to the promisor or promisee by the contract, but the drafters thought that the Act implicitly allows for it.[120] Finally, the English Act grants the court power to allow the variation of third-party rights without that party's consent, even beyond the cut-off point.[121] It is doubtful whether there is a need for such a provision, but if there is, then the wording of the English Act is problematic.

The general rules on revocation in Scotland,[122] South Africa[123] and PECL[124] also merely reflect the default position. In South Africa, for instance, a promisee may be given the power to rescind a third-party right after acceptance by that party, although acceptance by the third party establishes a separate contract between debtor and third party.[125] In Scotland a provision in the contract may grant powers of variation that go beyond, or are narrower than, those that will normally exist for the promisee.[126] In the comments to PECL[127] it is stated that the agreement may permit the promisee to rescind or amend third party rights beyond the cut-off point established by it.

---

118  Contracts (Rights of Third Parties) Act 1999, s 2(3); Merkin, *Privity*, paras 5.76–5.77.
119  Treitel, *Contract* at 659.
120  Merkin, *Privity*, para 5.77 (although problems may arise with the application of s 2(4), (5)).
121  Contracts (Rights of Third Parties) Act 1999, s 2(4)-2(5); Merkin, *Privity*, paras 5.87–5.93; Law Com CP 121, paras 5.32–5.33.
122  See the suggestion in *Carmichael* (CS) (note 3) at 653 per Lord Gurthrie, at 654–655 per Lord Skerrington; J T Cameron, *"Jus quaesitum tertio*: the true meaning of Stair, I.x.5" 1961 *JR* 103 at 116–117; McBryde, *Contract*, para 10-03.
123  Sutherland & Johnston, in Zimmermann, Visser & Reid, *Mixed Legal Systems* at 227–228, 230–232.
124  Although this issue is not dealt with expressly in PECL.
125  On how the connection between the contracts is made, see below, text accompanying note 161.
126  *Love v Amalgamated Society of Lithographic Printers of Great Britain and Ireland* 1912 SC 1078 at 1082; *Carmichael* (CS) (note 3) at 659; McBryde, *Contract*, paras 10-27–10-29; SME, vol 15, para 830; MacQueen (1997) *Edinburgh LR* 488 at 490.
127  Comment H (at 321).

## H. REMEDIES FOR ENFORCEMENT OF THIRD PARTY RIGHTS

The third party acquires rights from the third-party contract. Where the promisor does not adequately perform his duties in terms of the third-party contract, the third party will have the remedies for breach of contract that are ordinarily available to a contracting party.[128] In Scotland it was initially decided that a third party was not able to claim damages but this view apparently no longer holds true.[129] The English Act, correctly, states that the third party should not be able to cancel the contract or make use of restitutionary remedies.[130] The same principle should apply in Scotland and in terms of PECL. The South African two-contract approach calls for somewhat different rules. There acceptance by the third party brings into being a separate contract with the debtor. Often this contract will be reciprocal.[131] The third party should be able to cancel the contract for breach by the debtor in the usual manner.

As an alternative to a contract for the benefit of a third party, the law simply might allow the promisee to enforce a benefit in favour of a third party. Nevertheless, the English Law Commission has shown convincingly that this does not provide adequate protection to a third party. There is a need to grant direct rights to the third party.[132] The more complex question which then remains is whether the promisee should *also* be allowed to enforce third-party benefits.

Unless otherwise agreed, the promisee should indeed have such additional right against the promisor to force him to perform to the third party.[133] In South Africa the third party acquires no rights against the promisor before acceptance. The promisee is therefore the custodian of the third party's interests before acceptance, and is able to interdict the promisor against doing anything that would undermine the third party's benefit.[134] There are conflicting authorities in South Africa on whether the promisee can enforce a claim on behalf of a third party.[135] However, there is no reason why he should

---

128 Contracts (Rights of Third Parties) Act 1999, s 1(5). Treitel, *Contract* at 656, calls this a fiction.
129 Especially *Scott Lithgow Ltd v GEC Electrical Projects Ltd* 1989 SC 412 at 438; MacQueen, in Reid & Zimmermann, *History*, vol 2 at 233; SME, vol 15, para 837; Smith, 1956 *JR* 3 at 16–19; MacQueen (1997) *Edinburgh LR* 488 at 492–493.
130 See Merkin, *Privity*, para 5.49, and Law Com No 242, para 3.33(i), and the Law Commission's interpretation of s 1(5).
131 See above, text accompanying notes 30–37, 60–61, on the two-contract approach.
132 Law Com CP 121, para 5.3; Law Com No 242, para 5.12; Merkin, *Privity*, para 5.8.
133 Article 6:110 PECL, Comment E (at 319).
134 Sutherland & Johnston, in Zimmermann, Visser & Reid, *Mixed Legal Systems* at 219–220.
135 *African Universal Stores Ltd v Dean* 1926 CPD 390 at 395; *Gardner v Richardt* 1974 (3) SA 768 (C) at 770; *Cape Produce Co (PE) (Pty) Ltd v Dal Maso* 2001 (2) SA 182 (W) 189; McKerron

not be allowed to bring such a claim, especially where he has some interest in the performance. In other legal systems recognising true third-party contracts, the third party acquires rights directly under these contracts but the promisees will also be able to sue the promisor to perform to the third party.[136]

The next, and more controversial, question is whether the promisee should be allowed to sue the debtor to render the promised performance to him. In terms of the two-contract approach, this is not possible in South Africa, unless the parties have agreed differently. The true third-party contract introduced by PECL also does not allow it.[137] In Scotland the promisee will be able to claim performance before the *ius quaesitum tertio* becomes irrevocable. There appear to be good policy reasons for this approach.[138] The Law Commission in England similarly proposed that the "promisor's duty to perform is owed both to the third party and the contractual promisee";[139] but that performance to the third party should free the promisor from performance to the promisee. The Commission further stated that the debtor should be allowed to perform to the promisee, with the promisee being allowed to claim performance; and that there should be no priority of actions. The Commission also expressed the view that performance could only be made to the promisee up to the point when the third party's rights become settled.[140]

This broad approach is sophisticated and sensible. However, it will also cause difficulties. The English promisee, like his Scottish counterpart, will be able to deprive the third party of the benefit by claiming the right himself before it becomes settled. However, the English Act does not determine how

---

(1929) 46 *SALJ* 387 at 391–392; Christie, *Contract* at 309 regards an interdict as the appropriate remedy. De Wet & Van Wyk, *Kontraktereg* at 98, and D B Hutchison, "Unravelling the *stipulatio alteri*" (1974) 3 *Responsa Meridiana* 1 at 7, accept that the promisee will be able to force the promisor to perform to the third party, albeit not without the latter's co-operation.

136  Article 6:110 PECL, Comment E (at 319). It is suggested at 320 that the promisee will have to enforce the third-party right before he receives notice of it from the promisee but there is no justification for this interpretation: see above, text accompanying note 29. The Contracts (Rights of Third Parties) Act 1999 clearly foresees an important role for promisees within third-party contracts: see Merkin, *Privity*, para 5.60. See also the comment in Law Com No 242 at paras 11.1–11.10, 11.20–11.22.

137  Article 6:110 PECL, Comment E (at 319); but see Comment G where it is wrongly suggested that the promisee will be able to claim performance for himself before notice is given to the third party. This is not borne out by the PECL text. See the argument in South Africa in *Bursey v Bursey* 1997 (4) All SA 580 (E) at 592.

138  Sutherland & Johnston, in Zimmermann, Visser & Reid, *Mixed Legal Systems* at 228–229.

139  Law Com CP 121, para 5.34.

140  Law Com CP 121, para 5.34; Law Com No 242, paras 5.18, 11.1–11.4, 11.5–11.6, 11.11–11.15; Merkin, *Privity*, paras 5.58–5.60.

disputes between promisees and third parties should be resolved.[141] In Scotland it is quite clear that the promisee holds the trump card before the third party obtains an irrevocable right. The Law Commission did not regard it as necessary to have this complex set of rules set out explicitly in legislation; but it is impossible to see how they can be discerned from the common law and the broad provisions of the Act.[142]

Finally, it can be asked whether or to what extent the promisee can claim damages from the promisor for breach of his duty to the third party. When the privity of contract doctrine held sway in England, the promisee was sometimes allowed to claim for losses of a third party. The rules concerning these claims are sophisticated if somewhat muddled.[143] These rules in some ways were intended to resolve problems that arose because the common law did not allow third-party contracts. But, even after the coming into effect of the new Act, their continued application to cases where only third parties benefit from a contract but where, nonetheless, no third-party contract has come into existence, can be justified. Lord Clyde in *Panatown* has commented that "the doctrine of privity of contract … excludes the ready development of a solution along the lines of the *ius quaesitum tertio*".[144] But this statement should not be understood as meaning that there would not be a need for acknowledging such claims in legal systems that recognise third-party contracts.[145] Thus, they have also been applied in Scotland.[146] Otherwise, a substantial claim for damages might conceivably disappear down a "legal black hole",[147] although it has been correctly remarked that the black hole problem is reduced in countries like Scotland (and for that matter South Africa) where, unlike in England, specific implement is recognised as the primary

---

141  Law Com No 242, para 11.14; Merkin, *Privity*, paras 5.73–5.74, although Law Com CP 121, para 5.34, suggests that the third party should be given preference.

142  Reliance is probably placed on Contracts (Rights of Third Parties) Act 1999, s 4, see below, text accompanying note 154.

143  Especially *Linden Gardens Trust Ltd v Lenesta Sludge Disposal Ltd* [1994] 1 AC 85; *Panatown* (note 3), where the judges were unanimous on this point but disagreed on the exact rules to be applied here: Lord Clyde at 529 ff follows a narrow approach but Lords Jauncey, Goff, Millett and, more reluctantly, Lord Browne-Wilkinson take a wider view of the bases for such claims; Law Com CP 121, paras 3.39–3.44; Law Com No 242, paras 2.37–2.51, 5.15; Merkin, *Privity*, paras 1.34, 2.9–2.15, 5.1, 5.3; Treitel, *Contract* at 592–603.

144  *Panatown* (note 3) at 534.

145  *Panatown* (note 3) at 535. See also the Scottish case of *Clark Contracts*, at paras 31, 36–38.

146  *McLaren Murdoch & Hamilton Ltd v The Abercromby Motor Group Ltd* 2003 SCLR 323 (henceforth *McLaren Murdoch*) at paras 33–42, rejecting Lord Clyde's suggestion in *Panatown* (above text accompanying note 144) but otherwise accepting his approach. Compare the more conservative approach followed in *Clark Contracts* (note 24) at paras 23–30.

147  *Panatown* (note 3) at 529 per Lord Clyde; *McLaren Murdoch* (note 146) at paras 33, 42.

remedy for breach of contract.[148] So the more difficult question is whether these rules should apply to allow a promisee to claim damages that only the third party will suffer in cases where a true third-party contract has been concluded. The English Law Commission wanted to leave this issue to the courts and the common law.[149] The judgments of the majority in *Panatown*, decided after the Law Commission's report was published, but relating to a contract concluded before the coming into force of the Contracts (Rights of Third Parties) Act 1999,[150] are to the effect that a person will not be able to claim the damages suffered by another person if that person has a right to claim them himself.[151] This approach implies that a promisee in a true third-party contract would not, without more, be able to rely on *Panatown* in claiming damages suffered by the third party. This is how the *Panatown* case has been understood in Scotland.[152] Logically the promisee should only be allowed to claim for his actual loss. This point is made clearly in the commentary to PECL,[153] albeit not in the proposed rules themselves. The same logic should apply to a promisee in terms of the two-contract approach in South Africa.[154]

However, the English Act has complicated matters. The proposal of the Law Commission has been given statutory effect by section 4. It determines that the Act does not "affect any right of the promisee to enforce any term of the contract". This provision suggests that the third party's claim will have to be ignored in determining whether the promisee can claim damages. However, it would have been better to abandon the idea of indirect claims for damages where a third party has a claim in terms of the Act. At least the Act tries to protect promisors against double jeopardy in these situations.[155] However, these types of damages claims unnecessarily complicate matters,[156] and the third party may be left without indemnification where the promisee claims damages but for some reason is unable to pay them over to the third party.[157]

---

148  *McLaren Murdoch* (note 146) at para 40.
149  Law Com No 242, paras 5.12–5.18 (esp the reasons for this approach at para 5.15); Merkin, *Privity*, paras 5.59–5.60. See also the original suggestion, Law Com CP 121, para 5.34
150  *Panatown* (note 3) at 535, 543, 544, 551–552.
151  *Panatown* (note 3) at 531–532 at 536 per Lord Clyde; at 566–568, 574–575 per Lord Jauncey; at 577–578 per Lord Browne-Wilkinson; and apparently per Lord Millett at 584, 593–595; but see Lord Goff, esp at 551–552.
152  *McLaren Murdoch* (note 146) at para 42; *Clark Contracts* (note 24) at paras 31, 39–41.
153  This is also the implication of Article 6:110 PECL, Comment E (at 319).
154  *African Universal Stores Ltd v Dean* 1926 CPD 390 at 396; *Bagradi v Cavendish Transport Co (Pty) Ltd* 1957 (1) SA 663 (D) at 668; Kerr, *Contract* at 90.
155  Contracts (Rights of Third Parties) Act 1999, s 5(a); Law Com No 242, para 11.17; Merkin, *Privity*, paras 5.68, 5.70–5.72.
156  *Panatown* (note 3) at 534 per Lord Clyde.
157  Merkin, *Privity*, paras 5.68, 5.72.

Moreover, there is a possibility of double jeopardy where the promisee claims such damages, even if he is able to claim only his own loss. Where the promisee is obliged to indemnify the third party, for example in terms of a contract between them, the loss to the third party because of the promisor's breach will also be a loss to the promisee.[158] Where the promisee claims damages and pays, or is able to pay, damages to the third party, the third party has suffered no loss. But what happens if the promisee claims damages and thereafter fails to perform to the third party? In England, the Act explicitly avoids double jeopardy in these situations by placing the risk of ultimate loss on the third party.[159] PECL does not explicitly provide for this situation.

## I. HOW DO EVENTS THAT NORMALLY AFFECT ENFORCEMENT OF CONTRACTUAL PROVISIONS IMPACT ON RIGHTS OF THE THIRD PARTY?

A host of events may affect the validity or enforceability of obligations in a contract. It may be difficult to determine how such events impact on third-party rights.

In South Africa the two-contract approach implies that the offer, which the third party accepts, will stand separately from the original contract between the promisor and promisee.[160] The contract concluded with the third party may be valid despite the invalidity of the previous contract. All that is required is that the offer made by the promisor must be able to form the basis of a valid contract, once it has been accepted by the third party. In many cases, the invalidity of the first contract will merely deprive the third party of protection before acceptance. Acceptance by the third party will be ineffective only if the defect in the first contract also taints the offer made by the promisor. This will, for instance, be the case where the promisor is of unsound mind and therefore incapable of concluding a contract with the promisee or making an offer to the third party.

The parties to the underlying contract may create a link with the third-party contract.[161] They determine the terms of the offer that is made to the

---

158  See Article 6:110 PECL, Comment A (at 318).

159  Contracts (Rights of Third Parties) Act 1999, s 5(b); Law Com No 242, paras 11.18–11.19; Merkin, *Privity*, paras 5.69–5.72.

160  See *Ackermann v Burland and Milunsky* 1944 WLD 172, where the promisee could rescind a contract induced by the promisor's fraud: see Christie, *Contract* at 310. See on the consequences of cancellation for breach Kerr, *Contract* at 92. *Mpakathi v Kghotso* 2003 (3) SA 429 (W) at paras 17–19, is not entirely persuasive, although it illustrates the point to some extent.

161  Kerr, *Contract* at 93.

third party. If that offer is to the effect that the third-party contract will be void or will fall away if the underlying contract fails for a particular reason, the second contract will be subject to a resolutive condition that will make its existence subject to that of the first contract.

The two-contract approach is important in determining which part of a third-party contract has to comply with any formalities imposed by the law. Where the ultimate contract between the third party and promisee has to comply with formalities, it will be valid if the offer to the third party and acceptance by him comply with the formalities even if the contract between the promisor and promisee does not.[162]

In a true third-party contract, the relationship between the rights of the third party and the contract from which they derive will be more intricate.[163] It may be proposed that a third party should be isolated from failures of the third-party contract. But there are stronger policy reasons for not doing so. In the English Law Commission's consultation paper on third-party contracts, it was contended that the third party should be in the same position as an assignee,[164] but it was convincingly concluded in their final report that this is a dangerous analogy.[165] The third party receives a benefit that derives from a particular contract. Its existence and enforceability should depend on the continued validity[166] and enforceability of the contract, and should be determined in the context of that contract.[167] Like any normal contracting party, the third party should be conscious of this. Even the acceptance of the third party should not be able to change the position, as a separate second contract will not be created through it.

It is surprising that this topic is not addressed in PECL, but the difficulties with legislating for these situations are illustrated by the English Act. It determines that a promisor, confronted by a third party who tries to enforce a term in the contract, will have available to him by way of defence[168] or set-off any matter that (1) applies to the term[169] and arises from the contract; and

---

162  *Kynochs* (note 32) at 77; Malan (1976) 9 *De Iure* 85 at 88. See *Trever Investments v Friedhelm* 1982 (1) SA 7 (A), although this case was not expressly decided on the basis that the contract constituted a *stipulatio alteri*.

163  See *Goodwood Racecourse Ltd v Satellite Information Services Ltd* 2004 EWHC 2346 (Ch) at paras 41–42, on rectification of a third-party contract.

164  Law Com CP 121, para 5.24.

165  Law Com No 242, paras 10.8–10.16; Merkin, *Privity*, para 5.94.

166  Law Com CP 121, para 5.1; Law Com No 242, paras 10.1 (n 1), 10.4; Merkin, *Privity*, para 5.96.

167  Law Com No 242, paras 10.13–10.15. See for Scotland McBryde, *Contract*, para 10–09; SME, vol 15, para 839.

168  See how the defence is defined by Law Com No 242, para 10.2.

169  See on this phrase Law Com No 242, para 10.11; Merkin, *Privity*, para 5.97.

(2) would have been available against the promisee.[170] Moreover, it states that the promisor will have available by way of defence, set-off or counterclaim any matter that would have been available against the third party if that third party had been a party to the contract.[171]

It is not quite clear from the wording whether a personal defence against the promisee, such as estoppel, can be maintained against the third party.[172] The Act merely states that the defence must relate to the term that provides the third-party right; but this requirement does not produce a clear answer to the problem. Although it may be difficult to determine what a personal remedy is, the issue cannot be avoided. Defences that are personal to the promisee should not be available against the third party, and legislation on third-party contracts should make this clear.

The English Act correctly implies that a third party's right will fall away if the contract is cancelled by one of the contracting parties for breach by the other.[173] This may be a trap for unwary third parties. A third party may feel hard done by if the right, though it can no longer be varied by the contracting parties, is lost because one of the contracting parties has cancelled the contract due to breach of the other. However, the third party will not be entirely unprotected in these situations. He should be able to claim damages in contract from the promisor where the contract is cancelled because of his breach, and in delict (unless there is a specific contract between the promisee and third party[174]) from the promisee where the promisee's breach caused the termination of the contract.

Where the promisor has to perform the duty to the third party in exchange for performance by the promisee, it should be possible for the promisor to withhold performance to the third party until he has received counter-performance. This is the implication of the English Act and the law will probably be no different in terms of PECL. But can the third party force the promisee to perform to enable him to claim performance from the promisor? Perhaps the answer should be no, but then the promisor and promisee

---

170 Contracts (Rights of Third Parties) Act 1999, s 3(2), (3).
171 Contracts (Rights of Third Parties) Act 1999, s 3(4); Law Com No 242, paras 10.17–10.21; Merkin, *Privity*, para 5.103. The counterclaim would have to concern a matter not arising from the contract.
172 See the discussion and criticism in Merkin, *Privity*, paras 5.100–5.101; Law Com No 242, para 10.2; and the distinction that is drawn here.
173 See similarly in South Africa *Bagradi v Cavendish Transport Co (Pty) Ltd* 1957 (1) SA 663 (D) at 668; Christie, *Contract* at 311.
174 Compare Article 6:110 PECL, Comment H (at 321).

should not be allowed to use reciprocity as an instrument to defeat the rights of the third party.[175]

The contracting parties should be able to extend the defences which the promisor will have against the third party. The English Act determines that the promisor will have as a defence, or a right of set-off, any matter which the contract expressly provides should be available against the third party and which would have been available against the promisee.[176] This provision places an important limitation on agreements that extend the promisor's defences. They must be expressly set out in the third-party contract. There are good policy reasons for such a requirement since it allows third parties to determine the limits of their benefits. However, the second requirement, namely that the defence should be available against the promisee, creates problems because contrary to the wording of the provision but in line with the intention of the legislator the parties can also provide for defences against the third party that are not available against the promisee.

Conversely, it is conceivable that the parties may want to create rights for the third party that are not subject to the failures and limits of the contract, and the English Act allows for this, but only by express term.[177] Furthermore, there are limits to the efficacy of these clauses. If the exclusion provision itself is affected by the defect in the contract, for instance where the contract is rescinded for misrepresentation, or undue influence, the right of the third party will also be so affected.

## J. CONCLUSION

The South African *stipulatio alteri* is not a third-party contract at all. In South Africa there is a need for a true third-party contract alongside what is currently so described. Scots law has a true third-party contract but has been plagued by the delivery requirement. Legislative reforms along the lines of the English Act or PECL will be useful in both jurisdictions. Nevertheless, existing rules in the mixed legal systems should not simply be jettisoned. The South African two-contract option can be utilised fruitfully in the other legal systems under discussion. In several respects the Scots law on third-party contracts is very refined. Both mixed legal systems raise important issues that

---

175 Sutherland & Johnston, in Zimmermann, Visser & Reid, *Mixed Legal Systems* at 218.
176 Contracts (Rights of Third Parties) Act 1999, s 3(3); Law Com No 242, para 10.15; Merkin, *Privity*, para 5.102.
177 Contracts (Rights of Third Parties) Act 1999, s 3(5). Law Com No 242, paras 10.13–10.16; Merkin, *Privity*, para 5.99.

improve the overall understanding of these contracts.

The legal systems under discussion are far from homogenous when it comes to third-party contracts. However, they are not as far removed from one another as may appear at first glance. Similar trends, difficulties and policy problems can be discerned in all of them. The new English Act has erased many of the differences between the Common and the Civil laws, but cultural and, to a lesser extent, historical differences between the different legal families are still apparent.

Scotland and South Africa, the two mixed legal systems, require legislative reform, in the English style but without some of the odd rules that are the legacy of the English doctrine of privity of contract. PECL should be important in establishing the best sets of rules for these systems.

# 9 Payment

## Charl Hugo

A. INTRODUCTION
B. FORM AND MANNER OF PAYMENT
(1) South African and Scots law
(2) PECL compared to South African and Scots law
(3) Conclusion
C. PAYMENT BY THIRD PARTY
(1) Introduction
(2) South African law
(3) Scots (and some English) law
(4) PECL compared to South African and Scots law
(5) Conclusion
D. FINAL REMARKS

## A. INTRODUCTION

Chapter 7 of PECL deals with the performance of obligations. The focus of this contribution is on the performance of a particular type of obligation, namely the obligation to pay money, or, in other words, on payment.[1] Two questions relating to payment dealt with in PECL are considered here in comparative perspective namely: (1) the form and manner of payment; and (2) payment by a third party.[2]

---

1 This innocent-looking and apparently simple definition should be approached with care. It contains terms such as "performance" and "money" both of which are anything but simple. See, e.g., R M Goode, *Commercial Law*, 2nd edn (1995), 489 on "money", and J E du Plessis "Die regsaard van prestasie" (2002) 65 *THRHR* 59 on "performance". See also on the meaning of "money" and "payment" McBryde, *Contract*, paras 24-01, 24-07.
2 PECL deals with a number of further topics relevant to payment namely: (1) the place of performance (or payment) (Article 7:101 PECL); (2) the time of performance (Article 7:102 PECL); (3) early performance (Article 7:103 PECL); (4) currency of payment (Article 7:108 PECL); (5) appropriation of performance (Article 7:109 PECL); and (6) money not accepted (Article 7:111 PECL). The other provisions of Chapter 7 PECL relate mainly to other types of performance.

## B. FORM AND MANNER OF PAYMENT

### (1) South African and Scots law

The point of departure in both South African and Scots law is that payment must be in legal tender, i.e. notes and coins.[3] The amount that the creditor is compelled to accept in coin is, however, statutorily limited.[4] A creditor may reject payment in foreign currency unless otherwise agreed in the contract.[5] Despite being widely accepted in Scotland, Scottish bank notes are not legal tender, whether in Scotland or elsewhere in the United Kingdom.[6] They are promissory notes widely accepted and negotiated.[7]

Payment in cash, however, is very often unpractical and unusual. Various other manners of payment have developed in the course of time such as payment by cheque, credit card, and, mainly for payments in international contracts, letters of credit.[8] Due to the widespread use of such alternative methods of payment it is somewhat divorced from reality to regard them as the exception and legal tender or money as the rule.[9] Especially as regards payment by cheque, the South African courts have developed guidelines to prevent the embarrassment of debtors intending to pay in this way. As early as 1917 De Villiers JP stated as follows in *Schneider and London v Chapman*:

> Now it can be said at once that generally speaking … the tendering of a cheque is not payment. But having regard to the course of commercial dealings in the modern world, which is so very different from what it used to be two or three hundred years ago, the Court will not require very strong evidence to show that the parties in the particular transaction contemplated that payment might be made by cheque.[10]

3 On South African law see *B & H Engineering v First National Bank of SA Ltd* 1995 (2) SA 279 (A) (henceforth *B & H Engineering*) at 285G; Van der Merwe et al, *Contract*, 484, 486; F R Malan & J T Pretorius (assisted by S F du Toit), *Malan on Bills of Exchange, Cheques and Promissory Notes* 4th edn (2002) (henceforth Malan & Pretorius, *Bills of Exchange*), paras 40, 188. On Scots law see *Glasgow Pavilion Ltd v Motherwell* (1903) 6 F 116 at 119; Walker, *Principles*, vol 2, 140; McBryde, *Contract*, para 24–08; Gloag, *Contract*, 709.

4 See s 17(2) of the South African Reserve Bank Act, 90 of 1989. For a summary of the Scottish legislation in this regard see Walker, *Principles of Scottish Private Law*, 4th edn (1989) (henceforth Walker, *Principles*), vol 2, 140 n 85. See also Walker, *Contract*, para 31.30.

5 Van der Merwe et al, *Contract*, 484 n 16. The currency in which the debt must be paid is that of the *locus solutionis*. See *Joffe v African Life Assurance Society Ltd* 1933 TPD 189 at 195. Scots law appears to be the same; see McBryde, *Contract*, para 24–03 n 19.

6 Walker, *Principles*, vol 2, 140 n 85; McBryde, *Contract*, para 24–08.

7 *Leggat Brothers v Gray* 1908 SC 67 (henceforth *Leggat Brothers*) at 74; Walker, *Contract*, para 31.30.

8 For an overview of the development of methods of payment see C Visser, "The evolution of electronic payment systems" (1989) 1 SA *Merc LJ* 189 at 189–191.

9 Christie, *Contract*, 469 regards it as "almost an anachronism".

10 1917 TPD 497 at 500.

Factors that will assist a court to determine whether it is competent for a creditor in a particular transaction to reject payment by cheque, include the previous transactions between the parties, the purpose for which the cheque has been rejected, and whether the creditor has given a reasonable warning to the debtor that he will not accept payment by cheque.[11] Similarly, in Scots law, an authorisation of payment in a common form such as a cheque or Scottish bank notes "may easily be implied".[12]

The precise effect of giving a cheque in payment has received considerable attention in South African law. In *Gordon v Tarnow* it was regarded as "a conditional payment of the rent", the effect of which was "to suspend the respondent's right of action, not to extinguish the debt."[13] The most recent authoritative pronouncement on this matter is probably that of Grosskopf JA in *B & H Engineering v First National Bank of SA Ltd*:

> The giving of a cheque is normally intended, not to novate the debt for which it was given, but to discharge it by payment. Since the creditor only receives his money under the cheque when the drawee bank pays it, commercial sense requires that the underlying debt should continue in existence until the creditor actually receives the money. On the other hand, the creditor, having accepted a cheque, must normally defer action on his antecedent debt to allow the cheque to be met.[14]

Thus, when a debt is paid by giving a cheque, there are two obligations that co-exist. The original or underlying debt (which is the *causa* for the cheque) is suspended until the cheque is either honoured or dishonoured. If it is honoured, the original debt is discharged; if it is dishonoured the original debt is no longer suspended and may be enforced. There is no novation,[15] at least not as a rule.[16] Despite some early academic criticism,[17] this must now be regarded as settled law in South Africa.

---

11  Van der Merwe et al, *Contract*, 486; *Esterhuyse v Selection Cartage (Pty) Ltd* 1965 (1) SA 360 (W) at 361D–F. Even where the parties have agreed to cash payment, "cash" has been interpreted widely to include payment by cheque: see *Sibbald v Dakota Motors* 1956 (3) SA 203 (T) at 207A–B.

12  McBryde, *Contract*, para 24–08; Walker, *Contract*, para 31.31.

13  1947 (3) SA 525 (A) at 540.

14  1995 (2) SA at 279 at 285I–J. See also *Adams v SA Motor Industry Employers Association* 1981 (3) SA 1189 (A) at 1199H–1200C (although this case deals with promissory notes the principle is the same).

15  See note 14 above. See also L R Caney, *A Treatise on the Law of Novation including Delegation, Compromise and Res Judicata*, 2nd edn (1973), 26; Malan & Pretorius, *Bills of Exchange*, para 199.

16  In *B & H Engineering* (note 3) the court recognised that the intention of the parties may in a particular case be to novate the original debt but mentioned, correctly I would submit, that this would "seldom accord with the requirements of commercial practice or the expectations of businessmen" (per Grosskopf JA at 285H).

17  See W G Burger, "Payment by cheque: cash or credit" (1957) 74 *SALJ* 454 at 457; J C Stassen, "Betaling deur middel van 'n driepartykredietkaart" 1978 *De Jure* 134 at 138. In *Eriksen Motors (Welkom) Ltd v Protea Motors, Warrenton* 1973 (3) SA 685 (A) Holmes JA, with specific reference to the views advanced by the above authors, held that they must yield due to the weight of authority to the contrary (at 693H).

Recent Scots textbooks,[18] following English legal terminology, regard payment by cheque as "conditional payment" as opposed to "absolute payment". Different terminology in this case, however, does not mean difference in substance. Conditional payment, according to Chitty, simply means that although the original debt remains due during the currency of the cheque, the creditor's remedy is suspended until it is due, when it is either discharged (if the cheque is honoured) or revives (if it is dishonoured).[19] The acceptance of an instrument as absolute payment, on the other hand, according to Chitty,[20] means that the original debt is extinguished and the creditor has no remedy other than on the instrument itself. This would not appear to differ from the position in South African law.

As to whether accepting a cheque in payment constitutes a novation of the original debt, Scots law is not entirely clear. The classical exposition of the nature of cheque payment in Scots law is that of Lord President Dunedin in *Leggat Brothers v Gray*:

> It is … quite obvious that when a creditor takes a cheque he takes it on the hypothesis that the cheque is going to be honoured, but if when he goes to the bank the cheque is not honoured … then there is no question that he would still have an action against his original debtor. … I do not know that it is necessary to refer the matter to any particular legal category, but if it is, I should rather suppose that the honouring of the cheque was a condition resolutive, and that if payment of the cheque failed to be made, the effect would be that no payment had been made, and the original debt would be set up again. …[I]t seems to me that payment is complete the moment that the creditor has accepted the cheque as in payment, subject always to the condition that the cheque will be met when presented.[21]

The resolutive-condition construction employed here appears to me to lead to the conclusion that the acceptance of the cheque extinguishes the underlying debt (as opposed to merely suspending it) and that it comes to life again if the cheque is dishonoured.[22] This, to my mind, looks very much like novation (albeit a novation that can be resolved – a conditional novation). Thus MacQueen, with reference to the *Leggat Brothers* case, states categorically that payment by cheque discharges the underlying obligation from

---

18 Walker, *Contract*, para 31.31; McBryde, *Contract*, para 24–10, with reference to *Bolt & Nut Co (Tipton) v Rowlands, Nicholls & Co* [1964] 2 QB 10; Gloag, *Contract*, 709.

19 *Chitty on Contracts* 28th edn (1999) (henceforth Chitty) vol 1, para 22-074.

20 Para 22–077.

21 1908 SC at 67, 73–74. See also McBryde, *Contract*, para 24–09; Walker, *Contract*, para 31.31; Gloag, *Contract*, 709.

22 Note also the formulation that "payment is complete" on acceptance of the cheque.

the time of receipt of the cheque, but that the discharge is conditional.[23] It is suggested, however, that too much has been made of the resolutive-condition construction in the context of this case read as a whole. The Lord President's reluctance "to refer the matter to any particular legal category" should be noted. Moreover, it appears later in the judgment that the question whether or not "the delivery and acceptance of a cheque really extinguished the debt during the interval between its acceptance and the payment of the money by the bank" was argued before the court. The court termed this "an interesting discussion" but declined to express its views on this question which it regarded as "rather abstract and logical than practical".[24]

Embarking, as an academic, on the luxury of addressing this abstract question logically, it seems to me sensible to do so from the perspective of novation. Stair, in considering the discharge of an obligation by novation, states:

> Innovation is the turning of one obligation into another. … *Innovation is not presumed by granting a new obligation … but it is rather held to be as caution or corroboration of the former obligation,* consistent therewith; and in the civil law it is never esteemed innovation, unless it be so expressed … ; but with us, though it be not named, yet, if it appear to have been the meaning of the parties, not to corroborate, but to take away the former obligation, it is a valid innovation.[25]

An intention to (in)novate will not lightly be ascribed to the parties. It is suggested that the acceptance of a cheque is in the rule indeed a corroboration of the underlying debt and does not extinguish it. The debt merely cannot be enforced until the cheque has been dishonoured. It is accordingly suggested that the employment of the resolutive-condition construction in this context can be misleading.[26] The established law in England and in South Africa on this point appears to me to be more in line with the likely intentions of the parties. Moreover, at least one Scots authority has expressed the view that acceptance of a cheque in payment does not, in the rule, constitute a novation.[27]

---

23  H L MacQueen "Payment of another's debt" in D Johnston & R Zimmermann (eds), *Unjustified Enrichment: Key Issues in Comparative Perspective* (2002) (henceforth MacQueen, in Johnston & Zimmermann, *Unjustified Enrichment*), 458 at 480.

24  1908 SC at 76.

25  Stair, *Institutions*, 1.18.8 (emphasis CH).

26  It is interesting to note that the construction of a "resolutive condition" employed in the *Leggat Brothers* case was also taken up in the first edition of Malan's textbook, but appears to have been jettisoned in later editions. Compare F R Malan (assisted by C R De Beer), *Bills of Exchange, Cheques and Promissory Notes in South African Law* (1983), para 318, and Malan & Pretorius, *Bills of Exchange*, para 199.

27  Gloag, *Contract*, 709 (ironically with reference to, *inter alia*, *Leggat Brothers*).

It is submitted that some, but not all, of the reasoning pertaining to cheques can be extended to credit cards.[28] A credit card is clearly not cash in the sense of being legal tender. It has been held in England that when a person tenders a credit card in payment, the presentation of the card to the merchant is a representation by the cardholder that he has the actual authority of the bank to conclude a contract between the bank and the merchant under which the bank will honour the sales voucher for the goods or services on the presentation of the voucher to the bank.[29] This is probably good law also in South Africa.[30] Payment by credit card is widespread and generally very effective and convenient. As in the case of cheques, it will therefore not take much to convince a court that a creditor has agreed to be paid by credit card. It is suggested, for example, that a creditor who has the mechanical or electronic facilities necessary for credit card payments, will be hard-pressed to convince a court that he did not contemplate payment by credit card, especially, as is often the case, where the availability of credit card facilities is also advertised on the premises.[31] Thus, the position in this regard is similar to that in the case of cheques.

Payment by credit card differs in one important respect from payment by cheque. Although, in both cases, the creditor has to look to a third party for the money (the drawee bank and card issuer respectively), the relationship between the creditor and third party differs significantly. In the case of a cheque the creditor has no right as against the drawee bank to be paid. In the case of the credit card the card issuer itself becomes a debtor of the creditor by virtue of the contract between them.[32] What impact might this have on the underlying debt? There is academic support in South Africa for the view that

---

28  In *B & H Engineering* (note 3) at 285G–H Grosskopf JA states, somewhat vaguely, that the rules regarding the giving of cheques can be extended to "other instruments". See also Stassen, 1978 *De Jure* 134 at 137.

29  *R v Lambie* [1981] 2 All ER 776 (HL) at 780a–b, by analogy to cheque cards. The bank's contractual liability to pay arises against the background of a pre-existing contract between it and the supplier, in terms of which it undertakes to pay the supplier for goods delivered or services rendered to the cardholder. See *Re Charge Card Services Ltd* [1986] 3 All ER 289 (Ch D) (henceforth *Charge Card Services*) at 296b–d.

30  D v Cowen & L Gering, *Cowen The Law of Negotiable Instruments in South Africa*, vol 1, 5th edn (1985) (henceforth Cowen & Gering, *Negotiable Instruments*) at 269–270; Stassen, 1978 *De Jure* 134. Credit cards have only been considered in two South African cases, neither of which sheds light on this issue: *Western Bank Ltd v Registrar of Financial Institutions* 1975 (4) SA 37 (T); *Diners Club South Africa (Pty) Ltd v Durban Engineering (Pty) Ltd* 1980 (3) SA 53 (A).

31  The creditor will, in any event, most likely be bound contractually as against the card issuer to honour the card. See Stassen, 1978 *De Jure* 134 at 140–141; and, Stassen, "Payment by credit card" (1978) 7 *Businessman's Law* 12 at 13.

32  J C Stassen "Payment by credit card – cash or credit?" (1979) 8 *Businessman's Law* 183 at 184.

acceptance of a credit card as means of payment, as in the case of a cheque, is conditional and not a novation of the underlying debt between the cardholder and merchant unless a novation is clearly intended, and does not discharge the underlying debt.[33] This approach, however, was subsequently rejected in England in the case *Re Charge Card Services Ltd.*[34] A number of important principles emerged from the well-reasoned judgment of Millett J:

1. there is no general rule that whenever a method of payment is adopted which involves a risk of non-payment there is a presumption that it be taken as conditional as opposed to absolute payment;[35]
2. the proper approach, as each new method of payment emerges and its effect must be considered, is to examine its nature and the surrounding circumstances to see whether there should be a presumption of conditional payment;[36]
3. a blind following of principles relating to cheques or letters of credit is inappropriate;[37]
4. in the absence of indications to the contrary payment by credit card is not conditional for a number of reasons; *inter alia*, (a) it is typically used to facilitate payment of small consumer debts on terms which are not subject to negotiation; (b) the machinery for payment does not require the address of the cardholder (which would make it difficult for the service provider to find him); and (c) the terms on which the supplier is entitled to payment are quite different from those on which the card issuer is entitled to payment from the customer.[38]

Scots law appears to be at peace with the *Charge Card* case.[39] The reasoning in this case is compelling and it is submitted, despite the earlier academic opinion to the contrary referred to above, that South African courts are likely to follow the decision should the matter arise.

As regards payment by letter of credit, this is almost always in pursuance of an express payment clause in the contract. The legal-tender problem, which is sometimes present in the case of payment by cheque or credit card, therefore does not arise. As regards the effect of the creditor accepting payment by letter of credit, both the South African and Scots law are almost certainly the

33 Stassen, 1978 *De Jure* 134 at 136–139; Cowen & Gering, *Negotiable Instruments*, 270.
34 [1986] 3 All ER 289 (Ch D).
35 At 301f.
36 At 301g.
37 At 301h–303e.
38 At 303h–304b.
39 Walker, *Principles*, 141.

same as that which has developed in the English courts. The leading decision on the nature of payment by letter of credit is that of the Court of Appeal in *W J Alan & Co Ltd v El Nasr Export and Import Co*.[40] In his judgment Lord Denning MR recognised that it was possible in a special case that the creditor and debtor might have reached an agreement to the effect that the issuing of the letter of credit would constitute "absolute payment" discharging the debt.[41] In the rule, however, it amounted to "conditional payment" which means:

> [T]he seller looks in the first instance to the banker for payment: but, if the banker does not meet his obligations when the time comes for him to do so, the seller can have recourse to the buyer.[42]

So viewed, it must be clear that the underlying debt, as in the case of a cheque, is not discharged by accepting payment in terms of a letter of credit. There is no novation. The letter of credit, as in the case of a credit card, gives the debtor rights against a third party, but, unlike the position in the case of payment by credit card, if the third party does not perform, the debtor's suspended rights in terms of the underlying debt become effective.

## (2) PECL compared to South African and Scots law

The following principles emerge from the foregoing discussion of South African and Scots law:

1. South African and Scots law both proceed from the basis that, unless otherwise agreed, a creditor can insist on being paid in legal tender. However, in both systems, an agreement by the creditor to accept payment by other common means such as by cheque or credit card is lightly inferred.

2. Payment by cheque is regarded as conditional, as opposed to absolute, in both systems. In *general terms* this means that although the moment of delivery of the cheque is regarded as the moment of payment, if the cheque is dishonoured, there has been no payment and the creditor can sue the debtor either on the cheque or on the underlying debt.

3. In the more precise analysis of the legal effect of the creditor accepting payment by cheque the two systems may differ, although this is not entirely clear. Whilst it is clear in South Africa that acceptance of

---

40  [1972] 2 QB 189 (CA).
41  At 209E–210B.
42  At 210C.

the cheque is not in the rule a novation, there is support in Scotland for the view that it constitutes a conditional novation.

4. Payment by letter of credit is likely to be regarded as conditional in the same sense as payment by cheque in both systems.

5. As regards payment by credit card Scottish commentators support the English *Charge Card* case (to the effect that such payment is absolute and discharges the underlying debt). The courts have not yet pronounced on this issue in South Africa. There is academic opinion to the contrary.

Against this background it is of interest to note two important principles embodied in PECL. In the first place Article 7:107(1) PECL provides:

> Payment of money due may be made in any form used in the ordinary course of business.

This implies that the debtor may choose the form of payment. The creditor cannot unilaterally demand payment in a particular form or manner, not even in legal tender. If the form and manner of payment are important to him, the particular form or manner must be agreed in the contract.[43] However, the debtor does not have an unfettered choice: the choice must fall within the "ordinary course of business". This is necessary in order to protect the creditor from having to accept a "surprising, unusual or burdensome manner of payment".[44] There is much to be said for the way in which PECL addresses this matter. The anachronistic nature[45] of the legal-tender requirement still present in many legal systems in modern times is recognised. The solution adopted is a better reflection of the commercial reality in an increasingly cashless society. It is also more satisfactory than the rule adopted in the USA in terms of which a creditor, when offered payment in some other manner, can demand payment in legal tender but subject to a reasonable extension of time to enable the debtor to procure it.[46]

The second principle is formulated as follows:

> A creditor which, pursuant to the contract or voluntarily, accepts a cheque or other order to pay or a promise to pay is presumed to do so only on condition that it will be honoured.[47]

---

43  See Comments A and B to Article 7:107 PECL.
44  Comment B to Article 7:107 PECL where the delivery of a vast number of small coins is given as an example
45  See note 9 above.
46  See Note 1 to Article 7:107 PECL.
47  Article 7:107(2) PECL.

Thus, if a payment instrument such as a cheque, promissory note or letter of credit[48] is dishonoured, there has been no payment. This principle is in accordance with the principle common to South African and Scots law that payment by cheque or letter of credit is conditional payment. However, provided a credit card can be regarded as "a promise to pay", PECL does not reflect the *Charge Card* case. The card issuer having contractually bound itself as against the provider of services or goods to pay, it is difficult to escape the conclusion that acceptance of payment in this form is acceptance of "a promise to pay". Moreover, it would appear from the comments and notes[49] to Article 7:107(2) PECL that the drafters had a wide interpretation in mind so as to cover any form of substituted performance. However, in accordance with the principle, the consequence of accepting substituted performance merely gives rise to a presumption that the parties intended it to be conditional. The possibility accordingly remains, on the basis of considerations such as those which led to the *Charge Card* decision, to argue that there are sufficient grounds upon which the presumption may be discharged.

The principle of conditionality of acceptance of substituted performance is further entrenched by the second sentence of Article 7:107(2) PECL which reads:

> The creditor may not enforce the original obligation to pay unless the order or promise is not honoured.

The use of the words "may not enforce the original obligation" is significant. This phrase does not support the idea of the original obligation having been discharged by acceptance of the substituted performance, and then coming to life again if the substituted performance leads to nothing – i.e. the idea of the substituted performance constituting a conditional novation. The drafters, as is also borne out in the comments,[50] have in mind the suspension of the underlying debt until such time as the substituted performance has been dishonoured. The understanding of conditional payment under PECL is therefore the same as that of English and South African law. This approach, it is suggested, is also in accordance with the probable intention of the parties.

---

48 "Promise to pay", it is suggested, is wide enough to include payment by documentary credit.

49 This is my impression from a general reading of the Comments and Notes. However, see specifically Note 2 to Article 7:107(2) PECL which refers by name to payment by credit card.

50 Comment C states "that the original claim subsists until satisfaction of the substituted performance has in fact been achieved". This is then illustrated by the following example: "A owes B £3000. A accepts B's request to give it a promissory note payable two months later. B's remedies on the original contract are suspended until the promissory note is due but revive if the note is dishonoured". See also Comment D.

## (3) Conclusion

Article 7:107 PECL deserves to be supported. It is clear, and in general reflects both commercial reality and the probable intentions of the parties. In doing away with the traditional possibility of requiring payment in legal tender it is probably prophetic. The solution employed is more advanced than the law in most countries. Its clear rejection of the idea that the acceptance of substituted performance is novatory, by recognising a presumption to the contrary, is, as a general rule, satisfactory. In the specific instance of payment by credit card, PECL probably favours an outcome different from that in the *Charge Card Services* case. However, it may well be that the reasoning in that case is compelling enough to rebut the presumption.

## C. PAYMENT BY THIRD PARTY

### (1) Introduction

In dealing with the form and manner of payment above, it was noted that a creditor very often does not obtain payment from the debtor directly but from a third party, in the form of the bank on which a cheque has been drawn, or the bank that has issued a letter of credit or credit card. In these situations the creditor typically looks towards the bank for payment in accordance with an agreement with the debtor that he will do so. However, payment of another's debt can also arise in various non-consensual situations. A benefactor may, for example, simply pay the debt of a friend without his knowledge, or a sub-tenant may pay the rental of the tenant to prevent his eviction, or a bank acting without mandate may pay a cheque. Such third-party payments are considered below.

### (2) South African law

The South African law regarding third-party payments is largely settled. The Roman–Dutch authorities are pretty uniform. An exposition often encountered[51] is that of Pothier:

> It is not essential to the validity of the payment, that it be made by the debtor, or any person authorised by him; it may be made by any person without such authority, or even in opposition to his orders, provided it is made in his name, and in his discharge, and the property is effectually transferred; it is a valid payment, it

---

51  See *B & H Engineering* (note 3) at 292F; *Froman v Robertson* 1971 (1) SA 115 (A) (henceforth *Froman*) at 124G; *Commissioner for Inland Revenue v Visser* 1959 (1) SA 452 (A) at 458A.

induces the extinction of the obligation, and the debtor is discharged even against his will.[52]

These views have been applied consistently by the South African courts.[53] Recently, in *Info Plus v Scheelke* the Supreme Court of Appeal stated "[that] it is hardly necessary to say that a debt owing by A to B may be extinguished by a payment made by a stranger to B in discharge of that debt even if A is unaware of such payment".[54] These views are shared by contemporary authors.[55]

Thus, should the payment be subject to the creditor ceding his rights against the debtor to the third party, the payment was not made with the intention of discharging the debt, and it will accordingly remain intact.[56] However, payment tendered by a third party on behalf of the debtor with the intention of discharging the debt cannot be refused by the creditor.[57]

Whether the third party will have any claim against the debtor will depend upon the circumstances. Such a claim may lie in contract (for example where the third party is a mandatary of the debtor). Claims may also be possible on the basis of *negotiorum gestio* or enrichment.[58] A problematic question against this background is whether a bank can recover the amount of a cheque which it has mistakenly paid to the payee. This question arises, *inter alia*, when payment of the cheque was countermanded and the bank overlooks the countermand.[59] The matter has been the subject of a lively debate in South African law,[60] but now seems to have been authoritatively settled by the judgment of the Supreme Court of Appeal in the *B & H Engineering* case. In contrast to the decision of the court *a quo*, Grosskopf JA took the view that in this situation one is not dealing with third-party payments

52  R J Pothier, *Treatise on the Law of Obligations* (1826, transl W D Evans) (henceforth Pothier, *Obligations*), para 463. Van der Linden, *Institutes*, 1.18.1 is virtually identical. See also Voet, *Commentarius*, 46.3.1; Van Leeuwen, *Censura Forensis*, 1.4.32.3.

53  *Reliance Agencies (Pty) Ltd v Patel* 1946 CPD 463 at 472–473; *Froman* (note 51) at 124F–H; *Info Plus v Scheelke* 1998 (3) SA 184 (SCA) at 192D.

54  1998 (3) SA 184 (SCA) at 192D.

55  Van der Merwe et al, *Contract*, 492–493; Lubbe & Murray, *Contract*, 705–706 n 2; Christie, *Contract*, 472.

56  Van der Merwe et al, *Contract*, 492; *Shaw v Burger* 1994 (1) SA 524 (C); *HK Outfitters (Py) Ltd v Legal & General Assurance Society Ltd* 1975 (1) SA 55 (T); cf also Pothier, *Obligations*, para 464; Christie, *Contract*, 472.

57  Pothier, *Obligations*, para 464. The test according to Pothier is whether the payment is in the interest of the debtor. If it is, it must be accepted. If it is not (as in the case of payment subject to cession), it need not be accepted.

58  Van der Merwe et al, *Contract*, 493.

59  It can also arise when the bank pays a forged cheque: see Malan & Pretorius, *Bills of Exchange*, para 210.

60  For an excellent historical overview see Malan & Pretorius, *Bills of Exchange*, para 210.

as contemplated by the Roman-Dutch commentators, or, as he terms it, the "Pothier argument":[61]

> [T]he bank is not the drawer's agent, but a neutral payment functionary. It is consequently correct that the acts and intent of the bank, by themselves, cannot result in the payment of the debt owed to the payee. However, the acts and intent of the bank form only a part of the picture. They must be seen in the light of the debt-extinguishing agreement between the debtor and creditor. It is that agreement which defines the purpose for which the cheque is given, and for which payment is to be received from the bank. If that agreement provides that any payment by the bank, even an unauthorised one, would discharge the debt as between debtor and creditor, such an agreement would be valid *inter partes*. The fact that the bank does not know or care what the purpose of its payment is does not matter. Its function is neutral, almost mechanical. It performs the act which the parties have agreed would serve to complete the payment of the debt. It follows that the above passage of Pothier is not relevant in the present circumstances. We are not here dealing with a case where the bank pays somebody else's debt. In our case the debtor is paying his own debt through the instrumentality of the bank.[62]

Whether the unauthorised payment of the cheque has discharged the underlying debt therefore depends upon the debt-extinguishing agreement between the debtor and creditor. Here the agreement is normally that the underlying debt is extinguished on payment of the cheque irrespective of whether the payment has been authorised. Therefore the payment of the countermanded cheque discharges the underlying debt which implies that the creditor (or payee of the cheque) is not enriched by this payment. Due to the absence of enrichment, the bank cannot not succeed with a *condictio sine causa* to recover the unauthorised payment.[63]

### (3) Scots (and some English) law

Apart from a recent contribution by MacQueen,[64] payment by a third party does not appear to have attracted much attention in Scots law. There is a considerable similarity between the opinions of some of the Scottish Institutional Writers and their Roman–Dutch counterparts. Bankton states the rule as follows:

> [P]ayment may be made for one that is ignorant of it, or even against his will, because he cannot hinder the creditor to take his payment where he can find it.[65]

---

61  1995 (2) SA 279 (A) at 292E.

62  At 293E–G.

63  At 291F, 294G–J. In arriving at this conclusion the court expressly distanced itself from the judgment of Goff J in *Barclays Bank Ltd v W J Simms Son & Cooke (Southern) Ltd* [1979] 3 All ER 522 (QB). See also *Govender v Standard Bank of South Africa Ltd* 1984 (4) SA 392 (C).

64  MacQueen, in Johnston & Zimmermann, *Unjustified Enrichment*, 458, 470–471.

65  Bankton, *Institute*, 1. 24.1.

Bell is slightly more expansive:

> Payment, to the effect of extinguishing the obligation, may be made not only by the debtor himself, but by anyone acting for the debtor: or even by a stranger, where the debt is pecuniary, and due, and demanded; or where any penal effect may arise from delay; or where the creditor has no interest in demanding performance by the proper debtor.[66]

The early Scots authorities, however, are not uniform. Some take the view, which prevails in England, that third-party payment does not discharge a debt unless ratified by the debtor.[67]

There is also little on this topic in the modern Scottish texts. Walker states that payment by a third party on behalf of the debtor is valid, even if made without the debtor's knowledge or consent.[68] In the *Stair Memorial Encyclopaedia* a preference is expressed for the view that the unauthorised payment of a debt by a third party discharges the debt.[69] Gloag, with reference to early case law,[70] states that a creditor who is not taking active steps to enforce his debt, is not bound to accept payment from any person other than the debtor or someone having his authority. Should he, however, be taking measures to enforce payment, or to realise securities, "he is bound to accept payment and to grant an assignation to anyone who can show an interest to intervene, such as a friend of the debtor, or a postponed bondholder in subjects conveyed in security".[71] In coupling the obligation to accept payment by an interested stranger to assignation, it would appear that Gloag does not have a debt-extinguishing situation in mind. Scottish case law on this topic is sparse. One case holds that where a third party had paid the debt of another owed to a bank, the debtor's obligations to the bank were discharged, and that Scots law, in this regard, was Civilian in character.[72] MacQueen's conclusions that the Scots law in this regard is "remarkably unclear"[73] or "at best undeveloped"[74] appears to be apposite.

It is of interest that the Notes to PECL express the view that, as regards

---

66 I rely here on MacQueen, in Johnston & Zimmermann, *Unjustified Enrichment* at 470.

67 See MacQueen, in Johnston & Zimmermann, *Unjustified Enrichment*, 470, who refers to Lord Kames, *Principles of Equity*, 5th edn (1825), 330, 331; and to Hume, *Lectures*, vol 3, 16, 17.

68 Walker, *Contract*, para 31.29.

69 SME, vol 15, para 97.

70 *Smith v Gentle* (1844) 6 D 1164; *Cunningham's Trustees v Hutton* (1847) 10 D 307; *Fleming v Burgess* (1867) 5 M 856.

71 *Contract*, 710. See also Walker, *Principles*, vol 2 at 140.

72 See MacQueen, in Johnston & Zimmermann, *Unjustified Enrichment*, at 470, referring to *Reid v Lord Ruthven* (1918) 55 SLR 616.

73 MacQueen, in Johnston & Zimmermann, *Unjustified Enrichment* at 470.

74 MacQueen, in Johnston & Zimmermann, *Unjustified Enrichment* at 482.

payment by third-parties, Scots law is "probably the same" as English law.[75] In the light of the above discussion, this statement is somewhat surprising. In English law the rule of "vicarious performance" is that the creditor may not refuse performance tendered by a third party if the third party performs on behalf of the debtor and with his prior authority or subsequent ratification.[76] This type of payment will discharge the debt. Third-party payments that are unauthorised will, however, not discharge the debt. This rule rests on two early cases. In *Belshaw v Bush*[77] it was held that a payment by a stranger for the debtor and on his account, which was subsequently ratified by him, is a good payment, while in *James v Isaacs*[78] the principle was established that payment by a stranger without the authority, prior or subsequent, of the debtor was bad. A consolidated rule was formulated as follows in *Simpson v Eggington:*

> The general rule as to payment or satisfaction by a third party, not himself liable as co-contractor or otherwise, has been fully considered in the cases of ...; and the result appears to be, that it is not sufficient to discharge a debtor unless it is made by the third person, as agent, for and on account of the debtor and with his prior authority or subsequent ratification.[79]

A detailed analysis of the complex[80] English law in this regard falls outside the scope of this contribution.[81] The main difference between English and South African law is clearly that whereas an unauthorised third-party payment can extinguish the debt in South Africa (the typical position in the Civilian tradition), it does not in English law. The uncertainty in Scotland must be ascribed to the mixed nature of Scots law – in this case much more visible than in South Africa.

In evaluating the Civilian and English approaches MacQueen[82] advances three reasons for preferring the Civilian rule. First, there is the practical reason that a creditor who has been paid by a third party is not likely to seek payment again from the debtor: "[H]aving got his money, he will normally

---

75 See Note 2(b) to Article 7:107 PECL. Professor MacQueen advises me that this note was drafted in the mid-1990s before he had fully addressed his mind to the problems involved.

76 S Whittaker, "Performance of another's obligation: French and English law contrasted", in Johnston & Zimmermann, *Unjustified Enrichment*, 433, 445–446; Treitel, *Contract*, 755–756; Chitty, para 22-041.

77 (1851) 11 CB 191 (138 ER 444). For a discussion of the case see P Birks & J Beatson, "Unrequested payment of another's debt" (1976) 92 *LQR* 188 at 189–191.

78 (1852) 22 LJCP 73; 12 CB 791 (138 ER 1115).

79 (1855) 10 Ex 845 at 847 (156 ER 683 at 684). See also *Smith v Cox* [1940] 2 KB 558 at 560.

80 Whittaker, in Johnston & Zimmermann, *Unjustified Enrichment* at 447.

81 For detailed expositions and debate regarding this matter, see Birks & Beatson (1976) 92 *LQR* 188; D Friedman, "Payment of another's debt" (1983) 99 *LQR* 534.

82 MacQueen, in Johnston & Zimmermann, *Unjustified Enrichment* at 471.

rest content." Secondly there is the systematic reason that it would align Scots law with the other systems in the Civilian tradition. Finally, MacQueen argues that there is more clear authority for the Civilian rule in Scotland, than for the English rule. However, he subjects his preference to one reservation: the Civilian rule appears to be inappropriate to determine the question whether a bank paying a stopped cheque thereby discharges the underlying debt. In this regard he prefers the English rule.

The effect of payment by a bank of a stopped cheque in English law was considered in detail by Goff J in *Barclays Bank Ltd v W J Simms Son & Cooke (Southern) Ltd.*[83] In this case the bank was successful in recovering such a payment from the payee on the basis that since the payment was unauthorised, it did not discharge the debt. The payee was accordingly enriched and liable to the impoverished bank in restitution. Unlike the stance taken by Grosskopf JA in the South African *B & H Engineering* case, it is clear that Goff J regarded payment of a cheque by a bank as third-party payment. For this reason, on application of the English law relating to vicarious payments, it can only discharge the debt if it has been authorised, i.e. if the bank has paid within its mandate. A bank paying a stopped cheque therefore does not pay within its mandate and does not discharge the debt. The recipient of the payment is accordingly enriched and liable to the bank in restitution, at least in the absence of a change of position defence.[84]

MacQueen, having reviewed the South African law as well, regards the *Barclays Bank* case as good law also in Scotland.[85] His preference for the *Barclays Bank* approach is based on policy considerations. He argues that the bank paying on a countermanded cheque is paying without instruction; therefore it must be very dubious whether in the circumstances the customer's debt can be properly treated as discharged by the bank's payment. MacQueen points out that the reason for the countermand is often some claim which the drawer customer wishes to make against the payee of the cheque in the underlying relationship in which the cheque constitutes payment. The withholding of payment by this route is a useful and legitimate pressure tactic towards obtaining proper performance of the payee's obligation. The drawer's position would be even more problematic if, in addition to losing his effective remedy, it was also subject to the bank's claim in respect of its impoverishment (as suggested in the *B & H Engineering* case[86]).

---

83  [1979] 3 All ER 522 (QBD).
84  At 539b–g.
85  MacQueen, in Johnston & Zimmermann, *Unjustified Enrichment* at 477–478.
86  1995 (2) SA 279 (A) at 295A.

## (4) PECL compared to South African and Scots law

The foregoing discussion discloses two main issues of interest from a comparative perspective:

1. Payment by a third party discharges the debt irrespective of whether it has been authorised by the debtor in South African law. This differs from the English rule in terms of which the debtor must either authorise or ratify the payment for it to discharge the debt. The position in Scots law is uncertain, but is probably the same as in South Africa.

2. It would appear that South African and Scots law differ on the competence of an enrichment claim (or claim in restitution) by a bank that has paid a countermanded cheque. South African law disallows such a claim against the payee on the basis that the payee is not enriched (as the drawer's indebtedness to the payee has been discharged by the payment). A Scottish commentator, on the other hand, favours the English approach which allows such restitution.

Against this background it is interesting to note that PECL clearly opts for a *via media*. It differentiates between two categories of third parties. The first category consists of any third party who "acts with the assent of the debtor"[87] as well as a "third person [who] has a legitimate interest" in timeous performance of the debt.[88] Any other third party falls into the second category. As regards performance by third parties falling into the first category, PECL identifies two consequences: (1) the creditor cannot refuse performance by such a third party; and (2) such performance discharges the debt. These rules apply unless the contract requires "personal performance"[89] i.e. payment by the debtor himself – which is unlikely.[90] PECL has no provision as to the consequences of performance tendered by a third party falling within the second category, which is accepted by the creditor.[91]

The competence of performance by a third party with the assent of the debtor, i.e. by an authorised third party, is in accordance with the law of all

---

87 See Article 7:106(1)(a) PECL.
88 See Article 7:106(1)(b) PECL which reads: "The third person has a legitimate interest in performance and the debtor has failed to perform or it is clear that it will not perform at the time performance is due."
89 See the proviso to Article 7:106(1) PECL.
90 Contracts requiring personal performance typically relate to a different type of performance than payment, namely for the rendering of personal services such as the painting of a portrait, where the personal skill of the debtor is important to the creditor. See Comment D to Article 7:106 PECL.
91 See Comment D to Article 7:106 PECL.

the jurisdictions reviewed above.[92] The *via media* of PECL accordingly consists in the recognition of effective payment by an unauthorised third party, but only in some cases, namely where the third party has a legitimate interest. In their comments the drafters give the following examples:

> A surety pays a debt in order to avoid costly proceedings against the debtor which eventually the surety will have to pay. The tenant pays the mortgage in order to avoid a forced sale of the property. In the interests of the family, a wife pays the debt of her husband for which she is not liable. A parent company pays the debt of its subsidiary to save the latter's credit rating.[93]

This differs from Pothier's view,[94] which may have the support of Bell,[95] according to which the creditor cannot refuse payment by a third party if such payment would be in the debtor's interest (as opposed to the third party's interest).

Finally, it should be noted that PECL does not attempt to address the possibility of enrichment claims of the third party who has paid against the debtor. This is understandable in view of the fact that the question is not one concerning contract law. However, in ascribing to certain third-party payments the consequence of the debt being discharged, PECL would have an impact upon the question of whether an unjustified enrichment claim may have to be granted.

## (5) Conclusion

The law relating to third-party payments differs substantially in different countries, and in some, including Scotland, it is rather unclear. To draft principles for European contract law on this matter must necessarily be difficult. The *via media* adopted here appears to me to be a reasonably practical solution. It has, however, simply avoided some difficult questions, especially as to the effect of an unauthorised payment by a disinterested third party that has been accepted by the creditor. Apart from the fact that PECL clearly diverges from the strict English rule, it does not appear to have a striking resemblance to the law of either South Africa or Scotland.

---

92 See Note 1 to Article 7:106 PECL which states that although "expressed differently" in different legal systems, all legal systems "seem to agree" on this principle.

93 Comment B to Article 7:106 PECL. Another obvious example would be where the sub-tenant pays the rental owed by the tenant to prevent the eviction of the tenant.

94 See note 59 above.

95 See the text above at note 68 where the competence to pay arises, *inter alia*, "where any penal effect may arise from delay". It appears to me that this penal effect relates to the debtor. It can, however, possibly be interpreted as affecting the third party.

## D. FINAL REMARKS

South African and Scots law have a mixed character which, in both cases, they have developed over a long period of time. This has been well documented in two substantial works that have been published in the past decade.[96] PECL obviously also have a mixed character. However, the manner and process by which this mix has come to fruition are very different from what happened in Scotland and South Africa. In conclusion one might ask the question posed by Zimmermann, Visser and Reid, the editors of *Mixed Legal Systems in Comparative Perspective*: whether, in comparing the Scots and South African law with PECL, we find either the "comfort of corroboration" in similarity, or a "cause for reflection" in difference.[97]

In applying this question specifically to the payment issues considered above, two difficulties emerge: first, the mixed nature of South African law is not really evident on these points – its principles are very much Civilian; and, secondly, although Scots law shows clear signs of English legal influence, this has not resulted in a blend but has led to uncertainty as to what the law actually is. A more interesting question, against this background, may be whether PECL can serve as a fertile source for the future development of South African and Scots law. I believe that the way in which PECL has dealt with modern methods of payment constitutes a useful model for legislation both in Scotland and South Africa. In Scotland, where the effect of unauthorised third-party payments is still uncertain, PECL may well be influential in future cases. From a South African perspective, one might in the light of PECL reflect on whether unqualified acceptance of the rule that payment by a third party discharges the debt, is sensible.

---

96  See Zimmermann & Visser, *Southern Cross*; Reid & Zimmermann, *History*.
97  Reid & Zimmermann, *History*, preface.

# 10 Specific Performance and Special Damages

## *Sieg Eiselen*

## A. INTRODUCTION

The interplay and differences between Common Law and Civil Law in mixed legal systems are illustrated very clearly in two remedies commonly available after a breach of contract, namely specific performance, or specific implement, and the rules relating to special damages. Specific performance provides an instance where the Civil Law and the Common Law depart from directly opposing points of view. In Civil Law specific performance is regarded as the natural remedy after breach, whereas in Common Law it is regarded as exceptional, with damages being the prime remedy.

The rules on special damages, on the other hand, provide an instance where there is a large measure of convergence between Common Law and

Civil Law, due to the pervasive influence of Pothier in this field. The comparison of these two remedies of South African and Scots law provides an interesting backdrop for a consideration of the relevant provisions of PECL.

## B. SPECIFIC PERFORMANCE

### (1) Introduction

The issue of specific performance seems to draw a very definite dividing line between the Common Law and Civil Law traditions.[1] During the drafting process for CISG the question of specific performance presented an obstacle on which no *consensus* could be reached.[2] It resulted in a compromise which preserved the autonomy of the *lex fori* to apply its own specific rules.[3]

It is generally said that the point of departure in the Civil Law systems is that a party is in principle entitled to have its contract enforced as agreed unless there is some equitable reason for denying it such relief, whereas in English law the creditor is entitled to damages as the primary remedy for a breach of contract unless there is some equitable reason for granting it in equity.[4] The validity of these axioms will be discussed below in order to evaluate the approach followed in Articles 9:101 and 9:102 PECL.

### (2) South African law

#### (a) Roman and Roman-Dutch law

In Roman law a court was not entitled to make an order forcing a party to deliver a thing or to do something in terms of a contract. All claims in contract were claims for the payment of money. If the contract required a party to render performance other than payment of money, a court could only grant a claim for damages upon default.[5]

Although some writers of the Roman-Dutch law repeated the Roman law position, there seems to be little doubt that the majority of the writers

---

1 Joubert, *Contract*, 224; De Wet and van Wyk, *Kontraktereg*, 190; Christie, *Contract*, 605–606; PECL, vol 1, 399.
2 See U Huber in P Schlechtriem, *Commentary on the UN Convention on the International Sale of Goods (CISG)* 2nd edn (1998) (henceforth Schlechtriem, *CISG*), Article 28 n 5 at 200.
3 See Article 28 CISG; Huber in Schlechtriem, *CISG*, Article 28 n 5 at 200 .
4 Joubert, *Contract*, 224; PECL, vol 1, 395; A Cockrell, "Breach of contract" in Zimmermann & Visser, *Southern Cross*, 325; Treitel, *Contract*, 926; MacQueen & Thomson, *Contract*, para 6.6; H L MacQueen & L J Macgregor "Specific implement, interdict and contractual performance" (1999) 3 *Edinburgh LR* 239.
5 Zimmermann, *Obligations*, 770–772; cf Joubert, *Contract*, 223; De Wet & Van Wyk, *Kontraktereg*, 189.

accepted that courts had the power to order specific performance.[6] This happened under the influence of Germanic law which granted the non-defaulting party a choice as to whether it wanted to claim compliance *in forma specifica* or whether it would be content with damages.[7] This power was subject to two exceptions, namely instances where the performance had become impossible and where the estate of the debtor had been sequestrated.[8]

### (b) South African law

The divide between the majority Roman-Dutch approach and the English approach became evident from early on in the case law, where there were two clear camps.[9] In the cases which followed the English approach, the sub-rules of the equitable discretion exercised by English courts were introduced into South African law. These cases referred to English cases to refuse specific performance where it would be unjust,[10] where the court was unable to enforce such an order,[11] where damages would be an adequate remedy,[12] or in cases of employment.[13]

Cases in the Roman-Dutch camp rejected the relevance of the English cases, relying on the majority point of departure of the Roman-Dutch law that a party is in principle entitled to specific performance, except in cases of impossibility and insolvency.[14] This insistence can partly be ascribed to the emphasis in South African law on the principle of *pacta sunt servanda*.[15]

This dichotomy in the approaches to the remedy of specific performance introduced a tension into the judgments on this remedy, even amongst those

6  Joubert, *Contract*, 223–224; De Wet & Van Wyk, *Kontraktereg*, 189; Cockrell, in Zimmermann & Visser, *Southern Cross*.

7  De Wet & Van Wyk, *Kontraktereg*, 189.

8  Joubert, *Contract*, 224; De Wet & Van Wyk, *Kontraktereg*, 189.

9  Cockrell, in Zimmermann & Visser, *Southern Cross*, 326–327.

10  *Atkinson v Vause's Executors* (1892) 13 NLR 85; *Pauline Colliery and Developing Syndicate v Natal Land and Colonisation Co Ltd* (1902) 23 NLR 166.

11  *Ingle Colonial Broom Co Ltd v Hocking* 1914 CPD 495; *Barker v Beckett & Co Ltd* 1911 TPD 151; Christie, *Contract*, 615; Cockrell, in Zimmermann & Visser, *Southern Cross*, 327.

12  *Visser v Neethling* 1921 CPD 176; Cockrell, in Zimmermann & Visser, *Southern Cross*, 327.

13  *Schierhout v Minister of Justice* 1926 AD 99 at 108; Christie, *Contract*, 613–614.

14  *Norden v Rennie* (1879) Buch 155; *Cohen v Shires, McHattie and King* (1882) 1 SAR 41; *Van der Westhuizen v Velenski* (1898) 14 SC 237; *Fick v Woolcott & Ohlsson's Cape Breweries* 1911 AD 214; *Farmer's Co-operative Society (Reg) v Berry* 1912 AD 343; *Amoils v Amoils* 1924 WLD 88 at 98; *Shill v Milner* 1937 AD 101; J W Wessels, *The Law of Contract in South Africa*, 2nd edn by A A Roberts (1951), § 3122; De Wet & Van Wyk, *Kontraktereg*, 189; Joubert, *Contract*, 223; Christie, *Contract*, 607–608.

15  See *Wells v SA Alumenite Co* 1927 AD 69; *Brisley v Drotsky* 2002 (4) SA 1 (SCA) at 27; and esp *Basson v Chilwan* 1993 (3) SA 742 (A) at 777A-B; *Santos Professional Football Club (Pty) Ltd v Igesund* 2003 (5) SA 73 (C) at 86–87.

judges who adhered to the Roman-Dutch point of view. The English-orientated cases departed from the point of view that courts had an overriding discretion to refuse specific performance, as the remedy was exceptional rather than one a party was entitled to as of right, which represented the Roman-Dutch point of view. This eventually resulted in the decision in the *Berry* case[16] in 1912, in which the Appellate Division stated that the aggrieved party had a right to specific performance, but that that right was subject to the discretion of the court. This represented a fusion of the Roman-Dutch and English positions. Due to the structurally anomalous nature of this decision, there was no uniformity of approach in the decisions that followed.[17] This position was reaffirmed in the *Haynes* case,[18] which remained the leading case on this remedy for many years. The decision did, however, leave some uncertainties as a result of its reference to English authorities and rigid rules.[19] These uncertainties were cleared up to some extent by the decision in the *Benson* case in 1986.[20]

Here the court held that there is no doubt in South African law that the aggrieved party has a right to specific performance, but that this right is limited by considerations of equity or justice.[21] It rejected any notion that the right should be limited by rigid rules which would curtail the court's discretion and erode the right to specific performance.[22] Hefer JA also rejected any need for the use of the English categories where specific performance would be refused, as had been done in some earlier cases.[23] Cockrell quite correctly indicates that despite trying to re-establish the Roman-Dutch position, the court has simply perpetuated the internal incoherence in this area of the law, occasioned by the fusion of the remedy from two dissimilar systems of law.[24]

Joubert distinguishes three different situations concerning specific performance in modern South African law, namely claims for payment of money, claims to enforce a negative obligation or duty, and claims for some act other than the payment of money.[25]

---

16  *Farmer's Co-operative Society (Reg) v Berry* 1912 AD 343.
17  See Cockrell, in Zimmermann & Visser, *Southern Cross*, 329.
18  *Haynes v Kingwilliamstown Municipality* 1951 (2) SA 371 (AD).
19  The analysis of this case in *Benson v SA Mutual Life Assurance Society* 1986 (1) SA 776 (A) at 782F–783C can hardly be said to be "strenuous criticism" as claimed by Cockrell, in Zimmermann & Visser, *Southern Cross* at 329. The court simply cleared up specific uncertainties caused by the decision.
20  *Benson v SA Mutual Life Assurance Society* 1986 (1) SA 776 (A).
21  At 783B–C.
22  At 782H–783C.
23  At 785C–G.
24  Cockrell, in Zimmermann & Visser, *Southern Cross*, 330.
25  *Contract*, 222–224; Christie, *Contract*, 606–607.

A claim for the payment of money due under the contract is strictly speaking a claim for specific performance, although this term has become reserved for those instances where performance of a non-monetary obligation is claimed.[26] Joubert is of the opinion that although some courts have refused to order specific performance relying on the judicial discretion to refuse such orders,[27] these cases must be seen as an aberration.[28] According to him courts have no discretion to refuse specific performance for the payment of money. However, the case law on which he relies does not bear this out.

In the *Anastassiou* case[29] to which Joubert refers,[30] the issue of the court's discretion to refuse specific performance was expressly raised.[31] Davidson J reviewed the leading cases dealing with this issue[32] in order to establish the circumstances under which the court may refuse to exercise its discretion.[33] There is no indication that the court regarded its discretion as fettered in the case of the payment of money.

Where a contract contains a negative obligation (i.e. where the debtor promises not to do something), the creditor is entitled to an order restraining the debtor from performing that act.[34] The usual remedy of the creditor is to obtain an interdict restraining the debtor from breaching its obligations. The creditor must prove the usual requirements for an interdict, namely a clear right, a threat of interference with that right and the absence of similar protection by any other remedy.[35]

The enforcement of restraints of trade provides by far the most common occasion where negative obligations arise. Although the early South African cases followed English law in regarding restraints of trade as being *prima*

---

26 Joubert, *Contract*, 222; Christie, *Contract*, 606–607. See also *Gibson v Woodhead Plant Ltd* 1918 AD 308.

27 *Manasewitz v Oosthuizen* 1914 CPD 328; *Carpet Contracts (Pty) Ltd v Grobler* 1975 (2) SA 436 (T).

28 Joubert, *Contract*, 222; *Industrial & Mercantile Corporation v Anastassiou Bros* 1973 (2) SA 601 (W).

29 *Industrial & Mercantile Corporation v Anastassiou Bros* 1973 (2) SA 601 (W).

30 Joubert, *Contract*, 222.

31 At 606 ff.

32 *Shakinovsky v Lawson & Smulowitz* 1904 TS 326; *Farmers Co-operative Society (Reg) v Berry* 1912 AD 343; *Haynes v Kingwilliamstown Municipality* 1951 (2) SA 371 (AD); *R v Milne and Erleigh (7)* 1951 (1) SA 791 (AD).

33 See at 607–609.

34 Wessels, *Contract*, § 3139 ff; Joubert, *Contract*, 223. The remarks in *Longhorn Group (Pty) Ltd v The Fedics Group (Pty) Ltd* 1995 (3) SA 836 (W) at 843C–D, that this type of relief is not specific performance, are hard to explain or understand.

35 *Setlogelo v Setlogelo* 1914 AD 221 at 227; L T C Harms, "Interdict", in LAWSA, vol 11, First Reissue (1998) at 288. The requirement of irreparable harm as stated by Joubert, *Contract*, 223 is not correct.

*facie* void, thus placing the onus to prove reasonableness on the applicant,[36] the position was fundamentally changed in the *Magna Alloys* case.[37] The onus is now on the party under restraint to prove that the restraint is unreasonable.[38] The other party is therefore entitled in principle to a strict adherence of the contract.[39]

The focus in the restraint cases has interestingly shifted from the general enquiries for the granting of an interdict to the issue of legality and reasonableness. In the *Basson* case Botha JA remarked:[40]

> The effect of it in practical terms is this: the covenantee seeking to enforce the restraint need do no more than to invoke the provisions of the contract and prove the breach; the covenantor seeking to avert enforcement is required to prove on a preponderance of probability that in all the circumstances of the particular case it will be unreasonable to enforce the restraint; if the Court is unable to make up its mind on the point, the restraint will be enforced. The covenantor is burdened with the onus because public policy requires that people should be bound by their contractual undertakings. The covenantor is not so bound, however, if the restraint is unreasonable, because public policy discountenances unreasonable restrictions on people's freedom of trade.

It would seem that the usual requirements for an interdict have simply been subsumed in the four requirements set out in the *Basson* case:[41] namely (1) does the covenantee have an interest deserving of protection; (2) is that interest being prejudiced; (3) if so, how does that interest weigh up against the interest of the covenantor not to be economically inactive or unproductive; and (4) is there any other issue of public policy which requires the restraint to be enforced or disallowed? If these questions are answered in favour of the covenantee the restraint will be enforced. There is no reference to the usual exclusions when considering the enforcement of claims for specific performance as set out below.

In all other cases of claims for specific performance relating to non-monetary obligations, it has been accepted that a party is in principle entitled to an order for specific performance as the point of departure, but that there

---

36 *Katz v Efthimiou* 1948 (4) SA 603 (O); *Durban Rickshas Ltd v Ball* 1933 NPD 479 at 493; *Rogaly v Weingartz* 1954 (3) SA 791 (D) at 792G; *Cowan v Pomeroy* 1952 (3) SA 645 (C) at 649; *Arlyn Butcheries (Pty) Ltd v Bosch* 1966 (2) SA 308 (W) at 309H.

37 *Magna Alloys and Research (SA) Pty Ltd v Ellis* 1984 (4) SA 874 (A). See also *Sunshine Records (Pty) Ltd v Frohling* 1990 (4) SA 782 (A); *Basson v Chilwan* 1993 (3) SA 742 (A) at 767E–I.

38 *Magna Alloys and Research (SA) Pty Ltd v Ellis* 1984 (4) SA 874 (A) at 893A–B, 898C–D; *Basson v Chilwan* 1993 (3) SA 742 (A) at 768D–E; Christie, *Contract*, 422; Kerr, *Contract*, 211–212.

39 *Basson v Chilwan* 1993 (3) SA 742 (A).

40 At 776I–777B.

41 *Basson v Chilwan* 1993 (3) SA 742 (A) at 767G–H.

are some limitations which may restrict that right.[42] The principle was clearly stated in the *Berry* case by Innes JA:[43]

> Prima facie every party to a binding agreement who is ready to carry out his own obligation under it has a right to demand from the other party, so far as it is possible, a performance of his undertaking in terms of the contract. As remarked by KOTZÉ, C.J., in Thompson v Pullinger, 1 O.R. at p. 301, "the right of a plaintiff to a specific performance of a contract where the defendant is in a position to do so is beyond all doubt". It is true that Courts will exercise a discretion in determining whether or not decrees of specific performance should be made. They will not, of course, be issued where it is impossible for the defendant to comply with them. And there are many cases in which justice between the parties can be fully and conveniently done by an award of damages. But that is a different thing from saying that a defendant who has broken his undertaking has the option to purge his default by the payment of money. For in the words of Storey, Equity Jurisprudence, sec. 717 (a), "it is against conscience that a party should have a right of election whether he would perform his contract or only pay damages for the breach of it". The *election is rather with the injured party, subject to the discretion of the Court.*

Courts will refuse to order specific performance outright in two cases, namely where performance is impossible and where the estate of the debtor is in sequestration.[44] The rationale for the second instance is that the claim by the creditor is simply a personal right or obligation and therefore it cannot jump the queue in a sequestration by obtaining an order for specific performance. The creditor must make his claim against the insolvent estate along with all other concurrent creditors.[45]

The rationale for the first exception is quite clearly the principle of *lex non cogit ad impossibilia* courts will not order something which is impossible to perform, even if such impossibility is subjective, i.e. if it is impossible for the specific creditor to perform, but not impossible in general.[46] Thus, where a party has sold the same object to two different parties and delivered it to the

42 Joubert, *Contract*, 223–224.
43 *Farmers Co-operative Society (Reg) v Berry* 1912 AD 343 at 350. See also *Norden v Rennie* (1879) Buch 155; *Cohen v Shires, McHattie and King* (1882) 1 SAR 41; *Van der Westhuizen v Velenski* (1898) 14 SC 237; *Fick v Woolcott & Ohlssons's Cape Breweries* 1911 AD 214; *Shill v Milner* 1937 AD 101; *Haynes v Kingwilliamstown Municipality* 1951 (2) SA 371 (AD) at 378G; *Benson v SA Mutual Life Assurance Society* 1986 (1) SA 776 (A) at 782F–783C; Wessels, *Contract*, § 3122; De Wet & Van Wyk, *Kontraktereg*, 189; Joubert, *Contract*, 223; Christie, *Contract*, 607–608.
44 *Ward v Barrett NO* 1963 (2) SA 546 (A) at 552–553; *Rampathy v Krumm* 1978 (4) SA 935 (D) at 941; Joubert, *Contract*, 224.
45 *Ward v Barrett NO* 1963 (2) SA 546 (A) at 552–553; *Rampathy v Krumm* 1978 (4) SA 935 (D) at 941.
46 *Shakinovsky v Lawson & Smulowitz* 1904 TS 326; *Wheeldon v Moldenhauer* 1910 EDL 97 at 99; *Rissik v Pretoria Municipal Council* 1907 TS 1024; *Fick v Woolcott & Ohlsson's Cape Breweries Ltd* 1911 AD 214; *Jacobsz v Fall* 1981 (2) SA 863 (C) at 873; *Pretoria East Builders CC v Basson* 2004 (6) SA 15 (SCA).

second buyer, courts will not order specific performance unless the buyer knew of the first sale.[47] However, where delivery has not yet taken place, courts will interdict the seller from delivering to the second buyer and will order specific performance in favour of the first buyer according to the principle of *qui prior est in tempore potior est in iure* unless the second buyer can show a balance of equities in his favour.[48] Where a *res aliena* has been sold a court will not order specific performance unless the third party had agreed to such sale because it would be a futile order.[49]

It has been recognised from a very early point that although the creditor is in principle entitled to specific performance, such remedy will not necessarily be granted on demand and that it is subject to a judicial discretion.[50] Although not always explicitly stated in these early cases, it would seem that the necessity and introduction of such a discretion was heavily influenced by the provisions of English law.[51]

From the outset the Appellate Division made it clear that the discretion to refuse specific performance was a general judicial discretion and not limited to a specified *numerus clausus* of instances. In the *Berry* case Innes J explained the discretion as follows:[52]

> It is, however, equally settled law with us that, although the Court will as far as possible give effect to a plaintiff's choice to claim specific performance, it has a discretion in a fitting case to refuse to decree specific performance and leave the plaintiff to claim and prove his id quod interest. The discretion which a Court enjoys although it must be exercised judicially is not confined to specific types of cases, nor is it circumscribed by rigid rules. Each case must be judged in the light of its own circumstances.

The onus to raise impediments to an order for specific performance rests squarely on the defaulting party.[53]

---

47  *Shakinovsky v Lawson & Smulowitz* 1904 TS 326; *Wheeldon v Moldenhauer* 1910 EDL 97 at 99; Christie, *Contract*, 609–610.

48  *Pienaar v Van Lill* 1928 CPD 299; *Campbell v First Consolidated Holdings (Pty) Ltd* 1977 (3) SA 924 (W) at 928–929; *Miller v Spamer* 1948 (3) SA 772 (C); *Le Roux v Odendaal* 1954 (4) SA 432 (N); *Barnhoorn v Duvenhage* 1964 (2) SA 486 (A) at 494H–495A; Christie, *Contract*, 610.

49  *Pretoria East Builders CC v Basson* 2004 (6) SA 15 (SCA) at 21.

50  Even De Wet, who was generally very much opposed to the influences of English law, conceded this point, without, however, referring to English law – see De Wet & Van Wyk, *Kontraktereg*, 189.

51  See, e.g., *Thompson v Pullinger* (1894) 1 OR 298; *Manesewitz v Oosthuizen* 1914 CPD 328; *Re Coronation Syndicate* 1903 TH 254; *R v Milne and Erleigh* (7) 1951 (1) SA 791 (AD) at 873; Wessels, *Contract*, §§ 3113, 3118, 3119, 136, 3137. See also De Wet & Van Wyk, *Kontraktereg*, 190; Cockrell, in Zimmermann & Visser, *Southern Cross*, 328–330.

52  *Farmers' Co-Operative Society (Reg) v Berry* 1912 AD 343 at 350. This *dictum* was confirmed in *Haynes v Kingwilliamstown Municipality* 1951 (2) SA 371 (AD) at 378G; *Benson v SA Mutual Life Assurance Society* 1986 (1) SA 776 (A) at 782F–783C.

53  *Tamarillo (Pty) Ltd v BN Aitken (Pty) Ltd* 1982 (1) SA 398 (A) at 442B–443F.

Despite the generality of the judicial discretion, a number of specific instances where courts will consider the refusal of specific performance have been recognised and are discussed in academic writing, namely in the case of undue hardship, contracts for personal services, imprecise obligations and agreements to negotiate a contract.[54]

The suggestion of the English rule, that specific performance should not be ordered where damages would constitute an adequate remedy,[55] was rejected in the *Berry* and *Haynes* cases.[56] In the *Benson* case[57] Hefer JA rejected this proposition on the ground that such a rule would completely negate the plaintiff's right to the remedy while unduly restricting the court's discretion.[58] Rules to the effect that specific performance should be refused where ordinary goods or chattels are sold,[59] or shares which are on the daily market,[60] were similarly rejected.[61] All three of these rules which exist in English law therefore form no part of South African law.

Courts will refuse to order specific performance where the order will cause undue hardship to the defaulting party or even third parties as was the case in the *Haynes* decision.[62] In that case Haynes asked for an order compelling the municipality to release a fixed amount of water during a period of severe drought. Haynes did not provide any evidence that he would suffer hardship or damages due to not receiving such water, while the municipality and the community of Kingwilliamstown would suffer undue hardship. The relevant instances were summarised by the court[63] as being those

> where the [order for specific performance] would operate unreasonably hardly on the defendant or where the agreement giving rise to the claim is unreasonable, or where the decree would produce injustice, or would be inequitable under all the circumstances.

---

54  Christie, *Contract*, 611–615; Kerr, *Contract*, 680–682; Wessels, *Contract*, §§ 3117–3121; Joubert, *Contract*, 224–227.

55  See Wessels, *Contract*, § 3136.

56  *Farmers' Co-Operative Society (Reg) v Berry* 1912 AD 343 at 351; *Haynes v Kingwilliamstown Municipality* 1951 (2) SA 371 (AD) at 378.

57  *Benson v SA Mutual Life Assurance Society* 1986 (1) SA 776 (A).

58  At 783G–784C.

59  Wessels, *Contract*, § 3137.

60  *Thompson v Pullinger* (1894) 1 OR 298 at 301; *R v Milne and Erleigh* (7) 1951 (1) SA 791 (A) at 873.

61  At 784B–C.

62  *Haynes v Kingwilliamstown Municipality* 1951 (2) SA 371 (AD) at 378. See also *ISEP Structural Engineering and Plating (Pty) Ltd v Inland Exploration Co (Pty) Ltd* 1981 (4) SA 1 (A); *Benson v SA Mutual Life Assurance Society* 1986 (1) SA 776 (A).

63  At 378H–379A.

In *SA Harness Works v SA Publishers Ltd*,[64] it was held that a publisher was not entitled to proceed with publishing advertisements where the advertiser had repudiated the contract. The publisher should have cancelled the contract and claimed its damages consisting of the loss of profits which was considerably less than the contract price. This case is probably the high-water mark of the leniency of the courts in refusing specific performance. The *Anastassiou Bros* case,[65] on the other hand, probably represents the strictest approach. In that case the defendant had repudiated its contract for shop-fitting and had almost immediately employed another person to perform the work. Here it was held that although an order for specific performance would cause the defendant some hardship and damages, courts should not be "supine and spineless" in dealing with contract breakers; specific performance was consequently ordered.[66]

Following English law, it has often been stated that courts will not enforce an agreement for the rendering of personal services or employment.[67] The reasons offered are that such contracts call for the performance of personal services of a continuing nature and would therefore be in danger of constant disputes, which courts are ill equipped to supervise or prevent.

This point of departure was rightly rejected in *National Union of Textile Workers v Stag Packings (Pty) Ltd*,[68] where the court held that there was no reason why there should be a departure from the general rule that a party is entitled to enforcement of its contract, subject to the court's discretion. The reasoning that enforcement would be difficult is derived from English law and is not consonant with South African law.[69] Perhaps the most far-reaching decision to date is found in the *Igesund* case.[70] Here the court held that there would not be undue hardship or inequity in forcing the coach of a professional soccer team to fulfil his obligations in terms of the contract with his

---

64  1915 CPD 43.

65  *Industrial & Mercantile Corporation v Anastassiou Bros* 1973 (2) SA 601 (W).

66  At 609.

67  *Gracie v Hull Blythe and Co (SA) Ltd* 1931 CPD 539; *Beeton v Peninsula Transport Co (Pty) Ltd* 1934 CPD 53; *Rogers v Durban Corporation* 1950 (1) SA 65 (D); *Ngwenya v Natalspruit Bantu School Board* 1965 (1) SA 692 (W); *Haynes v Kingwilliamstown Municipality* 1951 (2) SA 371 (AD) at 378; *Schierhout v Minister of Justice* 1926 AD 99 at 107; *Roberts Construction Co Ltd v Verhoef* 1952 (2) SA 300 (W); Wessels, *Contract*, § 3124; Christie, *Contract*, 613; Kerr, *Contract*, 681. Cf *Myers v Abrahamson* 1952 (3) SA 121 (C).

68  1982 (4) SA 151 (T). See also *Chevron Engineering (Pty) Ltd v Nkambules* 2004 (3) SA 495 (SCA); *Santos Professional Football Club (Pty) Ltd v Igesund* 2003 (5) SA 73 (C).

69  *National Union of Textile Workers v Stag Packings (Pty) Ltd* 1982 (4) SA 151 (T) at 158. Confirmed in *ISEP Structural Engineering and Plating (Pty) Ltd v Inland Exploration Co (Pty) Ltd* 1981 (4) SA 1 (A) at 5B; *Santos Professional Football Club (Pty) Ltd v Igesund* 2003 (5) SA 73 (C).

70  *Santos Professional Football Club (Pty) Ltd v Igesund* 2003 (5) SA 73 (C).

original club (which he had left in order to coach another club in the same soccer league). The club could not be denied its ordinary remedy simply because of the possibility that the coach might no longer perform properly, which was a factual issue that might, or might not, arise only in the future.[71]

In terms of section 193 of the Labour Relations Act 66 of 1995 and section 77A(e) of the Basic Conditions of Employment Act, the Labour Court has the power to make an order of specific performance in relation to contracts of employment. These provisions further strengthen the direction the courts have taken since the *Stag Packings* case.

The third type of case where courts have refused to order specific performance deals with the enforcement of so-called imprecise obligations. As Christie points out, there is no sharp dividing line between issues raised by these cases and the enforcement of employment cases.[72] It is on this ground that specific performance of contracts to form syndicates, partnerships or companies, to appoint a director, or to repair or insure buildings, has been refused.[73] It would seem that the precedents relied on consist wholly of older cases heavily influenced by the position and reasoning of English law, and that the trend in later cases is to enforce contracts rather than rely on the grounds of imprecision or difficulty in enforcement.[74]

The decision and reasoning in *Ranch International Pipelines (Transvaal) (Pty) Ltd v LMG Construction (City (Pty) Ltd*[75] are certainly indicative of this trend.[76] The court pointed out that the granting of the order did not replace the contract and therefore did not introduce any new difficulties in deciding whether work had been properly performed. It must be seriously doubted whether imprecision or difficulty of enforcement will in future be regarded as sufficient ground for refusing this remedy.

Most recently the Supreme Court of Appeal has confirmed this trend in *Southernport Developments (Pty) Ltd v Transnet Ltd.*[77] The parties had concluded a lease agreement which, upon the fulfilment of a particular

71  At 86B–E.
72  Christie, *Contract* at 615.
73  See Christie, *Contract*, 615; Wessels, *Contract*, §§ 3117–3118; De Wet & Van Wyk, *Kontraktereg*, 190; Kerr, *Contract*, 680–681.
74  *Ranch International Pipelines (Transvaal) (Pty) Ltd v LMG Construction (City (Pty) Ltd* 1984 (3) SA 861 (W) at 880G–881F; *Southernport Developments (Pty) Ltd v Transnet Ltd* 2005 (2) SA 202 (SCA); Christie, *Contract*, 615.
75  1984 (3) SA 861 (W) at 880G-881F.
76  See also *ISEP Structural Engineering and Plating (Pty) Ltd v Inland Exploration Co (Pty) Ltd* 1981 (4) SA 1 (A) at 5B; *Santos Professional Football Club (Pty) Ltd v Igesund* 2003 (5) SA 73 (C); *Brisley v Drotsky* 2002 (4) SA 1 (SCA) at 35.
77  2005 (2) SA 202 (SCA).

suspensive condition, would entitle Southernport to lease the property "on the terms and conditions of an agreement ... negotiated between the parties in good faith and approved by each of the party's board of directors". The agreement further provided that in the event of the parties failing to reach agreement, any dispute would be referred to an arbitrator who would resolve such dispute with final and binding effect. Southernport brought an application for the enforcement of these terms.[78] On exception the Supreme Court of Appeal held that because the agreement contained a deadlock-breaking mechanism, there was no reason why the agreement to negotiate in good faith should not be enforced.[79]

The South African approach to the granting of orders of specific performance retains its hybrid character, despite attempts to move away from the strong influence of the English law to its Roman-Dutch roots. On the one hand the *right* to specific performance is emphasised, while on the other hand this right is eroded by a general discretion, on the part of the courts, to refuse the remedy by the courts, albeit that courts have become increasingly reluctant to do so. The point of departure is the principle of *pacta sunt servanda* and courts will only very hesitantly use their discretion to refuse the remedy. There are no defined categories of cases other than impossibility and insolvency. The English exceptions of imprecision of the obligation, obligations for personal services, damages as a sufficient alternative, or the inability of the court to enforce its order, all seem largely to have fallen by the wayside. The only real exception remaining seems to be undue hardship. The discretion remains a general one unfettered by specific rules. The case law, however, indicates a clear move away from the exceptions towards the strict enforcement of the contract.

### (3) Scots law

A clear distinction is made in Scots law between three remedies aimed at enforcing the contract after a breach, namely payment, specific implement and interdict.[80] The distinction between payment and specific implement is important because of the consequences of such decrees. A decree for payment of money is enforced by diligence which may include arrestment, poinding and sale, whereas a decree for specific implement is enforced at common law by imprisonment.[81] There are, however, now also other statutory alternatives.[82]

---

78  Paras [1]–[4].
79  Paras [17], [18].
80  MacQueen & Thomson, *Contract*, para 6.2; McBryde, *Contract*, para 23–05.
81  McBryde, *Contract*, para 23–05.
82  McBryde, *Contract*, para 23–05.

The decree of specific implement is used to enforce positive acts of performance whereas interdict is used to enforce negative performance, i.e. prohibiting actions. Interdict is not competent if it requires the defender to take positive steps. Very often a decree to refrain from doing something and a decree to do something positive simply represent opposite sides of the same coin.

The facts in *Grosvenor Developments (Scotland) plc v Argyle Stores Ltd*[83] provide an interesting illustration of the difficulty of distinguishing between negative and positive acts. An interdict was sought against tenants for "ceasing to continue to occupy premises" for certain agreed purposes. The court regarded the action as one for an order requiring the tenants to stay in occupation and to carry on business. Consequently the application crave for an interdict was incompetent.[84] The distinction is therefore important for procedural reasons, requiring the non-defaulting party carefully to consider the remedy it will choose.[85]

In Scots law it is sometimes said that specific implement is the primary or ordinary remedy in cases of a breach of contract in contrast to English law where it is an exceptional remedy,[86] but it is probably more accurate to say that the aggrieved party has a choice between the remedies of specific implement and damages. In practice specific implement is apparently rarely sought and even more rarely granted.[87]

The decision in *Retail Parks Investments Ltd v The Royal Bank of Scotland plc (No 2)*[88] provides a good example of the difference of approach between Scots and English law.[89] In the *Retail Parks Investment* case, an order was sought to force a tenant in a shopping centre to occupy its shop in the centre and conduct business from it. The tenant was content to pay the rent but did not want to conduct its business there any longer. The order was granted. In an English case[90] with similar facts the order was refused on the grounds that in English law the ordinary remedy was damages unless damages could not adequately compensate the aggrieved party.

83 1987 SLT 738.
84 Subsequently confirmed in *Church Commissioners for England v Abbey National plc* 1994 SC 651.
85 See N R Whitty, "Positive and negative interdicts" (1990) 35 *JLSS* 453 for a discussion of the difficulties in distinguishing between these remedies and applying the relevant rules.
86 MacQueen & Thomson, *Contract*, para 6.6.
87 MacQueen & Thomson, *Contract*, para 6.6.
88 1996 SC 227; MacQueen & Macgregor (1999) 3 *Edinburgh LR* 239.
89 See also *Highland and Universal Properties Ltd v Safeway Properties Ltd* 2000 SLT 414; MacQueen & Macgregor (1999) 3 *Edinburgh LR* 239.
90 See *Co-operative Insurance Society Ltd v Argyll Stores (Holdings) Ltd* [1998] AC 1; MacQueen & Macgregor (1999) 3 *Edinburgh LR* 239 at 241.

Even though a party is entitled to specific implement as of right, the enforcement of this right has been subject to judicial discretion since the late nineteenth century.[91] The rule was formulated as follows in *Grahame v Magistrates of Kirkcaldy*:[92]

> It appears to me that a superior court, having equitable jurisdiction, must also have a discretion, in certain exceptional cases, to withhold from parties applying for it that remedy to which, in ordinary circumstances, they would be entitled as a matter of course. In order to justify the exercise of a discretionary power there must be some very cogent reason for depriving litigants of the ordinary means of enforcing their legal rights.

This *dictum* seems to suggest that the discretion is rather limited, even to the extent that it has been remarked that considerations of what is equitable or not are quite irrelevant.[93] The rule has been refined and elaborated, however, to deal with specific situations when the remedy will be refused, without limiting the generality of the discretion.[94] The remedy may be refused:

1. when the performance is impossible. This logical exception is based on the rule *lex non cogit ad impossibilia.*[95]
2. when the performance would cause hardship to the defender out of all proportion to the benefit to the pursuer, i.e. is regarded as inequitable;[96]
3. where the subject matter is of no particular significance (no *pretium affectionis*) and money compensation would be adequate, i.e. the performance can reasonably be obtained from another source such as with generic goods;[97]
4. where the contract involves personal or intimate relationships (thus, a contract for employment, a contract to marry, or a contract to enter into a partnership will not be enforced;[98] this rule has come under

---

91 *Grahame v Magistrates of Kirkcaldy* (1882) 9 R (HL) 91; MacQueen & Thomson, *Contract*, para 6.6.
92 (1882) 9 R (HL) 91.
93 *Salaried Staff London Loan Co Ltd v Swears and Wells Ltd* 1985 SC 189.
94 MacQueen & Macgregor (1999) 3 *Edinburgh LR* 239 at 240.
95 *Grahame v Magistrates of Kirkcaldy* (1882) 9 R (HL) 91; MacQueen & Thomson, *Contract*, para 6.6; McBryde, *Contract*, para 23-18; Walker, *Contract*, para 33.21.
96 MacQueen & Thomson, *Contract*, para 6.6; McBryde, *Contract*, para 23-22; Walker, *Contract*, para 33.21.
97 MacQueen & Thomson, *Contract*, para 6.6; McBryde, *Contract*, para 23-21; Walker, *Contract*, para 33.21.
98 MacQueen & Thomson, *Contract*, para 6.6; McBryde, *Contract*, para 23-20; Walker, *Contract*, para 33.21. There are also statutory remedies which influence this approach, entitling employees to be reinstated in certain circumstances. See the Employment Rights Act 1996 in terms of which an employment tribunal has the power to make an order for reinstatement where an employee has been unjustifiably dismissed.

scrutiny, however, in some employment cases where interdicts were granted which had the effect of specific implement,[99] apparently under the influence of English law and statutory measures);[100]

5.  where the decree would be unenforceable[101] (the example mentioned by Walker, i.e. the case of a defender outside of Scotland seems severely to limit the remedy in respect of contracts with an international flavour);

6.  where the order cannot be formulated specifically enough or where the act to be performed consists of a general duty to be performed over a long period of time;[102]

7.  where the obligation is to pay money.[103]

There is some controversy as to what extent the exercise of the discretion has been influenced by English law and on how readily the courts will resort to it.[104] A case such as *Macarthur v Lawson*[105] does seem to come very close to the English approach.

MacQueen and Thomson indicate that there is a reluctance on the part of the courts to decree specific implement because of the sanction of imprisonment in cases of non-compliance.[106] The effect is that the practical position in Scots law is not all that different from the practical position in English law.[107] It is therefore usual to couple a request for specific implement with one for damages.[108] Where a court will not grant an order for specific implement, it will normally also not grant a decree of interdict which would have the same effect.[109]

The remedy of interdict is used to enforce a performance which is of a negative character such as an undertaking not to compete, restraints of trade or *solus* ties. Non-compliance, as in the case of specific implement, is simply by imprisonment. MacQueen and Thomson, however, indicate that much of the discussion on the problems of imprisonment as sanction for non-

---

99   *Anderson v Pringle of Scotland* 1998 SLT 754 and *Peace v City of Edinburgh Council* 1999 SLT 712.
100  MacQueen & MacGregor (1999) 3 *Edinburgh LR* 239 at 244-245.
101  MacQueen & Thomson, *Contract,* para 6.6; McBryde, *Contract,* para 23-20; Walker, *Contract,* para 33.21.
102  Walker, *Contract,* para 33.21.
103  McBryde, *Contract,* para 23–16; Walker, *Contract,* para 33.21.
104  McBryde, *Contract,* para 23–15. See, however, *Co-operative Insurance Society Ltd v Halfords Ltd* 1998 SC 212 at 229; MacQueen & Macgregor (1999) 3 *Edinburgh LR* 239 at 242.
105  (1877) 4 R 1134 at 1136.
106  MacQueen & Thomson, *Contract,* para 6.8. See also the extensive list of circumstances set out in Walker, *Contract,* para 33.21.
107  MacQueen & Macgregor (1999) 3 *Edinburgh LR* 239.
108  MacQueen & Thomson, *Contract,* para 6.7.
109  *Murray v Dunbarton County Council* 1935 SLT 39; Walker, *Contract,* para 33.21.

compliance has overlooked a piece of legislation, namely the Law Reform (Miscellaneous Provisions) (Scotland) Act 1940, which makes provision for alternative orders in lieu of imprisonment, such as fines or an order for the search of moveables. This provides courts with a lot of flexibility in these cases, which has not yet been adequately realised or exercised.

As in South African law, restraints of trade in Scots law form an important area for the application of interdicts enforcing negative obligations. Scots law follows English law in this respect of restraints of trade.[110] Based on the *dictum* in *Nordenfelt v Maxim Nordenfelt*[111] covenants in restraint of trade are regarded as *prima facie* unenforceable,[112] but if it can be proven that they are justifiable they can be enforced.[113]

The covenantee has to prove three requirements in order to have a restraint enforced:[114]

1. The covenant must be necessary to protect the legitimate interests of the covenantee. Mere avoidance of competition is insufficient to satisfy this requirement.
2. The restraint is reasonable as between the parties. Account must be taken of the area of the restraint, the duration of the restraint and the nature of the restriction in order to determine its reasonableness.
3. The restraint must be in the public interest.

Restraints of trade apart, it would seem that Scots law has retained much of its original character in respect of orders for specific implement. The influence of English law in expanding the discretionary powers of the courts is undeniable, but that influence has not changed the point of departure, namely that the aggrieved party is in principle entitled to choose between specific implement and damages.

## (4) Articles 9:101 and 9:102 PECL

The issue of specific performance is dealt with in Articles 9:101 and 9:102 PECL. The point of departure in both Articles is that the non-defaulting party is entitled to specific performance, either by payment of the amount

110　McBryde, *Contract,* paras 19-87, 19-91.
111　[1894] AC 535.
112　The controversy as to whether these contracts are void or merely unenforceable seems to have been settled in *Esso Petroleum Co Ltd v Harpers Garage (Stourport) Ltd* [1968] AC 269. See McBryde, *Contract,* paras 19-144–19-146.
113　MacQueen & Thomson, *Contract,* para 7.7; McBryde, *Contract,* para 23-20; Walker, *Contract,* para 33.21.
114　MacQueen & Thomson, *Contract,* para 7.7; Walker, *Contract,* para 12.26.

due under the agreement[115] or by performance of the obligation to do something or to give something.[116] This is based on the principle of *pacta sunt servanda*.[117] The formulation of Article 9:101(1) PECL is wide enough to include the enforcement of negative obligations such as restraints of trade although it is not mentioned specifically.[118] Specific provision is made for the case where there has been defective or part performance. The aggrieved party is entitled to have the shortfall or defect remedied.[119]

It is important to note also that a distinction is made in these Articles between monetary and non-monetary obligations. Although it would perhaps have been possible to consolidate the two provisions,[120] they do recognise that different considerations come into play when a court is dealing with the enforcement of these two types of obligations. The distinction and different treatment leads to greater clarity and ease of application than would have been the case with a consolidated Article.

In the case of monetary obligations a party is always entitled to specific performance, i.e. payment of the full amount, and not simply damages, provided it has itself already performed in full.[121] The exceptions in Article 9:101(2) PECL only become relevant in cases where the creditor has not yet performed in full and it is apparent that the debtor will be unwilling to receive performance. In that case he is obliged to make a substitute transaction if it can be done without significant expense or effort.[122] The Comments express the opinion that a creditor will be forced to make a cover sale where commercial usage requires it to do so.[123]

An order to make full payment may also be refused if the payment debtor can show that to foist performance on him will be unreasonable under the circumstances.[124] In both these cases the payment creditor will be limited to claiming damages as a result of the breach of the payment debtor.

In the case of non-monetary obligations PECL has opted for the Civil Law

---

115  Article 9:101 PECL.
116  Article 9:102 PECL.
117  PECL, vol 1, 391.
118  PECL, vol 1, 397–398.
119  PECL, vol 1, 395.
120  Both provisions recognise specific performance as the point of departure, subject to certain exceptions. The exceptions in Article 9:101 PECL could have been subsumed in the exceptions of Article 9:102 PECL. Article 9:101(2)(a) PECL accords with Article 9:102(2)(d) PECL, and Article 9:101(2)(b) PECL accords to some extent with Article 9:102(2)(b) PECL.
121  Article 9:101 PECL; PECL, vol 1, 391.
122  PECL, vol 1, 392.
123  PECL, vol 1, 392.
124  PECL, vol 1, 392–393.

approach, namely that the aggrieved party is entitled to specific performance, bar certain exceptions.[125] As a result of the controversial nature of the remedy, it has been designed to be a compromise.[126] The point of departure accords with the Civil Law tradition, whereas the exceptions limit it to the extent that it comes quite close to the English approach.[127] The biggest remaining difference is that the adequacy of damages to compensate the aggrieved party, as applied in English law, is not one of the limitations. However, the Notes state that the differences between the Common Law and Civil Law in this area are more important theoretically than practically.[128]

The limitations operate strictly. Courts have no discretion to grant specific performance where one of the limitations is present.[129] However, under limitation (b), which deals with unreasonable expense or effort on the part of the defaulting party, and exception (d), which refers to "reasonably" making a substitute transaction, a fair bit of leeway is granted to courts. What is unreasonable will depend very much on the facts of individual cases and the notions of national courts.[130]

The first limitation, namely that a court will not enforce impossible obligations, follows for obvious reasons. The Comments seem to suggest that impossibility refers both to objective and subjective impossibility.[131] Thus in the case of double sales, where the defaulting party has already delivered the goods to a third party who obtains priority, specific performance will not be ordered. Cases of commercial impossibility, however, need to be dealt with under exception (b), i.e. that performance will cause the obligor unreasonable expense or effort.[132]

The exception of unreasonable effort or expense is aimed at dealing with cases where under the specific circumstances it would be unreasonable to require the debtor to perform. The Comments quote the example of a ship which is to be delivered sinking on its way to the place of delivery. The cost of salvaging the ship being forty times her value, this provides an obvious instance of commercial impossibility where this exception ought to be

---

125  PECL, vol 1, 399.
126  PECL, vol 1, 395.
127  PECL, vol 1, 399–400.
128  PECL, vol 1, 400.
129  PECL, vol 1, 396.
130  See the examples quoted in PECL, vol 1, 396, 398.
131  PECL, vol 1, 396.
132  PECL, vol 1, 396. Cases of moral impossibility as known in German law are excluded by the provisions of subsection (c). See R Zimmermann, "Remedies for non-performance: the revised German Law of Obligations, viewed against the background of the Principles of European Contract Law" (2002) 6 *Edinburgh LR* 271 at 285.

applied.[133] The exception is very specific and does not grant a general remedy protecting the debtor against undue hardship, although there may be some overlap.

PECL strictly excludes the possibility of requiring specific performance for the provision of services or work of a personal nature.[134] This is based on three considerations, namely the severe interference with the personal liberty of the debtor, the fact that work under compulsion may often be rendered unsatisfactorily, and the difficulty for a court in controlling proper enforcement of its order.[135] Enforcement of restraints of trade may also fall foul of this exception if it would result in an indirect enforcement of the personal work or services.[136]

Exception (d) requires the aggrieved party to make a substitute transaction where it can reasonably be done. This can place the aggrieved party in an invidious position because of the legal uncertainty involved in the term "reasonably", the application of which will depend very much on the specific circumstances of the case. The position may be somewhat alleviated if the suggestion in the Comments is followed that the choice made by the aggrieved party affords *prima facie* proof that a substitute transaction would not be reasonable; this would place the onus on the defaulting party to show that the aggrieved party could obtain performance from other sources without any prejudice.[137]

There is a final limitation under Article 9:102(3) PECL, namely that the claim for specific performance must be made within a reasonable time after the creditor ought to have become aware of the non-performance. Once again the onus is on the non-performing party to show that an unreasonably long period has elapsed and, possibly in view of the objective of this exception, that it will suffer prejudice as a result of that.

Where the exception applies, the aggrieved party has to resort to other remedies at its disposal under PECL. Usually this will be a claim for damages.[138]

## (5) Comparative conclusion

On the issue of specific performance South African law, Scots law, and PECL depart from the point of view that a party is in principle entitled to specific

133   See Zimmermann (2002) 6 *Edinburgh LR* 271 at 281–283.
134   Article 9:102(2)(c) PECL.
135   PECL, vol 1, 397.
136   PECL, vol 1, 397–398.
137   PECL, vol 1, 398.
138   PECL, vol 1, 399.

performance, but that there are certain instances where it will not be granted. All three systems, it seems, have been influenced to some extent by English law. It is, however, in these exceptions that we find a clear distinction, in that the South African and Scots law grant a general judicial discretion to refuse specific performance whereas the PECL exceptions operate strictly: this means that on the one hand a court has no discretion to refuse specific performance where the exceptions are not present, while on the other hand it has no discretion to grant specific performance where the requirements of the exceptions have been met. In this sense South African and Scots law represent a more flexible approach than PECL, although Articles 9:101(2) and 102(2)(b) and (d) PECL afford some flexibility in the use of the terms "reasonable", "unreasonable" and "reasonably".

In clearly distinguishing between monetary obligations and non-monetary-obligations, the PECL approach provides a more nuanced and legal solution which is, at the same time, more conducive to legal certainty, than the South African position, which is to treat both types of obligations in the same manner and to subject them to the same general judicial discretion of undue hardship. This approach comes closer to the Scots approach, where, however, it appears to be based on different reasons.[139] The South African decision in *SA Harness Works*,[140] in turn, comes close to establishing a position in respect of the enforcement of payments similar to that under Article 9:101(2)(b) PECL.

So far as non-monetary obligations are concerned, there is a considerable difference between PECL and the South African approach. PECL provides for very specific circumstances where the remedy will be refused, whereas South African law uses a broadly defined judicial discretion which applies in all cases. Although certain types of exceptions or factual situations have been identified where the discretion will be applied, these do not form a *numerus clausus*. The position is similar in Scots law.

All three systems agree that performance will not be enforced where it is impossible to do so, whether such impossibility is objective or subjective. The South African exception with regard to the use of the remedy in cases of insolvency is not directly dealt with in PECL, although it can possibly be seen as a performance that would be unlawful if the applicable insolvency provisions forbid or restrict such performance.

PECL exception (b) is much more limited in its scope than the South African limitation of undue hardship, although there will probably be quite a

---

139  In Scots law the distinction is important due to the sanction of imprisonment following non-compliance with a decree for specific implement.

140  *SA Harness Works v SA Publishers (Pty) Ltd* 1915 CPD 43.

big overlap in their application to practical situations. The PECL provision provides more certainty, whereas the South African law, in this respect, provides more flexibility.

The biggest divergence between PECL and South African law, however, is found in the provisions dealing with the enforcement of contracts for services or work of a personal nature. At the same time, PECL is very similar to the Scots common law position in this regard. In terms of PECL a court has no option but to refuse such a claim. South African law, in contrast, will go quite far in requiring specific performance, as the discussion above of the *SA Harness*[141] and *Igesund*[142] cases shows. In view of the basic point of departure, the South African approach is to be preferred. The reasons for a general refusal, as set out in the Comments,[143] originate from English law and are unconvincing. The reasoning of the courts in the *Stag Packings*[144] and *Igesund*[145] cases is to be preferred. It is only where the personal liberty of the debtor is unreasonably limited that a restraint ought not to be enforced.

South African case law contains no instances similar to the exception in Article 9:102(d) PECL, but there is a parallel in Scots law. The availability of damages or of a substitute transaction provides no relief to the debtor unless the order of specific performance will cause undue hardship. The emphasis, however, is on the undue hardship of the debtor and not on the availability of alternative remedies. This rule of PECL and Scots law provides a fairer and more acceptable solution than the rather strict South African position.

The restriction under Article 9:102(3) PECL finds no direct corollary in South African or Scots law. There is apparently no time limitation on the aggrieved party in these systems to lodge its claim for specific performance other than that it must not cause undue hardship. However, if the application of this exception in PECL is restricted to cases where the debtor can show prejudice, as suggested in the Comments, the practical differences may not be all that big.

Although in respect of specific performance PECL, Scots law and South African law all start from the same principle, namely *pacta sunt servanda*, there are considerable differences in the way in which the restrictions to this principle operate. Due to the compromise character of PECL, there is much less flexibility in the application of the restrictions which are in some areas

---

141 *SA Harness Works v SA Publishers (Pty) Ltd* 1915 CPD 43.
142 *Santos Professional Football Club (Pty) Ltd v Igesund* 2003 (5) SA 73 (C).
143 PECL, vol 1, 397.
144 *National Union of Textile Workers v Stag Packings (Pty) Ltd* 1982 (4) SA 151.
145 *Santos Professional Football Club (Pty) Ltd v Igesund* 2003 (5) SA 73 (C).

more restricted (especially exception (d)), and in some areas much more restrictive, (especially (c)), than South African law. The strictness of the exceptions is more closely akin to the position in Scots law. PECL does, however, offer a limitation in (d) which is worthy of consideration in South African law.

## C. SPECIAL DAMAGES OR REMOTENESS OF DAMAGES

### (1) Introduction

It is generally recognised that mere factual causation of damages may lead to liability for the defaulting party that goes much too far; thus, in the interests of fairness, such liability should be limited in some way or another.[146] This was recognised even in Roman times.[147] But it was also recognised in the famous English decision of *Hadley v Baxendale.*[148] Here the court held:[149]

> Where two parties have made a contract which one of them has broken, the damages which the other party ought to receive in respect of such breach of contract should be such as may fairly and reasonably be considered either arising naturally, i.e., according to the usual course of things, from such breach of contract itself, or such as may reasonably be supposed to have been in the contemplation of both parties, at the time they made the contract, as the probable result of the breach of it.

That decision has also been influential in South African law,[150] Scots law[151] and the drafting of PECL.[152]

### (2) South African law

#### (a) Roman and Roman-Dutch law

In classical Roman law a difference was made between *actiones stricti iuris*, where a specific amount not exceeding the value of the object owed was claimed, and *actiones iudicia bonae fidei*, where judges awarded a sum estimated to be equitable under the circumstances, which amount did not

---

146  Joubert, *Contract*, 251; Wessels, *Contract*, § 3239; Christie, *Contract*, 637; MacQueen & Thomson, *Contract*, paras 6.31–6.38; Article 9:503 PECL, Notes 1–3.
147  Zimmermann, *Obligations*, 826–828.
148  (1854) 9 Ex 341 at 354.
149  At 351.
150  See *Holmdene Brickworks (Pty) Ltd v Roberts Construction Co Ltd* 1977 (3) SA 670 (A) at 687.
151  MacQueen & Thomson, *Contract*, para 6.33; McBryde, *Contract*, para 22-60; Walker, *Contract*, para 33.29.
152  See Article 9:503 PECL, Note 1.

necessarily reflect the objective value of the object of the performance. The *id quod interest* awarded to the plaintiff was based on subjective factors and constituted a flexible and equitable approach.[153]

By the time of Justinian this individualised method of assessing loss was extended to all cases. Justinian was not happy with the intricacies of the case law and introduced the *lex Sancimus* in terms of which the claim was limited to double the amount of the value.[154] This crude limitation of the liability of the defaulting party which baffled generations of jurists, was to remain influential well into the nineteenth century.[155]

The French writer Molinaeus in 1574 seems to have been the first commentator who tried to explain the *in duplum* rule in terms of foreseeability.[156] Pothier divorced this idea of foreseeability from the original provision in Codex 7.47.1 and explained it purely on the basis of reason and natural equity. It was deemed that the debtor would not have subjected himself to risks beyond those that were foreseeable at the time of the conclusion of the contract.[157]

Pothier's views were enthusiastically received by nineteenth-century English courts and provided the basis for the formulation of the rule in *Hadley v Baxendale* quoted above. It also forms the basis for the approach initially followed by South African courts.[158]

## (b) South African law

In *Emslie v African Merchants Ltd*[159] the rule in respect of causation was formulated as follows:

> It is plain that if a plaintiff claims damages he must not only prove to the satisfaction of the Court the actual amount of his loss through the defendant's failure to perform his contract, but he must further show either the damages he claims were in the contemplation of the parties at the time of entering into the contract, or are the direct, proximate and natural result of the breach of contract.

For this statement the court relied on passages of Voet, Domat and, above all, Pothier.[160] From Pothier's exposition it is clear that not only damages in the

---

153  Zimmermann, *Obligations*, 825–826.
154  C 7.47.1; cf Zimmermann, *Obligations*, 828; Joubert, *Contract*, 251.
155  Zimmermann, *Obligations*, 828–829.
156  Joubert, *Contract*, 252; Zimmermann, *Obligations*, 829.
157  Joubert, *Contract*, 252; Zimmermann, *Obligations*, 829; De Wet & Van Wyk, *Kontraktereg*, 205; Wessels, *Contract*, § 3305.
158  Wessels, *Contract*, §§ 3238; 3253–3257; Joubert, *Contract*, 252; De Wet & Van Wyk, *Kontraktereg*, 205.
159  1908 EDC 82 at 90.
160  At 91.

actual contemplation of the parties come into play, but also those damages that were foreseeable at the time of entering into the contract.

In *Victoria Falls & Transvaal Power Co Ltd v Consolidated Langlaagte Mines Ltd*[161] Innes CJ stated that although the non-defaulting party is entitled to full compensation for the damages, the reinstatement cannot be complete for it would be "inequitable and unfair to make the defaulter liable for special consequences which could not have been in his contemplation when he entered into the contract". He then went on to explain that the legal position in Holland and England is substantially the same, relying on the *Emslie* case, Voet, Pothier and *Hadley v Baxendale*.[162] This represented a simple restatement of the foreseeability test of Pothier, or the contemplation principle, as it has become known subsequently.[163]

The rule in *Hadley v Baxendale* is usually said to comprise two parts, namely a provision for liability for damages arising naturally from the breach, i.e. the "general" or "intrinsic damages", and a provision for liability for "special" or "extrinsic damages".[164] According to this division a party is always liable for *general* damages, whereas it is only liable for *special* damages where such damages may "reasonably be supposed to have been in the contemplation of both parties".[165]

This fairly concise and clear statement of the law, which is in accordance with the position favoured by Pothier and English law, was thrown into a state of confusion, still enduring in South African law, by the decision in *Lavery & Co Ltd v Jungheinrich*.[166] Curlewis JA started off by restating the contemplation principle, namely that special damages must have been in the contemplation of the parties and that this can be inferred from either the subject matter, the contract, or the knowledge of both parties of special circumstances.[167] He then, however, went on to require that the contract should have been entered into on the basis of the parties' knowledge of the special circumstances. This might have been an ambiguous explanation of the contemplation principle, but Wessels JA added his own gloss to this explanation by requiring that the knowledge of the special circumstances must be "so far

161  1915 AD 1 at 22.
162  (1854) 9 Ex 341.
163  *Shatz Investments (Pty) Ltd v Kalovyrnas* 1976 (2) SA 545 (A) at 552.
164  *Holmdene Brickworks (Pty) Ltd v Roberts Construction Co Ltd* 1977 (3) SA 670 (A) at 687; Christie, *Contract*, 637–639; Joubert, *Contract*, 251–252.
165  *Hadley v Baxendale* (1854) 9 Ex 341; *Holmdene Brickworks (Pty) Ltd v Roberts Construction Co Ltd* 1977 (3) SA 670 (A) at 687.
166  1931 AD 156.
167  At 169.

in the mind and contemplation of the parties as virtually to be a term of the contract". This was later referred to as the "convention principle".[168]

Although this statement is still ambiguous in using the term "virtually", the issue that there had to be actual consensus, either express or tacit, was put beyond doubt by the analysis of the decision in *Shatz Investments v Kalovyrnas*,[169] where the court accepted that the *Lavery* case authoritatively introduced the convention principle as part of the South African law. Although Trollip JA regarded its acceptance of the principle as suspect, and worthy of criticism, he was not prepared to jettison it in the fashion of English law, because the matter had not been fully argued before him.[170]

In two subsequent cases the Appellate Division has also declined to overturn the decision in the *Lavery* case despite cogent reasons to do so. In *Holmdene Brickworks (Pty) Ltd v Roberts Construction Co Ltd*[171] Corbett JA refused to resolve the controversy caused by the *Lavery* case, as the case under consideration was concerned with general damages. The court, however, did restate the law, albeit *obiter*, in the conventional manner referring to the actual or presumptive contemplation of the parties. In *Thoroughbred Breeders' Association v Price Waterhouse*,[172] however, Nienaber JA gave very strong indications that when the appropriate case came before the court it would most probably reject the discredited convention principle and develop the law along the lines recognised for the causation issue in other branches of South African law, such as crime, delict, insurance and estoppel.[173]

The convention principle is therefore still part of South African law. There seems little doubt that it will be rejected and that courts will return to some form of the contemplation or foreseeability principle developed in accordance with the principles of causation currently applied in other parts of the law.

Nienaber JA also made further important remarks in respect of the second leg of the rule in *Hadley v Baxendale* dealing with special damages. It raises for the first time in South African case law questions about the proper meaning of the word "probable" in the phrase "as a probable result of the

---

168  *Shatz Investments v Kalovyrnas* 1976 (2) SA 545 (A) at 552F; *Holmdene Brickworks (Pty) Ltd v Roberts Construction Co Ltd* 1977 (3) SA 670 (A) at 687; Christie, *Contract*, 640.

169  1976 (2) SA 545 (A) at 551–552; *Holmdene Brickworks (Pty) Ltd v Roberts Construction Co Ltd* 1977 (3) SA 670 (A) at 688.

170  Referring to *Victoria Laundry (Windsor) Ltd. v Newman Industries Ltd* [1949] 2 KB 528 (CA) and *Koufos v C Czarnikow Ltd, The Heron II* [1969] 1 AC 350. See also *Thoroughbred Breeders' Association v Price Waterhouse* 2001 (4) SA 551 (SCA) para [51] at 582.

171  1977 (3) SA 670 (A) at 687.

172  2001 (4) SA 551 (SCA).

173  Para [52] at 582–583.

breach".[174] The issue is whether "probable" has the meaning of "more likely to occur than not", or whether it has a more limited meaning.

These questions have been dealt with in a number of English cases.[175] In *The Heron II* case,[176] the House of Lords rejected the notion that the test was reasonable foreseeability if it meant the same low threshold of probability as that required in tort law.[177] Lord Reid ascribed the meaning of "not unlikely to occur" to the word.[178] This meant "a degree of probability considerably less than an even chance but nevertheless not very unusual and easily foreseeable".[179] Lord Upjohn used the terms "a real danger"[180] and "a serious possibility"[181] to describe the probabilities,[182] terms earlier used in the *Monarch Steamship Co Ltd* case.[183] The result of *The Heron II* is that a higher degree of probability is required to satisfy the test of remoteness in contract than in tort law.[184] The difficulty of applying the test is apparent from subsequent cases.[185]

Nienaber JA appears to favour a more moderate approach to this question. Foreseeability or remoteness, according to him, does not mean:[186]

> ... that the type of event or circumstance causing the loss will in all probability occur but minimally that its occurrence is not improbable and would tend to follow upon the breach as a matter of course.

The approach requires a "realistic possibility" that harm may occur, i.e. a test at the lower end of the scale of probabilities, rather than a "likelihood", i.e. a test at the upper end of the scale of probabilities.

---

174  Relying *inter alia* on the exposition of Kerr, *Contract*, 5th edn (1998), 700–701.
175  *Victoria Laundry (Windsor) Ltd v Newman Industries Ltd* [1949] 2 KB 528 (CA); *Koufos v C Czarnikow Ltd* [1969] AC 350; *Balfour Beatty Construction (Scotland) Ltd v Scottish Power plc* 1994 SC (HL) 20. See generally H McGregor, *McGregor on Damages*, 17th edn (2003), paras 248–274; M P Furmston, *Cheshire, Fifoot and Furmston's Law of Contract*, 13th edn (1996), 614–617; Treitel, *Contract*, 965–968.
176  *Koufos v C Czarnikow Ltd, The Heron II* [1969] 1 AC 350.
177  At 385, 411, 425.
178  At 383A.
179  At 397.
180  At 425.
181  At 414–415; *The Pagase* [1981] 1 Lloyd's Rep 175 at 182; *Malik v BCCI* [1998] AC 20 at 37.
182  At 414–415, 425.
183  *A/B Karlshamns Oljefabriker v Monarch Steamship Co Ltd* [1949] AC 196; 1949 SC (HL) 1.
184  Treitel, *Contract*, 967.
185  See the discussion of the decision in *H Parsons (Livestock) Ltd v Uttley Ingham & Co Ltd* [1978] QB 791 by Treitel, *Contract*, 967–968.
186  *Thoroughbred Breeders' Association v Price Waterhouse* 2001 (4) SA 551 (SCA) at 581F.

## (3) Scots law

Scots law deals with the issue of special damages under two distinct heads, namely general causation and remoteness. General causation is determined by the "but for" or *sine qua non* test. It is merely required that the breach must have been a material cause of the damages.[187] The extent of the liability of the defaulting party is limited by the principle of remoteness. The discussion here, however, is restricted to the issue of remoteness.

The principle of remoteness was well established in Scots law by the eighteenth century,[188] long before the decision in the English case of *Hadley v Baxendale*.[189] Scots law followed Pothier in this regard.[190] Despite this venerable historic fact, *Hadley v Baxendale* provides the point of departure for most discussions of this topic in modern Scots law, without appreciation of the Civilian roots of this doctrine.[191]

The position in modern Scots law is largely determined by five cases, namely *Hadley v Baxendale*,[192] *Victoria Laundry (Windsor) Ltd v Newman Industries Ltd*,[193] *A/B Karlshamns Oljefabriker v Monarch Steamship Co Ltd*,[194] the *Heron II*,[195] and *Balfour Beatty Construction (Pty) Ltd v Scottish Power plc*.[196] These have already been discussed above when dealing with the English influence on South African law.

It would seem that in Scots law the remoteness test in contract law is generally more restrictive than that in delict, being limited to what is reasonably contemplated rather than what is reasonably foreseeable.[197] The reason offered for this distinction is that contracts are usually planned relationships and parties can therefore regulate their liability, whereas in delict they cannot. But this reasoning is hardly convincing.[198] The leading Scottish case, *Balfour Beatty*, applied a reasonable contemplation standard.[199]

---

187  MacQueen & Thomson, *Contract*, para 6.31; McBryde, *Contract*, para 22-16 ff; Walker, *Contract*, para 33.26.
188  MacQueen & Thomson, *Contract*, para 6.33; McBryde, *Contract*, paras 22-01–22-03; Walker, *Contract*, para 33.21.
189  (1854) 9 Ex 341.
190  McBryde, *Contract*, para 22-01.
191  MacQueen & Thomson, *Contract*, para 6.33; McBryde, *Contract*, para 22-03; and 22-60.
192  (1854) 9 Ex 341.
193  [1949] 2 KB 528.
194  1949 SC (HL) 1.
195  [1969] 1 AC 350.
196  1994 SC (HL) 20.
197  MacQueen & Thomson, *Contract*, para 6.34.
198  MacQueen & Thomson, *Contract*, para 6.34.
199  McBryde, *Contract*, para 22-64.

In practice the differences in approach may be difficult to determine and are probably best summed up by Lord Denning:[200]

> I soon begin to get out of my depth. I cannot swim in the sea of semantic exercises – to say nothing of different degrees of probability – especially when the cause of action can be laid either in contract or in tort. I am swept under the conflicting currents.

MacQueen and Thomson indicate that there was a definite trend in Scots law to expand liability by relaxing the standard of contemplation, but that the trend was somewhat reversed in the *Balfour Beatty* case by the House of Lords.[201] In that case a contractor was constructing a concrete aqueduct which necessitated a process of continuous pouring of concrete. There was a power failure constituting a breach of contract on the part of the power company which resulted in a substantial part of the aqueduct having to be demolished and rebuilt. The court held that the damages were too remote, relying on the first leg of the *Hadley v Baxendale* test in that the damage did not arise in the ordinary course of events and was therefore too remote. It had also not been in the contemplation of the parties and the power company did not have any special knowledge about the business of the contractor.

*Cosar Ltd v UPS Ltd*[202] provides an interesting illustration of an instance where a contracting party was held to have had knowledge of special circumstances. The delivery company failed to deliver tender documentation in time with the result that the contractor's tender was not considered during the tender process. It was held that the information supplied to the courier was sufficient to provide it with the necessary knowledge that the loss of the opportunity to tender could lead to a loss of the contract, provided that that knowledge extended to the likelihood of the tender being successful.[203]

### (4) Articles 9:502 and 9:503 PECL

The point of departure in PECL is that a claim for damages is a remedy that is generally available unless non-performance is excused under Article 8:108 PECL. It can be brought in addition to any other remedies that a party may have, provided that actual damages have been suffered. The provisions aim at compensating the aggrieved party as fully as possible.[204]

---

200  In *H Parsons (Livestock)Ltd v Uttley Ingham & Co Ltd* [1978] QB 791 at 802.
201  MacQueen & Thomson, *Contract,* para 6.36; McBryde, *Contract,* para 22-68.
202  1999 SLT 259.
203  See MacQueen & Thomson, *Contract,* para 6.38.
204  Zimmermann (2002) 6 *Edinburgh LR* 271 at 288.
205  PECL, vol 1, 442.
206  *Thoroughbred Breeders' Association v Price Waterhouse* 2001 (4) SA 551 (SCA) at 582F.

PECL also recognises that the liability for damages cannot be unrestricted. Article 9:503 PECL therefore formulates a general test of foreseeability excluding the liability for damages that are too remote. The formulation of Article 9:502 PECL accords with the general principle recognised in many legal systems that the aggrieved party is entitled to its fulfilment (or expectation or performance) interest. Whether a party chooses to enforce the contract by specific performance, or to terminate it where there has been a fundamental non-performance in terms of Article 8:103 PECL, the aggrieved party can claim full damages, including a loss of profit, in order to be placed, financially, in a position as close as possible to the one if the contract had been properly performed. This is only limited by the provisions of foreseeability contained in Article 9:503 PECL.

The first important aspect to note in Article 9:503 PECL is that it focuses only on what the non-performing party actually foresaw or could have foreseen. It is therefore not necessary to ask whether the aggrieved party could have foreseen such loss. That question is irrelevant, and quite rightly so. The test is an objective one to protect the defaulting party from too wide a liability. It is therefore reasonable to restrict its liability to what a party in its position could reasonably have foreseen at the time of the conclusion of the contract.

The limitation on liability apparently does not operate in favour of the defaulting party where the breach of contract was intentional or grossly negligent. In these instances the only limitation would be normal factual causation, i.e. the defaulting party will be liable for all damages caused by its default, even those which would ordinarily be regarded as too remote.[205]

The reference to "as the likely result" of the breach at first blush seems to require a high degree of probability that such loss would result if regard is had to the discussion of the English law and *The Heron II* above. "Likely result" can either have the meaning of "a reasonable possibility" or "serious possibility" at the lower end of the scale of probabilities, or "more likely to occur than not" at the higher end of the scale of probabilities. In the Notes to Article 9:503 PECL the similarity of this provision with the rule in *Hadley v Baxendale* is discussed without reference to the subsequent difficulties in interpreting the word "probable" in English law.

Finally the foreseeability must be judged as at the time of the conclusion of the contract and not at the time of the breach. This is in line with the principle in many legal systems that a party should only be liable for the risks it actually undertook or should have foreseen at the time of contracting.

## (5) Comparative conclusion

Although South African and Scots law as well as PECL seem to depart from the rule in *Hadley v Baxendale* in respect of the causation of damages, there are important aspects in which these systems diverge from that early formulation. In addition South African law seems to have accepted the convention principle which is even more restrictive than the contemplation principle formulated in *Hadley v Baxendale*.

It would seem that there is general agreement between writers and courts in South Africa that the acceptance of the convention principle, requiring actual *consensus* between the parties on the possibility of remote damages, was a mistake and should be rejected. The proper occasion has just not yet arrived for the Supreme Court of Appeal to do so, leaving inferior courts to manipulate the facts to avoid the full consequences of the restriction. Obviously this is a highly unsatisfactory state of affairs. In reforming the law, the Supreme Court of Appeal may also reconsider the development of this part of the law, as is quite clear from the decision in the *Thoroughbred Breeders* case.[206] The court will be helped by having regard to either Scots law or the PECL in doing so.

PECL departs from the rule in *Hadley v Baxendale* in two important respects. It focuses solely on the foreseeability by the defaulting party and not by both parties, and it excludes the limitation in instances of intentional or grossly negligent non-performance. The underlying principle involved in this rule is that it would be manifestly unfair to subject the defaulting party to risks it did not or could not reasonably have foreseen at the time of the conclusion of the contract. What the aggrieved party foresaw or should have foreseen is therefore irrelevant and need not be considered. That departure from the rule in *Hadley v Baxendale* is therefore fully justified. Similarly, where a party is grossly negligent, or intentionally breaks the contract, it should not be entitled to rely on this restriction and should fully compensate the other party for damages. This is a policy decision and probably a commendable one. The only question is whether it should not have been restricted to intentional non-performance.

The use of the term "likely" in Article 9:503 PECL is unfortunate, as it apparently requires a degree of probability higher than the drafters may have had in mind. This should be clear from the discussion of this issue in English law. It would appear from the Comments that the term has the same meaning as "probable" in *Hadley v Baxendale* which still leaves courts with interpretational uncertainties. The approach as set out in English law, namely that it means "a serious possibility" without suggesting that there should be more than an even chance of it occurring, is probably also appropriate here.

The position of PECL in respect of remote damages and causation provides a good example of the rational and fair development of the rule in *Hadley v Baxendale*. It should be considered when South African law is reconsidered.

## D. CONCLUSION

It is clear that mixed legal systems can often draw upon the collective wisdom and divergent approaches contained in different legal systems to formulate their own approaches which may provide solutions that are superior, in the sense of being more developed and nuanced. However, the hybrid character or compromise nature of the solution may sometimes also lead to inferior solutions in the sense that they are too restrictive or limiting; or it may even lead to outright bad results. The rules relating to specific performance and special damages in PECL and South African law provide examples for both possibilities.

The provisions of PECL in respect of specific performance are probably more limiting than necessary when compared to South African and Scots law. They do, however, contain some solutions such as that in respect of substitute transactions which are worthy of consideration in both legal systems.

The acceptance of the convention principle in South African law, apparently under the influence of earlier English law, is simply bad law. Fortunately it has been universally recognised that it should be abandoned. The provisions of PECL may prove helpful in reformulating this area of South African law.

# 11 Termination for Breach of Contract

## Tjakie Naudé

# A. INTRODUCTION

The remedy of termination[1] for breach of contract was introduced into Scots and South African law under the influence especially of English law.[2] In neither Roman nor Roman-Dutch law was there a generalised remedy of termination for breach of contract, as it is known to modern law.[3] Scots and South African law do not, however, mirror English law on all aspects of termination. In a number of instances, the courts have refused indiscriminately to take over all of English law on the subject.[4]

It has been said that the rules on termination upon non-performance of PECL also follow the Common Law rather closely in a number of respects.[5] Similarities between PECL and Scots and South African law on termination are therefore to be expected.

One characteristic of the remedy of termination for non-performance under PECL which is not shared with the Common Law, is that the rules on termination apply equally to breach of contract[6] and to excused non-performance (excused as a result of an impediment beyond the debtor's control). In Scotland and South Africa, as in the Common Law, termination due to excused supervening impossibility of performance is regarded as a doctrinally distinct issue meriting separate treatment from termination as a remedy for breach of contract.[7] To keep this chapter within manageable bounds, only termination as a remedy for breach of contract, and only the following aspects thereof, will be considered:

1 "Rescission" is the preferred term in Scotland, and "cancellation" in South Africa. I prefer the term "termination" used also by PECL.

2 For South African law, see A Cockrell, "Breach of contract", in Zimmermann & Visser, *Southern Cross*, 303 at 308, 313, 314, 317, 321. The writings of Pothier also played a role in South Africa (J R Harker, "The nature and scope of rescission as a remedy for breach of contract in American and South African law" 1980 *Acta Juridica* 61 at 70). For Scots law, see W W McBryde, "The Scots law of breach of contract: a mixed system in operation" (2002) 6 *Edinburgh LR* 5 at 11; D Johnston, "Breach of contract", in Reid & Zimmermann, *History*, vol 2, 175; McBryde, *Contract*, 509. H L MacQueen, "Scots and English law: the case of contract" (2001) 54 *CLP* 205 notes that the principle of mutuality was also decisive.

3 *Stewart Wrightson (Pty) Ltd v Thorpe* 1977 (2) SA 943 (A) (henceforth *Stewart Wrightson*) at 953B; Zimmermann, *Obligations*, 800 ff; Harker, 1980 *Acta Juridica* 61 at 69; Cockrell, in Zimmermann & Visser, *Southern Cross* at 320.

4 Zimmermann & Visser, *Southern Cross* at 322. For example, the distinction between conditions and warranties and the doctrine of total failure of consideration do not form part of South African and Scots law.

5 H Beale, A Hartkamp, H Kötz & D Tallon, *Cases, Materials and Text on Contract Law* (2002), 756.

6 In the sense of non-justified failure or refusal to perform in terms of the contract.

7 See, e.g, Walker, *Contract*; McBryde, *Contract*; MacQueen & Thomson, *Contract*; Gloag, *Contract*; Christie, *Contract*; Kerr, *Contract*; and Van der Merwe et al, *Contract*, who discuss these two issues in separate chapters.

1.  grounds for termination (in other words, when the remedy is available);
2.  effect, on the availability of the remedy, of a tender to cure the breach; and
3.  consequences of termination.

## B. GROUNDS FOR TERMINATION

PECL provides for three instances in which a contract may be terminated for non-performance. First, the contract may be terminated if the non-performance is fundamental.[8] Second, an ultimatum procedure is provided for in the case of delay, which allows the aggrieved party to terminate where the delay is not in itself a fundamental non-performance.[9] Third, termination for anticipatory non-performance is possible.[10] Article 8:105 PECL provides for a fourth related instance in which a party may terminate: a party who reasonably believes that there will be a fundamental non-performance may demand adequate assurance of due performance, and may terminate where this assurance is not provided within a reasonable time. These four instances will now be compared with South African and Scots law. Of course, the parties themselves may also provide expressly for a right to terminate which will override the aforementioned residual rules.

### (1) Fundamental or material breach

#### (a) Unitary concept of non-performance

As far as cancellation for fundamental non-performance is concerned, PECL adopts a unitary or generalised concept of non-performance.[11] Any type of non-performance justifies termination, as long as it is fundamental. Scots law also holds that any material breach justifies cancellation, and thus has a unitary concept of breach.[12]

The unitary approach of PECL and Scots law contrasts with the South African approach, which at first glance is more fragmented. Courts and textbook writers hold that the breach must first be pigeon-holed into one of

---

8 Article 9:301(1) PECL.

9 Article 9:301(2) PECL read with Article 9:106(3) PECL.

10 Article 9:304 PECL.

11 Article 8:103 PECL. "Non-performance" is defined in Article 1:301 PECL as any failure to perform an obligation under the contract, "and includes delayed performance, defective performance and failure to co-operate in order to give full effect to the contract".

12 Walker, *Contract*, 524; MacQueen & Thomson, *Contract*, 205; Gloag, *Contract*, 602; McBryde "Remedies for breach of contract" (1996) 1 *Edinburgh LR* 43 at 55.

several categories of breach, each with its own test for when termination is allowed.[13]

Closer examination of South African law reveals, however, that the notion of materiality is important throughout. Thus, positive malperformance (defective performance) justifies termination when the breach is material.[14] Prevention of performance also only allows the debtor to terminate the contract, if it amounts to a material breach.[15] Apart from the case where the entire contract is repudiated, only the repudiation of a "material aspect" or "material term" allows an election to terminate.[16] It is not specifically stated that *mora* or delay justifies termination if it amounts to a material breach. Instead, a right to terminate exists (apart from the ultimatum procedure) only where "time is of the essence under the contract".[17] However, this may just be another way of saying that the delay constitutes a material breach.

It must also be noted that some writers on Scots law have found it useful to distinguish between different forms of breach, such as delay, defective performance, impossibility of performance and repudiation (conduct demonstrating an unequivocal intention no longer to be bound), when discussing the instances when termination will be permitted.[18] In addition, the English law criterion of time being of the essence of the contract is applied to delay only,[19] but that is simply a manner of saying that the delay has to be material. Textbook writers also generally treat anticipatory breach or repudiation separately.[20]

### (b) More detailed definition of fundamental breach

Both Scots and South African statements on the law relating to termination for material breach consist of vague tests, which do not give much guidance

---

13 The history of this development is sketched by Cockrell, in Zimmermann & Visser, *Southern Cross*, 304–319. See also, e.g, Van der Merwe et al, *Contract*, ch 10; Lubbe & Murray, *Contract*, ch 10.

14 De Wet & Van Wyk, *Kontraktereg*, 179; Van der Merwe et al, *Contract*, 328; Lubbe & Murray, *Contract*, 491–492.

15 *Grobbelaar v Bosch* 1964 (3) SA 687 (E) at 691; *Holgate v Minister of Justice* 1995 (1) SA 921 (E) at 937A–B; Lubbe & Murray, *Contract*, 483.

16 *Culverwell v Brown* 1990 (1) SA 7 (A); *Tamarillo (Pty) Ltd v BN Aitken (Pty) Ltd* 1982 (1) SA 398 (A).

17 See, e.g., Van der Merwe et al, *Contract*, 319; Joubert, *Contract*, 237 and cases there cited.

18 MacQueen & Thomson, *Contract*, 206 ff; Gloag, *Contract*, 603 ff; Walker, *Contract*, 523–524; cf *Edinburgh Grain Ltd v Marshall Food Group Ltd* 1999 SLT 15.

19 Walker, *Contract*, 523; Gloag, *Contract*, 615; McBryde (1996) 1 *Edinburgh LR* 43 at 65; *Ahmed v Akhtar* 1997 SLT 218.

20 McBryde, *Contract*, 485 ff; MacQueen & Thomson, *Contract*, 206.

to parties or courts on when a breach will be regarded as material.[21] In both countries one often encounters the metaphor of the breach going to the root of the contract[22] and other similarly imprecise tests.

By contrast, PECL defines "fundamental breach" with more precision. There are three instances when a breach will be fundamental. These are, first, where strict compliance with the obligation is of the essence of the contract; secondly, where the non-performance substantially deprives the aggrieved party of what it was entitled to expect under the contract, unless the other party did not foresee and could not reasonably have foreseen that result; and thirdly, where the non-performance is intentional and gives the aggrieved party reason to believe that it cannot rely on the other party's future performance.[23]

Closer examination of Scots and South African case law reveals, however, that the same considerations are in fact taken into account to establish whether a breach is material. Under both systems, for example, a delay warrants termination where "time is of the essence of the contract" (in other words where strict compliance is of the essence of the contract).[24] In addition, in many South African cases on positive malperformance (defective performance) and partial repudiation, the presence or absence of substantial detriment to the aggrieved party was of decisive importance for the court's conclusion on the materiality of the breach.[25] The impact of the breach on the aggrieved party has also been taken into account in Scottish cases to determine whether a breach is material.[26] The question whether the breach was intentional was considered relevant in *Aucamp v Morton*,[27] a South African case on positive malperformance.

21 T Naudé & G Lubbe, "Cancellation for 'material' or 'fundamental' breach: a comparative analysis of South African law, the UN Convention on Contracts for the International Sale of Goods (CISG) and the UNIDROIT Principles of International Commercial Contracts" (2001) 12 *Stellenbosch LR* 357 at 373; Cockrell, in Zimmermann & Visser, *Southern Cross*, 313; cf Harker, 1980 *Acta Juridica* 61 at 79.

22 Scottish Law Commission Discussion Paper on Remedies for Breach of Contract (Scot Law Com DP No 109, 1999) (henceforth Scot Law Com DP No 109 (1999)), 9; *Wade v Waldon* 1909 SC 571 at 576; Gloag, *Contract*, 602; *Oatarian Properties (Pty) Ltd v Maroun* 1973 (3) SA 779 (A) at 784G; *Elgin Brown & Hamer (Pty) Ltd v Industrial Machinery Suppliers (Pty) Ltd* 1993 (3) SA 424 (A) at 430I–J.

23 Article 8:103 PECL.

24 See note 7 above.

25 For details, see Naudé & Lubbe (2001) 12 *Stellenbosch LR* 357 at 382–385.

26 See, for example, *Macari v Celtic Football and Athletic Co Ltd* 1999 SC 628 at 635–636; *Ghaznavi v BP Oil (UK) Ltd* 1991 SLT 924 at 928, 931. The Scottish Law Commission has also said that the modern tendency is to focus on the materiality of the breach rather than simply on the term breached (Scot Law Com DP No 109 (1999), para 2.9).

27 1949 (3) SA 611 (A).

One lesson that Scots and South African law can therefore learn from PECL is to formulate more explicitly the factors that courts regard as relevant to establish the materiality of breach. PECL gives the courts some leeway to take account of the particular circumstances of the case, but it also provides guidance on the aspects to be considered, enabling parties properly to prepare for litigation on the materiality of the breach.[28] A failure to take account of all possibly relevant considerations may render a decision on the materiality of a breach less persuasive.[29]

In this regard, the approach adopted in the UNIDROIT PICC is perhaps closer to South African practice than that of PECL. PICC simply provides that a material breach justifies termination, but then adds an open-ended list of factors to be considered in order to establish whether a breach is material.[30] The three tests listed in PECL are part of this list, but another factor is added, namely whether the non-performing party will suffer disproportionate loss as a result of preparation or performance if the contract is terminated. It appears that PICC, albeit not expressly, grants courts an equitable discretion to decide whether termination is justified. That the court should have an equitable discretion to decide whether termination is possible has been accepted in two South African decisions of the Supreme Court of Appeal on positive malperformance, i.e. *Spies v Lombard*[31] and *Singh v McCarthy Retail Ltd (t/a McIntosh Motors)*.[32] The *Singh* decision speaks of a "value judgment" to be exercised and enjoins the court to consider the competing interests of both parties in order to treat them fairly.[33] Ultimately the test laid down in the *Singh* case is whether the breach is "so serious that it is fair to allow the innocent party to cancel the contract and undo all its consequences'.[34]

The difference in approach between PECL, with its *numerus clausus* of three alternative instances of material breach, and PICC is not enormous. The approach of PICC appears preferable as it enjoins the court to have regard to all relevant circumstances, including the interests of the party breaking the contract, and the seriousness of the breach, instead of focusing

---

28 For example, counsel for the aggrieved party in *Singh v McCarthy Retail Ltd (t/a McIntosh Motors)* 2000 (4) SA 796 (SCA) only addressed the court on the materiality of the term breached, whereas the court also considered the consequences of the breach.

29 See Naudé & Lubbe (2001) 12 *Stellenbosch LR* 357 at 389 for an example from the case law.

30 Article 7.3.1 PICC.

31 1950 (3) SA 469 (A).

32 2000 (4) SA 796 (SCA).

33 At 804F–G.

34 At 804G–H. See also *Ankon CC v Tadkor Properties (Pty) Ltd* 1991 (3) SA 119 (C) at 123A.

the court's attention on only any one of three tests. That termination takes place extra-judicially is not an obstacle to the view that a discretion is involved. The decision by the aggrieved party that the breach is serious enough to warrant termination is explicitly rather than merely implicitly subjected to a judicial discretion under PICC.[35] An objection that the PECL approach brings more certainty than a judicial discretion[36] can be met by the argument that a certain degree of vagueness is unavoidable in this area. As Treitel has stated, "the delicate balancing of interests that is required in this area is pre-eminently a matter for judicial discretion, and not one that can be determined in advance by fixed rules."[37] What should be avoided is an unfettered judicial discretion, where the factors which the courts should and do take into account are not formulated clearly.[38]

The acknowledgment by the drafters of PECL that a trivial breach should not warrant termination even where strict compliance is of the essence,[39] means that the detriment caused to the aggrieved party should in any event be taken into account in all cases, except, it is submitted, where the contract itself provides for a right to terminate upon breach. Thus the test in PICC more correctly reflects the reality that courts should consider the detriment caused in addition to whether strict compliance is of the essence of the contract.

The recognition of an equitable discretion to allow termination can also be extended to breach in the form of prevention of performance and *mora* (delay).[40] Or, at the least, foreseeable substantial detriment caused by the breach should also justify cancellation for delay, as is the case under PECL. The causation of foreseeable substantial detriment is probably the best explanation of the doctrine of "time being of the essence under the contract". Certainly such an explanation is superior to the strained argument that a tacit termination clause or *lex commissoria* is involved.[41] At present, there is a danger that the "time is of the essence" doctrine will only assist a South African creditor under a commercial contract subject to price fluctuations

---

35 Naudé & Lubbe (2001) 12 *Stellenbosch LR* 357 at 397.

36 This is implicit in the Scottish Law Commission's preference for the approach of PECL above that of PICC (Scot Law Com DP No 109 (1999), para 2.16) (although ultimately the Commission did not deem it necessary to implement either of the two approaches).

37 G H Treitel, *Remedies for Breach of Contract* (1988) (henceforth Treitel, *Remedies*), 350. See also Naudé & Lubbe (2001) 12 *Stellenbosch LR* 357 at 397; Harker, 1980 *Acta Juridica* 61 at 79.

38 Naudé & Lubbe (2001) 12 *Stellenbosch LR* 357 at 397.

39 Comment B to Article 1:201 PECL.

40 Naudé & Lubbe (2001) 12 *Stellenbosch LR* 357 at 394.

41 Naudé & Lubbe (2001) 12 *Stellenbosch LR* 357 at 394; cf Cockrell, in Zimmermann & Visser, *Southern Cross* at 309–310. The view that a tacit *lex commissoria* is involved is followed by, e.g., Harker, 1980 *Acta Juridica* 61 at 74.

and so on. That there is a need to protect the creditor in a wider ambit of cases, when late performance will lead to foreseeable substantial detriment, is demonstrated by the decision of *Cowley v Estate Loumeau*.[42] In this case the curators of an insolvent estate were allowed to terminate the sale of a farm on the basis of the buyer's failure to pay the price by a certain date. The court took into account the detriment caused by late performance, namely that the money was required for purposes of the estate, as mortgagees were demanding interest and other creditors were pressing their claims. A discretionary approach to termination for delay on the basis of foreseeable substantial detriment would also lay to rest Alfred Cockrell's criticism that "it is anomalous that a debtor who fails to perform a vital term is better placed than one whose timeous performance is materially defective".[43]

## (2) Ultimatum procedure in the case of delay

Like PECL, both Scots and South African law know an ultimatum procedure after which the aggrieved party may terminate for delay, regardless of the seriousness of the breach.[44]

One difference between South African and Scots law, on the one hand, and PECL, on the other, is that the ultimatum under PECL will be effective even if it stipulates an unreasonable period for performance. If the period stated is too short, the aggrieved party may still terminate after a reasonable period.[45] By contrast, a notice giving too short a period for performance will be invalid in South African law and apparently also in Scots law.[46]

## (3) Anticipatory breach

All three systems recognise that an anticipatory breach may justify termination. In this regard, Article 9:304 PECL provides that "[w]here prior to the time for performance by a party it is clear that there will be a fundamental

---

42 1925 AD 392.

43 At 319.

44 McBryde, *Contract*, 523; MacQueen & Thomson, *Contract*, 213; Walker, *Contract*, 557; McBryde (2002) 6 *Edinburgh LR* 5 at 18; *Rodger (Builders) Ltd v Fawdry* 1950 SC 483 at 492; *Johnstone v Harris* 1977 SC 365 at 370; Report on Remedies for Breach of Contract (Scot Law Com No 174, 1999) (henceforth Scot Law Com No 174 (1999)), para 7.38; Van der Merwe et al, *Contract*, 319; Christie, *Contract*, 590; *Microcoutsis v Swart* 1949 (3) SA 715 (A) at 730. Certainly in South Africa, this development is owed to English influence (Harker, 1980 *Acta Juridica* 61 at 74).

45 Article 8:106(3) PECL.

46 *Ver Elst v Sabena Belgian World Airlines* 1983 (3) SA 637 (A); McBryde (2002) 6 *Edinburgh LR* 5 at 18.

non-performance by it, the other party may terminate the contract."

There is some ambivalence under PECL and Scots law as to whether anticipatory non-performance is a breach in itself. The Comment to Article 9:304 PECL draws a distinction between "anticipatory non-performance" and "actual non-performance".[47] Some Scottish authors deny that anticipatory breach is a breach before its acceptance by the aggrieved party.[48] In this regard, Scots law and perhaps PECL are still more under the influence of English law, from whence the doctrine of anticipatory breach or repudiation derives.[49] By contrast, anticipatory breach is indeed regarded as an immediate breach under South African law.[50] "Acceptance" of the repudiation is not required to turn the repudiation into a breach of contract; it simply amounts to the exercising of an election to terminate the contract.[51] The English law language of offer and acceptance has been rejected in South Africa as inappropriate.[52]

Whereas traditionally repudiation was defined as an unequivocal indication that the contract will not be performed,[53] there is a modern tendency to allow termination where it is clear that a fundamental breach will occur, as under PECL.[54] For example, in *Datacolor International (Pty) Ltd v Intamarket (Pty) Ltd* the South African Supreme Court of Appeal held that "whether the innocent party will be entitled to resile from the agreement will ultimately depend on the nature and degree of the impending non- or malperformance".[55] As is the case under PECL, one is therefore enjoined to consider whether the forthcoming breach will be material. The implication may at first sight appear to be that if the party in breach intimates that he will

---

47  Comment D to Article 9:304 PECL.

48  MacQueen & Thomson, *Contract*, 206; McBryde (1996) 1 *Edinburgh LR* 43 at 57. The Scottish Law Commission has stated that repudiation, "a sort of 'inchoate breach'" creates an option to rescind, upon the exercise of which repudiation is treated "as if it were a breach" (Scot Law Com DP No 109 (1999), para 1.16).

49  McBryde (2002) 6 *Edinburgh LR* 5 at 21; Scot Law Com DP No 109 (1999), para 2.6.

50  *Datacolor International (Pty) Ltd v Intamarket (Pty) Ltd* 2001 (2) SA 284 (SCA) (henceforth *Datacolor International*) at 287J; *Tucker's Land and Development Corporation (Pty) Ltd v Hovis* 1980 (1) SA 645 (A) (henceforth *Tucker's Land and Development*); *Novick v Benjamin* 1972 (2) SA 842 (A) at 853H–854A; P M Nienaber, "Kontrakbreuk *in anticipando* in retrospek" 1989 *TSAR* 1; Van der Merwe et al, *Contract*, 332–333; Christie, *Contract*, 627.

51  *Datacolor International* (note 50) at 288B.

52  *Stewart Wrightson* (note 3) at 953; *Tucker's Land & Development* (note 50); *Datacolor* (note 50). See also Harker, 1980 *Acta Juridica* 61 at 80, on the artificiality of the "offer and acceptance" analysis of repudiation.

53  Gloag, *Contract*, 598–599; McBryde, *Contract*, 486; McBryde (2002) 6 *Edinburgh LR* 5 at 20; *White & Carter (Councils) Ltd v McGregor* (1962) SC (HL) 1 at 11–12; *GL Group plc v Ash Gupta Advertising Ltd* 1987 SCLR 149 (henceforth *GL Group plc*) at 152; *Street v Dublin* 1961 (2) SA 4 (W); Christie, *Contract*, 601.

54  Scot Law Com No 174 (1999), para 7.3.

55  *Datacolor* 2001 (2) SA 284 at 294I.

not perform at all, the aggrieved party will only be entitled to terminate if time is of the essence under the contract, since that is presently regarded under South African law as the only ground when a delay will justify cancellation in itself.[56] However, it appears that even where time is not of the essence under the contract, a total repudiation of the contract will justify termination, that is, where the debtor intimates that he will not perform at all. The test, added the court, is whether a reasonable person would conclude that proper performance will not be forthcoming.[57]

### (4) Termination for failure to give adequate assurance of performance

PECL allows a party who reasonably believes that there will be a material breach on the part of the other party a right to demand assurance of performance, and if this is not forthcoming within a reasonable time, a right to terminate the contract.[58] There is authority for a similar rule in South Africa.[59] In *Hayne NO v Narun Bros*[60] a buyer assigned his estate and the seller insisted on a bank guarantee. The court indicated that an aggrieved party was allowed in such circumstances to ask for security for due performance, failing which the aggrieved party may cancel the contract. Unlike under PECL, the South African principle is not expressly qualified by a requirement that a fundamental breach is to be feared, but such a requirement is sensible and logical.

The Scottish Law Commission considered the usefulness of such a rule, but declined to make a recommendation on the point as it received objections that more uncertainty would be created than would be removed.[61] In my view the PECL rule is a useful provision.

## C. EFFECT OF TENDER TO CURE ON REMEDY OF TERMINATION

A tender to cure a remediable breach can conceivably affect the aggrieved party's power to terminate in at least four different ways. First, a legal system may grant the party in breach a right to be given a second chance, or ultimatum, before the aggrieved party may terminate. A second, weaker, meaning of the

---

56 Apart from the case where a notice of intention to cancel (an ultimatum) is given or where the contract expressly provides for cancellation on delay.

57 *Datacolor* 2001 (2) SA 284 at 294G.

58 Article 8:105 PECL.

59 Van der Merwe et al, *Contract*, 360.

60 1926 OPD 207.

61 Scot Law Com No 174 (1999), para 7.37.

right to cure is that the aggrieved party has no obligation to give an invitation to cure, but the defaulting party has a right to cure, which overrides a purported termination. Thirdly, a tender of cure may merely lead to a loss of the right to terminate provided the tender to cure, or alternatively cure itself, occurs before termination. This is more akin to a possibility of cure than a right to cure.[62] A fourth manner in which a cure might affect the right to terminate is when a legal system recognises that a tender to cure may prevent the breach from being fundamental or material, so that no right to terminate arises at all.

The approach to cure diverges in the three systems under consideration.

## (1) PECL

Article 8:104 PECL provides that:

> [a] party whose tender of performance is not accepted by the other party because it does not conform to the contract may make a new and conforming tender where the time for performance has not yet arrived or the delay would not be such as to constitute a fundamental non-performance.

The right to cure under PECL is limited for a number of reasons. First, it is limited to instances where the party in breach has indeed made a non-conforming tender of performance. Delay appears to be curable only if the party in breach has indeed made a tender to perform late. The right to cure does not exist if the party in breach has not tendered to perform at all. Repudiation in the sense of a total refusal to perform is therefore not curable under this provision (it will be considered later whether it will be retractable for other reasons).

Secondly, a mere verbal statement of intention to cure will not be sufficient – a new and conforming tender must be made.

Thirdly, either the time for performance must not yet have arrived, or the resulting delay should not be such as to constitute a fundamental non-performance. This will depend on whether time is of the essence under the contract, or has become of the essence by the giving and expiry of an ultimatum notice under Article 8:104 PECL.[63] Of course, the delay can also constitute a fundamental non-performance if it would cause foreseeable substantial detriment to the aggrieved party.

It is unclear whether Article 8:104 PECL creates a right to cure which would override a purported notice of termination. The right to cure is not expressly limited to instances where notice of termination has not yet been

---

62 Cf Treitel, *Remedies*, 371.
63 Comment to this Article (PECL, vol 1, 368).

given.[64] By contrast, PICC, for example, specifically provides that the right to cure is not precluded by a notice of termination.[65]

Is there any right to retract a repudiation under PECL? The situation is not dealt with under Article 8:104 PECL. But the Comment to Article 9:304 PECL states that the aggrieved party may terminate on the basis of an anticipatory breach "at any time while it remains clear that there will be a fundamental non-performance".[66] This suggests that an anticipatory repudiation may be retracted with the resultant loss of the right to terminate, as it is then no longer clear that there will be a fundamental non-performance.

Article 9:303(3)(b) PECL also provides for loss of the right to terminate in the case of delay. It states that, if the aggrieved party knows or has reason to know that the other party still intends to tender within a reasonable time, and the aggrieved party unreasonably fails to notify the other party that it will not accept performance, it loses its right to terminate if the other party in fact tenders within a reasonable time. Therefore, when it knows that cure of delay is forthcoming, the aggrieved party must act swiftly if it does not wish to accept the cure, otherwise the party in breach will have the right to cure the delay within a reasonable time.

## (2) Scots law

Scots law does not have a rule identical to that of PECL. There is, however, authority to the effect that the right to terminate may be lost if the party in breach tenders proper performance of a remediable breach before termination has occurred.[67] Whether this also applies to breach in the form of a delay is somewhat controversial. The Scottish case of *Cumming v Brown* holds that

---

64 See also E Clive & D Hutchison, "Breach of contract", in Zimmermann, Visser & Reid, *Mixed Legal Systems*, 176 at 202.

65 Article 7.1.4(2) PICC.

66 At 418.

67 McBryde, *Contract*, 521; Scot Law Com DP No 109 (1999), para 4.26 ("Where a remediable material breach has occurred and, before the contract has been rescinded, effective performance is tendered then the right to rescind is lost"); *Cumming v Brown* 1994 SLT (Sh Ct) 11 (henceforth *Cumming v Brown*); Clive & Hutchison, in Zimmermann, Visser & Reid, *Mixed Legal Systems* at 203–204. Cf Walker, *Contract*, 525. McBryde (1996) 1 *Edinburgh LR* 43 at 63 has criticised *Cumming v Brown* on the basis that it overlooked *Ford Sellar Morris Properties plc v E W Hutchison Ltd* 1990 SC 34 which held that the right to resile could not have been taken away by belated performance of the condition involved; and also that *Cumming v Brown* actually encourages an innocent party to rescind before the right to terminate may be lost, which is not conducive to the implementation of contracts. However, the Scottish Law Commission finds the present law satisfactory and has pointed out that *Ford Sellar Motors* did not concern rescission for material breach, but a right for either party to resile if a landlord's consent was not obtained by a certain date (Scot Law Com DP No 109 (1999), 30). Lord Marnoch, who was in the minority in *J & H Ritchie Ltd v Lloyd Ltd* 2005 SLT 64, relied on *Ford Sellar Motors* to hold that a right to

a tender of performance after a delay causes the right to terminate to be lost even though time was expressly made of the essence.[68] Similarly, the Law Commission does not limit its statement that a tender to cure a remediable breach will affect the right to terminate to certain forms of breach, and it refers with approval to *Cumming v Brown* in this regard.[69] Although Eric Clive and Dale Hutchison agree that the right to terminate will be lost upon a satisfactory offer of conforming performance, they state that "[a]n offer of late performance, where time is of the essence, is not an offer of conforming performance" as "time cannot be recovered".[70] The question in all such cases will be whether the breach is still remediable. MacQueen and Thomson do not mention the principle that the right to terminate will be lost upon tender of a remediable breach. They explain *Cumming v Brown* on the basis that the aggrieved party was prevented from terminating on the basis of personal bar.[71]

Scottish writers accept that a repudiation may be retracted before termination has occurred.[72] Some explain this on the basis that there is no breach before acceptance of repudiation.[73]

There have also been suggestions that the defaulting party should first be given an ultimatum to cure,[74] but the Scottish Law Commission has rejected this proposition.[75] The Commission also held that, subject to exceptions,

---

reject cannot be taken away by the later renewed tendering of goods in a proper condition (paras 11, 12). He explained *Cumming v Brown* on the basis that the seller had not invoked his option to regard the delay as material (para 11). On the other hand, Lord Hamilton in the same decision declined to resolve the differences between *Ford Sellar Motors* and *Cumming v Brown,* but nevertheless held that the seller was no longer in breach after it repaired the equipment sold so that the buyer's attempted termination came too late (para 48).

68　The contract itself provided that timeous payment was an essential obligation and that there would be a right to terminate after late payment 1994 SLT (Sh Ct) at 12.

69　Scot Law Com DP No 109 (1999), para 4.26.

70　Clive & Hutchison, in Zimmermann, Visser & Reid, *Mixed Legal Systems* at 204 n 157. They do not refer to *Cumming v Brown* in this context. McBryde (1996) 1 *Edinburgh LR* 43 at 62, also argues that "performance after the specified date was not performance in terms of the contract".

71　MacQueen & Thomson, *Contract* at 214. The court stated, however, that personal bar did not apply in this case (at 213). The issue of personal bar was never raised and the court stated that the sharp and narrow question to be decided was "where one party … has acquired a right to resile, does that right remain effective and exercisable notwithstanding a tender of performance by the other party" (at 213). However, the court quoted Gloag, *Contract*, 620 who talks of the right to reject being barred if the aggrieved party is led to the assumption that the contract still exists.

72　McBryde, *Contract*, 490; Gloag, *Contract*, 600; McBryde (1996) 1 *Edinburgh LR* 43 at 57; MacQueen & Thomson, *Contract*, 206.

73　MacQueen & Thomson, *Contract* at 206.

74　*Lindley Catering Investments Ltd v Hibernian Football Club Ltd* 1975 SLT (Notes) 56 at 57; *Strathclyde Regional Council v Border Engineering Contractors Ltd* 1998 SLT 175 at 177; cf Clive & Hutchison, in Zimmermann, Visser & Reid, *Mixed Legal Systems* at 201–202; McBryde (2002) 6 *Edinburgh LR* 5 at 18–19; McBryde, *Contract*, 521–523. McBryde (1996) 1 *Edinburgh LR* 43 at 60, states that *Lindley Catering* may mean that a remediable breach is a non-material breach.

Scots law does not recognise such a right.[76] One such exception is found in Part VA of the Sale of Goods Act 1979, in terms of which a consumer must generally have resort to the remedies of repair or replacement before seeking rescission.[77] Another exception is that of a lessee in breach being granted the right to an ultimatum before the landlord may terminate for a monetary breach of the lease.[78]

There is some authority in Scotland that remediability should be considered in determining whether a breach is material;[79] this is the fourth sense identified above in which cure can be relevant to the right to terminate. Some authors explain the aforementioned cases that apparently accept a right to an ultimatum on this basis.[80]

## (3) South African law

South African authorities are generally less comfortable with the notion that a tender to cure should affect the right to terminate.

Like PECL, however, two South African cases allow the breaching party in breach to cure a non-conforming performance before the time for performance has passed,[81] although many South African writers either fail to mention[82] or criticise this rule.[83] The two South African cases in question suggest that the right to cure exists despite a purported notice of termination, so that it is a right to cure in the second sense mentioned above. One of these cases suggests, however, that the right to cure is possibly precluded if it would cause unreasonable inconvenience to the aggrieved party[84] or if the initial

---

75  Scot Law Com No 174 (1999), para 7.21.

76  Scot Law Com No 174 (1999), para 7.21.

77  Section 48C. The relationship between this provision and s 15B, which allows for rescission without the necessity of first seeking repair or replacement, is problematic, probably because it results from the European Consumer Sales Directive.

78  Law Reform (Miscellaneous Provisions) (Scotland) Act 1985, s 4. *McKimmie's Trustees v Armour* (1899) 2 F 156 also suggests that a lessor must be given a second chance to remedy damages in the leased premises (see Scot Law Com DP No 109 (1999), para 4.10).

79  MacQueen & Thomson, *Contract*, 211; cf McBryde (1996) 1 *Edinburgh LR* 43 at 60; Clive & Hutchison, in Zimmermann, Visser & Reid, *Mixed Legal Systems* at 201.

80  MacQueen & Thomson, *Contract*, 211.

81  *Leviseur v Scott* 1922 OPD 138 (henceforth *Leviseur v Scott*) at 141–143; *Inrybelange (Edms) Bpk v Pretorius* 1966 (2) SA 416 (A) at 427B–E. Cf Clive & Hutchison, in Zimmermann, Visser & Reid, *Mixed Legal Systems* at 203–204, stating that the right to terminate will be lost if, within the time available for performance, the breaching party makes a satisfactory tender of conforming performance.

82  Van der Merwe et al, *Contract*, 386; Lubbe & Murray, *Contract*, 583; Kerr, *Contract,* 703 ff.

83  De Wet & Van Wyk, *Kontraktereg*, 180. But see Harker, 1980 *Acta Juridica* 61 at 82; Christie, *Contract*, 491.

84  *Leviseur v Scott* (note 81) at 142. Cf in this regard Article 48(1) CISG which makes the right to cure dependent on the absence of unreasonable inconvenience to the aggrieved party.

tender of non-conforming goods has induced the aggrieved party to act to its own detriment (in which case an estoppel may arise).[85] The Appellate Division in *BK Tooling (Edms) Bpk v Scope Precision Engineering (Edms) Bpk*[86] relied on these cases to state that as long as performance remains possible and the contract is not cancelled, the other party can still perform, and that this possibility should be related to our doctrine of *purgatio morae*.[87]

There are conflicting views on whether a repudiation may be retracted.[88] Those against retractability point out that this proposition is supported merely by *obiter dicta*, and that it derives from the rejected notion of English law that repudiation is a thing writ in water, without any effect until accepted by the other party, as opposed to an immediate breach giving rise to an immediate right to cancel which should not be lost unless by the actions of the aggrieved party itself.[89] It has also been argued that allowing retraction of repudiation causes the very uncertainty which recognition of this type of breach aims to prevent.[90] Furthermore, it is pointed out that the aggrieved party may have acted in reliance on the power of termination, even though notice of termination has not yet been given.[91] Nienaber, on the other hand, provides a theoretical foundation for the doctrine of retraction of repudiation. He argues that, since the test for termination is whether the anticipated malperformance would justify cancellation, a retraction of repudiation causes the erstwhile right to cancel to disappear, as the anticipated malperformance will no longer occur.[92] This presupposes that the time of purported termination is decisive for establishing whether there is a right to terminate. There is some authority in South African law that repudiation may also be retracted after the date for performance has passed.[93] A fourth view is that

---

85  *Leviseur v Scott* (note 81) at 142.

86  1979 (1) SA 391 (A) (henceforth *BK Tooling*).

87  At 419B–C.

88  Authorities in favour of retractability include J W Wessels, *The Law of Contract in South Africa vol II*, 2nd edn by A A Roberts (1951), para 2955; De Wet & Van Wyk, *Kontraktereg*, 216; Nienaber, 1989 *TSAR* 1 at 3, 14; *De Wet v Kuhn* 1910 CPD 263 at 267 (*obiter*). Those against retractability include G Lubbe, "Retraction of repudiation: a doctrine writ in water?" (1996) 7 *Stellenbosch LR* 147; Kerr, *Contract*, 595–596; Christie, *Contract*, 627; Van der Merwe et al, *Contract*, 385.

89  Lubbe (1996) 7 *Stellenbosch LR* 147 at 159; Kerr, *Contract*, 596.

90  Lubbe (1996) 7 *Stellenbosch LR* 147 at 161.

91  Kerr, *Contract*, 596.

92  *Anticipatory Repudiation in English and South African Law of Contract: a Comparative Study* (1961), 432 (as cited by Lubbe (1996) 7 *Stellenbosch LR* 147 at 160).

93  See the cases cited by Lubbe (1996) 7 *Stellenbosch LR* 147 at 148 ff. De Wet & Van Wyk, *Kontraktereg*, 216, do not specifically limit their view that the repudiating party may perform in spite of the repudiation to cases where the date for performance has not yet passed.

repudiation can be retracted as long as the position of the aggrieved party has not been altered in any way.[94]

Apart from the cursory reference in *BK Tooling* to the doctrine of *purgatio morae*, there appears to be no South African authority holding that the right to terminate will be lost if the party in "ordinary breach" (as opposed to repudiation) purports to cure after the date for performance. Instead, some South African writers deny that the right to terminate should be affected by a tender to cure.[95] There is clear authority that a tender of full performance cannot affect a right to terminate derived from a *lex commissoria*,[96] inter alia because a party cannot lose the right to terminate except by its own act.[97] It is said that otherwise two competing rights[98] would be set up against each other, which would undermine the object of the *lex commissoria*.[99] It has been asked whether the same consideration should not also apply to the common law residual right to terminate for breach.[100]

South African law does not recognise a strong right to cure in the sense of a right to be given a second chance to perform before the aggrieved party may cancel. The only common law exception to the rule appears to be the lessor's right to be given an opportunity to cure defects arising in the leased property before the lessee may cancel.[101]

## (4) Conclusion

Scots law recognises that the right to terminate may be lost if the cure takes place before termination. In addition, cure is a factor affecting materiality. Repudiation may also be retracted, a notion that has found *obiter* support in South African cases. There are some Scottish legislative provisions, which oblige the aggrieved party to give the other party an opportunity to cure. In South African law, there is only clear authority for a right to cure other types of breach before the date for performance, although this has been criticised.

There are cogent policy arguments both in favour of and against allowing a tender to cure to affect the aggrieved party's right to terminate. In my view, these opposing policy arguments can most fairly be balanced by a rule that

---

94  *Langverwacht Farming Co v Sedgwick & Co Ltd (II)* 1942 CPD 155 (*obiter*).
95  Van der Merwe et al, *Contract*, 386; cf Harker, 1980 *Acta Juridica* 61 at 82.
96  *Schuurman v Davey* 1908 TS 664 at 671–672; *Pienaar v Fortuin* 1977 (4) SA 428 (T); *Moodley v Reddy* 1985 (1) SA 76 (D); cf *Boland Bank Ltd v Pienaar* 1988 (3) SA 618 (A).
97  *Boland Bank Ltd v Pienaar* 1988 (3) SA 618 (A) at 622 with reference to Voet, *Commentarius ad Pandectas*, 22.1.31.
98  The right to cure and the right to cancel.
99  *Moodley v Reddy* 1985 (1) SA 76 (D) at 81E–F.
100  Lubbe & Murray, *Contract*, 583.
101  W E Cooper, *Landlord and Tenant*, 2nd edn (1994), 100.

the right to terminate will be lost if a tender to cure has been made before termination has occurred, provided that:

1. the cure will cause no unreasonable inconvenience;
2. the resultant delay will not constitute a fundamental or material breach;
3. the aggrieved party has not yet acted in reliance on the breach;
4. damages and costs are tendered simultaneously; and
5. the cure is effected promptly.

A number of European systems recognise in some form the defaulting party's right to cure.[102] It is also consistent with the principle of Scots and South African law that the law should encourage performance of a contract,[103] and that termination is a drastic remedy which should not easily be granted. Allowing cure also reflects the policy of minimising economic waste.[104] The aggrieved party's interests are protected by the limitations on the right to cure set out above. The aggrieved party can make an end to the uncertainty of whether cure will take place by terminating the contract. Granting the party in breach a right to cure that overrides a purported termination or a right to an ultimatum goes too far in protecting the party in breach. A rule that an ultimatum should always be given does not give due consideration to the possibility that the aggrieved party may have lost confidence in the party in breach, and may also tempt unscrupulous parties to perform shoddily in the knowledge that they will be given a second chance.[105]

## D. CONSEQUENCES OF TERMINATION

The winding-up regime set out in Articles 9:305 to 9:309 PECL has been criticised on a number of grounds. These provisions are in some respects overly complex and yet in others too underdeveloped to provide clear solutions. The aspects that warrant criticism will now be compared with the position under South African and Scots law.

### (1) Mutual restitution not the point of departure under PECL

First, the PECL winding-up regime has been criticised on the basis that it would have been simpler to require mutual restitution[106] as the point of

102  See the Notes to Article 8:104 PECL.
103  Cf McBryde, *Contract*, 490. That this is a principle underlying PECL appears also from Articles 9:101 and 9:102 PECL, which grant a right to specific performance.
104  Cf Comment to Article 7.1.4 PICC.
105  Scot Law Com DP No 109 (1999), para 4.17.
106  The term "restitution" does not refer to a special type of enrichment action in this chapter, but simply describes the recovery of a performance.

departure, and then to provide for exceptions in the case of successive or divisible contracts such as lease, where termination only has prospective effect,[107] as well as for contractual provisions which are intended to operate even after termination, such as arbitration and penalty clauses. Instead, the PECL winding-up regime takes the continuous or successive contract as its point of departure, and only provides for restitution by way of a number of rather complicated exceptions set out in Articles 9:306 to 9:308 PECL. Essentially, these Articles provide that restitution is only called for when no counter-performance has been received or the counter-performance received has been rightfully rejected. According to some Scots authors, the same principle applies in Scots law: it is said that restitution depends on non-reciprocation.[108] By contrast, the point of departure in South African law is simply that cancellation of a reciprocal obligation causes the counter-obligation to be extinguished or undone, with the result that the parties must restore mutually.[109] South African law then provides for an exception where rights have accrued which are independent of any executory part of the contract so that the contract is divisible.[110] Of course, provisions which are intended to operate after termination, such as arbitration or penalty clauses, are also not affected thereby.[111] The approach of PICC is similar to South African law in this regard and appears to be preferable to PECL.[112]

107  R Zimmermann, "Restitutio in integrum: Die Rückabwicklung fehlgeschlagener Verträge nach den Principles of European Contract Law, den Unidroit Principles und dem Avant-projet eines Code Européen des Contrats" in H Honsell et al, *Privatrecht und Methode: Festschrift für Ernst A Kramer* (2004) (henceforth Zimmermann, in *Festschrift Kramer*), 735 at 741; P Hellwege, *Die Rückabwicklung gegenseitiger Verträge als einheitliches Problem* (2004) (henceforth Hellwege, *Rückabwicklung*) at 589.

108  H L MacQueen, "Contract, unjustified enrichment and concurrent liability: A Scots perspective" 1997 *Acta Juridica* 176 at 193–195; H L MacQueen, "Unjustified enrichment and breach of contract" 1994 *JR* 137 at 138, 145, 148; Scot Law Com DP No 109 (1999), paras 4.28–4.29; cf MacQueen & Thomson, *Contract*, 216–217; Hogg, *Obligations*, 199. A Scottish case which is at first glance contrary to the principle that restitution depends on non-reciprocation is *Connelly v Simpson* 1993 SC 391, where the court refused to order restitution of a purchase price of £16,000 for shares which were not delivered and which were worth only £400 at termination of the contract. This decision can possibly be explained on the basis that the shareholder got what he paid for, namely a right to claim the shares on demand and that he therefore by implication carried the risk of a drop in value (MacQueen, 1997 *Acta Juridica* 176 at 195–196; MacQueen, 1994 *JR* 137 at 145–146).

109  Van der Merwe et al, *Contract*, 376.

110  *Shelagatha Properties Investments CC v Kellywood Homes (Pty) Ltd* 1995 (3) SA 179 (A), summarising the principle in *Walker's Fruit Farms Ltd v Sumner* 1930 TPD 394. See also Van der Merwe et al, *Contract*, 379; Christie, *Contract*, 629.

111  *Atteridgeville Town Council v Livanos* 1992 (1) SA 296 (A) at 303I-306C; Christie, *Contract*, 629.

112  See Articles 7.3.5 and 7.3.6 PICC.

## (2) Article 9:306 PECL

Article 9:306 PECL provides that property previously received may be rejected by the party terminating the contract when the value of the property has been fundamentally reduced as a result of the other party's non-performance. This provision applies, for example, where a contract has been partially performed, but the performance received has become useless by reason of the breach in respect of the rest of the performance.[113] Article 9:306 PECL has been criticised for apparently excluding rejection of performance where a seller has delivered a different object from the one foreseen by the contract, which is of the same value as the promised performance.[114] For this reason, Article 9:306 PECL should rather have provided that performance may be rejected where it is defective or does not comply with the contract.[115]

## (3) Articles 9:307 and 9:308 PECL

Article 9:307 PECL provides that on termination of the contract a party may recover money paid for a performance which it did not receive or which it properly rejected. According to Article 9:308 PECL a party which has supplied property that can be returned and for which it has not received payment or other counter-performance may on termination of the contract recover the property.

Both Articles have been criticised for focusing on something similar to the Common Law requirement that the aggrieved party must have suffered a "total failure of consideration" before it may reclaim an advance payment.[116] This criticism is more cogent concerning Article 9:308 PECL as that Article does not provide for the possibility of rejection of defective performance with a resultant duty to make restitution as does Article 9:307 PECL. As Article 9:308 PECL reads now, only a total failure of counter-performance will lead to restitution.

In any event, the South African rule, which simply requires mutual restitution, is preferable.

---

113  Comment to Article 9:306 PECL.
114  Hellwege, *Rückabwicklung*, 590.
115  Hellwege, *Rückabwicklung*, 590.
116  Hellwege, *Rückabwicklung*, 590–591; Zimmermann, in *Festschrift Kramer* at 741; R Zimmermann, *Die Principles of European Contract Law als Ausdruck und Gegenstand europäischer Rechtswissenschaft* (2003) at 9.

## (4) Article 9:309 PECL

On termination of the contract a party which has rendered a performance that cannot be returned and for which it has not received counter-performance may recover a reasonable amount for the value of the performance to the other party. This is provided by Article 9:309 PECL. The impossibility of restitution may arise either because the benefit received was the result of work that cannot be returned or with regard to which restitution is too onerous,[117] or because property transferred has been used up or destroyed – but for which the receiving party has not been paid.[118]

It is clear that under Article 9:309 PECL an inability to restore, whether attributable to the acts of the recipient or not, is not a bar to termination.[119]

Article 9:309 PECL is somewhat underdeveloped, however, and does not provide a clear solution to the situation where non-conforming property which may be rejected has been destroyed. The following example illustrates the problem: suppose a boat owner has refrigeration equipment installed in his boat that is guaranteed to operate properly for a certain period of time. The equipment does not function at all upon the first attempt to use it out at sea, and the boat owner resolves to terminate the contract. However, before he is able to do so the boat sinks in an unexpected gale and the refrigeration equipment is lost. Suppose the breach is serious enough to justify termination. Since restitution is not a condition precedent for termination under PECL, the boat owner may terminate, but does he owe something to the person who installed the refrigeration equipment for its value?[120] It is not clear from Article 9:309 PECL at what stage the "reasonable amount for the value of the performance to the other party" must be determined.[121] On the one hand, Article 9:309 PECL may mean that even where the performance has been consumed, lost or destroyed, the value of the performance to the recipient at the time it was received must be returned.[122] In favour of this interpretation is the statement in the Notes to Articles 9:305 to 9:309 PECL that the Principles are broadly in accordance with systems which take a

117  Comment to Article 9:308 PECL.
118  Comment to Article 9:309 PECL.
119  Notes to Articles 9:305–9:309 PECL.
120  The example is based on the facts of *Hall-Thermotank Natal (Pty) Ltd v Hardman* 1968 (4) SA 818 (D) (henceforth *Hall-Thermotank*).
121  C Coen, *Vertragsscheitern und Rückabwicklung* (2003) (henceforth Coen, *Vertragsscheitern*) at 308.
122  Cf § 346 BGB, which also provides for "Wertersatz", and according to which the value of the performance at the time of performance must be restored (see A Teichmann, in O Jauernig (ed), *Kommentar zum BGB*, 10 edn (2003), § 346 Rn 4 and Rn 6).

liberal approach to restitution after termination and thus enable the court or arbitrator to order full restitution of benefits received. On the other hand, the value at termination may be intended, so that if the recipient has lost the performance without having received any benefit therefrom, he need not restore anything. Comment A to the Article refers to a party being *"left with a benefit which cannot be returned"* which seems to support this inter-pretation.[123] To similar effect is Comment B, which refers to the amount by which a party has been enriched.[124] Under the South African and Scots laws of enrichment, for example, there is a defence of change of position or loss of enrichment, which would put the risk of accidental destruction of property on the transferor, and thus on the person who installed the equipment in this instance.[125] Of course, had it been the party in breach who had destroyed or lost the property, a damages claim would compensate the aggrieved party for loss of his performance in such a case. But the position where it is the aggrieved party who has lost the property remains unclear under PECL.

Another aspect on which Article 9:309 PECL is unclear concerns the situation where the actual value of the performance to the recipient is much higher than the contract price – that is where the performing party has made a bad bargain. However, the example in the Comment makes it clear that in such case the recipient need only restore an appropriate part of the purchase price.[126] An important qualification such as this should rather have been contained in the Article itself.

### (a) Comparison with South African law

The South African rules dealing with an inability to return in kind are far more complex than Article 9:309 PECL.

It is trite that if by the very nature of the performance received, literal restoration is not possible, as where services have been rendered, the value of

---

123  Comment A to Article 9:309 PECL; Coen, *Vertragsscheitern* at 308.
124  Comment B to Article 9:309 PECL.
125  N R Whitty and D Visser, "Unjustified enrichment", in Zimmermann, Visser & Reid, *Mixed Legal Systems*, 399 at 435; Bell, *Principles*, § 537; *Cantiere San Rocco v Clyde Shipbuilding and Engineering Co* 1923 SC (HL) 105 at 111 per Lord Birkenhead. Eric Clive contends, however, that, contrary to what Bell and *Cantiere* hold, the risk of accidental destruction does, or should, lie with the transferee since ownership has passed to him and the owner bears the risk of loss (E M Clive, *Draft Rules on Unjustified Enrichment and Commentary*, prepared for Scottish Law Commission (1996) (henceforth Clive, *Draft Rules*), Schedule, para 2(2)(a) and (b), comment, example 3).
126  At 426.

the performance must be restored.[127] In other instances, there has been some support in South African law for a principle that the ability to restore performance is a condition precedent for termination.[128] This principle was then subjected to a number of qualifications based on the idea that restitution is required only as far as it is equitable.[129] However, in the context of rescission for improperly contained consent, the Supreme Court of Appeal has made it clear that restitution is not a condition precedent but rather a consequence for the act of rescission,[130] although a tender of restitution, or an explanation and excuse for its failure is a requirement for a claim for restitution.[131] This view should also apply in the breach of contract context.[132] As Clive and Hutchison point out, there is often no policy reason for denying termination provided that a suitable adjustment of economic imbalances by way of monetary compensation can be arranged.[133]

Examples of cases where the courts have held it to be inequitable to require restitution include the situation where the property received has perished as a result of the inherent defect complained of[134] or during the normal intended use of the property.[135] It has also been held to be inequitable to require restitution where it has become impossible through no fault of the aggrieved party, provided that that party does not gain an advantage from the performance.[136] Thus a boat owner in circumstances similar to those described above was held to be entitled to terminate without having to compensate the other party for the refrigeration equipment lost at sea.[137]

There are instances where the recipient must restore the value of a

---

127 Harker, 1980 *Acta Juridica* 61 at 100; *Spencer v Gostelow* 1920 AD 617. The claim has been said to be based on unjustified enrichment in that context (*BK Tooling* (note 86) at 424), but the better view is that it is contractual in nature (S Miller, "Unjustified enrichment and failed contracts", in Zimmermann, Visser & Reid, *Mixed Legal Systems*, 437–468). A full consideration of this controversy is beyond the scope of this chapter.

128 Van der Merwe et al, *Contract*, 374; Harker, 1980 *Acta Juridica* 61 at 100; *Uni-Erections v Continental Engineering Co Ltd* 1981 (1) SA 241 (W) at 247G, 248A. Cf Walker, *Contract*, 558 who states that where innocent third parties have acquired rights for consideration in the subject matter of the contract, e.g. where a buyer has resold goods, rescission is precluded in Scots law.

129 Van der Merwe et al, *Contract*, 374.

130 *Extel Industrial (Pty) Ltd v Crown Mills (Pty) Ltd* 1999 (2) SA 719 (SCA) at 731E–G, 732A–D.

131 At 732B.

132 Although Van der Merwe et al, *Contract*, do not mention the *Extel* case, they refer to other cases decided in the context of rescission for improperly obtained consent as if the same principles should apply in both contexts.

133 Clive & Hutchison, in Zimmermann, Visser & Reid, *Mixed Legal Systems* at 205–206.

134 Cf *Marks Ltd v Laughton* 1920 AD 12.

135 *African Organic Fertilizers & Associated Industries Ltd v Sieling* 1949 (2) SA 131 (W).

136 *Hall-Thermotank* (note 120); Van der Merwe et al, *Contract*, 374; Harker, 1980 *Acta Juridica* 61 at 100–101; Lubbe & Murray, *Contract*, 592.

137 *Hall-Thermotank* (note 120).

performance that cannot be returned. For example, if a party has gained an advantage from the performance which cannot be returned, he has to restore that benefit or a monetary substitute for it.[138] If owing to the fault of the aggrieved party restitution is not possible *in specie* but remains substantially possible, termination will be possible if the shortfall is supplemented by payment in money.[139] Some authors hold that where it is the party in breach who is unable to return the performance received, he must always pay a surrogate for the performance, regardless of whether he has obtained any benefit from the performance.[140] This duty is regarded as part of the process of restitution and not as ordinary damages.[141]

### (b) Comparison with Scots law

Apparently, restitution in kind is not generally considered to be a condition precedent for termination in Scots law, but merely as a consequence of termination.[142] Certainly, a substitutive claim for restitution of the value of a performance that cannot be returned by reason of its very nature is allowed.[143] Whether this claim is based on unjustified enrichment or the law of contract is controversial, but the better view is that it is a contractual claim,[144] despite the Law Commission's suggestion that enrichment analysis should govern the consequences of termination.[145]

---

138  *Harper v Webster* 1956 (2) SA 495 (FC); cf *Theron v Africa* 10 SC 246.

139  Van der Merwe et al, *Contract*, 375; *Harper v Webster* 1956 (2) SA 495 (FC).

140  De Wet & Van Wyk, *Kontraktereg*, 244 n 236; Lubbe & Murray, *Contract*, 593 n 5; Van der Merwe et al, *Contract*, 383.

141  De Wet & Van Wyk, *Kontraktereg*, 244 n 236; Lubbe & Murray, *Contract*, 593 n 5; Van der Merwe et al, *Contract*, 383.

142  Clive & Hutchison, in Zimmermann, Visser & Reid, *Mixed Legal Systems* at 206; McBryde, *Contract*, 480; Hellwege, *Rückabwicklung*, 346, 348, 354, 357, and P Hellwege, "*In integrum restitutio* and the requirement of counter-restitution in Roman Law" 2004 *JR* 165 at 171, 176, suggest that it is not a condition precedent, whereas P Hellwege "Unwinding mutual contracts: *restitutio in integrum v* the defence of change of position" in Johnston & Zimmermann (eds), *Unjustified Enrichment* at 255, states that it is a requirement in the case of defective goods sold. See also MacQueen, 1994 *JR* 137 at 148, cf at 138. According to Miller, in Zimmermann, Visser & Reid, *Mixed Legal Systems* at 449, Scots law prevents termination for breach when the aggrieved party cannot return a performance received, but there have been calls for restitution by way of monetary surrogate. However, the authorities Miller lists are concerned with reduction or rescission of a voidable contract and not with termination for breach.

143  See, e.g., *Ramsay v Brand* (1895) 25 R 1212.

144  See, e.g., Miller, in Zimmermann, Visser & Reid, *Mixed Legal Systems*; Hogg, *Obligations*, 201–202; J A Dieckmann and R Evans-Jones, "The dark side of *Connelly v Simpson*" 1995 *JR* 90 at 100; McBryde, *Contract*, 524–525; H L MacQueen, "Unjustified enrichment" in C Ashton et al, *Fundamentals of Scots Law* (2003), 267 at 306.

145  Scot Law Com No 174 (1999), paras 7.23–7.24. See also *Watson v Shankland* (1871) 10 M 142 at 152. A number of cases hold that the party in breach cannot sue on the contract but must

How would Scots law treat the example of the boat owner who has lost the performance received? Must he restore the value of the boat upon reclaiming the price? First, if the boat owner can be said to have had a reasonable opportunity to examine the equipment to ascertain its conformity, he would lose the right to reject the goods on the basis that he had accepted them as provided for in the Sale of Goods Act.[146] The buyer could probably have tested the equipment before going out to sea and on this basis has lost the right to reject.

Suppose, however, that the defect manifested itself before the buyer could be said to have accepted the goods, that it was serious enough to warrant rejection, but that the goods had been accidentally destroyed before termination took place. The majority view is that the risk of accidental destruction does not pass to the buyer where defective goods are delivered and then rejected by the buyer, and so the buyer would still be allowed to terminate.[147] Michael Bridge, however, argues that it would be fairer if the risk of interim loss arising from events unconnected with the non-conforming character of the goods should remain with the buyer, with the implication that the buyer may not terminate.[148] If one were to follow the former view it has to be asked whether the seller is entitled to the value of what he performed so that ultimately this is deducted from the purchase price claimed by the buyer. There seems to be no clear case law on this issue in the breach of contract context.

Robin Evans-Jones contends that a party who is unable to return the object itself upon termination has to offer its value.[149] This is based on the idea that the parties must be placed into the position in which they were before the transaction was performed (*restitutio in integrum*).[150] Since the purpose of the rules on restitution after termination is to prevent unjustified enrichment,[151] one answer might lie in the application of enrichment rules.[152] However, the weight of authority on restitution of corporeal property is to the

---

base its claim on unjustified enrichment (e.g. *Steel v Young* 1907 SC 360; *Forrest v Scottish County Investment Co Ltd* 1916 SC (HL) 28 at 39).

146   Sale of Goods Act 1979, s 35; see further P S Atiyah, J N Adams, H MacQueen, *The Sale of Goods*, 11th edn (2005) (henceforth Atiyah et al, *Sale of Goods*), 513–515.

147   Atiyah et al, *Sale of Goods*, 356.

148   M G Bridge, *The Sale of Goods* (1997), 125.

149   Robin Evans-Jones, *Unjustified Enrichment*, vol 1 (2003), 316–317; cf Hellwege, *Rückabwicklung*, 600.

150   Hogg also holds that a substitutive claim would lie if the property has been consumed or transferred to a third party (*Obligations*, 201–202).

151   MacQueen, 1997 *Acta Juridica* 176 at 192–193.

152   Clive & Hutchison, in Zimmermann, Visser & Reid, *Mixed Legal Systems*, at 206, suggest that contract law could usefully adopt or refer to enrichment rules to provide a solution in this context.

effect that the risk of accidental destruction lies with the transferor.[153] On this view, the seller would not have a claim for the value of the goods lost based on unjustified enrichment. Once again there is a contrary view: Eric Clive contends that the risk of accidental destruction should lie with the transferee since, first, ownership has passed to him and the owner, generally, bears the risk of loss and, secondly, the transferor would have acted reasonably if he cancelled his insurance.[154]

### (c) Evaluation

It is commendable that Article 9:309 PECL does not treat restitution in kind as a condition precedent for termination. Article 9:309 PECL operates fairly where the performance cannot be returned by reason of its very nature, such as in the case of services rendered.

The problem of accidental destruction of property in the hands of the aggrieved party, however, on which Article 9:309 PECL and Scots law are not clear, is not easily resolved.[155] On the one hand it may be argued that breach justifies a differential treatment of the party in breach and the aggrieved party, so that the aggrieved party should be excused from paying anything for the lost property, provided it has exercised the degree of caution which it would have exercised in its own affairs. On the other hand, breach is not always accompanied by fault and may not be a suitable reason to subvert the normal incidence of risk, which should run with physical control of the property involved.[156] This implies that the recipient should carry the risk of accidental destruction and should therefore compensate the performing party for the value of its performance if restitution in kind becomes impossible as a result of no fault of either party. Another argument in favour of the risk of accidental destruction resting on the recipient of the performance is that the recipient can be expected to insure the property, whereas the transferor may reasonably have cancelled his insurance.

On balance, the best solution would be for the recipient to carry the risk of accidental destruction so that he has to pay a monetary substitute if restitution in kind is not possible.[157] Accordingly, the recipient should always be

---

153 Bell, *Principles*, § 537; *Cantiere San Rocco v Clyde Shipbuilding and Engineering Co* 1923 SC (HL) 105 at 111 per Lord Birkenhead.
154 Clive, *Draft Rules*, Schedule, para 2(2)(a) and (b), comment, example 3.
155 Cf Miller, in Zimmermann, Visser & Reid, *Mixed Legal Systems* at 449.
156 Miller, in Zimmermann, Visser & Reid, *Mixed Legal Systems* at 449; Zimmermann, in *Festschrift Kramer* at 753.
157 Zimmermann, in *Festschrift Kramer* at 753. Hellwege, 2004 *JR* 165 argues that this was most likely the position in Roman law.

forced to restore the value of what he has received, except where, first, the impossibility to restore is attributable to the other party, i.e., for example, where an inherent defect for which that other party is responsible has led to the destruction, and, secondly, where the damage would have occurred anyway if the property had been in the hands of the claimant.[158] Article 9:309 PECL should be rewritten to provide for these exceptions.

### (5) Calls for unified winding-up regime

There have been calls for the same winding-up regime to apply to all instances where the contract is either void, or avoided, or terminated.[159] In my view, as in that of Saul Miller, there are valid reasons for distinguishing between these various instances of contractual failure. For example, in the case of voidable contracts, the fact that the aggrieved party is innocent whereas the other party is blameworthy may justify treating the aggrieved party who accidentally lost the property he had received more favourably than the other party. Breach, on the other hand, is not always accompanied by moral culpability.[160] The fact that the contractual nexus is not completely extinguished by termination for breach also justifies a different treatment from the case where the contract is avoided. Thus, the contract price should be the limit of the amount recoverable for the value of the performance upon termination for breach,[161] a principle which does not apply where the contract is voidable due to improperly obtained consent. There is also arguably a stronger argument for giving effect to the contractual allocation of risk in breach of contract cases.[162]

### E. CONCLUSION

The PECL provisions on termination for non-performance are similar to Scots and South African law in a number of important respects, not surprisingly in view of the Common Law influence in all three systems. The right to terminate is exercised by notice, and recourse to a court is not, therefore, required. In some respects termination only operates prospectively in all

---

158  Cf Zimmermann, in *Festschrift Kramer*, at 753–754.
159  Zimmermann, in *Festschrift Kramer* at 753–754; Hellwege, *Rückabwicklung*, 599; Hellwege, in Zimmermann & Johnston, *Unjustified Enrichment* at 262 ff.
160  Miller, in Zimmermann, Visser & Reid, *Mixed Legal Systems* at 468. Zimmerman mentions a possible exception to the duty to repay the value of a lost performance where the other party has fraudulently induced the recipient to enter into the contract (in *Festschrift Kramer* at 754). If this exception were allowed, there would essentially be two different regimes for winding up a contract.
161  Comment B to Article 9:309 PECL.
162  Miller, in Zimmermann, Visser & Reid, *Mixed Legal Systems* at 468.

three systems. All three systems know the concept of fundamental or material breach, although PECL defines this concept more clearly. Under all three systems a non-fundamental delay may be elevated into a fundamental one by an ultimatum, and all three know the concept of anticipatory breach.

However, the solutions adopted by PECL also differ from those of Scots and South African law in a number of respects. The most prominent examples are: the clearer and more extensive definition of "fundamental non-performance"; the validity of an unreasonable ultimatum in the case of delay that will simply become effective after a reasonable time;[163] the right to cure a delay of performance, provided that the delay does not constitute a fundamental breach; the acceptance of the receipt theory in respect of the notice of termination;[164] and the detailed rules on when a right to terminate will be lost by reason of the lapse of a reasonable time.[165]

In some instances, PECL and Scots law have similar rules whereas South African law displays a different approach. For example, the more fragmented concept of breach of contract under South African law is in contrast with the unitary concept of "material breach" known to PECL and Scots law. However, some Scots courts and lawyers also distinguish between different types of breach in their discussion of what constitutes material breach. In addition, Scots law and PECL are more comfortable with the notion that the cure of a breach may affect the right to terminate than is South African law. In both PECL and Scots law, there is a principle that restitution depends on non-reciprocation, whereas the point of departure in South African law is that mutual restitution must take place except where rights have accrued independently of the executory part of the contract.

In one instance it is Scots law that diverges from a solution found in both PECL and South African law, for Scots law alone does not allow the aggrieved party to demand an adequate assurance of performance, failing which the aggrieved party may terminate.

Concerning the issues on which the systems diverge, the solutions of PECL are certainly worth consideration, although in a number of instances some variation might make them more attractive for adoption in Scots and South African law.

---

163  Article 8:106(3) PECL.
164  Article 1:303 PECL.
165  Article 9:303 PECL. Scots and South African law, on the other hand, enquire whether the lapse of a reasonable time shows that the aggrieved party has made an election, or has waived the right to terminate or is barred from terminating on the basis of personal bar or estoppel. *Mahabeer v Sharma* 1985 (3) SA 729 (A) at 736; Van der Merwe et al, *Contract*, 384; Christie, *Contract*, 628; McBryde, *Contract*, 521; Walker, *Contract*, 521, 557–558; Gloag, *Contract*, 620; *Cumming v Brown* (note 67).

# 12 Assignment

## Gerhard Lubbe

## A. INTRODUCTION

Throughout Europe, assignment is understood as involving a transfer of a personal right of a creditor to a third party (the assignee), the latter, replacing the former (the assignor) as creditor in respect of the related obligation.[1] Common also is an understanding of assignment as an institution that straddles both the law of property and the law of obligations.[2] As a disposition by a creditor of an incorporeal asset, assignment is an institution of the law of property. Because it in addition effects a substitution of creditors, assignment also reveals affinities with the law of obligations. It is accordingly not surprising that although national solutions might differ in matters of detail, comparative treatments are readily able to deal with assignment in the European context by means of a common conceptual vocabulary.[3] The

---

1 H Kötz & A Flessner, *European Contract Law*, vol 1 (Formation, Validity and Content of Contracts and Third Parties) (1997) (henceforth Kötz & Flessner, *European Contract Law*), 265.
2 P Nienaber & G Gretton, "Assignation/Cession", in Zimmermann, Visser & Reid, *Mixed Legal Systems*, 788.
3 Kötz & Flessner, *European Contract Law*, 262–284.

assignment regimes of the various national systems also address common concerns of policy. The need to ensure that rights are freely disposable without having to obtain the consent of the debtor is balanced by a shared concern to ensure that the debtor's position is not rendered more burdensome by the assignment. The interests of would-be assignees must also be protected against subsequent disposals by the assignor and balanced against those of creditors seeking to attach the assets of the assignor and parties interested in his insolvency. There is, accordingly, some basis for a *presumptio simulitudinis* in respect of the broad outlines of the European understanding of this part of law.[4]

The assignment provisions of PECL (in Part III, Chapter 11) endeavour to provide a framework of basic, general doctrinal concepts (*Grundregeln*)[5] to address similar concerns.[6] A range of provisions providing for the free disposal by creditors of their claims untrammelled by formality or any veto by the debtor[7] are balanced by measures to ensure that the debtor's position is not prejudiced.[8] Although provisions along these lines are "commonplace" in other international instruments,[9] it is evident that PECL is not only fully abreast with international developments but sets a high standard for attempts at the development of a uniform law of assignment.[10]

These aspects will not be discussed here. Instead, the focus is on the tension between the basic themes of the mobility of claims and the need for debtor protection: the more readily claims are assignable untrammelled by formality, the greater the risk that the debtor might be compromised.[11] The balancing of these competing demands is traditionally effected by means of the basic understanding of what an assignment is (the *Abtretungsmechanismus*), i.e. how it is effected and its legal consequences.[12] The notion that rights are freely transferable by mere agreement results in a real risk that a debtor may be prejudiced by performing to the assignor, who, being a third party, is incapable of releasing the debtor. If, on the other hand, the debtor is

---

4  M W Hesselink & G J P de Vries, *Principles of European Contract Law* (2001) (henceforth Hesselink & de Vries, *European Contract Law*), 30.

5  R Zimmermann, *Die Principles of European Contract Law als Ausdruck und Gegenstand Europäischer Rechtswissenschaft* (2003) (henceforth Zimmermann, *Principles*), 13, 15.

6  PECL, vol 2, 85.

7  See H Eidenmüller, "Die Dogmatik der Zession vor dem Hintergrund der internationalen Entwicklung" (2004) 204 *Archiv für die civilistische Praxis* 457 at 463–473.

8  Eidenmüller (note 7 above) at 483–491.

9  Eidenmüller (note 7 above) at 498–499.

10  Eidenmüller (note 7 above) at 466 ff; cf 499–500; cf 501.

11  Eidenmüller (note 7 above) at 462; cf 483.

12  Eidenmüller (note 7 above) at 483.

to be protected by requiring notice as a formality, or even by making the assignment dependent on his or her consent, the mobility of claims will be adversely affected.[13] It is proposed to investigate the interrelationship between the mobility of claims and debtor protection on the one hand and the basic understanding of mechanisms of assignment and its effects on the other hand. It is precisely at this level that the treatment of assignment in PECL faces its greatest challenges.

The shared understanding in European legal systems of the theoretical nature of assignment and the agreement on the concerns to be addressed does not extend to the manner in which assignments are made. Although all systems agree that assignment has as its base an agreement to this effect between the assignor and assignee,[14] there is a fundamental divide between systems which regard such an agreement as sufficient to effect the transfer of the right and those which require a further formality, namely that the assignment should be intimated to the debtor, or in the absence thereof, be acknowledged by him or her.[15]

The challenge to the draftsmen of PECL of this dichotomy should not be underestimated. The divergence is of a fairly technical nature and so deeply embedded in the respective legal systems that a uniform approach will be hard to come by. It furthermore concerns matters of considerable practical importance. A wide range of assignment-based practices[16] is of enormous economic significance in the modern commercial context, especially as mechanisms for securing the extension of credit.[17] The emergence of a range of international instruments intended to provide uniformity in this area[18]

---

13 P M Nienaber, "The inactive cessionary" 1964 *Acta Juridica* 99.

14 The "cessionary act" (Nienaber & Gretton, in Zimmermann, Visser & Reid, *Mixed Legal Systems* at 789), which must be distinguished from an obligationary undertaking to assign.

15 For an overview, see Kötz & Flessner, *European Contract Law*, 263–284; F Ranieri, *Europaisches Obligationenrecht* (2003) (henceforth Ranieri, *Obligationenrecht*), 435–436; Nienaber & Gretton, in Zimmermann, Visser & Reid, *Mixed Legal Systems* at 790–791.

16 For an overview, see paras 7–13 of the UNCITRAL Secretariat's *Analytical Commentary on the Draft Convention on Assignment of Receivables in International Trade*, UN Commission on International Trade Law, 34th Session, UN Doc. A/CN/. 9/489 and Add 1 (2001) (*http://www.uncitral.org*); Eidenmüller (2004) 204 *Archiv für die civilistische Praxis* 457 at 458–459.

17 Eidenmüller at 458–459; S V Bazinas, "Lowering cost of credit: the promise in the future UNCITRAL Convention on the Assignment of Receivables in International Trade" (2001) 9 *Tulane Journal of International and Comparative Law* 259; G McCormack, *Secured Credit under English and American Law* (2004) (henceforth McCormack, *Secured Credit*), 209; I Davies, "The reform of English personal property security law: functionalism and Article 9 of the Uniform Commercial Code" (2004) 24 *Legal Studies* 295 at 296.

18 See, e.g., the UN Convention on Assignment of Receivables in International Trade 2001; the UNIDROIT Convention on International Interests in Mobile Equipment 2001 (Cape Town Convention); and the UNIDROIT Convention on International Factoring 1988 (Ottowa

bears witness not only to the significance of assignment practices in the transnational context and the need for the development of uniform rules in this regard,[19] but also to the reluctance to depart from national solutions.[20]

This contribution will in the first instance consider how an assignment is effected under PECL and its consequences and the extent to which the divergence between systems based on notice and those that do not require it is resolved. A second area of enquiry relates to the practical utility of the PECL chapter on assignment. Zimmermann has suggested that Part III of PECL, and in particular also the treatment of assignment, go beyond the tentative steps towards a codification of European contract law evident in Parts I and II. The question therefore is whether the PECL assignment regime can accommodate practical demands by establishing a doctrinal framework that rivals national legal systems in detail and the potential for practical application.[21] Finally, some remarks will be addressed to the implications of PECL's treatment of assignment for the theoretical understanding of this phenomenon.

These questions will be considered against the background of an overview of the manner in which the mixed legal systems of Scotland and South Africa have developed a synthesis between conflicting impulses and influences that inform the law of assignment.

## B. ASSIGNMENT UNDER SCOTS AND SOUTH AFRICAN LAW

Both Scots and South African law portray assignment as involving the transfer of a personal right from a creditor to a third party transferee. There are, however, marked differences about how this is to be achieved. Although both systems require a so-called "cessionary act", consisting of a transfer agreement, i.e. an agreement to make over and to receive the subject matter,[22] the significance attached to a notice to the debtor of the assignment is markedly different. According to South African law the debtor need not participate in or be aware of the cession of the right: the mere transfer agreement

---

Convention). Apart from PECL, restatements of the law of assignment are to be found in the UNIDROIT PICC 2004 and the draft European Contract Code of Academy of European Private Lawyers (Gandolfi Draft).

19  Zimmermann, *Principles*, 39.

20  See the overview of the drafting of the UN Convention on Assignment of Receivables in International Trade by M E Trager, "Towards a predictable law on international receivables financing: The UNCITRAL Convention" (1999) 31 *International Law and Politics* 611.

21  Zimmermann, *Principles*, 8.

22  Nienaber & Gretton, in Zimmermann, Visser & Reid, *Mixed Legal Systems* at 789–790, 791.

suffices to pass the right from the patrimony of the cedent to that of the cessionary (the proprietary aspect of cession), who thereby also becomes substituted as creditor in the cedent's stead (the obligationary aspect).[23]

In Scots law, on the other hand, the transfer agreement is not enough. According to Nienaber and Gretton:

> Notice to the debtor *is* a substantive requirement for the transfer of the right and the substitution of creditors. Absent such notice, the transfer as such is ineffectual and the claim remains vested in the cedent. It passes only when intimation is made to the debtor.[24]

As in South African law, an assignment has a dual effect, but both the obligationary operation of the assignment, i.e. the substitution of the creditor and its patrimonial effect, i.e. the transfer of the right, is triggered by intimation rather than the mere transfer agreement.

Importantly, the notion of a transfer of a right from the assignor to the assignee is, in both systems, a functional one, explanatory of the operation of the assignment. Because of the transfer of the right, the assignee becomes creditor, enjoying the title to sue and having the capacity to effect a discharge of the debtor by accepting performance, granting a release or concluding a compromise. This is also the case in respect of the patrimonial consequences of the assignment. Once a transfer has been effected, by mere agreement in South Africa or by intimation in Scotland, the assignee is protected against the attachment of the subject matter at the hands of a creditor of the assignor. Because there is nothing left in the hands of the assignor to be taken after a transfer has been effected, the assignee is, subject to the provisions of insolvency legislation, also insulated against the insolvency administrator of the assignor where sequestration intervenes after the assignment becomes effective. The notion of an assignment as a transfer of the right is also of decisive importance in respect of multiple disposals of the right by the assignor. In South African law, a full, out and out cession deprives the cedent of an interest in the subject matter of the cession, so that the same right cannot, in principle, be ceded twice over to different persons. In Scotland, the assignor remains creditor until intimation and accordingly still capable of a further assignment. The rule here is one of priority of intimation. Notice to the debtor extracts the right from the patrimony of the assignor so that there

---

23  S Scott, *The Law of Cession*, 2nd edn (1991) (henceforth Scott, *Cession*), 101–102, 103.

24  In Zimmermann, Visser & Reid, *Mixed Legal Systems* at 796; McBryde, *Contract*, paras 12-100, 12-104, 12-105. Alternatively, in the absence of intimation, the debtor is required to have acknowledged the assignment. See Nienaber & Gretton, in Zimmermann, Visser & Reid, *Mixed Legal Systems* at 790, 792; 801–802.

is thereafter nothing that a further assignee can acquire by intimation.[25]

In a seemingly axiomatic way, therefore, both systems use the notion of transfer to explain the consequences of assignment.

## C. ASSIGNMENT UNDER PECL

### (1) PECL's concept of assignment

Despite the assertion that the assignment of a contractual claim involves "a transfer of a right to performance",[26] there is in the General Principles, as elaborated in Section 1 of Chapter 11, no express statement to this effect. This proposition, and the corollary that an assignment is effected by agreement, is only obliquely apparent from Article 11:101 PECL.[27] The adherence to the transfer construction is made explicit only in Article 11:201(1) PECL, which provides that an assignment of a claim transfers to the assignee all the assignor's rights to performance in respect of the claim assigned. This provision, coupled with the assertion in the commentary that "[t]he assignee becomes the new holder of the claim",[28] and the provision that an assignment is effected informally,[29] project an image of assignment that is seemingly familiar to South African lawyers.

The assignment regime of PECL differs fundamentally from that of South African law, however. Article 11:201 PECL is applicable only to the relations between the assignor and assignee.[30] This is not apparent from the text of the provision, but follows from the fact that Article 11:201 PECL is placed under the rubric "Effects of Assignment as between Assignor and Assignee" in Section 2. The structure of Chapter 11, it seems, provides a key to an understanding of assignment under PECL. Section 3 deals with the effects of an assignment as between the assignee and the debtor, and the "Order of Priority between Assignee and Competing Claimants" is considered in Section 4. The latter two sections, respectively, reflect the obligationary and

---

25 See, generally Nienaber & Gretton, in Zimmermann, Visser & Reid, *Mixed Legal Systems* at 796–801.

26 PECL, vol 2, 85.

27 An assignment involves an "agreement" (Article 11:101(1) and (2) PECL), in respect of contractual and "other transferable claims" (Article 11:101(2) PECL). That it entails a transfer of a right is apparent from Article 11:101(3) and (4) PECL and the contrast in Article 11:101(5) PECL between assignments on the one hand and "grants by agreement" of a right of security over a claim.

28 PECL, vol 2, 98.

29 Article 11:104 PECL.

30 PECL, vol 2, 98.

proprietary dimensions of an assignment, i.e. consequences relating to the substitution of the creditor and the shifting of asset from the patrimony of the assignor to that of the assignee.

The substantive provisions of PECL as regards the effect of an assignment, therefore, operate in three dimensions. These sections must be considered *seriatim* and related to the basic points of departure in Section I in order to obtain a complete impression of assignment under PECL.

## (2) The obligationary aspect: effects of an assignment as between assignee and debtor (Section 3)

Despite the very general thrust of Article 11:201 PECL, the commentary asserts that "the assignment does not by itself oblige the debtor to perform in favour of the assignee", such an obligation arising "only where the conditions set in Article 11:303 are satisfied".[31] From the latter provision it is evident that a debtor "is bound to perform in favour of the assignee if and only if the debtor has received a notice in writing".[32] This is a formality in the true sense of the word, a "prerequisite to enforcement"[33] with substantive legal effect. Until notice, the obligationary nexus persists between the assignor and debtor, so that performance by the debtor to the assignor discharges the debt.[34] Prior to notice in terms of Article 11:303(1) PECL, the title to sue remains vested in the assignor and the assignee is a third party as regards the debtor. Although under PECL, either the assignor or assignee may give notice, it is only notice by the former that renders the debtor immediately liable to the assignee. Notice by the assignee is subject to the requirement that the debtor may, within a reasonable time, request the assignee to provide reliable evidence of the assignment. Until then the debtor is entitled to withhold performance from the assignee.[35] Notice, accordingly, substitutes the assignee as creditor in place of the assignor, but where notice is given by the assignee, the claim is suspended should the debtor require reassurance.

The impression, therefore, is that an assignment of itself merely vests in the assignee a power to substitute him or herself as a creditor by means of a notice to the debtor where the assignor does not do this.[36] Articles 11:301 and

---

31  PECL, vol 2, 98.
32  The effect of notice is subject to Articles 11:301, 11:302, 11:307, 11:308 (see Article 11:303(1) PECL).
33  PECL, vol 2, 111.
34  Article 11:303(4) PECL.
35  Article 11:303(2) PECL.
36  This is in accordance with Scots law: Nienaber & Gretton, in Zimmermann, Visser & Reid, *Mixed Legal Systems*, 790–791.

11:302 PECL confirm this. They deal, respectively, with contractual prohibitions of assignment and claims of a personal nature which cannot be assigned without the consent of the debtor. By providing that an assignment contrary to a contractual prohibition is "not effective against the debtor" (Article 11:301 PECL) and that absent the debtor's consent an assignment falling within the ambit of Article 11:302 PECL is "ineffective against the debtor", it is suggested that in other cases an assignment does have some effect as against the debtor even in the absence of notice. What this consists in, appears from the comment that "[t]he effect of a prohibition on assignment is that the debtor is not required to recognise the status of the assignee and can ignore any notice of assignment and give performance to the assignor".[37] Where, therefore, an assignment is effective, the debtor is required to recognise the status of the assignee, heed a notice of assignment and perform to the assignee.[38] This merely confirms that under PECL an assignee has a power to effect a substitution of the creditor unilaterally by means of proper notice to the debtor.

Irrespective of notice, knowledge of an assignment also affects the position. A debtor who has received a notice of assignment which is not in writing, or has by other means become aware of an assignment,[39] cannot discharge the debt by performance to the assignor,[40] but may elect either to withhold performance or to perform to the assignee.[41] Whether knowledge results in a substitution of the creditor is unclear. On the wording of PECL, there is nothing to indicate that a debtor who is aware of an assignment independently of notice is obliged to perform to the assignee. Performance to the assignee will presumably discharge the debtor, unless perhaps the debtor could not have been unaware that despite the assignment the assignee was not entitled to performance.[42]

Of importance also is a provision designed with a view to the protection of the debtor. In the case of competing demands for performance made of the

---

37  PECL, vol 2, 108 (Comment A).

38  PECL, vol 2, 108 (Comment B) on the exceptions to Article 11:301 PECL.

39  PECL, vol 2, 112.

40  Article 11:303(4) PECL. Despite indications to the contrary (*Libertas-Kommerz GmbH v Johnson* 1977 SC 191; F R Salinger, *Factoring Law and Practice* (with a contribution on "Special Considerations for Scotland" by R B Wood) 2nd edn (1995) (henceforth Salinger and Wood, *Factoring*), 151, the predominant view in Scotland still is that knowledge obtained otherwise than by formal intimation is irrelevant (Nienaber & Gretton, in Zimmermann, Visser & Reid, *Mixed Legal Systems* at 801; McBryde, *Contract*, para 12-114; Salinger & Wood, *Factoring*, 151).

41  Article 11:303(3) PECL.

42  By analogy to Article 11:304 PECL. The right to withhold performance under Article 11:303(3) PECL also cannot be an absolute one, but is presumably by analogy to Article 11:303(2) PECL subject to reliable evidence of the assignment being provided.

debtor, a debtor may by virtue of Article 11:305 PECL "discharge liability" by "conforming to the law of the due place of performance" or, "if the performances are due in different places, the law applicable to the claim". The purpose is clearly to avoid the possibility that "[a] debtor who gives performance to a claimant who has not the best right to receive it may have to perform again in favour of the person who has the best right".[43] So as not to involve the debtor in third party disputes and the attendant uncertainties, the provision seeks to insulate the debtor against the risk of having to pay twice. Of interest here is that PECL makes no attempt to resolve conflicts of this nature with reference to their own rule regarding obligationary substitution, and that the issue is also severed from the question as to which claimant is to be preferred according to the priority rules. Although the Comments refer in the abstract to the possibility that the national laws that are mentioned may provide procedural devices rendering it unnecessary for the debtor to make a decision as to which claimant has the best right to the proceeds of what is due,[44] the existence of such devices cannot be accepted as a given for all legal systems. The wording of Article 11:305 PECL is in any event broad enough to permit the release of the debtor who performs according to the provisions of the applicable national law contrary to the provisions of PECL regarding obligationary substitution and priority.

In taking this line, PECL avoids the difficulties experienced with the basic South African rule requiring the debtor to perform to the claimant with the best right from operating unfairly.[45] By acting in conformity with Article 11:305 PECL, the debtor will be released, leaving competing claimants to fight matters out in terms of the priority rules of the applicable law. The obligationary question of the debtor's release is by virtue of Article 11:305 PECL severed from the proprietary question as to who is entitled to the value locked up in the performance. The approach is consistent with the implication implicit in the formal structure of PECL, namely that the provisions of Section 3 concerning the effects of the assignment as between the assignee and the debtor are restricted to them.

---

43 PECL, vol 2, 115.
44 The applicable national law may provide for the consignation of the performance by the debtor or an application for a resolution of the dispute on the basis that the debtor will abide by the decision (PECL, vol 2, 115).
45 See e.g. Van der Merwe et al, *Contract*, 478 in respect of South African law.

## (3) Proprietary aspects: Priorities as between assignee and competing claimants

Priority concerns the question whether the assignee is entitled to assert a preferent claim to the proceeds of the right as against third parties who also claim to be entitled thereto. The question typically arises in conflicts between the assignee and a creditor of the assignor who seeks to attach the claim, an insolvency administrator appointed to administer the estate of an insolvent assignor, or a further assignee of the claim.[46] Legal systems differ in their treatment of the proprietary aspects of assignment. In Scots law, following the approach of French law, the rule is that priority depends on priority of intimation.[47] South African law on the other hand accords priority with reference to the time of the assignment.[48]

Article 11:401 PECL combines the principle of priority of assignment with a first-to-notify rule.

In respect of a conflict between the assignee and an attaching creditor of the assignor, the assignee takes priority over a third party who attaches the claim after the assignment takes effect, i.e. at the time of the assignment or such later time as determined by the parties.[49] Although this approximates the German rule, it must be remembered that contrary to the position under that law,[50] the assignee does not under PECL become a creditor until the formality of notice has been complied with. Under PECL, the absence of notice and any obligationary substitution is irrelevant for the priority conflict: an assignee may enjoy priority even though he is not a creditor of the debtor. This aspect of the priority issue has been severed from the obligationary effects of the assignment.

A similar approach is evident in the case of the bankruptcy of the assignor. Subject to peremptory rules of insolvency law pertaining to the publicity of assignments or security interests, the ranking of claims, and void and voidable transactions, the interest of an assignee, irrespective of whether it was established by an outright assignment or one made by way of security, is preferred over that of the insolvency administrator appointed after the assignment.[51] Subject to the aforementioned provisos, the time of the

---

46  See e.g. the definition of "competing claimant" in Article 5(m) of the UN Convention on the Assignment of Receivables in International Trade.
47  Nienaber & Gretton, in Zimmermann, Visser & Reid, *Mixed Legal Systems* at 797–798.
48  Nienaber & Gretton, in Zimmermann, Visser & Reid, *Mixed Legal Systems* at 797.
49  Article 11:401(3), read with Article 11:202 PECL in relation to future rights.
50  Kötz & Flessner, *European Contract Law*, 279.
51  Article 11:401(4) PECL. Cf PECL, vol 2, 123.

assignment is again decisive. Noteworthy is that the assignment is accorded a proprietary effect irrespective of whether notice has been given. The assignee may therefore enjoy priority even though no obligationary substitution has taken place.

The issue of priority in these two instances is severed from its traditional basis, namely the notion that as a result of the obligationary substitution of the assignee for the assignor the assignor is no longer the creditor so that there is nothing in his or her hands that can be attached or fall into the insolvent estate.

The priority of assignment approach holds even for a conflict between successive assignees of the same claim or claims but is in this instance qualified by a first-to-notify rule.

Where neither party has given notice (or could not have done so because there is as yet no debtor), "priority is determined by the order in which the assignments are made", so that the first assignee is in principle preferred over subsequent assignees.[52] The priority of the first assignee is provisional only and liable to be displaced if the second assignee is first to give notice.[53] Provided that such an assignee neither knew nor ought to have known of any earlier assignment, he or she will enjoy priority over any prior assignee.[54] Interestingly, the explanation for the first-to-give-notice rule is not that the right is immediately passed to the first assignee to give notice and that nothing remains that is capable of transfer to a subsequent transferee. Instead, the effect of notice is justified with reference to considerations appropriate to the law of property rather than the law of obligations. On the one hand, the giving of notice is portrayed as "the closest equivalent to taking possession, which is recognised as a way of obtaining priority in respect of movables". Notice to the debtor may also fulfil a publicity function in the sense that "an intending assignee, before giving value, can ask the debtor whether the debtor has received any prior notice of assignment".[55] A second assignee is accordingly entitled to assume that there is no earlier assignment if a first assignee has failed to give notice, unless he or she did not know and could not have been unaware of an earlier assignment.

The treatment of priority in the case of a double assignment is dealt with as an issue formally and conceptually distinct from the notion of transfer as between the assignor and assignee embedded in Article 11:201(1)(a) PECL,

52  Article 11:401(2) PECL.
53  PECL, vol 2, 122.
54  Article 11:401(1) PECL.
55  PECL, vol 2, 122.

and this applies also to the determination of the other aspects of the priority problem. Priority, according to PECL, is accordingly severed from what the comments style the "validity" of the assignment.[56] There is therefore a departure from the *nemo dat* rule as a rationale for according priority, and an express disjunction of the provision regarding the obligationary effect of an assignment *inter partes* between assignor and assignee and the issue of priority.[57]

## (4) Immediate effects of assignment as between assignor and assignee

In view of Sections 3.2 and 3.3 the assertion that by virtue of Article 11:201(1)(a) PECL the assignee "becomes the new holder of the claim" and that "the claim becomes vested in the assignee"[58] cannot be taken literally. The effect of Article 11:201(1)(a) PECL is restricted to the relation between assignor and assignee.[59] Article 11:303 PECL postpones the obligationary substitution until notice is given. Lest it be thought that the priority afforded a first assignee in the absence of notice is based on the notion that a transfer to such an assignee deprives the assignor of the ability to give a further assignment, the commentary points out that Article 11:201 PECL does not deal with priority issues either.[60] If the effect of an assignment is severed from the obligationary substitution of the assignor and is independent of the question of priority, the question arises as to the sense in which the notion of transfer is used in this connection.

Relevant in this regard is Article 11:203 PECL where, under the heading "Preservation of Assignee's Rights against Assignor", it is stated:

> An assignment is effective as between the assignor and assignee, and entitles the assignee to whatever the assignor receives from the debtor, even if it is ineffective against the debtor under Articles 11:301 or 11:302 PECL.

The proviso refers to cases where an assignment, even prior to and independently of notice, is said to be ineffective as against the debtor because of a contractual prohibition on assignment (Article 11:301 PECL) or the highly personal nature of the right (Article 11:302 PECL). Even in such cases, and therefore also in all others, an assignment according to the Comments to

---

56  PECL, vol 2,, 122 (Comment A to Article 11:401 PECL).
57  PECL, vol 2, Comment A on 121–122.
58  PECL, vol 2, 98.
59  The heading to Section 2 of Chapter 11; PECL, vol 2, 98.
60  PECL, vol 2, 98, 100.

Articles 11:301 and 11:302 PECL, "operates to *transfer* to the assignee the right to all benefits received by the assignor from the debtor".[61]

A transfer presupposes, however, that the subject matter should have been vested in the transferor. To portray the effect of an assignment as a transfer to the assignee of a right "to whatever the assignor receives from the debtor" is artificial in the extreme. This is not a right that the assignor ever had against the debtor, of course. It comes as no surprise that the text of Article 11:203 PECL does not speak of a transfer at all, but merely states that the assignment "entitles" the assignee to whatever the assignor receives from the debtor.[62] This casts doubt on the portrayal of the effect of the assignment as a transfer. If as between the assignor and the assignee the only effect of an assignment is that the assignee has a personal right as against the assignor to have the proceeds of performance by the debtor paid over, the notion of a transfer becomes redundant. One might equally well take the view that an assignment by operation of law creates a claim against the assignor for the assignee. This is very different from what is envisaged by Article 11:201 PECL, namely a transfer to the assignee of "all the assignor's rights to performance in respect of the claim assigned".

The severance of the effect of an assignment between the parties thereto and the priority question, coupled with the postponement of obligationary substitution until notice is given entails that an assignor retains the competence to make multiple assignment in respect of the same claims or otherwise to dispose of the claim in spite of having done so previously.[63] To do so might amount to a breach of contract against an earlier assignee.[64] It will not, however, preclude a later assignee from acquiring priority by being the first to notify the debtor.

## (5) PECL provisions in perspective

PECL does not stand alone in making a break with traditional views of assignment and its effects. The differentiation of the effects of an assignment *inter partes* from that between the assignee and third parties is also apparent from the UN Convention on Assignment of Receivables in International Trade[65]

---

61  PECL, vol 2, Comment D on 109 (emphasis GL).

62  See also PECL, vol 2 at 111 on Article 11:203 PECL.

63  This is also implicit in provisions of Articles 11:204(b) and 11:308 PECL, which presuppose that the assignor and debtor are in principle still entitled to agree to a modification of the contract, and hence to deal with the subject matter of the assignment.

64  Article 11:204(a)(i) PECL.

65  Adopted in 2001 after a gestation period of almost six years: see Bazinas (2003) 11 *Tulane Journal of International and Comparative Law* 275 at 277.

and Chapter 9 of the UNIDROIT PICC 2004.[66] While both instruments characterise assignment as a transfer by agreement of a contractual right,[67] it is made clear that an assignee does not derive priority over competing claimants from the mere assignment. Neither the PICC nor the Convention provides a substantive rule regarding the issue of priority. In the case of the PICC, the explanation for "this self-restraint" is that the priority question involves property rights which "can hardly be dealt with satisfactorily in a soft law instrument ... and are better entirely left to the otherwise applicable law".[68] In the case of the Convention, the inability of UNCITRAL to achieve consensus on a uniform substantive priority regime[69] resulted in the inclusion of conflict of law rules to identify the national legal system applicable to priority issues.[70] Under both these instruments, the position of an assignee as against competing claimants therefore depends on norms beyond their ambit which are not necessarily congruent with its provisions as to the relationship between the assignee and the debtor and that between the assignor and the assignee.

A further parallel is that both the PICC and the Convention regard notice to the debtor as decisive for the substitution of the assignee as creditor. Until the debtor is notified of the assignment, discharge is effected by payment in accordance with the original contract.[71] After notification the debtor is discharged only by paying the assignee[72] or, under the UN Convention if otherwise instructed by the assignee, in accordance with such a payment instruction.[73] Under the UN Convention, the assignee has the right as against the assignor to retain payment received from the debtor even before notification, and where payment is made to the assignor the assignee is entitled to payment of the proceeds.[74] The assignee's right to the proceeds is treated as

---

66 Cf M J Bonell, "UNIDROIT Principles 2004 – The New Edition of the Principles of International Commercial Contracts adopted by the International Institute for the Unification of Private Law" (2004) 9 *Uniform Law Review* 5.

67 Article 2(a) UN Convention; Article 9.1.1 PICC.

68 Bonell (2004) 9 *Uniform Law Review* 5 with reference to Comment 4 to Article 9.1.1 PICC.

69 Bazinas (2001) 9 *Tulane Journal of International and Comparative Law* 259 at 285–287.

70 Articles 22–25, 30. On the optional substantive priority regimes held out as models for possible adoption by member states, see Article 42 and Articles 6–9 of the Annex to the Convention. Cf Bazinas (2001) 9 *Tulane Journal of International and Comparative Law* 259 at 285; Eidenmüller (2004) 204 *Archiv für die civilistische Praxis* 457 at 474.

71 Article 17(1) UN Convention; cf Article 9.1.10 PICC.

72 UN Convention Article 17(2), cf the provisos in sub-paragraphs 3–8; Article 9.1.10 PICC. By virtue of Article 9.1.11 PICC in respect of successive assignments of the same right, payment according to the order in which the notices were received from the various assignees discharges the debtor. Importantly, this rule has no bearing on the resolution of priority conflicts. See Bonell (2004) 9 *Uniform Law Review* 5.

73 Article 17(2).

74 Article 14(1)(a), (b).

a contractual right against the assignor rather than a consequence of a transfer.[75] Principally therefore, the effect of the assignment under the UN Convention is to empower the assignee to send the debtor notification of the assignment and a payment instruction. The assignor may also notify, but after notification only the assignee may send a payment instruction,[76] so that notification establishes the assignee as the party entitled to the performance as against the debtor. Prior to the notification of the assignment the assignor and the debtor may by agreement modify the original contract. The provision that such an agreement "is effective as against the assignee" and that "the assignee acquires corresponding rights", presumably upon notification,[77] confirms that, to the extent that an agreement of assignment is immediately effective, its operation is restricted to the assignor and the assignee.[78]

The underlying assumption of both the PICC and the UN Convention, accordingly, is that the obligationary and proprietary aspects are separate issues capable of being divorced from one another and susceptible to regulation by means of different systems of rules not necessarily based on similar premises. This is also the approach of PECL.

## D. PRACTICAL UTILITY OF THE ASSIGNMENT REGIME OF PECL

The claim that PECL's assignment regime is sufficiently detailed to serve as the basis of a uniform law of assignment in the European context[79] raises a number of issues. While it can be assumed that PECL deals adequately with the mobility of claims and the protection of the debtor,[80] regard must be had to their priority regime as well as the extent to which they can accommodate modern assignment practices relating to the trade receivables of businesses.

These practices assume various manifestations,[81] but generally involve the global or bulk assignment of both existing and future claims generated by businesses by means of a single deed of assignment, often to provide a continuous, covering security to a financial institution in respect of a fluctuating

---

75 Bazinas (2003) 11 *Tulane Journal of International and Comparative Law* 275 at 289; cf Article 11:203 PECL.

76 Article 13(1).

77 Article 20(1). Subject to certain exceptions, an agreement concluded after notification of the assignment between the assignor and the debtor that affects the assignee's rights, on the other hand, is ineffective as against the assignee (Article 20(2)).

78 Article 11(1).

79 See note 21 above and the accompanying text.

80 See Eidenmüller (2004) 204 *Archiv für die civilistische Praxis* 457 at 483–491.

81 See note 16 above.

indebtedness of a client. Thus, under an invoice discounting or confidential factoring arrangement, a business, with a view to financing its business operations, assigns its present and future claims against trade debtors to a financial institution acting as factor in return for periodic financial advances. The so-called factor does not provide any of the credit control, debt collection and other administrative services typical of many factoring arrangements. The agreement envisages instead that the assignor conducts normal relations with its customer base, maintains the sales ledger, and collects from debtors, without informing them of the assignment and requiring them to pay directly to the factor.[82] It is of the essence that the transaction is concluded, quietly, without publicity in order not to disrupt the relations between the assignor and its customers and to maintain the creditworthiness of the assignor as against those who supply goods to it. The agreement accordingly envisages that the assignee will come to the fore and rely on the assignment as against the debtors only when the assignor fails to comply with the underlying contract.[83] Although the assignee's security will continually be diminished by payments to the assignor, it will be replenished because the prior assignment extends to all further claims generated by the assignor's business activities.

Assignment regimes based on the formality of notice to the debtor experience difficulties in accommodating practices of this kind.[84] Scots law provides an illustration. Although it has been asserted that Scots law is flexible enough to permit the assignment of future rights and that this can be done on a global basis,[85] the position is not altogether clear.[86] The requirement of intimation, for instance, presupposes that the debtor be in existence when notice is given,[87] so that the formality will have to be complied with in respect of each debtor as and when a particular debt is created.[88] This is not only cumbersome and costly, but precludes the possibility of a confidential or quiet assignation.[89] A further and even more fundamental difficulty is that

---

82 Salinger & Wood, *Factoring*, 18–19.

83 McCormack, *Secured Credit*, 225; cf 211–212 on the need to preserve the assignor's "management autonomy" in respect of its trade claims.

84 Kötz & Flessner, *European Contract Law*, 278; cf the amendment of para 3:94 of the Dutch BW (see (2004) *Staatsblad* 314 on the Law of 30 June 2004) to permit a cession without the usual requirement of notice to the debtor specifically to accommodate bulk assignments.

85 Salinger & Wood, *Factoring*, 150, 151.

86 Nienaber & Gretton, in Zimmermann, Visser & Reid, *Mixed Legal Systems* at 803–804 n 97.

87 Nienaber & Gretton, in Zimmermann, Visser & Reid, *Mixed Legal Systems*, 803–804 n 98.

88 Nienaber & Gretton, in Zimmermann, Visser & Reid, *Mixed Legal Systems* at 804, but see McBryde, *Contract*, paras 12–101, 12–108.

89 Nienaber & Gretton, in Zimmermann, Visser & Reid, *Mixed Legal Systems* at 804.

under Scots law an assignee does not derive any protection from an unintimated assignation.[90] Because "no title vests in assignment until the intimation has been given to the debtor",[91] the formality of intimation places the assignee under a confidential factoring arrangement at risk in respect of priority conflicts.

These difficulties are met by recourse to the institution of the trust. Although in the absence of intimation, an assignee enjoys no obligationary standing as against the debtor and no proprietary interest in the subject matter, it is said to be permissible for the assignor to undertake to hold the subject matter of the assignment on trust for the assignee. On the basis that the assignee is thereby constituted the beneficial owner of the claims, it has been held that the assignee is protected in the event of the insolvency of the assignor provided the constitution of the trust was notified to the assignee.[92] Although the correctness of this approach has been doubted,[93] it is said to be the normal practice in Scotland to obviate the need for intimation in respect of invoice discounting in this way.[94]

Under PECL, such expedients are unnecessary. The difficulties which the formality of intimation or notice poses for the recognition of the efficacy of a global assignment are overcome by the separation of the obligationary consequences of an assignment from the proprietary dimension. Priority dates from the time of the assignment when the assignee gives value to the assignor and becomes interested in the claim and not on the obligationary status of the assignee as against the debtor. The failure to notify cannot therefore detract from the position of the assignee. The same holds true of the case of a conflict between successive assignees where, as is often the case, notice cannot be given because the debtors have as yet not materialised. To the extent that notification could have been given, it is merely an option to be considered by the assignee in order to obtain preference over a competing assignee. This approximates the role of notice in South African law, where notice does not play a constitutive role. Because the assignee enjoys priority irrespective of notification, confidentiality can be maintained. The idea underlying practices such as invoice discounting, namely that the arrangement should not interfere with the business operations of the assignor and disturb its relations

90 Nienaber & Gretton, in Zimmermann, Visser & Reid, *Mixed Legal Systems* at 804.

91 Salinger & Wood, *Factoring*, 151.

92 *Tay Valley Joinery Ltd v CF Financial Services Ltd* 1987 SLT 207; Nienaber & Gretton, in Zimmermann, Visser & Reid, *Mixed Legal Systems* at 804; Salinger & Wood, *Factoring*, 152–153.

93 Nienaber & Gretton, in Zimmermann, Visser & Reid, *Mixed Legal Systems* at 804; Salinger & Wood, *Factoring*, 154.

94 Salinger & Wood, *Factoring*, 153.

with its clients, is arguably also better served by a system in which the assignor remains the creditor until notification. This obviates the need to resort to expedients, common in South Africa, such as an authorisation to the assignor to collect on behalf of the assignee as some sort of undisclosed principal.[95] Because the assignor remains creditor until notification, keeping the assignment quiet will also not present a false front, as is so often the case in systems such as South African law.[96]

The severance of the priority issue from the assignee's standing as creditor as a result of the move away from the *nemo dat* rule has a further important implication. It permits and facilitates multiple assignments by a creditor of the same claims, thus optimising the use businesses can make of their trade claims. In this way, problems experienced in South African law in respect of successive security cessions pertaining to the same rights are overcome.[97] Provided that the order of priority is clearly determined, such an approach is value maximising and on the face of it economically efficient.

Overall, the approach of PECL is functional and in harmony with that of the UN Convention and other international instruments.[98] By providing a basis for the regulation of practices such as invoice discounting, the PECL regime is responsive to the practical needs of a sophisticated financial environment such as the European Union.

The priority issue is one of the most complex and intractable facing attempts to establish a uniform law of international assignment. PECL, as indicated earlier,[99] opts for a regime combining a first-to-give-notice rule and a rule based on the priority of the assignment. Whether such a mixed system addresses all aspects of the priority issue adequately cannot be fully dealt with here. The approach, which is reminiscent of that established for English law in *Dearle v Hall*,[100] avoids the problems associated with according priority on the basis of the registration of the assignment in a public registry,[101] but

---

95  For example, *Densam (Pty) Ltd v Cywilnat* 1991 (1) SA 100 (A).

96  Cf Nienaber & Gretton, in Zimmermann, Visser & Reid, *Mixed Legal Systems* at 818.

97  Van der Merwe et al, *Contract*, 479.

98  See section C(5) above.

99  See section C(5) above.

100  (1828) 3 Russ 1; cf Bazinas (2001) 9 *Tulane Journal of International and Comparative Law* 259 at 285.

101  See Bazinas (2001) 9 *Tulane Journal of International and Comparative Law* 259 at 285; Davies (2004) 24 *Legal Studies* 295 at 308–311; but see Eidenmüller (2004) 204 *Archiv für die civilistische Praxis* 457 at 477–479, 500–501. See generally on the filing system of Article 9 of the US Uniform Commercial Code: H Kötz, "Rights of Third Parties – Third Party Benefici-aries and Assignment", 7 *International Encyclopedia of Comparative Law*, vol. VII/13 (1992), para 103 (henceforth Kötz, "Rights of Third Parties").

brings with it not only the advantages of each of its component elements, but also their disadvantages. The simplicity of the priority of assignment rule and the confidentiality which it permits[102] must be balanced against the possibility that the lack of publicity and the risk of harm to would-be assignees might raise the price at which the latter is prepared to extend credit to a level which would discourage transactions.[103] The supposed advantage of a priority regime based on the notification of the debtor is that an intending assignee is able to elicit information about prior assignments by enquiry from the debtor.[104] Apart from the fact that this provides no protection for third parties who supply to assignors on short-term credit,[105] an enquiry of this kind prior to taking an assignment is not equivalent to a notice of the assignment. The question in any event is whether a debtor would necessarily be aware of any prior assignment, and if so, whether he can be regarded as duty bound to inform a would-be assignee thereof.[106] Whatever the position might be in relation to existing claims of high value, the supposed publicity value of notice is illusory in respect of the global assignment of future rights and those comprising both existing and future rights. In such cases the debtors are either non-existent or unknown. Where the debtors are known, there might be so many of them that notification is impractical and costly, particularly where, as will often be the case, the assignment is of claims that taken singly are of relatively low value.[107] In the final analysis the very nature of the assignment might require that an assignee refrain from approaching the debtors of his assignor.[108] Although transaction costs are saved by the fact that in relation to the issue of priority notice is facultative and not a constitutive requirement,[109] the mixed system of PECL does not bring the certainty as to the

---

102  Bazinas (2001) 9 *Tulane Journal of International and Comparative Law* 259 at 284.

103  Bazinas (2001) 9 *Tulane Journal of International and Comparative Law* 259 at 284, and see Eidenmüller (2004) 204 *Archiv für die civilistische Praxis* 457 at 474–475 on the role of publicity in reducing transaction costs. Contra Davies (2004) 24 *Legal Studies* 295 at 309–310.

104  Bazinas (2001) 9 *Tulane Journal of International and Comparative Law* 259 at 285; cf PECL, vol 2, 122 ("an intending assignee, before giving value, can ask the debtor whether the debtor has received any notice of a prior assignment").

105  Eidenmüller (2004) 204 *Archiv für die civilistische Praxis* 457 at 476.

106  Eidenmüller (2004) 204 *Archiv für die civilistische Praxis* 457 at 476; Bazinas (2001) 9 *Tulane Journal of International and Comparative Law* 259 at 284–285; McCormack, *Secured Credit*, 245 ("the debtor is not a publicly commissioned official charged with the task of receiving or tracking notices"); cf F Oditah "Priorities: equitable versus legal assignments of book debts" (1989) 9 *Oxford JLS* 513 at 525–527.

107  Interestingly, Illustration 1 in PECL, vol 2, 122 makes no mention of an assignment of future rights or of bulk or global assignments.

108  Eidenmüller (2004) 204 *Archiv für die civilistische Praxis* 457 at 476.

109  Eidenmüller (2004) 204 *Archiv für die civilistische Praxis* 457 at 475–476.

entitlement to claims required by the principle of publicity.[110] The suggested regime would permit an assignee under a global assignment of all the present and future book debts of a business to establish priority without regard to the considerations which led German law to qualify its priority rule in favour of third party suppliers of goods to businesses,[111] or the publicity requirements of English law in respect of company charges.[112]

## E. THEORETICAL NATURE OF ASSIGNMENT UNDER PECL

The notion of assignment as a transfer of a claim from a creditor to a third party is a venerable and powerful idea. Since its inception in medieval mercantile practice, the transfer construction has superseded the Romanistic *procuratio in rem suam* as a method for substituting the creditor under an obligation.[113] The transfer construction remains the foundation of the understanding of assignment not only in European legal systems but also in mixed systems such as those of South Africa and Scotland.[114] In South African and Scots law, the transfer of the subject matter of the assignment is decisive for both the obligationary and proprietary consequences of the transaction.[115]

PECL also adheres to the transfer construction. Although the substitution of the assignor is made to depend on the formality of notification, it is clear that an assignee enjoys priority irrespective of whether he or she is a creditor of the debtor.[116] This renders the role of the transfer idea unclear. As has been pointed out, furthermore, there is on the face of it no discernible right or claim that can unambiguously be identified as the subject matter for the immediate transfer that supposedly operates as between the parties to the assignment.[117] In the absence of clarity in this regard the very understanding of an assignment as a transfer of a right and the need to retain it is thrown into doubt.

PECL also recognises the possibility of dealing with personal rights other than by way of assignment. Article 11:101 PECL extends, "with appropriate

110  Eidenmüller (2004) 204 *Archiv für die civilistische Praxis* 457 at 476; cf McCormack, *Secured Credit*, 244–245.
111  Eidenmüller (2004) 204 *Archiv für die civilistische Praxis* 457 at 480; Kötz, "Rights of third parties", para 105.
112  See McCormack, *Secured Credit*, 221–222, 224–225; M G Bridge, R A McDonald, R L Simmonds & C Walsh, "Formalism, functionalism and understanding the law of secured transactions" (1999) 44 *McGill LJ* 567 at 646–648.
113  Zimmermann, *Obligations*, 63–75; Ranieri, *Obligationenrecht*, 434.
114  See note 1 above and the accompanying text.
115  See section B above.
116  See section C(3) above.
117  See section C(4) above.

adaptations", the provisions of Chapter 11 "to the granting by agreement of a right in security over a claim otherwise than by assignment". Such a constitutive security agreement, which creates a real right of security in claims that remain in the patrimony of the creditor,[118] is not fully explored in PECL. It provides an alternative to the transfer notion in respect of what is probably the most important application of assignment in commercial practice.

In splitting off the obligationary from the proprietary aspects of assignment, PECL and other international instruments treat these aspects as functionally distinct problems. Rather than attempting to deal with them by means of rules seemingly derived from a general theoretical model of assignment, a choice has been made for a differentiated treatment of these areas by means of autonomous rules informed by policy considerations relevant to each.

There is of course no doctrinal necessity which renders the transfer construct axiomatic. The ambiguity of the text in relation to the subject matter of the supposed transfer between the assignor and the assignee under Article 11:203 PECL, when seen in conjunction with other provisions, provides a foundation for alternative models of an assignment, so that the possibility that PECL has made a decisive conceptual break with the past and the dogma of assignment as entailing the transfer of personal rights requires consideration.

The PECL provisions on assignment for instance provide some basis for the notion that an assignment vests in the assignee a power to effect a substitution of the creditor in relation to the obligation which is the subject matter of the transaction. In particular, provisions relating to the immediate effect of an assignment as against a debtor[119] are compatible with the view that the assignee (or for that matter the assignor) enjoys a legally recognised power (*Gestaltungsrecht*) to make him or herself into the creditor. On this basis, the imagery of transfer is rendered superfluous. The effect of an assignment can be understood merely as involving the substitution of a party rather than a transfer of a notional thing. If there is no logical necessity to tie priority to the idea of a transfer to the assignee of a notional beneficial ownership of a claim, it can certainly by legislative *fiat* be tied to a point in time at which the power of substitution was acquired by the assignee. Such a construction is conceivably better suited to explain the ability to deal by way of assignment with future rights, where the notion of a transfer is strained beyond the breaking point, and would also be consistent with the notion of a substitution of parties proposed in Chapter 12 of PECL. On this approach, the obligationary

---

118 By way of a charge or pledge: cf McCormack, *Secured Credit*, 210.
119 See above section C(2).

substitution that occurs on notice to the debtor facilitates the collection of what is due from the debtor and thus the realisation of the subject matter where the assignment is made for security.

The transfer construction is of course embedded in the text of PECL. It is apparent that the notion of a transfer can only be maintained if it is understood in a rather special way.

At first blush, the PECL regime appears reminiscent of a model of cession advanced for South African law by Susan Scott. Common to both PECL and Scott's vision of a cession is a separation of the proprietary and obligationary effects of a cession. Whereas according to Scott a "shifting of assets" occurs immediately upon the cession, the obligationary substitution of the cedent by the cessionary is regarded as complete only upon notice to the debtor.[120] This approach has been severely criticised in the South African literature and has not found acceptance in the case law.[121] It differs in any event from the approach of PECL and cannot serve to provide a theoretical explanation for it. According to PECL the supposed transfer agreement is effective only as between the assignor and the assignee and not per se as against third parties.[122] Scott, on the other hand, adheres to the *nemo dat* rule and regards the cessionary act as having an immediate proprietary effect not only as against the cessionary, but also as regards third parties.[123]

A closer approximation of the PECL position is provided by the view of some Scottish commentators that intimation serves to complete or perfect, as against third parties, a transfer that has already taken place as between the assignor and the assignee.[124] This view, which is not generally accepted for Scots law,[125] could conceivably provide an explanation for the effect of knowledge on the part of the debtor of an unnotified assignment.[126] The notion of an inchoate transfer is not fully consistent with the wording of Article 11:203 PECL, however. Here the emphasis is merely on the relationship of the assignee as against the assignor. The Article gives no indication that the assignment as such leaves the assignee with an inchoate or suspended claim against the debtor.

---

120  Scott, *Cession*, 96–105; see also Nienaber & Gretton, in Zimmermann, Visser & Reid, *Mixed Legal Systems* at 795 n 43.
121  Van der Merwe et al, *Contract*, 456.
122  See above section C(4).
123  Scott, *Cession*, 101–102, 103.
124  Nienaber & Gretton, in Zimmermann, Visser & Reid, *Mixed Legal Systems* at 790–791; Salinger & Wood, *Factoring*, 150.
125  Nienaber & Gretton, in Zimmermann, Visser & Reid, *Mixed Legal Systems* at 796.
126  See Article 11:303(4) PECL.

Yet another analysis could proceed from the view that has been advanced for South African law, that a creditor, as the holder of a personal right, enjoys not only a beneficial interest in the performance due from the debtor, but also a legally recognised capacity to enforce and otherwise to dispose of the right.[127] According to some, these components of a creditor's interest may be separated from one another by way of a cession, for example by a cession of the capacity to dispose of the right — or at least the capacity to enforce it — to a cessionary where a security cession is intended to effect a pledge of the right. Conversely, the cedent may cede the beneficial interest to the cessionary while retaining the capacity to dispose of and control the economic value inherent in the debtor's performance.[128] The notion of a transfer which involves a splitting of the claim so as to leave the assignor with the capacity to deal with the debtor as creditor (at least so long as no notice of the assignment is given) but to vest the assignee with the beneficial interest in the performance could conceivably provide a theoretical template for the relative effect accorded to an unnotified assignment under PECL. The claim of an assignee to whatever the assignor has received from the debtor under Article 11:203 PECL can be construed as resulting from a transfer to the assignee of the beneficial ownership in the claims. Interestingly, an analysis along these lines approximates the results reached in Scots law by the utilisation of the trust in order to invest the assignee with a proprietary interest in the subject matter of the assignment even though intimation has not yet been made.[129] If the notion of beneficial ownership in a claim is given legal recognition, an assignee will be protected on that basis irrespective of his standing as creditor. Article 11:203 PECL echoes the trust construction as far as the assignee, as beneficial owner of the claims of which the assignor is still formally the owner, is entitled to whatever has been received by the latter from the debtor.

## F. CONCLUSION

Whether there is a need to retain the transfer model – perhaps in an adapted form – or to develop some other theoretical construct as an overall theoretical framework of understanding is unclear. It is true, as asserted by Hesselink,[130] that conceptual jurisprudence has no place in the European context. The

---

127  Van der Merwe et al, *Contract*, 468, but see P M Nienaber, "Cession" in LAWSA, 2nd edn (2003), vol 2(2), para 53.

128  Van der Merwe et al, *Contract*, 468–469.

129  See notes 92–94 above and the accompanying text.

130  Hesselink & De Vries, *European Contract Law*, 89–90.

treatment of assignment under PECL and related international instruments calls to mind the functionalist approach adopted in respect of Article 9 of the UCC whereby transactions of divergent kinds are dealt with on the same juridical basis on account of a common underlying economic purpose.[131] From this perspective certainly, the obscurity regarding the basic understanding of an assignment under PECL does not necessarily amount to a major defect.

It should be borne in mind, however, that the experience with the functionalist approach of the UCC has not been a uniformly positive one.[132] The caveat against conceptual jurisprudence is in any event properly directed at legal formalism, i.e. the conviction that results can be achieved merely by inferences drawn from the seemingly self-evident content of concepts, such as the notion that assignment involves the transfer of a right.[133] Whether the rejection of formalism of this kind necessarily does away with the need for rigorous conceptual analysis of legal institutions designed to facilitate an understanding of the interests at stake in any particular field, and the balancing thereof, is a moot point. It is submitted that the regulation of an area as complex as that of assignment does require clarity as to the conceptual tools by means of which it is to be understood.

While some aspects of the PECL Chapter on assignment are in need of further elaboration and debate, this is, of course, a primary function of a restatement of law. Overall, Chapter 11 is of a high quality and provides a sound basis for future development.

---

131  Bridge et al (1999) 44 *McGill LJ* 567 at 572–573; Davies (2004) 24 *Legal Studies* 295 at 300–304.

132  Bridge et al (1999) 44 *McGill LJ* 567 at 573, 614–615, 662; Davies (2004) 24 *Legal Studies* 295 at 304–305.

133  H L A Hart, *The Concept of Law* (1961), 126.

# 13  Capitalisation of Interest

## *Max Loubser*

## A. INTRODUCTION

Distaste for interest has been pervasive in ethics, religion and law in all of recorded history. The rules against usury are rooted in the idea that interest is by its nature exploitative. If by this reasoning interest is bad, then the taking of interest on interest – that is compound interest or anatocism (the archaic and almost obsolete term for compound interest) – is worse.[1] The word anatocism has a ring about it of something unpleasant.

From an economic and mathematical point of view it does not matter whether compound interest is seen as the adding of accrued interest to a debt as interest or as capital, the effect is the same. In legal terminology, almost as if by verbal sleight of hand, the lawful taking of compound interest becomes capitalisation – the process whereby accrued interest is merged with the principal or capital, so as then to generate further interest on the increased capital amount.

The legal rules on capitalisation indicate circumstances where the taking of interest on interest is tolerated in terms of a statute, agreement or trade usage. Research projects in various countries over the last twenty years or so have indicated that such tolerance has been generally limited and that the law on capitalisation or compound interest has lagged behind economic and commercial realities.[2] In this chapter the focus is on Article 17:101 PECL, which provides for the annual capitalisation of interest for certain types of debt.[3] This provision will be compared with the position in Scotland and South Africa, to assess to what extent it provides a suitable model for reform of the law.

---

1 See A S Hartkamp, *Asser's Handleiding tot de Beoefening van het Nederlands Burgerlijk Recht Verbintenissenrecht* Deel I, 11th edn (2000), 463: "Bestond er reeds outijds zekere afkeer tegen het bedingen van rente, nog groter was de weerzin tegen het berekenen van rente over vervallen, doch achterstallig gebleven rente."

2 See generally on various European legal systems the notes to Article 17:101 PECL, vol 2, 241; and see the Law Reform Commission of Manitoba's Report on Pre-judgment Compensation on Money Awards (1982); the Law Reform Commission of British Columbia's Report on the Court Order Interest Act LRC 90 (1987); the Law Reform Commission of Ontario's Report on Compensation for Pesonal Injuries and Death (1987); the Law Reform Commission of Hong Kong's Report entitled Interest on Debt and Damages (1990); the New Zealand Law Commission's Report on Aspects of Damages: The Award of Interest on Money Claims, No 28 (1994); the Law Commission of England's Report on Pre-judgment Interest on Debts and Damages, Law Com No 287 (2004); and the Scottish Law Commission's Consultation Paper on Interest on Debt and Damages, Scot Law Com DP No 127 (2005).

3 Article 17:101 PECL provides as follows:
   (1) Interest payable according to Article 9:508(1) is added to the outstanding capital every 12 months.
   (2) Paragraph (1) of this Article does not apply if the parties have provided for interest upon delay in payment.

Where the taking of interest on interest is tolerated as lawful capitalisation, the merger of interest into capital does not necessarily remove the taint of interest. For example, South African law allows banks to capitalise interest, but, as will be shown below, the original nature of the capitalised interest is not forgotten and when an overall limitation on interest is enforced in terms of the *in duplum* rule, capitalised interest is taken into account as interest and not as capital.[4]

The lingering aversion to compound interest or anatocism is reflected in the practice of courts in Scotland normally to award only simple interest on unpaid debt, whereas compound interest will be considered where the debtor's conduct has been particularly offensive, such as in cases of fraud or misappropriation of funds held in a fiduciary capacity. On the practice in Scotland Lord Justice-Clerk Patton put it as follows in *Douglas v Douglas's Trustees*:[5]

> A claim for compound interest, with annual rests, is a demand which can only be maintained, either in the case of a fixed usage in commercial dealings, or where there has been an abuse in a party trusted with funds, and violating his trust.

In the Scottish case *Maclean v Campbell*[6] the Inner House of the Court of Session distinguished between interest on arrears of interest (once-off capitalisation of interest) on the one hand and compound interest (involving "rests", i.e. compounding at specified intervals) on the other. The court allowed the former, but not the latter, describing it as being of a "penal nature".[7]

The long-standing distaste for interest generally and compound interest in particular is rooted in the rules on usury. To discuss capitalisation in context it is necessary first to clarify the terms "interest" and "usury" and second to refer briefly to the history of usury and the policy considerations that have impacted on this area of the law.

## B. THE NATURE AND FUNCTION OF INTEREST

The meanings of the terms "interest" and "usury" have changed over time. Historically these terms were often equated and usury indicated any payment

4  See section F(2) below.
5  (1867) 5 M 827 at 836. See also on the practice in England, Lord Browne-Wilkinson in *Westdeutsche Landesbank Girozentrale v Islington London Borough Council* [1996] AC 669 at 701 : "In the absence of fraud, courts of equity have never awarded compound interest except against a trustee or other person owing fiduciary duties who is accountable for profits made from his position."
6  (1856) 18 D 609.
7  See further Scot Law Com DP No 127 (2005), para 8.4.

for the use of money, whereas today the term usury is used to indicate an exorbitant payment for the use of money. Historically the term interest primarily indicated compensation for non-payment of money due, whereas today it indicates payment for a number of reasons, including compensation for unpaid debt; payment for the use of money in terms of a contract or trade usage; and payment specifically provided for by statute.[8]

According to Keynes the rate of interest is the "price" which "equilibrates the desire to hold wealth in the form of cash with the available quantity of cash".[9] The rate of interest thus represents the price at which there is equilibrium between the demand and supply of loans of money.[10] The rate of interest can also be said to represent "the percentage excess of a sum of money contracted for forward delivery, e.g. a year hence, over what we may call the 'spot' or cash price of the sum thus contracted for forward delivery".[11] In functional terms interest is the price a borrower has to pay for the use of money and, conversely, the return obtained by a lender for parting with liquidity and deferring consumption of money.[12] Interest therefore indicates a time preference for money and could be described as the price that borrowers are willing to pay to have money now rather than having it later. The Scottish Law Commission in its Discussion Paper on Interest on Debt and Damages[13] notes that interest can be divided into different elements: an element accounting for the time value of money, or inflation; an element for reward for not having the use of money; and an element accounting for the risk of non-payment.

Simple interest is calculated on the principal sum only, whereas compound interest is calculated on the principal plus any interest due at a date when by agreement or operation of law interest can be added to the principal (capitalised).[14]

The effective interest rate determines the future value of a payment that includes interest or, conversely, the present (discounted) value of an entitlement to receive a future payment that includes interest. For instance,

8　P S Atiyah, *The Rise and Fall of Freedom of Contract* (1979), 65; English Law Com CP No 167 (2002), para 2.2.

9　J M Keynes, *The General Theory of Employment Interest and Money* (1949) (henceforth Keynes, *General Theory*), 167.

10　Keynes, *General Theory*, 186 fn 1.

11　Keynes, *General Theory*, 222.

12　See P Mohr, *Economic Indicators* University of South Africa (1998) (henceforth Mohr, *Economic Indicators*), 179.

13　Scot Law Com DP No 127 (2005), para 7.13.

14　See Mohr, *Economic Indicators*, 179.

the future value of £100, one year from now, at 5 per cent simple interest, is £105; and the present value of the entitlement to receive £100 now instead of one year from now, calculated at 5 per cent interest, is £95.23.

The rate of interest is determined by a variety of factors, including the chance of making profit, the rate of inflation, current and anticipated, and concomitant fall in the purchasing power of money, the risk of payment-default, the preference of owning rather than renting an asset and the strength of borrowers' time preference for consumption. These factors reflect that in modern economic theory interest is a fundamental price mechanism.

Legally the function of interest is to provide compensation for being deprived of the use of money. Liability to pay interest may be pre-determined as in the case of a loan agreement or contingent upon the failure of a debtor to pay money on the due date, whatever the cause of the indebtedness. Bell in his *Commentaries*[15] says: "In the ordinary case the damage due for delay in payment of money is nothing but interest." The Scottish Law Commission in its Discussion Paper on Interest on Debt and Damages comments as follows on the function of interest:[16]

> 3.1 The primary purpose of an award of interest is to acknowledge the fact that by being deprived of the use of money, a creditor has either lost an opportunity to benefit from the use of the money or, alternatively, has suffered a further loss as a consequence of not having it to hand.
>
> . . .
>
> 3.2 Similar considerations apply to a sum claimed by way of damages: so long as the damages remain unpaid the claimant is deprived of that sum of money. If the claim is for losses incurred in the past, the claimant is in a position analogous to that of the creditor of an unpaid contractual debt. The effect of an award of interest is to compensate the creditor by redressing the balance and, in theory, leaving both parties in the same position as if the debt had been paid when it fell due or, in the case of damages, as if reparation had been made as soon as the loss was sustained. Neither the claimant nor the debtor benefits from delaying settlement or judicial determination of the dispute.

In the comment on Article 17:101 PECL it is said that the obligation to pay interest upon delay in payment is functionally equivalent to an obligation to pay damages: "The interest can be regarded as a form of abstract damages, although it is not ordinary damages."[17]

The South African Supreme Court of Appeal has held that the economic function of interest (to provide compensation for being deprived of the use of

15 Bell, *Commentaries*, I, 691, as cited in SME, vol 12, para 1018.
16 Scot Law Com DP No 127 (2005), paras 3.1 and 3.2.
17 PECL, vol 2, 240.

money) is the same for both interest *ex contractu* and interest *ex mora*. In *Linton v Corser*[18] Centlivres CJ said in this regard:

> The old authorities regarded interest *a tempore morae* as "poenaal ende odieus", vide *Utrechtsche Consultatien* 3, 63, p 288. Such interest is not in these modern times regarded in that light. Today interest is the life-blood of finance, and there is no reason to distinguish between interest *ex contractu* and interest *ex mora*. ... The question that now arises is whether we should apply the old Roman-Dutch law to modern conditions where finance plays an entirely different rôle. I do not think we should. I think that we should take a more realistic view then in a matter such as this than to have recourse to the old authorities.

In *Bellairs v Hodnett*[19] the function of interest is described as follows:

> under modern conditions a debtor who is tardy in the due payment of a monetary obligation will almost invariably deprive the creditor of the productive use of the money and thereby cause him loss. It is for this loss that the award of mora interest seeks to compensate the creditor.

The quantification of the loss compensated for by interest should be determined according to the notional proceeds of "productive use of the money" in the market. The rates offered in the market and in particular the possibility of obtaining compound interest on an investment should therefore be taken into account. However, as will be shown below, there is often an imperfect correlation between the capitalisation of interest in the commercial markets and interest allowed by way of compensation.

## C. HISTORY OF RULES ON CAPITALISATION

### (1) Roman law

The history of the regulation of interest in Roman law goes back to the XII Tables, which already prescribed a ceiling rate in respect of contracts of loan, albeit in enigmatic fashion on the basis of *unciarium fenus* (interest of $\frac{1}{12}$ of the capital).[20] This restriction has left modern scholars puzzling over the ceiling rate intended, i.e. $8\frac{1}{3}$ per cent, 10 per cent, $83\frac{1}{3}$ per cent, or 100 per cent, depending on whether the interest had to be calculated per year or per month, and for a ten-month or twelve-month year.[21]

Originally compound interest or anatocism may not have been regulated in Roman law, but in the Republican era it was established that interest on

---

18  1952 (3) SA 685 (A) at 695H.
19  1978 (1) SA 1109 (A) at 1145G.
20  K Verboven, "The Sulpicii from Puteoli and usury in the early Roman empire" (2003) 71 *TR* at 7.
21  See Zimmermann, *Obligations*, 166–167.

overdue interest could be charged only after one year. Cicero, in a letter to Atticus, refers to both the initial legality of *anatocismus anniversarius* and its subsequent prohibition.[22] In 51 BC the senate decreed that interest would be reduced to 1 per cent per month (*usura centesima*) and that compound interest (*anatocismus*) would not be allowed. This limit seems to have remained in force under Caesar.[23] In the early Empire rules on interest involved three basic principles: (1) Interest rates were fixed and the general limit was 1 per cent a month (*usura centesima*). Simple interest was available in a variety of situations, such as in the case of late payment of a debt.[24] Higher interest rates were allowed in respect of enterprise-lending, as in the case of *foenus nauticum* and loans for the training and development of professional sportsmen.[25] (2) Compound interest (*usurae usurarum*) was not permitted.[26] (3) The total sum of interest paid by the debtor to his creditor could not exceed the original amount of the loan (*usurae supra duplum*). The origins of these three principles, however, and their practical effectiveness are not clear.[27]

The restrictions on interest rates and compound interest in Roman law, as set out above, were exceptional in the context of a legal system that generally favoured freedom of contract. Free Roman citizens were supposed to be able to look after their own interests and the *paterfamilias* was supposed to protect the weak and the vulnerable such as women, children and slaves.[28] Generally in contracts of sale whatever price was agreed upon could be taken to represent a fair price in the particular circumstances. Sharp practice was moderated by remedies such as those based on *dolus* or latent defects. Generally, therefore, Roman law recognised the autonomy of contracting parties to construct their own deals. Prominent exceptions to the general absence of price-control measures in the Roman law of contract were the restrictions on interest rates and the *laesio enormis* doctrine.[29] Restrictions on interest rates applied to the contract of loan (*mutuum*), where interest, the price element of *mutuum*, had to be promised by way of a separate *stipulatio*.[30]

22 Cicero, *Ad Atticum*, V 21, [11], [12], [13]. The Latin text is available at *http://web.tiscali.it/latino/ Cicerone_epistole/ad_atticum_5.1.htm* (accessed 30 March 2005); and for a translation see D R Shackleton Bailey, *Cicero Letters to Atticus*, vol 2 (1999), 98–103.

23 Verboven (2003) 71 *TR* at 8.

24 D 22.1.32.2.

25 Zimmermann, *Obligations*, 181–187.

26 D 22.1.29; C 2.11.20; C. 4.32.28.

27 Verboven (2003) 71 *TR* at 7, 8.

28 Zimmermann, *Obligations*, 256.

29 See Zimmermann, *Obligations*, 166.

30 Zimmermann, *Obligations*, 258.

The restrictions in Roman law on interest generally and compound interest specifically were later adopted and reinforced in the doctrine of the Christian Church on usury, dealt with in the following section.

## (2) Policy on interest and capitalisation

Restrictions on the recovery of interest by means of usury laws are among the oldest and most prevalent forms of economic regulation.[31] In the notes to Article 17:101 PECL, dealing with the capitalisation of interest, it is stated that the basis of differences in national rules on capitalisation or "interest for delayed payment of interest" is "the differing impact of religious and ideological conceptions".[32] Some of the considerations underlying the historically perceived illegitimacy of interest (and therefore of compound interest) are briefly referred to below. The purpose is only to indicate certain themes that form the background to the lingering reluctance in modern legal systems to accept compound interest or capitalisation. Religious and emotional factors have been at play in this ancient debate and some of these factors exert influence up to the present day.

The taking of interest is of course a precondition to the taking of compound interest. If interest is bad, then compound interest is worse. The English Law Commission in its 2002 Consultation Paper on Compound Interest noted the common policy concerns in this regard:[33]

> Compound interest being interest on interest, it is hard to think of any principled argument against the legitimacy of compound interest that does not also impugn interest as such.

A prominent theme in this debate has been that interest necessarily involves the exploitation of the poor by rich and powerful creditors and that the taking of interest is therefore unjust and sinful, flouting the virtues of humility and charity.[34]

Another theme has been that money is sterile and that the "breeding" of money from money is unnatural.[35] The visible, calculable and progressive "growth" of a loan carrying interest appeared to be something unnatural and

---

31 See Keynes, *General Theory*, 351: "Provisions against usury are amongst the most ancient economic practices of which we have record."

32 PECL, vol 2, 241.

33 Law Com CP No 167 (2002), para 4.12.

34 N N Bowsher, "Usury laws; harmful when effective" *Federal Reserve Bank of St Louis Review* (Aug 1974), 16.

35 E L Glaeser & J Scheinkman, "Neither a borrower nor a lender be: an economic analysis of interest restrictions and usury laws" (1998) 41 *Journal of Law and Economics* 1.

distasteful. The taking of interest appeared to be an illegitimate way of earning income without labour.[36]

Also influential was the idea of a "just price" (*pretium iustum*); that price should be a construct of social will and not private will; and that interest is also a price that should be subject to objective criteria of justice.[37]

The essence of usury was seen as being "pure interest" that was stipulated in advance for a loan of money or wares. The objectionable nature of this kind of interest was that it was pre-determined, certain and, whether the borrower gained or lost, the usurer took his pound of flesh, so to speak.[38]

The Christian Church has been the most powerful force in the shaping of law and practice on interest in Europe. The restrictions in Roman law on interest generally and compound interest specifically were adopted and reinforced by the Christian Church in medieval times, leading up to the Third Lateran Council of 1175, which provided for the excommunication of usurers.[39]

Certain passages in the five books of Moses (Pentateuch) and also in Psalm 15 explicitly forbid the charging of interest, but some of these passages suggest that the ban on interest only applied among the Jews ("brothers") and that it was aimed primarily at loans to the indigent. The passages occur among other appeals to social justice and appear to be aimed at protecting the poor, so that they do not reduce themselves to a further level of poverty where they would be burdens on the community.[40] In the New Testament the parable of the talents suggests the condonation of interest and much has been written on reconciling this message with Christian doctrine.[41]

Usury laws were primarily intended to curb wasteful and extravagant consumption. In Christian doctrine, as in Roman law, restrictions on lending at interest were primarily focused on consumption loans, where the cost to the borrower was not offset by production benefits.[42] In the Vulgate version of Luke's prohibition on lending, the word *mutuum* was chosen to refer to the prohibited loans, suggesting that the focus was on consumption loans. Aquinas,

---

36 See H G Ulrich "Das Zinsnehmen in der Christichen Ethik", in M Vollkommer (ed), *Der Zins in Recht, Wirtschaft und Ethik* (1989), 61.

37 See Ulrich (note 36 above) at 63.

38 See R H Tawney, *Religion and the Rise of Capitalism* (1938, reprint 1948) (henceforth Tawney, *Religion and Rise of Capitalism*), 54–55.

39 Tawney, *Religion and the Rise of Capitalism*, 58.

40 Glaeser & Scheinkman (1998) *Journal of Law and Economics* 1 at 21.

41 E Kerridge, *Usury, Interest and the Reformation* (2002) (henceforth Kerridge, *Usury, Interest and the Reformation*), 6–7.

42 Tawney, *Religion and the Rise of Capitalism*, 50–51.

one of usury's harshest critics, differentiated between consumption and production loans.[43]

The motives of the Christian Church in respect of interest may not have been entirely pure. It has been argued that usury restrictions were kept in place because the Christian Church, a prominent borrower, wanted to lower the price of goods it needed to buy. The Church could also have had an incentive to support strict usury laws because it often seized the assets of convicted usurers on their death.[44] The formal legal position of the Church on usury was in any event by no means adequately reflected commercial reality.[45] Errant members of the Church often charged usurious rates and so did the Jewish lenders, who were immune to threats of excommunication.[46]

Protestant reformers made a distinction between sinful usury and legitimate interest and the Reformation led to widespread liberalisation of the usury laws. Christian doctrine in fact had never involved a blanket ban on the taking of interest on loans.[47] Kerridge argues that inconsistent terminology was the cause of much confusion on doctrine.[48]

Anti-interest sentiments are by no means restricted to the Christian faith. In India early Vedic law restricted interest rates and condemned usury as a major sin. Interest rates were set according to the level of risk involved (loans for forest or sea travel attracted higher rates of interest); and there was also a clear distinction between production-related and consumption-related loans.[49]

A common practice to avoid usury laws for productive loans was to incorporate the lender into the productive enterprise with an equity stake. The Talmud specifically allows and regulates this form of finance and, on account of the aversion to interest in the Islamic religion, Islamic banking is based almost entirely on the creation of lender equity rather than debt.[50]

Interest and usury have featured prominently in philosophy and literature. Plato and Aristotle both viewed money lending as immoral and Dante placed

---

43  Glaeser & Scheinkman (1998) 41 *Journal of Law and Economics* 1 at 23.

44  Tawney, *Religion and the Rise of Capitalism*, 41–42; Glaeser & Scheinkman (1998) 41 *Journal of Law and Economics* 1 at 2, 25.

45  Tawney, *Religion and the Rise of Capitalism*, 56–57.

46  Tawney, *Religion and the Rise of Capitalism*, 42, 49; Glaeser & Scheinkman (1998) 41 *Journal of Law and Economics* 1 at 24.

47  Tawney, *Religion and the Rise of Capitalism*, 54.

48  Kerridge, *Usury, Interest and the Reformation*, Introduction, 5–6.

49  Glaeser & Scheinkman (1998) 41 *Journal of Law and Economics* 1 at 19 n 33.

50  On the lending practices of Islamic banks see *Carrim v Omar* 2001 (4) SA 691 (W), where the nature of the Shariah-compliant "unrestricted Mudhaarabah contract" is examined. See further generally Glaeser & Scheinkman (1998) 41 *Journal of Law and Economics* 1 at 23.

the usurers of Cahors in the same area of hell as the denizens of Sodom.[51] Shakespeare's Shylock has become the metaphor for greed and the immorality of moneylending.[52]

From a political point of view the pervasive restriction on interest over the centuries is somewhat surprising. It seems to indicate that borrowers often possessed more political power than lenders, which seems implausible.[53] This is exemplified by the special interest rate restriction applicable in the time of Justinian to the Roman political elite, the senators, many of whom had thriving moneylending businesses. At work may have been Justinian's Christian beliefs, moving him to act as a benevolent dictator and to enforce exemplary commercial behaviour on the part of the ruling political elite, who had to accept 4 per cent instead of the usual 6 per cent interest on their moneylending operations.[54]

Theories on the time value of money and inflation were late in developing and the historical arguments on interest and usury generally fail to explain why the charging of a price for money is any different from the charging of a price for other goods. Viewed retrospectively in terms of modern economic theory usury laws over the centuries may have intended, at least partially, to narrow the income gap between rich and poor; and consequently interest rate restrictions were enforced more rigidly when income inequality was high and growth rates were low.[55] Another aim could have been to curb interest rates which, in a world generally regarded as highly unsafe, would have risen too high to permit borrowing for investment.[56]

## D. MODERN THEORY ON REGULATION OF INTEREST

Whereas the law on interest and usury was historically based primarily on moral and religious considerations one would expect modern law on interest to be consistent with current economic policy and commercial realities. The prevailing view in modern economic theory is that governments do well to refrain from controlling prices in most markets, because experience has shown that in free competitive markets more goods are produced at lower prices

---

51 See Tawney, *Religion and the Rise of Capitalism*, 42; Glaeser & Scheinkman (1998) 41 *Journal of Law and Economics* 1, nn 40, 41, 42.

52 On the terminology associated with Shylock see Kerridge, *Usury, Interest and the Reformation*, Introduction and 8.

53 Glaeser & Scheinkman (1998) 41 *Journal of Law and Economics* 1 at 2–3.

54 See Zimmermann, *Obligations*, 168.

55 Glaeser & Scheinkman (1998) 41 *Journal of Law and Economics* 1 at 26–27.

56 See Keynes, *General Theory* at 351.

than in markets subject to price controls. This approach applies also to the price of credit in the market and underlies the absence of usury legislation in many countries, as in Europe generally and in Scotland specifically. South Africa is a mixed system in respect of interest regulation, as will be shown below.

The economic argument for restrictions on compound interest is that such restrictions at least assist in staving off the disproportionately oppressive effect of exponential growth of interest costs on poorer borrowers. Where compound interest is charged, and the borrower becomes unable even to service the loan, the effect is destructive. An exponential increase in interest is more frightening and unpredictable than a linear increase, and liability for compound interest might be a slippery slope to hopeless debt. This is said to be the consideration underlying the prohibition of compound interest in the developing world, particularly in some Latin American countries.[57]

The current policy approach in South Africa is to protect consumers against extortion by setting rate ceilings where these can be enforced relatively successfully. The system is a mixed one. In the small or "micro-lending" loans sector, where rate ceilings cannot be enforced effectively and where normal market-related rate ceilings would in any event be economically unrealistic in view of high transaction costs, the policy since 1992 has been to exempt defined small loans from the application of the Usury Act 73 of 1968 (referred to below as "the Usury Act"). Such loans were made subject to other regulatory measures, including registration of "micro-lenders" and the prohibition of certain lending and collection practices.[58] In respect of consumer credit contracts governed by the Credit Agreements Act 75 of 1980 (below referred to as "the Credit Agreements Act") and the Usury Act, involving medium-size consumer debt (loans, credit sales and leases of between R10,000 and R500, 000) compound interest is prohibited, except in case of default (mora).[59]

Most medium-sized consumer transactions governed by the Usury Act involve pre-calculated monthly instalments, providing lenders with a monthly interest income corresponding to or surpassing that available in the commercial investment market. In this context the commercial need for compound interest or capitalisation arises mainly in cases of default (mora), where it is

---

57  Law Com CP No 167 (2002), para 4.10.

58  See generally *Report on Costs and Interest Rates in the Small Loans Sector*, published as Government Notice No 706 of 21 July 2000 in Government Gazette No 21381 of 21 July 2000 at 11–13, 18.

59  Section 4 of the Usury Act 73 of 1968 provides for the recovery of additional finance charges in case of payment default.

allowed in a limited form, as indicated in the preceding paragraph. In the case of debts not covered by consumer protection legislation no ceiling rates apply and compound interest is in principle allowed, subject to the *in duplum* rule and to common law rules on extortionate interest, as detailed in section E(3) below. The policy on capitalisation in cases of default (*mora*) is consistent with the economic reality that compensation for being deprived of the use of money should be calculated according to the compound interest rates offered in the commercial investment market.

## E. REGULATION OF CAPITALISATION BY CONTRACT AND TRADE USAGE

### (1) Enforceability of agreements on capitalisation

Article 17:101(1) PECL provides for annual capitalisation in respect of certain types of debt; and Article 17:101(2) PECL makes the capitalisation provision in Article 17:101(1) PECL subject to a specific contract between the parties. In some European systems parties are free to agree in advance on capitalisation of interest. In others, for instance in Germany, an agreement on capitalisation is given effect only if entered into after interest has fallen due, although financial institutions are exempted. In other systems an agreement on capitalisation is only permitted after a specific period has elapsed since the interest first fell due, the period being a year in some cases and six months in others. Italy requires that in agreements on capitalisation of interest in credit and savings contracts the rest period and interest rate be specifically agreed upon.[60]

In Scotland compound interest is allowed where a contract or trade usage specifically provides for it.[61] Lord Justice-Clerk Inglis put it as follows in *Douglas v Douglas's Trustees* in 1867: "A claim for compound interest, with annual rests, is a demand which can only be maintained, either in a case of fixed usage in commercial dealings, or where there has been an abuse in a party trusted with funds and violating his trust."[62]

The situation in South Africa is similar and has been described as follows:[63]

Our usury legislation has never outlawed the charging of compound interest. Although such a prohibition is mentioned in the old authorities, it has been held to

60  PECL, vol 2, 242 (national notes).
61  SME, vol 12, para 1038; Scot Law Com DP No 127 (2005), para 8.7.
62  Quoted by Gloag, *Contract*, 683 n 13.
63  In *Standard Bank of SA Ltd v Oneanate Investments (Pty) Ltd* 1995 (4) SA 510 (C) at 566D–F.

have been abrogated by disuse in the modern law. ... Compound interest will be admitted provided only that it has been agreed to either expressly or by custom. ...

In South Africa the common-law rule against compound interest was held to have been abrogated precisely because of evidence that it was the universal practice of banks in South Africa to charge compound interest.

There is recognition in Scotland[64] and South Africa[65] that the operation of current accounts involves an implied agreement on capitalisation of interest. There is a distinction in banking practice between accrual of interest and capitalisation.[66] Banks customarily calculate interest on overdrawn current accounts on a daily basis and debit the accumulated total to the account, usually on a monthly basis. The entries passed to the account and the running balance which they generate are reflected in a bank statement which is usually sent to the customer at regular intervals.[67] However, the daily debiting of interest does not constitute capitalisation or compounding. It is only at the agreed rests or intervals, usually monthly, that the accrued interest is treated as an accretion to the capital, with the effect that interest is from then on taken on the total sum.

## (2) Unconscionability standards

In the United Kingdom the Consumer Credit Act prohibits "extortionate" and "grossly exorbitant" interest pricing. Extortionate credit bargains can be re-opened under section 137 of the Consumer Credit Act, 1974. The Act defines a credit bargain as extortionate if it "(a) requires ... payments ... which are grossly exorbitant, or (b) otherwise grossly contravenes ordinary principles of fair dealing." Courts take into account factors such as the following: the standard of sophistication of the borrower and financial necessity or pressure. Borrowers for business speculation do not qualify for assistance.[68] The Consumer Credit Act directs the court to evaluate the rate charged in relation to prevailing interest rates and the borrower's risk. It is apparent from English cases that almost anything goes when the debtor has a bad credit history, minimal collateral, or both. Rates of 177 per cent, 120 per cent and 80 per cent have been upheld in such cases.[69]

---

64 Gloag, *Contract*, 684.

65 *Senekal v Trust Bank of Africa Ltd* 1978 (3) SA 375 (A) at 384C–G.

66 See generally R M Goode, *Consumer Credit Law* (1989) (henceforth Goode, *Consumer Credit Law*), 310–311.

67 *Standard Bank of SA Ltd v Oneanate Investments (Pty) Ltd* 1995 (4) SA 510 (C) at 568E–I.

68 See generally Goode, *Consumer Credit Law*, 756–762.

69 S W Bender, "Rate regulation at the crossroads of usury and unconscionability: the case for regulating abusive commercial and consumer interest rates under the unconscionability standard" (1994) 31 *Houston LR* 721 at 781–787.

In Germany extortionate interest bargains are void where there is substantive disparity between the benefit of the parties to the credit transaction and the borrower's weakness has been exploited. Gross pricing disparity alone may be actionable under the general prohibition of transactions contrary to public policy in terms of §138(2) of the BGB. German courts look at interest rates with reference to comparable market transactions, borrower risk, and the effects of inflation.[70]

The case law on §138(2) of the BGB in respect of extortionate interest rates has been summarised as follows:

> A creditor loses all claims to the payment of interest and other cost elements if in a consumer credit contract as it is regulated by the Consumer Credit Act the annual percentage rate of charge (APR) as defined by the Consumer Credit Act lies more than relatively 100 per cent or absolutely 12 per cent over the average interest rate of instalment credit published monthly by the central bank. If other harsh conditions burden the consumer 90 per cent will suffice. In cases of refinancing into a worde credit contract a ceiling of 70 per cent for the new credit leads to the same effect.[71]

In Germany an extortionate interest rate was initially a bar to recovery of both principal and interest, but courts now allow recovery of the principal in such a case. The lender cannot recover any interest, not even interest reduced to a fair rate. In contrast, English courts reduce an excessive rate to a fair one. Commentators criticise Germany's denial of all interest as harsh and inflexible, but others in England feel that merely reducing the rate does not deter unfair pricing, and advocate reform to render the whole bargain unenforceable.[72]

In South Africa general rules on public policy can be invoked in respect of agreed interest in contracts not governed by consumer credit legislation (generally contracts where the principal exceeds R500,000). Excessive interest can be regarded as extortionate and therefore against public policy or good morals. There is no such thing as a "common law rate of interest" (*certum modum usurarum*), but the circumstances of a particular case could indicate that the stipulated interest is extortionate or usurious.[73] In *Reuter v Yates*,[74] for instance, it was held that interest at 60 per cent on a small loan for a short period was not usurious. Agreement on a usurious interest rate does not

---

70 Bender (1994) 31 *Houston LR* 721 at 783–787.

71 U Reifner "Good faith: interpretation or limitation of contracts? The power of German judges in financial services law", in R Brownsword, N J Hird & G Howells (eds), *Good Faith in Contract: Concept and Content* (2000), 269 at 295.

72 Bender (1994) 31 *Houston LR* 721 at 783–787.

73 See the summary of the position in common law by N J Grove, "Klein Lenings en die Woekerwet" (1993) 56 *THRHR* 657 at 662–663.

74 [1904] TS 855.

necessarily make the contract void in its entirety. Arguably a court has the power to declare a contract partially enforceable to the extent that the interest is not usurious, so that the creditor may claim his capital and so much of the interest which is not usurious and can be regarded as reasonable.

### (3) Capitalisation under the Usury Act in South Africa

The Usury Act applies to credit transactions, leasing transactions and money-lending transactions. A moneylending transaction is widely defined, to include credit card transactions, certain sales of immoveable property and improvements to immoveable property.

The Act has two main purposes: to limit "finance charges" (a defined concept including interest and costs) and to ensure adequate disclosure of all the terms of the contracts governed by the Act, in particular payment terms and interest. Finance charges are calculated on the "principal debt". Any item, expenditure or amount which is not covered by the definition of "principal debt" or "finance charges" will be recoverable only if it constitutes a cost item specifically authorised in terms of section 5 of the Act.

Section 2 of the Act provides for maximum rates in respect of the different transactions governed by the Act. Rates vary according to the value of the transaction. The registrar has the power to determine rates by notice in the *Government Gazette* in accordance with the directions of the responsible minister (who in the past had to publish it himself). This is done frequently to adjust maximum finance charge rates to the interest rates prevailing in the market.

It has been held that section 5 of the Usury Act does not prevent the recovery of compound interest (capitalisation) if an agreement to that effect exists.[75] However, the correctness of this decision is open to question, in view of the provision in section 2(6)(a) of the Usury Act that a creditor may not levy finance charges calculated according to shorter or more periods than those according to which instalments or the outstanding balance of the principal debt must be paid.[76] This section prevents a creditor, for instance, from

---

75  *Interaccess (Pty) Ltd v Van Dorsten* [1999] 2 All SA 561 (C) at 574. The court held that s 5 of the Usury Act does not specifically preclude the charging of compound interest and that compound interest is claimable provided there is agreement between the parties to that effect (referring to *National Bank of South Africa v Graaf* (1904) 2 SC 457 at 462).

76  There is one exception, namely in the case of a moneylending transaction where finance charges may be *recovered* on a monthly basis if instalments are paid at intervals of longer than a month. It would seem that s 2(7) allows the moneylender to recover his finance charges in shorter periods, but that the rate must still be calculated in accordance with s 2(1)(a). In other words, s 2(7) permits him to obtain his interest sooner, but at no higher a rate than that allowed by s 2(1)(a).

levying interest on a weekly basis where instalments are payable monthly in order to earn more interest. Furthermore, in terms of section 5(1)(c) finance charges are recoverable only on the principal debt and on certain specified disbursements and therefore not on other finance charges.

The Usury Act requires pre-calculation and specific disclosure of instalments, on the basis of simple interest over intervals corresponding with the instalment payments. Under this system capitalisation occurs on a one-off basis upon default, where further interest is taken on both the outstanding principal and the outstanding interest, as indicated below in section G(3).

## (4) Small loans in South Africa

South Africa has an advanced financial services sector, but it provides banking services and credit to not more than half of the population. Others depend on traditional savings and loan institutions and providers of small loans, known as micro-lenders. Small loans overwhelmingly finance consumption or servicing of other debts, rather than production.[77]

Extortionate lending practices feeding on adverse socio-economic conditions create massively excessive indebtedness among lower-income groups. An exemption notice under section 15 of the Usury Act exempts loans of less than R10,000 from compliance with the maximum interest rates set under the Act, provided certain conditions are met. These conditions involve increased administrative regulation of lenders and detailed regulations on lending and enforcement practices have also been enacted.

A survey of registered short-term cash lenders in South Africa in 2000 shows that, on average, these lenders charge an interest rate of 30 per cent per month, all fees included. Interest rates vary according to the term of the loan.[78]

Many retail stores have entered this market. After small loans were deregulated in terms of the Usury Act many furniture dealers and other retail stores have entered the lending market by registering as micro-lenders and promoting loans to their regular clients. In this manner they provide finance at much higher rates, bypassing the Credit Agreements Act and the Usury Act.[79]

*Mashonisas*[80] are lenders who operate in the townships of South Africa, providing short-term loans, mostly for no longer than a month. Interest rates

---

77 See generally *Report on Costs and Interest Rates in the Small Loans Sector*, published as Government Notice No 706 of 21 July 2000 at 35.

78 See generally *Report on Costs and Interest Rates in the Small Loans Sector* at 28, 33.

79 See Examination of Costs and Interest Rates in the Small Loans Sector, 34–35.

80 The term is of Zulu origin and means "those who bring you down".

average about 50 per cent per month and *mora* interest is capitalised. *Stokvels*,[81] burial societies and rotating savings and credit associations are informal savings and loan organisations that receive savings from members and then invest the funds or make loans to members on a rotating basis. The repaid capital and interest go back into the group fund for redistribution to the members. Interest on loans is taken as a form of additional forced saving by the borrower. There are an estimated 800,000 of these institutions with more than 8 million members. Funds are normally distributed to members on a rotating basis at group meetings, as a form of dividend. Little is known about enforcement procedures of these lenders, but there is no reported judgment involving any of these lenders and no indication that normal legal processes are involved for collection of debts.[82]

## F. CAPITALISATION AND THE *IN DUPLUM* RULE IN SOUTH AFRICA

### (1) General nature, effect and rationale of in *duplum* rule

The effect of the *in duplum* rule (a rule deriving from Roman law[83] and still forming part of South African law but not of Scots law) is that interest stops running when the unpaid interest equals the outstanding capital.[84] When the debtor repays a part of the interest, so that the outstanding interest amount drops below the outstanding capital amount, interest again begins to run until it once again equals the capital amount. This rule applies not only to moneylending transactions, but to any kind of transaction involving the payment of interest on an amount due in terms of the transaction.[85] The rule applies only to interest outstanding at a particular time and does not limit the total amount of interest payable by the debtor by way of instalments or in piecemeal fashion for the duration of a particular transaction.[86]

The rationale for the rule is simply to protect the debtor against liability for an accumulated interest debt that exceeds the outstanding capital debt. The rule and the policy considerations underlying it were simply described by

---

81  The term "stokvel" is said to have originated in the Eastern Cape area as a black version of the periodical "stock fairs" held by white farmers.

82  See generally *Report on Costs and Interest Rates in the Small Loans Sector* at 35–36.

83  See section C(1) above.

84  See generally M M Loubser & M A Muller "Bank overdrafts: Limitation of interest by the in duplum rule; and prescription" (1998) 115 *SALJ* 598–612.

85  *LTA Construction Bpk v Administrateur, Transvaal* 1992 (1) SA 473 (A) at 482.

86  *LTA Construction Bpk v Administrateur, Transvaal* at 480.

Joubert JA in *LTA Construction Bpk v Administrateur, Transvaal*[87] as being part of daily life; not an anachronism; and serving a useful purpose to protect debtors.

The rule therefore remains part of South African law and it is most likely to find application where a debtor has an open account with a trader or a current account with a bank, allowing the purchase of goods or withdrawal money, subject to a certain credit limit, without the obligation to pay regular instalments. Should the interest debt become equal to the capital debt (even though the overall credit limit has not been reached) the creditor could find himself unable to recover all the interest that has accumulated in the account.

## (2) Capitalisation

Because of the fluctuating balance of an open account with a trader or a current account with a bank, interest is often calculated daily on the outstanding balance of the account as at close of business on that day. At the end of each month the individual amounts of daily interest for that month are added to the outstanding amount.

In *Standard Bank of South Africa Ltd v Oneanate Investments (Pty) Ltd (In liquidation)*[88] the Supreme Court of Appeal considered the effect of the banking practice of capitalising interest on a current account on the operation of the *in duplum* rule. The court held that the parties cannot by agreement or conduct waive or alter the effect of the *in duplum* rule. The rule is based on public policy and is designed to protect borrowers from exploitation by lenders. As such it cannot be waived by borrowers and cannot be altered by banking practice.[89]

The Supreme Court of Appeal also held that the practice of capitalisation of interest by bankers does not result in the interest losing its character as such for the purposes of the *in duplum* rule. If lenders were entitled to employ the expedient of a book entry to convert what is interest into capital, this would afford an easy way to avoid not only the *in duplum* rule but also prescription and usury legislation.[90]

To apply the *in duplum* rule, the outstanding capital amount of the debt must be determined, and this in turn could depend on how credits to the account have been allocated or appropriated. In the *Standard Bank* case the

---

87 At 482F–H.
88 1998 (1) SA 811 (SCA).
89 At 828C–D.
90 At 828I–J.

court held the rule to be that payments should be allocated first to interest and then to capital.[91]

On the application of the rule *pendente lite* the court in the *Standard Bank* case held that the purpose of the rule is to protect borrowers from exploitation where lenders permit interest to accumulate excessively. A creditor who has instituted action cannot be said to exploit a debtor if the latter, assisted by the delays inherent in legal proceedings, keeps the creditor out of his money. The court held that therefore no principle of public policy justifies providing the debtor with protection *pendente lite* against interest in excess of the outstanding capital amount. A creditor can control the institution of litigation and can, by timeously instituting action, protect himself against loss of interest by operation of the *in duplum* rule. However, the creditor has limited control over delays caused by the litigation process and the rule should therefore be suspended as soon as the legal process begins, i.e. upon service of the initiating process. The result is that the outstanding interest, frozen at the level of the outstanding capital amount, then begins to run again at the applicable rate of interest, up to the time of judgment. Once a judgment has been delivered interest begins to run on the judgment debt, which may already contain a component of accumulated interest equal to the capital component, or exceeding the capital component as a result of the suspension of the *in duplum* rule *pendente lite*. The judgment reinforces the existing debt by affording the creditor the right to implement a process of execution and interest begins to run from the date of the judgment on the judgment debt as a whole, irrespective of the size of its interest component. The *in duplum* rule then applies again to the judgment debt as a whole, the policy consideration being that after obtaining judgment the creditor is in duty bound to execute and bring to a close the further accumulation of interest. The effect is that interest may again accumulate on the judgment debt, but only until the interest equals the amount of the judgment debt.[92]

Arguably the *in duplum* rule is arbitrary in simply limiting outstanding interest to double the capital and its reception into modern South African law has been sparsely and unconvincingly justified. It takes no account of the effect of fluctuating interest rates on the time that it takes for unpaid interest to equal the outstanding capital and, insofar as it is supposed to penalise a tardy creditor it usurps the function of prescription.

---

91  At 831I–832C.
92  At 834B–H.

# G. *MORA* INTEREST

## (1) Entitlement to *mora* interest

In Roman law simple interest was available in a variety of situations, such as in the case of late payment of a debt,[93] but interest on interest was from 51 BC and still under Justinian forbidden in all circumstances.[94] Medieval lawyers argued that interest payable on account of delayed payment (*mora*) was not subject to usury rules, because such interest serves to compensate the creditor for damages.[95] *Mora* thus became one of the most important causes for awarding interest.

In both Scotland and South Africa the courts accept without requiring special proof that a party who has been deprived of the use of his capital for a period of time has suffered a loss. At the same time it is accepted that in the normal course of events such a party will be compensated for his loss by an award of *mora* interest. Scots law has distinct rules on what constitutes "wrongful withholding" of payment, to create a liability for interest.[96]

On the purpose of *mora* interest the comment on Article 17:101 PECL states that the obligation to pay interest upon delay in payment is functionally equivalent to an obligation to pay damages. "The interest can be regarded as a form of abstract damages, although it is not ordinary damages."[97] Interest is not a species of ordinary damages and the general rules on damages do not apply. Interest is owed without proof of loss and the aggrieved party is entitled to it without regard to whether reasonable steps were taken to mitigate loss.[98] Although the creditor cannot claim damages for any loss already compensated for by the payment of interest, he or she is entitled to additional damages not compensated for by the interest.[99]

## (2) *Mora* interest and capitalisation

Article 17:101 PECL provides for the capitalisation of interest every twelve months and the comment on this Article states that the capitalisation of interest is justified by the fact that delay in the payment of interest to which the creditor is entitled deprives the creditor of a due benefit as much as delay in the payment of the capital itself. Such delay often has a highly detrimental

93  D 22.1.32.2.
94  D 22.1.29; C 2.11.20; C 4.32.28.
95  Zimmermann, *Obligations*, 799–800.
96  Scot Law Com DP No 127 (2005), para 2.23.
97  PECL, vol 2, 240.
98  PECL, vol 1, 451.
99  PECL, vol 2, 240–241.

effect on creditors, especially smaller businesses dependent on cash flow. Article 17:101 PECL is intended as a sanction for late payment of interest. In the comment to this Article it is said that capitalisation is "an effective sanction because of its gradually increasing effect".[100]

Article 6:119 of the Dutch Civil Code is of particular interest in relation to Article 17:101 PECL, because it is the most recent of the major European Codes (the new Code came into force in 1992) and because of its similarity to Article 17:101 PECL. It also provides for automatic capitalisation at the end of each year while the interest remains outstanding. It differs from Article 17:101 PECL in that the creditor is not entitled to prove additional loss as a result of the delay in payment.[101] Like Article 17:101 PECL the Dutch Code allows the parties to agree on a higher or lower rate than that prescribed by the Code.[102]

The New Zealand Law Commission in its Report on Aspects of Damages: The Award of Interest on Money Claims[103] says the following:

> As a matter of general principle, therefore, people kept out of pocket should be able to recover interest on money owed to them from the date they were entitled to the money until it is paid in full. The law should compensate plaintiffs realistically for the loss they suffered (para 10).
>
> Simple interest does not reflect business practice. When money is borrowed, interest accrues on outstanding balances which include interest charges already incurred. For example, where a bank lends money to a customer, there will normally be regular payments of interest during the term of the loan. If payments are not made, the outstanding interest is capitalised and interest charged upon it. Where interest does not compound, it fails to compensate adequately the person to whom money is owed (para 24).
>
> The object of an award of interest in court proceedings is to compensate the plaintiff for not having the money during the period for which it is due and unpaid (para 32).

The Scottish Law Commission in its Discussion Paper on Interest on Debt and Damages[104] likewise accepts that interest serves to compensate a creditor for being deprived of the use of money. By payment default the creditor either loses an opportunity to benefit from the use of the money or, alternatively, suffers a further loss as a consequence of not having it to hand.

---

100  PECL, vol 2, 240.
101  See Hartkamp *Asser's Handleiding tot de Beoefening van het Nederlands Burgerlijk Recht Verbintenissenrecht* Deel I, 11th edn (2000), 461.
102  See Hartkamp *Asser's Handleiding tot de Beoefening van het Nederlands Burgerlijk Recht Verbintenissenrecht*, 464.
103  New Zealand Law Com No 28 (1997).
104  Scot Law Com DP No 127 (2005), para 3.1, 3.2.

The South African Supreme Court of Appeal has held in *Bellairs v Hodnett*[105] that the function of interest is to provide compensation to a creditor who is deprived by the debtor's default of the productive use of the money. Capitalisation of interest on unpaid debt is allowed in principle, but not expressly provided for by the Prescribed Rate of Interest Act 55 of 1975. In *Davehill (Pty) Ltd v Community Development Board*[106] the South African Appellate Division considered whether it was permissible, in the absence of agreement, to award interest on statutory interest payable in terms of legislation on expropriation. The court held that the rule against interest on interest in Roman and Roman-Dutch law has become obsolete in modern South African law. Commercial agreements involving compound interest are commonplace and on principle *mora* interest (a species of damages) could also be claimed on unpaid interest, statutory interest payable for loss of possession and fruits of land. The wording of the legislation in question will determine whether it allows for such compound interest.[107]

In Scotland the Late Payment of Commercial Debts (Interest) Act 1998 covers business debts for the supply of goods and services. If the Act applies to a contract the "qualifying debt" created by the contract carries simple interest. The Act provides for a particularly high rate of interest, but the rate is simple rather than compound, a situation clearly not in accordance with commercial realities.[108]

In Scotland the general rule, as set out in *Nash Dredging (UK) Ltd v Kestrel Marine Ltd,*[109] is that interest is not allowed on interest, but there are occasions where accumulation of principal and interest (capitalisation) is allowed. A claim for compound interest with annual rests is seldom allowed, but in some cases it may be legitimate to accumulate outstanding interest with the principal, and then to claim interest on the whole sum outstanding. The position in Scotland is complicated by the rule that mere non-payment of a debt is not sufficient to create a liability for interest. Payment must be "wrongfully withheld".[110]

In *Maclean v Campbell*[111] the court accumulated the principal and the

---

105  1978 (1) SA 1109 (A) at 1145G.
106  1988 (1) SA 290 (A).
107  In *Boland Bank Ltd v The Master* 1991 (3) SA 387 (A), e.g., it was held that s 103(2) read with s 95(1) of the Insolvency Act 24 of 1936, providing for interest "calculated at the rate of eight per cent per annum", payable on a secured claim after date of sequestration, is simple interest, not compound interest.
108  See McBryde, *Contract*, paras 22-131–22-135.
109  1987 SLT 67.
110  See on the origins of this rule J Murray, "Interest on debt" 1991 *SLT (News)* 305 at 306–307.
111  (1856) 18 D 609.

interest found due as at the date of citation, and allowed interest on the accumulated sum from that date, but without rests, which were regarded as being of a penal nature.

In the *Nash Dredging* case the court found that both the principal and the outstanding interest had been wrongfully withheld by the debtor. When the principal sum was paid the interest remained outstanding and the dispute between the parties concerned the rate of interest to be applied. The defenders were not entitled to withhold payment of the interest and so to avoid paying interest on interest. A defender may be regarded as wrongfully withholding payment even if no decree had been pronounced for payment.

Lord Ross concluded as follows:[112]

> It appears to me that a distinction requires to be drawn between interest on arrears of interest on the one hand and compound interest on the other hand. It is highly unusual for compound interest to be allowed. "A claim for compound interest, with annual rests, is a demand which can only be maintained, either in the case of a fixed usage in commercial dealings, or where there has been an abuse in a party trusted with funds, and violating his trust." (*Douglas v Douglas's Trustees* (1867) 5 M 827, per Lord Justice-Clerk Patton at p 836). Compound interest proper does include rests, but interest on arrears without rests may be allowed when the arrears of interest are treated as the equivalent of the principal sum (*Napier v Gordon*; *MacClean v Campbell*).

The practical effect of both the South African *Davehill* case and the Scottish *Nash Dredging* case is that arrear interest is at one point (and only once) added to the principal and from then on simple interest runs on the total. Lord Ross in the *Nash Dredging* case specifically made the distinction between the taking of interest on arrear interest on the one hand and compound interest on the other hand. The former indicates a once-off approach, whereas the latter indicates recurrence of capitalisation at regular intervals or rests, i.e. annual or monthly. In terms of this distinction Article 17:101 PECL would qualify as a provision for compound interest with annual rests. The South African *Davehill* case professes to support the taking of compound interest on arrear debt, but applied only a single or once-off capitalisation. Lord Ross in *Nash Dredging* stuck firmly to a once-off capitalisation in a case where it was clear that both principal and interest were at a particular point being wrongfully withheld.

If interest is to be regarded as a remedy equivalent to damages for the non-payment of money due, it is difficult to see how a debtor could successfully argue on principle that his creditor should not be put into the position

112   At 68.

that he would otherwise have been in had he had the use of his money time-ously.[113] The reasonable approach would then be to allow compound interest with recurrent capitalisation, at least annually, as provided for by Article 17:101 PECL.

### (3) Additional finance charges under South African Usury Act 73 of 1968

Section 4 of the Usury Act provides for three situations where additional finance charges may be recovered. They are where a debtor fails to pay any amount which is owing "in connection" with a contract on the date when the amount is payable; where the parties agree that the debtor may defer the payment of an amount; and where the debtor notifies the creditor of his intention to pay the outstanding debt in one amount before the due date and he subsequently fails to pay it on that date. When additional finance charges are recovered in any of these instances it is calculated on the total amount which is payable but unpaid, for the time of the default or deferment, at the rate applicable to the principal debt in terms of the instrument of debt.

It was decided in *Ex parte Minister of Justice*[114] that additional finance charges may be calculated not only on that part of the principal debt which is owing but also on finance charges which are owing but unpaid. Section 4(2) of the Usury Act now specifically provides that additional finance charges are recoverable on "the total amount which is payable but unpaid". This provision amounts to a once-off capitalisation of the interest component of every arrear instalment, not to compound interest with periodic rests. After capitalisation simple interest runs on the total amount outstanding until date of payment. The process is repeated in respect of every new instalment that falls in arrear.

A trade usage is recognised in respect of a debit balance on a current or cheque account to the effect that arrear interest is capitalised monthly and further interest is recoverable on the capitalised amount. Additional finance charges may therefore be capitalised periodically without any express agreement to the effect and without any instrument of debt having been executed.[115]

One of the questions which the court had to answer in *Ex Parte Minister of Justice*[116] was how the additional finance charges are to be calculated, particularly from what date until what date. The court held that the period during

---

113 See SME, vol 12, para 1038.
114 1978 (2) SA 572 (A).
115 *Senekal v Trust Bank of Africa Ltd* 1978 (3) SA 375 (A).
116 1978 (2) SA 572 (A).

which additional finance charges may be recovered in the case of breach of contract "is the periods *commencing* on the day *after* the date on which the amount in question is *payable* and *ending* on the date of *payment* thereof".

## (4) *Mora* interest on damages

Article 17:101 PECL is based on Article 9:508 PECL and confers a right to capitalisation in respect of an unpaid primary contractual debt and not in respect of secondary obligations such as damages for breach of contract.[117]

Under common law in both Scotland and South Africa a debtor was not liable for interest on damages.[118] In respect of a claim for unliquidated damages where the amount is only ascertainable through "a long and intricate investigation", the debtor could not be in *mora* and therefore could not be held liable for interest on the damages prior to judgment.[119]

In South Africa the introduction of section 2A of the Prescribed Rate of Interest Act,[120] under the heading "Interest on unliquidated debts", changed the law in this regard. Section 2A, in abbreviated form, provides as follows:

(1) Subject to the provisions of this section the amount of every unliquidated debt as determined by a court of law ... shall bear interest as contemplated in section 1.
...

(2)(a) Subject to any other agreement between the parties the interest contemplated in subsection (1) shall run from the date on which payment of the debt is claimed by the service on the debtor of a demand or summons, whichever date is the earlier.
...

(5) Notwithstanding the provisions of this Act but subject to any other law or an agreement between the parties, a court of law ... may make such order as appears just in respect of the payment of interest on an unliquidated debt, the rate at which interest shall accrue and the date from which interest shall run.

The new section was obviously aimed at alleviating the plight of a plaintiff who has to wait a substantial period of time to establish his claim, through no fault of his own, and is paid in depreciated currency.[121] Section 2A(2)(a) lays down what is to be the general position, namely that interest runs from date of demand or summons. If a plaintiff seeks interest from an earlier time then the court must be urged to exercise its discretion under subsection (5). To obtain a favourable discretionary decision a plaintiff must discharge the onus of establishing facts justifying such decision. There is no authority in section

---

117  PECL, vol 1, 451.
118  SME, vol 12, para 1032.
119  *Standard Chartered Bank of Canada v Nedperm Bank Ltd* 1994 (4) SA 747 (A).
120  55 of 1975.

2A or in case law for capitalisation or the granting of compound interest on damages.

The position in Scotland is similar. Under the Interest on Damages (Scotland) Act 1958, as amended by the Interest on Damages (Scotland) Act 1971, a court may grant interest on damages. The court has a discretion to award interest from the date the right of action arose. It appears, however, that there must be special circumstances before this discretion will be exercised.[122] The Interest on Damages (Scotland) Act expressly provides that it of itself does not authorise the granting of interest on interest,[123] but also that it does not affect the running of interest which otherwise would run by virtue of any enactment or rule of law.[124]

As noted above, Article 17:101 PECL is based on Article 9:508 PECL and confers a right to capitalisation in respect of an unpaid primary contractual debt and not in respect of secondary obligations such as damages for breach of contract.[125] There is also an economic and commercial justification for capitalisation in respect of debts for damages, as will be suggested below.

## H. CAPITALISATION AND INTEREST AS DAMAGES

In both Scotland and South Africa interest as a form of special damages for breach of contract is recoverable where such damages flow naturally from the breach or may reasonably be supposed to have been in the contemplation of the contracting parties as likely to result therefrom. Article 17:101 PECL is based on Article 9:508 PECL and deals with primary contractual debts and not with secondary obligations such as damages for breach of contract.[126]

In the South African case of *Thoroughbred Breeders' Association v Price Waterhouse*[127] the plaintiff claimed for losses suffered as a result of thefts by a bookkeeper, which losses and thefts remained undiscovered as a result of negligence of accountants. The main claim for interest was calculated at the rate of interest levied by its banker on every individual amount stolen from the date upon which that particular amount was stolen. Because of the thefts the claimant's overdraft, so it was contended, was inflated and the excess attracted interest at the higher rates charged by a banker to its customer on

---

121  *Adel Builders (Pty) Ltd v Thompson* [2000] 4 All SA 341 (A).
122  See McBryde, *Contract*, para 22–129.
123  Section 1(2)(a).
124  Section 1(2)(c).
125  PECL, vol 1, 451.
126  PECL, vol 1, 451.
127  2001 (4) SA 551 (SCA).

overdraft. Thus formulated, the claim was one not for ordinary *mora* interest but for additional damages in the form of interest. The court referred with approval to the following description of such a claim in *Bellairs v Hodnett*:[128]

> As previously pointed out, mora interest in a case like the present constitutes a form of damages for breach of contract. The general principle in the assessment of such damages is that the sufferer by the breach should be placed in the position he would have occupied had the contract been performed, so far as this can be done by the payment of money and without undue hardship to the defaulting party. Accordingly, such damages only are awarded as flow naturally from the breach or as may reasonably be supposed to have been in the contemplation of the contracting parties as likely to result therefrom (*Victoria Falls and Transvaal Power Co Ltd v Consolidated Langlaagte Mines* Ltd 1915 AD 1 at 22). In awarding mora interest to a creditor who has not received due payment of a monetary debt owed under contract, the Court seeks to place him in the position he would have occupied had due payment been made. The Court acts on the assumption that, had due payment been made, the capital sum would have been productively employed by the creditor during the period of mora and the interest consequently represents the damages flowing naturally from the breach of contract.

The court in the *Thoroughbred Breeders' Association* case decided that the claim for interest *qua* damages, be it general or special, could not succeed, because it was not proved that the claimant became liable to its banker for the additional interest claimed. The claimant had failed to prove that, had it not been for the thefts, its overdraft would have been reduced by the exact amounts of the thefts and would not, for instance, have been employed for another purpose.

In Scotland interest may be recovered as a loss for breach of contract in terms of the principle established by *Hadley v Baxendale*.[129] This means that liability for interest or loss of interest on money invested must be capable of being fairly and reasonably considered as arising in the usual course of things from the breach of contract, or of being reasonably supposed to have been in the contemplation of both parties at the time they made the contract, as the probable result of the breach of contract.[130] Courts in Scotland have been reluctant to award interest in terms of these principles in some cases involving cost overruns or late payment in building disputes.[131] This gives rise to

128 1978 (1) SA 1109 (A) at 1146H–1147C.
129 (1854) 9 Ex 341.
130 See Murray, 1991 *SLT (News)* 305 at 309–311.
131 See Murray, 1991 *SLT (News)* 305 at 309–311; and see subsequently *Margrie Holdings Ltd v City of Edinburgh District Council* 1994 SC 1; *Ogilvie Builders Ltd v City of Glasgow District Council* 1995 SLT 15. In the *Ogilvie Builders* case it was held that in the construction industry delay in payment to the contractor might naturally result in the ordinary course of things in his being short of working capital and so having to incur finance charges as those claimed in this case in the form of "direct loss and / or expense" under the contract.

the question whether it is not "in the usual course of things" for a creditor in such cases either to have to borrow money on which interest would have to be paid, or to divert funds from other sources on which interest is then lost? Professor F A Mann has asked rhetorically in this regard: "Who would venture to suggest that a defaulting debtor could not reasonably foresee interest as the creditor's loss flowing from the failure to pay?"[132] Professor John Murray has suggested that the answer to this rhetorical question could be: "The Scottish Judiciary".[133]

An example cited in this regard by the English Law Commission[134] is the case of *Hartle v Laceys*,[135] where a solicitor knew that his client had borrowed heavily from the bank at relatively high compound rates of interest and that he needed to sell property to reduce his borrowing. The solicitor acted negligently, and so lost his client the opportunity to sell. The court found that interest could be claimed at compound rates as special damages, because the issue was in the contemplation of both parties. Where such interest is claimed it must be specifically pleaded as special damage.

Modern commercial realities indicate that a creditor, who is out of pocket as a result of breach of contract and has to borrow money on which compound interest would have to be paid, or to divert funds from investments on which compound interest is then lost, should be compensated accordingly.

## I. CONCLUSIONS

The following are some conclusions on the need for reform of the law on capitalisation of interest in Scotland and South Africa, with reference to Article 17:101 PECL as a possible model for reform.

### (1) Lack of uniformity

The law in both Scotland and South Africa lacks uniformity and consistency in its approach to capitalisation of interest. On the position in Scotland Lord Craighill said more than a century ago in *Blair's Trustees v Payne*[136] "nothing can be conceived less amenable to a settled general principle than our law upon a creditor's right to interest", a view still supported by some modern

132  F A Mann, "On interest, compound interest and damages" (1985) 101 *LQR* 30.
133  Murray, 1991 *SLT (News)* 305 at 310.
134  Pre-judgment Interest on Debts and Damages Law Com No 287 (2004).
135  [1999] Lloyd's Rep PN 315, CA; see Law Com No 287, summary, para 2.21.
136  (1884) 12 R 104.

commentators.[137] In this regard the Scottish Law Commission has pointed out significant differences between interest on contractual debts and interest on damages (injured parties suing for damages may be awarded interest from a date prior to the date osf judicial demand); differences in the date of commencement of a creditor's entitlement to interest depending on the nature of the claim; anomalies and uncertainties with regard to the awarding of interest for wrongful withholding of payment;[138] and a persisting reluctance to allow capitalisation or "interest upon interest."[139]

The South African system likewise lacks a uniform approach. There is no effective enforcement of rate ceilings or limitations on capitalisation in respect of small loans, a market where the exploitation of the poor appears to be the most likely. Mid-size consumer debt is strictly regulated in terms of the Usury Act 73 of 1968, by enforcement of rate ceilings and prohibition of capitalisation, except in case of payment default. Larger commercial debts fall outside the ambit of the Usury Act and capitalisation by agreement is allowed, both for regular repayments and in case of default. The application of the *in duplum* rule to all debts appears to be an arbitrary and anachronistic blunt instrument for debtor protection.

## (2) Economic and commercial realities

A recurrent theme in the Report of the English Law Commission on Pre-judgment Interest on Debts and Damages[140] and the Discussion Paper of the Scottish Law Commission on Interest on Debt and Damages[141] is that a restriction on compound interest or capitalisation ignores commercial realities, under-compensates the creditor, and therefore reflects poorly on the legal system, particularly in large commercial disputes. If a claimant should have had the money earlier, and in fact had it later, he or she has either missed an opportunity to invest it, or had to borrow to cover the shortfall, in either case at compound interest. Compound interest is particularly important in long-running claims. The English Law Commission stated that the introduction of a power to award compound interest would "remove one of the blots on the English civil justice system".[142]

The New Zealand Law Commission has expressed similar views:

---

137  See McBryde, *Contract*, para 22–118; Murray, 1991 *SLT (News)* 305.
138  Scot Law Com DP No 127 (2005), paras 3.7 – 3.19.
139  Scot Law Com DP No 127 (2005), para 8.11.
140  Law Com No 287 (2004).
141  Scot Law Com DP No 127 (2005).
142  Law Com No 287, summary, para 4.3.

Simple interest does not reflect business practice. When money is borrowed, interest accrues on outstanding balances which include interest charges already incurred. For example, where a bank lends money to a customer, there will normally be regular payments of interest during the term of the loan. If payments are not made, the outstanding interest is capitalised and interest charged upon it. Where interest does not compound, it fails to compensate adequately the person to whom money is owed.[143]

The Law Reform Commission of British Columbia[144] has found that compounding pre-judgment interest is theoretically desirable in that it would more accurately reflect both the behaviour of investors in the marketplace and the cost of delay to successful plaintiffs. The Commission accepts that the basic rationale for making an award of interest is that the defendant has kept the plaintiff out of his money and should compensate him accordingly. This objective cannot be achieved adequately if courts are limited to awarding simple interest rather than compound interest. At higher interest rates and in cases where the delay between the due date of payment and the date of judgment is greater, the degree of under-compensation becomes more acute. Commentators have decribed the antipathy of courts and legislatures to compound interest as "a relic from the days when interest was regarded as necessarily usurious".[145]

### (3) Capitalisation in respect of both debts and damages

Article 17:101 PECL is based on Article 9:508 PECL and confers a right to capitalisation in respect of an unpaid primary contractual debt and not in respect of secondary obligations such as damages for breach of contract.[146] The Principles do not apply to debts for damages in the law of delict. Neither in Scots law nor in South African law is there authority in statute or case law for the award of compound interest on damages. The underlying consideration appears to be that compound interest should only run on fixed sums. Where the court has not yet determined the amount to be paid, the defendant cannot be said to be wrongfully withholding the money and should not have to pay compound interest.

The Law Commission of England regards this argument as a misunder-

---

143 Aspects of Damages: The Award of Interest on Money Claims, NZ Law Com No 28 (1994), para 24.

144 Report on the Court Order Interest Act, LRC 90 (1987).

145 R Bowles & C J Whelan "The law of interest: dawn of a new era?" (1986) 64 *Canadian Bar Review* 142 at 143. See also Bowles & J Whelan, "Compound interest: could multipliers be the way forward?" (1986) 136 *New LJ* 876.

146 PECL, vol 1, 451.

standing of the nature of the interest award, which is to compensate the claimant for the delay, rather than to penalise the defendant. The Commission has therefore recommended that no distinction be made between debts and damages.[147] The Scottish Law Commission agrees, because if it is acceptable to charge interest on damages, such interest becomes a debt like any other and should therefore attract interest like any other debt.[148]

Should a distinction be made between pecuniary and non-pecuniary damages? Non-pecuniary damages are awarded in a variety of different actions, including personal injury claims and defamation. Such damages are assessed as lump sums to provide a rough approximation for losses that cannot be fully quantified in monetary terms. Non-pecuniary damages are assessed to be broadly correct at the time of the award, to cover both past and future loss. The award is not necessarily the same as the sum that should have been paid at the time the cause of action arose. It is suggested, therefore, that damages for non-pecuniary losses should generally not carry interest, either simple or compound.

### (4) Should consumer debts be excluded?

Compound interest "evokes deep-seated fears", according to the English Law Commission.[149] Where interest increases in an exponential rather than a linear way, the outcome may appear to be frightening and unpredictable. However, in the United Kingdom consumers in many cases already pay compound interest, often at high rates. Contracts for mortgages, bank loans, credit cards and store cards routinely charge compound interest. As pointed out by the English Law Commission,[150] in most small to medium cases the difference between simple and compound interest will be relatively small. This was the basis for its recommendation that a distinction should be drawn between awards of less than £15,000 and those above £15,000. For those of less than £15,000 the Commission recommended that there should be a presumption that interest should be simple. This could be rebutted if the claim has been particularly long-running, or the creditor can show special reasons for compound interest, such as having to borrow money at compound rates. In claims of £15,000 or more, the Commission recommended that there should be a presumption in favour of compound interest. The Scottish Law

---

147  Law Com No 287 (2002), summary, para 5.9; and see also Scot Law Com DP No 127 (2005), para 8.29.
148  Scot Law Com DP No 127 (2005), para 8.38.
149  Law Com No 287 (2002), summary, para 5.16.
150  Law Com No 287 (2002), summary, para 5.31.

Commission has indicated disagreement, stating persuasively that compound interest is either fair and correct, or it is not; and if there is no advantage to compounding on small sums of money, it seems odd that all major financial institutions charge compound interest on any sum, however small.[151]

Article 17:101 PECL does not distinguish between different kinds of debt or on the basis of the size of the debt. In South Africa, as shown above, there is no effective enforcement of rate ceilings or limitations on capitalisation in respect of small loans, while mid-size consumer debt is strictly regulated in terms of the Usury Act 73 of 1968, by enforcement of rate ceilings and prohibition of capitalisation, except in case of payment default.

It is suggested that the view of the Scottish Law Commission in this regard is logical and fair, namely that with regard to capitalisation no distinction on the basis of the size of the debt should be made.

### (5) Contractual provisions

Article 17:101 PECL recognises the primacy of contractual ordering. It provides for annual capitalisation as a remedy for payment default, but this provision is subject to whatever agreement on capitalisation is concluded between the parties, for instance on monthly instead of annual capitalisation.

Under Article 6:119 of the Dutch Code, to which Article 17:101 PECL corresponds closely, the prescribed rate of interest for payment default applies subject to contractual ordering, but the statutory provision constitutes a minimum, so that an agreed lower rate is upon delay replaced by the statutory rate.[152]

The English Law Commission[153] has also recommended that its proposed general statutory provision for compound interest should be subject to contractual regulation of interest.

It seems logical and fair that no contract providing for compound interest should be interfered with, unless it could be considered unconscionable or extortionate with reference to standard indicators.

### (6) Interest as damages

A general statutory provision on capitalisation of interest in respect of delayed payment, on the model of Article 17:101 PECL, would not affect the

151  Scot Law Com DP No 127 (2005), para 8.16.
152  See Hartkamp, *Asser's Handleiding tot de Beoefening van het Nederlands Burgerlijk Recht Verbintenissenrecht* Deel I, 11th edn (2000), 464.
153  Law Com No 287 (2002), summary, para 5.46.

courts' existing powers to award interest as damages. Special damages are recoverable where such damages flow naturally from the breach or may reasonably be supposed to have been in the contemplation of the contracting parties as likely to result therefrom. In these cases judges would continue to be able to award the actual interest lost – at whatever compounding rate and interval might be deemed appropriate.

Compound interest would only be recoverable as special damages in the limited circumstances where liability for compound interest or loss of compound interest on money invested could be fairly and reasonably considered as arising in the usual course of things from the breach of contract, or of being reasonably supposed to have been in the contemplation of both parties at the time they made the contract, as the probable result of the breach of contract.

Modern commercial realities indicate that a creditor having to incur a debt bearing compound interest as a result of breach of contract, or having to divert funds from investments on which compound interest is then lost, should be compensated accordingly.

## (7) Calculation – undue complexity?

Calculation of compound interest can be complex, particularly over a lengthy period with fluctuating rates of interest. Ucòike simple interest calculations compound interest can be calculated in several different ways. The outcome will depend, for example, on whether one uses annual, quarterly or monthly rests, and whether rests occur on a set date (such as the first of January of each year), or on the anniversary of the start of the debt. Entitlement to compound interest therefore has the potential to generate disputes. However, this does not justify restricting or excluding the right to such interest.

The conclusions of the English Law Commission in this regard are convincing. The Commission considered the only realistic possibility to be that the parties should calculate compound interest, either themselves or through their legal representatives.[154] Where the claimant seeks a judgment for compound interest, the onus should be on it to present the calculations to the court. The Commission also recommended that the Court Service should produce a computer program to calculate compound interest and make it readily accessible on its website. An appropriate set of tables covering periods up to twenty years would be about twenty pages long and the Commission felt that it would not be an unduly cumbersome document for judges to keep

---

154   Law Com No 287 (2002), summary, para 4.19.

on their shelves, or for advocates to take to court. It noted that judges would probably benefit from some training in using the tables.

## (8) Intervals for capitalisation

Article 17:101 PECL provides that capitalisation should occur only after twelve months; and thereafter every twelve months while the debt remains unpaid. If annual intervals or rests for capitalisation or compounding are used, there is of course no capitalisation during the first year. The period of grace of one year before capitalisation occurs replicates the *anatocismus anniversarius* of Roman law,[155] but it is a questionable practice for the modern commercial environment.

Annual rests simplify calculations in short-running cases by removing the need for capitalisation whenever the debt remains unpaid for less than a year. On a debt that remains unpaid for less than a year compound interest with monthly rests does not produce results dramatically different from simple interest. To illustrate, a simple interest rate of 8 per cent would be the equivalent of a compound rate of 7 per cent after five years, and the equivalent of a 6 per cent compound rate after eleven years. After nineteen years, a simple rate of 8 per cent becomes the equivalent of 5 per cent compound.

More frequent rests would be consistent with current commercial practice in respect of loans and investments. The main argument in favour of annual rests is that this may simplify calculation. However, as indicated by the English Law Commission,[156] for debts of over a year, a computer program or tables using monthly rests would be no more complicated to use than those for annual rests. The Commission found that the balance of convenience lies with monthly rests. The aim should be to reflect commercial reality, in particular normal banking practice, which involves for both the lender and the borrower that interest is usually compounded at least monthly. This is also the view adopted by the Scottish Law Commission.[157]

## (9) Reform in Scotland and South Africa

The main criticism that can be levelled at the current legal position in Scotland and South Africa is the lack of uniformity in the rules on capitalisation in respect of different kinds of debt and the inconsistency in the application of capitalisation where it is allowed. This is the product of piecemeal

155   See section C(1) above.
156   Law Com No 287 (2002), summary, para 6.21.
157   Scot Law Com DP No 127 (2005), para 8.43.

development that historically has been shaped partly by religious doctrine and emotional aversion to interest generally and compound interest in particular. The current position does not adequately reflect economic and commercial realities. In South Africa the general application of the *in duplum* rule appears to be arbitrary and anachronistic.

In both Scotland and South Arica there is a need for reform and there should be a general entitlement to compound interest, as recommended by the Scottish Law Commission.[158] Article 17:101 PECL provides a useful starting point, but reform should go further, to include capitalisation in respect of all debts. The frequency of capitalisation should reflect current commercial practice, which usually involves capitalisation on a monthly rather than on an annual basis. If it is acceptable to charge interest, it becomes a debt like any other when it is charged. Interest should therefore attract interest like any other debt.[159]

---

158  Scot Law Com DP No 127 (2005), para 8.15.
159  Scot Law Com DP No 127 (2005), para 8.38.

# The Principles of European Contract Law[*]

## *Prepared by the Commission on European Contract Law*

### CHAPTER 1: GENERAL PROVISIONS

**Section 1: Scope of the Principles**

**Article 1:101: Application of the Principles**

(1) These Principles are intended to be applied as general rules of contract law in the European Union.

(2) These Principles will apply when the parties have agreed to incorporate them into their contract or that their contract is to be governed by them.

(3) These Principles may be applied when the parties:
  (a) have agreed that their contract is to be governed by "general principles of law", the "lex mercatoria" or the like; or
  (b) have not chosen any system or rules of law to govern their contract.

(4) These Principles may provide a solution to the issue raised where the system or rules of law applicable do not do so.

**Article 1:102: Freedom of Contract**

(1) Parties are free to enter into a contract and to determine its contents, subject to the requirements of good faith and fair dealing, and the mandatory rules established by these Principles.

(2) The parties may exclude the application of any of the Principles or derogate from or vary their effects, except as otherwise provided by these Principles.

**Article 1:103: Mandatory Law**

(1) Where the law otherwise applicable so allows, the parties may choose to have their contract governed by the Principles, with the effect that national mandatory rules are not applicable.

---

[*] This reproduction of the text of the Principles of European Contract Law appears with the kind permission of the Commission on European Contract Law.

(2) Effect should nevertheless be given to those mandatory rules of national, supranational and international law which, according to the relevant rules of private international law, are applicable irrespective of the law governing the contract.

## Article 1:104: Application to Questions of Consent

(1) The existence and validity of the agreement of the parties to adopt or incorporate these Principles shall be determined by these Principles.
(2) Nevertheless, a party may rely upon the law of the country in which it has its habitual residence to establish that it did not consent if it appears from the circumstances that it would not be reasonable to determine the effect of the party's conduct in accordance with these Principles.

## Article 1:105: Usages and Practices

(1) The parties are bound by any usage to which they have agreed and by any practice they have established between themselves.
(2) The parties are bound by a usage which would be considered generally applicable by persons in the same situation as the parties, except where the application of such usage would be unreasonable.

## Article 1:106: Interpretation and Supplementation

(1) These Principles should be interpreted and developed in accordance with their purposes. In particular, regard should be had to the need to promote good faith and fair dealing, certainty in contractual relationships and uniformity of application.
(2) Issues within the scope of these Principles but not expressly settled by them are so far as possible to be settled in accordance with the ideas underlying the Principles. Failing this, the legal system applicable by virtue of the rules of private international law is to be applied.

## Article 1:107 : Application of the Principles by Way of Analogy

These Principles apply with appropriate modifications to agreements to modify or end a contract, to unilateral promises and other statements and conduct indicating intention.

## Section 2: General Duties

## Article 1:201: Good Faith and Fair Dealing

(1) Each party must act in accordance with good faith and fair dealing.
(2) The parties may not exclude or limit this duty.

## Article 1:202: Duty to Co-operate

Each party owes to the other a duty to co-operate in order to give full effect to the contract.

## Section 3: Terminology and Other Provisions

### Article 1:301: Meaning of Terms

In these Principles, except where the context otherwise requires:

(1) "act" includes omission;

(2) "court" includes arbitral tribunal;

(3) an "intentional" act includes an act done recklessly;

(4) "non-performance" denotes any failure to perform an obligation under the contract, whether or not excused, and includes delayed performance, defective performance and failure to co-operate in order to give full effect to the contract.

(5) a matter is "material" if it is one which a reasonable person in the same situation as one party ought to have known would influence the other party in its decision whether to contract on the proposed terms or to contract at all;

(6) "written" statements include communications made by telegram, telex, telefax and electronic mail and other means of communication capable of providing a readable record of the statement on both sides

### Article 1:302: Reasonableness

Under these Principles reasonableness is to be judged by what persons acting in good faith and in the same situation as the parties would consider to be reasonable. In particular, in assessing what is reasonable the nature and purpose of the contract, the circumstances of the case, and the usages and practices of the trades or professions involved should be taken into account.

### Article 1:303: Notice

(1) Any notice may be given by any means, whether in writing or otherwise, appropriate to the circumstances.

(2) Subject to paragraphs (4) and (5), any notice becomes effective when it reaches the addressee.

(3) A notice reaches the addressee when it is delivered to it or to its place of business or mailing address, or, if it does not have a place of business or mailing address, to its habitual residence

(4) If one party gives notice to the other because of the other's non-performance or because such non-performance is reasonably anticipated

by the first party, and the notice is properly dispatched or given, a delay or inaccuracy in the transmission of the notice or its failure to arrive does not prevent it from having effect. The notice shall have effect from the time at which it would have arrived in normal circumstances.

(5) A notice has no effect if a withdrawal of it reaches the addressee before or at the same time as the notice.

(6) In this Article, "notice" includes the communication of a promise, statement, offer, acceptance, demand, request or other declaration.

## Article 1:304: Computation of Time

(1) A period of time set by a party in a written document for the addressee to reply or take other action begins to run from the date stated as the date of the document. If no date is shown, the period begins to run from the moment the document reaches the addressee.

(2) Official holidays and official non-working days occurring during the period are included in calculating the period. However, if the last day of the period is an official holiday or official non-working day at the address of the addressee, or at the place where a prescribed act is to be performed, the period is extended until the first following working day in that place.

(3) Periods of time expressed in days, weeks, months or years shall begin at 00.00 on the next day and shall end at 24.00 on the last day of the period; but any reply that has to reach the party who set the period must arrive, or other act which is to be done must be completed, by the normal close of business in the relevant place on the last day of the period.

## Article 1:305: Imputed Knowledge and Intention

If any person who with a party's assent was involved in making a contract, or who was entrusted with performance by a party or performed with its assent:

(a) knew or foresaw a fact, or ought to have known or foreseen it; or

(b) acted intentionally or with gross negligence, or not in accordance with good faith and fair dealing,

this knowledge, foresight or behaviour is imputed to the party itself.

## CHAPTER 2: FORMATION

### Section 1 : General Provisions

### Article 2:101: Conditions for the Conclusion of a Contract

(1) A contract is concluded if:
  (a) the parties intend to be legally bound, and
  (b) they reach a sufficient agreement
  without any further requirement.
(2) A contract need not be concluded or evidenced in writing nor is it subject to any other requirement as to form. The contract may be proved by any means, including witnesses.

### Article 2:102: Intention

The intention of a party to be legally bound by contract is to be determined from the party's statements or conduct as they were reasonably understood by the other party.

### Article 2:103: Sufficient Agreement

(1) There is sufficient agreement if the terms:
  (a) have been sufficiently defined by the parties so that the contract can be enforced, or
  (b) can be determined under these Principles.
(2) However, if one of the parties refuses to conclude a contract unless the parties have agreed on some specific matter, there is no contract unless agreement on that matter has been reached.

### Article 2:104: Terms Not Individually Negotiated

(1) Contract terms which have not been individually negotiated may be invoked against a party who did not know of them only if the party invoking them took reasonable steps to bring them to the other party's attention before or when the contract was concluded.
(2) Terms are not brought appropriately to a party's attention by a mere reference to them in a contract document, even if that party signs the document.

### Article 2:105: Merger Clause

(1) If a written contract contains an individually negotiated clause stating that the writing embodies all the terms of the contract (a merger clause), any prior statements, undertakings or agreements which are not embodied in the writing do not form part of the contract.

(2) If the merger clause is not individually negotiated it will only establish a presumption that the parties intended that their prior statements, undertakings or agreements were not to form part of the contract. This rule may not be excluded or restricted.

(3) The parties' prior statements may be used to interpret the contract. This rule may not be excluded or restricted except by an individually negotiated clause.

(4) A party may by its statements or conduct be precluded from asserting a merger clause to the extent that the other party has reasonably relied on them.

### Article 2:106: Written Modification Only

(1) A clause in a written contract requiring any modification or ending by agreement to be made in writing establishes only a presumption that an agreement to modify or end the contract is not intended to be legally binding unless it is in writing.

(2) A party may by its statements or conduct be precluded from asserting such a clause to the extent that the other party has reasonably relied on them.

### Article 2:107: Promises Binding without Acceptance

A promise which is intended to be legally binding without acceptance is binding.

### Section 2 : Offer and Acceptance

### Article 2:201: Offer

(1) A proposal amounts to an offer if:
  (a) it is intended to result in a contract if the other party accepts it, and
  (b) it contains sufficiently definite terms to form a contract.

(2) An offer may be made to one or more specific persons or to the public.

(3) A proposal to supply goods or services at stated prices made by a professional supplier in a public advertisement or a catalogue, or by a display of goods, is presumed to be an offer to sell or supply at that price until the stock of goods, or the supplier's capacity to supply the service, is exhausted.

### Article 2:202: Revocation of an Offer

(1) An offer may be revoked if the revocation reaches the offeree before it has dispatched its acceptance or, in cases of acceptance by conduct, before the contract has been concluded under Article 2:205(2) or (3).

(2) An offer made to the public can be revoked by the same means as were used to make the offer.

(3) However, a revocation of an offer is ineffective if:
    (a) the offer indicates that it is irrevocable; or
    (b) it states a fixed time for its acceptance; or
    (c) it was reasonable for the offeree to rely on the offer as being irrevocable and the offeree has acted in reliance on the offer.

### Article 2:203: Rejection

When a rejection of an offer reaches the offeror, the offer lapses.

### Article 2:204: Acceptance

(1) Any form of statement or conduct by the offeree is an acceptance if it indicates assent to the offer.

(2) Silence or inactivity does not in itself amount to acceptance.

### Article 2:205: Time of Conclusion of the Contract

(1) If an acceptance has been dispatched by the offeree the contract is concluded when the acceptance reaches the offeror.

(2) In case of acceptance by conduct, the contract is concluded when notice of the conduct reaches the offeror.

(3) If by virtue of the offer, of practices which the parties have established between themselves, or of a usage, the offeree may accept the offer by performing an act without notice to the offeror, the contract is concluded when the performance of the act begins.

### Article 2:206: Time Limit for Acceptance

(1) In order to be effective, acceptance of an offer must reach the offeror within the time fixed by it.

(2) If no time has been fixed by the offeror acceptance must reach it within a reasonable time.

(3) In the case of an acceptance by an act of performance under Article 2:205 (3), that act must be performed within the time for acceptance fixed by the offeror or, if no such time is fixed, within a reasonable time.

### Article 2:207: Late Acceptance

(1) A late acceptance is nonetheless effective as an acceptance if without delay the offeror informs the offeree that he treats it as such.

(2) If a letter or other writing containing a late acceptance shows that it has

been sent in such circumstances that if its transmission had been normal it would have reached the offeror in due time, the late acceptance is effective as an acceptance unless, without delay, the offeror informs the offeree that it considers its offer as having lapsed.

## Article 2:208: Modified Acceptance

(1) A reply by the offeree which states or implies additional or different terms which would materially alter the terms of the offer is a rejection and a new offer.

(2) A reply which gives a definite assent to an offer operates as an acceptance even if it states or implies additional or different terms, provided these do not materially alter the terms of the offer. The additional or different terms then become part of the contract.

(3) However, such a reply will be treated as a rejection of the offer if:
   (a) the offer expressly limits acceptance to the terms of the offer; or
   (b) the offeror objects to the additional or different terms without delay; or
   (c) the offeree makes its acceptance conditional upon the offeror"s assent to the additional or different terms, and the assent does not reach the offeree within a reasonable time.

## Article 2:209: Conflicting General Conditions

(1) If the parties have reached agreement except that the offer and acceptance refer to conflicting general conditions of contract, a contract is nonetheless formed. The general conditions form part of the contract to the extent that they are common in substance.

(2) However, no contract is formed if one party:
   (a) has indicated in advance, explicitly, and not by way of general conditions, that it does not intend to be bound by a contract on the basis of paragraph (1); or
   (b) without delay, informs the other party that it does not intend to be bound by such contract.

(3) General conditions of contract are terms which have been formulated in advance for an indefinite number of contracts of a certain nature, and which have not been individually negotiated between the parties.

## Article 2:210: Professional's Written Confirmation

If professionals have concluded a contract but have not embodied it in a final document, and one without delay sends the other a writing which purports to be a confirmation of the contract but which contains additional or different terms, such terms will become part of the contract unless:

(a) the terms materially alter the terms of the contract, or

(b) the addressee objects to them without delay.

## Article 2:211: Contracts not Concluded through Offer and Acceptance

The rules in this section apply with appropriate adaptations even though the process of conclusion of a contract cannot be analysed into offer and acceptance.

## Section 3: Liability for negotiations

### Article 2:301: Negotiations Contrary to Good Faith

(1) A party is free to negotiate and is not liable for failure to reach an agreement.

(2) However, a party who has negotiated or broken off negotiations contrary to good faith and fair dealing is liable for the losses caused to the other party.

(3) It is contrary to good faith and fair dealing, in particular, for a party to enter into or continue negotiations with no real intention of reaching an agreement with the other party.

### Article 2:302: Breach of Confidentiality

If confidential information is given by one party in the course of negotiations, the other party is under a duty not to disclose that information or use it for its own purposes whether or not a contract is subsequently concluded. The remedy for breach of this duty may include compensation for loss suffered and restitution of the benefit received by the other party.

## CHAPTER 3: AUTHORITY OF AGENTS

### Section 1 : General Provisions

### Article 3:101 : Scope of the Chapter

(1) This Chapter governs the authority of an agent or other intermediary to bind its principal in relation to a contract with a third party.

(2) This Chapter does not govern an agent's authority bestowed by law or the authority of an agent appointed by a public or judicial authority.

(3) This Chapter does not govern the internal relationship between the agent or intermediary and its principal.

## Article 3:102: Categories of Representation

(1) Where an agent acts in the name of a principal, the rules on direct representation apply (Section 2). It is irrelevant whether the principal's identity is revealed at the time the agent acts or is to be revealed later.

(2) Where an intermediary acts on instructions and on behalf of, but not in the name of, a principal, or where the third party neither knows nor has reason to know that the intermediary acts as an agent, the rules on indirect representation apply (Section 3).

## Section 2 : Direct Representation

## Article 3:201: Express, Implied and Apparent Authority

(1) The principal's grant of authority to an agent to act in its name may be express or may be implied from the circumstances.

(2) The agent has authority to perform all acts necessary in the circumstances to achieve the purposes for which the authority was granted.

(3) A person is to be treated as having granted authority to an apparent agent if the person's statements or conduct induce the third party reasonably and in good faith to believe that the apparent agent has been granted authority for the act performed by it.

## Article 3:202: Agent acting in Exercise of its Authority

Where an agent is acting within its authority as defined by Article 3.201, its acts bind the principal and the third party directly to each other. The agent itself is not bound to the third party.

## Article 3:203: Unidentified Principal

If an agent enters into a contract in the name of a principal whose identity is to be revealed later, but fails to reveal that identity within a reasonable time after a request by the third party, the agent itself is bound by the contract.

## Article 3:204: Agent acting without or outside its Authority

(1) Where a person acting as an agent acts without authority or outside the scope of its authority, its acts are not binding upon the principal and the third party.

(2) Failing ratification by the principal according to Article 3:207, the agent is liable to pay the third party such damages as will place the third party in same position as if the agent had acted with authority. This does not apply if the third party knew or could not have been unaware of the agent's lack of authority.

## Article 3:205: Conflict of Interest

(1) If a contract concluded by an agent involves the agent in a conflict of interest of which the third party knew or could not have been unaware, the principal may avoid the contract according to the provisions of Articles 4:112 to 4:116.

(2) There is presumed to be a conflict of interest where:

    (a) the agent also acted as agent for the third party; or

    (b) the contract was with itself in its personal capacity.

(3) However, the principal may not avoid the contract:

    (a) if it had consented to, or could not have been unaware of, the agent's so acting; or

    (b) if the agent had disclosed the conflict of interest to it and it had not objected within a reasonable time.

## Article 3:206: Subagency

An agent has implied authority to appoint a subagent to carry out tasks which are not of a personal character and which it is not reasonable to expect the agent to carry out itself. The rules of this Section apply to the subagency; acts of the subagent which are within its and the agent's authority bind the principal and the third party directly to each other.

## Article 3:207: Ratification by Principal

(1) Where a person acting as an agent acts without authority or outside its authority, the principal may ratify the agent's acts.

(2) Upon ratification, the agent's acts are considered as having been authorised, without prejudice to the rights of other persons.

## Article 3:208: Third Party's Right with Respect to Confirmation of Authority

Where the statements or conduct of the principal gave the third party reason to believe that an act performed by the agent was authorised, but the third party is in doubt about the authorisation, it may send a written confirmation to the principal or request ratification from it. If the principal does not object or answer the request without delay, the agent's act is treated as having been authorised.

## Article 3:209: Duration of Authority

(1) An agent's authority continues until the third party knows or ought to know that:

(a) the agent's authority has been brought to an end by the principal, the agent, or both; or

(b) the acts for which the authority had been granted have been completed, or the time for which it had been granted has expired; or

(c) the agent has become insolvent or, where a natural person, has died or become incapacitated; or

(d) the principal has become insolvent.

(2) The third party is considered to know that the agent's authority has been brought to an end under paragraph(1) (a) above if this has been communicated or publicised in the same manner in which the authority was originally communicated or publicised.

(3) However, the agent remains authorised for a reasonable time to perform those acts which are necessary to protect the interests of the principal or its successors.

## Section 3: Indirect Representation
## Article 3.301: Intermediaries not acting in the name of a Principal

(1) Where an intermediary acts:

(a) on instructions and on behalf, but not in the name, of a principal, or

(b) on instructions from a principal but the third party does not know and has no reason to know this,

the intermediary and the third party are bound to each other.

(2) The principal and the third party are bound to each other only under the conditions set out in Articles 3:302 to 3:304.

## Article 3:302: Intermediary's Insolvency or Fundamental Non-performance to Principal

If the intermediary becomes insolvent, or if it commits a fundamental non-performance towards the principal, or if prior to the time for performance it is clear that there will be a fundamental non-performance:

(a) on the principal's demand, the intermediary shall communicate the name and address of the third party to the principal; and

(b) the principal may exercise against the third party the rights acquired on the principal's behalf by the intermediary, subject to any defences which the third party may set up against the intermediary.

## Article 3:303: Intermediary's Insolvency or Fundamental Non-performance to Third Party

If the intermediary becomes insolvent, or if it commits a fundamental non-performance towards the third party, or if prior to the time for performance it is clear that there will be a fundamental non-performance:

(a) on the third party's demand, the intermediary shall communicate the name and address of the principal to the third party; and

(b) the third party may exercise against the principal the rights which the third party has against the intermediary, subject to any defences which the intermediary may set up against the third party and those which the principal may set up against the intermediary.

### Article 3:304: Requirement of Notice

The rights under Articles 3:302 and 3:303 may be exercised only if notice of intention to exercise them is given to the intermediary and to the third party or principal, respectively. Upon receipt of the notice, the third party or the principal is no longer entitled to render performance to the intermediary.

## CHAPTER 4: VALIDITY

### Article 4:101: Matters not Covered

This chapter does not deal with invalidity arising from illegality, immorality or lack of capacity.

### Article 4:102: Initial Impossibility

A contract is not invalid merely because at the time it was concluded performance of the obligation assumed was impossible, or because a party was not entitled to dispose of the assets to which the contract relates.

### Article 4:103: Fundamental Mistake as to Facts or Law

(1) A party may avoid a contract for mistake of fact or law existing when the contract was concluded if:
  (a) (i) the mistake was caused by information given by the other party; or
      (ii) the other party knew or ought to have known of the mistake and it was contrary to good faith and fair dealing to leave the mistaken party in error; or
      (iii) the other party made the same mistake,
  and
  (b) the other party knew or ought to have known that the mistaken party, had it known the truth, would not have entered the contract or would have done so only on fundamentally different terms.
(2) However a party may not avoid the contract if:

(a)  in the circumstances its mistake was inexcusable, or

(b)  the risk of the mistake was assumed, or in the circumstances should be borne, by it.

### Article 4:104: Inaccuracy in Communication

An inaccuracy in the expression or transmission of a statement is to be treated as a mistake of the person who made or sent the statement and Article 4:103 applies.

### Article 4:105: Adaptation of Contract

(1)  If a party is entitled to avoid the contract for mistake but the other party indicates that it is willing to perform, or actually does perform, the contract as it was understood by the party entitled to avoid it, the contract is to be treated as if it had been concluded as the that party understood it. The other party must indicate its willingness to perform, or render such performance, promptly after being informed of the manner in which the party entitled to avoid it understood the contract and before that party acts in reliance on any notice of avoidance.

(2)  After such indication or performance the right to avoid is lost and any earlier notice of avoidance is ineffective.

(3)  Where both parties have made the same mistake, the court may at the request of either party bring the contract into accordance with what might reasonably have been agreed had the mistake not occurred.

### Article 4:106: Incorrect Information

A party who has concluded a contract relying on incorrect information given it by the other party may recover damages in accordance with Article 4:117(2)and (3) even if the information does not give rise to a fundamental mistake under Article 4:103, unless the party who gave the information had reason to believe that the information was correct.

### Article 4:107: Fraud

(1)  A party may avoid a contract when it has been led to conclude it by the other party's fraudulent representation, whether by words or conduct, or fraudulent non-disclosure of any information which in accordance with good faith and fair dealing it should have disclosed.

(2)  A party's representation or non-disclosure is fraudulent if it was intended to deceive.

(3)  In determining whether good faith and fair dealing required that a party

disclose particular information, regard should be had to all the circumstances, including:

(a) whether the party had special expertise;

(b) the cost to it of acquiring the relevant information;

(c) whether the other party could reasonably acquire the information for itself; and

(d) the apparent importance of the information to the other party.

## Article 4:108: Threats

A party may avoid a contract when it has been led to conclude it by the other party's imminent and serious threat of an act:

(a) which is wrongful in itself, or

(b) which it is wrongful to use as a means to obtain the conclusion of the contract,

unless in the circumstances the first party had a reasonable alternative.

## Article 4:109: Excessive Benefit or Unfair Advantage

(1) A party may avoid a contract if, at the time of the conclusion of the contract:

   (a) it was dependent on or had a relationship of trust with the other party, was in economic distress or had urgent needs, was improvident, ignorant, inexperienced or lacking in bargaining skill, and

   (b) the other party knew or ought to have known of this and, given the circumstances and purpose of the contract, took advantage of the first party's situation in a way which was grossly unfair or took an excessive benefit.

(2) Upon the request of the party entitled to avoidance, a court may if it is appropriate adapt the contract in order to bring it into accordance with what might have been agreed had the requirements of good faith and fair dealing been followed.

(3) A court may similarly adapt the contract upon the request of a party receiving notice of avoidance for excessive benefit or unfair advantage, provided that this party informs the party who gave the notice promptly after receiving it and before that party has acted in reliance on it.

## Article 4:110: Unfair Terms not Individually Negotiated

(1) A party may avoid a term which has not been individually negotiated if, contrary to the requirements of good faith and fair dealing, it causes a significant imbalance in the parties' rights and obligations arising under the contract to the detriment of that party, taking into account the nature

of the performance to be rendered under the contract, all the other terms of the contract and the circumstances at the time the contract was concluded.

(2) This Article does not apply to:

(a) a term which defines the main subject matter of the contract, provided the term is in plain and intelligible language; or to

(b) the adequacy in value of one party's obligations compared to the value of the obligations of the other party.

## Article 4:111: Third Persons

Where a third person for whose acts a party is responsible, or who with a party's assent is involved in the making of a contract:

(1) (a) causes a mistake by giving information, or knows of or ought to have known of a mistake,

(b) gives incorrect information,

(c) commits fraud,

(d) makes a threat, or

(e) takes excessive benefit or unfair advantage,

remedies under this Chapter will be available under the same conditions as if the behaviour or knowledge had been that of the party itself.

(2) Where any other third person:

(a) gives incorrect information,

(b) commits fraud,

(c) makes a threat, or

(d) takes excessive benefit or unfair advantage,

remedies under this Chapter will be available if the party knew or ought to have known of the relevant facts, or at the time of avoidance it has not acted in reliance on the contract.

## Article 4:112: Notice of Avoidance

Avoidance must be by notice to the other party.

## Article 4:113: Time Limits

(1) Notice of avoidance must be given within a reasonable time, with due regard to the circumstances, after the avoiding party knew or ought to have known of the relevant facts or became capable of acting freely.

(2) However, a party may avoid an individual term under Article 4:110 if it gives notice of avoidance within a reasonable time after the other party has invoked the term.

## Article 4:114: Confirmation

If the party who is entitled to avoid a contract confirms it, expressly or impliedly, after it knows of the ground for avoidance, or becomes capable of acting freely, avoidance of the contract is excluded.

## Article 4:115: Effect of Avoidance

On avoidance either party may claim restitution of whatever it has supplied under the contract, provided it makes concurrent restitution of whatever it has received. If restitution cannot be made in kind for any reason, a reasonable sum must be paid for what has been received.

## Article 4:116: Partial Avoidance

If a ground of avoidance affects only particular terms of a contract, the effect of an avoidance is limited to those terms unless, giving due consideration to all the circumstances of the case, it is unreasonable to uphold the remaining contract.

## Article 4:117: Damages

(1) A party who avoids a contract under this Chapter may recover from the other party damages so as to put the avoiding party as nearly as possible into the same position as if it had not concluded the contract, provided that the other party knew or ought to have known of the mistake, fraud, threat or taking of excessive benefit or unfair advantage.

(2) If a party has the right to avoid a contract under this Chapter, but does not exercise its right or has lost its right under the provisions of Articles 4:113 or 4:114, it may recover, subject to paragraph (1), damages limited to the loss caused to it by the mistake, fraud, threat or taking of excessive benefit or unfair advantage. The same measure of damages shall apply when the party was misled by incorrect information in the sense of Article 4:106.

(3) In other respects, the damages shall be in accordance with the relevant provisions of Chapter 9, Section 5, with appropriate adaptations.

## Article 4:118: Exclusion or Restriction of Remedies

(1) Remedies for fraud, threats and excessive benefit or unfair advantage-taking, and the right to avoid an unfair term which has not been individually negotiated, cannot be excluded or restricted.

(2) Remedies for mistake and incorrect information may be excluded or restricted unless the exclusion or restriction is contrary to good faith and fair dealing..

## Article 4:119: Remedies for Non-performance

A party who is entitled to a remedy under this Chapter in circumstances which afford that party a remedy for non-performance may pursue either remedy.

# CHAPTER 5: INTERPRETATION

## Article 5:101: General Rules of Interpretation

(1) A contract is to be interpreted according to the common intention of the parties even if this differs from the literal meaning of the words.

(2) If it is established that one party intended the contract to have a particular meaning, and at the time of the conclusion of the contract the other party could not have been unaware of the first party's intention, the contract is to be interpreted in the way intended by the first party.

(3) If an intention cannot be established according to (1) or (2), the contract is to be interpreted according to the meaning that reasonable persons of the same kind as the parties would give to it in the same circumstances.

## Article 5:102: Relevant Circumstances

In interpreting the contract, regard shall be had, in particular, to:

(a) the circumstances in which it was concluded, including the preliminary negotiations;

(b) the conduct of the parties, even subsequent to the conclusion of the contract;

(c) the nature and purpose of the contract;

(d) the interpretation which has already been given to similar clauses by the parties and the practices they have established between themselves;

(e) the meaning commonly given to terms and expressions in the branch of activity concerned and the interpretation similar clauses may already have received ;

(f) usages; and

(g) good faith and fair dealing.

## Article 5.103: Contra Proferentem Rule

Where there is doubt about the meaning of a contract term not individually negotiated, an interpretation of the term against the party who supplied it is to be preferred.

### Article 5:104: Preference to Negotiated Terms

Terms which have been individually negotiated take preference over those which are not.

### Article 5:105: Reference to Contract as a Whole

Terms are to be interpreted in the light of the whole contract in which they appear.

### Article 5:106: Terms to Be Given Effect

An interpretation which renders the terms of the contract lawful, or effective, is to be preferred to one which would not.

### Article 5:107: Linguistic Discrepancies

Where a contract is drawn up in two or more language versions none of which is stated to be authoritative, there is, in case of discrepancy between the versions, a preference for the interpretation according to the version in which the contract was originally drawn up.

## CHAPTER 6: CONTENTS AND EFFECTS

### Article 6:101: Statements giving rise to Contractual Obligations

(1) A statement made by one party before or when the contract is concluded is to be treated as giving rise to a contractual obligation if that is how the other party reasonably understood it in the circumstances, taking into account:

  (a) the apparent importance of the statement to the other party;
  (b) whether the party was making the statement in the course of business; and
  (c) the relative expertise of the parties.

(2) If one of the parties is a professional supplier who gives information about the quality or use of services or goods or other property when marketing or advertising them or otherwise before the contract for them is concluded, the statement is to be treated as giving rise to a contractual obligation unless it is shown that the other party knew or could not have been unaware that the statement was incorrect.

(3) Such information and other undertakings given by a person advertising or marketing services, goods or other property for the professional supplier, or by a person in earlier links of the business chain, are to be treated as giving rise to a contractual obligation on the part of the

professional supplier unless it did not know and had no reason to know of the information or undertaking.

## Article 6:102: Implied Terms

In addition to the express terms, a contract may contain implied terms which stem from

(a) the intention of the parties,
(b) the nature and purpose of the contract, and
(c) good faith and fair dealing.

## Article 6:103: Simulation

When the parties have concluded an apparent contract which was not intended to reflect their true agreement, as between the parties the true agreement prevails.

## Article 6:104: Determination of Price

Where the contract does not fix the price or the method of determining it, the parties are to be treated as having agreed on a reasonable price.

## Article 6:105: Unilateral Determination by a Party

Where the price or any other contractual term is to be determined by one party whose determination is grossly unreasonable, then notwithstanding any provision to the contrary, a reasonable price or other term shall be substituted.

## Article 6:106: Determination by a Third Person

(1) Where the price or any other contractual term is to be determined by a third person, and it cannot or will not do so, the parties are presumed to have empowered the court to appoint another person to determine it.
(2) If a price or other term fixed by a third person is grossly unreasonable, a reasonable price or term shall be substituted.

## Article 6:107: Reference to a Non Existent Factor

Where the price or any other contractual term is to be determined by reference to a factor which does not exist or has ceased to exist or to be accessible, the nearest equivalent factor shall be substituted.

## Article 6:108: Quality of Performance

If the contract does not specify the quality, a party must tender performance of at least average quality.

## Article 6:109: Contract for an Indefinite Period

A contract for an indefinite period may be ended by either party by giving notice of reasonable length.

## Article 6:110: Stipulation in Favour of a Third Party

(1) A third party may require performance of a contractual obligation when its right to do so has been expressly agreed upon between the promisor and the promisee, or when such agreement is to be inferred from the purpose of the contract or the circumstances of the case. The third party need not be identified at the time the agreement is concluded.

(2) If the third party renounces the right to performance the right is treated as never having accrued to it.

(3) The promisee may by notice to the promisor deprive the third party of the right to performance unless:

(a) the third party has received notice from the promisee that the right has been made irrevocable, or

(b) the promisor or the promisee has received notice from the third party that the latter accepts the right.

## Article 6:111: Change of Circumstances

(1) A party is bound to fulfil its obligations even if performance has become more onerous, whether because the cost of performance has increased or because the value of the performance it receives has diminished.

(2) If, however, performance of the contract becomes excessively onerous because of a change of circumstances, the parties are bound to enter into negotiations with a view to adapting the contract or terminating it, provided that:

(a) the change of circumstances occurred after the time of conclusion of the contract,

(b) the possibility of a change of circumstances was not one which could reasonably have been taken into account at the time of conclusion of the contract, and

(c) the risk of the change of circumstances is not one which, according to the contract, the party affected should be required to bear.

(3) If the parties fail to reach agreement within a reasonable period, the court may:

(a) end the contract at a date and on terms to be determined by the court ; or

(b) adapt the contract in order to distribute between the parties in a just and equitable manner the losses and gains resulting from the change of circumstances.

In either case, the court may award damages for the loss suffered through a party refusing to negotiate or breaking off negotiations contrary to good faith and fair dealing.

## CHAPTER 7: PERFORMANCE

### Article 7:101: Place of Performance

(1) If the place of performance of a contractual obligation is not fixed by or determinable from the contract it shall be:

(a) in the case of an obligation to pay money, the creditor's place of business at the time of the conclusion of the contract;

(b) in the case of an obligation other than to pay money, the debtor's place of business at the time of conclusion of the contract.

(2) If a party has more than one place of business, the place of business for the purpose of the preceding paragraph is that which has the closest relationship to the contract, having regard to the circumstances known to or contemplated by the parties at the time of conclusion of the contract.

(3) If a party does not have a place of business its habitual residence is to be treated as its place of business.

### Article 7:102: Time of Performance

A party has to effect its performance:

(1) if a time is fixed by or determinable from the contract, at that time;

(2) if a period of time is fixed by or determinable from the contract, at any time within that period unless the circumstances of the case indicate that the other party is to choose the time;

(3) in any other case, within a reasonable time after the conclusion of the contract.

### Article 7:103: Early Performance

(1) A party may decline a tender of performance made before it is due except where acceptance of the tender would not unreasonably prejudice its interests.

(2) A party's acceptance of early performance does not affect the time fixed for the performance of its own obligation.

## Article 7:104: Order of Performance

To the extent that the performances of the parties can be rendered simultaneously, the parties are bound to render them simultaneously unless the circumstances indicate otherwise.

## Article 7:105: Alternative Performance

(1) Where an obligation may be discharged by one of alternative performances, the choice belongs to the party who is to perform, unless the circumstances indicate otherwise.

(2) If the party who is to make the choice fails to do so by the time required by the contract, then:

    (a) if the delay in choosing is fundamental, the right to choose passes to the other party;

    (b) if the delay is not fundamental, the other party may give a notice fixing an additional period of reasonable length in which the party to choose must do so. If the latter fails to do so, the right to choose passes to the other party.

## Article 7:106: Performance by a Third Person

(1) Except where the contract requires personal performance the creditor cannot refuse performance by a third person if:

    (a) the third person acts with the assent of the debtor; or

    (b) the third person has a legitimate interest in performance and the debtor has failed to perform or it is clear that it will not perform at the time performance is due.

(2) Performance by the third person in accordance with paragraph (1) discharges the debtor.

## Article 7:107: Form of Payment

(1) Payment of money due may be made in any form used in the ordinary course of business.

(2) A creditor who, pursuant to the contract or voluntarily, accepts a cheque or other order to pay or a promise to pay is presumed to do so only on condition that it will be honoured. The creditor may not enforce the original obligation to pay unless the order or promise is not honoured.

## Article 7:108: Currency of Payment

(1) The parties may agree that payment shall be made only in a specified currency.

(2) In the absence of such agreement, a sum of money expressed in a currency other than that of the place where payment is due may be paid in the currency of that place according to the rate of exchange prevailing there at the time when payment is due.

(3) If, in a case falling within the preceding paragraph, the debtor has not paid at the time when payment is due, the creditor may require payment in the currency of the place where payment is due according to the rate of exchange prevailing there either at the time when payment is due or at the time of actual payment.

## Article 7:109: Appropriation of Performance

(1) Where a party has to perform several obligations of the same nature and the performance tendered does not suffice to discharge all of the obligations, then subject to paragraph 4 the party may at the time of its performance declare to which obligation the performance is to be appropriated.

(2) If the performing party does not make such a declaration, the other party may within a reasonable time appropriate the performance to such obligation as it chooses. It shall inform the performing party of the choice. However, any such appropriation to an obligation which:

    (a) is not yet due, or

    (b) is illegal, or

    (c) is disputed,

is invalid.

(3) In the absence of an appropriation by either party, and subject to paragraph 4, the performance is appropriated to that obligation which satisfies one of the following criteria in the sequence indicated:

    (a) the obligation which is due or is the first to fall due;

    (b) the obligation for which the creditor has the least security;

    (c) the obligation which is the most burdensome for the debtor

    (d) the obligation which has arisen first.

If none of the preceding criteria applies, the performance is appropriated proportionately to all obligations.

(4) In the case of a monetary obligation, a payment by the debtor is to be appropriated, first, to expenses, secondly, to interest, and thirdly, to principal, unless the creditor makes a different appropriation.

## Article 7:110: Property Not Accepted

(1) A party who is left in possession of tangible property other than money because of the other party's failure to accept or retake the property must

take reasonable steps to protect and preserve the property.

(2) The party left in possession may discharge its duty to deliver or return:

   (a) by depositing the property on reasonable terms with a third person to be held to the order of the other party, and notifying the other party of this; or

   (b) by selling the property on reasonable terms after notice to the other party, and paying the net proceeds to that party.

(3) Where, however, the property is liable to rapid deterioration or its preservation is unreasonably expensive, the party must take reasonable steps to dispose of it. It may discharge its duty to deliver or return by paying the net proceeds to the other party.

(4) The party left in possession is entitled to be reimbursed or to retain out of the proceeds of sale any expenses reasonably incurred.

### Article 7:111: Money not Accepted

Where a party fails to accept money properly tendered by the other party, that party may after notice to the first party discharge its obligation to pay by depositing the money to the order of the first party in accordance with the law of the place where payment is due.

### Article 7:112: Costs of Performance

Each party shall bear the costs of performance of its obligations.

## CHAPTER 8: NON-PERFORMANCE AND REMEDIES IN GENERAL

### Article 8:101: Remedies Available

(1) Whenever a party does not perform an obligation under the contract and the non-performance is not excused under Article 8:108, the aggrieved party may resort to any of the remedies set out in Chapter 9.

(2) Where a party's non-performance is excused under Article 8:108, the aggrieved party may resort to any of the remedies set out in Chapter 9 except claiming performance and damages.

(3) A party may not resort to any of the remedies set out in Chapter 9 to the extent that its own act caused the other party's non-performance.

### Article 8:102: Cumulation of Remedies

Remedies which are not incompatible may be cumulated. In particular, a party is not deprived of its right to damages by exercising its right to any other remedy.

### Article 8:103: Fundamental Non-Performance

A non-performance of an obligation is fundamental to the contract if:

(a) strict compliance with the obligation is of the essence of the contract; or

(b) the non-performance substantially deprives the aggrieved party of what it was entitled to expect under the contract, unless the other party did not foresee and could not reasonably have foreseen that result; or

(c) the non-performance is intentional and gives the aggrieved party reason to believe that it cannot rely on the other party's future performance.

### Article 8:104: Cure by Non-Performing Party

A party whose tender of performance is not accepted by the other party because it does not conform to the contract may make a new and conforming tender where the time for performance has not yet arrived or the delay would not be such as to constitute a fundamental non-performance.

### Article 8:105: Assurance of Performance

(1) A party who reasonably believes that there will be a fundamental non-performance by the other party may demand adequate assurance of due performance and meanwhile may withhold performance of its own obligations so long as such reasonable belief continues.

(2) Where this assurance is not provided within a reasonable time, the party demanding it may terminate the contract if it still reasonably believes that there will be a fundamental non-performance by the other party and gives notice of termination without delay.

### Article 8:106: Notice Fixing Additional Period for Performance

(1) In any case of non-performance the aggrieved party may by notice to the other party allow an additional period of time for performance.

(2) During the additional period the aggrieved party may withhold performance of its own reciprocal obligations and may claim damages, but it may not resort to any other remedy. If it receives notice from the other party that the latter will not perform within that period, or if upon expiry of that period due performance has not been made, the aggrieved party may resort to any of the remedies that may be available under chapter 9.

(3) If in a case of delay in performance which is not fundamental the aggrieved party has given a notice fixing an additional period of time of reasonable length, it may terminate the contract at the end of the period of notice. The aggrieved party may in its notice provide that if the other party does not perform within the period fixed by the notice the contract

shall terminate automatically. If the period stated is too short, the aggrieved party may terminate, or, as the case may be, the contract shall terminate automatically, only after a reasonable period from the time of the notice.

### Article 8:107 Performance Entrusted to Another
A party who entrusts performance of the contract to another person remains responsible for performance.

### Article 8:108: Excuse Due to an Impediment
(1) A party's non-performance is excused if it proves that it is due to an impediment beyond its control and that it could not reasonably have been expected to take the impediment into account at the time of the conclusion of the contract, or to have avoided or overcome the impediment or its consequences.
(2) Where the impediment is only temporary the excuse provided by this Article has effect for the period during which the impediment exists. However, if the delay amounts to a fundamental non-performance, the creditor may treat it as such.
(3) The non-performing party must ensure that notice of the impediment and of its effect on its ability to perform is received by the other party within a reasonable time after the non-performing party knew or ought to have known of these circumstances. The other party is entitled to damages for any loss resulting from the non-receipt of such notice.

### Article 8:109: Clause Excluding or Restricting Remedies
Remedies for non-performance may be excluded or restricted unless it would be contrary to good faith and fair dealing to invoke the exclusion or restriction.

## CHAPTER 9: PARTICULAR REMEDIES FOR NON-PERFORMANCE

### Section 1 : Right to Performance

### Article 9:101: Monetary Obligations
(1) The creditor is entitled to recover money which is due.
(2) Where the creditor has not yet performed its obligation and it is clear that the debtor will be unwilling to receive performance, the creditor may nonetheless proceed with its performance and may recover any sum due under the contract unless:

(a) it could have made a reasonable substitute transaction without significant effort or expense; or

(b) performance would be unreasonable in the circumstances.

### Article 9:102: Non-monetary Obligations

(1) The aggrieved party is entitled to specific performance of an obligation other than one to pay money, including the remedying of a defective performance.

(2) Specific performance cannot, however, be obtained where:
   (a) performance would be unlawful or impossible; or
   (b) performance would cause the debtor unreasonable effort or expense; or
   (c) the performance consists in the provision of services or work of a personal character or depends upon a personal relationship, or
   (d) the aggrieved party may reasonably obtain performance from another source.

(3) The aggrieved party will lose the right to specific performance if it fails to seek it within a reasonable time after it has or ought to have become aware of the non-performance.

### Article 9:103: Damages Not Precluded

The fact that a right to performance is excluded under this Section does not preclude a claim for damages.

### Section 2 : Withholding Performance

### Article 9:201: Right to Withhold Performance

(1) A party who is to perform simultaneously with or after the other party may withhold performance until the other has tendered performance or has performed. The first party may withhold the whole of its performance or a part of it as may be reasonable in the circumstances.

(2) A party may similarly withhold performance for as long as it is clear that there will be a non-performance by the other party when the other party's performance becomes due.

### Section 3 : Termination of the Contract

### Article 9:301: Right to Terminate the Contract

(1) A party may terminate the contract if the other party's non-performance is fundamental.

(2) In the case of delay the aggrieved party may also terminate the contract under Article 8:106 (3).

## Article 9:302: Contract to be Performed in Parts

If the contract is to be performed in separate parts and in relation to a part to which a counter-performance can be apportioned, there is a fundamental non-performance, the aggrieved party may exercise its right to terminate under this Section in relation to the part concerned. It may terminate the contract as a whole only if the non-performance is fundamental to the contract as a whole.

## Article 9:303: Notice of Termination

(1) A party's right to terminate the contract is to be exercised by notice to the other party.

(2) The aggrieved party loses its right to terminate the contract unless it gives notice within a reasonable time after it has or ought to have become aware of the non-performance.

(3) (a) When performance has not been tendered by the time it was due, the aggrieved party need not give notice of termination before a tender has been made. If a tender is later made it loses its right to terminate if it does not give such notice within a reasonable time after it has or ought to have become aware of the tender.

   (b) If, however, the aggrieved party knows or has reason to know that the other party still intends to tender within a reasonable time, and the aggrieved party unreasonably fails to notify the other party that it will not accept performance, it loses its right to terminate if the other party in fact tenders within a reasonable time.

(4) If a party is excused under Article 8:108 through an impediment which is total and permanent, the contract is terminated automatically and without notice at the time the impediment arises.

## Article 9:304: Anticipatory Non-Performance

Where prior to the time for performance by a party it is clear that there will be a fundamental non-performance by it the other party may terminate the contract.

## Article 9:305: Effects of Termination in General

(1) Termination of the contract releases both parties from their obligation to effect and to receive future performance, but, subject to Articles 9:306 to

9:308, does not affect the rights and liabilities that have accrued up to the time of termination.

(2) Termination does not affect any provision of the contract for the settlement of disputes or any other provision which is to operate even after termination.

## Article 9:306: Property Reduced in Value

A party who terminates the contract may reject property previously received from the other party if its value to the first party has been fundamentally reduced as a result of the other party's non-performance.

## Article 9:307: Recovery of Money Paid

On termination of the contract a party may recover money paid for a performance which it did not receive or which it properly rejected.

## Article 9:308: Recovery of Property

On termination of the contract a party who has supplied property which can be returned and for which it has not received payment or other counter-performance may recover the property.

## Article 9:309: Recovery for Performance that Cannot be Returned

On termination of the contract a party who has rendered a performance which cannot be returned and for which it has not received payment or other counter-performance may recover a reasonable amount for the value of the performance to the other party.

## Section 4 : Price Reduction

## Article 9:401: Right to Reduce Price

(1) A party who accepts a tender of performance not conforming to the contract may reduce the price. This reduction shall be proportionate to the decrease in the value of the performance at the time this was tendered compared to the value which a conforming tender would have had at that time.

(2) A party who is entitled to reduce the price under the preceding paragraph and who has already paid a sum exceeding the reduced price may recover the excess from the other party.

(3) A party who reduces the price cannot also recover damages for reduction in the value of the performance but remains entitled to damages for any

further loss it has suffered so far as these are recoverable under Section 5 of this Chapter.

## Section 5 : Damages and Interest

### Article 9:501: Right to Damages

(1) The aggrieved party is entitled to damages for loss caused by the other party's non-performance which is not excused under Article 8:108.
(2) The loss for which damages are recoverable includes:
    (a) non-pecuniary loss; and
    (b) future loss which is reasonably likely to occur.

### Article 9:502: General Measure of Damages

The general measure of damages is such sum as will put the aggrieved party as nearly as possible into the position in which it would have been if the contract had been duly performed. Such damages cover the loss which the aggrieved party has suffered and the gain of which it has been deprived.

### Article 9:503: Foreseeability

The non-performing party is liable only for loss which it foresaw or could reasonably have foreseen at the time of conclusion of the contract as a likely result of its non-performance, unless the non-performance was intentional or grossly negligent.

### Article 9:504: Loss Attributable to Aggrieved Party

The non-performing party is not liable for loss suffered by the aggrieved party to the extent that the aggrieved party contributed to the non-performance or its effects.

### Article 9:505: Reduction of Loss

(1) The non-performing party is not liable for loss suffered by the aggrieved party to the extent that the aggrieved party could have reduced the loss by taking reasonable steps.
(2) The aggrieved party is entitled to recover any expenses reasonably incurred in attempting to reduce the loss.

### Article 9:506: Substitute Transaction

Where the aggrieved party has terminated the contract and has made a substitute transaction within a reasonable time and in a reasonable manner, it may recover the difference between the contract price and the price of the substitute transaction as well as damages for any further loss so far as these are recoverable under this Section.

### Article 9:507: Current Price

Where the aggrieved party has terminated the contract and has not made a substitute transaction but there is a current price for the performance contracted for, it may recover the difference between the contract price and the price current at the time the contract is terminated as well as damages for any further loss so far as these are recoverable under this Section.

### Article 9:508: Delay in Payment of Money

(1) If payment of a sum of money is delayed, the aggrieved party is entitled to interest on that sum from the time when payment is due to the time of payment at the average commercial bank short-term lending rate to prime borrowers prevailing for the contractual currency of payment at the place where payment is due.

(2) The aggrieved party may in addition recover damages for any further loss so far as these are recoverable under this Section.

### Article 9:509: Agreed Payment for Non-performance

(1) Where the contract provides that a party who fails to perform is to pay a specified sum to the aggrieved party for such non-performance, the aggrieved party shall be awarded that sum irrespective of its actual loss.

(2) However, despite any agreement to the contrary the specified sum may be reduced to a reasonable amount where it is grossly excessive in relation to the loss resulting from the non-performance and the other circumstances.

### Article 9:510: Currency by which Damages to be Measured

Damages are to be measured by the currency which most appropriately reflects the aggrieved party's loss.

## CHAPTER 10: PLURALITY OF PARTIES

### Section 1: Plurality of debtors

### Article 10:101: Solidary, Separate and Communal Obligations

(1) Obligations are solidary when all the debtors are bound to render one and the same performance and the creditor may require it from any one of them until full performance has been received.

(2) Obligations are separate when each debtor is bound to render only part of the performance and the creditor may require from each debtor only that debtor's part.

(3) An obligation is communal when all the debtors are bound to render the performance together and the creditor may require it only from all of them.

### Article 10:102: When Solidary Obligations Arise

(1) If several debtors are bound to render one and the same performance to a creditor under the same contract, they are solidarily liable, unless the contract or the law provides otherwise.

(2) Solidary obligations also arise where several persons are liable for the same damage.

(3) The fact that the debtors are not liable on the same terms does not prevent their obligations from being solidary.

### Article 10:103: Liability under Separate Obligations

Debtors bound by separate obligations are liable in equal shares unless the contract or the law provides otherwise.

### Article 10:104: Communal Obligations: Special Rule when Money claimed for Non-performance

Notwithstanding Article 10:101(3), when money is claimed for non-performance of a communal obligation, the debtors are solidarily liable for payment to the creditor.

### Article 10:105: Apportionment between Solidary Debtors

(1) As between themselves, solidary debtors are liable in equal shares unless the contract or the law provides otherwise.

(2) If two or more debtors are liable for the same damage under Article 10:102(2), their share of liability as between themselves is determined according to the law governing the event which gave rise to the liability.

### Article 10:106: Recourse between Solidary Debtors

(1) A solidary debtor who has performed more than that debtor's share may claim the excess from any of the other debtors to the extent of each debtor's unperformed share, together with a share of any costs reasonably incurred.

(2) A solidary debtor to whom paragraph (1) applies may also, subject to

any prior right and interest of the creditor, exercise the rights and actions of the creditor, including accessory securities, to recover the excess from any of the other debtors to the extent of each debtor's unperformed share.

(3) If a solidary debtor who has performed more than that debtor's share is unable, despite all reasonable efforts, to recover contribution from another solidary debtor, the share of the others, including the one who has performed, is increased proportionally.

### Article 10:107: Performance, Set-off and Merger in Solidary Obligations

(1) Performance or set-off by a solidary debtor or set-off by the creditor against one solidary debtor discharges the other debtors in relation to the creditor to the extent of the performance or set-off.

(2) Merger of debts between a solidary debtor and the creditor discharges the other debtors only for the share of the debtor concerned.

### Article 10:108: Release or Settlement in Solidary Obligations

(1) When the creditor releases, or reaches a settlement with, one solidary debtor, the other debtors are discharged of liability for the share of that debtor.

(2) The debtors are totally discharged by the release or settlement if it so provides.

(3) As between solidary debtors, the debtor who is discharged from that debtor's share is discharged only to the extent of the share at the time of the discharge and not from any supplementary share for which that debtor may subsequently become liable under Article 10:106(3).

### Article 10:109: Effect of Judgment in Solidary Obligations

A decision by a court as to the liability to the creditor of one solidary debtor does not affect:

(a) the liability to the creditor of the other solidary debtors; or

(b) the rights of recourse between the solidary debtors under Article 10:106.

### Article 10:110: Prescription in Solidary Obligations

Prescription of the creditor's right to performance ("claim") against one solidary debtor does not affect:

(a) the liability to the creditor of the other solidary debtors; or

(b) the rights of recourse between the solidary debtors under Article 10:106.

### Article 10:111:  Opposability of other Defences in Solidary Obligations

(1) A solidary debtor may invoke against the creditor any defence which another solidary debtor can invoke, other than a defence personal to that other debtor. Invoking the defence has no effect with regard to the other solidary debtors.

(2) A debtor from whom contribution is claimed may invoke against the claimant any personal defence that that debtor could have invoked against the creditor.

### Section 2 : Plurality of creditors

### Article 10:201:  Solidary, Separate and Communal Claims

(1) Claims are solidary when any of the creditors may require full performance from the debtor and when the debtor may render performance to any of the creditors.

(2) Claims are separate when the debtor owes each creditor only that creditor's share of the claim and each creditor may require performance only of that creditor"s share.

(3) A claim is communal when the debtor must perform to all the creditors and any creditor may require performance only for the benefit of all.

### Article 10:202:  Apportionment of Separate Claims

Separate creditors are entitled to equal shares unless the contract or the law provides otherwise.

### Article 10:203:  Difficulties of executing a Communal Claim

If one of the creditors in a communal claim refuses, or is unable to receive, the performance, the debtor may discharge the obligation to perform by depositing the property or money with a third party according to Articles 7:110 or 7:111 of the Principles.

### Article 10:204:  Apportionment of Solidary Claims

(1) Solidary creditors are entitled to equal shares unless the contract or the law provides otherwise.

(2) A creditor who has received more than that creditor's share must transfer the excess to the other creditors to the extent of their respective shares.

### Article 10:205: Regime of Solidary Claims

(1) A release granted to the debtor by one of the solidary creditors has no effect on the other solidary creditors

(2) The rules of Articles 10:107, 10:109, 10:110 and 10:111(1) apply, with appropriate adaptations, to solidary claims.

## CHAPTER 11: ASSIGNMENT OF CLAIMS

### Section 1:  General Principles

### Article 11:101:  Scope of Chapter

(1) This Chapter applies to the assignment by agreement of a right to performance ("claim") under an  existing or future contract.

(2) Except where otherwise stated or the context otherwise requires, this Chapter also applies to the assignment by agreement of other transferable claims.

(3) This Chapter does not apply:

  (a) to the transfer of a financial instrument or investment security where, under the law otherwise applicable, such transfer must be by entry in a register maintained by or for the issuer; or

  (b) to the transfer of a bill of exchange or other negotiable instrument or of a negotiable security or a document of title to goods where, under the law otherwise applicable, such transfer must be by delivery (with any necessary indorsement).

(4) In this Chapter "assignment" includes an assignment by way of security.

(5) This Chapter also applies, with appropriate adaptations, to the granting by agreement of a right in security over a claim otherwise than by assignment.

### Article 11:102:  Contractual Claims Generally Assignable

(1) Subject to Articles 11:301 and 11:302, a party to a contract may assign a claim under it.

(2) A future claim arising under an existing or future contract may be assigned if at the time when it comes into existence, or at such other time as the parties agree, it can be identified as the claim to which the assignment relates.

### Article 11:103:  Partial Assignment

A claim which is divisible may be assigned in part, but the assignor is liable to the debtor for any increased costs which the debtor thereby incurs.

## Article 11:104: Form of Assignment

An assignment need not be in writing and is not subject to any other requirement as to form. It may be proved by any means, including witnesses.

## Section 2: Effects of Assignment As Between Assignor and Assignee

## Article 11:201: Rights Transferred to Assignee

(1) The assignment of a claim transfers to the assignee:
  (a) all the assignor's rights to performance in respect of the claim assigned; and
  (b) all accessory rights securing such performance.
(2) Where the assignment of a claim under a contract is associated with the substitution of the assignee as debtor in respect of any obligation owed by the assignor under the same contract, this Article takes effect subject to Article 12:201.

## Article 11:202: When Assignment Takes Effect

(1) An assignment of an existing claim takes effect at the time of the agreement to assign or such later time as the assignor and assignee agree.
(2) An assignment of a future claim is dependent upon the assigned claim coming into existence but thereupon takes effect from the time of the agreement to assign or such later time as the assignor and assignee agree.

## Article 11:203: Preservation of Assignee's Rights Against Assignor

An assignment is effective as between the assignor and assignee, and entitles the assignee to whatever the assignor receives from the debtor, even if it is ineffective against the debtor under Article 11:301 or 11:302.

## Article 11:204: Undertakings by Assignor

By assigning or purporting to assign a claim the assignor undertakes to the assignee that:
(a) at the time when the assignment is to take effect the following conditions will be satisfied except as otherwise disclosed to the assignee:
  (i) the assignor has the right to assign the claim;
  (ii) the claim exists and the assignee's rights are not affected by any defences or rights (including any right of set-off) which the debtor might have against the assignor; and
  (iii) the claim is not subject to any prior assignment or right in security in favour of any other party or to any other incumbrance;

(b) the claim and any contract under which it arises will not be modified without the consent of the assignee unless the modification is provided for in the assignment agreement or is one which is made in good faith and is of a nature to which the assignee could not reasonably object; and

(c) the assignor will transfer to the assignee all transferable rights intended to secure performance which are not accessory rights.

### Section 3: Effects of Assignment As Between Assignee and Debtor

### Article 11:301: Contractual Prohibition of Assignment

(1) An assignment which is prohibited by or is otherwise not in conformity with the contract under which the assigned claim arises is not effective against the debtor unless:

(a) the debtor has consented to it; or

(b) the assignee neither knew nor ought to have known of the non-conformity; or

(c) the assignment is made under a contract for the assignment of future rights to payment of money.

(2) Nothing in the preceding paragraph affects the assignor's liability for the non-conformity.

### Article 11:302: Other Ineffective Assignments

An assignment to which the debtor has not consented is ineffective against the debtor so far as it relates to a performance which the debtor, by reason of the nature of the performance or the relationship of the debtor and the assignor, could not reasonably be required to render to anyone except the assignor.

### Article 11:303: Effect on Debtor's Obligation

(1) Subject to Articles 11:301, 11:302, 11:307 and 11:308, the debtor is bound to perform in favour of the assignee if and only if the debtor has received a notice in writing from the assignor or the assignee which reasonably identifies the claim which has been assigned and requires the debtor to give performance to the assignee.

(2) However, if such notice is given by the assignee, the debtor may within a reasonable time request the assignee to provide reliable evidence of the assignment, pending which the debtor may withhold performance.

(3) Where the debtor has acquired knowledge of the assignment otherwise than by a notice conforming to paragraph (1), the debtor may either withhold performance from or give performance to the assignee.

(4) Where the debtor gives performance to the assignor, the debtor is discharged if and only if the performance is given without knowledge of the assignment.

### Article 11:304: Protection of Debtor

A debtor who performs in favour of a person identified as assignee in a notice of assignment under Article 11:303 is discharged unless the debtor could not have been unaware that such person was not the person entitled to performance.

### Article 11:305: Competing Demands

A debtor who has received notice of two or more competing demands for performance may discharge liability by conforming to the law of the due place of performance, or, if the performances are due in different places, the law applicable to the claim.

### Article 11:306: Place of Performance

(1) Where the assigned claim relates to an obligation to pay money at a particular place, the assignee may require payment at any place within the same country or, if that country is a Member State of the European Union, at any place within the European Union, but the assignor is liable to the debtor for any increased costs which the debtor incurs by reason of any change in the place of performance.

(2) Where the assigned claim relates to a non-monetary obligation to be performed at a particular place, the assignee may not require performance at any other place.

### Article 11:307: Defences and Rights of Set-Off

(1) The debtor may set up against the assignee all substantive and procedural defences to the assigned claim which the debtor could have used against the assignor.

(2) The debtor may also assert against the assignee all rights of set-off which would have been available against the assignor under Chapter 13 in respect of any claim against the assignor:

   (a) existing at the time when a notice of assignment, whether or not conforming to Article 11:303(1), reaches the debtor; or

   (b) closely connected with the assigned claim.

### Article 11:308: Unauthorised Modification not Binding on Assignee

A modification of the claim made by agreement between the assignor and the debtor, without the consent of the assignee, after a notice of assignment, whether or not conforming to Article 11:303(1), reaches the debtor does not affect the rights of the assignee against the debtor unless the modification is provided for in the assignment agreement or is one which is made in good faith and is of a nature to which the assignee could not reasonably object.

## Section 4: Order of Priority between Assignee and Competing Claimants

### Article 11:401: Priorities

(1) Where there are successive assignments of the same claim, the assignee whose assignment is first notified to the debtor has priority over any earlier assignee if at the time of the later assignment the assignee under that assignment neither knew nor ought to have known of the earlier assignment.

(2) Subject to paragraph (1), the priority of successive assignments, whether of existing or future claims, is determined by the order in which they are made.

(3) The assignee's interest in the assigned claim has priority over the interest of a creditor of the assignor who attaches that claim, whether by judicial process or otherwise, after the time the assignment has taken effect under Article 11:202.

(4) In the event of the assignor's bankruptcy, the assignee's interest in the assigned claim has priority over the interest of the assignor's insolvency administrator and creditors, subject to any rules of the law applicable to the bankruptcy relating to:

    (a) publicity required as a condition of such priority;

    (b) the ranking of claims; or

    (c) the avoidance or ineffectiveness of transactions in the bankruptcy proceedings.

## CHAPTER 12: SUBSTITUTION OF NEW DEBTOR: TRANSFER OF CONTRACT

### Section 1: Substitution of New Debtor

### Article 12:101: Substitution: General Rules

(1) A third person may undertake with the agreement of the debtor and the creditor to be substituted as debtor, with the effect that the original debtor is discharged.

(2) A creditor may agree in advance to a future substitution. In such a case the substitution takes effect only when the creditor is given notice by the new debtor of the agreement between the new and the original debtor.

### Article 12:102: Effects of Substitution on Defences and Securities

(1) The new debtor cannot invoke against the creditor any rights or defences arising from the relationship between the new debtor and the original debtor.
(2) The discharge of the original debtor also extends to any security of the original debtor given to the creditor for the performance of the obligation, unless the security is over an asset which is transferred to the new debtor as part of a transaction between the original and the new debtor.
(3) Upon discharge of the original debtor, a security granted by any person other than the new debtor for the performance of the obligation is released, unless that other person agrees that it should continue to be available to the creditor.
(4) The new debtor may invoke against the creditor all defences which the original debtor could have invoked against the creditor.

### Section 2: Transfer of Contract

### Article 12:201: Transfer of Contract

(1) A party to a contract may agree with a third person that that person is to be substituted as the contracting party. In such a case the substitution takes effect only where, as a result of the other party's assent, the first party is discharged.
(2) To the extent that the substitution of the third person as a contracting party involves a transfer of rights to performance ("claims"), the provisions of Chapter 11 apply; to the extent that obligations are transferred, the provisions of Section 1 of this Chapter apply.

## CHAPTER 13: SET-OFF

### Article 13:101: Requirements for Set-Off

If two parties owe each other obligations of the same kind, either party may set off that party's right to performance ("claim") against the other party's claim, if and to the extent that, at the time of set-off, the first party:
(a) is entitled to effect performance; and
(b) may demand the other party's performance.

### Article 13:102: Unascertained Claims

(1) A debtor may not set off a claim which is unascertained as to its existence or value unless the set-off will not prejudice the interests of the other party.

(2) Where the claims of both parties arise from the same legal relationship it is presumed that the other party's interests will not be prejudiced.

### Article 13:103: Foreign Currency Set-Off

Where parties owe each other money in different currencies, each party may set off that party's claim against the other party's claim, unless the parties have agreed that the party declaring set-off is to pay exclusively in a specified currency.

### Article 13:104: Notice of Set-Off

The right of set-off is exercised by notice to the other party.

### Article 13:105: Plurality of Claims and Obligations

(1) Where the party giving notice of set-off has two or more claims against the other party, the notice is effective only if it identifies the claim to which it relates.

(2) Where the party giving notice of set-off has to perform two or more obligations towards the other party, the rules in Article 7:109 apply with appropriate adaptations.

### Article 13:106: Effect of Set-Off

Set-off discharges the obligations, as far as they are coextensive, as from the time of notice.

### Article 13:107: Exclusion of Right of Set-Off

Set-off cannot be effected:

(a) where it is excluded by agreement;

(b) against a claim to the extent that that claim is not capable of attachment; and

(c) against a claim arising from a deliberate wrongful act.

## CHAPTER 14: PRESCRIPTION

### Section 1: General Provision

### Article 14:101: Claims subject to Prescription
A right to performance of an obligation ("claim") is subject to prescription by the expiry of a period of time in accordance with these Principles.

### Section 2: Periods of Prescription and their Commencement

### Article 14:201: General Period
The general period of prescription is three years.

### Article 14:202: Period for a Claim Established by Legal Proceedings
(1) The period of prescription for a claim established by judgment is ten years.
(2) The same applies to a claim established by an arbitral award or other instrument which is enforceable as if it were a judgment.

### Article 14:203: Commencement
(1) The general period of prescription begins to run from the time when the debtor has to effect performance or, in the case of a right to damages, from the time of the act which gives rise to the claim.
(2) Where the debtor is under a continuing obligation to do or refrain from doing something, the general period of prescription begins to run with each breach of the obligation.
(3) The period of prescription set out in Article 14:202 begins to run from the time when the judgment or arbitral award obtains the effect of res judicata, or the other instrument becomes enforceable, though not before the debtor has to effect performance.

### Section 3: Extension of Period

### Article 14:301: Suspension in Case of Ignorance
The running of the period of prescription is suspended as long as the creditor does not know of, and could not reasonably know of:
(a) the identity of the debtor; or
(b) the facts giving rise to the claim including, in the case of a right to damages, the type of damage.

### Article 14:302: Suspension in Case of Judicial and Other Proceedings

(1) The running of the period of prescription is suspended from the time when judicial proceedings on the claim are begun.

(2) Suspension lasts until a decision has been made which has the effect of res judicata, or until the case has been otherwise disposed of.

(3) These provisions apply, with appropriate adaptations, to arbitration proceedings and to all other proceedings initiated with the aim of obtaining an instrument which is enforceable as if it were a judgment.

### Article 14:303: Suspension in Case of Impediment beyond Creditor's Control

(1) The running of the period of prescription is suspended as long as the creditor is prevented from pursuing the claim by an impediment which is beyond the creditor''s control and which the creditor could not reasonably have been expected to avoid or overcome.

(2) Paragraph (1) applies only if the impediment arises, or subsists, within the last six months of the prescription period.

### Article 14:304: Postponement of Expiry in Case of Negotiations

If the parties negotiate about the claim, or about circumstances from which a claim might arise, the period of prescription does not expire before one year has passed since the last communication made in the negotiations.

### Article 14:305: Postponement of Expiry in Case of Incapacity

(1) If a person subject to an incapacity is without a representative, the period of prescription of a claim held by or against that person does not expire before one year has passed after either the incapacity has ended or a representative has been appointed.

(2) The period of prescription of claims between a person subject to an incapacity and that person's representative does not expire before one year has passed after either the incapacity has ended or a new representative has been appointed.

### Article 14:306: Postponement of Expiry: Deceased's Estate

Where the creditor or debtor has died, the period of prescription of a claim held by or against the deceased's estate does not expire before one year has passed after the claim can be enforced by or against an heir, or by or against a representative of the estate.

## Article 14:307:  Maximum Length of Period

The period of prescription cannot be extended, by suspension of its running or postponement of its expiry under these Principles, to more than ten years or, in case of claims for personal injuries, to more than thirty years. This does not apply to suspension under Article 14:302.

## Section 4: Renewal of Periods

## Article 14:401:  Renewal by Acknowledgement

(1) If the debtor acknowledges the claim, vis-à-vis the creditor, by part payment, payment of interest, giving of security, or in any other manner, a new period of prescription begins to run.

(2) The new period is the general period of prescription, regardless of whether the claim was originally subject to the general period of prescription or the ten year period under Article 14:202. In the latter case, however, this Article does not operate so as to shorten the ten year period.

## Article 14:402:  Renewal by Attempted Execution

The ten year period of prescription laid down in Article 14:202 begins to run again with each reasonable attempt at execution undertaken by the creditor.

## Section 5: Effects of Prescription

## Article 14:501:  General Effect

(1) After expiry of the period of prescription the debtor is entitled to refuse performance.

(2) Whatever has been performed in order to discharge a claim may not be reclaimed merely because the period of prescription had expired.

## Article 14:502:  Effect on Ancillary Claims

The period of prescription for a right to payment of interest, and other claims of an ancillary nature, expires not later than the period for the principal claim.

## Article 14:503:  Effect on Set-Off

A claim in relation to which the period of prescription has expired may nonetheless be set off, unless the debtor has invoked prescription previously or does so within two months of notification of set-off.

### Section 6: Modification by Agreement

### Article 14:601:  Agreements Concerning Prescription

(1)  The requirements for prescription may be modified by agreement between the parties, in particular by either shortening or lengthening the periods of prescription.

(2)  The period of prescription may not, however, be reduced to less than one year or extended to more than thirty years after the time of commencement set out in Article 14:203.


## CHAPTER 15: ILLEGALITY

### Article 15:101:  Contracts Contrary to Fundamental Principles

A contract is of no effect to the extent that it is contrary to principles recognised as fundamental in the laws of the Member States of the European Union.


### Article 15:102:  Contracts Infringing Mandatory Rules

(1)  Where a contract infringes a mandatory rule of law applicable under Article 1:103 of these Principles, the effects of that infringement upon the contract are the effects, if any, expressly prescribed by that mandatory rule.

(2)  Where the mandatory rule does not expressly prescribe the effects of an infringement upon a contract, the contract may be declared to have full effect, to have some effect, to have no effect, or to be subject to modification.

(3)  A decision reached under paragraph (2)  must be an appropriate and proportional response to the infringement, having regard to all relevant circumstances, including:

   (a)  the purpose of the rule which has been infringed;
   (b)  the category of persons for whose protection the rule exists;
   (c)  any sanction that may be imposed under the rule infringed;
   (d)  the seriousness of the infringement;
   (e)  whether the infringement was intentional; and
   (f)  the closeness of the relationship between the infringement and the contract.


### Article 15:103:  Partial Ineffectiveness

(1)  If only part of a contract is rendered ineffective under Articles 15:101 or 15:102, the remaining part continues in effect unless, giving due con-

sideration to all the circumstances of the case, it is unreasonable to uphold it.

(2) Articles 15:104 and 15:105 apply, with appropriate adaptations, to a case of partial ineffectiveness.

## Article 15:104: Restitution

(1) When a contract is rendered ineffective under Articles 15:101 or 15:102, either party may claim restitution of whatever that party has supplied under the contract, provided that, where appropriate, concurrent restitution is made of whatever has been received.

(2) When considering whether to grant restitution under paragraph (1), and what concurrent restitution, if any, would be appropriate, regard must be had to the factors referred to in Article 15:102(3).

(3) An award of restitution may be refused to a party who knew or ought to have known of the reason for the ineffectiveness.

(4) If restitution cannot be made in kind for any reason, a reasonable sum must be paid for what has been received.

## Article 15:105: Damages

(1) A party to a contract which is rendered ineffective under Articles 15:101 or 15:102 may recover from the other party damages putting the first party as nearly as possible into the same position as if the contract had not been concluded, provided that the other party knew or ought to have known of the reason for the ineffectiveness.

(2) When considering whether to award damages under paragraph (1), regard must be had to the factors referred to in Article 15:102(3).

(3) An award of damages may be refused where the first party knew or ought to have known of the reason for the ineffectiveness.

## CHAPTER 16: CONDITIONS

## Article 16:101: Types of Condition

A contractual obligation may be made conditional upon the occurrence of an uncertain future event, so that the obligation takes effect only if the event occurs (suspensive condition) or comes to an end if the event occurs (resolutive condition).

## Article 16:102: Interference with Conditions

(1) If fulfilment of a condition is prevented by a party, contrary to duties of

good faith and fair dealing or co-operation, and if fulfilment would have operated to that party's disadvantage, the condition is deemed to be fulfilled.

(2) If fulfilment of a condition is brought about by a party, contrary to duties of good faith and fair dealing or co-operation, and if fulfilment operates to that party's advantage, the condition is deemed not to be fulfilled.

### Article 16:103: Effect of Conditions

(1) Upon fulfilment of a suspensive condition, the relevant obligation takes effect unless the parties otherwise agree.

(2) Upon fulfilment of a resolutive condition, the relevant obligation comes to an end unless the parties otherwise agree.

## CHAPTER 17: CAPITALISATION OF INTEREST

### Article 17:101: When Interest to be Added to Capital

(1) Interest payable according to Article 9:508(1) is added to the outstanding capital every 12 months.

(2) Paragraph (1) of this Article does not apply if the parties have provided for interest upon delay in payment.

# List of Cases

# Index

The Index is arranged letter by letter. References are to page numbers. References to footnotes are in the form of page number followed by 'n': 36n refers to a footnote on page 36. Names are indexed if they are discussed or quoted in the text.